The Heart of Northwest Climbing

NORTHWEST OREGON ROCK

Hugh Brown climbing on the *E Ridge of South Chamber, Illumination Rock*

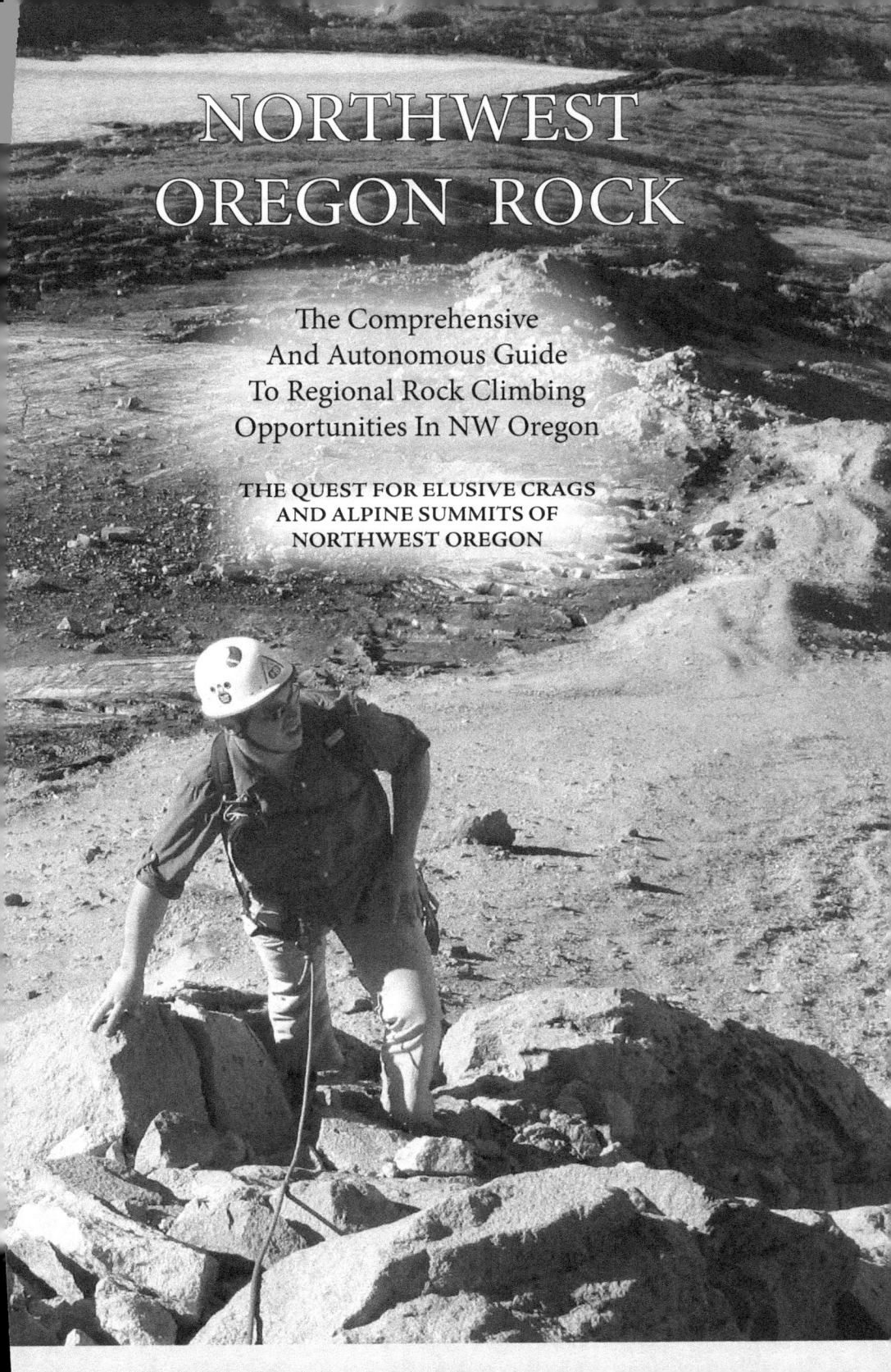

NORTHWEST OREGON ROCK

The Comprehensive
And Autonomous Guide
To Regional Rock Climbing
Opportunities In NW Oregon

THE QUEST FOR ELUSIVE CRAGS
AND ALPINE SUMMITS OF
NORTHWEST OREGON

Northwest Oregon Rock™
© 2021 East Wind Design

All rights reserved. No part of this book may be reproduced or transmitted in any form by any means, electronic or mechanical, including photocopying and recording, or by any information storage system, except as may be expressly permitted by the Copyright Act. Requests for permission must be made in writing to the author and publisher.

Book Design: East Wind Design
Technical Maps and Illustrations: East Wind Design
Cover Design: East Wind Design
Cover Photograph: *Hugh Brown on Needle Rock*
Frontispiece: *Hugh Brown on East Ridge South Chamber, Illumination Rock*

www.portlandrockclimbs.com

Library of Congress Card Number: 2010902673
Northwest Oregon Rock (NWOR)

NWOR2 (v2.5)
ISBN-EAN: 978-0-9997233-3-3

Manufactured in the United States of America

Table of Contents

Introduction 1
- General History 2
- NW Oregon Climate 9
- Geology Of NW Oregon 10
- Climbing Route Ratings 17
- Equipment And Specialized Gear 19

Mt. Hood Regional Climbs 21
- French's Dome 21
- Salmon River Slab 28
- Illumination Rock 29
- Razorblade Pinnacle 34
- Hunchback 36
- Enola (The Swinery) 47
- Kiwanis Crag 56
- Castle Canyon 58
- Kinzel Tower 60
- Mosquito Butte 61

East side Rock Climbs 65
- Newton Pinnacle 69
- Lamberson Butte 69
- Pete's Pile 74
- Klinger Springs 88
- Bulo Point 99
- Heliotrope 106
- Area 51 107
- Hood River Pinnacle 120

Columbia Gorge Rock 125
- Rooster Rock 125
- Crown Point 127
- Pillars of Hercules 129
- The Rat Cave 130
- Little Cougar Rock 134
- St. Peters Dome 136
- Little St. Pete's 138
- Katanai Rock 138
- Apocalypse Needles 139
- Cape Horn 140
- Rabbit Ears 141
- Jimmy Cliff (Twilight Zone) 142
- Rock Creek Crag 145
- No Star Slab 149
- Skookum Pinnacle 149
- Wind Mountain 151
- Windy Slab 152
- Dog Spine 154
- The Bypass 156
- Wankers Column 159
- OH8 162
- Lyle West Crag 169
- Lyle Tunnel Crag 170
- Horsethief butte 171

Monte Cristo Slab	185
Gorge Ice	**211**
Crown Jewel Area	218
Mist Falls Area	223
Benson Ice Area	225
Horsetail Falls Area	229
Starvation Creek Area	235
Cape Horn Area	237
SW Washington	**243**
Chimney Rocks	243
LaCamas PLug	251
Tower Rock	252
Sunset Bluff	255
Clackamas & Molalla	**261**
Coethedral	261
Collawash Cliff	266
Rooster Hen & Chicks	267
Wild Boar Crag	269
Santiam Summits	**279**
Needle Rock	279
Little Needle Rock	280
Elephant Rock	281
Dog Tooth Rock	283
Spire Rock	285
X-Spire	288
Breitenbush Ears	288
Thor's Hammer	289
Stack Rock	291
Pika Rock	293
The Menagerie	297
Santiam Pinnacle	314
Iron Mountain Spire	315
Smokestack	316
Twin Sisters Pinnacle	317
Two Girls Mtn	317
Pirates Pinnacle	319
Horse Rock Pillar	320
Southern Willamette	**321**
Skinner Butte Columns	321
Wolf Rock	326
Moolack	337
Central Oregon	**373**
Steins Pillar	373
Twin Pillars	381
Gothic Rock	382
Trout Creek	384
Shepard Tower	388
Ne Oregon Rock	**389**
Spring Mountain	393
The Dikes	418
High Valley	422

Caution

Rock climbing contains certain inherent risks that may be dangerous to your health. The sole purpose of this book is to inform rock climbers of the many wonderful crag climbing opportunities available in and around our corner of northwest Oregon. Before attempting any climb described in these pages, you should first be proficient in the use of modern rock climbing equipment. These climbs, for the most part, are not for beginners.

This guidebook is not a substitute for personal insight, time-learned skills, or lessons taught by climbing instructors. There are no warranties, neither express nor implied, that this book contains accurate or reliable information. As the user of this or any guidebook, you assume full responsibility for your own safety. Because the sport is constantly evolving, the author cannot guarantee the accuracy of any of the information in this book, including the location of bolts, pitons (or other hardware), route names and route ratings, route descriptions, or approach trails. No one can offer you any assurance against natural hazards such as lightning or other weather phenomena, loose or poor quality rock, or the risk of equipment failure.

Only you can know the scope and the upper limit of your rock climbing abilities. Assess your prospective climb shrewdly, and make prudent decisions based on your strengths and weaknesses. If you have any doubt concerning your ability to safely ascend a climbing route today, then stop and consider a climb that is less difficult or dangerous.

This is not a how-to guide but rather a where-to book. *Northwest Oregon Rock* explains where to rock climb, but you must honestly determine whether you have mastered the most important aspects of the sport before embarking on any rock climbing adventure before you use this book.

Consult other climbers about the adventure or rock climb you are planning to embark upon. A skilled climber who knows the crag can give quality advice and insight as to proper gear placement as well as impart ideas about climbing technique and balance that will surely be beneficial to you.

Wisely seek assistance, and attain good instruction from others, such as a diligent climbing instructor who will teach you how to become a safe, intuitive climber.

Consider with suspicion all fixed protection, such as bolts and pitons. Weathering, metal quality, and impact stress loading are some of the variants that can cause fixed gear to fail. Placing additional equipment, such as cams or wires as your safety backup, is a good precaution.

Exercise good judgment as to where the climbing route ascends the cliff face, and learn to quickly perceive subtle variants you will likely encounter in route difficulty. Ask yourself if the route is an off-width, or has run-out sections, or are portions of the wall damp? Know your own strengths and weaknesses; develop a competent understanding of your route-finding abilities and safety skills, for these and the right equipment are your best protection against the hazards of climbing. Confidence and ability gained through many hours of physical and mental preparation are perhaps the most valuable skills you and your climbing partner will need when managing the degree of risk you both are willing to accept.

Chad Ellers climbing *The Watchman*

Preface

This edition of *Northwest Oregon Rock* fulfills requests from close friends who expressed their desire for a truly diversified guidebook that covers the entire scope of rock climbing throughout this region with articulate precision. Their words of encouragement provided the motivation to achieve that goal.

Their invaluable ideas and fruitful suggestions were essential in helping to bring an otherwise impossible project to the light. From a large collection of maps, illustrations, and climbing related documents that lay deep upon my desk, came this reformulated guidebook that I hope you find useful for many years to come.

Ideally, this edition will encourage you to seek your own bold new frontier. A world full of discovery and possibilities awaits the adventurous climber, and these pages reveal but a tiny fragment of the whole.

Throughout your quest, remember that our rock climbing actions today impact and influence the future decisions of property owners and land managers alike. We are responsible for keeping ours a friendly, self-managed sport and for acting in full cooperation with land managers so that rock climbers will continue to be welcomed for generations to come. By developing a perceptive, respectful awareness of the environment around us, from the peregrine falcon to *Sedum integrifolium*, we ultimately discover that we are entrusted with the keys to provide a legacy for tomorrow.

With some reservation I still see this guide book as an incomplete thesis. Therefore, fully knowing its shortcomings and not expecting perfection, but merely lacking certain extended resources by which one might attain a more thorough documentation of northwest Oregon rock climbing, I submit to you this partial exploratory analysis of climbing, knowing that it is less complete than that which I desired to see. Even so, we are instilled with a sense of commitment that what is bound herein these pages you will find both rewarding and fulfilling.

Dedication

Many years ago, while solo rock climbing at Rocky Butte, I had the good fortune of meeting Robert McGown and Wayne Wallace, two remarkably talented climbers whose expertise and insights helped transform the direction and expectations concerning the sport of rock climbing in Portland. These extraordinary men have impacted and shaped the core values of not one but two sports in the Northwest: rock climbing and mountaineering.

Robert McGown's imprint on the sport has spanned many years, from the early 1970s into the 1990s. Bob's vibrant enthusiasm for the hunt in those early climbing days was inspirational, and his is a truly remarkable legacy. I wish him continued success as he reaches for the most distant stars.

Wayne Wallace is known for his savvy adventures along the crest of the Picket Range in northern Washington State. Wayne's boldness throughout his quest to conquer the vast unknown and his seemingly endless strength are in a universal first degree of their own.

With gratitude I thank both Wayne and Bob for their amazing friendships and for providing the courage to develop this edition of *Northwest Oregon Rock*.

Mike Schoen has been another courteous and ardent fellow adventurer—one who has excelled far beyond many of us and is worthy of the highest respect. Mike's creative short stories enlivened each climbing adventure, and his timeless wit and humor have made each enjoyable outing even more memorable. Because of his friendship I have learned to understand the brilliant nature of the "Light" more clearly. I wish him strength and fortitude in his ongoing quest for discovery!

All three of these climbers know how to enjoy each adventure to the fullest. They all possess scholarly intuition, strength, and discipline, yet each has a boldness that we all may aspire to.

And lastly, to the memory of Don Gonthier, a friend who greatly enjoyed all aspects of rock climbing as well as exploring the hills of NW Oregon.

Acknowledgments

During the long hours of formulating a giant project of this kind, I learned that the end result, which you now see, can only come into existence through the shared knowledge and guidance of many individuals. Thank you all for sharing your expertise and wisdom.

This guidebook to rock climbing opportunities in Northwest Oregon is the end formulation of insight from many mountaineers, rock climbers and historical research writers. Their notes, small articles and short but authoritative published journals provide the foundation stones upon which this book is based.

The tremendous efforts of Carl Neuberger who summarized quite effectively the early climbs of the Gorge published his work in 'A Climber's Guide to the Columbia Gorge', in the December 1958 issue of the Mazama Annual Volume XL, Number 13.

The twice published book 'A Climber's Guide to Oregon' by Nicholas Dodge contains a wealth of interesting content from the earlier years of climbing and mountaineering and describes many fascinating areas in Oregon from Katanai Rock to Wolf Rock. It was great to talk with him briefly about the essence of encompassing various select parts of his guide into this guide.

The following individuals were highly instrumental in sharing knowledge and ideas that have helped to strengthen the quality and vibrance of this book.

Jim Nieland shared considerable insight about his climbing history, verified route beta, and loaned a fine selection of historical images for inclusion, including a rare photo of Eugene Dod.

Paul Waters provided a superb detailed analysis of Moolack (one of his favorite climbing areas) and took special efforts to communicate closely with his friends about the desire to release a positive study (photographic, topographic and written) to this site (action photo credits are listed with each image); David Sword provided the key to unlocking the mysteries at Pete's Pile by writing a superb history and beta list for that site; Paul Cousar and Kay Kucera were very kind in providing a viable solution for Area51 and OH8; Tymun Abbott shared his in-depth insight on the powerful list of routes at French's Dome; Dain Smoland generously allowed us to utilize aspects of his data for Bulo Point; Chip Miller, Gavin Fergusan and Kent Benesch were all instrumental in the crucial data for Steins Pillar. We are grateful for the opportunity to include Kevin Pogue's excellent beta list compilation on Spring Mtn crag; thanks to Allen Sanderson for his analysis of High Valley crag; Greg Lyon's long out-of-print knowledge to Horsethief Butte helped to start a new chapter of analysis for that climbing site; Tymun Abbott's thorough bouldering knowledge of Horsethief Butte proved instrumental toward developing a refined beta list; Wayne Wallace and Steve Elder both provided valued information on their conquests in the mountains, Brad Englund shared a detailed analogy to his Detroit Rock City adventures, and Kelly Hann kindly shared certain aspects of beta about Enola. Miles Noel contributed by writing an excellent introduction and beta list for Skinner Butte; Jeff Wenger wrote a stellar introduction for Trout Creek. George Beilstein graciously provided insight about some of his early climbing forays. John Rust and associates helpfully clarified certain first ascent aspects at French's Dome. Special thanks to Jim Tripp for providing a personal guided beta tour of The Swine.

Individuals like Dave Sowerby, Norm Watt, Scott Peterson, Karl Helser and others provided highly valued bits of data. Thanks to Mike Schoen who provided the energy to carry the ropes to conquer many of these routes. We are indebted to the impressive strength and courage of all climber's who first touched these summits and established these routes.

Dave Sowerby at *The Rat Cave*

..."we have ceased to be slaves and have really been men.
It is hard to return to servitude."
~Lionel Terray

ALL FOR THE SPORT OF CLIMBING

INTRODUCTION

The Ongoing Quest for Elusive Summits, Alpine Pinnacles and Other Climbing Opportunities in Northwest Oregon

NW Oregon Rock provides an extensive analysis of the sport of rock climbing throughout Northwest Oregon. From rock pillars to alpine pinnacles, from tiny bluffs to huge vertical rock walls this guidebook expands upon the Portland Rock Climbs theme by taking you on a grand tour of the great and unique treasures well beyond our local city crags. This book is intended to bridge the gap between old information and new as well as provide the skilled climber with a valuable tool to use throughout his or her quest in the sport of rock climbing.

Our corner of the Pacific Northwest offers numerous tantalizing climbing destinations, from diverse Columbia Gorge rocky summits and ice climbs in winter, to stellar hidden climbing sites found on the eastern slopes of Mt. Hood.

The original heart of this guidebook came from a rather brief analysis which began in the 1993 edition of *Portland Rock Climbs* called 'Cragging Options'. Several previous authors have laid the groundwork for making portions of *Northwest Oregon Rock* a successful guidebook. Carl A. Neuberger's "A Climbers Guide to the Columbia Gorge," was published in the December 1958 issue of the *Mazama Annual* Volume XL, Number 13. Neuberger's article provided the first comprehensive guide detailing the great Columbia River Gorge classics. He described key features of the gorge that were of great interest to climbers—objectives like St. Peter's Dome, Rabbit Ears, Little Cougar Rock, and other famous Columbia River Gorge climbs—all within a compact, well-written guide.

The other Oregon guidebook with a compilation of climbing history and route statistics was the twice published *A Climber's Guide to Oregon* by Nicholas Dodge. Printed in 1968 and 1975, Dodge's book contains a wealth of interesting content from the earlier years of climbing and mountaineering and describes many fascinating areas in Oregon from Illumination Rock to Wolf Rock. These guidebook authors have helped to draw considerable climber

Rebecca Gibson leading *Blind Ambition 5.10b*

and community attention to some of these climbing destinations, not only for continued access but also for their natural preservation.

Northwest Oregon Rock incorporates a broad selection of rock climbing opportunities available within relatively easy one-day drive (approximately 80 mile radius) from Portland, Oregon.

The chapter on Columbia Gorge Ice explores a bold new frontier of adventure climbing. This fascinating sport is popular due to easy roadside access to the ice routes in the Gorge. Everyone should visit the Gorge when a cold winter storm encases the waterfalls in ice. The wild vertical world of Gorge ice is spectacular to climb and to photograph.

Each NWOR chapter provides an in-depth analysis of the regional rock climbing opportunities from sites near Mt. Hood, to excellent places of interest on the North and South Santiam Rivers that will certainly appeal to everyone. These sections are a colorful, quality mixture of activity that encompasses a variety of challenges such as total off trail bushwhack scrambles to forgotten classic pinnacles, to energetic and beautiful summit climbs on higher altitude spires such as the Razorblade. The guidebook also includes a brief selection of Columbia Gorge rock climbing summits that are within the scope of most seasoned rock climbers who are comfortable climbing over some loose rock terrain.

Wayne Wallace during an October ascent of Eliott Headwall

GENERAL HISTORY

Every generation of rock climbers strives to reach out and discover bold new horizons that prove both challenging and rewarding. Rock climbers today have great access to a myriad of alpine summits and backwoods cragging opportunities. But the exploring and scrambling idea has been a gratifying pursuit in northwest Oregon since before the turn of the twentieth century. In the Columbia River Gorge, interest for exploration expanded in part because of the building of the Columbia River Highway, which began in 1913. Recreational pursuits in northwest Oregon have continued to become focused and energized ever since.

In the Gorge one wave of exploration began in earnest when turn of the 20th century pioneer photographers and explorer-geologists, men like Benjamin Gifford, G. M. Weister, the Kister Brothers and Ira A. Williams reached places that are extremely difficult to access, even today.

The first recorded ascent of Beacon Rock occurred on August 24, 1901 by Frank Smith, George Purcell, and Charles Church. The route ascended steep brush slopes and exposed 4th and low 5th class corner systems on the west side of the rock formation.

Back in the 1880s high upon the slopes of Mt. Hood, the renowned O.C. Yocum began guiding his guests up to the summit of the mountain, one of them being a young man of 16 years age. This legendary young man, Elijah [Lige] Coalman, is remembered for his strength and zeal. He was instrumental while working for the Forest Service as a lineman striving to establish a lookout station on the summit of Mt. Hood, which he manned for a short time when it was completed. His abilities quickly gained a reputation among the all the great climbers and mountain guides in the Northwest.

"The great vitality of Coalman was demonstrated by one day he spent in 1910. He and a climbing client ate breakfast at the hotel in Government Camp. They then climbed to the summit of Mount Hood and down to Cloud Cap Inn, where the client wanted to go. After lunch at Cloud Cap, Lige climbed back over the summit and arrived for dinner at Government Camp at 5:00 p.m." [Quote from *Mount Hood, A Complete History*, by Jack Grauer.]

In the years from 1913 to 1930 T. Raymond Conway is said to have ascended Illumination Rock nearly a dozen times. From August 1933 to 1936, Gary Leech, another virtual climbing legend in his own right, recorded climbing numerous routes on Illumination Rock, many of these solo, including a solo traverse from the south side up and over the summit and down the East Ridge to the saddle.

In the 1930s another generation of adventures began to take on the serious rock summits of the Gorge, and also high on Mt. Hood. With tremendous vitality Don Onthank, Lee Darling, Ray Conkling, John Ohrenschall, Carl Neuberger, Joe Leuthold, Bill Cummins, Art Maki, the Darr's, Don Comer and many others were instrumental in exploring and conquering some of those great classics. The summits they ascended are unique, tantalizing, and serious in every way, and yet are still available to climb with caution.

Eugene Dod near *Gothic Rock*

These early era rock and mountain climbing pioneers found that by their tremendous endeavors they could go to the edge and beyond.

Beginning in December 1930 an elite mountaineering fraternity was formed known as the Wy'East Climbers. The original founding members were: Don Burkhart, Ray Atkeson, James Harlow, Ralph Calkin, Barrie James, Alfred Monner, Norman O'Connor. Other members who quickly joined the ranks were Joe Leuthold, Olie Lien, James Mount, Everett Darr, Bob Furrer, Ray Lewis, Henry Kurtz, Curtis Ijames and others. This group was known for bold adventures, but also showing community founded generosity.

They were highly successful in pioneering a number of new routes on Mount Hood, including Eliot Glacier Headwall. They were instrumental in establishing a First Aid & Rescue equipment cache at a rock shelter near the base of Crater Rock.

Jim Nieland on *Lower Twin Pillar*

On September 28, 1937 Timberline Lodge was formally dedicated by Franklin D. Roosevelt. In 1938 the Wy'East Climbers were instrumental in forming Ski Patrol. This organization initially focused on Search & Rescue emergencies, accident prevention, training, and public education, but has today expanded into the National Ski Patrol Association.

After the Second World War, the fraternity gained new members such as the Petrie brothers, Richard Pooley, David Nelson, James Angell, the Levin brothers, Richard Dodd, John McCormick, Ray Conkling, Al, Kirnak, Albert Weese and others.

In the early 20th century interest for a round-the-mountain trip at the 9,000' elevation level among the glaciers of Mt. Hood was suggested. It was first mentioned by Will Languille. Lige Coalman and O.C. Yocum took a personal 2-day excursion and found an adventure filled with light-

Bob McGown on *Turkey Monster*

ning storms, rockfall, and collapsing glacial serac walls. In later years, a very select group of skiers have continued this adventure by skiing from Timberline Lodge up to Illumination Rock saddle, then across the Reid Glacier and around the mountain (Previous seven paragraphs based on brief articles in *Mount Hood: A Complete History*, by Jack Grauer, 1975).

One of the early conquests by some of these historical climbers was on St. Peters Dome in the Columbia River Gorge. On June 23, 1940 a team consisting of Eldon Metzger, Everett and Ida Darr, Glen Asher, James Mount, and Joe Leuthold made the first ascent of St. Peters Dome. Due to the extreme difficulty of succeeding on a wall of loose rubble the number of summit ascents on St Peters Dome gradually grew smaller; in 1963–64 there were five groups; from 1965–68 just three groups; in 1972 one group; in 1977 one group; in 1994 one person (Wallace's roped solo ascent). In early 2008 Radek & Shirley Chalupa, and Jeff Thomas accomplished another rare ascent of this spire, then in 2011 Scott Peterson and partner summited on it, as well.

Alpine exploring, rock climbing, and adventure driven spire climbing quickly became popular again after World War II. Don Comer and friends took to exploring the Crown Point West Chimney in 1950. Ray Conkling and Bud Frie made a second ascent (and likely the first, too) of the minor Conklings Pinnacle in 1951 near Kinzel Tower.

John Ohrenschall (a Swiss guide) and Gene Todd completed the first ascent of the south face of Beacon Rock in 1952. To this day the SE Face route (5.7) is the most frequently climbed technical route on the river face at Beacon. Ray and Leonard Conkling teamed up later to establish the ever popular Giants Staircase in 1958, the first technical route at French's Dome. Dave Bohn and partners explored a new variant in 1958 on St Peters Dome.

In 1961 Eugene Dod, Bob Martin, and Earl Levin teamed up to explore a particularly steep crack system near the third tunnel at Beacon Rock leading up to Big Ledge.

The development of "Dod's Jam" route is particularly interesting in that it began as a mixed aid and free climb from the railroad tracks at the bottom of the face. On one of the early attempts (in 1961) Earl Levin recalled evaluating a 65-foot overhanging jam crack, which would probably have been aided, but for Eugene Dod, who insisted on flailing away at it, with all his might. "Starting out was most difficult, as Eugene had to stand on my shoulder to work his way into the crack. Up he went and struggling every inch of the way. At the halfway point he was almost completely exhausted and felt that he would fall any moment. Somehow he made his way to the top where he rested before setting up a third belay position on a tiny ledge appropriately named "The Perch". At the same time I belayed Bob Martin to my position. Bob then decided to go on to Eugene and received a belay to "The Perch". He was so tired at this point that Eugene took the next lead. Through a tree growing inconveniently in our path and sixty-five feet higher up an overhanging face (A1) we found ourselves on 'Big Ledge' and peaceful serenity (Nick Dodge, *A Climbing Guide to Oregon* (1975), pg 26).

Starting in the early 1960s Kim Schmitz, Dean Caldwell, Bob Martin, Charles Carpenter, Wayne Arrington, Alan Kearney and others forged alliances to continue exploring the bold new frontier of Beacon Rock. Schmitz and Levin extended the Dod's Jam route with a variation in 1965 that ends by rappeling onto Grassy Ledges above Flying Swallow. Wayne Arrington and Jack Barrar developed a direct finish variant in 1972 that follows close to the upper headwall and lands on the trail near an overlook.

More climbers met and forged formidable climbing teams during the 1960s-70s. Jim Nieland, Bill Cummins, and Dave Jensen formed climbing partnerships with the indefatigable Eugene Dod as they succeeded on numerous bold ascents throughout northwest Oregon and southwest Washington. Some of their contributions include the Zucchini Route (NE Face route) in 1968 on Crown Point, three routes on Twin Pillars in the Ochoco Mtns also in 1968, and Needle Rock near Detroit, Oregon also in September of 1968.

Jim Nieland traveled often, and this afforded the opportunity to explore rock pillars even in the remote hinterland of southeast Oregon. He still found untraveled rock climbs closer to Portland. He and Francisco Valenzuela completed the first ascent of the northwest face Tower Rock on June 19th & 20th, 1982. His remembrance about the ascent, "...[we] started the climb thinking it would take 5-6 hours to complete. At dark we found ourselves in the middle of the face, with no easy way to retreat down the overhangs below. We spent a cold night on a ledge. We reached the top early afternoon the next day, a little dehydrated but none the worse for wear..." Though an impressive plainly visible roadside wall, Tower Rock is a seldom repeated climb to this day.

The Columbia Gorge seems to have its own share of mysterious places, too. Jim Davis and Wayne Haack attempted the West Face of Wind Mtn during the summer of 1975. The goal was to reach the prominent upper left leaning corner system. They rapped after placing some fixed gear on the initial technical lead at the top of the main ravine after an encounter with rockfall. Davis returned a year or two later with friends Priest and Tyerman determined to succeed, but still could not surmount the friable R/X section above the initial ravine. Years later Jim Nieland and Francisco Valenzuela completed a 3-pitch route in 1984 immediately to the right of the West Face crack in another deep corner system. As a low elevation backup plan Wallace and Olson opted to try the West Face crack in 1994, but the adventure was cut short when Wayne took a leader fall on the X-rated pitch. Later that same season, Steve Elder completed the first ascent of the West Face crack by rope-soloing the route in September 1994 in his usual daring style.

The original half dozen routes on Illumination Rock were established prior to the second world war. In relatively recent days, and after honing ice climbing skills in the Columbia Gorge, another generation of climbers found the rime ice gullies on I-rock to be stellar when the conditions are good. Wayne Wallace teamed up with Richard Ernst, Lane brown and Leesa Azaar to punch a stout string of extreme mixed ice routes up the face left of the South Chamber. Steve Elder quietly shook the scene and made a rope-solo run on the northeast face in his typically classic style (he is also the only person known to have soloed Yocum Ridge in summer and winter). Nate Farr and Collin Bohannon found the stone cold icy northwest face of I-rock to their liking, and added to the spectrum of minimalist routes on that shaded side.

The north western portion of Oregon state has a great variety of rock bluff formations ranging from basalt to andesite, as well as a few minor andesitic bouldering opportunities which have boosted the sport of rock climbing in all aspects. A broad group of individuals from the 1960s onward took great interest in rock climbing near their home base whether that was Portland, Hood River or Government Camp. Each little core group, driven by team members in a closely knit, and sometimes exclusive enclave, set

Kim Krihfield at Horsethief Butte

6 INTRODUCTION ✦ NWOR

Portland Metro:
1. Broughton Bluff
2. Rocky Butte
3. Carver Bridge Cliff
4. Madrone Wall

Mt Hood Region:
5. French's Dome
6. Salmon River Slab
7. Hunchback
8. Enola
9. Kiwanis Crag
10. Illumination Rock
11. Razorblade Pinnacle
12. Mosquito Bluff
13. Lamberson Butte
14. Newton Pinnacle
15. Pete's Pile
16. Klinger Springs
17. Bulo Point
18. Area51
19. Collawash Cliff
20. Coethedral

Columbia Gorge:
21. Rooster Rock
22. Crown Point
23. Pillar of Hercules
24. St Peters Dome
25. Katanai Rock
26. Apocalypse Needles
27. Ozone Wall
28. Cigar Rock
29. Beacon Rock
30. Jimmy Cliff
31. Rock Creek Wall
32. Wind Mtn
33. Windy Slab
34. Wankers Column
35. OH8
36. Little Lyle Wall
37. Lyle Tunnel
38. Horsethief Butte
39. Monte Cristo Slab

Southwest Washington:
40. Chimney Rocks
41. Tower Rock
42. Shark Rock
43. Pinto Rock

North Santiam Region:
44. Thor's
45. Dog Tooth Rock
46. Needle Rock
47. Spire Rock
48. Breitenbush Ears

South Santiam Region:
49. Menagerie
50. Santiam Pinnacle
51. Iron Mtn Spire
52. Two Girls Mtn
53. Smokestack

Southern Willamette:
54. Wolf Rock
55. Skinner Butte
56. Moolack

Central Oregon:
57. Trout Creek
58. Smith Rock
59. Steins Pillar
60. Twin Pillar
61. Gothic Rock
62. Shepard Tower

Northeast Oregon:
63. Spring Mtn
64. The Dikes
65. High Valley
66. Burnt River
67. Hell's Canyon

new trends by exploring and establishing a string of fine climbing areas in this region that continues even to this day. Idealistic teams such as the legacy of Paul LaBarge and Jim Tripp have brought great little climbing sites like The Swine (Enola) to the forefront of regional climbing. Even the minor Misty Slab outcrop above French's Dome was rumored by Bob McGown to offer a nice 5.9 crack climb. Enticing rumors make it all a worthy hunt.

At French's Dome, climbers like Hermann Gollner, Vance Lemley, Pat Purcell, Tom Kingsland, and other coaches from the Mt Hood Summer Ski Camps found the dome perfect for their first ascent climbing purposes beginning in the late 1990s. Tymun Abbott and Dave Sowerby added a string of powerful quality routes during that same period. The Dark Side (aka The Siege) carries a unique bit of history. The route was bolted by Hermann who shortly later departed out of state. The route was cleaned and projected by Florjan Jagodic but he could not do it. Florjan, still eager to attain the first ascent on the route asked Hermann, who is a training master, "How to attain the 5.13 mark." Hermann said, "Just loose a few pounds." So, Florjan feverishly worked the route all the while dieting, but down south Hermann also got still stronger. As he subtly put it, "He surrounded the castle and starved him out," like a Seige. The next spring Hermann came back to work at the Ski School and sent it sometime in the late spring of 1997. But oddly enough, during the very same months a local Scotsman (Dave Sowerby) began working the project and also managed to free it. So the FFA saga, whoever might have sent it free still makes a great saga in classic European style.

Menagerie hardman Jim Anglin departed from the Sweet Home area for finer climes, and quickly took to helping with route development at Area51 in the year 2003. Paul Cousar and Kay Kucera, a team filled with virtually infinite energy, have taken giant steps from the years 2001-2005 to set Area51 and OH8 firmly on this regions climbing map. Their strong emphasis on biodiversity dynamics, user impact, and trail maintenance (as well as rock climbing) keep these sites readily accessible, while bringing various ethical awareness considerations to all visitors.

The Wolf Rock massif is an imposing feature subtly inviting to adventure climbers who like forging new routes. Wolf Rock saw a wide variety of climbers such as Gil Staender, John Barton, Nick Dodge and others forged climbs up the steep moss ravines of the north side during the '60s and early '70s. Yet it was Wayne Arrington, Mike Seeley who during a two-day effort that they established the classic Barad-Dûr route, punching a line through the improbable great roofs on the southeast face of Wolf in June 1972. The 1970s-'80s brought Dean Fry, John Barrar, Jeff Thomas, Doug Phillips and Jay Peterson to Wolf's south face scene where the rock was suitable to their taste, though still occasionally friable with runout sections. Wolf Rock continues to be popular, especially for those of us who are determined to walk in the footsteps of Mr. Arrington by repeating his great 900' long Barad-Dûr route. The monolith attained greater interest from a widely diversified generation of climbers who arrived on the scene from early 2000s onward to establish a stellar string of high quality bolt routes near the Conspicuous Arch. Some of those players were John Rich, the Fralick brothers, Jim Anglin, and Kent Benesch.

The Menagerie Wilderness climbing area offers an extensive selection of rock bluffs and spires, from an enjoyable mix of moderate climbs around Rooster Rock in the lower area, and the very bold spicy flavored climbs with plenty of serious leading endeavors in the upper Menagerie area on tuffaceous rhyolite formations. Rooster Tail was initially explored in 1949 by Bill Sloan and Byron Taylor. In the 1950s energetic climbers like Pat Callis and associates, quickly joined by the Bauman brothers starting in the early '60s the vertical edge trend of climbing at the Menagerie continued unabated well into the early 2000s. Tom and Bob Bauman are certainly the two most prolific Menagerie climbers who began exploring here, finding its steep spires and cliff formations an exhilarating worthy objective. The Bauman brothers were also highly instrumental toward encouraging the formation of this small Wilderness area. Pat Callis, Willi Unsoeld, Bob Ashworth, Eugene Dod, Jim Nieland, Dave Jensen, Wayne Arrington, and Jeff Thomas (Oregon Rock and Oregon High author) were a few of the contenders from the 1960s and onward. The Dod-Jensen-Pratt team succeeded in summiting on the infamous Turkey Monster spire in 1966. Pat Callis and Soren Norman teamed up the conquer the North Rabbit Ear in 1960, quickly followed by the Bauman brothers on the South Rabbit Ear in 1966. Jim Anglin teamed up with the Bauman brothers to establish a tremendous selection of additional climbs. Jim was certainly one of the primary players who helped place the Menagerie firmly on the modern rock climbing map. The Menagerie site is quite possibly the single most diverse (from quality to friable rock) place in the mid-western Cascades that has over 150 climbing routes on rock 40+ formations.

The central Cascade range of western Oregon have long been a suitable back door haunt for the OSU Mtn Club at the University in Corvallis. This club, initially founded by Willi Unsoeld and associates, became an energetic club where students could mix a bit of studies with the great outdoors. Members of the club explored and climbed a variety of spires in the Menagerie and Detroit areas and well beyond, often leaving a powerful climbing legacy in their own time.

Southern Willamette climbers such as Dave and Dee Tvedt, Mark Ashworth, Randy Rimby and the Fralick brothers enjoyed establishing climbs at Hills Creek Spires from 1995 onward. This odd cluster of steep tuffaceous volcanic spires lay perched on the south facing ridge crest slopes of Kitson Ridge near Oakridge, Oregon. Flagstone climbing site provides a tremendous selection of fine climbing opportunities on a steep slab of snow and ice polished densely compact fine-grained andesitic rock formation. Initially explored in the late 1970s, the site eventually experienced a surge of activity from the mid-1980s onward. Alan Amos, Walt Corvington, the Tvedt's, the Fralick brothers, and many other climbers helped establish the 70 odd fine quality slab climbs. The route Hydrotube (5.9) first climbed by Corvington and Amos in the late 1980s is certainly one of the great classic gems at Flagstone and likely to be one of your fist leads if you visit there.

Although this book details some of these fascinating old summit rock climbs, today's trend toward climbing on solid rock is beneficial to the sport, for it has opened a great new door to back forest rock climbing opportunities at excellent, high quality rock crags in a fresh air environment that benefits everyone.

Most climbers visiting these crags described in this book find great satisfaction visiting these quiet forested crags that are within a relatively easy 1-day outing from the city of Portland.

NW OREGON CLIMATE

The northwest U.S. has a temperate climate that receives an abundance of precipitation mainly because a warm subtropical air mass and a cold polar front jet stream air mass intermix producing variant seasonal changes in the climate. The Oregon climate west of the Cascade Range is predominantly wet for most of the year. Pacific marine air weather systems bring an abundance of rainfall that saturates the region, especially from late-October through May. Most rock climbers in northwest Oregon generally seek the local crags during the warm season (May through October). During this portion of the year mild marine air often mixes with inland Great Basin hot weather to bring a climber-friendly cycle that keeps the region quite comfortable.

During the summer months, temperatures will average in the seventies to mid eighties (Fahrenheit) with occasional short peaks of hot, sunny days in July and August reaching the nineties. Temperatures above 100°F are infrequent.

By late October, the Pacific marine air storm tracks become more active, usually bringing a consistent series of rain showers. The typical winter storm systems generate frequent cold, rainy days with average temperatures in the 35–50°F range. Infrequently, a severe storm track from the inland polar region may produce short periods of intense cold in the upper twenties to mid thirties east of the Cascade Range, but these brisk temperatures seldom penetrate into the valleys of western Oregon. Average annual precipitation in the Willamette Valley near Portland is about 40 inches; at times the winter weather is prohibitively wet. During these periods, many climbers seek the refuge of a local rock gym or sports gym for fitness continuity.

Lower elevation (3,000' to 4,000') rock climbing sites west or east of the Cascade mountain range such as French's Dome or Pete's Pile are usually accessible as early as mid-May through October. Expect heavy snow pack to hinder easy access to high-altitude (5,000' to 6,000') pinnacles or climbing sites such as Lamberson Butte or Needle Rock until mid-July.

Certain summits like Illumination Rock offer winter mixed alpine climbing opportunities which yields a year-round opportunity for those dedicated to the extreme sport of rime ice climbing. In spite of regional rain showers, the spires and cliffs generally dry out quickly during the seasonally mild May through October temperatures.

POLAR JET STREAM

The polar jet stream gradually descends southward each month in the Fall and Winter; Ketchikan Alaska in October, near Vancouver, British Columbia in November, Astoria in December, and Eureka, California in January.

When this jet stream develops a sharp southward swing over the mid-continent some of this Arctic cold air mass will pour over the Cascades from the east (and through the Columbia Gorge). Initially is produces a mix of snow or freezing rain, but if the Arctic air mass if strong enough it can provide a term of intense cold (20° F – 30° F) but otherwise sunny weather in the Columbia Gorge and slightly warmer temperatures in the northern Willamette Valley. A Gorge wind chill factor (30+ mph) increases the sense of cold and assists in distributing water droplets on cliff scarps that freeze quickly in two to three days. Local ice climbers usually will closely watch for this weather pattern.

TRIP PLANNING

How does this data break down for quick use by a rock climber? If it is not raining, go climbing. Is the forecast on the west side of the Cascades predicting gray skies and showery conditions in May and June? Then consider driving to an east side destination where you can often find sunnier skies and certainly less rain than the west side climbing sites.

Unique places such as Pete's Pile or the remote well-concealed Bulo Point climbing crag make great drier climbing destinations because of the effect of the rain shadow created by the Cascade mountain range. In essence, your visit to east side climbing destinations for rock climbing opportunities is sure to be a success, although during summer thunderstorm activity can develop rapidly along the eastern slope of the High Cascades on a hot summer afternoon.

GEOLOGY OF NW OREGON

A formative discussion on the physical geology and natural processes of rock structures is beneficial to all climbers by providing a better understanding of the cliffs and mountains we climb on. This analysis is a brief summary of Plate Tectonics and continental volcanism designed to enhance your understanding of localized geologic characteristics of rock stratum and lava formation.

PLATE TECTONICS

The geological landscape of Oregon, like a thin fabric has been stretched and reshaped by continental and oceanic movements described systematically as Plate Tectonics. This diverse region of volcanic activity is structurally composed of igneous, sedimentary, and metamorphic rock formations creating an interwoven and complex matrix. Though our lowlands and valleys of northwestern Oregon (including the northern Coast Range) are commonly formed of sedimentary rock, much of the Cascade Mountain Range is built on multiple layers of basalt (~50% silica), andesite (~60% silica), some dacite, and infrequent formations of welded tuff rhyolite (~70%+ silica) stratum such as Steins Pillar.

The lithosphere between the upper plates and the earth's mantle moves in relation to deep ocean volcanism, while the oceanic and continental plates ride piggyback on top. Plate tectonics gradually shift and build all rock formations into similarly understandable patterns and concepts.

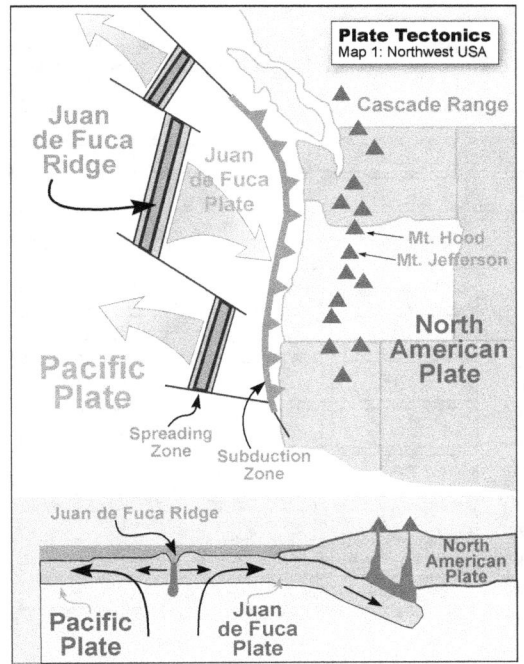

The thicker continental plate is composed of very old granitic stock surrounded by younger uplifted sediment, and when it collides with the offshore oceanic crustal plate the heavier (denser) plate is subducted beneath the former. Some of the compositionally lighter weight sedimentary rocks (oceanic & continental) that are subducted back down into the earths mantle will melt and remix with the magma pool or core, then rise as infrequent magma intrusions through fissures or fault lines in the continental crust. Most oceanic seafloor sediment accumulates from organic marine animals and plants, as well as from terrigenous (land) or submarine volcanic sources. If the magma congeals underground it is referred to as intrusive igneous rock in the form of dikes, sills or batholiths, but when the magma erupts volcanically through breaks or fissures in the earths surface it is known as extrusive igneous volcanism.

When the magma breaks the continental crust they are observable as volcanic vent openings which can develop into mountains that expel material composed of lava flows, flood basalts, lava domes, explosive pumice, ash or tuff clouds, and debris formations. This offshore fault line subduction zone folds and warps the sedimentary perimeter continental landscape creating our coastal range. These coastal foothills of sedimentary rock are folded and uplifted by the oceanic plate to form the low profile Coast Mountain range.

Certain mountain ranges such as the Olympics in Washington state are created less by volcanism and more by the ongoing tectonic folding and faulting process. The northern Cascade Mountain range of Oregon has a series of major strato-volcanoes (i.e. Mt. Hood, Mt. Jefferson) but also shield volcanoes (Newberry Crater in central Oregon) and numerous smaller cinder cones such as Olallie Butte.

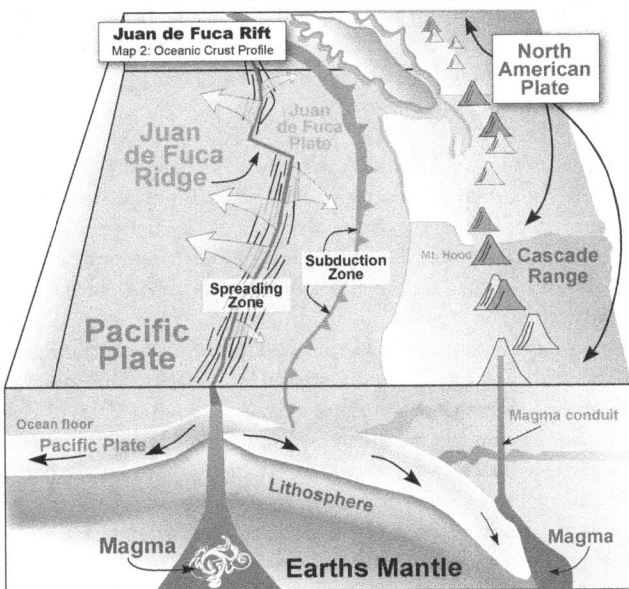

THREE TYPES OF ROCK

Igneous rock formations are classified geologically into three main groups to emphasize the mode of origin: igneous, metamorphic, and sedimentary.

Intrusive or plutonic rock forms as magma migrates upward from Earth's mantle, but cools and solidifies slowly at depth to form subsurface rock masses. Extrusive volcanic rock forms when the magma breaks out upon the Earth's surface and cools quickly. The principal forms of hardened extrusive igneous rock are basalt, andesite, dacite, and rhyolite, while intrusive igneous magma congeals below the surface slowly to form granite, diorite, and gabbro.

Metamorphic rock is formed when deeply buried, then folded and compressed by stresses, high temperatures, and chemical conditions. Sedimentary rocks are formed by processes that are active at the earth's surface. These are usually formed by erosion, decay, breakdown of other rock material, or an accumulation or buildup of rock, shells, or corals that over time are compacted and hardened to form sedimentary rocks. Examples are limestone, gypsum, flint, conglomerate, sandstone, and shale.

Igneous Rock Classifications				
	Felsic	Intermediate	Mafic	Ultramafic
Fine Grain	Rhyolite	Andesite	Basalt	
Intermediate		Dacite	Diabase	
Course Grain	Granite	Diorite	Gabbro	Peridotite
Glassy	Obsidian			
Frothy	Pumice		Scoria	

SiO_2 Content	Magma Type	Volcanic Rock
~50%	Mafic	Basalt
~60%	Intermediate	Andesite
~65%	Felsic (low Si)	Dacite
~70%	Felsic (high Si)	Rhyolite

Most magmas are composed of ten elements: Oxygen (O), silicon (Si), aluminum (Al), iron (Fe), magnesium (Mg), titanium (Ti) calcium (Ca), sodium (Na), potassium (K), and phosphorous (P). Oxygen and silicon are by far the two most abundant elements, thus for clarity the different magma types are described by their silica content (SiO_2).

The primary factors affecting the melting ratio of rock structures are water (volatiles), changes in pressure, and heat. Partial melting occurs when the rocks melting point breaks down certain silica-rich minerals first, then stops the process by a shift or change in parameters. As magma cools and solidifies two groups of silicate mineral elements form; dark and light silicates.

Dark silicates are rich in iron and magnesium (prevalent in olivine, pyroxene, amphibole, biotite, garnet), and light silicates are rich in potassium, sodium, and calcium (prevalent in quartz, muscovite, feldspar). The formation of dark or ferromagnesian basaltic (mafic) magma is composed from dry, silica-poor ultramafic rock of the Earth's upper mantle peridotite, which contains mostly olivine and pyroxene. Ultramafic rock is uncommon at Earth's surface, but is thought to be the primary constituent of the upper mantle. Light granitic (felsic) magma is likely composed from the crystallization of silica-rich andesitic magma or continental rocks.

BORING LAVA FORMATION

The low silica basalt lava cliff formations in and around Portland were deposited from a flow called the Boring Lava Flow. Prominent hills such as Mount Scott, Mount Tabor, Rocky Butte, Chamberlain Hill, and buttes near the town of Boring are cinder cone volcanoes part of the Boring Lava Field formation which generally deposited cinder, ash and lava flows. Larch Mountain, further to the east is a shield volcano which allowed for fluid lava to travel along a gentle gradient slope to deposit alternating layers of basalt and debris.

The degree to which the Boring Lava formation congealed resulted in deep layers of compact basalt with broad smooth surfaces with widely-spaced generally vertical joint cracks. The flow was deposited upon the Troutdale Conglomerate formation, a mixture of well-rounded pebbles of water transported volcanic material. The slope below the north face of Broughton Bluff reveals some of this layer of pebbled product. Thick sheets of this low silica basaltic lava flow also exist on Mount Sylvania, as well as near Oregon City. Broughton bluff, Carver cliff, and Madrone wall are part of this extensive formation. Surface color striations, such as at the Madrone Wall show a distinctly golden-tan undertone with a smattering of artistic yellowish-brown, red, orange, and gray painted upon the surface of the rock cliff caused from iron oxidation interaction with water.

COLUMBIA GORGE BASALT GROUP

Highly fluid dense black magma erupted as flood basalts during the middle Miocene Epoch in southeast Washington and northeastern Oregon. These very active flows traveled laterally for hundreds of miles eventually covering extensive portions of southeast Washington and much of eastern Oregon. The cumulative effect of the CGBG deposited lava formation varies from 2,000' thick to a thickness in excess of 5,000' near Tri-Cities. This basalt formation, when deposited congealed quickly to form dense dark-colored 6-, 5-, 4-sided vertically oriented polygonal structured columns (6 inches to 2 feet in diameter) of dark colored basalt capped with an entablature on top of each flow. Each individual lava flow has congealed in distinct layers commonly 40' to 200' thick and is readily visible on numerous cliffs throughout the Columbia River Gorge and eastward to Wallula Gap, the lower Palouse River, and the channeled scablands of central Washington. The largest of these flood basalts formations is known as the Grande Ronde flow.

The cliffs in the Gorge near Yeon Mountain reveal well over 2,000 feet of horizontal layered bands of this basalt flow, bringing beauty and rugged harmony to this scenic area. The vertical beauty of the Gorge terrain was enhanced by Columbia River erosion processes, by multiple Missoula Flood inundations, and a gradual uplift of the Cascade Range. Although some rock climbing is possible on these flood basalt formations (such as Horsethief Butte) the nature of the narrow columnar rock formations, decomposition, and weathering processes tends to limit rock climber interest.

The outstanding exception in the gorge of course is Beacon Rock, an old volcanic neck core that is the second largest monolith in the world after the Rock of Gibralter. The volcano, originally erupted and built in a distant Epoch was weathered by erosional processes and flood waters of ancient Lake Missoula, leaving this prominent remnant core neck in the central Gorge. The 848-foot high monolith is composed of a medium-colored, vesicular andesite and is steeply featured on all sides. On the south face massive vertically-jointed columns make this site a perfect haven for skilled rock climbing enthusiasts. Today, the mile-long zigzag trail leading to the top of Beacon provides hikers with one of the finest panoramic views of the Columbia River Gorge.

CASCADIAN MOUNTAINS

The Cascade range is formed from these active plate tectonic movements and typically align roughly parallel to the general off-shore descending oceanic plate. Andesite and basalt formations are common in the northern part of the High Cascades while rhyolite, andesite, and basalt formations surface south of the Three Sisters peaks.

The northern Oregon coastline rock formation, though often sedimentary in nature has prominent headland basalt formations as well. The impressive mass of Onion Peak near Nehalem (including Saddle Mtn. and Humbug Mtn.) is an intrusive body of submarine pillow basalt. North of Mt Hebo old flows, tuffs, and breccia formations are common in the hills, while the central Oregon Coast Range south from Mt Hebo reveals a greater percentage of sandstone formations. The crest of certain prominent peaks west of Salem, Corvallis and Eugene have gabbro, diorite, syenite and basalt caps. These usually formed as dikes or sills and have eroded into minor rock outcrops and an occasional boulderfield some of which is viable for climbing. The southern Oregon Coast range has a large percentage of volcanic

Hugh climbing at Trillium

and sedimentary seafloor uplifted rock formations strongly metamorphosed into schist, sandstone, serpentine, some limestone, and in the Klamath Mountains outcrops of granite.

CASCADE MOUNTAIN RANGE

The Cascade Mountain range can be structurally divided into two north-south oriented regional masses; the older or Western range which have low hills near 1700' at the western margin and 5800' near the eastern margin, and the presently existing High Cascades with 10,000'+ tall peaks. The High Cascade formation contains the series of peaks climbers often ascend, such as Mt. Hood, Mt. Jefferson, 3-Sisters, etc.

The volcanic history of the Cascades can be sub-divided further into three general building phases: a coastline Klamath-Blues-Wallowas lineament, the Western Cascade gradient, and the High Cascade fault zone lineament.

The original phase of volcanic activity began during the Eocene Epoch built a mountain chain from the Klamath's to the Wallowas, including the Ochoco Mountain remnant in central Oregon. Once completed sometime in the Pliocene Epoch most of this series of very old coastal range (prior to the existence of the Willamette Valley) produced major granitic peak formations on a scale rarely seen since in Oregon.

After considerable inactivity, the next eruptive phase in the Miocene Epoch produced the old Western Cascade mountain range, some of which fell as ash-tuff deposits in Central Oregon of which the John Day ash formation is a primary example.

This Western range of mountains gradually reduced in size through weathering and glacial processes, now look like mere foothills or ridge crests cut by deep ravines nearly lacking in visible summits showing volcanic origin. But the evidence is in the rocks.

Oregon's northwestern Cascade province are separated by three major river drainage valleys; the Clackamas River, the Santiam Rivers, and the McKenzie River. This diverse region is a heavily forested eco-system that lies entirely below timberline, but do occasionally provide sub-alpine craggy peaks and pinnacles, thin-soiled steep slopes covered with Bear-grass (Xerophyllum tenax) and beautiful scenic views. Some of the low foothills southeast of Stayton and south past Eugene are composed of tuffaceous sandstone, rhyolite and basalt formations.

Our present High Cascade skyline is the result of relatively recent Pliestocene Epoch activity in the timeline of eruptive cyclical volcanism. Initially, this final eruptive phase produced Shield or low-profile mountains. Belknap Crater and Newberry Crater are several classic examples of low-profile shield volcanoes that produced much cindery tuffaceous material, including high silica content obsidian flows.

Soon the conical stratovolcanoes built much larger (and taller) andesitic-dacitic mountains intermixed with basalt lava flows as well as considerable tuff ash fall deposits. Several late stage High Cascade volcanoes have produced some rhyolite, but this is usually found south of the 3-Sisters region, while Andesite formations are commonly found in the northern part. The southern Oregon volcanoes seem to be using a silica-rich but water-poor coastal subduction material which is remixed with magma and resurfaced as light-colored rhyolite-andesite lava.

Rhyolitic volcanism can be violently explosive though. Mt. Mazama, our present day water filled Crater Lake is an example of an old rhyolitic volcano that was comprised of sufficient quantities of water and gasses to produce a highly explosive tuff explosion.

MISSOULA FLOODS

Broughton Bluff and even Rocky Butte Quarry were partially exposed by dramatic erosional processes of the Missoula Flood (see J. Harlen Bretz papers 1923, 1925, & 1956) which scoured the Columbia River Gorge and east side regions with 400' to 1000' high inundations of flood waters emanating originally from near the northeastern Idaho-Montana border. These flood waters occurred during the last Ice Age when lobes or tongues of the Cordilleran Ice Sheet extended across the Clark Fork River drainage channel blocking and forming the infamous Lake Missoula in western Montana. The ice dam broke repeatedly sending powerful forces of water moving abruptly southwestward along the river system all the way to the Pacific Ocean.

Fine examples of the effects of this flood are Lake Pend Orielle, the channeled Scablands, Grand Coulee, and the steeply scoured walls of the Columbia River Gorge. Numerous large erratic boulders rafted on icebergs were left scattered along the entire route and in the northern Willamette Valley.

The Sandy River carved additional steepness into Broughton Bluff, while erosional processes on the Clackamas River exposed the mighty cliffs of the Madrone Wall and Carver Bridge Cliff.

GEOLOGIC NATURE OF VARIOUS CLIMBING SITES

Mt. Hood volcanism is composed of andesitic rock with medium silicon content 57-62% (SiO_2) mostly in the nature of lava flows, domes and pyroclastic deposits. The south debris slope fan from Crater Rock (a hornblende dacite dome) down past Timberline Lodge is composed mostly of dacite and andesite debris material. Illumination Rock and Steele Cliffs are andesite flows that congealed abruptly due to surrounding abstract terrain movement limitations. Mt. Hood is a composite or stratovolcano which has alternating layers of lava flows and pyroclastic deposits.

French's Dome is a fine example of a late stage 'plug' dome neck core of an old volcano that was likely a 'satellite' vent of the larger very old Sandy Glacier Volcano on the west flank of Mt. Hood. The ancient flows of this volcano exist below the Sandy River Glacier at the 1,650 meter elevation as a narrow profile dike or core composed of olivine andesite lava. Additional satellite vents are the Pinnacle and Cloud Cap.

The andesite lava of Enola (the Swinery) east of Rhododendron is a moderately porphyritic (58.7% SiO_2) formation.

The Pete's Pile bluff is a widely joint-spaced 60-meter high columnar andesite formation that is a moderately porphyritic lava flow exposed on the east canyon wall of East Fork Hood River near Polallie Creek. The bluff was exposed by the effects of avalanche flood debris and river cutting forces from Mt. Hood eruptive volcanic cycles. Compositionally the Pete's Pile bluff has an abundance of 2-3mm blocky plagioclase phenocrysts of silicate mineral (5-10%) with traces of olivine and amphibole in a dense medium-gray colored groundmass.

Porphyritic andesite with various sized phenocryst minerals in a dense mesocratic matrix of medium gray to light gray colored rock are quite common in the northern part of the state. The Cascade mountain geographic zone experiences a continuous cycle of seasonal hot and cold temperate fluctuations that strongly influence the process of mechanical and chemical weathering.

At Bulo Point chemically active water solutions increased the process of granular decomposition of the superficial structures. Rock formations in the 15-mile creek watershed are

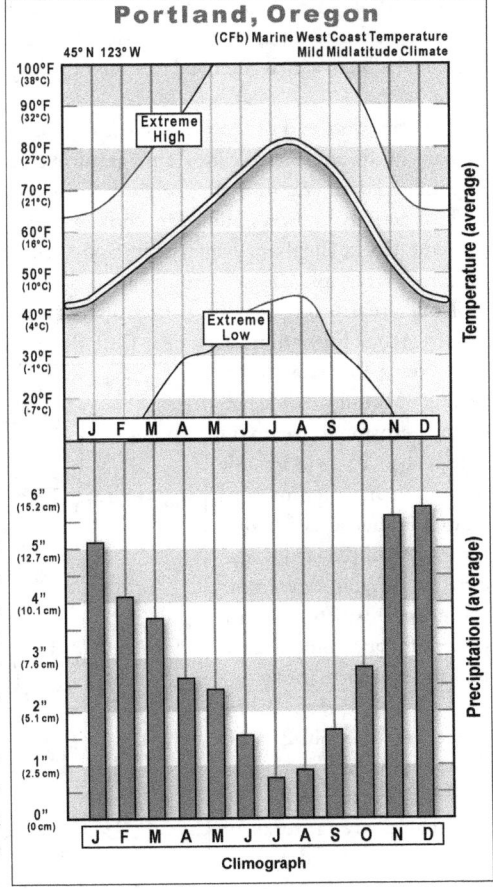
Climograph

porphyritic silicic andesite (62.6% SiO_2) in a blocky plagioclase phenocryst matrix of light and dark-colored minerals. The Bulo Point formation is likely an extrusive lava flow or intrusive near-surface sill later exposed through erosional processes that removed the less resilient layers. A steady weathering process from water, heat and other factors gradually rounded the overall cliff features. Bulo Point has a course-grained surface texture akin to a particularly rough grade of sandpaper that increases friction ability so long as you are careful with how you jam your fingers or fists into rough-edged cracks.

Crown Point is a CGBG flood basalt formation with some conglomerate and Boring Lava formations at the top near Vista House.

Skinner Butte is polygonal sided steeply oriented columnar course-grained basalt that formed from a congealed near-surface intrusive flow and is likely a laccolith (the tip of a larger batholith) that is weathered erosionally along with limited quarrying activity.

Spire Rock and X-Spire, which are located near Triangulation Peak east of Detroit, Oregon are likely old basalt volcanic necks or feeder vents of resilient rock that resisted erosional effects which removed the surrounding softer landscape.

At the west end of Detroit Lake is a small granitic stock or core of an ancient volcano. This granitic structure about one mile in diameter near the dam was formed by subsurface magma activity and crystallized by cooling slowly at great depth. The summits above Tumble Lake (Needle Rock, Elephant Rock, Split Spire, Tumble Rock) are likely fissures or vents from a deep volcanic formation. These summits are basaltic formations heavily weathered by the elements, but still offer reasonably massive outcrop structures ideal for adventure climbers. Other subsurface granitic stock formations exist near Blue River on the McKenzie and near Leaburg Dam.

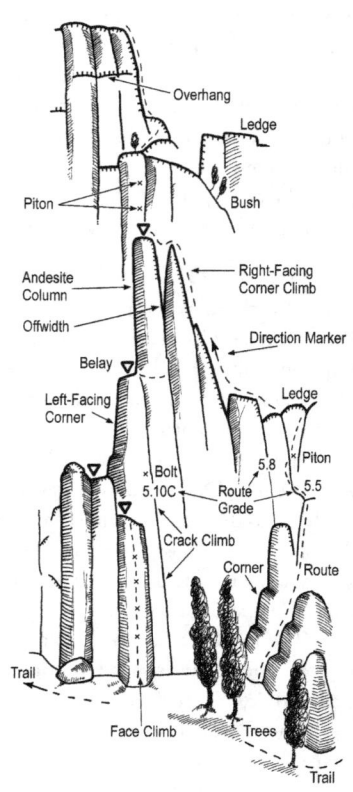

Steins Pillar is an imposing 350' tall (with a 120' girth) erosional remnant composed of moderately welded tuff (ignimbrite) from hot pyroclastic flows typically vented from dacite or rhyolite volcanic ash eruptions. This natural pillar of light-colored rock and the two formations immediately to the south are silicic (65%+ SiO_2) tuff flow remnants from the John Day Formation.

There are a total of three distinct banding col-

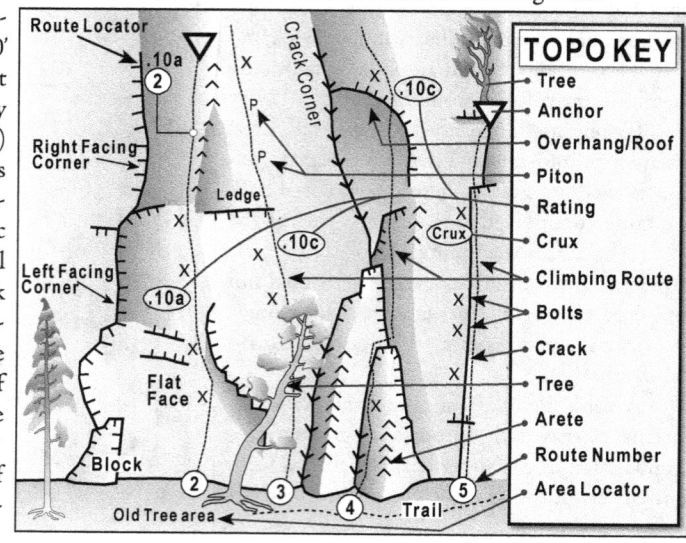

orations due to three violent eruptive volcanic phases of silica-rich hot pumice fragments, ash, and glass shards built upon the other is short succession. Nearby buttes such as Forked Horn Butte are the likely former sources of these eruption cycles. Each distinct layer of the ash eruption was still hot when the next eruptive phase deposited additional frothy fragments. The pumice, readily altered by compression, heat, and chemical agglutination, flattened the fragments and gaseous pockets, thus cementing the crystaline ash elements together. Steins Pillar is capped with a weathering-resistant fourth layer of reddish hardened ash giving the spire a pronounced steeply overhung feature. The pillar walls have a notable hardened yellow-brown stain from the oxidation process of iron bearing minerals in the tuff.

If you are looking for big granite alpine spires Oregon is not the place. The sand dunes on the Oregon coast are closer to Portland than the nearest outcrop of pure granite. But, Silver Star Mtn does have some granodiorite related formations in the 3,500'-4,500' elevation, such as Chimney Rocks.

CLIMBING ROUTE RATINGS

This guide uses the well-known Yosemite Decimal System (YDS) as the standard method for rating rock climbs. This system, first developed at Tahquitz in the 1950s, is a two-system concept connecting a Difficulty Grade and a Free Climbing Class.

Difficulty Grades

A Difficulty Grade (Roman numerals I through VI) indicates how long it will take to climb a route and is determined by the difficulty, the involvement, and the length of a route. For example:

- Grade I   Can be climbed in a few hours.
- Grade II   Can be climbed in a half day or less.
- Grade III   Can be done in less than a day.
- Grade IV   One long, hard day. Hardest pitch is no less than 5.7 in free climbing difficulty.
- Grade V   In one long day if the climbers are experienced and fast, otherwise 1½ days plus should be expected while the hardest pitch is usually at least a 5.8 difficulty.
- Grade VI   Requires multiple days to ascend and often includes extreme mixed free climbing and/or difficult nailing.

The Yosemite Decimal System concept, though designed to assist, is highly subjective and will vary from area to area. Some climbers may be able to climb very efficiently on two Grade IV routes while others may barely manage a Grade II without bivouacking. Most of the climbs found in this guide are Grade III or less in difficulty.

Free Climbing Difficulty Class

The Free Climbing Difficulty Class is based on an ascending scale from 1 to 5 and is then subdivided into an open-ended scale from 5.0 to 5.14 and beyond. This scale is designed to reflect the hardest free move on a pitch or the overall sustained character of the pitch. See the graph in Appendix B for detailed comparisons with other international ratings.

This open-ended scale allows for future routes of increasing difficulty. If a particular pitch contains a series of moves of the same difficulty, a higher rating is usually assigned. Further sub-grading separates the easier 5.10s from the harder 5.10s by using the letters A, B, C and D (or as .10- and .10+). Some free-climbing routes at the local crags are underrated due to top-roping before leading. The best solution is to rate the climb according to an on-sight lead by a climber unfamiliar with the route in question.

Aid Climbing Difficulty

The art of modern nailing, Aid Climbing Difficulty or Class 6, is quite unlike its neighbor mentioned above. Both the technical severity of the piton or pro (protection) placement and the climber's security are linked to the same rating. In the sport of nailing, the letter A indicates aid climbing, while the number, (0 through 6 and higher), indicates the degree of nailing. The letter

C indicates that it can be ascended clean without the need for pitons or other gear driven with a hammer. All of Class 6 aid climbing uses equipment as the means for progressing up the rock scarp to a higher point.

- **A0** Pendulum, shoulder stand, tension rest, or a quick move up by pulling on protection.
- **A1** Solid equipment placements.
- **A2** Is more difficult to place but offers some good protection.
- **A3** Involves marginal placements and the potential for a short fall.
- **A4** Frequent marginal placements; will only hold body weight.
- **A5** Pro supports body weight only; risk of 50-foot-plus fall.
- **A6** Involves full pitch leads of A-4 and serious ground fall potential.

Modern nailing equipment has profoundly changed the way in which climbers approach a prospective route. Knifeblades, RURPs, Bird Beaks, and a variety of hooks and ultrathin wires offer new ways to aid climb at the extreme edge. Since free climbs are often maintained as free climbs, certainly some nailing routes should be maintained as nailing routes.

For those routes requiring a "seriousness" rating, they are as follows:

- **PG**: Protection may be adequate near the difficult sections, yet involve risky or runout sections which can increase the potential for an accident.
- **R**: A bold lead with a serious fall potential; may involve questionable or poor protection; serious injury is likely.
- **X**: Involves high risk of ground fall potential; very poor to no protection available; serious or fatal injury possible.
- **TR**: Indicates the route is generally a top-rope climb, although the climb may have been free climbed in the past.

The climbing difficulty class rating listed in this guide is not an absolute. All climbing routes are subject to unforeseen challenges that can quickly make the climb inherently dangerous.

Confidence, ability, intuition, and good judgment are crucial for managing the degree of risk that you and your climbing partner are willing to accept. Develop those invaluable skills so that you can foresee your risks or liabilities, because careless judgment becomes a harsh learning curve. Proceed with caution; climb at your own risk!

The "Star" or Quality Rating used throughout this book is designed to help climbers selectively choose the more aesthetic climbs. This is a highly subjective system, for many of the un-starred routes are worthy of attention. Do seek out the lesser-known climbs, especially if you have an extra hour.

- **No Stars**: An average route.
- **One Star** (★): Good quality route, better than the usual.
- **Two Stars** (★★): Excellent route, good position with quality rock climbing, a highly recommended route.
- **Three Stars** (★★★): Superb position, a classic line on excellent rock, a must-do route on everyones list.

Of these starred routes, not all will be bolted face climbs. Some will be crack climbs, several will be short but worthy, and a few will be two routes connected together making an even better classic climb.

The star ratings for a climb at Broughton Bluff will vary from the quality routes at Beacon Rock or Smith Rock as they represent the favorable, interesting routes at that particular cliff.

EQUIPMENT AND SPECIALIZED GEAR

Both personal safety and your quality of enjoyment depend on your being adequately prepared with the appropriate gear when rock climbing at the crags. Essential equipment such as locking carabiners, belay-rappel devices, and even double ropes will help to ensure that your outing is a successful one.

In recent years, climbers have seen quality improvements in rock climbing equipment, both innovative and beneficial to the sport. Standard rock gear protection ("pro") such as spring-loaded camming devices (Camalots, Friends, TCUs, etc.), HBs, RPs, curved wired stoppers (I often refer to these as wires), bolts, and tailored rock shoes have contributed greatly to climbers' overall safety and climbing enjoyment . The following gear recommendations should be used as a broad list from which you can generally determine your needs for a specific climb. Gear sizes appear under each route name as a guideline, but choose your gear by analyzing your skills and needs for each rock climb *before* ascending it. Ask other climbers what they may have used for route protection, and be willing to take extra equipment and perhaps even larger-sized gear.

For traditional free climbing you will likely need a variety of the following gear: A single 60-meter rope, helmet, a set of 12–15 quick draws (QDs), wired stoppers up to 1½ inches, small camming devices like TCUs up to 1½ inches, and larger spring-loaded camming devices ranging from 1–4 inches.

It is wise to bring extra slings as well as some of the big stuff like Hexcentrics or Big Bro, especially if a particularly fine off-width crack is your challenge. Tiny specialized pro (like HBs, RPs, or Steel Nuts) may be useful on a few of the desperately thin routes.

You are likely to need a rock hammer and a selection of pitons (Lost Arrows, Knifeblades, angles, etc.) for ascending some of the spires or pinnacles described in this guidebook.

For the climbing enthusiast who needs the latest new gear products (or even quality used equipment) there are many sources available that offer competitive prices.

Remember, wherever you climb, always exercise good judgment before and during the climb. Practice route analysis, ask for consultation and advice from others, develop foresight, and when you begin your ascent, climb with a reasonable degree of caution, fully aware of the risks of this sport!

WILDERNESS ETHICS & RESOURCE MAPS

When traveling into the wild areas of Northwest Oregon always strive for a minimal form of impact travel, using good judgement skills, and wilderness values. Just a short distance from our homes we have a vast and diverse ecosystem in a unique temperate rain forest climate. Forest management agencies have readily available information that promote resource concepts such as backcountry preparation and safety, leave no trace (LNT) ethic, and other guidelines useful for wilderness travel. Analysis, consultation, foresight, and preparation are wise steps that should be taken before you venture into wilderness areas.

If you are planning to travel into the wilderness or other back country areas, a wide variety of invaluable maps are available concerning your area of exploration. Some of these are national forest maps, topographic maps (USGS or private source), or the highly useful digital maps now available on a CD disk.

ABOUT THIS GUIDEBOOK

This books goal is to educate users about long-term stewardship of our natural resources we enjoy climbing upon. Our purpose is to provide information that will help influence rock climbing for the public good. This material helps teach us where to park our vehicle, seeks to identify the proper trail to the crag (avoiding a braided network of shortcuts), informs you if the site is not suitable for large groups (or if there is a USFS memorandum effecting groups), explains regulations such as seasonal raptor/flora closures, suggests where overnight camping options may exist, and points out basic community and emergency services at nearby towns.

This guidebook aims to give insight about the nuances of each different climbing site, route development limitations (cliff top vegetation, LNT ethics, bolting and anchors), private property or ownership issues, discuss issues that effect access by providing a written communication bridge to rock climbers in the hopes of eliminating or reducing potential friction with area residents, and encourages users to become involved in trail maintenance and other crag stewardship opportunities. This book reminds climbers about showing respect for a neighbor or owner of private land, about being visitors on various public utility based lands, and about being courteous when using leased or owned timber entity lands where multi-use access is allowed. On state or federally managed lands, you are not merely a visitor, but a valued partaker with an interest in how these public lands are being managed.

We aim to broaden user interest throughout the entire region, avoiding overuse of any one single area, seeking results that bring beneficial tourism-based stimulus to our local economies. This book is all about creating a good public resource that will be helpful toward preserving access in both public and private venues, and brings crucial reference material forward for public officials, and is highly useful with emergency response agencies for developing emergency rescue or evacuation plans.

In summation: "...the essential self-interest of any person, or nation, is not what he/she takes away from life, but what that persons developed talents give to humanity at large."

West Side Climbing Opportunities

CHAPTER 1

MT. HOOD REGIONAL CLIMBS

Mt. Hood is a picture perfect jewel and a dominant feature of our northern Oregon Cascade mountain range. This mountain is the states highest summit, and also the states most frequently climbed peak.

Surrounding this majestic mountain is a forested landscape which provides local rock climbers with a multitude of opportunities from extreme precipitous pinnacles to quiet enjoyable wooded crags. This extensive variety of high altitude and sub-alpine climbing destinations along the Mt. Hood scenic highway corridor provides a virtual year-round source for exceptional outdoor adventure of inherent value. These rock climbing sites encompass a well-established core selection of regional favorites you are certain to find rewarding.

Your Gateway to Adventure

This chapter details a variety of fine rock climbing sites beginning near ZigZag, Oregon along the smaller tributary forks of the Sandy River, Salmon River, with highlights about the wild routes on Illumination Rock.

FRENCH'S DOME

Though tiny in comparison to many crags, the merits of French's Dome should not be overlooked. Many Portland area rock climbers have discovered that this miniature crag's rare qualities give it an enduring appeal. A visit to French's is sure to spark your enthusiasm, as well.

This unique and easily accessible dome of rock lies amongst a tall canopy of evergreen trees along the lower west side of Mt. Hood. There are at least a dozen climbing routes available ranging from 5.6 to 5.12. Most of the climbs are fixed with bolts, practically eliminating the need for natural protection. The overall height is 160 feet from the longest side and 80 feet on the road face.

The dome itself is not visible above the forest of Douglas fir trees, but it is just a short, one-minute walk to the crag. French's Dome is an interesting geological wonder of the Oregon woods and a perfect little area to escape from the city. Misty Slab is the visible sloping buttress of rock located 40 minutes uphill from French's, yet because of the approach, ascents there have been kept to a minimum.

The Dome seemed to languish for years after the initial four original routes were established. In the 1980s local summer ski school coaches became enthralled by the place and sought to establish a string of new routes that has literally set the place on edge. Hermann Gollner, Vance Lemley, Pat Purcell, Tom Sell, John Rust, Joe Reis, Tymun Abbott and Dave Sowerby put considerable time into cleaning and establishing the 5.11/.12 grade at the Dome. Their route development energy helped tremendously to make the Dome a premier climbing destination in the Mt. Hood National Forest.

Effective erosion control platforms have been built along the cliff base of French's Dome providing a long-term solution to a hillside that had been rapidly sliding away. With Forest Service trail building guidance and a volunteer workforce locals have built a legacy that will keep this place a perfect little Mt. Hood gem!

The routes at French's Dome are de-

scribed symmetrically clock-wise, which you will find quite beneficial because the trail first encounters the crag at the routes facing the road. Beginning with the road face the list shown below details each rock climb as if you were to descend the perimeter trail around the crag to the left from the road face. Then from the lowest portion of the Dome the routes are described uphill ending with the Yellow Brick Road route as the last climb to be mentioned.

French's Dome is composed of olivine basalt and is a tall remnant of an old volcanic neck core after the surrounding softer material eroded away exposing the rock knob.

Directions

Drive east from Gresham/Portland on U.S. Hwy 26. Continue through Sandy, Oregon until you are near the small community of Zigzag at the base of Mt. Hood. Turn north on the Lolo Pass Road. The crag is located 6¼ miles up the Lolo Pass road (NF 18) from its junction with U.S. Hwy 26 at Zigzag. Look for an unobtrusive dirt pullout on the right and the NW Forest Pass sign. A vehicle parking pass is required for all users at this site. You can obtain a daily or annual Northwest Forest Pass parking permit at their office in the small community of Zigzag.

Since French's is literally a giant round spherical dome you can always find a way to be climbing in the shade, especially if you are a .12 climber. This site is encapsulated deep within a substantial green forest so there is generally no need for sunscreen lotion here, unless you plan to have lunch at the summit anchor. French's Dome is a sport crag haven because the nature of the rock (crackless) lends itself to bolt protected climbing.

The routes in this section are numbered according to a descent made clockwise to the left from the road face area to the lowest portion of the Dome, and up the south side on the perimeter trail.

1. High Voltage (aka Rhoid Rage) 5.12 b ★★
Length: 60' (18m), Pro: 5 QD's
This line lies a few feet immediately right of the Road Face climb. The steepest hung route at French's, with large edges and sidepulls, pumpy climbing that leads up to a big overhung bouldery crux bulge that ends on a final finishing jug. A very good climb.

2. Road Face 5.12a ★★★
Length: 60' (18m), Pro: 6 QD's
Classic route, originally an aid line, but now a popular free climb. The route involves a moderate variety of powerful thin crimp movement, a full shake hold out at mid-height, followed by some stout movement at a crux overhanging bulge section near the top just below the belay.

3. Road Kill 5.12a ★★
Length: 60' (18m), Pro: 5 QD's
Techy slightly overhung face climb. This is the upper direct finish from Road Rage that leads up to its own separate anchor. Where RR moves left at the jug, Road Kill goes up and right slightly.

4. Road Rage 5.12a ★★
Length: 60' (18m), Pro: 5 QD's
Climb the first 2 bolts

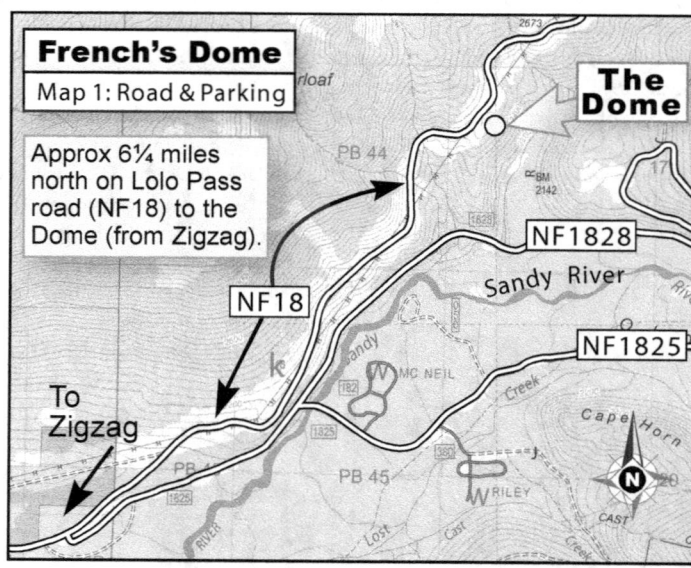

French's Dome
Map 1: Road & Parking

Approx 6¼ miles north on Lolo Pass road (NF18) to the Dome (from Zigzag).

then traverse left and continue up.

5. **BSD 5.12b** ★
   Length: 60' (18m), Pro: 6 QD's (BSD & Road Rage merge at 3rd bolt)
   A direct start. Initial sequential movement on thin techy crimps (risky second bolt clip) with numerous holds for about 18' till it connects with RR at the fourth bolt.

6. **Jackie Chan 5.12b** ★★★
   Length: 60' (18m), Pro: 5 QD's
   This route begins on Tier #8. A steep thin crimp climb entailing considerable technical movement and endurance. Begin with a series of initial tough crux opening boulder moves to get to the first bolt, then easier movement to an odd natural feature at mid-height, then finish with a series of moves on steep terrain to an anchor. *Note:* You can clip the first bolt from atop the upper tier, or you can bypass the initial opener moves entirely via an 5.11d variation by cutting in from off the upper edge of the top tier.

7. **China Man 5.11b** ★★★
   Length: 60' (18m), Pro: 7 QD's
   The route begins on Tier #7. An excellent climb on a slightly overhanging face with many small edges and finger holds. Powerful pumpy climbing on the lower section leads to a nice mid-height shake out rest point. More pumpy climbing on the upper section that ends with a good jug at the anchor.

8. **The Dark Side (aka The Siege) 5.12b** ★★
   Length: 60' (18m), Pro: 6 QD's
   Initial moderate opening moves lead to a lower crux section, followed by a series of continuously pumpy climbing all the way to the anchor.

8b. **Philanthropy 5.12c**
   Length: 60' (18m), Pro: 8 QD's
   A powerful variation that splits off from either POR or TDS. Via the POR start gets you 5.11+. Via TDS start gets you 5.12c.

9. **Pump-o-rama 5.12a/b** ★★
   Length: 60' (18m), Pro: 6 QD's
   An interesting, well named route that offers challenging sequential movement up steep overhanging and pumpy

Alan leading at French's Dome

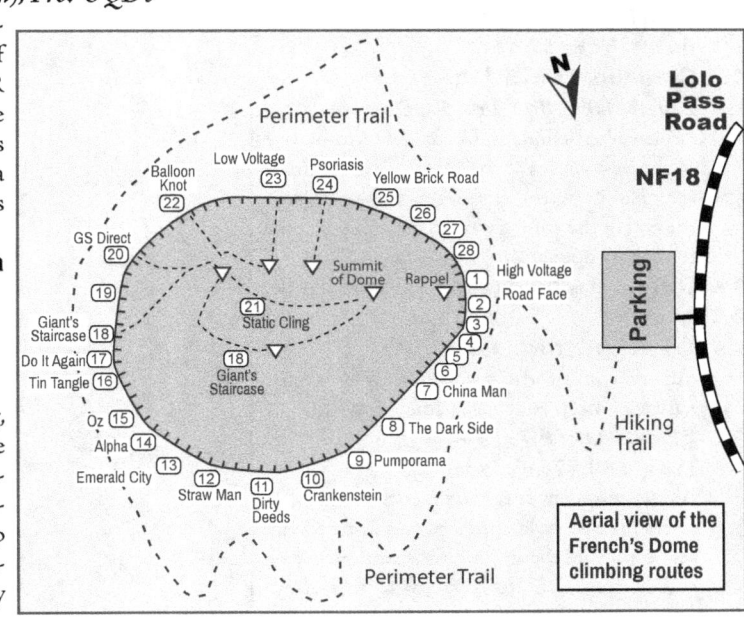

Aerial view of the French's Dome climbing routes

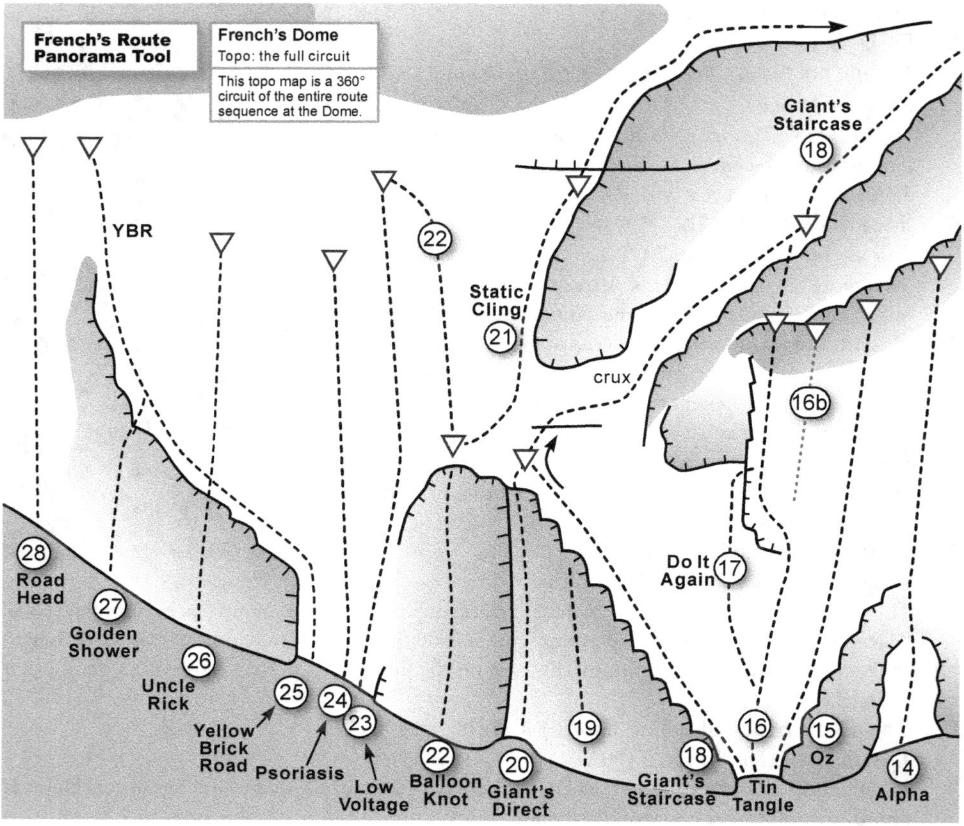

24 CHAPTER 1

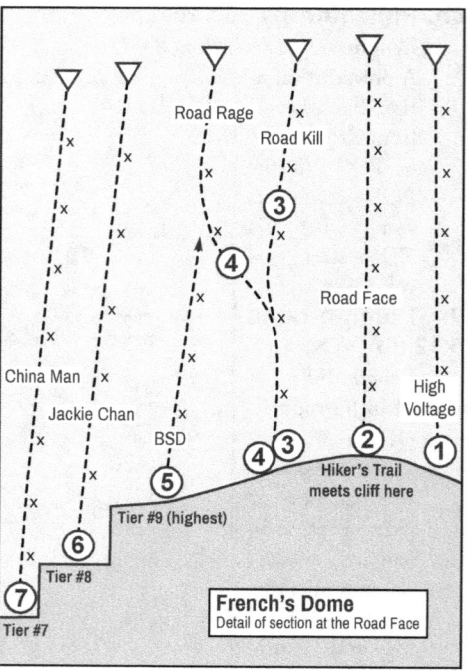

terrain that ascends along an obvious black water streak. A series of thin holds low on the climb lead to a difficult sequence of moves at the 4th - 5th bolts.

10. Crankenstein 5.11c ★★★
Length: 60' (18m), Pro: 5 QD's
An excellent climb and considered to be one of the best routes at the Dome. The technical crux is low on the climb, but the bulge near the end of the climb is surprisingly formidable to most people.

11. Dirty Deeds (aka Silverstreak) 5.10c ★★★
Length: 60' (18m), Pro: 6 QD's
Superb climb to help you quickly grasp the nature of steep edgy face climbing at FD.

12. Straw Man 5.7 ★★★
Length: 80' (24m), Pro: 9 QD's
A very popular and classic rock climb that starts up easy holds, then passes a steep crux section near the 5th bolt. Additional new closely spaced bolts have made this climb

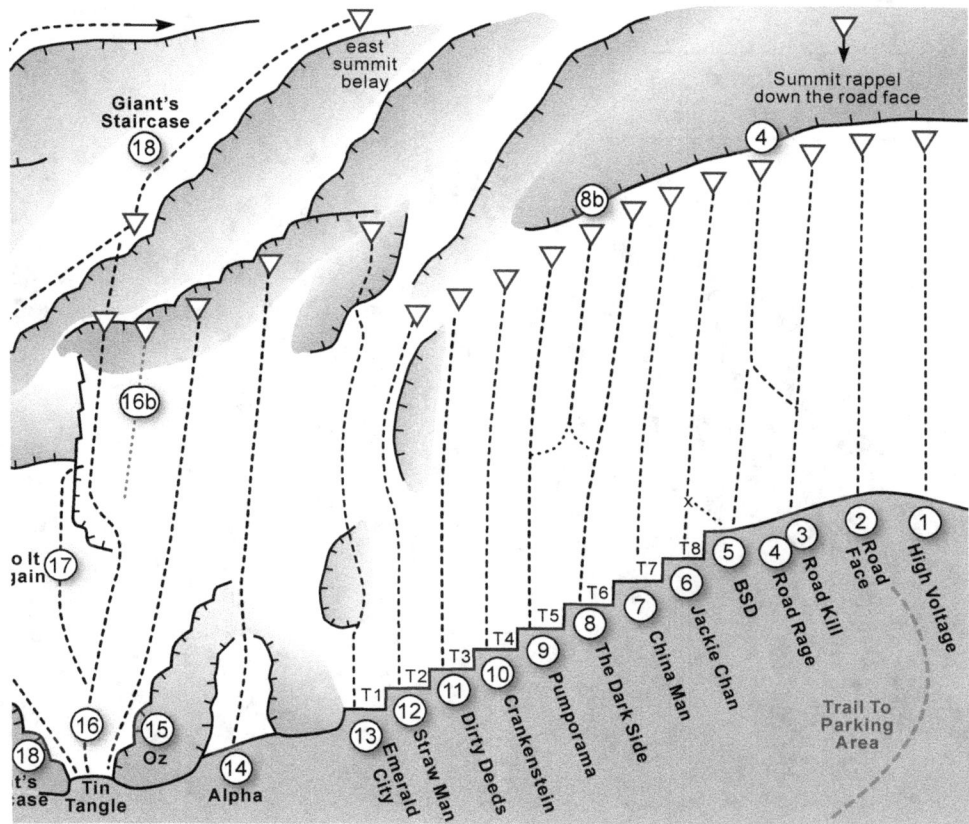

more reasonable in nature.

13. Emerald City 5.8 ★★
Length: 60' (18m), 9 QD's
A steep enjoyable face climb located between Straw Man and Alpha. Surmount an initial bulge crux, then cruise up moderately easy terrain. The climbing steepens, then passes a pumpy lip section before the holds get bigger and difficulty eases near the belay station.

14. Alpha 5.8 ★★★
Length: 80' (24m), Pro: 8 QD's
A great climb with a variety of small ledges, face climbing, and positive knobby hand holds near the crux. Climb up easy steps in a gully, then continue up a steep face to a short vertical section. The original left start is seldom climbed. Rappel from bolt anchors.

15. Oz 5.8 ★★
Length: 60' (18m), Pro: 8 QD's
Ascends a ramp of large steps then embarks up and left on a steep face to a crux near the 4th bolt. and then large hand holds and edges on the upper portion near the bolt anchor.

16. Tin Tangle (aka Tin Man) 5.8 ★★★
Length: 60' (18m), Pro: 8 QD's
This excellent and popular route climbs directly up a subtle blocky flat buttress starting at the lowest point of the east face of French's Dome (where Giant's Staircase begins). Ascend up the initial big holds till the face steepens. Gingerly work up just right of the vertical flat rib. The best holds are situated on the vertical blocky flat rib, but the first three bolts are located a long reach out to the right. From about the third bolt angle slightly left onto the flat rib buttress then up

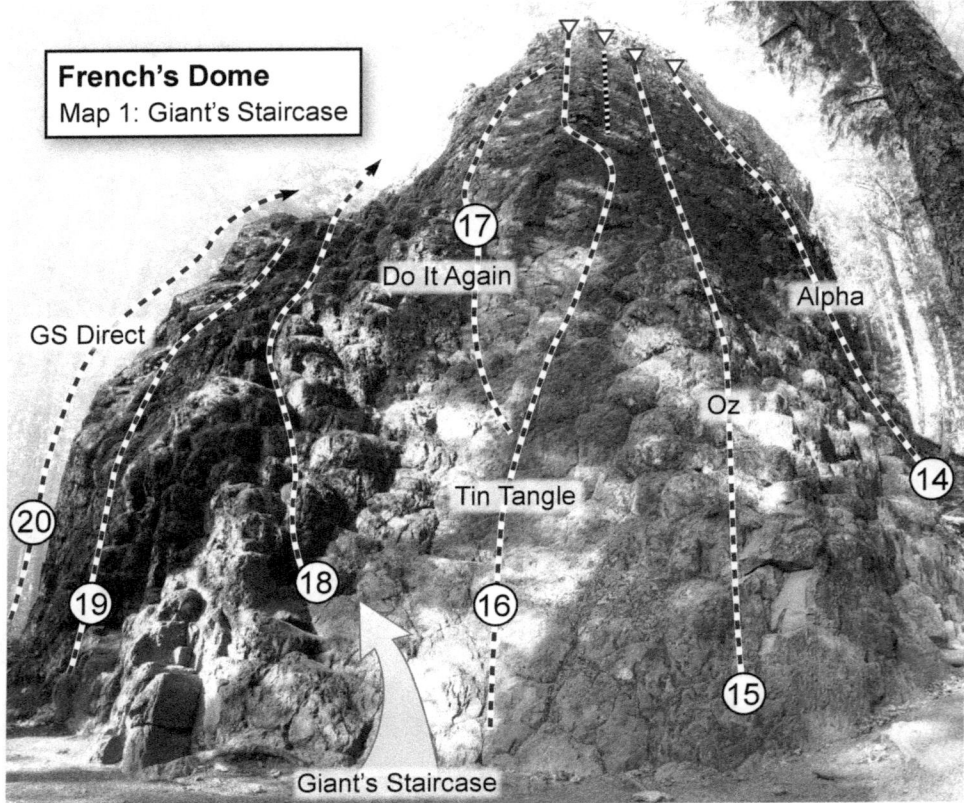

easier terrain to the belay station.

Note: a recent 2-bolt extension (#16b) continues up right-ish (from the third bolt) into a weak corner ending at a belay station. You might use that variant but it's not the original route.

17. Do It Again 5.9
Length: 50' (15m), Pro: 8 QD's
This route travels up on the left side of the blocky flat ribbed buttress called Tin Tangle. Start at the same place as you would for Giant's Staircase at the lower eastside dirt landing but climb directly up to the first bolt, staying just to the left side of the inobvious flat ribbed buttress. At a small lip overhang, move abruptly right to merge in with Tin Tangle, then continue up easier terrain to the belay station. Rap or continue up to merge with Giant's Staircase route. This is a variation route left of Tin Tangle but is quite popular today.

18. Giant's Staircase 5.6 ★★★
Multi-pitch climb, about 6 QD's per pitch
This is a classic and original climb that ascends steps and ledges starting from the lower or longest side of the pinnacle. From the lowest point in the trail ascend up easy steps leftward (bolts) to a ledge and a bolt belay anchor. From the first belay traverse right (bolts) to bypass a vertical section, till you pass a minor ridge. Climb upward on good holds (bolts) into a large gully and belay at an anchor. Continue up the gully to the summit of the pinnacle and belay at a bolt anchor. To rappel descend west down to the road face 80-foot rappel station. This rappel descends down a section of cliff that is substantially overhung.

19. Park Her Here 5.4
Length: 30' (9m), 3 QD's
Something minor tucked just left of the famous Giant's Staircase route. This lil' minor route jogs

up a pile of steps to its own belay. Bring more quickdraws if you're going above it.

20. Giant's Direct 5.7
Length: 30' (9m), Pro: 5 QD's
This is a short vertical bolted direct start alternative route that merges with Giant's Staircase at the first belay station. Bring more QD's if climbing another route above this.

21. Static Cling 5.10b ★★
Length: 60' (18m), Pro: about 4-5 QD's (if doing two short leads)
Interesting route with a short steep crux right out of the gate. From the westmost first belay on the Giant's Staircase route, commence directly up right-*ish* into a vertical bolted scoop (5.9 if using the right part of scoop), which lands at another belay, then goes over a horizontal crumbly seam up a minor steep face to easier terrain on top. If doing one long lead bring about 8+ QD's.

22. Balloon Knot 5.9 ★
Length: 80' (23m), 5 QD's (P1)
An initial steep section (5.9 crux) which soon lands at the belay ledge (used by Giant's Staircase). P2: step up left and climb airy 5.8 moves till it merges at the Low Voltage belay.

23. Low Voltage 5.11a ★
Length: 60' (18m), 7-8 QD's
An interesting long climb which is a bit easier (.10-) if you are climbing on the big holds over to the right of the bolts. A bit gravelly on the upper section near the anchor.

24. Psoriasis 5.13a ★★★
Length: 60' (18m), 5 QD's
This route and the previous share the same initial opening bolt. A true power-enduro route that lacks a comfort jug. The business begins at 3rd bolt so get your rests where you can find them. Crux between 4th and 5th bolt, but pumpy to the anchor.

25. Yellow Brick Road 5.10b PG ★
160' (50m) in length, QD's mostly, and minor pro to 1"
Less frequently climbed in the past, but with the addition of newer stainless bolts (and bolts added where there used to be odd gear placements) this route should certainly gain in popularity in the years ahead. Brief minor runout exists near the top of the route. Located on the southwest side of the Dome on a surprisingly overhang aspect of the wall. Begin at a vertical right facing corner, clamber up, then traverse left on a slowly rising ramp that also narrows the further you go up it. As the ramp fades to a vertical corner, ascend up a steep slightly hung section of cliff face (bolts at the crux) till the terrain eases to a belay anchor. The route is one single lead. Rappel.

26. Uncle Rick 5.12d ★
Length: 60' (18m), 7 QD's
Begin to the immediate left of the initial start of the Yellow Brick Road route. Climb a series of difficult steep moves, then cross over the ramp of the YBR route, and continue to climb up a powerful and crimpy substantial overhung cliff face. Somewhat pumpy .11+ climbing gets you to the second to last bolt.

27. Golden Shower 5.11a ★
60' (18m) in length, 6 QD's
A direct start variant to the renowned Yellow Brick Road route. Ascend up a slightly overhung cliff face (3 bolts at 5.11-) by going up right till it merges onto the narrow YBR ramp. Continue up left-ish as the YBR ramp steepens to a vertical corner (3 bolts) taking you to the high belay doing some laybacking and pumpy climbing (YBR 5.10- crux is just before the belay).

28. Road Head 5.11d ★
Length: 60' (18m), 6 QD's
Road Head is actually immediately right of High Voltage route which faces west toward the parking lot. This route is a powerline involving long moves between good holds, and pumpy climbing on a substantial overhung section of wall. The climbing is slightly right of the bolt line.

SALMON RIVER SLAB

Salmon River Slab is a steep slice of exposed rock face located at a small road side pullout just a few short miles south of the tiny community of Zigzag. The rock climbs here provide a comprehensive cluster of well-bolted sport routes on a smooth flakey rock.

The rock bluff faces west and is shaded during the morning hours. The best time to visit here to climb is from May to October (on a sunny day!) so you can take advantage of the great Salmon River swimming hole just a few steps across the road from the rock climbs.

Directions

Drive east from Sandy, Oregon on US Highway 26 to the tiny community of Zigzag. Turn south onto the Salmon River Road (NF2618) and continue due south on this for 4 miles. The popular summer time swimming hole is on the west side of the road, while the tiny bluff is located on the left (east side) of the road at a small dirt pullout.

1. **Climbing Theme 5.6**
   Length: 45'; Pro: 6 QD's
   A basic minor rock climb, but it crosses several brief sections of hollow or slightly loose rock.

2. **Brown Rice 5.9 ★★**
   Length: 50'; Pro: 8 QD's
   Considered to be one of the better climbs here. The crux is at the small overhung lip a few moves below the belay anchor.

3. **Camel Back 5.9 ★**
   Length: 50'; Pro: 8 QD's
   A popular climb and an interesting lead on the long central part of the slab.

4. **Caveman 5.7 ★**
   Length: 50'; Pro: 7 QD's
   Pull past a steep short bulge section for the initial opening moves, then cruise up a moderately easy steep slab using numerous edges to the belay anchor at the top of the cliff.

5. **Salmon 5.5**
   Length: 45'; Pro: 6 QD's
   Start on the right side of the cliff. Power up an initial steep section while angling up leftward

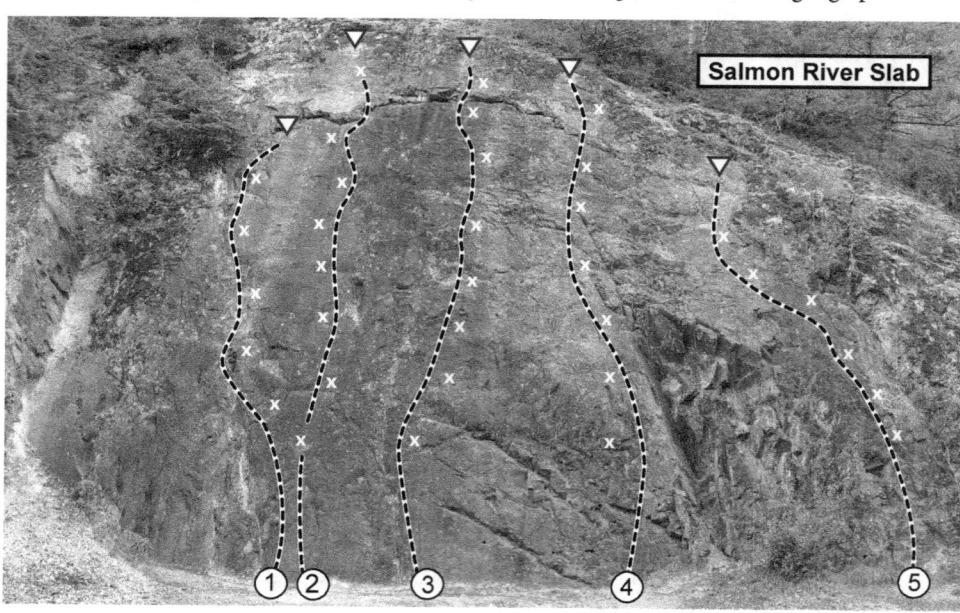

to easier ground. Route has numerous edges (some minor dirty sections to contend with).
South of the main cliff about 200' are several very short low angle slab routes.

The left shorty slab route: **Spawning Sockeye 5.4**, length 30', 3 QD's.
The right shorty slab route: **Moist Minow 5.3**, length 30', 4 QD's.

ILLUMINATION ROCK

This challenging sharp profiled high altitude pinnacle is situated at the 9643' level on the SW slopes of Mt. Hood. Illumination Rock is deeply cut by glaciers on all sides yielding a three-sided sharp profiled fin of rock. This unusual rock formation represents some of the most difficult and committing alpine climbing in the entire State, and in recent years I-Rock has become the central scene of a whole new dimension in technically demanding alpine routes in Oregon.

During the summer months after the snow and rime melts off from the pinnacle, a somewhat reasonable ascent can be made on this wind-swept challenging pinnacle. All routes to the summit are 5th class rock climbs. After all of your hard effort to conquer I-Rock you will find that the summit block is a teetering boulder that few climbers will venture to stand upon.

Winter Alpine Ice Routes

During Oregon's long winter months, when Mt. Hood is covered in a mantle of ice and snow, Illumination Rock offers the totally honed alpine climber numerous exhilarating rime ice ridges and alpine ice gullies to ascend. This is the core attraction to Illumination Rock and provides quite possibly Oregon's only all-winter site for difficult rime ice ravine climbing of an extraordinaire degree. This type of steep ice climbing requires exceptional stamina, strength, and commitment, as well as proper equipment in order to succeed.

Beware of the hazards typical of high altitude climbing which are rapid changes in the weather, potential rock fall, and ledges that are covered with loose rock or debris. Protect yourself adequately by wearing a helmet and setting belays in a protected place. If you plan to climb here, face it; this is very bold climbing. For those who are mysteriously drawn to I-Rock,

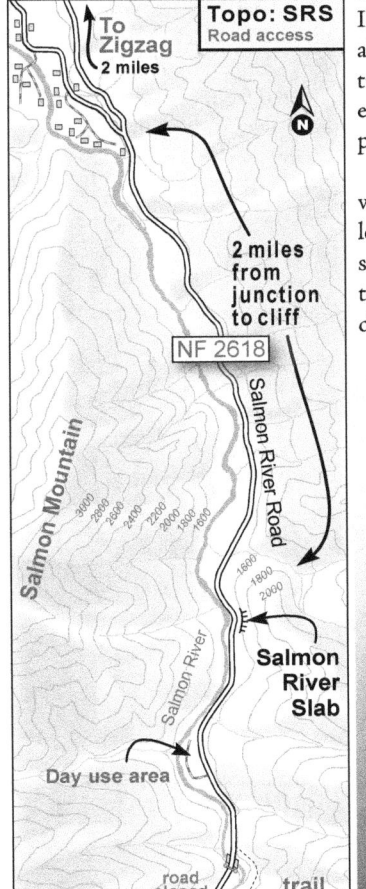

Summit ridge on Illumination Rock
Inset: I-Rock profile

you are certain to find many challenges and rewards. The mountaineers who helped pioneer most of the original routes on I-Rock between 1913 - 1938 were Gary Leech, Bill Blanchard, and Ray Conway. Without doubt I-Rock, Steel Cliff, Eliot Glacier Headwall, and the Black Spider (east face of Mt. Hood) will put a spark in the wildest dreams of any local ice climber. Some original routes have changed radically over the years so the beta provided is consolidated from present day ascents.

The five-pitch route called **Castle Crag's Direct** route rides the crest of the rotten ridge immediately northeast of Illumination Rock. Rated at III 5.7X this notorious rock spine provides high-altitude precarious a summer time adventure for a well-seasoned climber. First climbed in 1994, the route proved surprisingly feasible given the overall odd nature of the rock. One must wonder why no one had crossed this wild ground before. The climbing has been reported as being stable for the 5th class sections, and rotten for the 3rd and 4th class sections.

To access Illumination Rock drive up to Timberline Lodge and park at the parking area. Fill out a wilderness day-use permit. The approach hike from Timberline Lodge to the base of the rock generally takes about 3 hours.

1. **West Arête II 5.1 R** *(summer rating)*

Ascend up a broad scree-dirt gully up onto the long west ridge. Continue up easy but loose 5th class terrain lead-

MT HOOD ROCK 31

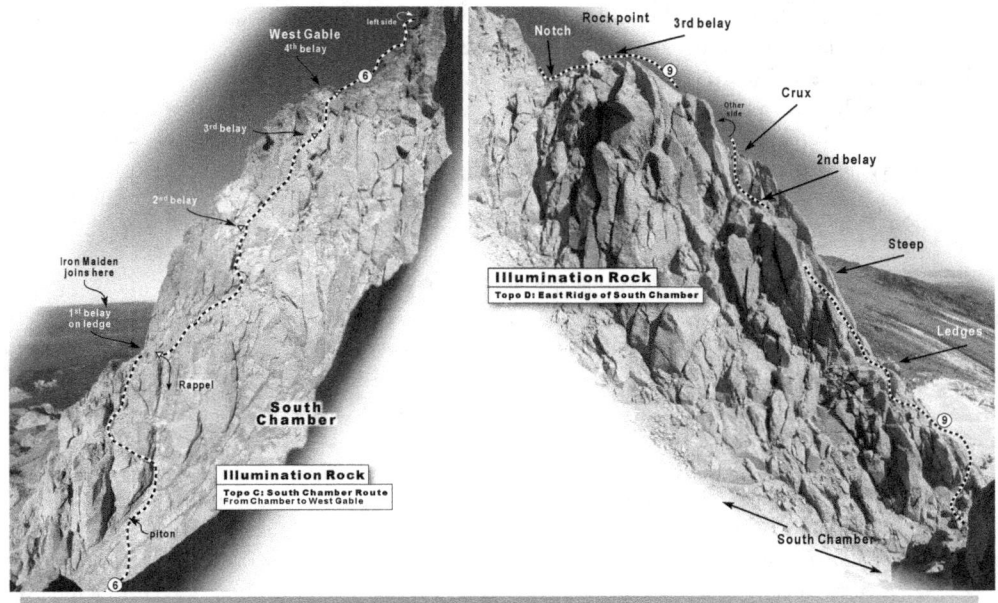

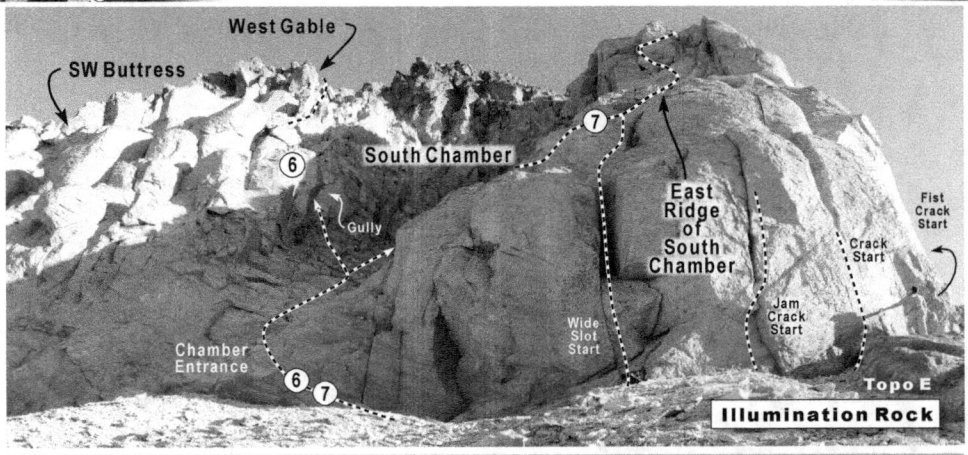

ing to the saddle of the West Gable. A plethora of routes top up at the West Gable. For the continuation of this route see the South Chamber route beta details.

2. **South West Ridge IV 5.9 AI2** *(5.9R summer)*
SW Ridge is climbed in early winter conditions usually when the route is generally exposed rock and feathers of rime ice intermixed. A difficult climb that is focused on or near the buttress ridge utilizing crack and corner features.

The South West Ridge is a six pitch route generally starting at a steep ravine and making use of the prominent buttress. Use a variety of dihedral corner crack systems at or near the ridge crest or utilize the main rib.

As you near the West Gable you can still use the left side of the main rib or venture over right to bypass some odd sections. Expect a liberal amount of loose rock as always.

Winter foray? Well...expect putting in some serious mega-power climbing like a bad dude on tenuous rime ice during the winter season. From West Gable the usual is to bail off down one of the rappel routes. *Summer Gear:* Nuts, pitons, hexes, and a few cams.

3. **April Insanity IV 5.9+ AI4 M4+**
An extreme winter climb that utilizes a prominent ravine on the south buttress wall left of Iron Maiden. The upper headwall just below the West Gable is difficult to get past.

4. **Iron Maiden III 5.7 AI2**
Iron Maiden starts the same as Rime Dog, but does not exit left at the stance. Iron Maiden stays in the deep corner system directly up staying near the general prow of the Standard Chamber Route. It parallels closely the summer route much of the way to West Gable while making ready use of the rime ice filled ravines.

5. **Rime Dog III 5.8 AI3 M5 200m+**
P1 165' (50m): Climb a mixed corner (5.7) for 80' to a stance, then move left to the next corner system. Ascend a right-leaning ramp to a belay at the top of the ramp at the base of a wide gully. **P2 150' (45m):** Ascend the wide gully on the right side, surmounting occasional ice steps till you reach the base of a headwall. **P3 165' (50m):** Ascend a wildly steep corner for 50' (5.8) and then traverse right to an exposed ramp and set a belay at the base of a corner. Note: Pitch 3 & 4 follow the same general area as the **South Chamber** (P2, P3, P4) route. **P4:** Ascend the short (20')tricky corner (5.7) and ascend open snow and rime slopes (80') to West Gable. Rappel into South Chamber to descend.

Note: Gary Leech's 7-1936 ascent of the **South Wall** likely follows a similar ravine as Rime Dog or Iron Maiden and merges onto the standard South Chamber route as it draws near to the West Gable.

6. **South Chamber II 5.4 R** (summer rating)
This is the '*standard*' method by which climbers make an ascent of Illumination Rock. It is also the standard rappel route for getting off this choss pile. The route climbs the inner left side of the South Chamber to the West Gable then along the upper West Arête to the summit. Its a bigger world than it looks from a book.

P1 200' (60m): Scramble up into

Hugh following P2, East Ridge South Chamber

the South Chamber along the left side and locate an easy groove that wanders (5.4) up onto the ridge crest to a saddle. **P2 & P3 165' (50m):** From a sling belay at the saddle march (5.4) up steep slabs and steps to another belay. **P4 100' (30m):** Surmount a steep step and scramble up over loose debris to the West Gable. **P5 & P6:** From the Gable scramble up low 5th class steps and large blocks turning the left side of a short vertical prow and set a belay at 100'. Climb carefully along the ridge crest (200'+) passing the skylight to the summit block.

7. East Ridge of South Chamber III 5.6 R

The East Ridge is a visually fascinating rib on the right side of the south chamber. The East Ridge offers wildly exposed climbing on moderately steep terrain and is a viable summer rock climb or a winter mixed climb (III 5.6 R AI3 M2). **P1 180' (54m):** Scramble into right side of the South Chamber onto (5.1 R) the ridge crest of the East Ridge. Waltz up easy but loose terrain to a belay stance. **P2 120' (36m):** Climb variable steep corners and steps (5.5) to a small belay ledge with steep-sided walls. **P3 180' (54m):** This lead starts immediately out of the gate with a punchy 5.6 crux. Stem a short vertical tight crack corner from the belay and then up basic steps and edges to a long scramble on low angle wide ledge along the crest to a belay. **P4 180' (54m):** Step down to the notch, then ascend a broad flat face (5.4) with edges and breaks that is difficult to protect due to the nature of the rock. Delicately dance up this broad face, then exit up left onto the ridge line to a belay. **P5 40' (12m):** Scramble over easy terrain to the summit ridge.

8. Abracadabra 5.10c
9. March Madness II AI4 or WI4

This is a desperate two pitch frozen waterfall when it fully forms. See diagram.

10. Northeast Face (aka Northeast Ridge) II 5.8 R

From Illumination Rock saddle climb up along the ridgecrest over large boulders to the base of the main cliff. Climb up to a bolt anchor on a ledge. Traverse a short distance to the right and climb a crack corner system to the ridge crest.

11. North Face II 5.5 R *(summer)*

From Illumination Rock saddle climb up along the ridgecrest over large boulders to the base of the main cliff. Climb up to a bolt anchor on a ledge. Traverse far to the right along a wide ledge till you are on the exposed north face above the Reid Glacier. Once you are directly under the skylight ascend steep ledges and cracks to the natural skylight on the summit ridge.

12. Northern Skylight II AI3 M5+ *(winter)*

Descend around to the north side of Illumination Rock on snow to the first buttress toe. Tackle the steep mixed terrain directly to the northern skylight. The two 60-meter pitches start about 250' left of the Southern Skylight route. The 2nd pitch offers some burly mixed climbing followed by half a pitch of mostly vertical rime ice.

13. Southern Skylight II AI3 M5 *(winter)*

Descend around to the north side of Illumination Rock on snow past the first buttress toe to a snow slope at a minor ravine. This will place you directly under the southern natural skylight. Ascend minor crack corners and steep ledges aiming for the natural skylight along the ridgecrest. Expect a wild ride on rock covered rime and ice choked corners for two 60-meter pitches. Rappel the route or descend down the south side. A direct start variation (Skylight Direct M5) starts about 150' left of the regular start for Southern Skylight.

Illumination Rock rappel routes

The following is a brief analysis of the descent options on Illumination Rock. Only two descent routes are viable depending on your time commitment and the sweat collecting on your brow. The most commonly used rappel is also known as the South Chamber route. The other alternative is the NE Ridge descending down to Illumination Saddle. Neither is simple and both have inherent risks. Always bring a sufficient quantity of webbing for your planned descent. If in doubt about the safety of the rappel anchor consider bringing pitons or perhaps a bolt kit.

South Chamber rappel:

From the leaning summit block (highest point) follow the ridge crest southwest descending down around the massive gaping 'skylight' hole. Crawl back up onto the ridge crest and continue southwest to the very tip (200'+). Set up a sling belay/rappel point at the far west end of this ridge crest where it drops off into the void. The West Gable is visible from here.

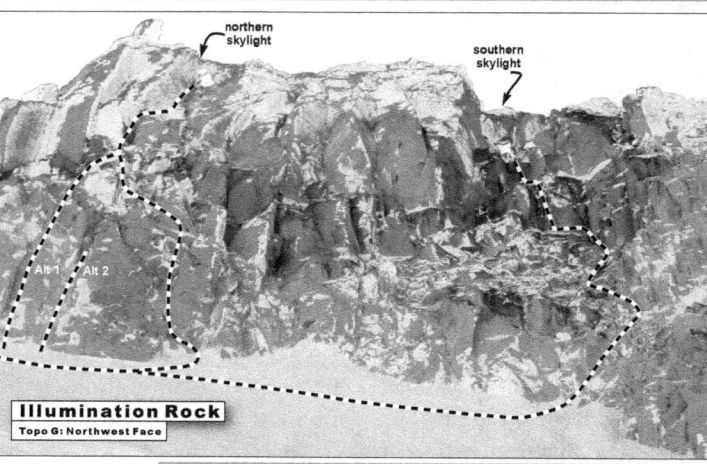

#1 Rappel 100': Rappel down toward West Gable, but initially aiming over toward the Reid Glacier side. Once around the very tip of the crest it will be quite apparent how easy it is to continue down direct to the West Gable. It is a 100' rappel down to the saddle at West Gable. **#2 Rappel 70':** Descend down toward the south chamber to a small stance at a rock horn. **#3 Rappel 70':** From the horn of rock rappel to a ledge with another sling festooned block. **#4 Rappel 80':** Descend down the ridge through a minor slot past a slab to a large ledge with a sling festooned block. **#5 Rappel 80':** Descend 80' to the inner left side of the South Chamber. Scramble down easy steps from here back to your packs at the base of the cliff. Or make another minor 80' rappel from blocks on the east side of the South Chamber.

NE Ridge rappel:

From the leaning summit block rappel or down scramble along the ridge crest toward Illumination saddle to an obvious sling festooned rock horn. Rappel onto the vertical Reid Glacier side (100') to a fixed bolt anchor on a ledge. Rappel again (150') along the ridge crest toward the saddle, down scrambling where feasible for the remaining portion.

RAZORBLADE PINNACLE

This superb isolated mountain jewel is a true alpine experience located at the 5700' level just below the Sandy Glacier. Separated by two deep river chasms, the profile of the Blade captivates all who tread near, while giving the climber a postcard perfect view of the stark west face of Mt. Hood.

Separated by two deep tributary chasms, the profile of the 'Blade' captivates all who tread near, while giving the climber a postcard perfect view of the stark west face of Mt. Hood. The first ascent was on 9-29-91 and the initial party was surprised to discover that this major summit deep in the heart of the Mt. Hood wilderness had never been climbed.

Directions
Approach by way of the Lolo Pass road (NF18). Take NF1828 near the McNeil-Riley campgrounds. The road winds uphill to a graveled side road leading to the Top Spur trailhead.

Hike the Top Spur trail, and then follow the Bald Mountain (Round the Mountain) trail south into the vast Sandy River basin. Take the southernmost drainage of the Muddy North Fork Sandy River. Follow the stream upward until the foreboding canyon walls steepen. Angle leftward up the steep hillside to the SW base of the Blade. To descend from the summit, rappel via an easy tree-to-tree descent on the south face of the crag (this can be done with a single 50m (165') rope. Expect a minimum of 3 hours to reach the base of the Razorblade Pinnacle.

1. **Gillette Arête (West Arête) 5.10b** ★ ★ ★
    Pro to 2" including cams
    Ascends the outer right corner of the western arête, and is a classic multi-pitch alpine climb. **P1 80':** Start by scrambling up a brushy leftward leaning ramp on the south face to a large fir tree, then step around tree 20' to the main notch that overlooks the north side chasm. **P2 90':** Embark straight up the prow following a crack system, and then surmount a slight overhanging bulge that has a good jam crack in it. Belay just above on a small ledge. **P3 100':** Step up right onto the next ledge, then up a slightly hung crack on a face (5.10b) then work up the outer edge of the arête, then on the right again to make the final step onto a ledge. Belay from a small fir tree located near the edge of the north face up near the summit. Rappel down the south face by using the Machete route anchors.

2. **Machete 5.8**
    Pro to 2" including cams
    This is an interesting climb that ascends the sunny south side of the pinnacle and it is also the rappel route. **P1 80':** Start by scrambling up the obvious brushy ramp (mentioned above) to the large fir tree belay. **P2 70':** Step up right on steep ground (fixed pins) that quickly eases to a slab. Then angle up right ward, then smear directly right (crux) and up through some prickly bushes to the next belay just above a small cedar tree. **P3 40':** Zigzag directly up the wall above using a minor ramp to the next tree belay. **P4 30':** Then up an easy low angled chimney with steps in it that ends at the summit anchor.

3. **Leadhead 5.7 A3**
    Pro: Pitons, nuts, and small cams
    This is the outside left corner of the major west facing arête on the Razorblade. Begin at the notch on Gillette Arête, and step down and across an exposed traverse to a stance on a small pedestal. Belay here. Ascend the north face of this slightly overhanging outside corner via thin cracks and edges. Potential free route at 5.11.

4. **Indirect East Arête 5.8 R**
    An unappealing, exposed meandering line, though feasible if you are desperate.

5. **East Arête 5.8 X**
    The lower ¼ portion of this route has loose rock.

6. **Desert of Reason IV 5.4 A4**
    *Pro: Nuts to 1½", cams to 2",
    LA, KBs, Bugaboos, RURP's,*

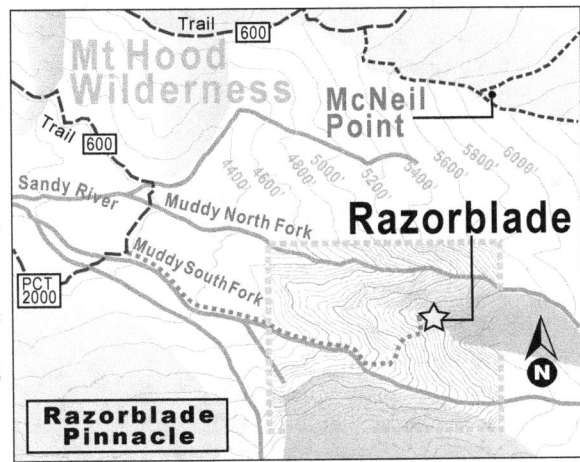

hooks, and hangers

This is an exhilarating, and fascinating ultra extreme nailing route that ascends the fabulous overhanging north face of the Blade. To the right of the route and high on the face is a blown out donut shaped rock scar. The Desert of Reason ascends the blank, overhung face to the left of this scar. The climb begins near the center of the north face in a short left leaning, left facing corner. Exit the corner onto a thin seam rightward that leads to a narrow left leaning ramp. Nail up left to the top of the ramp then upward to a hanging belay. The next lead continues up mostly blank sections of wall that offer hollow flakes, loose blocks, and incipient seams for nailing. Free the last 15' to the main ledge and rappel. Estimated height to the upper belay ledge is approximately 200'. The summit leans out from the base of the wall near the start of the route approximately 20'. The last 50' above the belay ledge is a steep unclimbed dirty corner system that leads to the summit.

Note: The extensive boulder field below the north face has slide downhill into the north Muddy Fork creek drainage. Expect difficult access to north side routes and expect the routes to be 25'+ longer.

HUNCHBACK

The Hunchback Wall is an excellent rock climbers haven offering good climbs on a vertical 100' high wall composed of andesite rock. The technical nature of the rock climbing routes tend to make the place primarily suitable for experienced hard

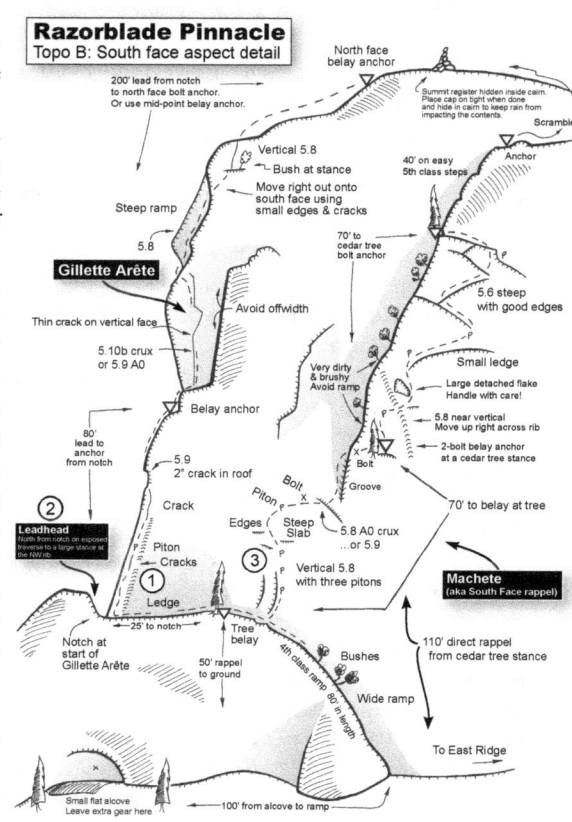

core face or crack climbers who are well honed at long, stout, sustained climbing. The site has a plethora of steep rock with powerful leads ranging from 5.10 to 5.13. The cracks luckily clock in at moderate ranges from 5.8 to 5.10 but are generally long and sustained in nature (and often very wide). The crag is convenient in its near proximity to Portland (1 hour drive) and has paved road access.

Hunchback Wall is nestled quietly in a tall wonderfully serene Douglas fir forest locale, sitting amongst tall 180' fir trees, never getting the direct blazing hot sunshine as other crags do. A gentle breeze generally keeps the place comfortable even on hot summer days (even when its 90°F) when other places are simply too muggy. This is a place where the sounds of nature predominate; no highway noise, and no boom box noise; instead you will find a quiet setting designed for those who relish quiet back woods climbing while still seeking high-end technical enduro rock climbs.

A Brief History:

The site was initially explored by Don Gonthier, Craig Murk and friends in the early 90's. Craig and Don referred to the place as the Hunchback secret. Upon arrival during their first exploration of the crag they were impressed with the potential scope of the massive wall. They recruited several buddies, but kept the place in general secrecy. Some additional early partners were Clif and Justin. Don also invited several other folks to the cliff to join the adventure. Some of the friends in this original crew cut the original rough path all the way up to this wall, using a deer trail for minor portions of the approach hike. They climbed a few routes, partly rap cleaned 1-2 other lines, and rappeled down other sections of the bluff. The initial team though parted ways soon thereafter, and the place sat quiet until late 2010 when higher grade level of rock climbers found interest in the place. That crew found the Hunchback Wall to be a su-

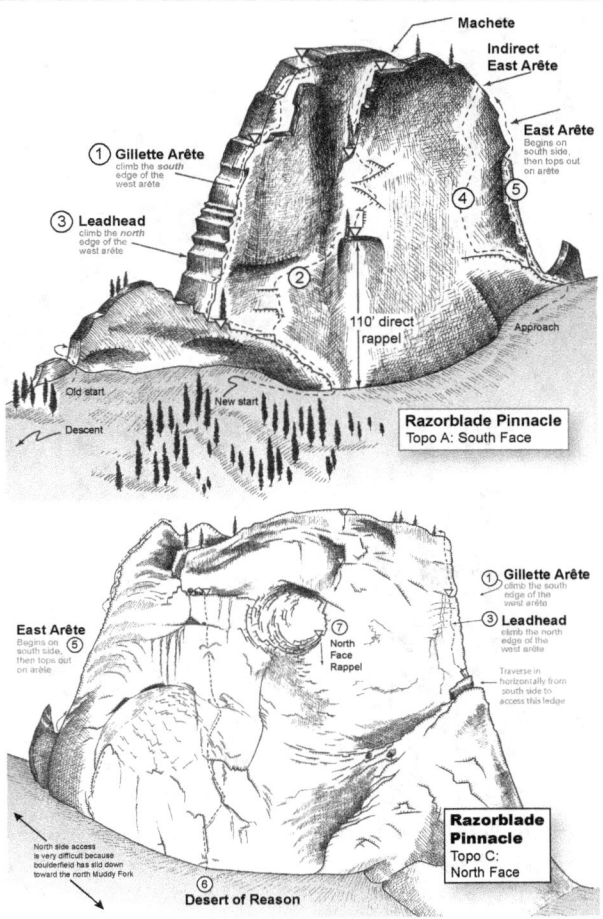

Top left: Pete G. on *Machete*
Top right: Base of *Gillette Arête*
Center: Kyle L. on *Machete*
Top center: Wayne on *Gillette Arête*
Left: Steve on the *North Face*
Right: Wayne on *Leadhead*

perb crag to fit their expectations of power climbing. Today [2020] another young generation of climbers have begun tackling HW anew.

Route development:

Route development requires patience because the cliff is tall and a bit mossy or dirty in places. Often the route project will be much harder than it appears, so if it seems like it might be a 5.10- anticipate it being a 5.10+. Fixed gear (bolts) are a common necessity if you plan to develop a new rock climb at Hunchback Wall.

Only route developers should use the sloped tricky midway terrace for access purposes (and be in direct communication with your friends below when doing so). That terrace has loose rock which can jeopardize folks standing at the base of the wall. Most routes are designed to end below the top lip of the main lower wall. By placing the belays on the steep face 10'-15' below the terrace it avoids displacing excessive amounts of dirt and moss from the terrace. Stay off the upper tier wall entirely; though it may be tall and appear visually appealing, significant loose rock would be a potential hazard to climbers using the main lower wall.

Directions:

Drive east on U.S. 26 from Sandy, Oregon till you reach Welches. Turn south at the Subway store onto Salmon River Road (NF 2618). Continue about 9/10 mile south passing a guardrail on the right and a small rotten roadside bluff on the left, then a deeply cut water ravine exists also on the left. Park immediately on the west side of the road at a minor pullout. Step into the dry waterless ravine for a few yards, then angle up right onto the south slope into a grove of cedar trees. A faint path begins there and zigzags gently uphill, and gradually steepens for the remainder of the hike. The uphill hike is 25-minute approach time to reach the base of the wall so pace your hike well to avoid a sweaty over exuberant experience getting up there.

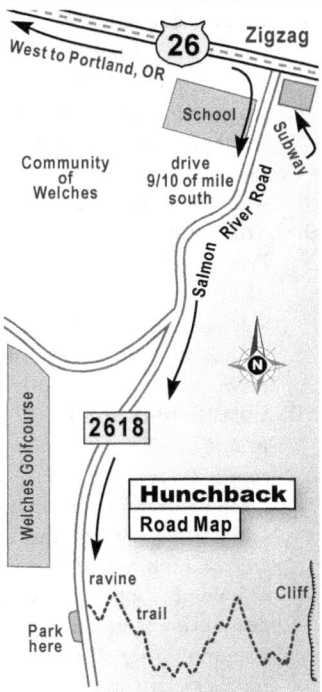

Notre Dame Wall

This very long main wall travels from the Central Ravine northward for roughly 725' and gradually fades to low angle mossy sloped sections of bluff at the far north end of the main wall. The beta is described Left to Right (north to south):

1. **Critical Conundrum 5.10b/c ★★★**
   Pro: 9 QD's, height 70'
   Climb out an initial crux overhung bulge, up a brief short slab, then up through a vertical second crux (bulge on your left), and up another brief short slab. At a slight overhung lip, power up onto a vertical final face on a minor prow that has incuts and positive holds all the way to the belay. Rap from belay.

2. **Tilting at Windmills 5.9**
   Pro: Nuts (to 1") and Cams (to 2.5"), height 70'
   Climb a prominent crack corner system (5.8) to a small midway stance (also used by next route), then bust out left over the crux bulge into the upper quality crack system.

3. **Metamorphosis 5.11c/d ★**
   Pro: 9 QD's, height 70'
   Start up initial easy small edges over the first bulge (5.8), then power over a second larger (crux 5.11d) overhung bulge. Continue up a rounded low angle prow (5.8) to a small flat stance (recompose your energy here), then power out a brief crux overhang (5.10c) up a vertical prow with incut edges to a high belay. Rappel. Note: 5-bolts on lower, and 4-bolts on upper section.

4. **_____ P1 5.7, P2 5.8 [?]**
   Pro: __", height 40' (P1), height 70' (P1 & P2 total)
   Right angled crack system starting at the foot of a notable buttress. P1: Climb the crack to a very large midway ledge (belay). P2: Climb a short steep deep corner to another ledge belay. Rappel. **Note:** Route 4b is an alternate start leading up into the same double cracks [5.9?].

5. **Mothership Supercell 5.11a/b ★★**
   Pro: 4 QD's, height 40'
   Step left to first bolt, then climb overhung face up past a giant gas pocket. Top half is delicate left handed side pulls, then easier exit moves to a large sloped ledge (belay). Direct is 5.11+.

6. **Meister Brau 5.6 ★**
   Pro: gear to 3.5" (or clip bolts), height 35' (P1), height 70' (P2 total from ground)
   Climb a short fun fat offwidth crack to a very big ledge and belay. Continue up the fat offwidth corner system to another higher belay. Rappel.

7. **Mirage 5.7 ★★**
   Pro: gear to 2", height 50'
   Climb initial step, then (bolt) tricky right trending tiny ramp to stance (bolt), then up left via a thin face and crack to big ledge and belay.

8. **Oasis 5.10d** ★★
   Pro: 5 QD's, height 45'
   A thin techical face climb that stays sustained all the way to the ending on a small perched ledge. A quality route in a forested oasis. Shares same belay anchor with the next route..

9. **The Tallest Pygmy 5.11c** ★★★
   Pro: 4 QD's, height 45'
   The prominent and stellar overhung wild arête ending on a small perched ledge. Shares the same belay with the previous route.

10. **Lord Frollo 5.10a**
    Pro: .5" to 5" cams and nuts, height 65' (upper belay)
    Deep corner (5.9) crack offwidth system immediately behind the wild overhung arête. Climb up till it exits left at midway point to a belay. The full length lead deal option: continue up and power out a crumbly roof (5.10a) then up a short small crack to another higher belay.

11. **Axe with a Passion [AWAP] 5.8** ★★
    Pro to 3" including cams, height: 65'
    Start up onto a small stance, then climb up right on a thin jam crack passing a crux. At the first roof (bolts) the crack widens to a chimney. Finish up the chimney (bolts) to the belay anchor.

12. **Abby Normal 5.9** ★
    Pro: same gear as the Axe plus 3 more QD's, height 70'
    This extension launches off from the last bolt on AWAP and steps right out onto the vertical face and finishes to the upper belay.

13. **Peloton 5.11b/c** ★
    Pro: same gear on Axe (plus 5 QD's for Peloton), height 60'
    Climb AWAP, then at midway bust left (at 2nd AWAP bolt it's 5.11) and climb past a small lip up a vertical face. Note: If you move left at the 3rd AWAP bolt it's 5.10+.

14. **Magician 5.12+** ★★
    Pro: 6 QD's, height 65'
    Fasinating technical, thin crimps face route that merges left onto AWAP crack at mid height.

15. **Magic 5.12+** ★★
    Pro: 9 QD's, height 75'
    Prominent flat buttress formation near belay anchor. A powerful superb face route that begins on a broad face immediately left of S&E and launches up a flared crack on the vertical upper buttress face. Thin technical holds for a 10' crux section before easing slightly to better holds above a series of small lips. Continue up the final moderate terrain to the belay.

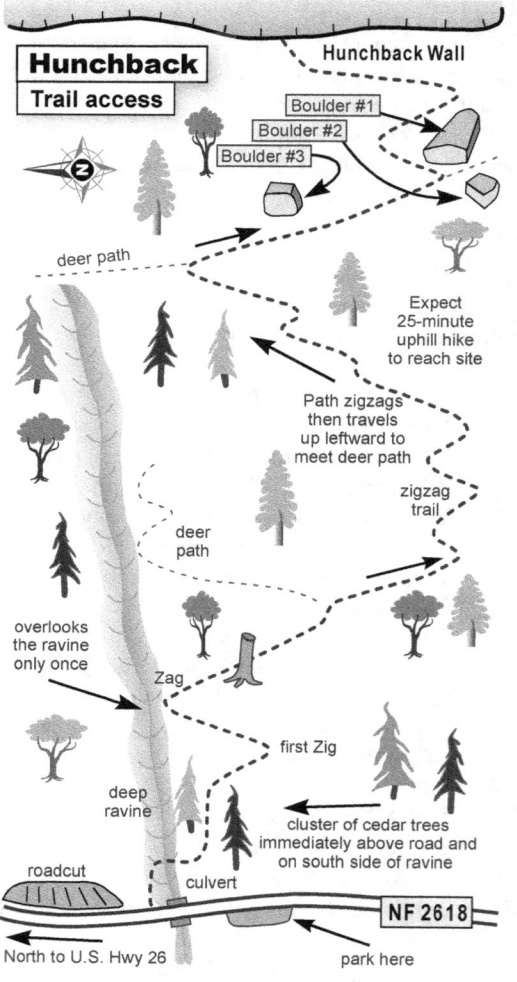

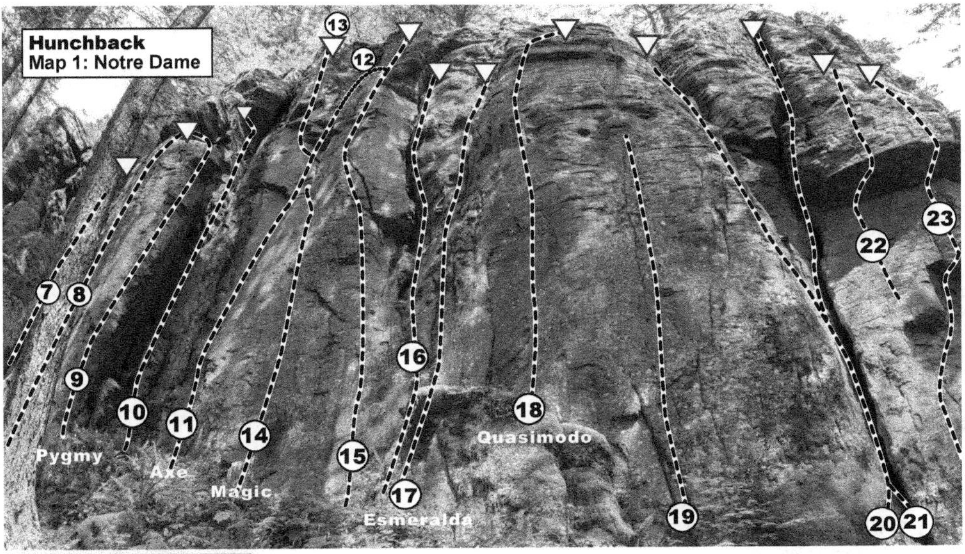

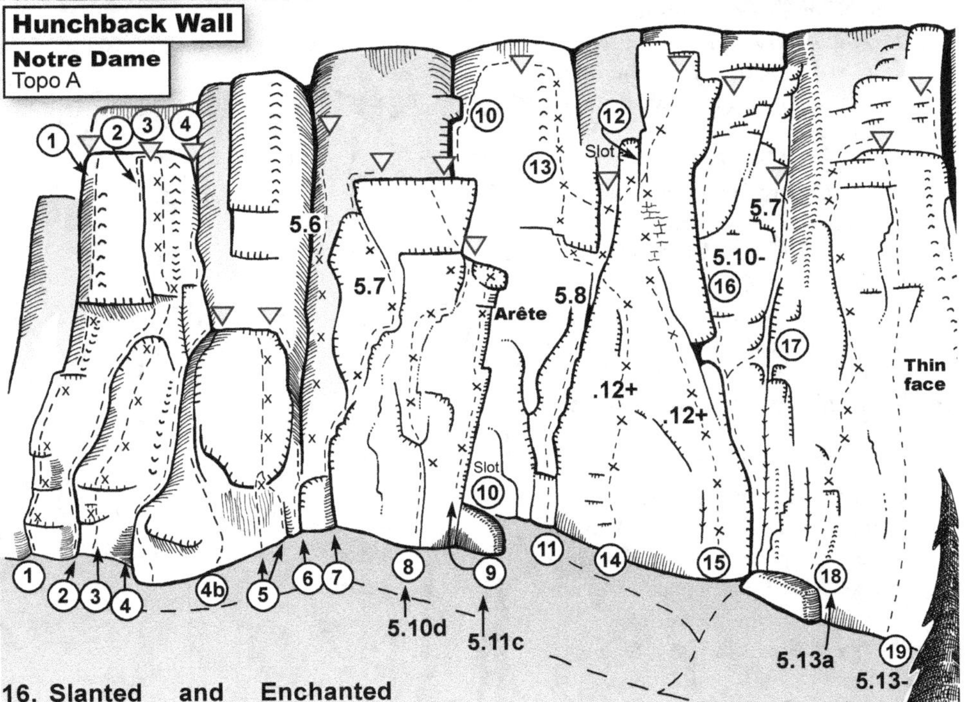

MT HOOD ROCK 41

Hunchback
Map 1: Notre Dame

Hunchback Wall
Notre Dame
Topo A

16. Slanted and Enchanted
5.10b ★★

Gear to 4" including cams (optional to 5"), (Singles up to .5 inch, triples 1 and 2 inch, otherwise doubles), height 65'

Climb up the leftward angling crack to a good rest stance. Power over a steep crux flared slot, and continue up past several more small lips to an anchor. Crux is wide, but the upper portions are nice hand jams to a technical face finish.

17. Esmeralda 5.7 ★★
Gear to 2" mostly nuts and TCU's, height 55'
A nice fun corner crack system that starts at the same as SE. March about 20' up SE, then bust off right into the crack and climb this to an anchor. Takes excellent bomber gear placements. A first class route for sure.

18. Quasimodo 5.12d ★★★
Pro: 8 QD's, Height 60'
A burly techy thin face climb that starts with a stunning 4.5' long reach off a flake. Then very tricky balancy movement, followed by a snappy final crux at the lip where it is quite deceptive to line up for the final sequence.

19. _____ 5.13-
Pro: __ QD's
Another superb quality technically stout face route, one of the hardest routes at HBW.

20. Gypsy Dance 5.9 ★
Pro: .5" to 6" cams, Nuts to 1", height 90'
Nice long offwidth jam crack that angles up leftward on steep terrain. Good pro and mostly moderate 5.7 climbing except for a short crux section at the upper last part.

21. Archdeacon 5.10c
Pro: .5" to 7" cams, Nuts to 1", height 90'
Ascends a very wide vertical corner system. Eases at mid-height, then steepens again in a deep easy slot corner on the upper portion of the route. Rappel from a high belay.

22. _____ 5.12+ [?]
Potential over the left part of the upper large roof (well...maybe).

23. _____ 5.12c/d [?] ★★
Pro: 6 QD's, height 60'
A superb technical power crimps face climb that goes through two large roofs.

24. Hangin' with the Hunch' 5.11b/c ★★
Pro: 7 QD's. Height 60'
On the immediate right side of the double roof is a thin seem. A tough climb with powerful moves passing two roofs. The last portion eases but has a tricky exit to the anchor.

25. Murky Waters 5.10a ★
Pro: gear to 4" (includes cams), height 60' (P1)
One of the original routes established by the crew way back in the 1990s. A fine long technical and occasionally flared crack system with a belay at the mid-point on the cliff scarp. Rappel. Upper section is not clean (though it's been led to Zeno's belay).

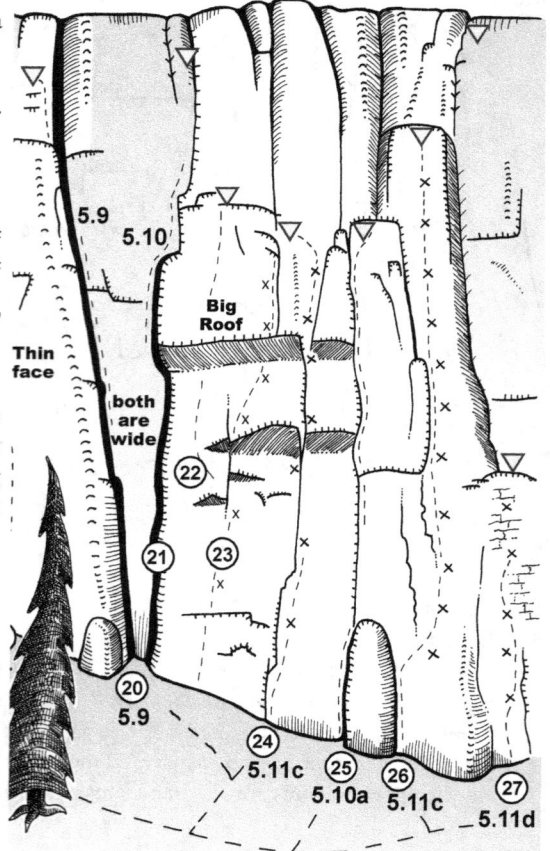

26. **Zeno's Paradox 5.11c** ★★
    Pro: 11 QD's, height 75'
    A stellar technical climb. Start up the right side of a small pillar, then step onto the face and finesse through a very techy crux section till it eases at a flared crack. Prance up the flared crack using mostly nice edges and round features to a small perch below a minor lip (the Murky Waters route anchor immediately to the left). Step right (crux) onto a vertical face and send a double arete face that offers unique box-shaped flared seams for hand and foot holds.

27. **Persistence Is Futile 5.11d** ★
    Pro: 5 QD's, height 40'
    A short 40' very oddly techy climb on very flared box-shaped surface textured rock. Layback, then smear, layback then smear. Considered to be a unique challenge.

28. **Plaid's Pantry 5.10b/c**
    Pro .5" to 6" cams, Nuts to 1", height 80'
    A long crack with a prominent large ledge about 35' up, then continues up a long wide slot crack system to a belay near the top of the cliff. A midway belay and upper belay exist.

29. **Phoebus 5.10- / .11a** ★★
    Pro: .5" to 6" cams, Nuts to 2", height 80'
    Mixed gear/bolt free route. Climb initial part of the previous crack route to the ledge, then embark up right (bolts/gear) on a long face section with occasional gear placements

30. **Achilles 5.9** ★★
    Pro: .5" to 6" cams, Nuts to 1", length 60'
    A steep cool jam crack that punches over a small lip, and continues up a steep crack section on a high rounded rock pedestal ending at a belay anchor at 60'. Wide pro at top. Rappel.

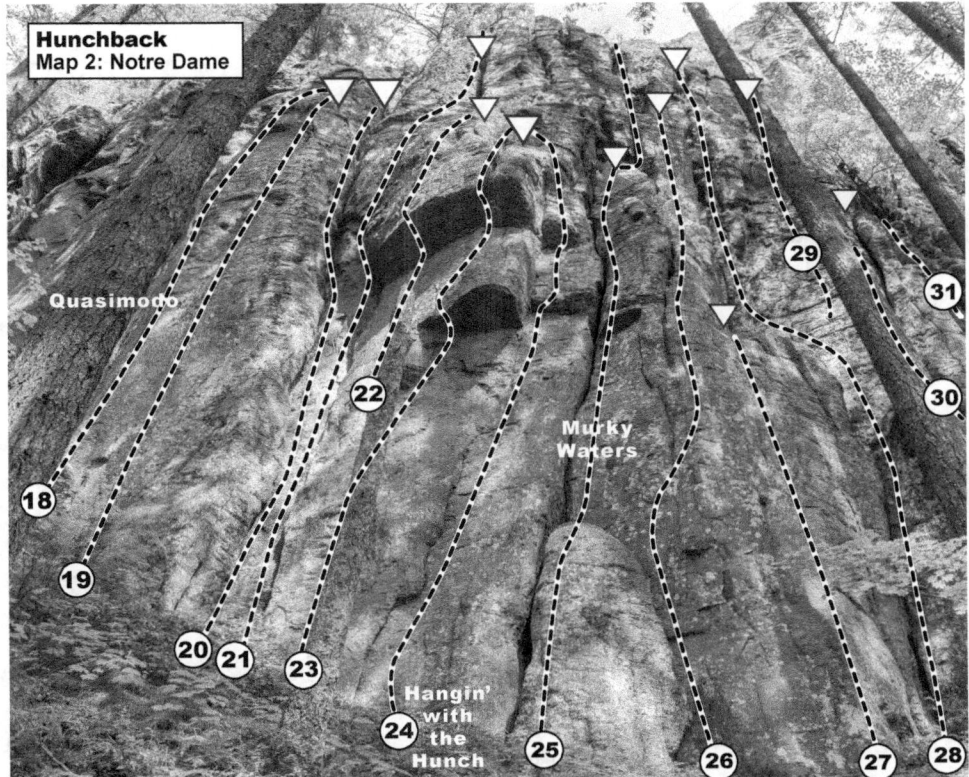

Hunchback
Map 2: Notre Dame

31. Djali 5.10b/c ★★
Pro: .5" to 4", Nuts to 1", length 60'
A excellent quality vertical jam crack ending at same belay as the previous route. An alternate direct boulder move face start is 5.11-.

32. Ho' Lotta Shakin' 5.11a ★★★
Pro: to 3.5" for main crack, then 4 QD's to finish, length 80'
Climb a cool right facing corner crack system that ends at a roof. Bust out right at the roof up past a stout crux (first bolt), continue up tricky face climbing (bolts) to the belay anchor.

33. Notre Dame 5.12b ★
Pro: 9 QD's, length 80'
Face immediately right of the wide jam crack.

34. _____ 5.9 (P1 & P2)
Pro: .5" to 6" cams (plus doubles large sizes), Nuts to 1", slings for blocks, length 100'
Climb a wide mossy corner that lands on a midway ledge (belay), then embarks up a second even wider chimney system to the top. Belay/rap using the Plaid's belay.

35. _____ 5.11+ [?]
Pro: 4 QD's, minor gear to .5", length 40'
Climb a short crack (use gear here), then move up right onto a face (bolts) as it ascends a slight overhung crimp featured scoop and bulge. Rappel from belay.

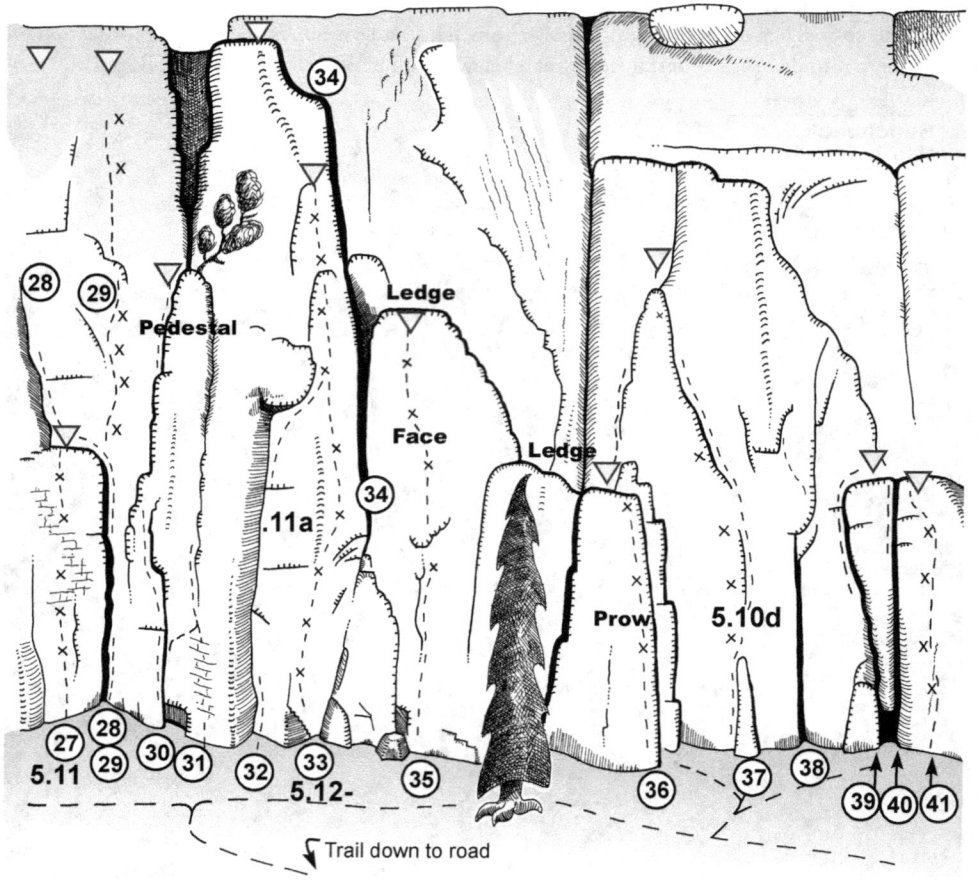

Notre Dame Wall - Southern Section

36. Three Martini Lunch 5.10d ★
Pro: 3 QD's
A minor 35' long short arête that lands on a large belay ledge. This route gains quick access to the potential face routes above the ledge.

37. Cathedral 5.10d ★★
Pro: 4-5 QD's (plus 2" gear), length 50'
Quality route starting with a series of powerful face moves. The power crux climbing eases for a short bit at the short crack, then gets energetic for a final punchy ending near the belay.

38. _____ 5.__ [?]
Pro:
Short vertical jam crack that abruptly exits right and lands on a large belay ledge. An alternate second pitch will eventually embark up left onto a tall prominent face prow.

39. Victor 5.8 ★★
Pro: 2" to 6" cams, Nuts to 1", length 40'
This is a popular left deep flared crack (with a few aid bolts). The route ends on a large ledge with a belay station. Rappel.

40. Hugo 5.10c/d
Pro: 1" to 6" cams, Nuts to 1", length 40'
This is the right fat offwidth crack, of the two side-by-side flared offwidth cracks.

41. Laverne 5.10b/c ★★
Pro: 4 QD's , length 40'
Power crimping on the flat vertical left aspect of a prominent tall rock outcrop formation with a large ledge. Rappel from belay.

Central Ravine

The Central Ravine gains access to several minor short lead routes scattered along the inner aspects of the ravine system.

South Wall

From the Central Ravine southward is the grand South Wall, a very vertical formation with potential for single and multi-pitch lead routes, easy and stout.

South Amphitheater

At the far south end of the South Wall you will find a superb major amphitheater for the grand finalé. Some routes in this giant alcove lean in your face 5°-15°, leaving a very naturally clean wall of hard core face, crack and incipient seam routes, perfect

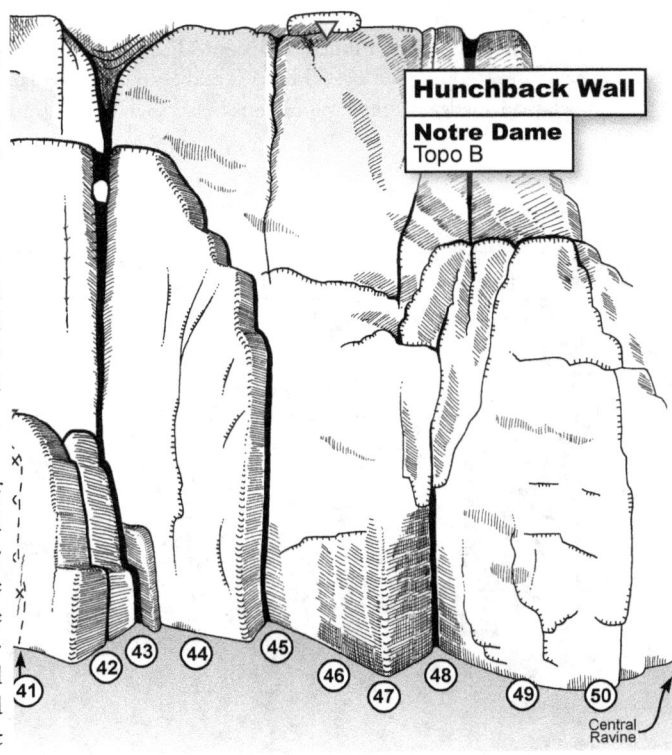

Hunchback Wall
Notre Dame
Topo B

for a string of classic hardman climbs.

1. **Hunch Sack 5.10d / 5.11a** ★ ★ ★
   Pro: 10-11 QD's
   Superb climb on the left side of the stunning narrow fin arête. A low crux around the 4th bolt and a high crux on the last 2 bolts. Harder if you stay left, easier if you embrace the exposure and hang over the arête.

2. _____
   An unfinished project. The right side and overhung aspect of the fin arête.

3. _____
   A deep crack corner on left face of the amphitheater.

4. _____
   A crack on the center face of the amphitheater.

5. _____ **5.12- [?]**
   An impressive extreme looking seam on vertical face.

6. **Mellow Drama 5.10c** ★
   Gear to 2", has 7 bolts
   Start up an easy wide crack ramp to where the headwall steepens following discontinuous cracks and ledges. Follow the thin steep crack to the top, avoid the overhang on the top by going to the right through the narrow chimney to the rap anchors. A 60-meter rope will just barely get you back to the ground.

Upper Southern Tier

This is a brief upper tier section above the South End Amphitheater, thus it offers second pitch leading options above certain amphitheater routes, if you are so inclined.

7. **Jon Pussman 5.9**
   Pro: 3 QD's, height 30'
   This is located above the Hunch Sack route. From that belay embark up right for some exciting exposure stepping out over the abyss and onto the short face above the massive roof. Ends at a belay on a ledge. Rappel to previous belay, then to the ground.

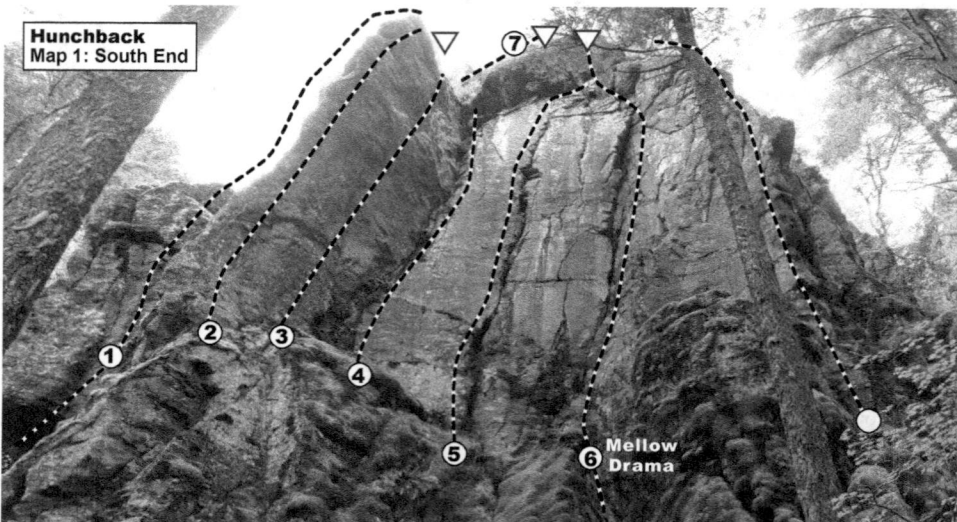

✦ MT HOOD ROCK 47

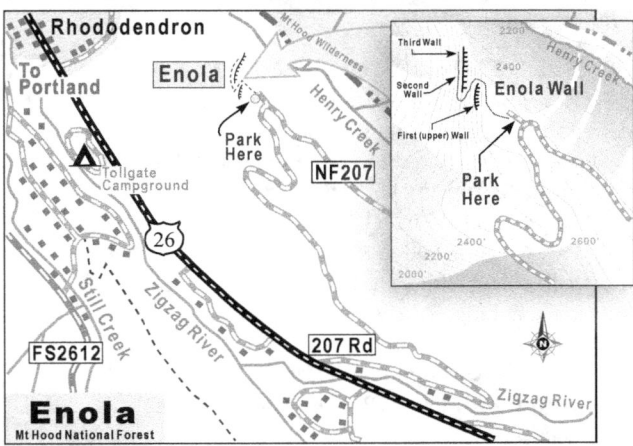

Dave leading Burning Tree, Enola Hill

ENOLA (THE SWINERY)

Primary beta by Jim Tripp, Tymun Abbott and associates

Enola (aka The Swine, and the Swinery) is a well-established crag that holds a sizable selection of steep rock climbs on a bluff that faces directly west overlooking the tiny community of Rhododendron.

The bluff is composed of Tertiary pliocene andesite (Ta1) and is surprisingly steep in places. The rock climbing routes and quality vary from small finger edge face climbs to sloping pocketed sections interspersed with larger edges. A variety of climbing routes exist such as pure face routes while others are traditional crack climbs using natural/mixed pro. The climbing routes are typically 50' to 100' in length. The crag is well-suited for climbers who have solid 5.10 to 5.11 leading capabilities. The lesser traveled 5.9-and-under routes (and there are plenty) tend to be a bit mossy and dirty from lack of use. A few route names and ratings are not known at this time.

Seasonally the crag is generally limited to Oregon's reasonably good summer weather (May to late October) as it receives the brunt of most weather systems arriving from the west. Yet a mild breeze rolls up through the trees from the valley below the crag keeping the temperatures comfortable all season while generally keeping various pesky insects away.

Cliff Sections

This guide sub-divides the entire wall into recognizable sections for easy reference. The initial upper wall at the overlook is called Sunset Wall. The popular middle wall (with its stellar classics) is the Moonshine Wall (the alcove). A hidden Bench Area branches up left from the alcove on a steeply zigzagging trail. The North Point Wall is located about 400' northward along a path from the second wall.

Directions

Drive east of Rhododendron 1¼ miles, then turn left onto road 27. Follow the paved portion east, then back up west on a very rough gravel road to the upper west most bend in the road at the 3000' elevation (total of 2⅓ miles from highway). Park on a small dead-end side spur road in a thick stand of fir trees.

From the forested parking area follow a level trail one minute west to a viewpoint overlooking the community of Rhododendron. Immediately below your feet is the Sunset Wall. Follow a narrow descending trail northward that zigzags down

Dave leading a *Too Cool* at Enola

below the Sunset Wall.

SUNSET WALL (UPPER WALL)

The climbing routes are listed as if you are descending the trail. The first route described is the long arête climb on the left of the Sunset Wall.

1. **Pig's Knuckles 5.11d** ★★
   Length: 100', Pro: 8 QD's
   This is the bolted arête on left side of the wall. Great climb involving technical steep face climbing. Reachy mid section, and balancey on upper arête.

2. **Pigs Nipples 5.11a** ★★
   Length: 100', Pro to 2½" including cams & doubles
   This is a stellar crack that climbs a corner system to the immediate right of the arête. Route involves a tenuous layback through the middle crux section.

3. **Forbidden Zone 5.10a**
   Length: 90', Pro: nuts and cams to 2"
   This is the left direct crack leading up and right to merge with Tibbets.

4. **Tibbet's Crack 5.12a**
   Length: 90', Pro: nuts and cams to 2"
   A deceptively difficult crack system that starts under the left corner of a roof and powers up a tenuous thin crack. Merges with FZ.

MOONSHINE WALL

Continue to descend steeply down a narrow trail to the next wall. The first climb is next to a large maple tree. A short distance further lands at the main area. This wall offers a comprehensive selection of routes ranging from quality 5.9 routes, pumpy 5.10 routes, to stellar crimper 5.12 face routes. The alcove is the place where most first-time climbers come in order to experience the invigorating flavor of Enola.

5. **Calm Before The Storm 5.7**
   Length: 40' Pro: 4 QD's
   This is a nice climb on a fairly steep face that follows next to a minor crack on the upper part. Start behind a large maple tree.

6. **Granny's Got A Gun 5.12b**
   Length: 75' Pro: 8 QD's
   This climb is located to the immediate right of the toe of a minor sunny buttress that overlooks a boulder field. This climb zooms up positive holds to a 'knock-you-in-the-head' powerful crux move punching through the outer right edge of the overhang then

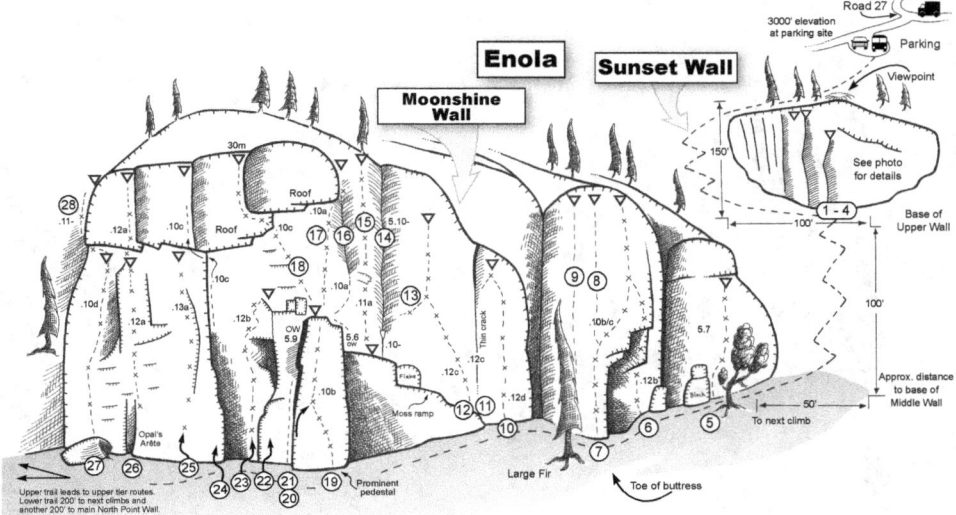

merges into the classic Burning Tree route.

7. **Burning Zone 5.10c ★★★**
Length: 75' Pro: 8 QD's
This is considered to be one of the best routes at Enola. This stellar line gets plenty of sunshine in the afternoon hours. Climb starts at the toe of a minor buttress and ascends tricky face edges then angles up right above the lip of the large roof on good holds. Finish up a very steep rounded nose on interesting face holds.

8. **Samurai 5.10c ★★**
Length: 75' Pro: 8 QD's
This fine route branches up left from Burning Zone at the 3rd bolt, and continues directly straight up to its own belay. The crux is on BZ so this variant offers interesting face climbing that eases as you get near the belay station.

9. **Meatloaf 5.10c ★★**
Length: 75' Pro: 8 QD's
This high quality climb is completely independent to its anchor. Start just left of Burning Zone and climb up next to a bush, then gingerly surmount the wobbly block, and continue up sustained face climbing to a belay station.

10. **Hillbilly Hot Tub 5.12c ★**
Length: 45' Pro: 4 QD's
An extreme thin face climb immediately to the right of Scorpion.

11. **Scorpion BBQ 5.12c ★★★**
Length: 45'
Pro: #3 TCU, #1 WC rock, #00 TCU (opt.), #5 nut, #0 TCU, 1½" Cam
A powerful thin seam lacking in real holds this quality climb is composed of painful side pulls, smears, crimps and long reaches. The climb eases at the bolt so don't peel off during the last few moves. Just use a biner on each pro piece.

Dave leading *Fifty-seven*

Tymun leading Grits & Gravy 5.12b

12. Fifty-seven 5.12c ★★
Length: 70', Pro: 7 QD's
As in AGE fifty-seven not Heinz. A fierce edgy face climb that powers up left from the seam. Merges with the next route. Starts at the base of the grass ramp. The rating is based upon avoiding the thin vertical seam of Scorpion BBQ. This route merges into the upper portion of route #10.

Access the next three climbs on a long grass ramp ledge system by utilizing a belay anchor at a stance immediately above the large flake.

13. Serpentine Arête 5.10a
Length: 60', Pro to 2" then QD's
Scramble up the grass ramp past the large flake to a belay stance. Power up a vertical crack over the chock stone (crux)wedged in the crack, and then angle up RIGHT on the bolt line that ascends a vertical face. This route merges with the route Fifty-Seven.

14. The Easy Way 5.10a
Length: 60', Pro to 3" including small cams & nuts
Walk up the ramp and hop up past the large flake to a belay stance at a single bolt. Power past the initial chockstone (crux) wedged in the crack. Finish directly up the vertical minor crack corner system (5.9) on good edges and smears.

15. Calf's Gash 5.10c
Length: 60', Pro: QD's
From the same ramp belay stance power up past two bolts on a vertical flat face (crux), then power over a large block with a crack in it. Balance up a steep smooth face using delicate smears (bolts) to the belay anchor.

Access the next three climbs from the belay anchor on top of the prominent pedestal.

16. **Mr. Hair of the Chode 5.10a PG**
Length: 60', Pro to 2"
From the belay anchor at the top of the pedestal, step hard right and climb a poorly protected crack system with jug holds. The protection gets better the higher you climb. Exit past the right side of the roof to a belay anchor.

17. **Jugalicious 5.10a** ★★★
Length: 60', Pro: 5 QD's
One of the great quality routes at Enola totally worth doing. From the belay anchor at the top of the pedestal climb up RIGHT (bolts) using positive holds. Exit past the right side of the roof (crux) to a belay anchor.

18. **SOTT P2 5.10c** ★★★
Length: 60', Pro: 6 QD's & minor cams to 2"
This is P2 of Swine of the Times. From the belay anchor at the top of the pedestal climb up LEFT (bolts) on vertical terrain. Balance out left through the upper roof (some minor hollow rock) then continue climbing a vertical face (cam pro) to a belay anchor. A classic warm-up route when connected with the face climb on the outer side of the prominent pedestal.

The following two routes start at the base of the prominent pedestal at the 'Cove.

19. **Jethro 5.10b** ★
Length: 50', Pro: 6 QD's
Face climb on the outer portion of the prominent pedestal. Climb direct from the ground on vertical face edges (bolts) all the way to the belay at the top of the pedestal. The first move can be protected with a small cam if needed.

20. **Swine of the Times 5.10b** ★
Length: 50', minor pro to 2" & QD's
This starts up Fat Crack, then steps right to send the last 3 bolts on the outside of the pedestal. Continue up to the ledge on a pedestal. SOTT pitch two launches off the top of the pedestal up left through a series of overhangs. Last moves need minor 2" pro.

21. **Fat Crack 5.9**
Length: 50', Pro: 2½"
Climb the obvious off-width on the left side of the pedestal. Usually top-roped. Another top-rope on a flat face just left of Fat Crack is called **Prohibition** 5.12c (TR).

22. **Tipsy McStagger 5.11d**
Length: 50', Pro: gear to 1", including micro-cams
Climb the wide broken corner to a short left facing corner capped by a roof. Power over the lip and up a very thin crack (crux) till it eases onto a small ledge

Brian is in for another Twenty Years 5.10b

at a belay.

22b. Fortune Cookie 5.12b
Length: 50', *Pro:* 5 QD's
Climb a face immediately right of the previous route. Thin crux face sequence on upper ¼.

23. Grits & Gravy 5.12b
Length: 50'
A wild face climb that balances up delicate face moves to a slight lip. The 'gravy' portion is below the small lip. The grits potion ensues at the lip where you must pull on small rounded edges and non-existent foot smears (crux).

This area is the very heart of the Alcove where most climbers congregate for action.

24. Too Cool 5.10c ★★★
Length: 90', *Pro:* 3"
This is the stellar and obvious dihedral corner crack climb in the very center of this wall. The route powers directly up the crack on relatively holds, then launches into a small overhang. Move out and up left on precarious terrain to a tight stance, then out left again through the giant roof and then finish up a vertical corner groove to the anchor. Easy to get flamed out by the end of the climb at the top.

25. Psycho Billy Cadillac 5.13a ★★★
A powerful series of committing sequential moves utilizing the outer arête edge of a nearby dihedral. A strenuous series of crimps through the crux require excellent body core balance to connect the difficult string of moves.

26. Opal's Arête 5.12a ★★★
Length: 60' (P1), *Pro:* 7 QD's
Opal's Arête is considered to be one of the great classic routes at Enola. It is a tribute to the late Opal who owned what used to be called the "Food & General Store" in Rhododendron. Ascend an initial short slot then launch up on a vertical smooth face using tiny edges and sharp knobby pockets. Use one of the methods listed below to power through the crux, then from a nice stance move either up right or up left for one move then clip into the belay anchor. Rappel. Opal's Arête has several methods for ascent, so pick your style and go for it.
From the fifth bolt plant your right foot high onto a long narrow rail and using the right facing vertical rib pull up by rocking up onto your right foot.
Other option: From the fifth bolt plant an initial right foot on something, then reach out LEFT to the left arête. Slap up both blunt arêtes until you can stand on a narrow sloping right foot edge to clip the next bolt. Use the method that best suits your skill level, core body strengths and structure.
From the sixth bolt lean out left to use the left arête, or stay in close to the right rib.
Sea Hag Roof extension (5.12a) is the roof above Opal's Arête.

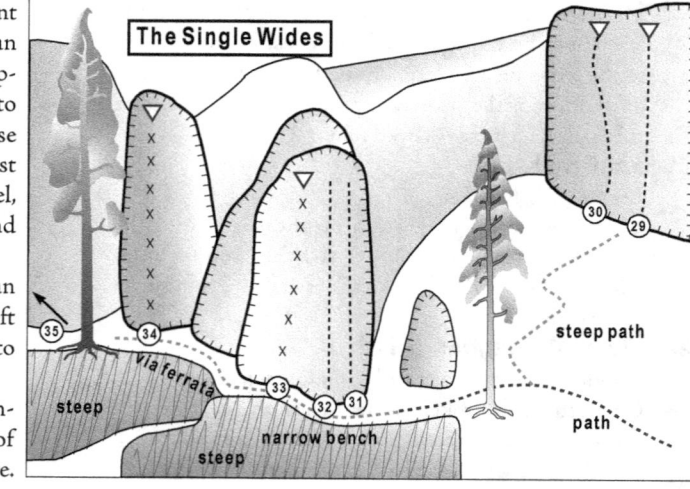

Continue a few moves up from the belay anchor and climb out a large roof past 3 bolts.

27. Twenty Year Hangover 5.10d ★★★
Length: 60', Pro: 5 QD's
Twenty Year Hangover is certainly one of the more popular climbs at Enola. The route uses a minor crackless corner immediately left of Opal's Arête. The route has many unique face edges and pockets.

28. _____ 5.11a
Length: 25', Pro: 4 QD's
This route launches out up left from the belay anchor on 20YH around the left edge of the large upper roof to an upper anchor.

The Bench

This section can be accessed by a steep trail which starts next to Twenty Year Hangover. The trail zigzags uphill to a shaded steep wall (80' tall) with the following two routes on it.

29. _____ 5.11 [?]
Length: 80', Pro to [?]
Climbs up steep face and crack corners, then powers through a bulge.

30. The Fang 5.10a
Length: 80', TR
Climbs up a steep face using minor seams, and then cruises up a crack on the left side of the overhang to the belay anchor.

The Single Wides Area

A string of routes along a narrow Via Ferrata ledge system are available by walking halfway up toward the Bench area and then stepping to the left. Each buttress along this ledge is tall like a bunch of single wide trailers stood up on end.

31. Shine 5.12d ★
Length 60', Pro: 5 QD's
A technical thin face climb on the right south facing aspect. The OW to its right has been TR'd and goes at 5.8.

32. White Lightning 5.11c ★★★
Length 60', Pro: 7 QD's
Climb past a prominent pocket up a rounded face through a techy thin crux at mid-height. Thought to be one of the best routes here. FA: TA 2012.

33. Single Wide 5.12a ★★
Length 60', Pro: 6 QD's
A difficult face climb on the left side of the first tall buttress along this narrow ledge system.

34. Moonshiners Arête 5.13b/c
Length 60', Pro: 7 QD's
A face climb on the second pillar along this ledge. Start next to a large fir tree. Ascends a series of strenuous wave shaped features on the steep buttress. FA: TA 2012.

35. Tailgater 5.12a
Length 60', Pro: mixed QD's and gear to 2"
This is on the far left end of the Via Ferrata. Climb corner crack, step left to ramp, climb up ramp to upper left corner of ramp, then around a corner crux to nice crack on left headwall, then up crack to belay.

NORTH POINT WALL
Walk north from the middle wall for about 200' on a flat trail that follows the base of a mossy rock bluff. The trail ends at a steep rock scarp (see diagram). It has a small selection of climbing

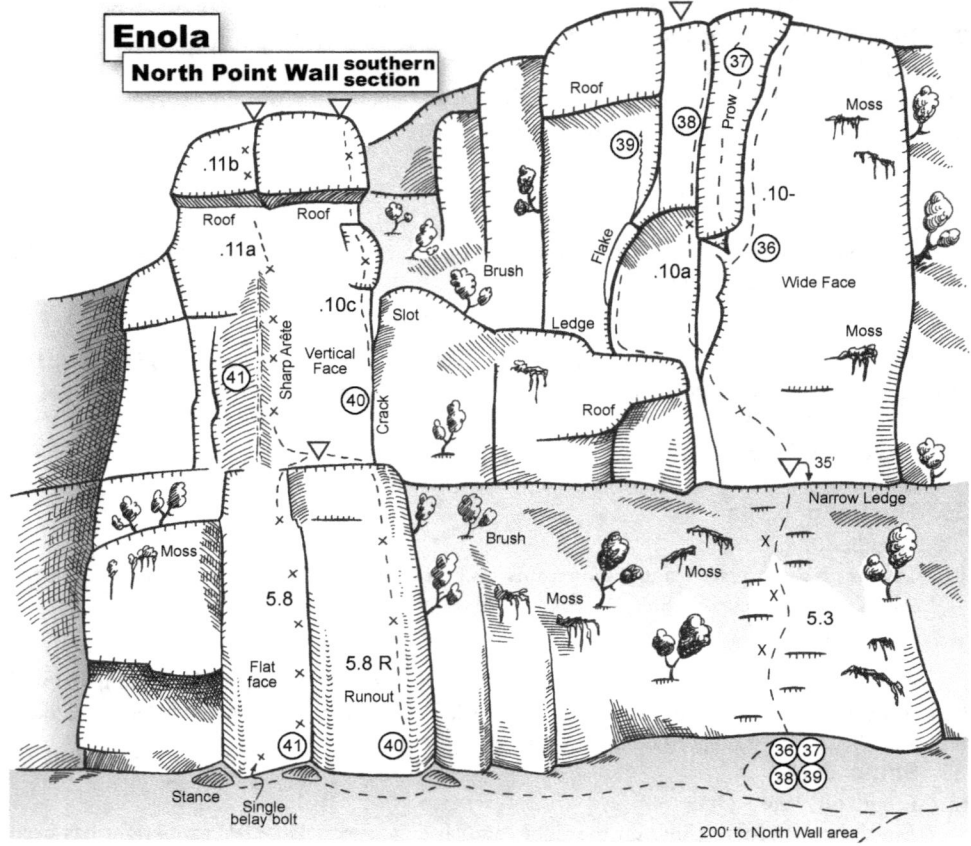

options that guide you up to several belay anchors on a higher ledge.

Reach the next three rock climbs via 5.4 easy steps to a belay anchor.

36. King of the Moes 5.9 ★★
Length: 120', Pro to 2½" including cams
Dash up the easy steps to the ledge anchor. Embark up left (bolts) then move up right under a large nose-shaped prow, and continue up a right facing thin crack system to the top. Rap from anchor.

37. _____
Length: 60'
A potential route that can tackle the overhanging prow.

38. Dismantled Fears 5.10a ★★
Length: 60', Pro to 3"
From the ledge belay anchor launch up left on a face past 3 bolts to a crack, then climb up under a large roof (bolt). Power out the roof and up the double cracks above to an anchor.

39. _____
A potential thin seam starts up a right arching crack then punches up onto a steep blank face, but awaiting a potential buyer.

Access the next two climbs at the furthest point on this cul-de-sac trail.

40. Tres Hombres P1 5.8 R (avoid), P2 5.10+
Length: 40' 1ˢᵗ pitch (avoid), 50' 2ⁿᵈ pitch, Pro to 3" including cams
The first 40' is a mossy runout 5.8 R to the ledge with an anchor. Avoid this first pitch until someone safely fixes and cleans the climb better. Best to use the next 5.8 route to access a midpoint belay ledge (see topo). From the belay launch up right in a stiff 5.9 flared crack to a stance, then onto an odd arête (bolt) over a crux bulge (bolt) to the anchor.

Access the next climb from a single bolt belay stance on the ground at the very end of a narrow trail.

41. Welcome to the Swine P1 5.8, P2 5.11c ★★★
Length: P1 40', P2 50', Pro: P1 has 5 QD's, P2 has 8 QD's
A stellar arête climb considered to be one of the better routes at Enola. Walk out to the very end of the narrow trail to an exposed belay perch stance at a single bolt. The belayer should set up a belay here. Ascend up a delicate steep 5.8 face climb (bolts) to a large ledge with a belay anchor. Power up left onto the arête (5.11a) to a tiny no-hands rest stance under the roof. The crux roof is a height dependent (5.11c) inobvious riddle to solve. After you surmount the roof continue to an anchor at the top of the cliff.

The trail descends northward at an angle for about 100' then continues horizontally another 100' to a main amphitheater.

NORTH POINT WALL - MAIN AMPHITHEATER
The base of this wall has an open slightly contoured amphitheater with a string of twelve steep crack and face routes to select from (see topo). This section is broken by a midway horizontal ledge system which is very narrow on the left but is a wider ledge system for the routes on the upper right. The routes on the upper right tier can be accessed by several gear lead starts (see topo).

42. PB Direct 5.10c
Length: 40', Pro to 2"
Start up a 2" wide jam crack (5.10c) on the lower tier to a ledge & belay. Or squeeze up behind

some blocks (5.4) just to the left of the thin crack.

43. Plum Butt 5.10d
Length: 40', QD's
From the midway ledge climb the quality bolted route on a double arête.

44. Thin & Lovely 5.10b
Length: 40', Pro to 1"
A thin seam crack corner system near a large maple tree.

45. This ain't yo momma's five-nine 5.9
Length: 40', Pro to 2½"
A vertical crack corner system.

46. The Plum Arête 5.10d
Length: 40', Pro: 5 QD's & gear
A bolted arête face climb with minor gear placements at the last move near a tree belay.

47. Plumberette 5.10+
Length: 40', QD's
A nice bolted climb on a minor rounded prow.

48. _____
Length: 60', Pro ___
A steep crack corner system.

49. _____
Length: 60'
A deep corner crack system immediately above the initial rock step. Not developed.

50. EMF middle 5.9
Length: 60', Pro to 3"
This line ascends a thin 1" crack to a minor stance, and then launch into a slight bulge following a wide crack corner.

51. EMF left 5.9
Length: 60', Pro to 3"
A nice long wide jam crack on the left side of the main arena that ascends a thin 1" crack then powers into a wider crack on a vertical wall.

Tymun leading the classic route *Psycho Billy Cadillac*

KIWANIS CRAG

KC is truly a roadside crag with zero hiking distance. Composed of vertical Andesite the crag offers climbers a smattering of a dozen 40' tall top-ropes or lead climbs ranging in difficulty from 5.6 to 5.11+. The climbs are mostly crimpy face climbs or positive incut jug holds. Some routes take reasonable gear placements, while others are fully bolted routes or mixed bolt/gear leads. There are plenty of belay anchors, but for some routes you will need to sling a tree to belay.

The nature of the bluff is a short flat slice of well-worn smooth surfaced Andesite that is quite solid, but has a bit of moss on the infrequently traveled routes. Perhaps more climbers visiting KC will help to make this site more user friendly. The entire main wall tilts in-your-face about 2°, but each routes difficulty really depends on the size and quantity of holds. This particular grade of grainy surfaced Andesite is great for friction. Do not drop any gear (water bottles, belay device) because a roaring little stream (south fork Little Zigzag creek) is just beneath your feet a few steep yards away from the crag.

Directions

Drive east of Rhododendron on US 26. Take #39 Road which travels east along the north side of Laurel Hill. Drive 1 mile along this road. Before you reach the Kiwanis Campground a small

◆ MT HOOD ROCK 57

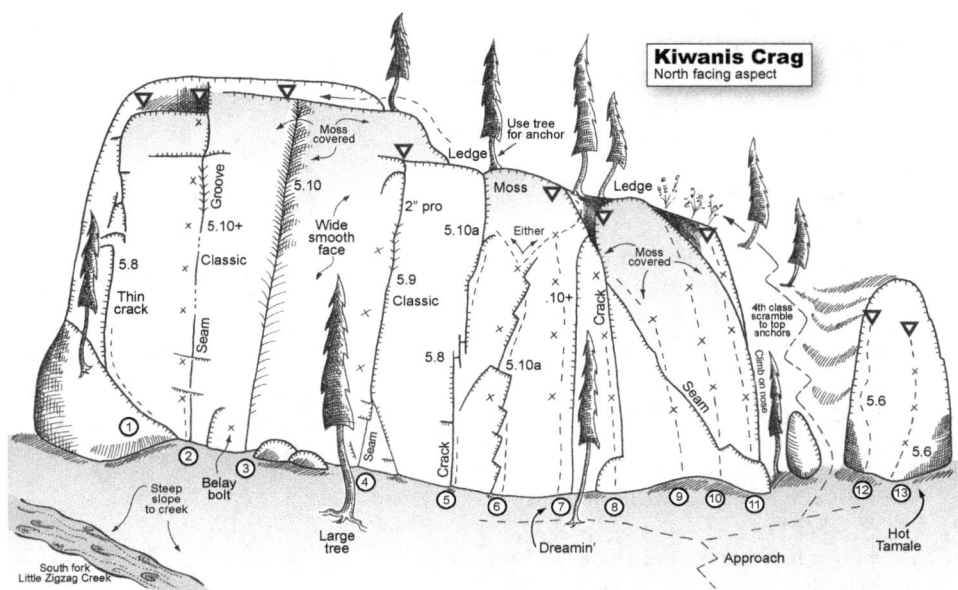

stream splits and runs under the road. The crag is located immediately south of the road next to the stream culvert. The site is ½ mile west of Kiwanis Campground, and ¼ mile east of the gravel road for Paradise Park Trailhead #778. Park alongside the road in a wide spot and have at it.

If you drove right past the little bluff on the way up #39 Road, don't be surprised. If you drive away even after locating the crag…again, don't be surprised. KC is not a destination crag, but the climbs will certainly keep you focused for a few hours.

The routes are described from left to right (see diagram).

1. **Newlywed 5.8** ★
   The far left route smears up to a tiny tree, then dances up small edges (crux) to an anchor on a ledge. Using the tree reduces the rating to 5.8. It might be 5.9 without it. The crack is not easy to protect so leading it is not logical.

2. **Kiwanis Klassic 5.10c/d** ★★★
   Pro: 7 QD's and optional pro to ¾" (cams)
   THE classic climb at KCC and a must-do for everyone. Starts with balancy 5.9, then powers up a slightly hung face crux. As you near the upper pod slot do a crossover, then walk up into the pod. The final bulge is 5.9 and can be pinch smeared on the right to avoid the mantle onto the belay ledge.

3. **_____ 5.10-** ★
   Pro:
   A steep crack, but usually damp because of moss near the top (so clean it out).
   There is a single belay bolt at the start of this crack climb.

4. **_____ 5.9** ★★★
   Pro to 2"
   Excellent lead route that starts with bolts and ends of natural gear. Powers up mostly positive jug holds and incuts on steep ground to a challenging ending.

5. **Sumthng Mssing 5.10c** ★★
   Pro to 1½" (cams are helpful)
   Starts as a great solid 5.8 then punches into a .10+ near the top. A bit mossy at the top.

58 CHAPTER 1

6. **Kosmos 5.10b/c** ★★
   Pro: QD's (minor gear to 1½" if exiting left)
   A great starting climb with positive holds. At the third bolt you either break left (gear) or break right to #7 route to finish. Both exits are powerful and difficult.

7. **Dreamin' 5.10+**
   Pro: 4 QD's
   Although not a logical line, the difficulty focuses on a difficult series of balancy moves. Not easy to consistently stay with the line of bolts, but that's what makes it .10+. And the tree is very close!

8. **_____ 5.9+**
   Pro: 3 QD's and minor gear to 2"
   A prominent bolted closed up crack system that powers up good holds but ends in a widening slot with a bit of moss groveling to finish.

9. **_____ 5.9 [?]**
   A two bolt line that catches a seam mid-way up the face, then angles left to join route #8. Too much moss.

10. **_____ 5.9 [?]**
    A three bolt line that aims directly up through the dense moss madness.

11. **_____ 5.7 [?]**
    A three bolt line that aims directly up the nose at the far right edge of the cliff formation. Too much moss.

The last two climbs are on a small rounded knoll

12. **_____ 5.6**
    A project or perhaps it is already done?

13. **Hot Tamale 5.6** ★
    Pro: 3 QD's
    A surprisingly reasonable short route.

CASTLE CANYON

Castle Canyon trail #765 is a mere .9 mile gentle uphill hike (400' elevation gain) in a nice forested setting ending at a cluster of pinnacles composed of light colored volcanic breccia ash flow conglomerate. The rock is a sandy matrix with various sized rocks and boulders embedded with ledges covered in moss and grass. Potential hand holds simply come loose in your hand. The pinnacles are not your typical formations that one might desire to climb due to the detachable nature of the holds.

For those desperate few who relish the adventure

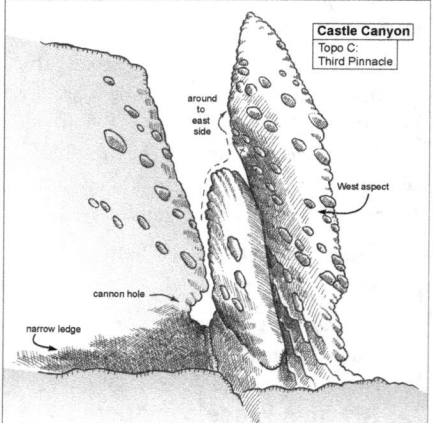

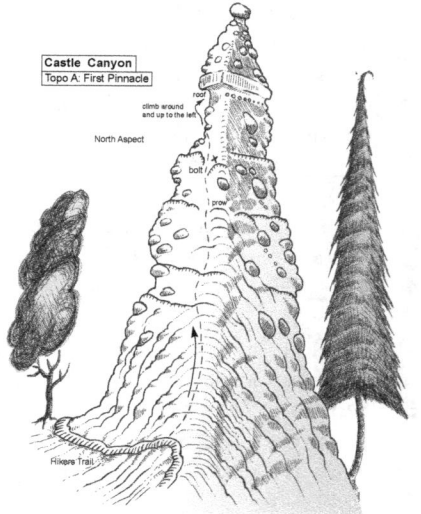

MT HOOD ROCK

Libby Kramm on the Second Pinnacle (Castle Canyon)

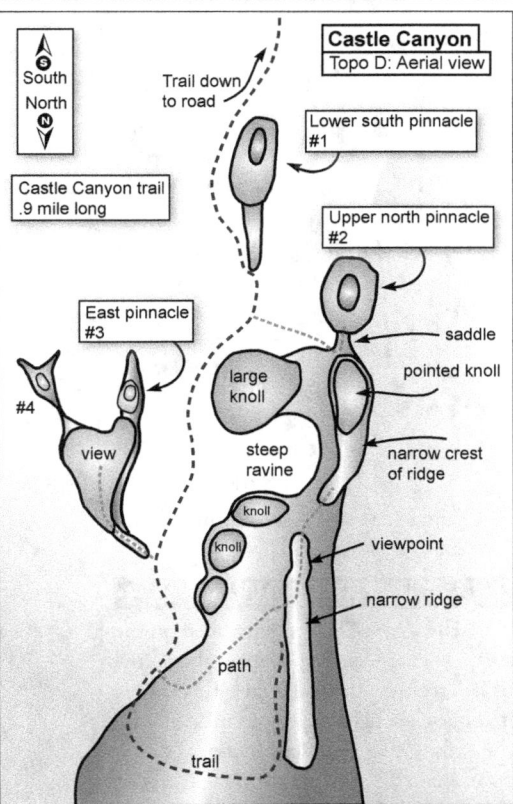

here is some beta.

There are three primary pinnacles. There are narrow ridge features that provide tricky traversing along for views and some of these might offer further exploratory climbing. The First Lower Pinnacle is obvious as the trail weaves around its east flank and up to the saddle on the uphill side. The Second Pinnacle is just west of this first pinnacle, and is rather massive in size, standing nearly 150' on its longest side. The Third Pinnacle is a few steps up the trail and is quite apparent to the immediate east of the trail. It is like a cigar standing on end with a cannonhole next to it. Another minor point of rock exists on the far side of the third pinnacle. The trail ends on a narrow rib that overlooks the Second Pinnacle and offers great views of the valley.

Drive on U.S. 26 to Rhododendron, Oregon and then take a narrow paved road northwest of the community for ½ mile to the trailhead. A few yards up the trail you will enter the wilderness boundary. Since these rock pinnacles lack cracks (for gear) and has very, very old fixed gear, you might consider bringing an adequate selection of tools to get you up the pinnacles.

Zac Reisner climbing on Conkling's Pinnacle

First Pinnacle 5.6 X
FA: Jim Nieland and Libby Kramm in 1969
Jaunt up the north rib past a bulge and cut up around left to top up.

Second Pinnacle 5.4 X
FA: Bill Cummins, Janet Marshall and Jim Nieland in 1968
Their original method of ascent was from the viewpoint but it is also feasible from as shown in the diagram to the saddle with the tree.

Third Pinnacle 5.4 X
FA: Jim Nieland and Libby Kramm in 1969
Start at the cannonhole and chimney up the space between the main wall and the cigar shaped

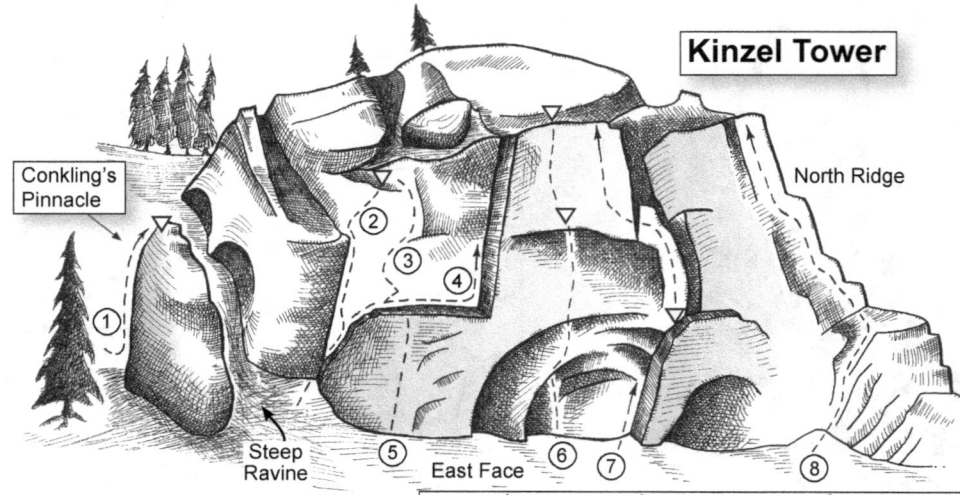

pinnacle to a stance. Cut up around the east side to top up.

KINZEL TOWER

The Kinzel Tower is perched on the steep spruce covered slopes above the Still Creek drainage. Kinzel Tower area has been used lightly by climbers since the early 1950s. The second ascent of the cigar shaped Conkling's Pinnacle was in October 1951 by R. Conkling and Bud Frie.

To get there from Government Camp take the first road east of the State maintenance yard that leads down toward Trillium Lake. Take the surprisingly bumpy road F.S. #2613 southwest past Veda Lake trail, and on toward Kinzel Lake. The road is 10 long, slow miles, so expect 45-60 minutes driving time from Government Camp. Follow the trail toward Devil's Peak about 10 minutes till you see the tower of your right. The main wall is on the east side including Conkling's Pinnacle. The tower is vertical on the east side, even radical in places. Most of the routes are ground-up affairs, and protection can be quite minimal at times so bring pins and bolts. The scramble to the summit from the south has a short 5.3 vertical section.

1. **Conkling's Pinnacle 5.8+**
   Length: 35' Pro: 4 QD's and minor gear to 1"
   A great, little thumb of rock with a few dicey moves near the top. A worthy ascent for everyone.
2. **Squeaky Alibi 5.8+**
   Length: 120', Bring hangers and pro to 3" including cams
   Ascends the right facing corner on the overhung NE face of the main tower, 50' from Conkling's Pinnacle. Excellent corner climbing that leads to a section of face climbing on delicate moves near the anchor.
3. **Butterfly 5.9**
   Length: 120', Bring hangers and pro to 3½" including cams
   Nice route that starts same as SA, then angles up right to a belay on a ledge. Step up left, meander up technical ground then finish up 5.*easy* terrain near the anchor.

4. _____
   Unclimbed steep dihedral corner.
5. _____ **Top-rope**
6. _____ **5.12 project**
7. **Ripples 5.9 PG**
   Length: 100', Bring hangers and pro to 3" including cams
   Nice face climbing on round fat like pinches. Ascends a right leaning corner to a small belay ledge, then exits up left on ripples, crossing an wide odd balancy corner and up steep ground to the top.
8. **North Rib 5.__ [?]**
   An old anchor at top of rib indicates this may have been ascended.

MOSQUITO BUTTE

With a name like 'mosquito' it must be good. This site offers a very small but fine selection of climbing opportunities from 5.6 to 5.11, and fits a general theme suitable to most climbers: quick access, a nearby camping area, and a nice lake for swimming. An idyllic weekend retreat.

Mosquito Butte (aka Trillium) lightly forested rounded rock knoll is an eroded short steep little bluff composed of grainy textured Tertiary andesite (Ta1) from an old lava flow, eroded gradually to expose a steep little cliff. Route offer steep knobby holds or small edges for crimping.

This secluded west-facing bluff is situated in the high cascades in a quiet lightly forested slope, but is often sunny and climbable throughout the summer season from mid-May to October. The primary nuisance you can expect is the pesky mosquito during early summer. The bluff is about 40' tall but yields a cool selection of climbs from 5.6 to 5.11. Not all the climbs are described so you will find other fairly clean climbs in the area, because this small bluff has been utilized as a rock

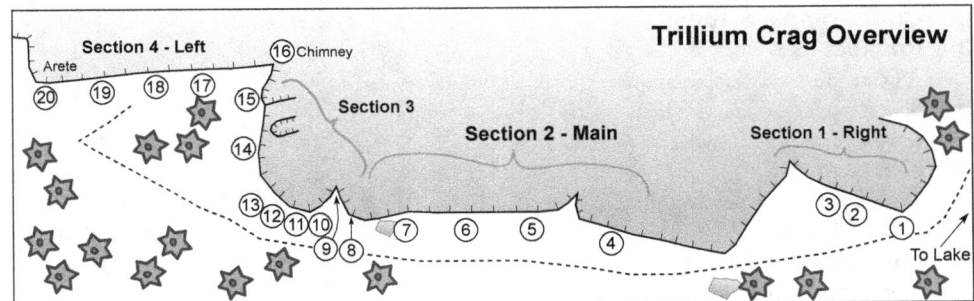

Trillium Crag
Main Wall
Section 2

climbing site for well over 25 years. A short rock wall on the east side of this rounded butte also may yield 6-8 additional potential rock climbs, but has only been minimally used to date. Enjoy the scenic nature of this site; do not litter, and maintain the site for future generations. This site is best for small teams (1-4 persons), but is NOT viable for large groups.

Directions

Drive east from Government Camp on U.S. 26, and turn south on FS 2656. Park near the Trillium Lake Campground and walk to the north end, then follow a well-maintained round-the-lake trail. Near the northeast edge of the lake angle up toward a small bluff but angle around to its lower west side to access this small crag.

1. **Classic Arête 5.10c ★★★**
   A superb arête climb. Power start under an overhanging nose of rock. Reach around left then continue up using pockets and the arête. Ends on pumpy sloped holds near the top. Exit left along the rim to the anchor.
2. **Cool Crimps 5.10b/c**
3. **Pockets 5.8 ★★★**
   A great route with sloping pockets (crux) at the start on a steep face, then ends by using the left edge near top just before you reach the anchor.
3b. **Mosquito 5.5**
   On left flat face aspect is a minor bolt route.
4. **Easy Slab 5.3**
5. **Fun Slab 5.7 ★★★**
   The standard popular route and a good introduc-

Peter Neff at Trillium

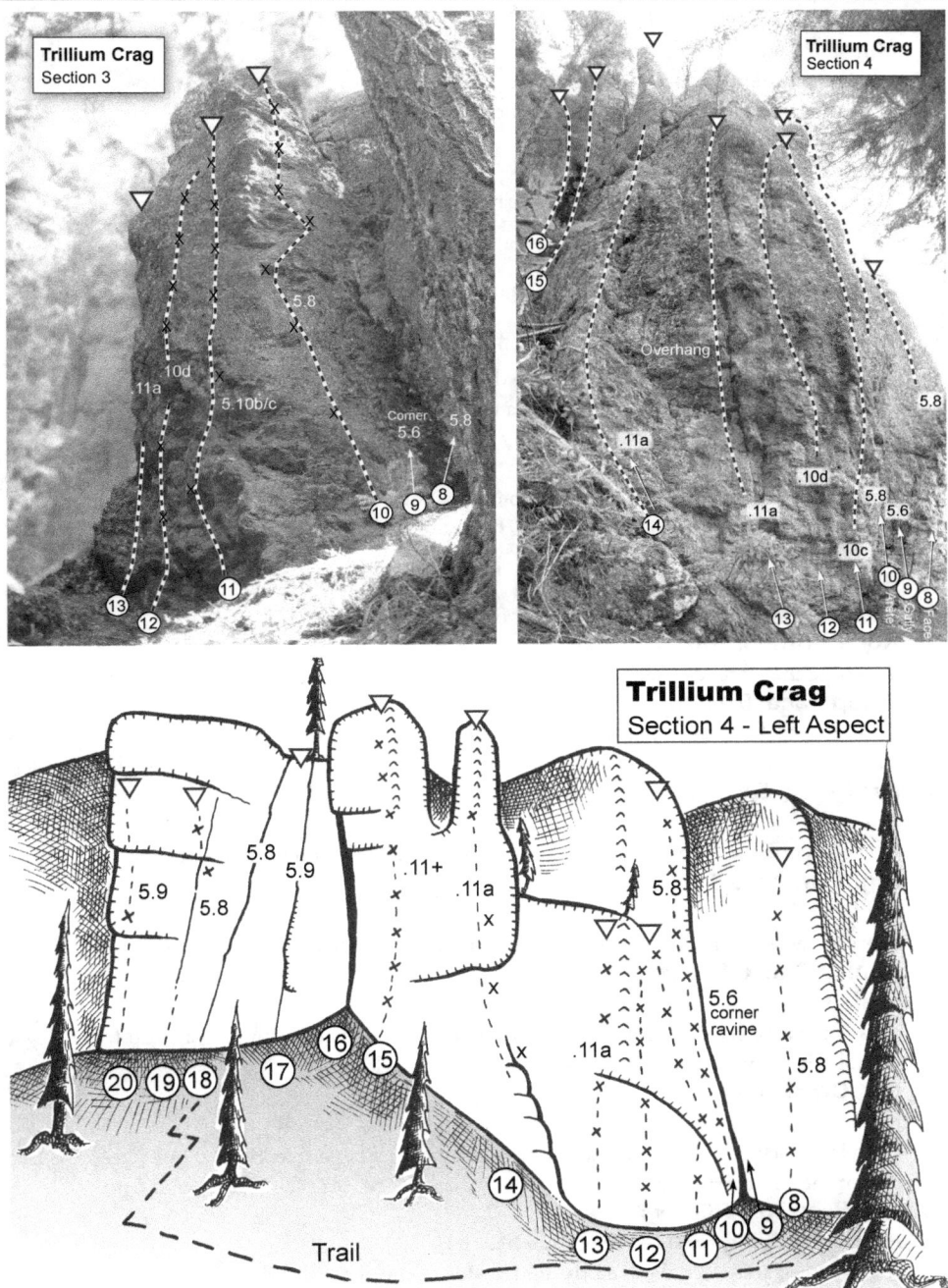

6. **Fun Run 5.7** ★★
   A bit steeper for the first portion of the climb.
7. **Two Small Lips 5.7** ★★
   Two variations on the lower part of this climb. Both are nearly identical in difficulty but most

people enjoy the right variation.
8. **Minor Prow 5.8**
Located on the right face of a deep wide corner system. Starts up a steep slightly hung section but quickly eases.
9. **The Ravine 5.6**
Pro to 3"
Wide corner system (a bit mossy). Pro can be found on left side and in small cracks.
10. **Classic Tall Prow 5.8** ★★★
A roman nose rock feature that is an enjoyable surprisingly steep face climb.
11. **Nubbins 5.10b/c** ★★★
Great climb that starts up a slight bulge then dances up plentiful small chickenhead nubbins on a very steep face to the anchor.
12. **Crimper 5.10d** ★★★
Power up the initial jugs then crimp the remainder of the overhung moves in a timely fashion, then gingerly exit up right onto small knobs on the final slab.
13. **Steep Crack 5.11a**
Balance up an odd steep crack in a slight overhang till it eases some.
14. **Rock Horn 5.11a**
Top-rope that ascends a face busting over a lip onto a steep prow on a tall rock horn.
15. **Steep Face 5.11c/d**
A very steep face climb that ascends up the wall immediately right of a vertical off-width corner system.
16. **Fat Crack 5.9**
Pro to 4"
Obvious gutter ball mossy off-width corner system slightly hung near the top.
17. **Right Crack 5.9**
Pro to 3"
A overly mosssy thin crack next to the chimney corner system. The right most thin crack.
18. **Center Crack 5.9** ★★★
Pro to 3"
This is the area classic and a must for every hunter who enjoys climbing a steep face using a variable sized thin crack on a flat face. The middle crack.
19. **Left Crack 5.8** ★★
Pro to 2½"
Long left crack system that angles up to a belay near a large tree. Several bolts keep the last part of the climb reasonable.
20. **Left Prow 5.8 PG** ★★
Pro to 3" including cams (4" cam if you have it)
A great steep arête face climb on the far left side of this flat wall. Climb over two slight bulges to a stance. Wrap a very long sling around the large fir tree at this stance, otherwise it is a heady unprotected move to the belay anchor.

Hugh leading at *Trillium*

East Side Climbing Opportunities

CHAPTER 2
EAST SIDE ROCK CLIMBS

East side rock provides a formidable wealth of beta suitable to the needs of regionally based rock climbing enthusiasts. This information avenue to good east side rock climbing opportunities is a positive bridge that analyzes the sheer breadth, bulk and beauty of some of these favorite climbing crags situated in the rain shadow of the Cascade Mountain range east of Mt. Hood.

This open-air theater is an ideal forested climate that provides people with a significant opportunity to learn environmental awareness and good stewardship practices on valuable public lands. Through an ongoing level of commitment and cooperation, climbers who developed these climbing sites are interacting with Forest management agencies to ensure that long-term harmonized relationships are established to allow continuous recreational use at these rock climbing sites.

Thanks to this talented group of dedicated climbers, through their energy and momentum the fascinating climbing sites in this east side climbing chapter provide quality destination crags, each in their own reckoning.

Everyone who has visited the Hood River valley knows that this region offers a plethora of extreme sport opportunities at your doorstep from windsurfing to skiing, from mountain biking to rock climbing; all in an area that boasts an ideal mix of sunshine and blue skies. This valley is your gateway to accessible climbing sites in the Cascade Mountain range east of Mt. Hood.

Geology of east side formations

The northern Cascade mountain geographic zone with its eastern sloping incline tends to experience a continuous cycle of seasonal hot and cold temperate fluctuations that strongly influence the process of mechanical and chemical weathering.

At Bulo Point in particular, chemically active water solutions tend to increase the process of granular decomposition of the superficial structures. Bulo Point fits the parameters of the typical northern state rock, igneous andesite, but with a visible dacitic-porphyritic twist in a plagioclase matrix with phenocryst variances of light and dark-colored minerals. The formation is likely an extrusive lava flow or intrusive near-surface sill to be later exposed through erosional processes that removed the less resilient layers. A steady weathering process from water, heat and other factors gradually rounded the overall features of Bulo Point.

Bulo Point has a course-grained texture which, after

Nicole leading the classic route *Jet Stream* 5.9

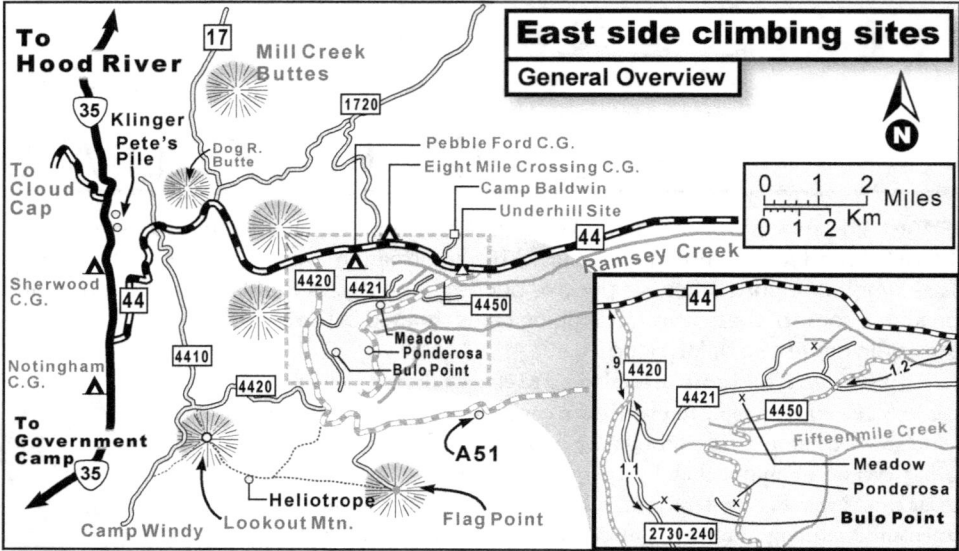

weathering tends to make the overall bluff features well-rounded and the surface akin to a particularly rough grade of sandpaper. This does not necessarily make poor rock, but surprisingly increases edging friction ability so long as you are careful with how you jam your fingers or fists into rough-edged cracks.

Area 51 is composed of porphyritic andesite with large white crystals of plagioclase in a dense mesocratic matrix of light gray colored rock. It has weathered to a steep, slightly overhung bluff with angular layered strata rock cleavage.

Pete's Pile cliff formation is an andesitic formation with an abundance of large clear phenocrysts of plagioclase feldspar in a dense ground mass of medium-gray colored rock.

Seasonal Climatic Variances

The northwest U.S. has a temperate climate that receives an abundance of precipitation mainly because a warm subtropical air mass and a cold polar front jet stream air mass intermingle producing variant seasonal changes in the climate. This climatic diversity of marine and polar air, in conjunction with high mountain barriers provides prominent seasonal contrasts that make rock climbing on the east side of the mountains more attractive.

The western side of the Cascades tends to experience the greatest variance of rainfall. The Willamette Valley sees about 40 inches of rainfall yearly average, the northern Oregon Cascades 80 inches or more, while immediately east of the range in north central Oregon it decreases substantially to about 16+ inches per year.

The effective rain shadow created by the Cascade mountain range allows east side climbing destinations to be your gateway to extended recreation opportunity.

Aside from the winter months when the cold jet stream funnels a steady series of winter snow and rain storms across the region you can find feasible rock climbing opportunity at some of the sites in this guide.

Bulo Point and Area 51 receive similar seasonal weather patterns and are usually inundated with deep winter snow from about November to mid-May, although it is possible to

Wayne on *Bag of Tricks*

access A51 a bit earlier via county roads and FS-2730 west from Friend, Oregon. Once the snow pack fully retreats sunny warm weather conditions usually prevail during much of the mid-May through October climbing season.

Bulo and A51 are ideally situated for rain shadow (in the shadow of Mt. Hood) climbing. Summer daytime temperatures peak in the 70°F - 90°F range. Night time summer temperatures can be cool (40°F +/-) and usually freezing (25°F - 35°F) in the Spring and Fall season because of clear skies and a relatively dry atmosphere typical of higher altitudes.

Since these climbing sites are situated close to the semi-arid Intermontane plateau of The Dalles-Madras-Bend region they tend to share similar daytime temperature characteristics, but are generally cooler than the usual boilerplate summer temperatures found further to the east of the range.

Barney leading at Bulo

This region does enjoy a considerable amount of yearly sunshine and is highly favored by many rock climbers who enjoy venturing beyond the limiting confines of an urbanized rock climbing scene. Even with a tremendous number of sunny days it does occasionally rain even on the eastern sloping Cascade incline, particularly if a mid-summer thunderstorm develops.

So, if you live on the west side of the Cascades and the forecast calls for rain (you know the tune), consider driving east to the rain shadow of the Cascade Range to escape wet weather conditions. In essence, your visit to east side climbing destinations for great rock climbing opportunities is sure to be a success.

Biodiversity dynamics of east side flora communities

East side climbing sites offer climbers a quality climbing experience, and each visitor is encouraged to be an ecological partner. Responsible climbing on our part, in harmony with our natural surroundings, encourages good relations with the Forest managers. Become familiar with plant species at the local climbing sites you are visiting. Vibrant floral species provide beautiful blooms throughout the season, perfect for photographic opportunities.

This region holds a richness of flora diversity worthy of our commitment to study to understand the environs in which these plants thrive. By developing greater knowledge about indigenous plant species of the region in which we rock climb we gain a greater appreciation for environmental values at the rock climbing crags we treasure.

These east side climbing sites provide a life-cycle to all floras in a very short seasonal window of time before the snow returns. Plants bloom and propagate during these short warm months. As a visitor our duration is merely for a day or weekend, while the east side landscape is a year-round flora home.

The relatively dry rain-shadow climate of the eastern Cascade Range has a unique quantitative botanical diversity that helps to sustain this dynamic ecological landscape with a vibrant genetic population of species particularly suitable to this region. The fir-pine-oak woodland zone of the eastern Cascades sustains this network in a balanced structure for flora and fauna communities.

Land managers believe that a balance can be maintained between the regional ecological value and recreational integrity of these climbing sites. You are our partner in this endeavor and through your diligence we hope to promote a legacy of low impact activity vital to the long-term ecological sustenance of these sites.

Management plans are designed to promote a cohesive harmonic ecological balance in conjunction with rock climbing at these sites. Help be a part of the process to ensure a balanced coexistence between climber access and long-term habitat protection.

Environmental Considerations

The lightly forest covered riparian zone of this east sloping Cascade incline is extensively rugged and wilderness-like, except perhaps for the numerous roads that bisect the area. This entire regional resource is a popular destination for many visitors.

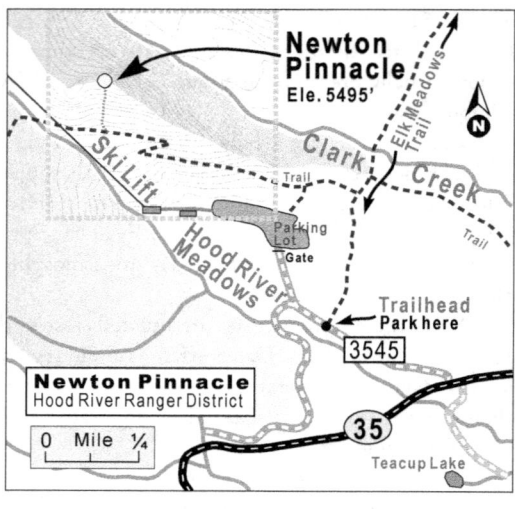

Low-growing vegetation and cliff dwelling plants are surprisingly fragile and visitors are encouraged to treat this vital region with care while climbing at these crags. There is much beauty to enjoy while walking in a forest of tall ponderosa pine. Mountain hemlock can be found at Bulo Point area, while gnarly Oregon White Oak or the bright colored leaves of the Douglas Maple can readily be seen at lower elevation climbing sites.

Many types of native micro-habitat flora inhabit this region, such as Balsamroot and purple Larkspur. The Microseris, Suksdorf's Desert Parsley, and certain Aster's compose just some of the species that make their niche in this ecological riparian zone between the semi-arid desert and high Cascade peaks.

Access and User Impact

Special efforts have been taken to provide a network of established user trails and base areas. Most foot trails are very well marked and have been creatively engineered with stone steps and stone belay platforms to minimize the erosional impact of visiting climbers in a dry, fragile environment. Please utilize the well-developed foot trails (no short-cutting) which provide convenient access to each climbing site and avoid unnecessary trampling of the local plant species. Concerned climbers have taken great strides to create trails designed to limit erosion problems.

Do not remove rare indigenous flora from the cliff, from the rock climb, or along the cliff base. Previous climbing route developers have occasionally left flora and moss in place on certain climbs because of the importance of the species. Certain sections of a bluff may be closed (such as at Pete's Pile) to protect and enhance the flora community. A low impact concept is encouraged for long-term viable use at these sites. Do your part to keep these sites a rare treasure for all climbers by packing out what you pack in.

Please seriously consider leaving your pets at home. A loose, rowdy dog is not everyone's best friend. It can cause more damage in five minutes than twenty climbers in a month, thus it is best to leave the pup at home.

Ethical Continuity

Pre-inspecting routes via rappel is normal business, so rappel bolting is the usual method (though not always) for route development at these crags. Removal of poor quality loose rock is a necessity for future climber safety. Refrain from chopping fixed gear, chiseling or altering holds, retro-bolting existing lines without permission, placing bolts next to quality gear placements, avoid developing 'R' or 'X' rated routes.

It is recommended to wear climbing helmets while leading or belaying. Some of the rock is less than stellar, even at Area 51. Use caution so as to keep your visit a safe journey free of an encounter with unidentified falling objects.

NEWTON PINNACLE

This secluded alpine rock pinnacle, is perched high along a forested ridge above the Hood River Meadows parking lot. From the community of Government Camp, drive 2 miles east on US Hwy 26, then at the three-way highway junction take state Hwy 35 toward Hood River. One mile east of Bennett Pass turn left onto the old Sahalie Falls road. Park near the entrance gate leading to the Hood River ski area. The small pinnacle is visible on the skyline northeast of the entrance gate. Hike northeast along an access road to trail #667 and follow this trail uphill to the ski run, then directly uphill through open forest to the pinnacle along the ridgecrest. A 30-minute approach hike. The northwest face is approximately 60' high, 150' wide and slightly overhung, but offers a liberal amount of hand holds. This site has been frequented for various climbing activity likely since the '50s-'60s based on several old hand-forged pitons found there.

1. **Wage Slave (aka Entropic Gravity) 5.11a** ★★
   A great short lead (QD's) on a crimpy face.
2. **Poison Pill 5.10c**
   Clamber up past a big wedged block.
3. **Logisticon 5.11a** ★★★
   Follow the thin seam using tiny incuts. Great TR.
4. **Neophytes 5.9** ★★★
   Stellar climb that power straight up a vertical face to the large ravine.
5. _____ 5.10+ TR
6. _____ 5.10 TR
7. _____ 5.10+ TR
8. **Gravity Waves 5.9**
   On the far west end is this mixed gear-bolt route sending a face/crack corner past a hang. FA by McGown and partner in early '90s.

LAMBERSON BUTTE

This extensive climbing area stands like a castle wall overlooking the majestic alpine slopes of the wooded Newton Creek drainage. Sheer rock cliffs, green forests of mountain hemlock, glacial moraines ablaze in red heather, and a view of the fearsome Black Spider combine to make Lamberson a remarkable destination for the veteran climber. The wall averages 150' to 200' high and is broken into several major sections offering rock climbing opportunities ranging from 5.8 to 5.12.

By far the most visible, and perhaps the most staggering is the **Great Pig Iron Dihedral**

(5.12a, or 5.10 A2+). Like ocean waves this 160-foot undulating dihedral glimmers in the sunlight, even from afar. Another super classic is **Bag of Tricks** (5.10c), which ascends up ledges, thin corners, and face climbing next to a large slice of rock.

There are routes of every make and color: smooth-as-glass dihedrals, lightning bolt cracks, arête's, flake cracks and high-angle face routes.

Several routes were accomplished by a ground-up means of ascent at Lamberson. Thin pitons, and bolts are usually necessary for success. Ground-up leading is bold, but also rewarding for those who like a fine mixture of free and nailing options. Beware of friable rock when you are exploratory climbing.

Directions

Park at the Hood River Meadows trailhead and hike toward Elk Meadows on trail #645. Take trail #646 following Newton Creek uphill to the Round-the-Mountain trail #600. A viable shortcut exists by hiking along the creek through light brush for the last ½ mile of the approach. Ford the stream and angle up toward one of the crags. The southwest-facing wall lies partway uphill overlooking the Newton Creek drainage. The hike is an easy 1½ hour 3-mile approach.

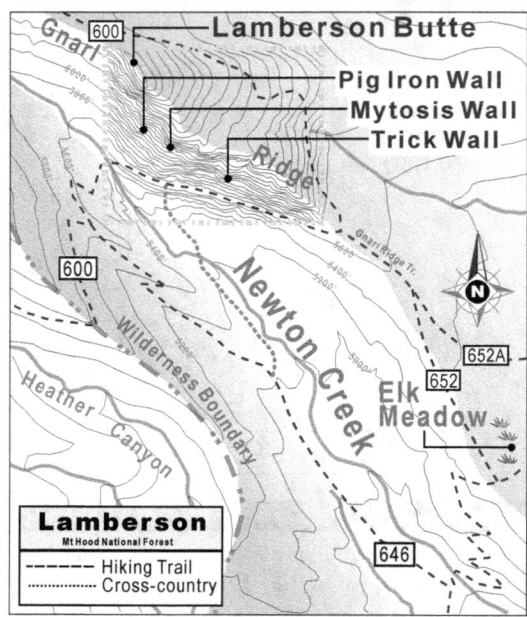

PIG IRON WALL

1. _____ **5.10+**

   A decent 150' top-rope climb if someone is into placing some fixed gear. Climb the main corner then launch out left into a long steep crack system.

2. **Pig Newton 5.10d**

   Length: 120', Pro to 2"

   A fine punchy line just left of Pig Iron. Wander up weird rock and corners, then out left (crux) and up right into the finishing crack to an anchor at a tiny perch.

3. **Great Pig Iron Dihedral 5.12a** ★★★

   Length: 150'

   Pro: KB, LA, TCU's and pro to 1"

   The Great Pig Iron is the most captivating corner climb at Lamberson. It radiates with a glimmer in the mid-day sunlight from afar. And it is certainly a must-do for any aid climber or free climber. The nailing line (5.10 A2) is a thin seam on the left face, but utilizes

✦ EAST SIDE ROCK 71

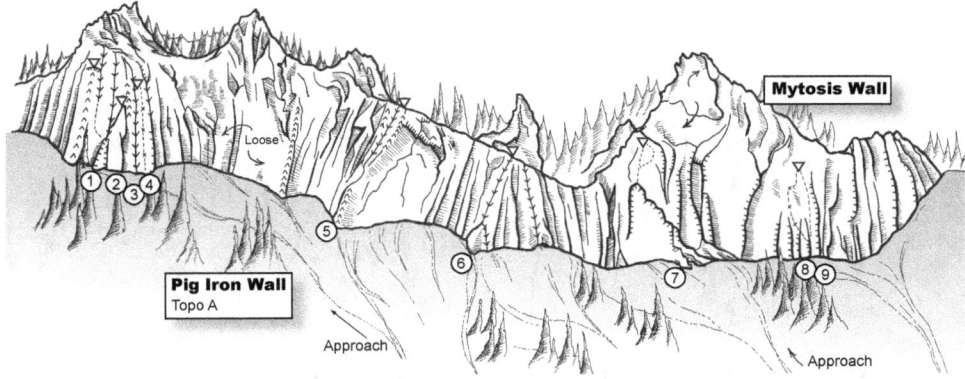

the lower and upper portion of the main corner. If you plan to free the dihedral (5.12a) just power your way directly up the corner past several bolts and gear placements to a belay anchor.

4. **Headhunters 5.11b PG** ★★★
Length: 150'
Pro to 1½" & TCU's, RP's
Quite possibly the finest route at Lamberson. Climbs the very nose of the long buttress immediately right of Pig Iron. A stellar power packed line with many tenuous challenging sections and one very tricky crux move at about mid-height.

5. **Panorama 5.8**
Length: 165', Pro to 3"
Ascends a rock rib then follows a crack corner to the top of the bluff.

MYTOSIS WALL

6. **Trafficosis 5.8**
Length: 150', Pro to 2"

7. **Mytosis 5.10c**
Multi-pitch, Pro to 2" Cams recommended
Aim up left past a tree along a series of steps in a corner to an airy stance. Continue onto the flat face above using thin cracks that angle up right. Power past a final small roof to a belay.

8. **Thirty-six Light Years 5.11b or 5.9 A2**
Length: 155', Pro to 2" TCU's suggested
A wild climb if you can locate it. Start just right of a broken corner system. Climb up to a long right facing thin corner crack till it ends. Power up right using face holds and thin seams on a wide flat face (bolts) till you reach easier terrain. Rappel.

9. **Catch Me If I Fall 5.11**
Length: 165', Pro to 2½" & pitons

TRICK WALL

1. **Poultry Picnic 5.9**
Length: 60', Pro to 3"
Way over on the left end of Trick Wall is a fine little climb on the right side of a steep minor nose. Aim for the notch to a tree belay on a ledge. Rappel.

Wayne nailing *Pig Iron Dihedral*

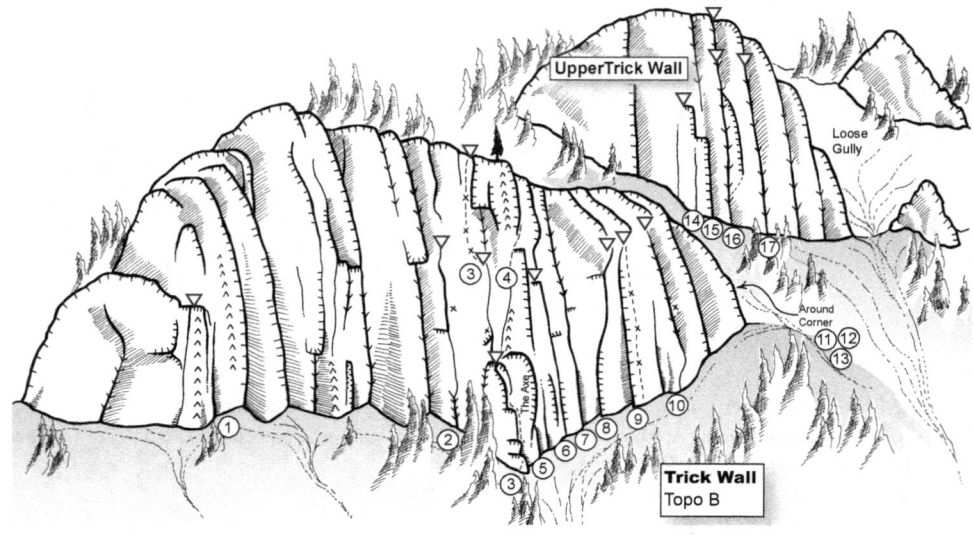

Trick Wall
Topo B

2. **Crash of the Titans 5.10c** ★★
    Length: 100', Pro to 2½" & cams
    A stellar climb punching up a thin seam corner past a flake on a flat face. Rappel anchor.
3. **Bag of Tricks 5.10c** ★★★
    Multi-pitch, TCU's, RP's and pro to 3"
    This superb climb starts on the left side of the sharp blade-like rock feature at the base nose of a prominent buttress on the Trick Wall. **P1 60':** Begin up numerous steps and ledges to a ledge belay near the notch. **P2 50':** Power up left into a minor crack corner that runs up to a nice perch belay under a small roof at a small tree. **P3 50':** Smear up left (bolts) onto the blank face and continue (crux) up a thin crack to a left facing corner to exit onto the top of the bluff at a large tree. Walk off.
4. **Upper Prow 5.10+**
    This is an interesting variation that ascends a thin crack up right from just above the first belay and above the 'axe' rock rib feature. Unconfirmed rating.
5. **Variation Start 5.10a**
    Length: 60', Pro to 1½" including pitons
    This starts on the south side of the blade-like rock feature by ascending a crack weakness to the notch. Merge with P2 Bag of Tricks and continue up.
6. _____ **5.11+ ?**
    Length: 80' TR
    Interspersed with a few ledges but has a long sustained smooth crux corner system.
7. _____
8. **Trafalgar 5.10c** ★
    Length: 80', TCU's, Friends to 3" required
9. **Arête 5.11b** ★★
    Length: 80', Pro: QD's
    A quality face climb that ascends a steep crimpy face on a minor rib.

Wayne on *Momma Bo Jomma*

10. Test Tube 5.10a A0 R
Length: 80', Pro to 2" & pitons
A long corner groove climb with some runout.

11. Quantum Gravity 5.8 ★★
Length: 60', Pro to 3"
QG and the next two climbs are situated on the uphill southeast facing side of this wall. It faces toward the Upper Trick Wall.

QG is a nice thin corner crack to a notch, where you face climb up another short distance to the bolt belay anchor shared by all three routes.

12. Pushover 5.10c ★★
Length: 60', Minor pro to 2"
Pushover is the center face climb immediately right of the crack corner.

13. Sunset Bowl 5.9
Length: 80', Pro to 3"
SB takes on the right side of this flat face mainly following the rib using some minor cracks along the way.

UPPER TRICK WALL
14. Lightning Bolt Crack 5.12 TR
15. Momma Bo Jomma 5.10c ★★
Length: 80', Pro to 3" & cams
A stellar climb. A deep dihedral corner system powers straight up with wide stems. As the crack widens place a piece high in the thin right crack, then launch out left into the offwidth moves and exit onto a stance where the Lightning Bolt Crack meets. Continue up a short chimney move to the bolt anchor and rappel.

Wayne on *Crash of the Titans*

16. **World is Collapsing 5.10c** ★
    Length: 150', Pro to 3" & cams
    Immediately right of Mamma.

17. **Sanctum 5.10b** ★★★
    Length: 165', Pro to 3" & cams
    Another stellar climb. A powerful steep corner stemming and face climbing extravaganza.

PETE'S PILE

Written by David Sword (Introduction and Beta)
History of the Area

Kendall Karch on For Pete's Sake

It was the summer of 1984, and I was on the hunt for a job before ski season rolled around. I was sitting on the porch outside of the Mt. Hood Country Store when a baby blue '67 Nomad rolled up. A friendly faced Newfoundland stuck his head out the passenger window, and a stringy blonde haired man with Popeye sized forearms jumped out, fired me a quick handshake and said, "Pete's the name, and danger's my game." Two things I quickly learned about Pete Rue were that he was always game for climbing, and he was rarely seen without his dog, Andy.

Pete's early explorations took him all across the Hood River valley in search of climbing possibilities. One day he asked me along to explore a crag across from Pollalie creek. The rock here was messy and frightening. Broken, fractured, and unstable basalt was the norm, but plumb sections of pure joy offered a respite from the pain. Many near misses came during these initial outings, with both emotional and physical scars to prove it. During one first ascent, Pete lead through a tough vertical hand crack. "Watch the loose flake!", he yelled. Even twenty five years later I can see that flake buzzing past my head as my girlfriend climbed ahead of me. We finished the route at sunset and rappelled to the ground without headlamps. As with many of our early ascents, the route itself still stands, but the quick sketch topo made on the inside of a matchbook on the car ride home was lost long ago. Most of the early ascents were never recorded, and many of the original lines lay in repose, awaiting new motivations and adventurers to make their mark.

Later, we continued to the south and began to explore the vertical columns of what we now know as Pete's Pile. Any vision for an accessible climbing area came from Pete, and his obsessive bond with the Pile became almost legendary. Pete single-handedly put the crag on the map while most of us were driving to Smith Rocks or doing crack laps at Beacon Rock. Establishing a climbing area can be an arduous task. For some time Pete did much of the laborious work himself, including hauling in secretly quarried rock for the stairs. Eventually he found he could motivate locals by offering up lunch and beers in return for physical labor; and sometimes even a shot at a new FA.

EAST SIDE ROCK

David Sword leading at Pete's Pile

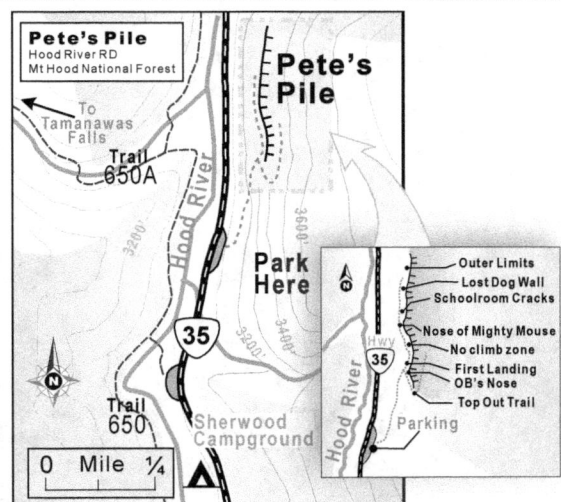

The name Pete's Pile became the local's reference for the outcrop, but other names, such as Pollalie Crags, Sunset Dihedrals, and East Fork Columns were discussed in the early development stages.

Surely ascended before the mid 1980's, climbers from the past left only tattered slings and a handful of fixed pitons; not exactly a clearly marked road map. There were rumors that some famous names had stopped by, and we wondered if perhaps Fred Beckey or Yvon Chouinaird ever graced the crag. Most likely however, the fixed remnants were left by local pioneers who used the outcrop for aid climbing and rescue practice.

We taught ourselves how to aid climb and to rope solo from a well worn copy of Robbins' Advanced Rockcraft. Where the book fell short we would fumble around with the intricate details until it felt good. When a solid stance was reached, or when we ran out of rope or motivation to continue the grind, piton and stopper belay stations were built. As the sport climbing movement in America was still young and extremely controversial, most all the early ascents were accomplished from the ground up. The first permanent top anchors were placed at the top out of Pop Bottle (.10a), by Pete using a 22 ounce framing hammer and a handful of Rawl bolts poached from a construction job. Pounding anchor bolts into the hard Oregon Basalt led to severely blistered hands, but the man would not be swayed by such trivial set-backs. We taped over the wounds so Pete could top-rope the route later that same day.

As is common at climbing areas, there were controversies at the crag. When talks of further crag development evolved, area naturalists were worried about the effect it would have on a plant species known as Suksdorf Violet Rock-Brake (Suksdorfia violacea). At the time, the violet flowers were only found growing on a handful of northwest facing rock abutments. Active local climbers met face to face in an attempt to find common ground, and in conjunction with local USFS personnel, a climbers association was developed. One of the main tenants of the now defunct group, was to protect this rare flora. Even greater alarm developed when locals devised a powerful route cleaning technique for the dirt and moss choked dihedrals. By securing a fire hose to a seasonal drainage atop the crag, new routers could quickly pressure wash the rock, virtually eliminating the gargantuan efforts required previously. Clearer thinking, and more ecologically forward minds prevailed, and only a few routes sprouted from the Firehose era.

Climber's from the past and present who helped shape the crag include Pete Rue, Dr. Roger Stewart, JD Decker, Stewart Collins, Emily Kohner, Jim Thornton, Susan Nugent, Jim Opdyke, Deno Klein, David Sword, Reed Fee, Elmo Mecsko and the late Jeremy Flanigan. With the continued efforts of USFS personnel, and the continued adherence to local guidelines from the climbing

Pete's Pile
Route analysis for the upper cliff face

community, the balance of recreation and preservation has been created and continues to move forward. As of today, the Suksdorf Violet Rock-Brake at Pete's Pile is growing stronger than ever, and has botanists reviewing its status as a sensitive species.

Dimensional Scope of the Crag

Pete's Pile is a hidden gem and one of only a handful of traditional climbing areas in the region. The crag is an excellent multi-season climbing area generally free of snow from April through October. Kept secret for a few decades, only recently has Pete's seen much traffic from outside the local community. Even today the crag remains a quite place to get your crack climbing skills up to par, and the scenic beauty is well worth the price of entry. Amazing views of the eastern and north slopes of Mt. Hood await you while climbing here. As the base of the crag sits a couple of hundred feet above the East Fork of the Hood River, once you climb to tree top level, the sense of exposure is spectacular. Most of the current routes are moderate (5.10 and under), and the potential exists for dozens of more climbs of various grades.

Guidelines for climbing here are straightforward and simple; 1) If you pack it in, you pack it out. This includes cigarette butts, food wrappers, TP, and tape; 2) Do not remove dirt or vegetation from cracks unless it is necessary to provide safe hand-holds, steps, or for placement of protection. The Suksdorf Rock-brake has continued to grow for years even in some of the established climbing areas because climbers have left the soils surrounding the plant intact. Suksdorfia violacea is found throughout the climbing area, and is most easily identifiable by it's puffy, round violet flowers that are reminiscent of something from the pages of Dr. Suess; 3) Stay on the established trail system to avoid soil erosion. This includes the access trail, the base area trail beneath the climbs, and the descent trail from the top of the cliff.

Geology Of Pete's

The exposed cliff line making up Pete's Pile is basalt made up from ancient flows originating from the Cloud Cap area of Mt. Hood. Geologist refer to the columnar formations as olivine-bearing basaltic andesite, which is common on the northern flanks of Oregon's largest volcano. Although vertically sliced, the broad band of basalt has many features conducive to climbing. The steep and sustained nature of the rock is softened slightly by incut edges, ledges and pockets, and the soaring cracks accept a multitude of traditional protection. Adding to the challenge are overhanging roof sections, which become more prominent as you move northward. Sections of loose rock exist and necessary precautions should be followed. A 60-meter rope is standard here, but 70m ropes are handy. A standard free climbing rack is sufficient for most climbs. Don't forget a nut

✧ EAST SIDE ROCK 77

Pete's Pile Route Overview

Legend: Trees, Boulders, Trail

Labels on overview: Top of Cliff, Cliff base, Outer Limits, Boulder field, 27, 26, 25, 24, 18 to 23, 17, 3rd landing, 11 to 16, Schoolroom Cracks, 7 to 10, OB's Nose, No climb zone, 2 to 6, 1st landing, 1, OB's Nose, Top of Cliff, Lounge Chair, Top out trail, Approach Trail

Pete's OB's Nose Map 1

5.8

1

Beer Garden

tool for the gear gobbling cracks, and long runners or cordelette, which are useful for belays and top anchors.

Some routes can be approached from the top of the crag by setting up rappels and top ropes. The top of the crag is sloped and tiered, and anchors are neither marked, nor necessarily convenient for setting up top ropes. Extreme care should be taken for your own safety and for the safety of those below you! Route numbers begin at the right most portion of the crag (OB's Nose) where the approach trail first meets the rock, and proceed northward (left).

Directions

Drive south from Hood River on Hwy 35 for 23¼ miles toward Mt. Hood. Park at a dirt pullout on east side of the highway (the pullout is ¾ mile south of the Cooper Spur Road and ¼ mile north of the East Fork Trail #650).

From Portland follow Hwy 26 to Government Camp. Take the Hwy 35 exit towards Mt. Hood Meadows ski area and Hood River. Park at a dirt pullout on east side of the highway located 0.6 miles north of Sherwood campground.

Parking and Approach

At a small pullout on the east side of the highway access a parking area made from an old section of roadway. An unmarked trail ascends towards the crag. As you near the cliff, sign posts directs you to the left (base of the crag) or to the right (top access). Once at the base of the crag, the trail follows the cliff band, terminating at the northern end of the established climbing area (Sandbox). The climbing routes are listed from right to left as you first encounter the cliff.

SOUTH END

The first climb you encounter on the approach trail is the Beer Garden located on a minor nose of rock at the sound end of the main bluff.

1. Beer Garden 5.8 ★★
Length: 80' (30m), Pro to 2½"
Beer Garden is a clean blocky route punctuated with plenty of steps and edges on the lower portion, and ending in a steep crack corner for the finale. It is a well traveled climb and rightly so because it protects reasonably well.
Belay from the trail or 3rd class to a higher platform. Wander around on slabby moves until it gets steep, and then stick to the right side. Anchors at top sit back from the lip so bring cordelette for a TR or be mindful for rope cuts.

78 CHAPTER 2

THE FIRST LANDING

As you ascend the trail northward you first encounter the cliff scarp at a large dusty landing spot at the base of a series of popular rock climbs.

2. For Pete's Sake 5.8 ★★★

Length: 92' (28m)
Pro to 2½" including cams

Another great moderate climb whose attention is well deserved. Although it starts up odd blocks and steps it quickly fires into a superb steep

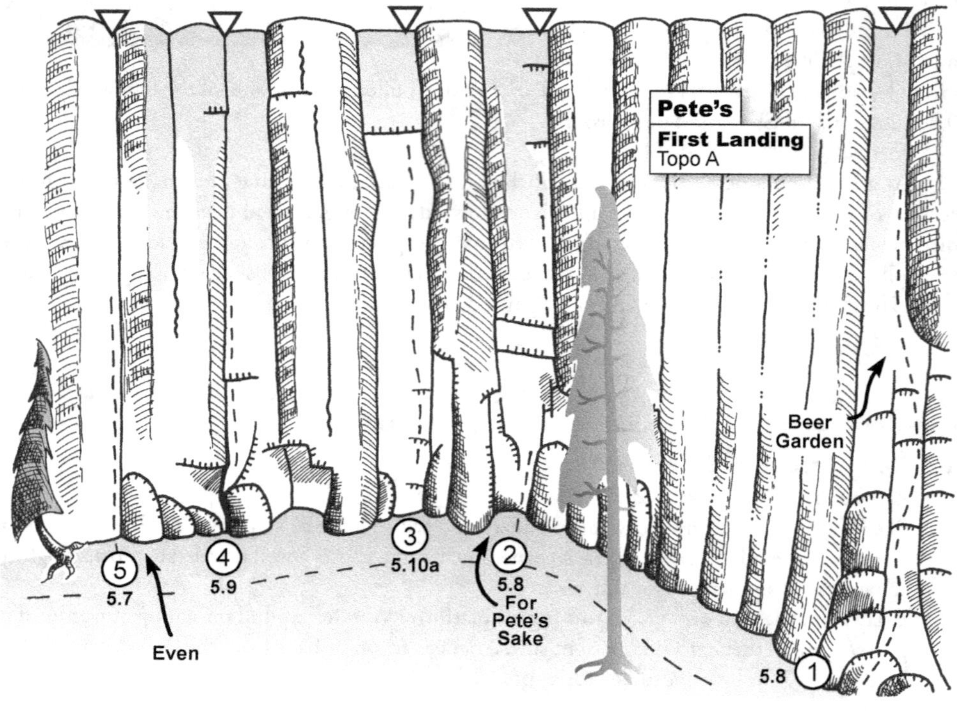

Pete's First landing Map 2

③ Guillotine

② For Pete's Sake

Pete's First Landing
Topo A

⑤ 5.7 — Even
④ 5.9
③ 5.10a
② 5.8 For Pete's Sake
① 5.8
Beer Garden

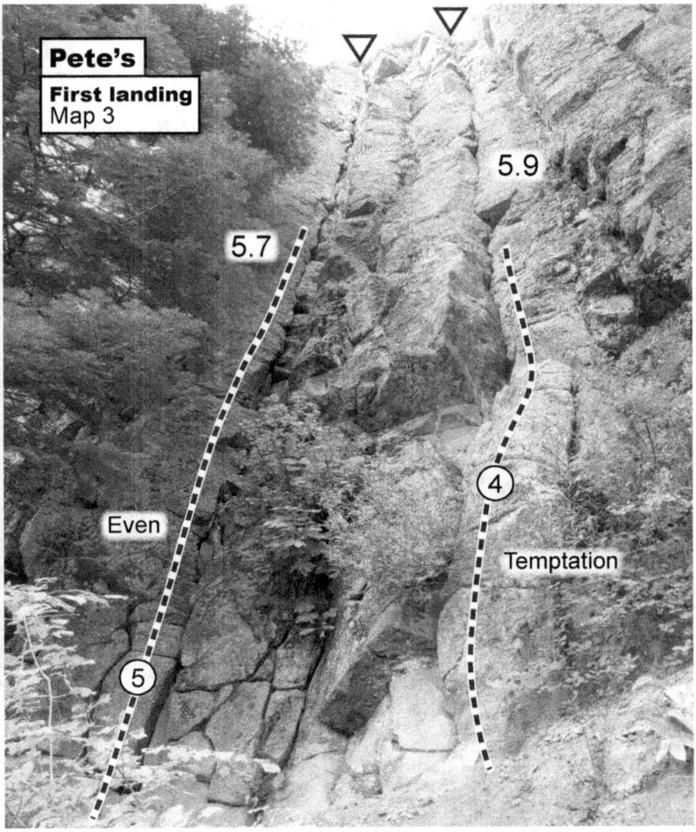

corner crack that jams well and protects very well. This route is entertaining all the way to the very end with diverse moves on steep basalt with a crux section up high on the route.

3. **Guillotine 5.10a** ★★
   Length: 92' (28m), Pro to 2"
   A brilliant climb that tackles a steep dihedral and small roof resembling a guillotine, A great rest on the left welcomes you about 35' up the route, just before you pull over the roof and climb up the smooth surfaced crux section just above. A long section of sustained climbing with great jams takes you to the top of the bluff.

4. **Temptation 5.9** ★★
   Length: 92' (28m), Pro to 2½"
   With a crux close to the ground this steep 'niner is another gear gobbler worth its weight. The triangular roof visible from the ground is the crux. Diverse and challenging climbing all the way to the anchors.

5. **Even 5.7** ★★★
   Length: 92' (28m), Pro to 3"
   A high quality moderate and certainly a must do route for every visitor. The route offers good protection with ample rest stances between the crux sections. Belay tree marks the beginning of the right facing book. Be mindful of some minor loose rock below and left of the belay bolt anchor.

NO CLIMB ZONE

80 CHAPTER 2

Between the route called 'Even' and the route 'Mighty Mouse' but before you reach the Schoolroom Cracks, there is a protected riparian zone that is set aside for flora preservation purposes. The Suskdorf Violet Rock-Brake grows well in this dark water stained cliff scarp. Signage placed at both ends of this section reminds climbers that this is preserved as a 'no climb zone'.

NOSE OF MIGHTY MOUSE

A prominent feature at Pete's Pile is a buttress formation that dips low along the entire stretch of the trail just before you reach the Schoolroom Cracks area. This is the Nose of Mighty Mouse which provides a haven of classic lines that will surely challenge the crack climbing aficionado.

6. Mighty Mouse 5.10b ★★
   Length: 165' (50m), Pro to 2"
   This is a long steep sustained crack corner climb starting at the base of a sunny buttress of rock. Start up steps and launch into a long crack system to a bolt belay at mid-height. Continue up another crack system to the top of the cliff. Rappel from anchors. Originally given a sandbag rating of 5.9.

Mighty Mouse Rappel

The Mighty Mouse rappel is a single 60-meter rope rappel for descending down from the top of Pete's Pile. A cliff top anchor and a mid-point anchor offer a convenient means to rappel if you have only one rope and you have topped out on a nearby route.

7. Stinger 5.10b
Length: 82' (25m) TR

A wild top-rope problem on the nose of MM buttress. Start at absolute toe of the buttress and work thin moves up to the protruding arête. Climb the arête using smears and side pulls for 70'. Access to the black painted rappel anchors by climbing nearby routes or from lowering in from top of cliff.

8. Tribes 5.10b
Length: 165' (50m), Pro to 2"

Long steep sustained climb.

9. S.T.A.R.D. (aka Pedestal) 5.10a
Length: 82' (25m), Pro to 2"

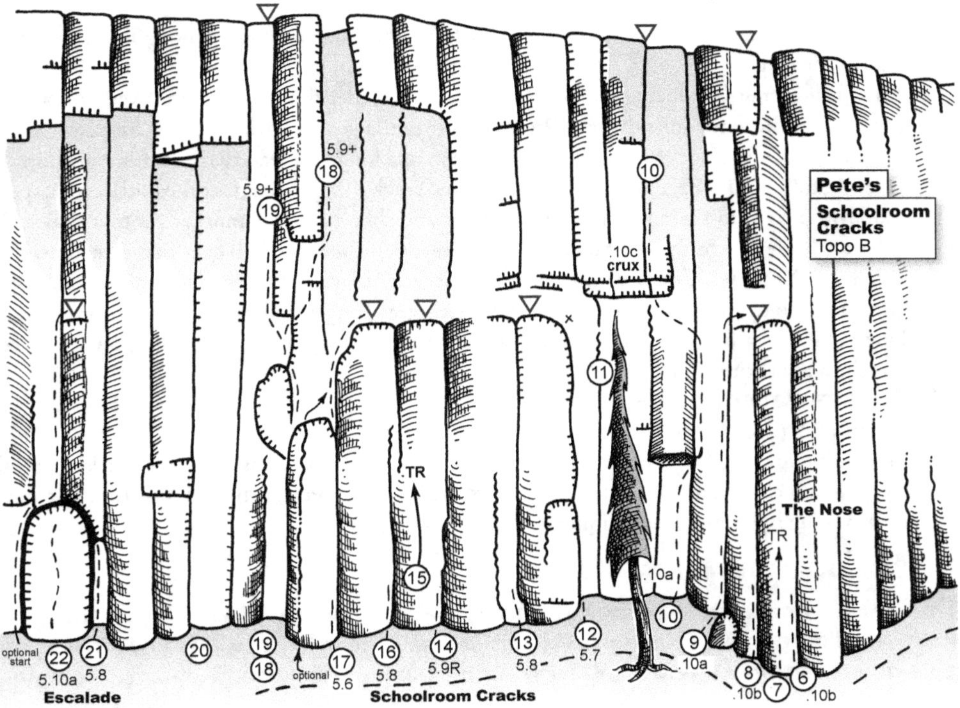

STARD is an acronym for short, thin and hard. An apt description for this seldom traveled

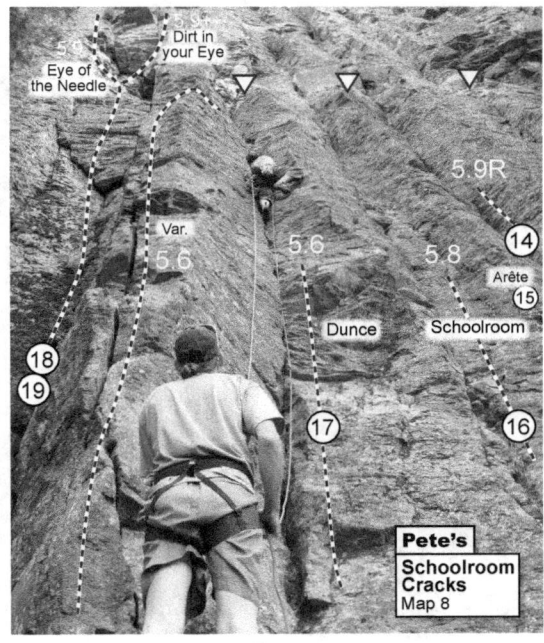

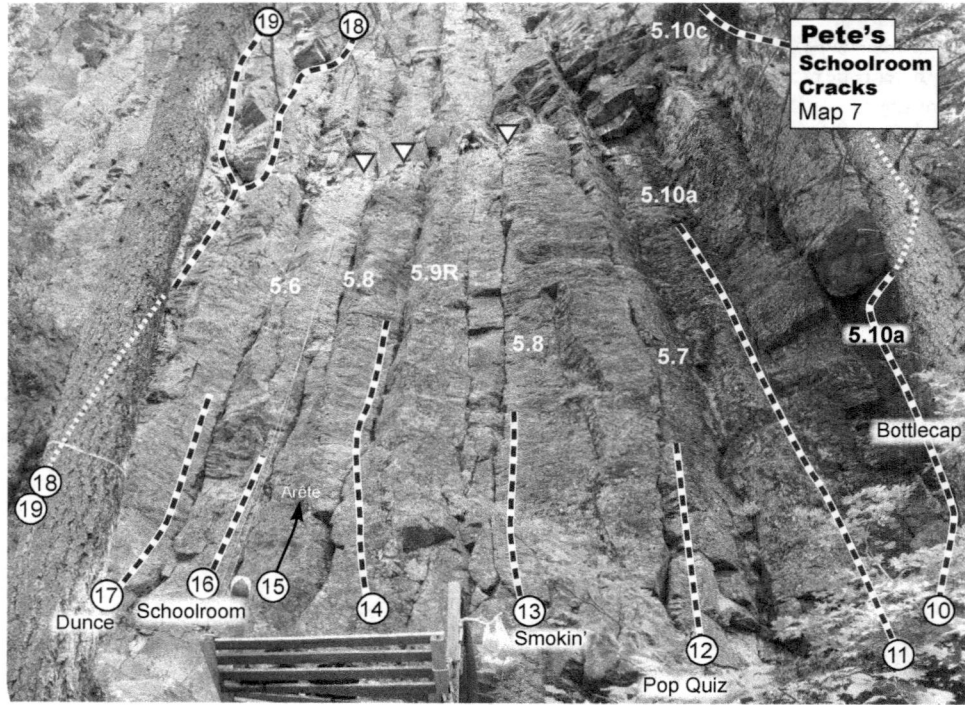

route. Begin up the shallow left facing dihedral with the pencil thin detached flake.

10. **Bottlecap P1 5.10a, and P2 5.10c** ★★★
    Length: 165' (50m), Pro to 2½"
    You can recognize this route by the dark 'bottlecap' shaped overhanging roof 35' up the initial part of the climb.
    An old slider nut left during the FA remained fused under the crux roof for over a decade; a testament to both its difficulty and few ascents over the years. Bottlecap is the first 5.10 route established at the crag. This climb can be done in one long 165' lead to the summit anchors.
    Pitch 1 (82') 5.10a: Begin by climbing up a steep crack till you are under the bottlecap shaped roof. Move right to surmount past this feature, and then continue another 20' to a stance. A belay anchor exists to the right on the next route if you choose to bail over that direction.
    Pitch 2 (82') 5.10c: Continue up left to another smaller roof. Pull through this second roof and continue up very steep sustained crack with great finger and hand jams. If done in one long pitch it is a full 165' long. A great welcome-to-the-crag route with solid power packed punch to the entire climb.

11. **Doctors Patient 5.10a**
    Length: 82' (25m), Pro to 2"
    Start in mossy corner left of the Bottlecap roof. Ascend a mossy corner to the bottlecap roof, step left and climb a dirty crack to a cluster of broken roofs. Power through this roof and continue via jug holds and crack climbing to the belay anchors.

SCHOOLROOM CRACKS

The Schoolroom Cracks is the second large flat dirt landing area, and this section provides the most popular selection of climbs at Pete's Pile. A large wooden bench is available here to sit on while you are relaxing between climbs. The belay anchors (three total) for the next six climbs are located 70' up the cliff face. You can access all three belay anchors by leading up the route of your choice and traverse left or right to access the other anchors. By far the most ascended zone at the crag, many of these cracks were climbing in the 1980's, and have been named and renamed more than once.

12. Pop Quiz 5.7
Length: 70' (21m), Pro to 2½"
Though very dirty it is a seemingly viable method to the schoolroom cracks bolt belay anchors. Follow low angle crack up and left to anchors above Smokin'.

13. Smokin' 5.8 ★★★
Length: 70' (21m), Pro to 3"
A superb moderate climb that is totally worth leading. Though most first time climbers start with Dunce, Smokin' is an optimal warm-up climb with a plethora of edges, great jams and good protection placements. A second pitch ascends the slightly overhanging left facing dihedral to top of the cliff. It's rating is unknown, but is certainly a couple of grades harder.

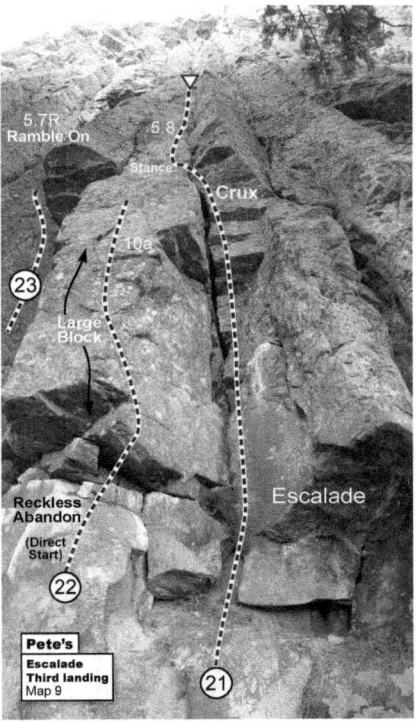

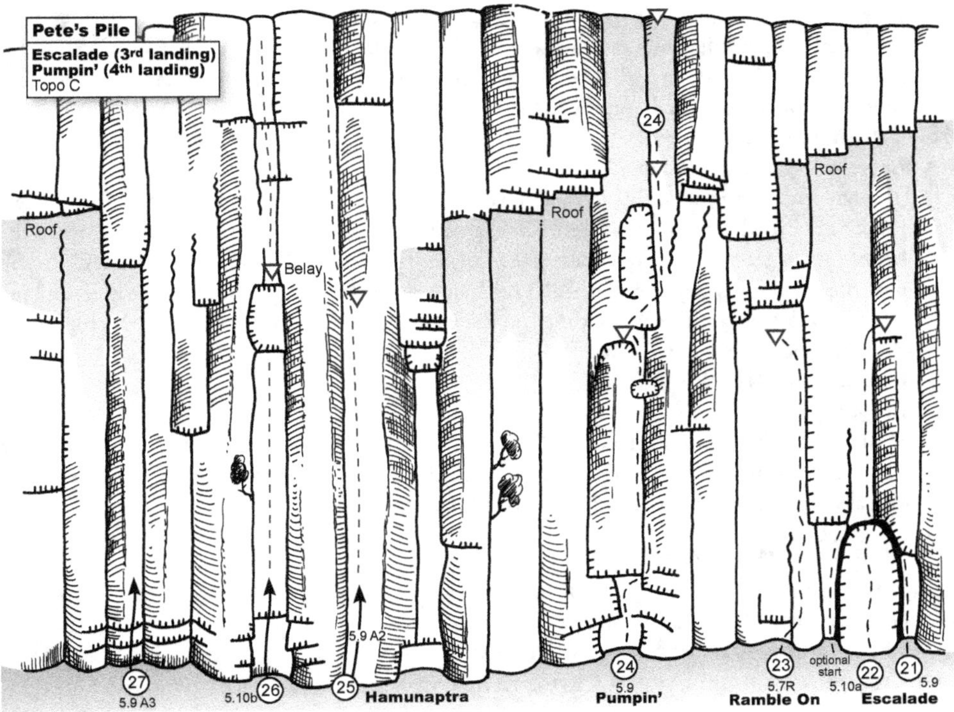

14. Not For Teacher 5.9R ★★
Length: 70' (21m), Pro to 2"
Though less often led this shallow open book crack climb is great even as a top-rope. The route is unusually tricky with odd smears and small featured edge holds that keep climbers challenged all the way to the anchors.

15. Times Tardy 5.10a
Length: 70' (21m) TR
An eliminate top rope effort between Smokin' and Not For Teacher. Edge, smear, pinch and layback up the arête. Using crack on either side lowers the grade to 5.8

16. Schoolroom 5.8 ★
Length: 70' (21m), Pro to 2"
Schoolroom is no less challenging than its immediate neighbor to the right (Not for Teacher). A challenging shallow open book crack climb filled with jams, smears and tiny edge features. A route that will challenge your balance.

17. Dunce 5.6 ★★★
Length: 70' (21m), Pro to 3"

The most frequently climbed route at Pete's Pile since most visiting climbers head straight to the Schoolroom Cracks area first. Wander up a crack 15' and pull past the small roof, and then zen your way through a few tenuous moves to easier terrain and a wider crack. Large edges and steps make the last few moves a cruise to the bolt anchors. Climbers often traverse from this bolt anchor over to the next bolt anchors to set up a top-rope for all the Schoolroom Cracks routes, but if you do watch out for rope drag!

18. Dirt In Your Eye 5.9+
Length: 165' (50m), Pro to 4"
Though seldom ascended this is a unique climb with great history and character. The earliest route established to the top and Pete Rue's favorite. Begin by jamming up a crack corner to the left of Dunce targeting the obvious right facing chimney capped with a chockstone. Once you near the small roofs step over to the RIGHT side of the detached pillar and continue climbing a wide crack (beware the chockstone) on the right side of the long column to the top of the cliff. Fun and diverse movement.

19. Eye Of The Needle 5.9+
Length: 165' (50m), Pro to 3½"
EOTN takes the same start as Dirt in your Eye up to the roofs. From there it stays on the LEFT side of the detached rock pillar using hand jams and edges to ascend a wide crack dihedral system to the top of the cliff. Use a tree for a belay anchor.

THE SECOND LANDING

A few yards further along the trail past the Schoolroom Cracks is another large flat dirt landing area. A series of fine quality routes begin here including the classic and popular Escalade. After Ramble One the trail dips down a bit past another small cluster of routes before aiming north out onto an open boulder field slope below the Sandbox

P2 5.8
P3 5.9
Triangular Roof
P1
5.9
Roof
Pete's Pile
Pumpin' for the Man
Map 11
24

K9 roof
27
Acoustic Kitty
5.10a/b
5.10b
Pete's
Map 12
Cryan's Shame
26
25
Hamunaptra

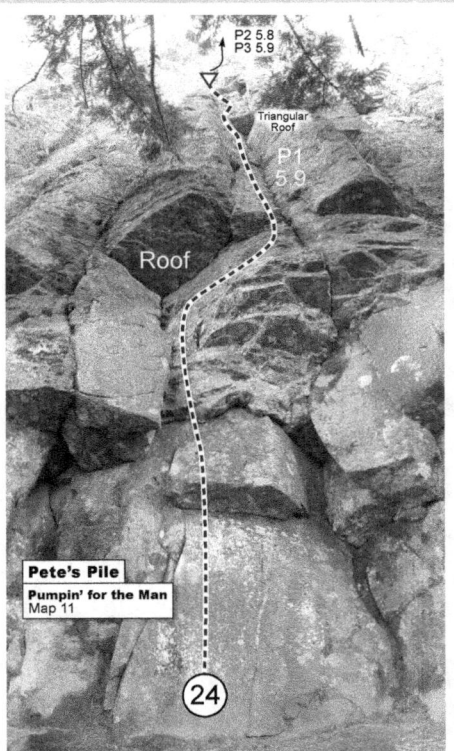

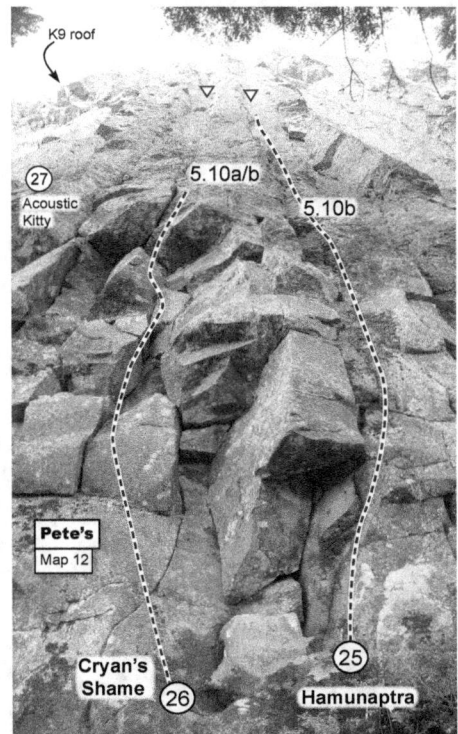

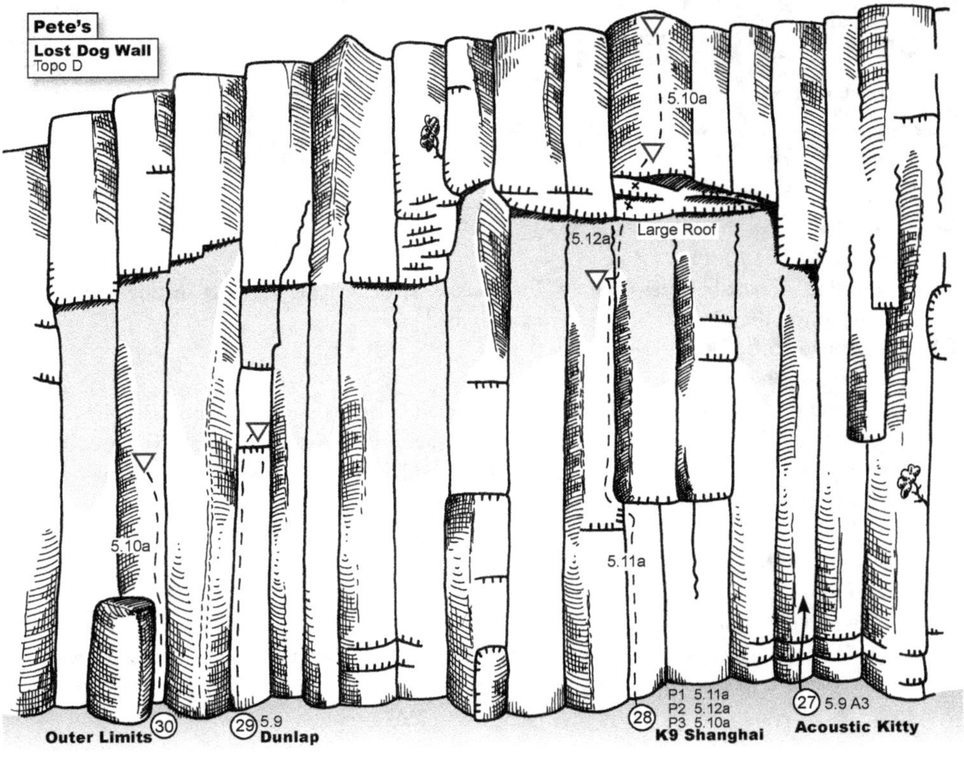

Pete's
Lost Dog Wall
Topo D
5.10a
5.12a
Large Roof
5.11a
5.10a
5.9
Outer Limits
30
29
Dunlap
28
P1 5.11a
P2 5.12a
P3 5.10a
K9 Shanghai
27
5.9 A3
Acoustic Kitty

Area.

20. Unknown
Length: 70' (21m), Pro to 2"
Ascending a crack between Eye Of The Needle and Escalade, a 2 bolt anchor awaits those willing to roll the dice on this mysterious climbed route.

21. Escalade 5.8 ★★
Length: 70' (21m), Pro to 3"
A fun and challenging route also known as Abandonment Issues. Start on the right side of a large tall detached block. Stem up the corner, place wide pro to protect the slight bulge, and then slide out up left onto the top of the detached block to a nice stance. Continue to cruise up steep terrain with great pro and good edges to the bolt anchor. An alternative 5.6 start is on the LEFT side of the block which protects better and with smaller pro.

22. Reckless Abandon 5.10a
Length: 70' (21m) TR
This is the direct start to Escalade (outside face of large block). The bolts were removed by angry locals shortly after the first ascent. Climb a series of thin, bouldery moves past two bolts to the stance atop the large boulder, and then continue up the route Escalade.

23. Ramble On 5.7R

Length: 70' (21m), Pro to 1¾"

Another fun route that needs more traffic. A bit runout with some dirty sections, lead climbers should take caution. Begin up a short crack corner to a small overhanging roof, step left and continue to climb up the slabby column. Amble up left from the crack to reach the rappel anchors on a flat face.

THE THIRD LANDING

A few yards further north along the trail is a third flat landing platform. Pumpin' for the Man begins here.

24. Pumpin' For The Man 5.9 ★★★

Multi-pitch 195' (59m)
Pro to 2" on P1, to 3" for P2, and to 5" for P3

Pumpin' is a quality three pitch lead with energizing technical pitches from bottom to top.

Pitch 1 (60') 5.9: Begin out of the gate with a crux move off the deck by powering over the initial bulge to a stance under the larger roof. Carefully place some pro, then balance right and up into the long steep crack corner system. The first lead takes good small cams and nut protection. Power past a second small triangular roof, and then exit up left to a bolt belay anchor at a small perch.

Pitch 2 (50') 5.8: From the anchor continue up right in a crack past a small roof and 20'+ to a large ledge and belay at a bolt anchor. You are standing next to a long detached pillar.

Pitch 3 (90') 5.9: From the belay ascend a long sustained offwidth by climbing on the left side of the huge columnar pillar of rock. This lead is very wide and requires large width protection devices. Tremendously exposed! Belay anchor at summit.

Rappel route, walk off, or descend down the Might Mouse rappel.

25. Hamunaptra 5.9 A2

Multi-pitch 200' (60m), Pro to 3"

Originally climbed by aid and top roped, this multi pitch outing awaits insitu belays. Ascend left facing corner surmounting roof on the left side. Continue up ever-steepening crack to the cliff top.

26. Cryan's Shame 5.10b (2 pitches)

Multi-pitch 200' (60m), Pro to 2½"

Pitch 1 100' (30m): Start by climbing up on edges and thin finger jams below a broken series of small roofs. Surmount the small roof and climb up to a bolt anchor on a sloping ledge.

Pitch 2 100' (30m): Follow shallow open book to top of cliff. Use tree for anchors. A great route that could use some cleaning.

27. Acoustic Kitty 5.9 A3

Multi-pitch 200' (60m), Pro to 2½"

Another steep outing that awaits permanent belays and an all free ascent. Begin in crack system to the right of the large, red roof complex which houses K-9 Shanghai. Zig zag leftwards over a series of roofs with jams and footwork.

LOST DOG WALL (aka SANDBOX)

A large open boulder field is at the extreme north end of Pete's Pile. A vast sweep of vertical cliff scarp here provides some of the most challenging climbing at Pete's Pile, including the stellar K9 Shanghai route. Jeremy Flanigan nailed 5-6 unrecorded routes on the long crack systems, but little record remains of the original ascent.

28. K-9 Shanghai   P1 5.11a, P2 5.12a, P3 5.10a   ★★★
Multi-pitch 240' (73m)
Pro to 3½" including cams, doubles small & medium cams P1
FFA: Elmo Mecsko, Reed Fee 8-2008

K9 is one of the newer challenging climbs at Pete's Pile, putting into perspective the vertical possibilities for the ultra-initiated. The route is long, sustained and technical with demanding crux sections. The classic crux second pitch punches OUT and over a massive improbable looking yet surprisingly well featured overhanging double tiered roof.

Pitch 1 (100') 5.11a: The first lead is technically thin but fun with interestingly steep crack climbing that increases in difficulty the higher you climb. Climb past a small overhanging crux near the anchor.

Pitch 2 (60') 5.12a: From the belay ascend steep thin jams and smears, then launch out the double tiered overhanging roof using a variety of face holds and a finger-hand jam crack. Strength and pure thuggery will get you through the giant roof crux. Need a 3½" cam for crux (A2).

Pitch 3 80') 5.10a: From the belay anchor above the crux pitch, move right and climb the steep arête upwards with mixed gear. Finish through a small overhang moving up left to bolted anchors on a big ledge. An outstanding climb with unmatched position!

Rappel with two ropes only...or walk south and descend via another standard rappel.

29. Dunlap 5.9
Length: 80' (25m), Pro to 1½"

Follow the shallow face between 2 steeps cracks. Left crack accepts protection more readily. Sustained climbing eases as you near the anchors. Dunlap and its neighbor Outer Limits were developed by a gregarious and prolific local outdoorsman, the late Jeremy Flanigan...Good on ya' mate.

30. Outer Limits 5.10a
Length: 80' (24m), Pro to 1½"

The left most climb at Pete's Pile located at the northernmost end of the Sandbox area. Begin on the right side of a series of stacked blocks and ascend up easy terrain to a crack immediately above the blocks. Power up the short flat face via a nice jam crack and exit left to the belay bolt anchors. Rappel the route.

KLINGER SPRINGS

Klinger Springs is the next door kissing cousin to Pete's Pile, so if you like long columnar crack systems found at Pete's you are sure to like the nature of the routes here. The rock type is the same as Pete's, but the textural nuances are slightly different. There are a fair number of the quality climbs, both bolted and trad gear leads.

The site has held intrigue to local Hood River climbers for a long time (see Pete's Pile intro), but recently Klinger has gained increased activity and popularity. The core route development enthusiasts are Elmo Mescko, Reed Fee, Rick Harrell and numerous others who have also found this place fascinating and enjoyable for climbing. The crag presently yields rock climbs ranging from 5.8 to 5.11 and there is certainly room for more. Seasonally the crag is great for rock climbing from May through October climbing under frequently sunny skies, but expect cold temperatures and snow in the winter months. As with many of the crags found of the east side of Mt Hood read the biodiversity section at the beginning of this chapter to familiarize yourself with the ecological nature of this region.

Review the local ethics concerning new anchor placements before starting a new project. Bring a trad gear rack if planning to climb here because about half of the routes are either trad gear leads or mixed gear/bolt leads.

Directions

Drive south of Hood River on highway 35 (about 20 minutes) till you pass NF3511 road that leads to Tilly Jane/Cooper Spur. Just as the highway crosses a small bridge, park at a small trailhead for Clinger Springs. Hike up this one minute, then take a faint path that continues upward steeply for about 15 minutes till you encounter the cliff. The rock climbing routes are located southward from the point where the trail first meets the crag.

North End

1. **Hanging Chad 5.7**
   Pro 6 QD's, Length 35'
   Bolted face climb (utilizing odd rock flakes). This route exists where the trail initially meets the wall at the north end.
2. **Hatchet Job 5.10-**
   6 QD's, length 45'
   Just right of Hanging Chad on the same outcrop formation. Climb a series of underclings/sidepulls on flakes (first bolt is a tough clip to the far left). Continue via stem moves, then angle up left to a roof, then up a brief headwall, moving up right to meet the belay.

Land of Shadows

3. **Hot Pockets 5.9**
   Pro 8 QD's, Length 50'
   Easy climbing and shallow cracks. About 40' south of 'Hanging Chad' route.
4. **Signs Preceding the End of the World 5.10**
   10 QD's, length 70'
   Located at a cave-like section with numerous hanging blocky roofs. Begin below the blocks, power underclings/sidepulls past it till it eases to edge climbing for the remainder of route.
5. **Cerberus 5.9**
   12 QD's, Length 80'
   Long bolt face climb, but has optional trad start on left (5.9) and on the right (.10a).
6. **It's All Good 5.7 PG/R**
   Pro to 1½", Length 80'
   Climb 25' of Trad Dad route, step left (2 bolts), then climb a thin crack. Clip bolts for safety, or if not (gets R).
7. **Trad Dad 5.7**
   Pro to 3" (+ QD's), Length 80'
   Sustained 5.7 climbing for about 2/3 of route, then it eases. Located about 15' left of Bulge Boogy. Start in a low point in the trail.
8. **Bulge Boogie 5.10b**
   Pro: about ½" nuts and cams, 9 QD's, length 90'
   Start at a ground belay bolt. Climb fun moves through several crux bulges.

Aviary Zone

9. **Eaglet 5.10**
   9 QD's, Length 70'
   Start near Kestrel, climb easy slab to small lip (above 4th bolt), then climb to belay underneath a giant roof. Rap.

10. **Golden Eagle 5.12c (the extension)**
    Pro 2 QD's, Length 16'
    From top belay of Eaglet, climb up over the giant horizontal roof. An extension.

11. **Kestrel 5.10c**
    9 QD's, Length 70'
    Climb up thru a crux balancy crimpy large plate of rock. The upper portion of route can be low-mid 10's depending on what part of the face you're climbing on.

12. **Osprey 5.10**
    13 QD's, Length 80'
    Start just to the right of large roof leaning out over the path. Has unique climbing style with crux puzzle.

13. **Felsschlüpfer (aka Rock Wren) 5.10d**
    10 QD's, Length 70'
    Techy climbing initially, thin crux at 4th bolt, and finish with face climbing to the belay.

14. **Blue Grouse 5.9**
    11 QD's, Length 70'
    Easy route involving a mix of underclings, laybacks and sidepulls. Located on same column as Rock Wren (to its right).

EAST SIDE ROCK 91

15. You Me & Everyone We Know 5.10d
12 QD's, Length 85'
Look for the first bolt pointing straight down under a low roof. Pull over the roof, and climb 45' of low-5.10's till you reach a stance below a slab. Climb the blank slab to a belay.

Wolf Point
16. No Balls 5.10a
Pro a few cams 2-4", (8 QD's), Length 75'
Move initially up left to the first bolt, climb up thru an easy roof, and continue up to a ledge, then (with pro) climb a wide crack to a belay.

17. John Harlin II 5.11a
11 QD's, Length 90'
Find a tall arête with 3 small lips on its right side. Climb the left side (bolts) of arete (crux at midway), pumpy to end it to large ledge. From ledge continue up another 25' on a minor pinnacle to a belay. Shares belay with Ego Ex.

18. Ego Extension 5.10+
13 QD's, Length 90'
Climbs the right side of the same arête. Power thru the three small lips, continue up to a ledge, then up a final minor pinnacle formation to a shared belay (with previous route).

19. Bollocks 5.8
Pro to 5" (double rack), Length 90'
This is the crack next to Ego Ex. Reasonable climbing past several small lips. Shares belay with Ego Ex.

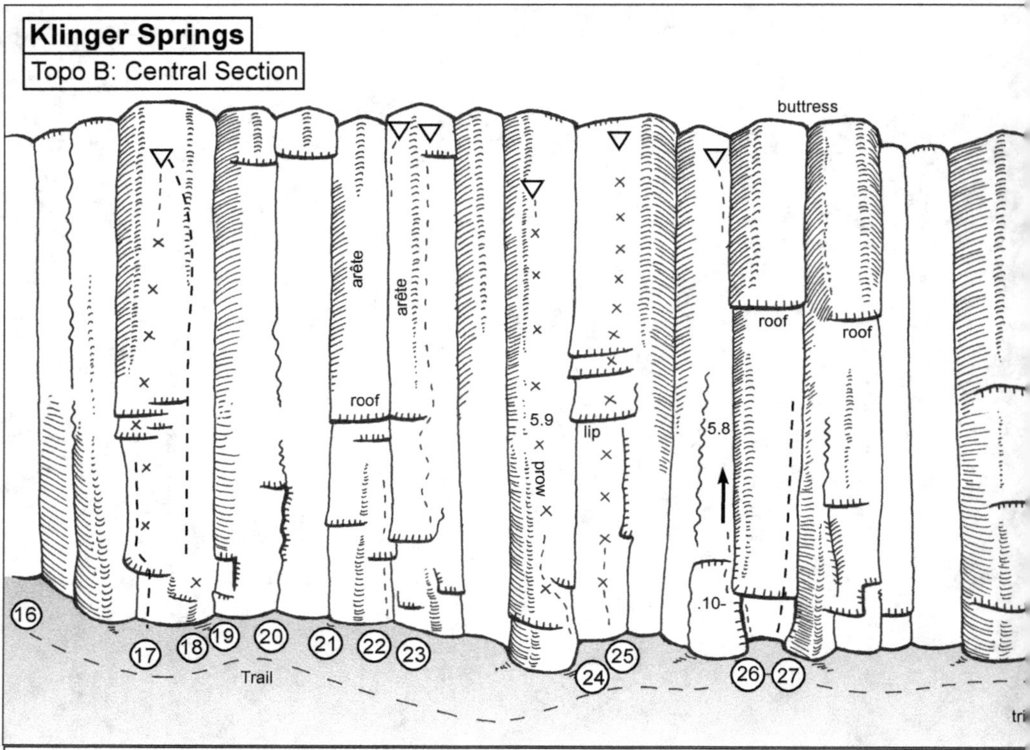
Klinger Springs
Topo B: Central Section
buttress
arête
arête
roof
roof
roof
5.9
prow
lip
5.8
.10-
16
17
18
19
20
21
22
23
24
25
26
27
Trail
tr

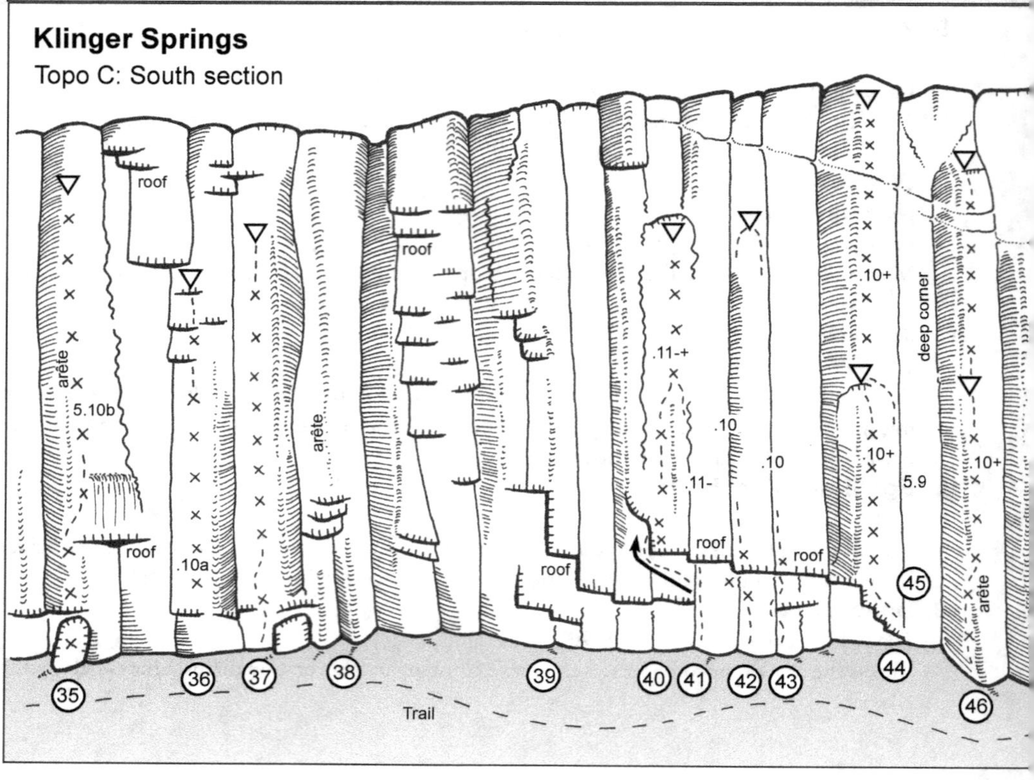
Klinger Springs
Topo C: South section
roof
roof
arête
5.10b
roof
.10a
arête
.11-+
.10
.10
.11-
roof
roof
roof
.10+
deep corner
.10+
5.9
.10+
arête
35
36
37
38
39
40
41
42
43
44
45
46
Trail

EAST SIDE ROCK

20. **Good Sport Route (GSR) 5.7**
    16 QD's, Length 90'
    Climb up to an arête (on its left side), continue up a face to a small lip, then move under the roof till you can pull over the lip using big sidepulls/jugs. Easiest route at KS.
21. **Funkytown 5.9**
    Pro to 1", Length 70'
    Stemming for the entire route. At top move left to attain GSR belay, then rap.
22. **Shorty Got Wolf 5.9R**
    Pro to 4", Length 70'
    Climb steep crack to a broken loose zone (sling a horn or runnout), continue with more steep variable sized crack climbing. Just left of Wolf Gang.
23. **Wolf Gang 5.12**
    15 QD's, Length 80'
    Initial odd opening sequential moves, then jugs run, and then power crimps to the belay. Located about 10' left of Wolf Point.
24. **Wolf Point 5.9**
    9 QD's, Length 80'
    Nice route on right side of arête. Climb face, then transition to the arête, and finish to a belay.
25. **Bone-Eata' 5.10+**
    13 QD's, Length 90'
    Power thru three roofs (in-a-row) using jugs. Located immediately right of Wolf Point.
26. **Jugular Vein 5.10+**
    Pro to 4½" (+ cams), Length 90'
    Initial crux moving under small roof-ish overhung section, then climb a steep corner, several minor bulges, to finish up a crack dihedral.
27. **Bear Claw 5.10a PG**
    Pro to 5" (the wide stuff), Length 80'
    Start same place as Jugular Vein. Initial opening roof crux section to start via edges and layback. The remainder of climb is a bit easier (wide pro is a +). Can avoid initial move by starting over on Jugular Vein route.
28. **Lean On Me 5.10a**
    8 QD's, Length 75'
    Start at the base of a leaning combination block tower. Climb the outside of the blocks, then continue up a brief bolted face above to reach a belay station.
29. **Point of Diminishing Returns 5.9**
    10 QD's, Length 90'
    Long sport route face (with a crux that can be negated by moving left around it).
30. **Solstice 5.10b**
    12 QD's, Length 90'
    Bouldery moves then jugs to a small rook, then move to the right side on a prow using crimps to finish on the prow.
31. **Dog Day Getaway 5.9**
    Pro to 3", Length 90'
    Quick start leads to a finger/hand jam crack. Move left at end to same belay as Solstice.
32. **Moss Covered Funk 5.10c/d**
    Pro to 3", Length 100'
    Pumpy crack climbing with stemming and finger jamming (a slight overhung section near top) and finish past a 'cap-stone' to a shared belay station (with Equinox).

33. **Equinox 5.10d**
    Pro 14 QD's, Length 90'
    Punch past an overhang to an arête, then up the arete on crimps till the holds fatten. A bit spacey near upper end.
34. **Delicate Sound of Falling 5.11a**
    Pro to 3" + QD's, Length 100'
    Crack punches past several small lips, then climbs up left under a large lip (bolts), then up left to an arte and face to reach the belay.

Roof Utopia Zone
35. **RIP Kurt Albert 5.10b**
    13 QD's, Length 80'
    A thin, sustained balancy lead on a bolted arête left of Wet Spot.
36. **Wet Spot 5.10a**
    12 QD's, Length 80'
    A discolored wet spot area that is wet in late spring and early fall. Power face climbing with a finale crux roof to surmount.
37. **Campus Wolfgang Gullich 5.11-**
    12 QD's, Length 80'
    Climb the face (avoid crack & nearby arête) to get full deal. Begin on a shattered block about 10' up the cliff at an open book (left side of column). Belay shared with next route.
38. **Todd Skinner 5.10c/d**
    13 QD's, Length 80'
    Initial section of broken rock (15') then quality sustained face climbing all the way. Belay same as previous route. Aka the Right Arête.
39. **Twitch 5.11b**
    Pro to 3", Length 80'
    Begin climbing a crack, then switches to crimp edge face climbing for the upper part. Mixed bolt/gear lead.

The next three routes climb up, then out of the same broad big roof system.

40. **Blockbuster 5.10a**
    ___ QD's, Length 95'
    Climb up to the big jutting roof, move left around the roof, and climb a long flat face.
41. **Sequel 5.10b**
    Pro to ___" (+ ___ QD's), Length 95'
    Climb up to and punch directly out the roof, then up a vertical face above.
42. **Roofatopia Dope 5.10b**
    Pro to 3" (+ QD's), Length 90'
    Climb through the initial hung roof (bolts) then up a long crack. Mixed bolt/gear lead.
43. **_____**
    Pro to _"
    Xxxx.

Gods and monsters zone
44. **Taken 5.10c**
    Pro 20 QD's, Length 115'
    A long arête with some tricky crimp climbing broken into to short leads (or 1 long lead).

45. Shaken 5.9
Pro to __", Length 65'
Long finger crack climb landing at the P1 'Taken' belay station.

46. Power Child 5.10d
Pro 18 QD's, Length 115'
Long sustained powerful stellar bolted arête.

47. Oroboros 5.8
Pro to 4" (+ large cams), Length 60'
Climb a crack till it splits (and use either split), then continue up crack until you can peer right to find the belay station (also used by 'Dragon' route.

48. Morosoarus 5.10a
Pro to 3" + QD's, Length 60'
A second pitch of Oroboros. Ascend the 'Dragon' P2 to a trad gear spot, then move up left along a crack and face (left of the rock protrusion). Shares belay with next route.

49. Crouching Climber Ridden Dragon 5.11c
P1 = __ QD's, Length 60'. P2 = Pro is small cams, Length 60'
A 2-pitch sport route that climbs a prow. P1 (5.12): start in BotB, then move left into a crux and climb powerful overhung moves to a belay. P2 (5.11c): Quick climbing gets you to a difficult rock protrusion, then finish across face to a belay.

50. Belly of the Beast 5.9
Pro to 3", Length 65'
Popular hand/fist crack to first roof, then left to a belay.

51. In Godzilla We Trust 5.10d
Pro to 3", Length 70'
Climb a crack up rightward through a difficult pumpy roof, then jams to finish to the belay.

52. Buddha Belly 5.10c
10 QD's, Length 65'
Second pitch option for previous route. Overhanging juggy sport route.

53. Getting It Up for the Crack of Dawn 5.10+
Pro to 3", Length 120' (total)
Just left of the tall rock pedestal is a long thin finger crack corner. P1 is 5.10c/d, and P2 is 5.10b/c.

54. Goddess of Virtue 5.11a
5 QD's, Length 40'
Short crimps face climb on the outside of the rock pedestal.

55. Monster Crack 5.9
Pro to 4" (5" is optional), Length 55'
Offwidth on the right side of the rock pedestal (with some tunneling for the last moves).

56. Medussa 5.9+
Pro to 2", Length 70'
Do a few moves of 'T.I.T.', then climb a small crack up left to shared belay.

57. Trapped in Time 5.9
Pro to 4", Length 70'
The second pitch of Monster Crack, offering a long crack with plenty of finger to hand jams.

58. Nosferatu 5.10-
Pro to 3" (optional to 4"), Length 110'
Long crack climb. Seam to start, then widens to fingers and hands, then widens to fist jams at a small roof (at 90'). The crack system widens to arm-bar status near the belay.

59. **Sphinx 5.10c**
    Pro 17 QD's, Length 100'
    Long steep sustained bolted arête with a small jug roof up high.
60. **Red-headed Yeti 5.10+ PG/R**
    Pro to 2", Length 120' (total)
    A multi-pitch lead. Long corner crack climb ending by climbing the big rock protrustion. Pitch 1 (5.8) and Pitch-2 (5.10c/d).
61. **Yeti's Betty 5.7+**
    Pro to 3" (+ doubles), Length 110'
    Long crack lead on a flat face.
62. **Primal Institution 5.10b/c**
    12 QD's, Length 100'
    Sustained face and arête climb.

South End of Crag
63. **Crackalicious 5.9**
    Pro to 2" (small cams and nuts), Length 75'
    Nice corner crack with finger to hand jams, and bulge finish near top.
64. **Know What I Mean 5.8**
    Pro to 3" (small cams and nuts), Length 75'
    A corner crack climb that shares same belay as previous route.

BULO POINT

The rocky crag of Bulo Point is a fascinating group of steep bluffs with quality rock climbing opportunities for leading and top-roping from mid-May to late October. Located roughly ten air miles east of Mt. Hood and a few miles south of FS44 this site offers enjoyable climbing from 5.6 to 5.11+. The site qualifies as one of the better backcountry climbing crags nestled in the ponderosa pine covered eastside crest of the Cascade mountains incline.

Nestled on the sunny eastern facing slopes overlooking the Fifteen Mile Creek watershed west of the small town of Dufur, Bulo Point offers visitors a quality selection of routes on surprisingly steep, 80' high rough-textured rock.

Although many of the rock climbs are sport routes, a fair selection of routes are traditional natural gear routes. Bring an adequate selection of cams and wires if you plan to lead any of the traditional climbs. Most of the climbing routes have fixed belay anchors which can be accessed from above for top-rope purposes.

Geological characteristics

The rock at Bulo is composed of heavily-weathered course-grained rock from old lava flows originating from the vicinity of Lookout Mountain. The outcrop is revealed later when the surrounding softer earthen layers are eroded away, leaving exposed bedrock that experiences chemical and mechanical decomposition from the principal reacting agents oxygen, water, and carbon dioxide.

The rough surface texture of the rock provides positive smearing friction opportunities along with numerous hand or finger edges. Moderate routes from 5.6 to 5.10 are plentiful, but the cracks tend to be shallow and flared, which can be challenging while placing protection on lead. The Point is a good place suitable for moderate to expert climbers.

These forested slopes provide recreational opportunities for hunters, hikers, mountain bikers,

as well as rock climbers who find the Ponderosa pine covered Dufur watershed a delightful haven far from the madding crowd.

Many individuals were dynamically instrumental in developing this climbing site. Bulo Point has long been an established historical climbing site prior to the 1980s and a number of the routes were top-roped and some were lead climbs long before the era of fixed bolts. Do your part to keep this site a rare treasure for all climbers by packing out what you pack in.

Directions

To visit Bulo Point, drive south from Hood River, Oregon on Hwy 35. Drive east on FS44 for 8¼ miles and turn south (right) onto FS4420. Follow the paved road initially for ¾ mile. At the Dufur Watershed sign take a gravel road on the left onto FS 4421-240, which is a narrow dirt road. This road splits again within a few hundred feet. Take the right fork and drive for 1 mile to Bulo Point. Park at the roads end (being decommissioned beyond this point), and walk east down a footpath that leads out through the forest to the top of the crag. The crag is a one minute walk from your vehicle to the bluff top

CHAPTER 2

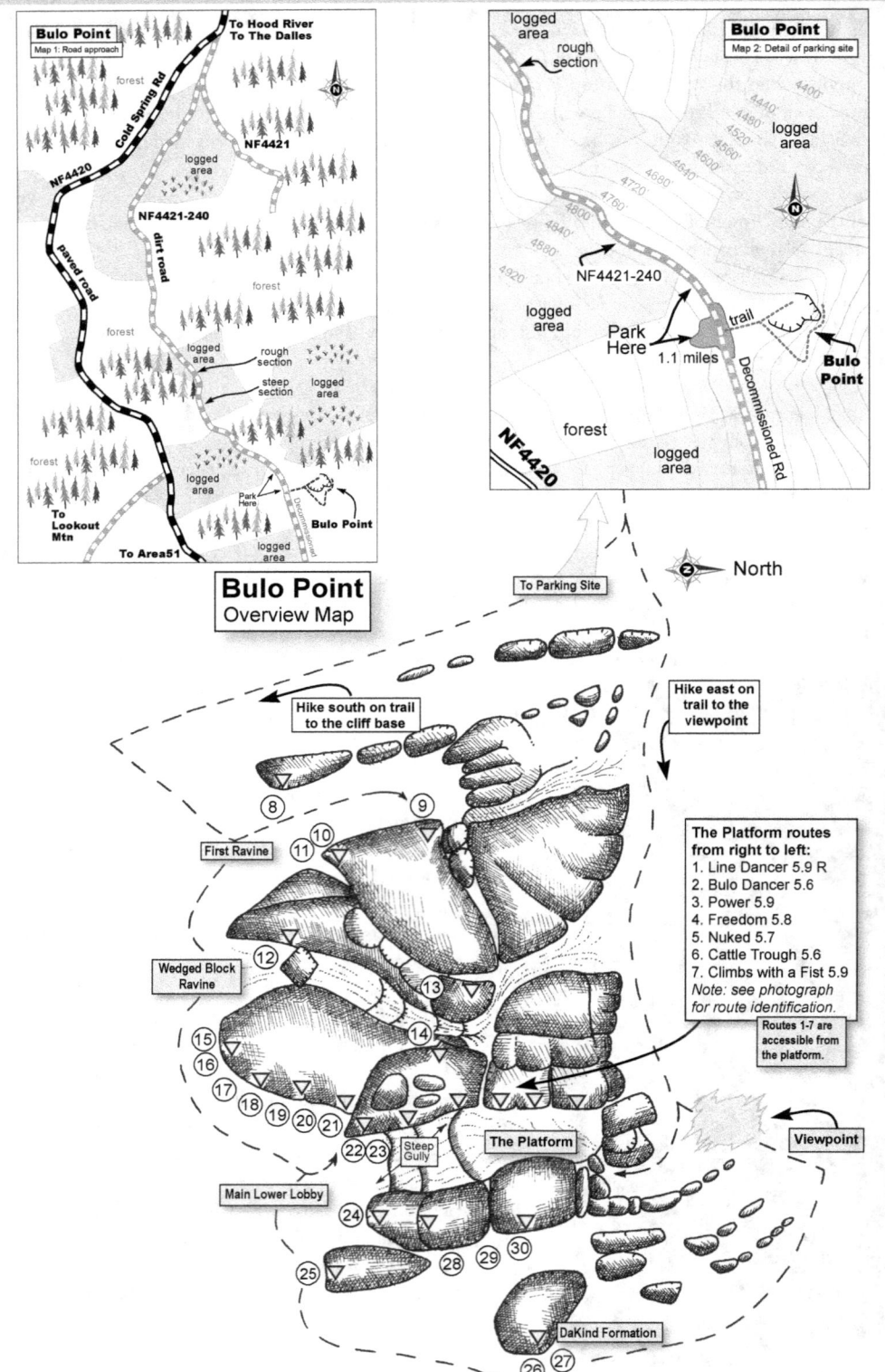

viewpoint.

The Viewpoint

The first string of routes begin at the Platform which is a common starting place where people arrive on their first visit to Bulo. Take the main trail out to the scenic viewpoint at the top of the bluff. Immediately downhill on your right side is an alcove platform with a short vertical east-facing wall. The routes at the Platform are listed from right to left. Only routes accessible from the Platform are listed here. **Jet Stream** and **Jet Wind** are listed in the Main Lower Lobby area.

To access the Platform routes scramble down exposed 4th class ramps to the alcove. Or climb up onto the top of the higher bluff, set a top-rope and rappel down to the Platform. Be cautious if scrambling down to the alcove platform as it is surprisingly steep.

Nicolle leading at *Bulo Point*

1. **Line Dancer 5.9 R ★★**
   Pro: Thin gear to 2"
   A sustained tricky thin crack on the upper right end of the Platform. This is the nearest route to the scenic viewpoint at the top of the bluff.

2. **Bulo Dancer 5.6**
   Pro: Behemoth gear to 5" or 6"
   This is the fat wide crack which is easier to just TR.

3. **Power & Politics 5.9 ★★★**
   Pro: Gear to 2"
   Starts the same as Freedom, but launch up into the right thin finger crack. This line is a bit more difficult to lead. Does not need the additional bolts other than the first bolt to protect the initial starting move off the ground.

4. **Cattle Guard. 5.8 ★★★**
   Pro to 2"
   One of the best short face climbs at Bulo Point. Climb the steep edgy face past a bolt then up to the left jam crack. Only the first bolt is necessary. The remaining portion of the climb protects well using natural pro and does not need the other bolts.

5. **Nuked 5.7**
   Pro: QD's
   A minor face climb on the extreme left end and facing toward Cattle Trough.

6. **Cattle Trough 5.6**
   Pro: Behemoth gear
   A large chimney separating the outer buttress from the main flat faced wall.

7. **Climbs with a Fist 5.9 ★★**
   Pro: QD's
   A face climb on the outer buttress immediately right of Jet Wind and facing Cattle Trough.

FIRST RAVINE

First Ravine offers four routes. You can access this ravine as you descend the hiking trail before you reach the Lower Lobby.

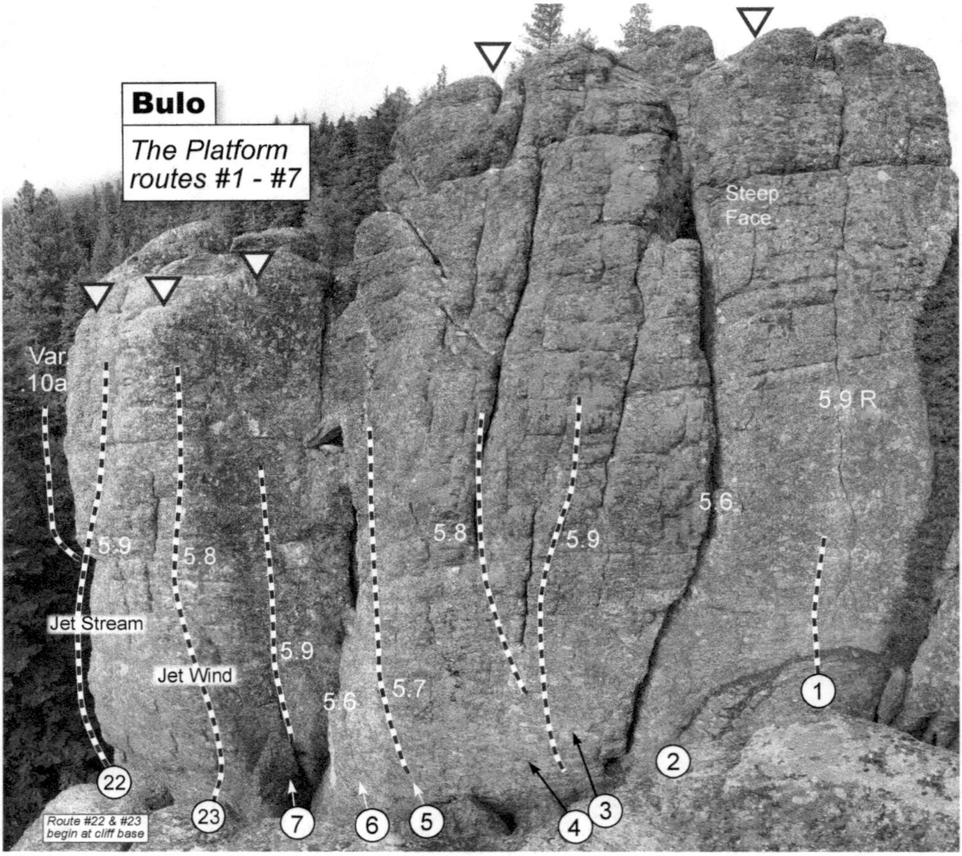

Bulo
The Platform routes #1 - #7

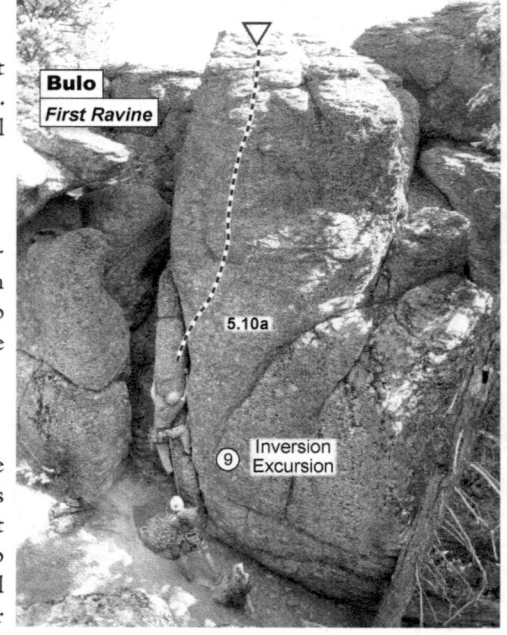

Bulo First Ravine

8. **Silence of the Cams 5.9 ★★**
   Pro: QD's
   Located on the immediate left in the First Ravine as you descend the hiking trail. Climbs a short vertical face using small edges and finishing on jug holds.

9. **Inversion Excursion 5.10a ★**
   Pro: QD's
   Located at the upper end of the same ravine as Silence of the Cams. Begin up an initial steep off-width crack, then step up right to finish up a low angle face to the belay anchor.

10. **Awesome Possum 5.11+/.12-**
    Pro: QD's
    An improbable face climb ascending the arête and ending at the same anchor as Separated at Birth. Located on the right side of the First Ravine. A powerful climb using small sloping holds on a substantial overhang. The upper bulge has another

thin crux section on small edges just before you reach the anchor.

11. Separated at Birth 5.10b R
Pro: QD's
Located in the First Ravine on the right and utilizes the same anchor as Drawin' a Blank. This route stems up the large deep chimney using positive face holds. Move up left on good face edges to a short hard steep face just before the belay anchor.

WEDGED BLOCK RAVINE

As you descend the hikers loop trail to the lower lobby you will see a narrow ravine with a massive wedged block in it. Atomic Dust Buster is next to the wedged block.

12. Atomic Dust Buster 5.10c
Pro: QD's
Starts on the left next to the huge wedged chockstone. Climb the short vertical face past a small lip to the anchor.

The next two climbs are visible uphill behind the giant wedged block. You can access both routes from several different places.

13. Barking Spider 5.8
Pro: QD's
14. Slice of Pie 5.9
Pro: Nuts to 2"
This is a crack climb located up left of Nook and Cranny on the upper west side of the buttress with a belay anchor at the top.

Main Lower Lobby is the primary destination for climbers because the popular Jet Stream is a must-lead route of stellar proportion.

15. Alice 5.9
Pro: Some gear and QD's
Located on the far left side of a lower lobby. Climb a flat face broken with cracks to a boorish one-move wonder over a bulge.

16. JRat Crack 5.8 ★
Pro: Wires and cams to 4"
The broad face is broken by a wide zigzagging flared crack. That's it.

17. Raiders of the Lost Rock 5.9 ★
Pro: Nuts to 2"
Immediately right of JRat is a low angle bolted face. Ascend easy steps to first bolt, then smear delicately up small sloping edges till it

eases.

LOWER LOBBY

18. Fat Rabbit 5.12b/c
Pro: 3 QD's
An very difficult route on a short vertical face.

19. Plumbers Crack 5.6 ★★★
Pro to 3"
An enjoyable deep corner crack system and a suitable lead for everyone.

20. Return of Yoda 5.10c ★★
A great balancy face climb with thin sloped edges that will keep you gripped. The final crux moves use some of the Nook & Cranny holds so in essence it is a bit squeezed at the end.

21. Nook and Cranny 5.8 ★★★
Pro to 2" including small cams
A popular crack climb immediately left of the long vertical arête. Rappel from belay anchor. Or if you are inclined step up around the corner to access an upper 5.8+ crack lead (Slice of Pie) that ends at the top of the bluff.

22. Jet Stream 5.9 ★★★
Pro: 10 QD's
Jet Stream is considered to be the best route at Bulo. When standing at the main Lower Lobby you can easily spot Jet Stream because it is the long bolted arête route on the tallest buttress.
Ascend the prominent arête on small but positive face edges. Power through the first over-

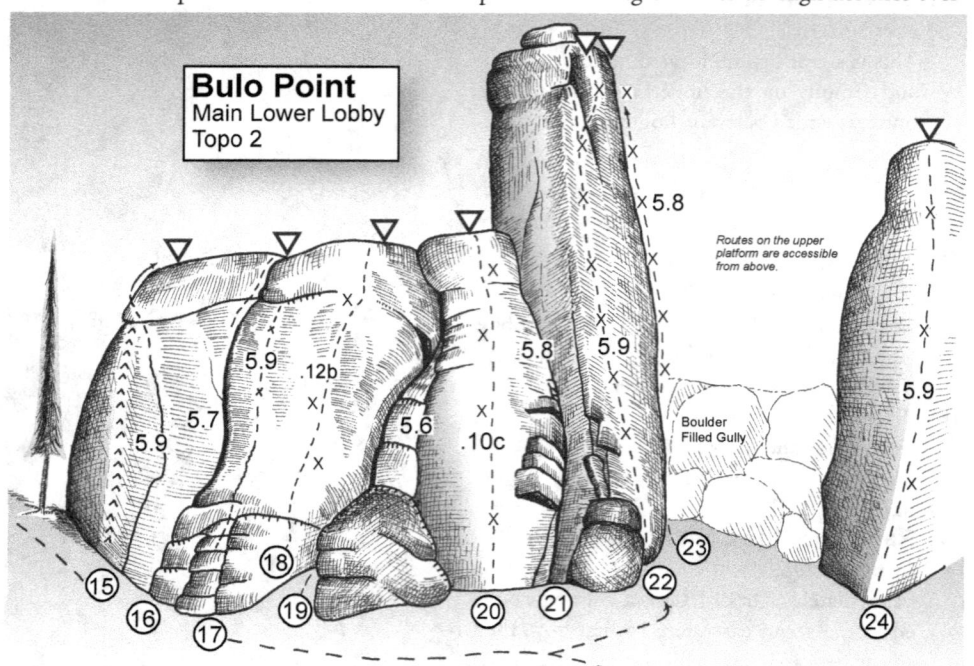

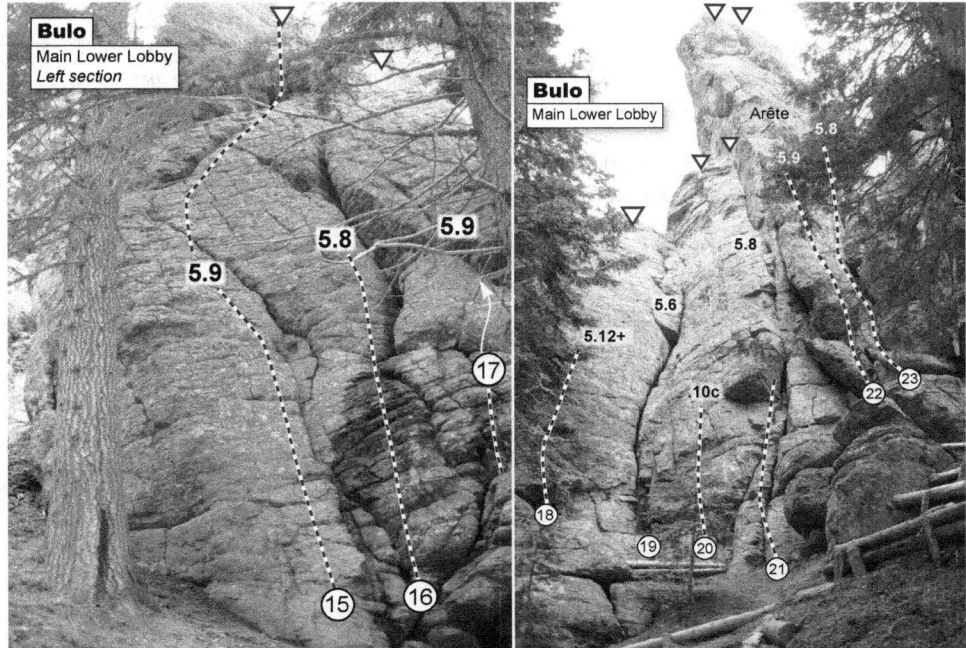

hanging bulge crux section. Cruise up to the second overhanging crux section and aim right to get through this bulge (avoid the variation exit crack on the left). Finish on easier holds to the anchor at the top of the cliff.

Alternative route ending variation: If you plan to exit up *left* using the upper left exit crack variation it is called **Jet Stream Variation** (5.10a). Bring minor gear to 2" including cams. Climb Jet Stream, but at the second overhanging crux bulge jaunt up left in a minor crack to the top.

23. Streamlined (aka Jet Wind) 5.8 ★★★
Pro: 10 QD's (minor gear to 2")
A stellar long climb immediately right of Jet Stream on the same tall buttress formation. Start up a corner to a short crack (minor gear to 2") on a face, then continue to face climb up right (bolts) around a minor bulge on positive holds to the top of the cliff formation.

24. Black Market 5.10a
Pro: QD's
A insignificant climb on a minor arête on a minor bluff. The first several moves are awkward, but the rest of the climb is basic and in some ways a bit runout.

25. Don't Call Me Ishmael 5.11b ★★
Pro: QD's
At the far lower right end of the Lower Lobby is a wildly overhanging formation leaning out over the trail. This is Ishmael, a short but stiff seam/face climb that often gets free climbed, but also frequently gets 'dogged' by pumped climbers. Clipping the belay anchor is difficult.

DAKIND BUTTRESS

26. Scene of the Crime 5.10 C ★★★
Pro: QD's
Located on the left side of the DaKind Buttress formation, which is a large rock formation separated from the main bluff. Power up into a vertical short crack using face holds, then balance up right (crux) under an overhang. Attain better hand edges past the roof and cruise on up the belay anchor. Shares the same anchor with the DaKind route.

27. DaKind 5.9 ★★★
Pro: Minor gear to 3"
Located on the right side of the DaKind Buttress formation. Step up under an overhang using a crack, then lean out the slight bulge (pro) to grasp the edges above the overhang. Power past this initial overhang to better holds, and continue up slightly right on steep terrain with good holds to an anchor.

The last three routes are located uphill behind the DaKind Buttress formation. These routes are seldom climbed.

28. Who's the Choss? 5.9
Pro to 2"
This and the next two routes are located to the right and uphill on the east side of the same bluff of rock. Scramble up a steep dirt gully around DaKind to approach these routes.

29. Big Al 5.7 TR
A top-rope next to the previous route.

30. Rock Thugs 5.9
Pro to 3"
A crack climb tucked uphill and behind the DaKind rock outcrop formation.

Coyote Flat

Coyote Flat (aka The Meadow) provides a nice selection of 'bumps' or minor rounded rock knobs and short bluffs composed of gritty sandpaper textured rock. The site has a minor string of bouldering opportunities and a few very short lead climbs. The knobs are scattered on a sunny Ponderosa forested slope, but is a reasonable place to escape the cloudy Spring weather of western Oregon. A little exploration and you will find other forested bouldering sites and minor rock bluffs.

To experience the flavor of this little area drive eleven miles east from Highway 35 on FS44, then take a sharp right turn (SW) onto FS4450. At 1¼ mile the Dufur City watershed sign will be visible at a 4-way intersection. Turn right on graveled road FS4421 and drive approximately 1 mile (elev. 3700').

HELIOTROPE

Another fascinating objective is this minor pinnacle located on a scenic hike east of Lookout Mountain on trail #458. About 1 mile east of the peak, and on the south-facing slope that drops into Badger Creek Wilderness is the **Heliotrope Pinnacle** (5.7) an 80' high pillar of rock that has a vertical aspect on all sides. The area is quite scenic and can be combined as a day hike in the area by starting at High Prairie, or at trail #456A, which starts at Fifteen Mile campground just south of Bulo Point. You can also hike the entire length of this trail starting from the east end near Flag Point.

AREA 51

Beta written by K. Kucera & P. Cousar

Area 51 is a great climbing crag that packs an energetic list of powerful rock climbs, all on a convenient south facing bluff. The site boasts unique advantages over other east side crags; it is great for early or late season climbing, and is conducive for rock climbers who are seeking a place to expand their skill level into the solid 5.11 range. The site tends to be dryer on overcast cold cloudy days when Bulo Point is too damp after a brief summer shower.

Area 51 is cast in a similar light as Bulo Point (proximity and seasonal temperatures) nestled in a forest of pine trees at the 4100' (1250m) elevation. Its southern exposure is advantageous in early Spring or late Fall. Area 51 is definitely a step beyond in terms of leading ability because the site has no easy routes under 5.9. Many of the climbs range in difficulty from 5.10c to 5.11+ and beyond, all on a very steep 80' high bluff. Many of the routes are mixed-sport routes in that you do need some specialized equipment (cams, nuts, etc.) to ascend the route without undue risk. The upper fixed belay anchors are not accessible from the top of the bluff so avoid trampling the fragile soils on the top of the bluff.

Area 51 was initially tapped as a climbing resource in the late '90s by several regional climbers. Others soon followed. Finding the site suitable for steep relentless climbing, they and friends quickly embarked onto creating a cliff where they could refine their climbing skills while enjoying the sport with friends. Paul Couser, Kay Kucera, and Jim Anglin were the primary route developers. They refined and enhanced the trail network, created stabilized platforms at the base of many routes, and placed an importance on climber awareness toward the ecological biodiversity of the Area 51 site.

Individuals who helped carry the dynamics of climbing into the 21st century were Dave Boltz, Jai Dev, Steve Mrazeck, Reed Fee, Matt Spohn, Adam McKinley, Kent Benesch, Elmo Mecsko, and other Portland

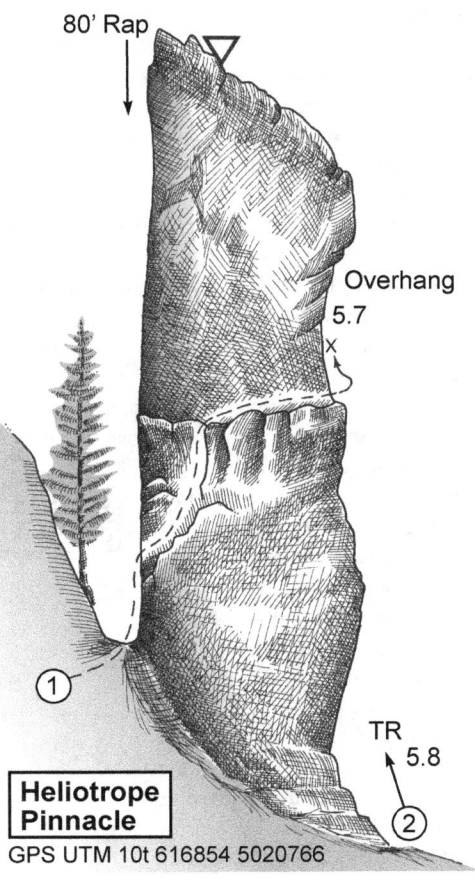

80' Rap

Overhang
5.7
x

①

Heliotrope Pinnacle
GPS UTM 10t 616854 5020766

TR
5.8

②

area climbers.

Read the entire section on *Biodiversity Dynamics of East Side Flora Communities, Access and User Impact* and *Ethical Continuity* at the beginning of this chapter. With your dedication this partnership of low impact rock climbing activity continues to be an ecological legacy. Several Area 51 reminder points from that article are:

1. Utilize the well-developed foot trails (no short-cutting). These user trails are well marked with stone steps and belay platforms to minimize the erosional impact.

2. The top anchors are not accessible from above so avoid walking on the fragile soils at the top of the bluff. Avoid unnecessary trampling of the local plant species. Do not remove indigenous flora from the cliff, from the rock climb, or along the cliff base.

3. Seriously consider leaving your pets at home. A loose, rowdy dog is not everyone's best friend. It can cause more damage in five minutes than twenty climbers in a month, thus it is best to leave the pup at home.

4. Pre-inspecting routes via rappel is normal business, so rappel bolting is the usual method (though not always) for route development here. Refrain from chopping fixed gear, chiseling or altering holds, retro-bolting existing lines without permission, placing bolts next to quality gear placements, avoid developing 'R' or 'X' rated routes.

5. It is recommended to wear climbing helmets while leading or belaying.

Directions

Area 51 has good paved road access to the trail parking site. The site, though nestled in a pine forest at an elevation of 4,000' is often dry on cool rainy overcast days of Spring or late Fall.

Directions from Hood River: Drive south from Hood River, Oregon on Hwy 35. Drive east on FS44 for 8¼ miles and turn south (right) onto FS 4420.

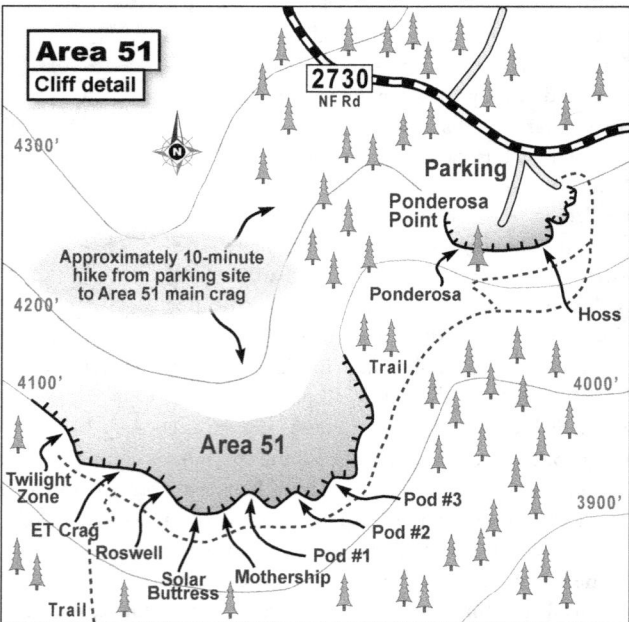

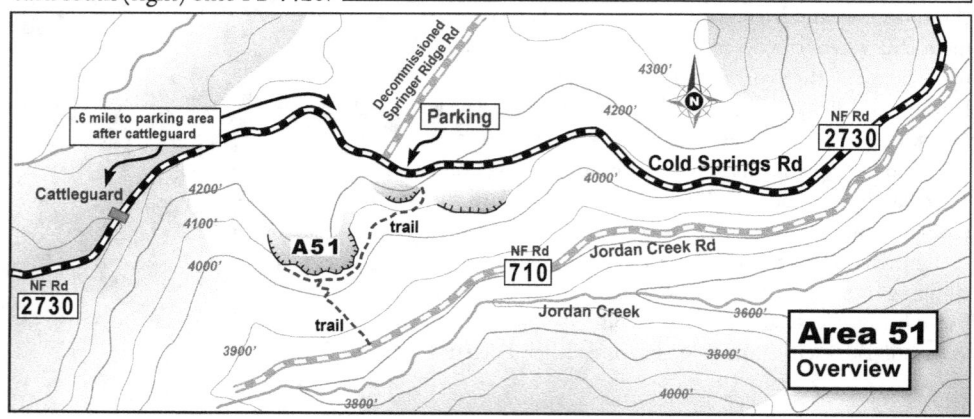

Drive south on paved road FS 4420 past the Bulo Point turnoff. At a three-way junction drive south on FS 2730 past Fifteen-Mile Campground. The road descends eastward several miles and will cross a cattle guard. Continue for ½ mile and park in a large pullout on the south side of the road at Ponderosa Point. Take the descent trail as it drops downhill south below the parking site and aim west below Ponderosa Point. A ten minute walk will take you to the east end of the main A51 formation.

Directions from The Dalles: Area 51 can also be approached by driving south from The Dalles through Friend, Oregon and drive west on FS 2730 (see overview diagram).

Trail Approach: A fast ten-minute walk down below Ponderosa Point and along a path to the west will bring you to the east edge of the main A51 wall. An alternate but lesser used lower trail approach begins on FS 710 road and hikes uphill in 5-10 minutes to the base of the routes called Friend or Alien.

Mackenzie Jones leading at A51

THE TWILIGHT ZONE

1. **Young Jedi 5.10a**
   Pro: 3 bolts and assorted gear
   Furthest west climb located 12' right of the "colonette cave". Start in crack left of Dreamland. Head right out crack through bolted bulge to common anchor.

2. **Dreamland 5.10b** ★
   Pro: 8 QD's
   Farthest left (west) bolted route on crag. Face climbing finishes out crack through bulge.

3. **War of the Worlds 5.11a** ★
   Pro: 7 QD's
   WOTW is 15' right of Dreamland. Follows right side of slab to steeper overlaps up higher.

4. **Men in Black 5.10b**
   Pro: 6 QD's
   MIB is 25' right of Dreamland. Funky face climbing with a slab finish.

5. **Crash Landing 5.12c** ★
   Pro: 8 bolts, and gear to 1.5"
   CL is 15' right of MIB. Start left of wide crack. Increasingly difficult face climbing with overlaps that leads up to a 'crash landing' finish (.11d AO).

6. **Earth First 5.11a** ★
   Pro: 8 QD's
   Pocketed face right of crack. Begin in overhanging corner, and move right to face. Finish up steeper bulge.

7. **Shape Shifter 5.11a** ★
   Pro: 6 QD's
   Obvious right facing dihedral with steep start and involves technical stemming.

Gabriel leading *Wormhole*

8. **Alien Lunacy 5.11b**
   Pro: 6 QD's
   Contrived variation of Luna. Stay left of bolts, and the crack is out of bounds. Crosses to right on upper face.
9. **Luna 5.10c** ★★
   Pro: 6 QD's
   Face climb 10' right of Shapeshifter. Balancy crux at bolts #3-#4.
10. **Take Me To Your Leader 5.10a**
    Pro: 3 bolts, and gear to 2"
    Description: Broken arête and crack system right of wet streak. Mixed ice in winter.
11. **Cattle Mutilation 5.11a** ★★
    Pro: 7 QD's
    About 60' east of TMOYL. Crimp up sunny face with ledge midway.
12. **The Eagle Has Landed 5.10a**
    Pro to 3" [?]
    About 10' right of CM is a sharp edged left leaning crack. Ends at CM anchor.
13. **Erased Memory 5.10b**
    Pro: 5 bolts, and gear to 1.5"
    About 12' right of CM. Start on 'eagle' crack, move up and right to finish on a narrow pinnacle.

ET CRAG

14. **ET (Extra Trad) 5.9**
    Pro to [?]
    Start from top of boulder 5' left of Phone Home. Follow the crack system.
15. **Phone Home 5.12b** ★★
    Pro: 9 QD's
    Striking red arête. Steepening crimps to obscure finish.

Jim Anglin leading at *Area 51*

Photo courtesy of Paul Couser

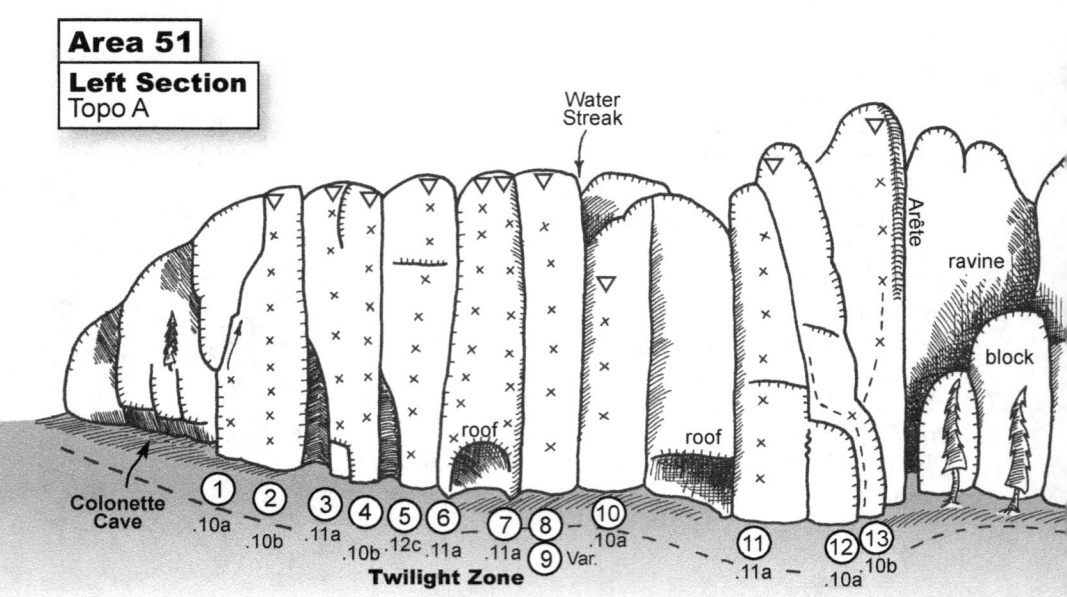

Area 51
Left Section
Topo A

✦ EAST SIDE ROCK   111

16. **Little Gray Men 5.11b** ★
    Pro: 5 QD's
    Short face between Phone Home and Mars.

17. **Mars 5.10d** ★★★
    Pro: 7 QD's
    Beautiful red face on the right wall of open book that is broken by large horizontals. This route is west facing and involves 5.10d stemming, and offers a 5.11b direct finish.

18. **Crop Circles 5.12c**
    Pro: 8 QD's
    Located 6' right of Mars above lower approach trail. Start on left arête with smooth blank band. Stick clip past missing first bolt.

19. **Friend or Alien 5.11a** ★★
    Pro: 8 bolts and gear to 2"
    At the top of lower approach trail and 12' right of CC. Has some height dependent reachy moves.

20. **Trouble With Tribbles 5.12a** ★
    Pro: 8 bolts and gear to 2"
    Easy crack to bolted face with small overlaps.

21. **The Cover Up 5.12a/b**
    Pro: 8 QD's
    Start up a slab 5' right of Tribbles. Move up right and work through bulge to featured face above.

22. **Out Of This World 5.9+** ★★
    Pro: 9 QD's
    Located 7' right of 'Cover Up'. Climb 20' of wide fist crack to heavily featured slab above. Route is best accessed from off of the Rocketman platform.

Tomma leading *Alien Observer*

ROCKETMAN FORMATION

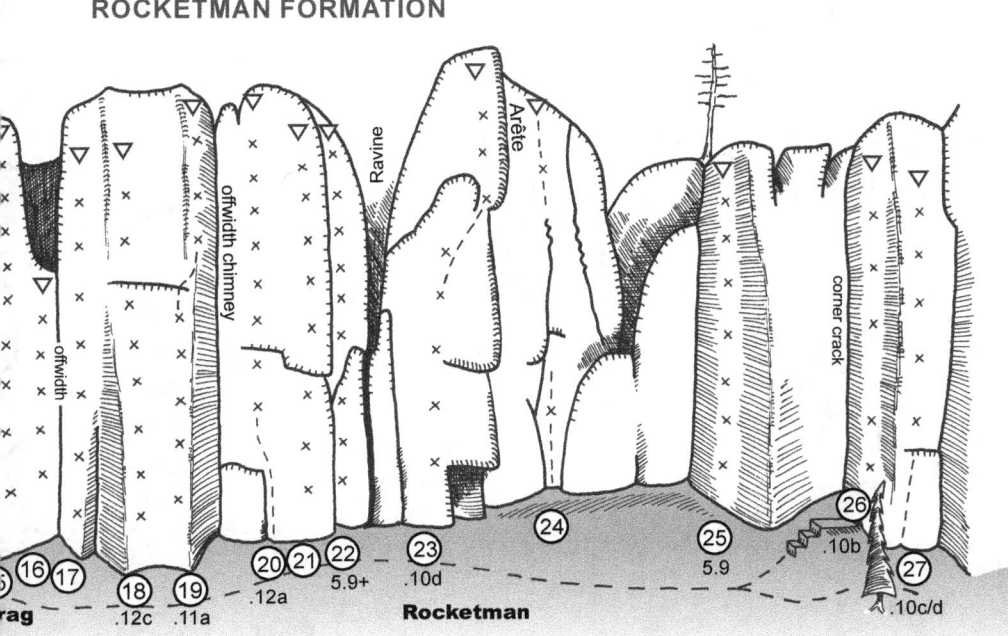

23. Rocketman 5.10d
Pro: 8 QD's
Located 45' left of First Contact above and right of the 'Cover Up'. Climbs slabby face, then moves right to a wide crack up to a pedestal. Step right and finish on fun arête.

24. Major Tom 5._ [?]
Pro: [?] bolts [?]
Discontinuous cracks to the right of a steep arête to a thin face.

25. Cosmic Debris 5.9
Pro: 6 QD's
A minor face climb on the left side of a steep rounded rock slab.

26. First Contact 5.10b ★★★
Pro: 6 QD's
Short stairs just behind a huge stump takes you up to a platform at the base of this route.

27. UFO 5.10c/d ★
Pro: 5 QD's
Located 10' right of First Contact. Climb up a hand crack left of some ledges and up to balancy moves on a bolted face above.

28. Roswell 5.9+ ★★
Pro: 5 bolts and gear to 2"
Located 20' right of UFO. Start up a 25' tall finger crack. Move left, and face climb to a bivy ledge, and then continue up the small pedestal to a chain anchor.

29. Uranus Has Rings 5.10c ★
Pro: 4 bolts and gear to 2"
Located 8' right of Roswell. Balancy moves down low on the lead, but casual climbing up top.

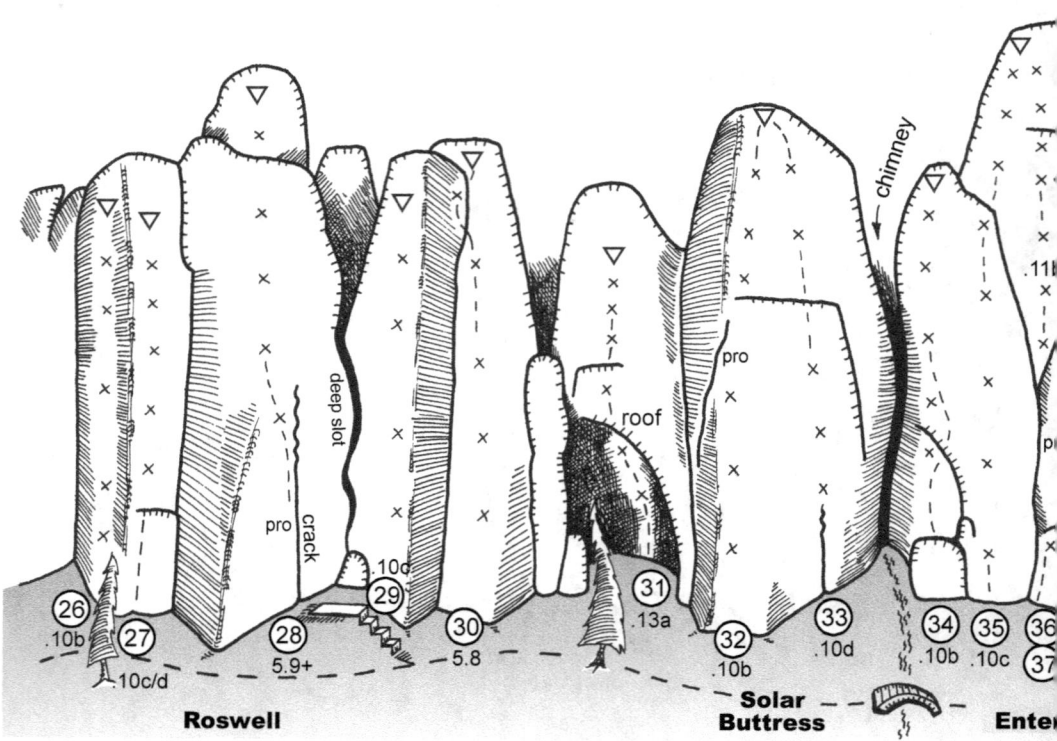

30. It Taint Human 5.8
Pro: 5 QD's

Located 8' right of UHR. Climb a slabby face on the right up to a dihedral using juggy crack holds. A bit dirty but will improve with use.

SOLAR BUTTRESS FORMATION
31. Journey To The Sun 5.13a
Pro: 6 QD's

Steep route in a short cave follows a bolt line to pull the lip and onward to a slabby face finish. There is an easier variation right of the bolt line.

32. Solar Flair 5.10b ★
Pro: 6 bolts and gear to 3"

Climb arête 15' right of JTTS. Finish on a steep face which quickly ends at the Sunspot belay anchor.

33. Sunspot 5.10d ★
Pro: 5 bolts and gear to 2"

Located on a sunny face 10' right of Solar Flair. Follow up some discontinuous cracks to cruxy face climbing above a ledge. The climb is a bit easier if you are tall.

THE ENTERPRISE
34. Vulcan Mind Meld 5.10b
Pro: 9 QD's

Located to the right of a drainage gully. Climb up large blocks to a roof. A vulcan mind meld might help with the perplexing moves above the roof. Finishes with adventurous climbing through questionable rock on blunt arête. Belayer should stay alert for flying objects.

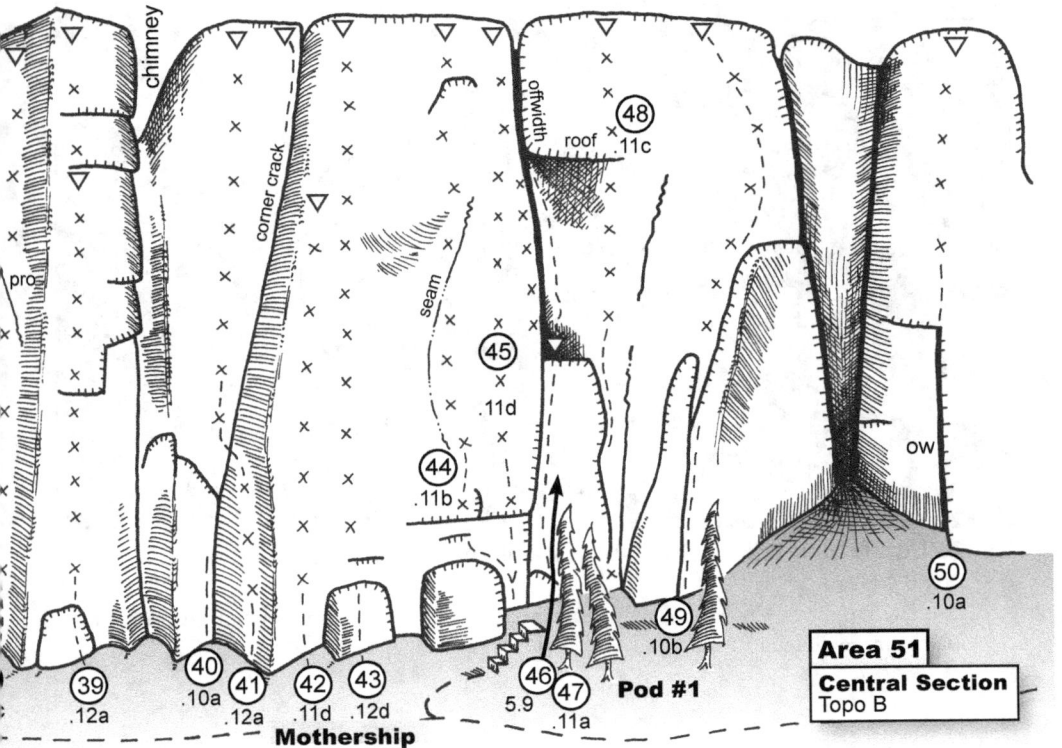

Area 51
Central Section
Topo B

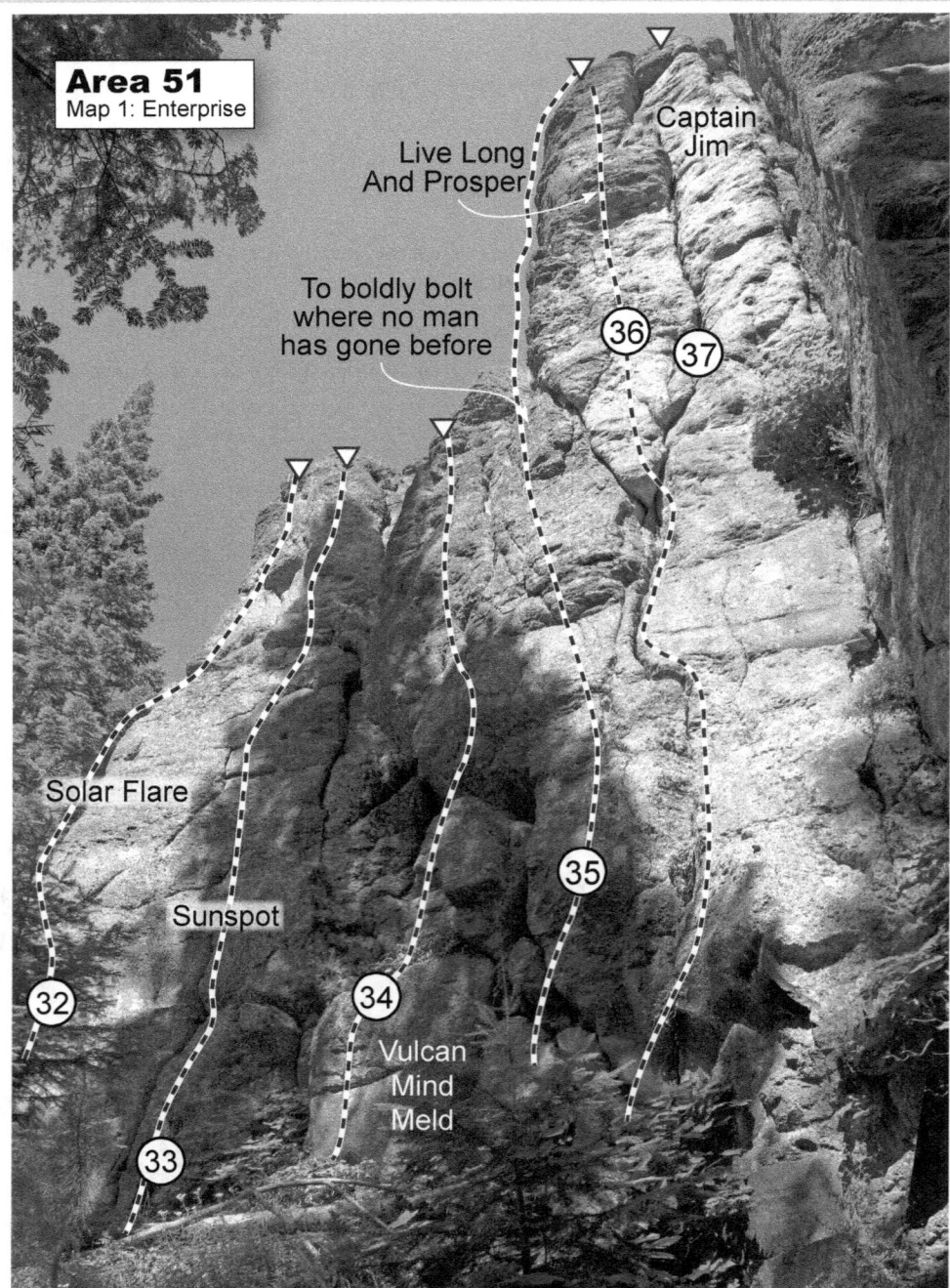

35. To Boldly Bolt Where No Man Has Bolted Before 5.10c ★
Pro: 8 QD's
Located 5' right of VMM. Follow discontinuous cracks to finish on a blunt buttress. Route may be more difficult if you are short.

36. **Live Long and Prosper 5.11b** ★
   Pro: 7 bolts and gear to 3"
   Located uphill about 6' left of AA. Climb to the right of a vegetated crack up to another hand crack. At the 'Y' continue straight up on crimpy orange face holds to end at the belay anchor for TBBWNMHBB.

37. **Captain Jim 5.10+**
   Pro to 3"
   Start as for LLP but follow up a right trending crack to the anchors.

MOTHERSHIP

38. **Alien Autopsy 5.10c** ★★★
   Pro: 7 bolts and gear to 2.5"
   Located on an obvious west facing wall. Bolts and gear will protect a delicate series of face moves between discontinuous cracks.

39. **Close Encounters 5.12a** ★★★
   Pro: 12 QD's
   Located 10' right of AA. Multiple crux sections with varied climbing. It takes 10 clips to reach the first anchor, or continue past the first anchor by climbing through the roof past two more bolts to a short headwall to the upper anchor.

40. **Black Ops 5.12a** ★★★
   Pro: 11 bolts and gear to 2"
   Located 20' right of Close Encounters. Locate HAL which is the long right leaning crack corner. Black Ops start on a steep technical slab immediately right of HAL, and then cross over the crack onto the left where Black Ops powers up a vertical slightly hung bolted face with reachy, fun moves.

41. **Open the Pod Bay Door HAL 5.10a** ★★
   Pro to 3"
   This is the obvious long right leaning crack corner system starting next to the trail.

42. **The Truth Is Out There 5.11d** ★★
   Pro: 7 QD's
   Fun shallow dihedral that leads up to technical moves above a good rest.

43. **Death Star 5.12d** ★★
   Pro: 11 QD's
   Attacks multiple crux bulges on left side of a tall face with light colored rock.

44. **Mothership 5.11b** ★★★
   Pro: 9 QD's
   This is THE classic at A51. Located 18' right of HAL and to the left of Pod #1 at the base of the stairs. Clamber up onto the top of a large detached boulder. Step up to a bulge and power through an awkward crux mantle move. Delicate face climbing leads up left to a thin seam. Follow the vertical seam (crux) past a slight bulge to juggy holds. A few final face moves lands at an anchor.

45. **Even Horizon 5.11d** ★★★
   Pro: 9 QD's
   Start at the top of the stairs which leads to Pod #1. Climb far right side of light colored face just left of the blunt arête. Stay left at the 7th bolt for the full tick. Short aliens might not achieve liftoff.

POD #1

46. The Wormhole 5.9 ★
Pro to 3" (possible gear to 4" on upper part)
Climb a wide crack immediately right of EH to a large ledge called Denial Pedestal. Continue up the deep overhanging offwidth corner system up out left to an anchor at top of Stargate.

47. Stargate 5.11a ★
Pro: 7 bolts and gear to 2"
Walk up the stairs to Pod #1. Climb the first part of Wormhole to the large ledge. Stargate powers up a deceptively pumpy thin face off the ledge side of the ledge and merges in with the upper part of the wide Wormhole near the anchor.

48. Lies and Deception 5.11c ★★★
Pro: 7 bolts and gear to 3"
Walk up the stairs to Pod #1. A bolt protects the opening moves to an easy crack on the right side of Full Denial flake. Avoid Denial Pedestal, and climb a vertical reddish face to pass a roof on the right. Finish on technical crimps to an anchor.

49. Alien Observer 5.10b ★★★
Pro: 6 bolts and gear to 2"
Locate the Pod #1 area by walking up the stairs to the right to the landing. Start up a 30' hand jam crack that quickly widens as you near the flat top of a minor pedestal. Power off from the top of the pedestal up overhanging jug holds up right, and then up left to the anchor.

50. Probe 5.10a
Pro: 4 bolts and gear to 4"
Located on the right side of Pod #1 via the upper belay platform.

51. Dilithium Crystals 5.11b ★
Pro: 8 QD's
Crystal crimping up an obvious blunt face/arête. Start on main trail.

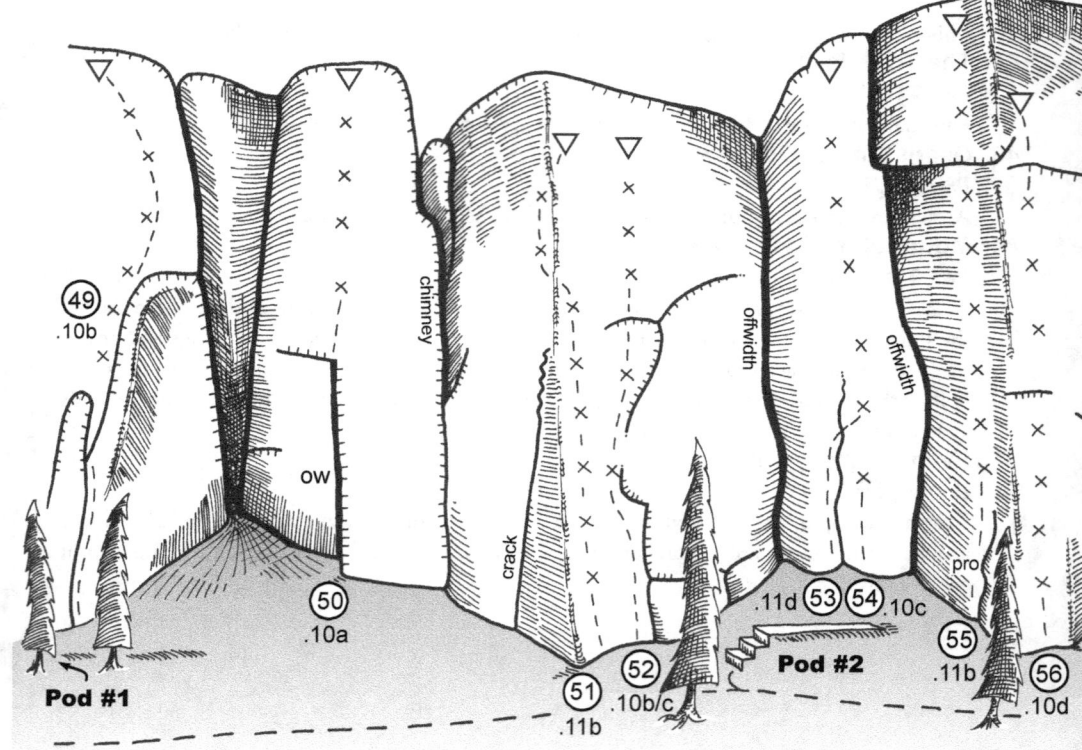

POD #2

52. Alien Invasion 5.10b/c
Pro: 5 bolts and gear to 2"
Located 9' right of DC in a right facing dihedral. Initial awkward moves lead to a finger crack passing a small roof on the left and ends on a fun slab above.

53. Abducted 5.10c ★
Pro: 6 bolts and gear to 1.5"
Begin on the highest platform between two wide cracks. Climb face and chimney (runout).

54. Taken 5.11d
Pro: 6 QD's
This is the direct no-stemming variation of Abducted. More difficult if you are short.

55. Glue Me Up Scotty 5.11b ★★
Pro: 8 bolts and gear to 2"
Located 30' right of AI. Usually starts from the low belay platform on the main trail. Climb a hand crack to the 'transporter' hold. Will Scotty beam you to the anchors? Stay tuned...

POD #3

56. We Are Not Alone 5.10d / .11a ★
Pro: 7 QD's
Located 5' right of 'Glue Me Up'. This route is the other side of the arête. Stay right of the bolts by using the pockets at start for the full value 5.11a stylin'.

57. The Borg 5.11a PG
Pro: 3 bolts and gear to 2"
Start on lower belay platform about 7' right of WENA. Belay on the trail. Starts in the crack/flake and ascends the bolted face above.

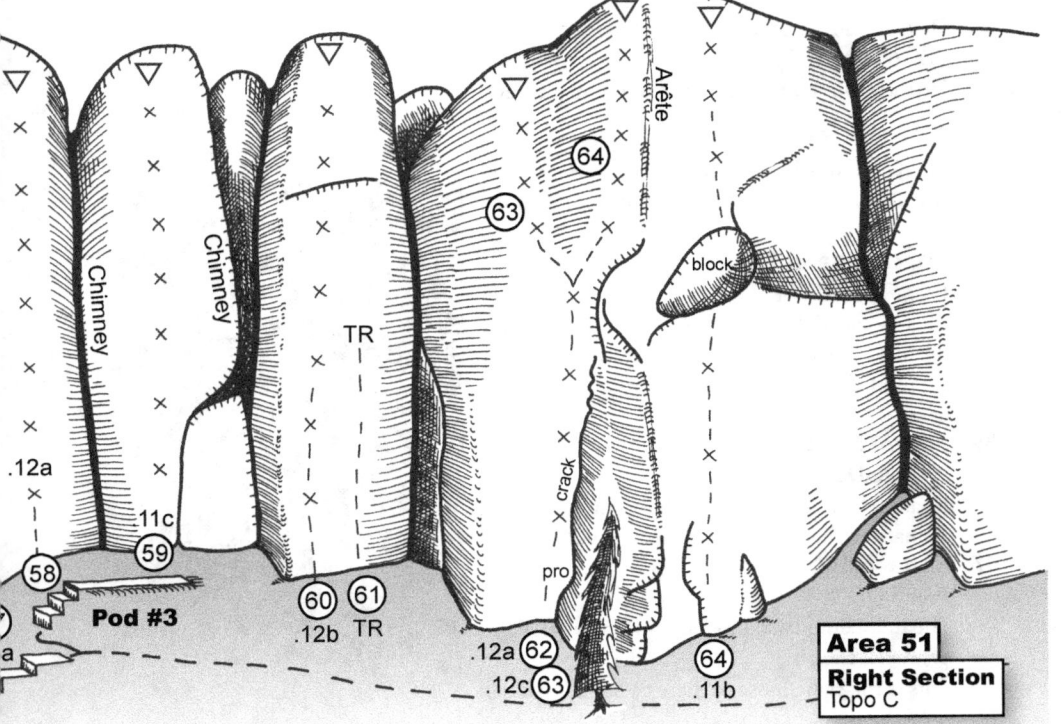

58. Lights Over Phoenix 5.12b ★
Pro: 7 QD's
Start on the upper belay platform 10' right of The Borg and left of the chimney. Technical climbing up a blunt arête.

59. Resistance Is Futile 5.11c ★★
Pro: 7 QD's
Located 8' right of LOP, but right of a mossy chimney on the upper platform. Mantle onto ledges leading up to a discontinuous crack system on a slightly overhanging face.

60. Covert Research 5.12b ★
Pro: 7 QD's
Located 14' left of Conspiracy Theory between two wide cracks. Surmount sloping ledge to a blank face above. Dude, if yo 6' or taller take off a letter grade!

61. Groom Lake (top-rope)
Pro: Top-rope
Located 5' right of Covert Research, and 5' left of Conspiracy. Power up a crack at the start which quickly leads to a hard boulder problem and micro flakes to an anchor.

62. Conspiracy Theory 5.12a ★★
Pro: 9 QD's
Begins on the far right wall in a steep, yellow dihedral. Climb up left past a small blocky roof to balancy moves on a blunt arête.

63. Conspiracy Lake 5.12c ★★
Pro: 7 QD's
Follows the initial part of Conspiracy Theory to the 5th bolt. Then it crimps out left and up a blank face past 3 more bolts to finish on the Groom Lake anchor.

OUTER LIMITS
Only one route, but with cleaning there could be more.

64. Dark Side of the Moon 5.11b
Pro: 6 QD's and pro
Furthest climb at the east end of the main crag.

PONDEROSA POINT
There are four known climbs here, but since the wall is 150' long it could certainly stand to see a few more.

65. Ponderosa 5.10b ★
Pro: 6 QD's
This is the right route on the buttress behind the BIG ponderosa pine. Climb up a shallow, featured dihedral and move up right around the flake.

66. Adam 5.10b
Pro: 6 QD's
Adam is the left climb on the right end of the formation. Shares the belay anchor with Hoss.

67. Hoss 5.10b ★
Pro: 6 QD's
The first climb encountered on Ponderosa Point approach trail.
This is the right-most of these two. Pull through

a fun bulge at the start. Follow discontinuous cracks and finish with exciting moves on slightly overhanging face moves near the top.

THE LINK-UPS
Here are some wild link-ups to mix some flavor into your venue on your next visit to A51.

A. Men Are From Mars 5.11b ★

Pro: 7 QD's

Climb up 5 bolts on Little Gray Men, clip the anchor with a long QD, and then step right to finish on fun headwall of mars past 2 more bolts.

B. Alien Encounter 5.11b ★★

Pro: 8 bolts and gear to 2"

Climb to 5th bolt on the Autopsy, then traverse right to Close Encounters. Finish through the roof to the headwall clipping three more bolts.

C. Black Truth 5.11c ★

Start on Black Ops slab (.11c), and finish on 'The Truth' as belay anchors.

D. Starship 5.11b ★★★

Pro: 11 QD's

Climb past 4 bolts on Death Star, and then trend right onto Mothership. Long slings reduce rope drag. Clip 7 more bolts on your way to the anchor on Mothership.

E. Event Gate 5.11c ★★

Pro: 9 QD's

Start at the top of the stairs leading to Pod #1. Follow 'Event Horizons' route to the 7th bolt. Move right onto easier terrain to finish on Stargate. Short stature aliens may not achieve liftoff.

Karl leading at *Hood River Pinnacle*

Climbing at *The Meadow*

HOOD RIVER PINNACLE

The elusive Hood River Pinnacles group has qualitative uniqueness that an adventure climber will relish with delight. This group of oddly shaped plugs and pinnacles are formed of slightly porphyritic dacite or ryhodacite material (generally solid on the bolted routes). The pinnacle group has remained well hidden and totally overlooked by generations of rock climbing adventurers until just recently. Only the famous Hood Pinnacle breaks through the towering forest canopy (the other plugs and pinnacles are shorter), yielding a short north side and a long back side. All the pinnacles are gargoyle knobby twisted volcanic creations with a plethora of crimps, edges and ledges. Virtually all of the routes are protected with 3/8" bolts (seldom is there any option for gear) so its quite possible to adventure here with just a set of QD's and a single light rope. Due to the friable nature of some of the rock a helmet is wise.

The first several teams to tackle this group of minor pinnacles are: Mr O, Mr B, Mr H, and Mr F, and they team climbed the various summits from 2015-2018. The upper Hood River valley has a brief selection of other minor odd rock plugs and pinnacle shaped outcrops scattered in several locales, most of which have been explored in one form or another. All summits tend to be helmet adventure climbing of one kind or another.

Directions:

From Portland drive I-84 east to Hood River, then south on Hwy 35 for 25.7 miles, and turn east onto NF44 road. Drive NF44 for 3.8 miles uphill. Turn right (south) onto NF4410 and drive 1.5 miles. Turn right (west) onto an old logging grade road NF4410-630. A tall dirt berm exists here (but at the moment AWD vehicles can get over the berm and all the way down this road to its end in .7 mile. Park where the road is overgrown and blocked by debris.

Hike south on the old road grade for .8 mile (it gradually descends). Bust off from the roadbed and descend in a tall forest downhill about 400' to the pinnacles (none are visible from the road so get a GPS lock on it). The site is at the headwaters of Culvert Creek.

GPS Info (using GoogleEarth technology):
Hood River Pinnacle: **GPS UTM 10t 613719 5025627**
Spire Desire: **GPS UTM 10t 613658 5025707**

Beta and Orientation:

The main HRP is about 70' tall on the north side and about 130' tall on the south side with a substantial girth of about 100' width. Its the ultimate goal if visiting here. It has more future route potential. It has two summits - the main and the lower west summit (which is seperated by a deep slot). The Rocktober Surprise is the standard original route to the top.

The beta begins on the main HRP, then details the next pinnacle uphill (Warp) to the north, then Weeble, then Foo Pinnacle. Then the beta jumps over to the other big pinnacle called Spire Desire, and finally mentions briefly the last tiny plug called Atomic. See diagram.

Hood River Pinnacle

1. Rocktober Surprise
Rating: 5.5
Pro: 9 QD's *(use long slings)*

The original east face FA route to get to the top and a nice fun line. Start at the north side saddle, traverse leftward onto the east side (past the initial bolt) and climb up left on steps and ledges to a stance on a narrow rib at a notch. Directly above is a large rock knob with a smooth chute on its left and a series of ramp steps on its right. Go up right via steps and a crux move (some chossy rock) till you are on top of the rock knob. Brief easy 4th class final moves near the summit. Rappel 70' northward down to the saddle.

2. **Chaco (multi-pitch)**
   Pro: P1 80' 5.6 (9 QD's), P2 70' 5.7 (6 QD's), P3 40' 5.4 (3 QD's)
   This climb involves ascending the West Face & West Summit. It's a unique and fun multi-pitch endeavor. P1: Climb 80' up a broad gully and where it gets vertical it angles slightly left past a tricky crux 5.6 section to attain a saddle belay station. P2: Climb the lower west summit via a steep sunny 5.7 face (70'). There are two belays on this west summit (use the eastmost one. Rappel down into a notch 20' below. P3: Climb a 5.5 section (3 bolts) to the main summit and belay. Rappel 70' northward down to the saddle.
   Note (see topo): if your not into harder leading, there is a 3-bolt alternate way to bypass the vertical P2 by marching up the wide ravine system to the slot saddle between the upper main summit and the lower west summit.

3. **SW Rib**
   Pro:
   Future wow potential.

4. **South Face**
   Pro:
   Future wow potential.

5. **SE Rib**
   Pro:
   Future wow potential.

6. **Warp Pinnacle 5.5**
   Rating: 5.5
   Pro: minor gear ½" to 3"
   The front uphill side of this small stretched pinnacle is about 40' tall while the lower back side is a bit taller. The regular route is all natural gear, and makes for a brief bit of entertainment.
   From the north (uphill side) move along a very narrow rock ridgecrest (sling 2 knobs). Or climb up a short 5.5 direct west face access point onto the crest. Then climb a steep vertical rock crack till you can slide left onto the east side ledge. A belay station exists here. Rappel down the route. The pinnace is about 40' tall max.

7. **Weeble Pinnacle 5.5 (free var.)**
   Pro: 4-5 QD's
   A tiny bowling pin shaped plug of rock plug that has a basic bit 'o entertainment on it.

122 CHAPTER 2

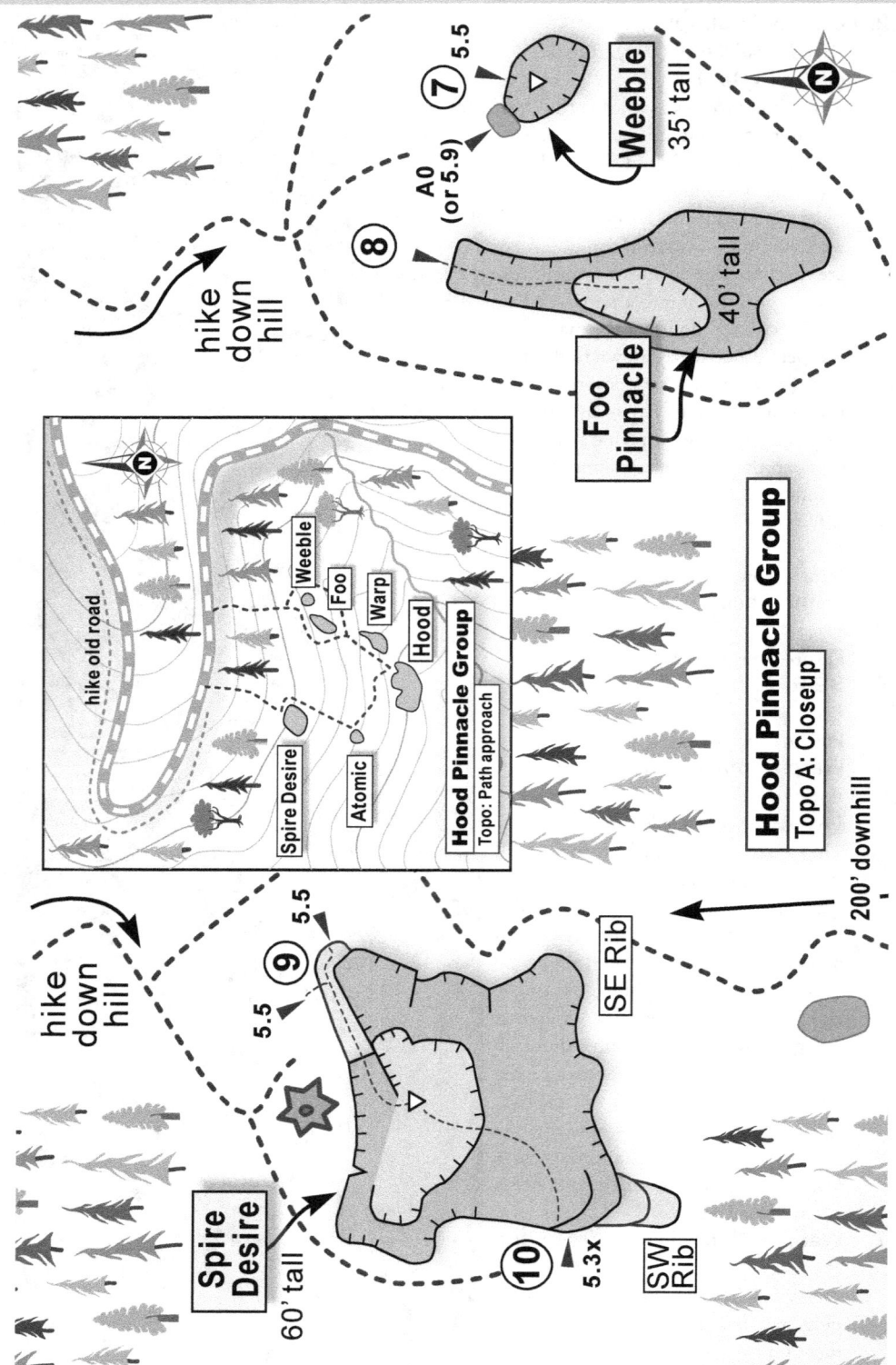

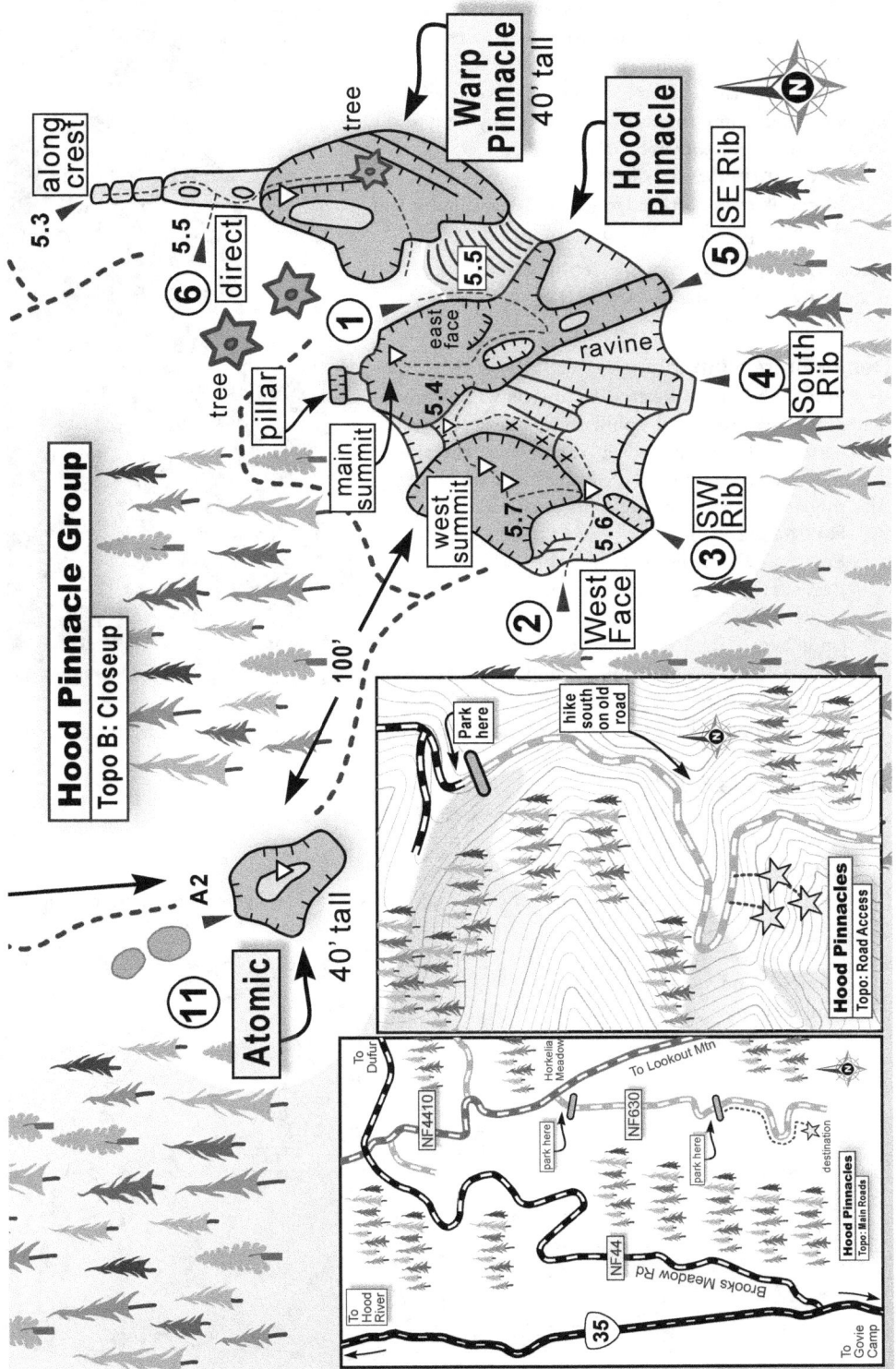

The rating is 5.5 via the left free route, or you can do A0 via the direct aid line (which is also free at 5.9 TR).

Start at its saddle on a rock stance, traverse left past a piton, then up the east side of this tiny plug to the summit. Approximately 35' tall.

8. **Foo Pinnacle 4th class**

    Minor 4th class north ridge gets onto the summit, but the entire plug is unappealing.

Note: The upper list of outcrops are all in a line (from low to high on same crest).

Desire Spire Pinnacle

This is the upper westmost pinnacle with a prominent corner system on the uphill north side at the saddle. A majestic tall fir tree spreads its canopy over this side of the pinnacle. The common NE route is well worth doing. This pinnacle has more future route potential.

9. **Razmataz 5.5**

    Pro: 6 QD's (for entire buttress)

    Begin at the lowest point of the NE buttress. Climb a series of steps to a large landing (the direct start crack lands here). Then step around a big 4' tall block to reach a crack corner system. Climb the crack corner system to the top. The route is all bolts. Note: At the third bolt a short alternate direct start crack jumps into the climb if you want to skip the longer start.

10. **South Face 5.3 R/X**

    The first original route used to reach the summit. Risky venture on poor rock.

11. **Atomic Garbage Can**

    Rating A1-A2

    Aid (bolts) from the notch up onto the left side. Starts rotten and gets more rotten the higher you aid up. It all might crumble and tumble soon.

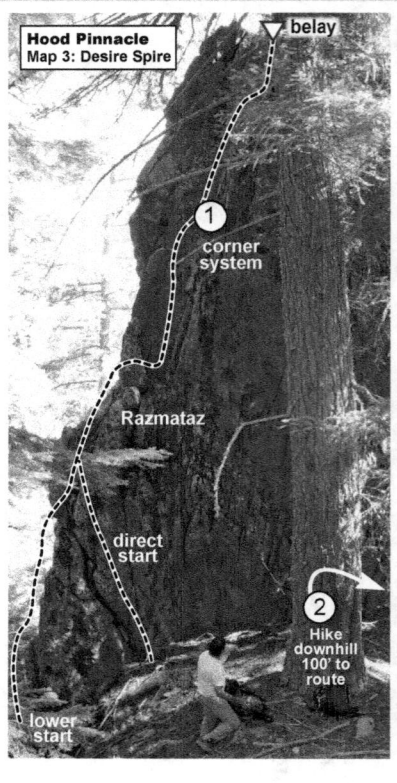

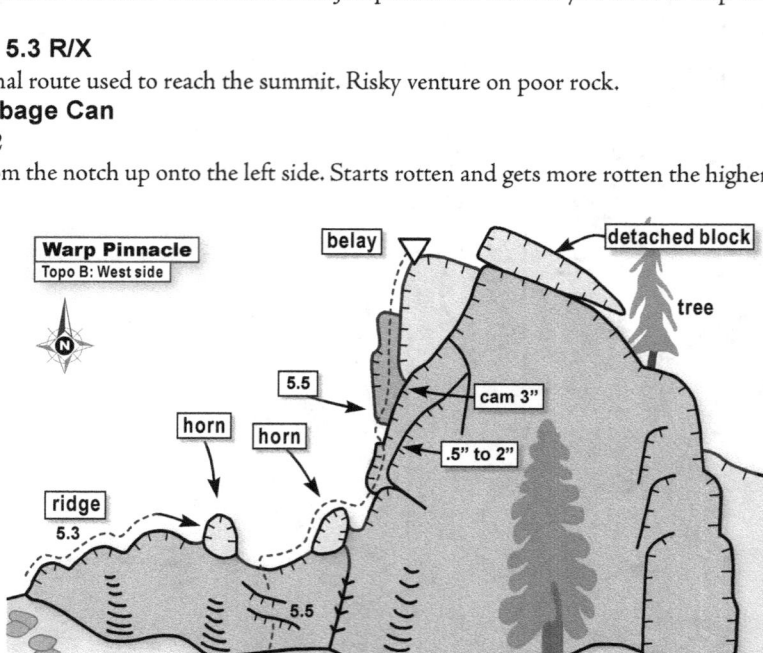

Rock climbing in the Columbia Gorge

CHAPTER 3

COLUMBIA GORGE ROCK

THIS SECTION provides an in-depth constructive research treatise concerning the natural value and historical aspect of rock climbing in the Columbia River Gorge. These pages are designed to serve as a utilitarian archival reference source for continuous long-term viable exploration of the Gorge.

The first section provides an inquiry about rock climbing summits on the south side of the Columbia River beginning near Rooster Rock State Park. The south side, of course, is the primary area of interest for research as it holds some of the greatest uplift of vertical terrain easily accessible from the roadside. This section ends with the Apocalypse formation east of The Dalles.

The second section details historical facts concerning places of interest starting near Cape Horn on the north side of the Gorge then proceeds eastward to Horsethief Butte at Columbia Hills State Park.

ROOSTER ROCK

Rooster Rock is a popular tooth shaped basalt pinnacle on the south side of the Columbia River Gorge located immediately west of the boat launch area at Rooster Rock State Park. Drive east on I-84 from Portland and take exit #25 at the State Park. Pay the daily user fee and park your vehicle at the State

Hugh near the top of *Rabbit Ears*

Park, then walk around the south side of the small boat moorage lagoon to access the rock pinnacle which is located on the west side of the lagoon. From the freeway walk north along a nice dirt path that soon angles directly over to the start of the popular South Face route. Just before you reach the base of the cliff another steep dirt path wanders directly up to the seldom climbed East Face area.

Crediting the first ascent of this pinnacle is rather dubious but yields an interesting history. As recorded in 'A Climber's Guide to the Columbia River Gorge' by Carl A. Neuberger, "...about 1910, a sailor from a Swedish ship undertook the climbing of the rock when challenged by other members of the crew. When nearing the summit he lost his nerve and would neither go further or back down. However, he was finally persuaded by companions from below to go on to the summit. He was too frightened by the experience to descend and it was necessary to shoot a line to him before he could be brought down." And so perhaps it is possible for those Swedes to climb just about anything.

1. **South Face 5.4**

    Pro: Nuts and Hex's to 3" and two 60m ropes for rappel
    Vertical Height of Route: 165'

    A popular and enjoyable rock climb. The approach trail leads directly to the base of the pinnacle and up to a small level dirt stance next to a large fir on the SW shoulder of the pinnacle. Lead up easy 4th class steps on the SW shoulder and after you surmount several steep spots belay (2-bolt belay anchor) at a small stance below a slight overhang (60' lead). Traverse right 15' to the base of the obvious diagonal ascending corner system. Ascend this corner system (crux) for 70' till you attain the southeast ridge. Scramble up the exposed ridge crest 30' to the summit. Rappel with two ropes down the south face (165' vertical).

2. **East Face Route 5.6 R**

    To approach the East Face route scramble up the steep dirt path to the east face of the pinnacle. Begin by leading up rightward on steep dirty steps 30' to a sling belay in the top of a large fir tree that leans up against the pinnacle. Climb to a shelf above the snag tree then continue directly to the summit using nailing gear by means of direct aid. Alternative B: Another route option is to angle leftward from the snag tree sling belay on poorly protected, and

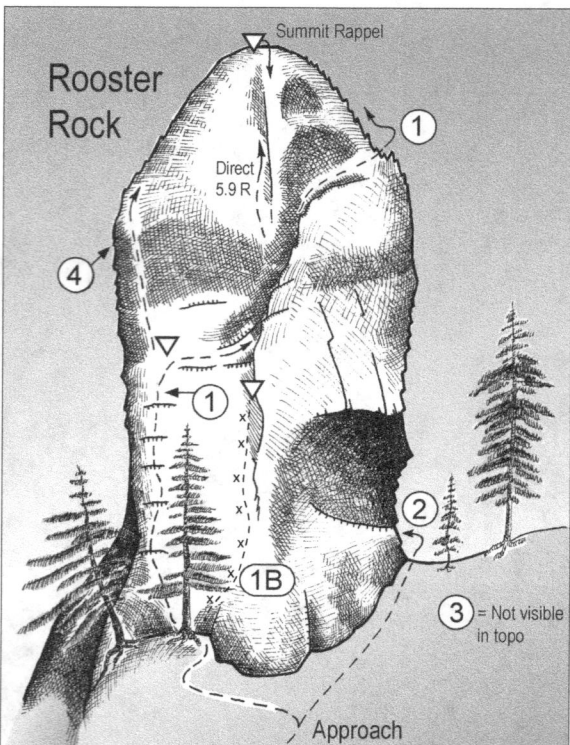

Mike & Hugh at 1st belay, West Chimney

steep moss-covered terrain up to a point where it joins with the South Face route at the southeast ridge. Scramble up 30' to the summit.

3. **North Face II 5.6 A3 (or 5.8 R)**
The route is reached by starting at the base of the east face, then dropping down 25' to a ledge. Follow this west till you can belay at one of several trees. Climb diagonally up left 25' and continue straight up through a notch in the first overhang. Ascend over the second overhang to a vertical slab, then up grass slopes to the top. It is ninety feet from the original tree belay up past the vertical slab, and then 45' up the grass slope to the summit.

4. **Southwest Face II 5.6 A2 (or 5.9 R)**
Ascends directly up the vertical rock on the SW shoulder above the first belay on the South Face route.
Note: All climbing routes other than the regular South Face route on Rooster Rock are infrequently climbed friable, mossy adventures.

Deep in the West Chimney

CROWN POINT

Crown Point is the prominent 500' north-facing scarp immediately south of Rooster Rock. The historic and panoramic Vista House is situated upon its summit. There are several known routes located on the north face, but expect to find difficult climbing on well vegetated steep friable

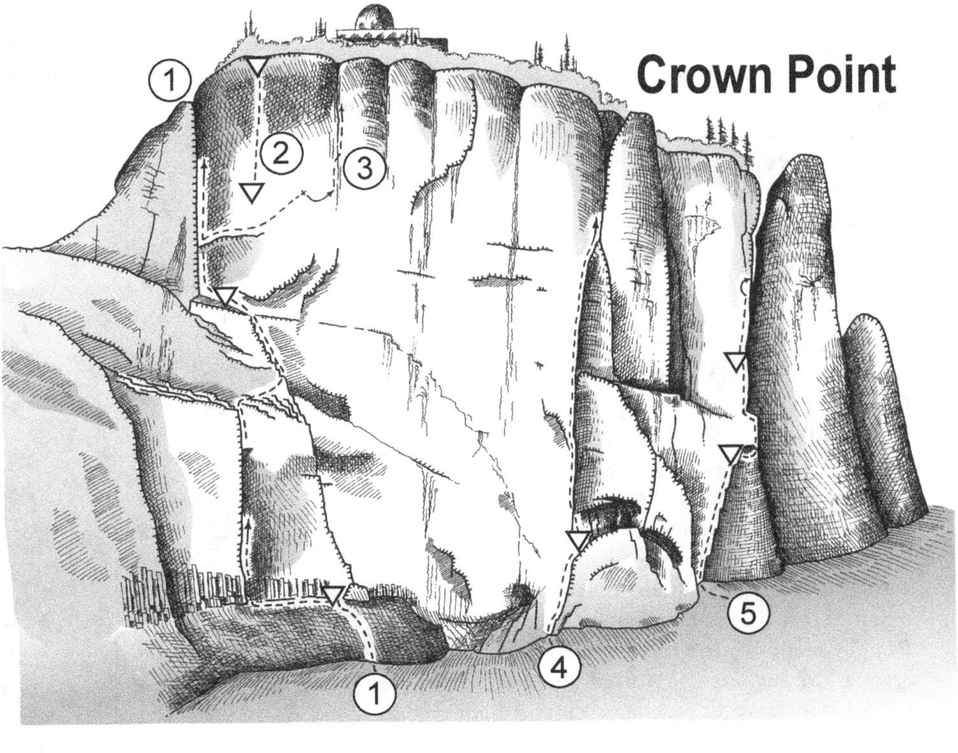

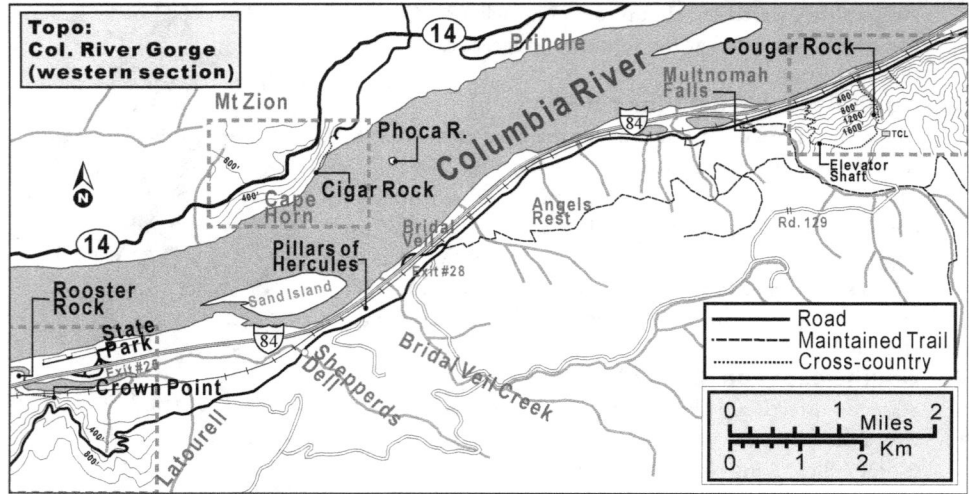

Topo: Col. River Gorge (western section)

rock. The climbs on this historical scarp are seldom ascended.

1. **Zucchini Route (NE Face)   III 5.6 A2 or 5.10a R**
   Multi-pitch climb, Pro: Nuts and cams to 3" including pitons
   To reach the Zucchini Route scramble up the talus slope to the base of the face directly below Vista House. Ascend up leftward on easy 5th class moss ledges 60' to a belay on a ledge system. Traverse east 30' to the base of a steep crack system and belay. Climb up the crack for 165' but do expect friable rock on the second half of this lead. Continue up right on poor rock to a left leaning diagonal system, following this up left 90' to the 'zucchini ledge'. This ledge is a small triangular ledge beneath the major chimney system at the upper east portion of the northeast face. If you are hungry and it is mid summer you can survive on wild zucchini for lunch. Climb 40' of corner crack into the chimney, and then squeeze up the chimney 50' to a notch belay. Walk up to the road and descend by scrambling down a steep western gully past the Alpenjager. There may be other variations on the first part of this route.

2. **Jewel in the Crown   5.12a**
3. **RURP Traverse   III 5.10 A2+ X**
4. **Unknown**
5. **West Chimney   II 5.4**
   Multi-pitch climb, Pro: Nuts and cams to 3"
   On the far right side of Crown Point a dark gash separates the main massif from a cigar-shaped dome of rock called **Alpenjager** in Nick Dodge's book. The deeply sliced corner system is called West Chimney. Although seldom climbed it is an impressive feature and a unique Gorge chimney route. To approach ascend a ravine in a forested slope just beyond the western edge of Crown Point wall. When you are level with the base of the wall scramble left through thick brush to the base of the route. Look for a diagonally rightward leaning brush corner system with grass steps (some fixed pins) that leads up into the main chimney far above.
   P1: The first pitch is a 150' lead up easy 5th class grass and moss steps to a fixed pin belay on a good grassy stance. Expect lots of grass hummock

Hugh on crux pitch on *West Chimney*

climbing on this lead.

P2: Traverse right 12′ on steep thin edges (fixed piton) to attain a prominent corner system. Work up and left around a slight bulge, then stem up a vertical crux section avoiding the loose rock. The climbing difficulties quickly ease as you enter into the main *deeeeeeeep* chimney system. Belay at 90′ at a good fixed piton belay just below a large rock wedged in the chimney.

P3: The next 150′ is a classic slightly smaller than shoulder-width chimney squeeze. You are certain to hear burly yet festive pig-like grunting sounds while in the depth of this great chimney. The adventure will take you literally right through the darkness of this rock wall chasm, and out the other side into the sunlight. Descend the west side of Alpenjager in a ravine.

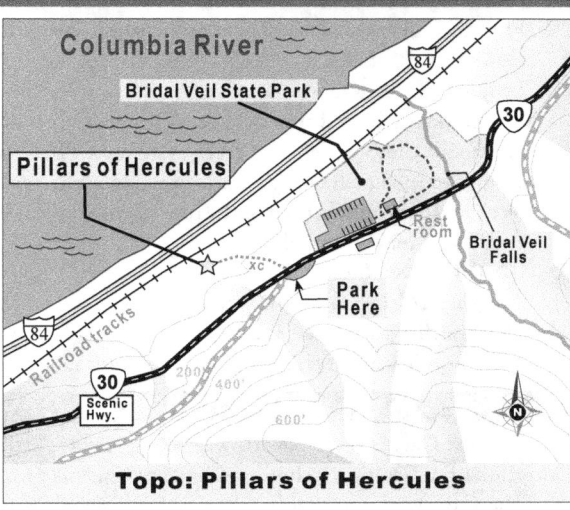

Topo: Pillars of Hercules

6. **Alpenjager 5.4 R**
The summit of **Alpenjager** is a harrowing feat, because steep dirt and friable rock make this a rather challenging undertaking. It can be ascended by a small ledge system on the south side near a tree. Or...halfway through the third pitch (P3) on the **West Chimney** you can ascend directly up vertically following several old fixed pitons. Expect runout sections on dubious rock to attain the top of **Alpenjager**.

PILLARS OF HERCULES

Although the pillars (aka Speelyei's Columns) are readily accessible and technically reasonable to climb, this formation is seldom ascended because the rock is mossy and friable. The West Arête, the Northwest Face and its variation, and the North Face Traverse are not climbed these days. This cobblestone basalt formation is located approximately 3 miles east of Rooster Rock State Park on the south side of the freeway, but west of Bridal Veil exit #28 about ½ mile. If the Pillar is your goal consider parking at a dirt pullout immediately west of Shepperds Dell State Park rest facility on old

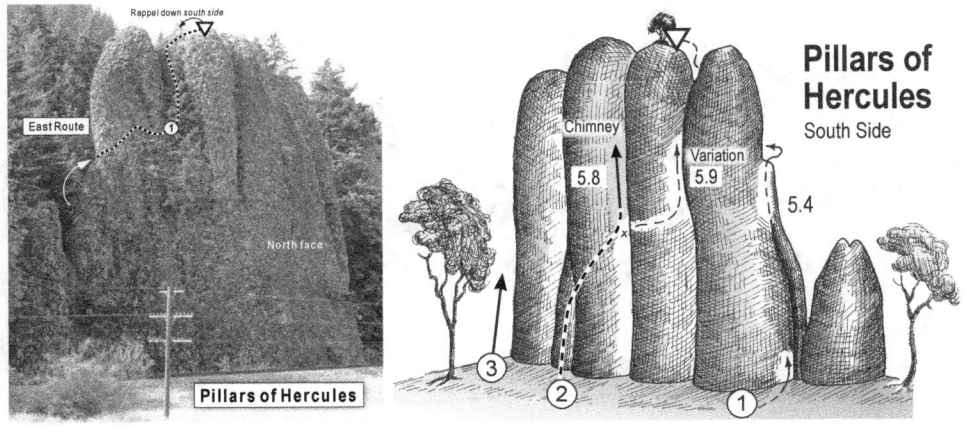

U.S. Hwy 30 and cross-country over to the south side of the pillar. Bring a helmet.

1. **East Route 5.4**
   Length: 120', Pro to 3½"
   The standard East Route begins on the *south side* of the pillar. Step up under a prominent notch and climb up left in a crack system for 60'. Traverse fifteen feet right on a minor ledge around to the north face. A tree is growing at the base of a wide corner crack. Climb the wide crack up to the notch, then to the top where a cable is wrapped around a large bush. Two ropes are needed for the rappel.

2. **South Face 5.8 R**
   Length: 120', Pro to 3" and pitons
   The **South Face** route ascends a vertical cobblestone face for 30', then traverses right 10' to climb a wide vertical chimney to the summit. Dirty and loose in places.

THE RAT CAVE

The Rat Cave is one of Northwest Oregon's rare little gems in that it sports the highest concentration of difficult rock climbs within a reasonable proximity to Portland metro area.

The Cave is an unusual basalt rock feature with a wildly overhung 30' horizontal cave roof surrounded with a 50' steep overhanging outer face. The routes provide an intense opportunity to experience beta-intensive rock climbing requiring endurance, power and movement. The routes are beta intensive, because every single knob looks like a hold. An initial foray might leave you with a sense of being sandbagged but local climbers who know the routes very well can provide great guid-

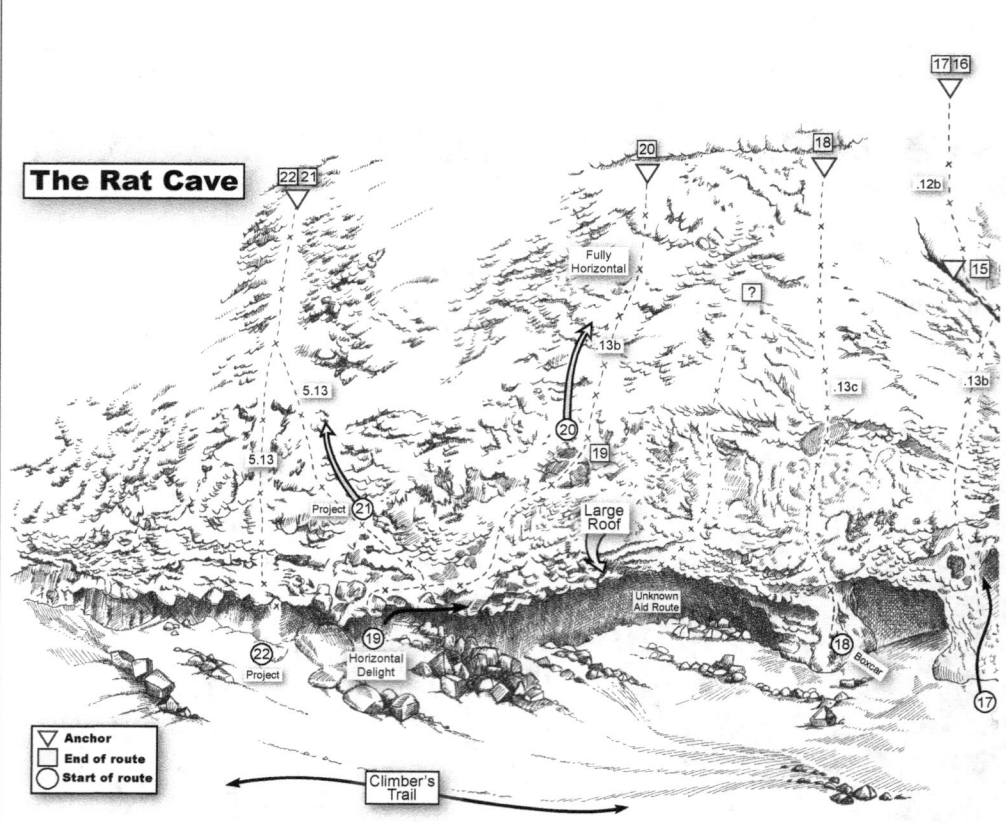

ance to each climb. The grades are based on a red-point lead, not an on-sight lead, because of the difficulty to identify which is a real hold and which is not. The listed ratings are 2-3 letter grades harder based on this red-point method. Beta was compiled by Tymun Abbott.

Seasonal variables

Climbing at the Cave is feasible for 12 months of the year, but the best time to climb here is generally from September till February. March and April bring considerable rain showers and warmer temperatures that allow steady seeps to occur along portions of the walls of the Cave, hindering access to certain climbs. June through August is typically humid (not like the east coast) and can lower your ability to effectively cling to pinches and tiny grips. Yet even during the long sultry days of summer you can find many days where climbing at the Cave is great and summer lighting colorfully photogenic. For climbers who already know where the Cave is...have fun! The Rat Cave is located about ¼ mile west of the Multnomah Falls parking lot directly across from

Dave leading Dork Boat, The Cave

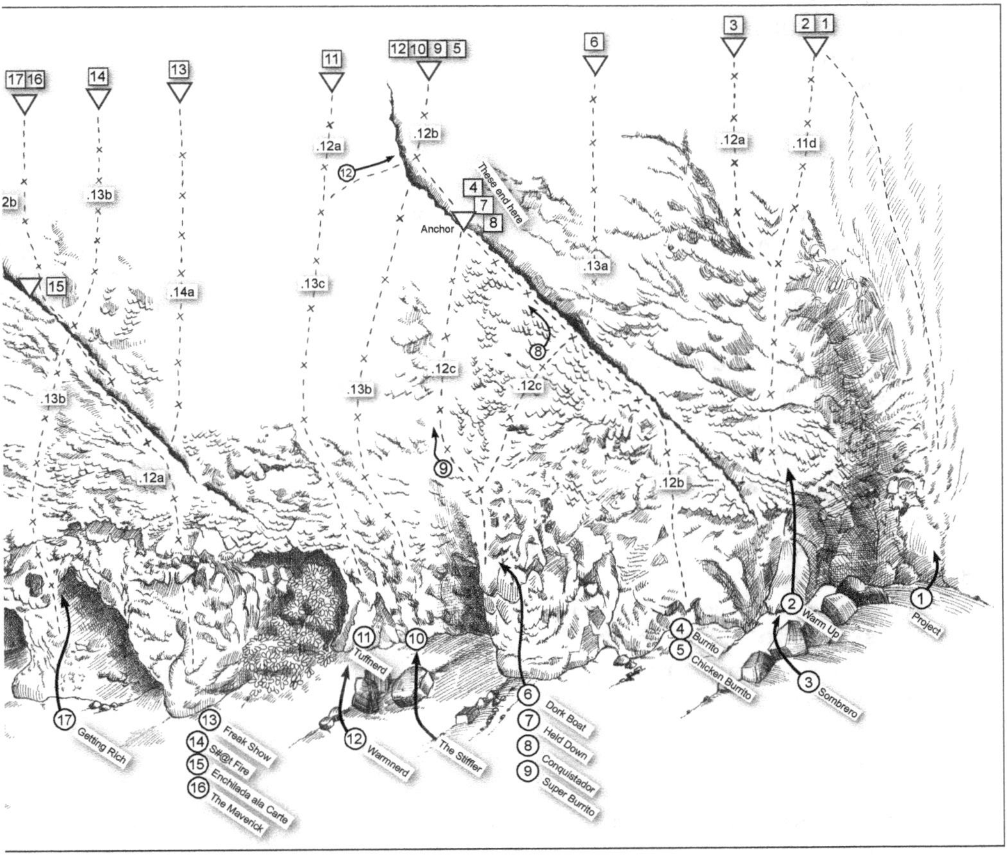

Benson Lake at a small gravel pullout.

1. **_____ (Project)**
   Starts on the outside wall of minor buttress and merges with the next route at anchor.

2. **Pissfire (aka Warm Up)   5.11d / 5.12a** ★
   Length: 70', Pro: 8 QD's
   This route has been cleaned up considerably and is a viable initial route to warm-up lead. Start on the far right side of the cave. Climb through a hard move to start then continue on big holds to a rest. Climb past a second hard section to reach the anchor.

Wolfgang leading *Horizontal Delight*

3. **Sombrero   5.12a**
   Length: 60', Pro: 7 QD's
   Clip first 3 bolts of warm-up route, then aim up left (4 more bolts) in a groove to the anchor.

4. **Burrito (aka Warm Up)   5.12b** ★★
   Pro: 7 QD's, Usually fixed draws on the second half
   This route is still considered to be the original 'Warm Up' route at the Rat Cave. The crux comes at the beginning which is a long lock-off utilizing an under cling pinch to another pinch which continues up left through more pumpy climbing. The route follows a small left leaning channel to the first set of anchors in the middle of the face.

5. **Chicken Burrito   5.12d** ★★
   Start on Burrito and end at the top of the wall on Super Burrito.

6. **Dorkboat   5.13a** ★★
   Length: 70', Pro: 9 QD's
   This route starts just left of Burrito on the same start as Held Down, and climbs straight to the top of the wall. Punch through an early crux move after the first bolt, which involves a tricky sequence of pinches utilizing a well placed drop knee. Hard moves continue until the 4th bolt where the Warm Up route crosses at the good pinch jug rest. Continue straight up using decent pinches and under clings passing through a crux at mid-height. A small Gaston at the 7th bolt lets you get just enough strength back to push through the next two clips. Endurance is the key to sending this line.

7. **Held Down   5.12c** ★★★
   Length: 70', Pro: __ QD's
   Held Down is the next logical route to climb after the Warm Up route. It starts the same as Dorkboat moving left at the first bolt to finish at the anchor in the middle of the wall. Begin up a small pillar to the face. Punch through a couple of long moves to set up the crux, which is a long lock-off to the second bolt followed by a reach to a small triangle and undercling requiring a back-step and lock-off. Expect another under-cling lock-off before you reach the anchor.

8. **Conquistador   5.12c** ★
   Start on Dorkboat and end on Held down.

9. **Super Burrito   5.12d** ★★★
   Start on Held down. After clipping the anchor for Held Down continue on up the top of the wall with a surprise waiting at the end.

10. **The Stiffler   5.13b** ★
    Length: 65', Pro: __ QD's
    The business begins early on this route. Start just left of Held Down. Climb through a small roof past a horn which entails a knee-bar followed by tenuous lockoffs. Continue through a

series of sloped holds, lockoffs and pinches to the anchor.

11. Tuffnerd 5.13c ★★★
Length: 70', Pro: __ QD's
Start just left of The Stiffler under a small roof. Begin with double hands and double heels on a hanging block-shaped rock feature followed by a series of side pulls using reasonable edges. The crux is moving off of two sloped holds at midway to a reasonable under-cling, followed by a series of lockoff Gaston moves. The climbing remains very sustained all the way to the anchor. You can find several useful knee-bar placements on this route. Some have the guns to make it to the end…some don't.

10. Warmnerd 5.13d ★★★
Length: 70', Pro: 8 QD's, mostly fixed Quick-Draws
This route starts on Tuffnerd and finishes on the Chicken / Super Burrito anchor. Pull the first three cruxes of Tuffnerd which take you to the 7th bolt. At the 7th bolt bust hard right by traversing through a series of sloped holds till you reach the last few bolts on the next route to the right. Make a powerful transition onto the under-cling to clip, then fire through a powerful pinch to sloped side pull crux and finish to the anchor.

13. Freak Show 5.14a ★★
Length: 65', Pro: __ QD's. There is a midway anchor at the 5th
Start up Enchilada ala Carte for the first three bolts (.12-), the head straight up instead of following the left leaning weakness. The first few moves off the seam involve a tough sequence of powerful crimper lockoffs to a desperate toss to a marginal sloped hold (V7ish). Make a clip off an OK under cling, and then enter the crux. A series of desperate pulls off sloped holds on a 30° overhang. This follows for two bolts (roughly V8). Unlike Tuffnerd this route lacks a decent rest before its pumpy headwall. Finish on sustained 5.12 for the last 5 bolts. This follows the second left leaning weakness from the right.

14. S#@t Fire 5.13c ★★
Length: 70', Pro: __ QD's. The second half has fixed quick-draws on it
Begin up Enchilada ala Carte and climb along the left leaning ramp/channel. At the 5th bolt transition to the upper wall. The climb kicks back dramatically here involving intense power climbing through three consecutive bulge sections. Expect long reaches in spots to marginal holds; however the occasional good pinch or crimp appears just when you need them most.

15. Enchilada ala Carte 5.12a ★
Length: 50', Pro: __ QD's
This route provides access to one of the rat caves finest routes (S#@t Fire). Start just left of Tuffnerd and climb out a short but powerful overhang crux section, and then angle up left along a left-leaning ramp/channel. The climb is roughly 5.11- climbing for the last part to the RC mid-height anchor.

15b. Kings of Rat 5.13b
Length: __', Pro: __ QD's (fixed)
From the Enchilada belay, reach right and clip a bolt, then climb directly up a series of under-clings and steep dynamic climbing till you reach a belay jug.

16. The Maverick 5.12b ★★
Pro: 10 QD's
Start just left of Tuffnerd using the same start as for Enchilada ala Carte. Climb out the roof and follow a left-leaning ramp/channel to the 6th bolt where the climbing eases near the anchor at mid-height. Continue past this anchor by making a long high clip, and then engage in a series of powerful pinches (2 bolts total) to the upper anchor.

17. Getting Rich Watching Porn 5.13c
This line punches out of the right edge of the main overhanging roof of the cave.

18. Boxcar 5.13c ★★★
Length: 45', Pro: Sports long fixed draws
Boxcar is a wildly overhanging route that begins at the very back of the cave. Move up on hanging blocks of rock using marginal pinches, and then climb horizontally for 30' out the roof using a variety of crucial opposition hand holds and knee-bars. Power past a 'pod' at the lip of the cave roof, then finish by climbing up the outer upper wall without getting too pumped.

18b. Boxtop 5.13d ★★
Length: 70', Pro: 16 QD's
Start on Boxcar, and climb out to the lip, then continue directly up after pulling the lip ending at a new set of belay anchors (left of Maverick belay).
Note: An unknown bolt line exists just left of Boxcar in the very back portion of the cave, but it is generally not used for free climbing purposes. Boxcar is the right bolt line.

19. Horizontal Delight 5.12d ★★★
Length: 35', Pro: 6 QD's, two bolt rap anchor
A stellar route that begins on the far left side of the cave. Climb out horizontally toward the center of the cave using a variety of oppositional counter pressure and knee-bars to finish in a 'pod'. Lower off here for just the .12d portion. Bolts have fixed chains and carabiners for the first 6 bolts to facilitate efficient climbing. The upper portion ascending the outer wall to the upper anchor is 5.13+.

20. Fully Horizontal 5.13b ★★★
This is the continuation of Horizontal Delight and it ascends the outer face past six more bolts with a crux at the upper bolt anchor. Has one reasonable rest point on the upper wall, but beware when clipping the anchor, especially if you line up backward for it.

21. Project 5.13?
This project branches directly up from the third bolt on Horizontal Delight.

22. Project 5.13?
This project is located at the very left edge of the cave.

LITTLE COUGAR ROCK

Little Cougar Rock (Winema Pinnacles) protrudes from the south wall of the gorge one mile east of Multnomah Falls at the 1683' level. This rocky promontory juts out against the green forest and can be seen from the Multnomah parking area when looking east. Located immediately above it is the forested Big Cougar Rock. Though Cougar Rock is a seldom traveled summit for the off-trail gorge rock climbing hound this is a great objective.

The origin of the name of this pinnacle is mentioned in the Crown Point Country Historical Society's 2006 newsletter as follows. "An early settler in the area in the 1890's named George Pau was trying to climb to the viewpoint of the Columbia River Gorge. He found a tree lodged against the rock which afforded him handholds to do so. As he neared the summit, he spotted three cougar kittens in a den in the rocks. The kittens' mother came out of the trees at him trapping him at the top. The cougar slashed at him and finally lunged for him. Pau used the cougar's momentum to fling it off the cliff. Bleeding from several wounds, he was able to climb down and make his way back to help. The next day, he and some fellow loggers went back, rescued the kittens which were taken to the Portland zoo. After this, it was named Cougar Rock."

Three different approaches are available.

Option #1: Park at Multnomah Falls and ascend the Larch Mountain trail. Then hike the Multnomah Basin trail to the Trails Club's Nesika Lodge, then descend a trail immediately west of the lodge down to Big Cougar. Descend down east under BC to access LC.

Option #2: Park in a small pullout ½ mile east of Multnomah creek and ascend the Elevator Shaft trail which zigzags up a long talus field east of the falls, then cross-country to the main trail, then follow the same descending trail toward Big Cougar. Descend east off from the ridge, skirting the base of Big Cougar to access the saddle between BC and LC.

Option #3: Take the 2½ hour grunt directly up the stream drainage immediately east of the pinnacle. This drainage is exactly 1 mile east of Multnomah creek and is best when you park on the shoulder of the I-84 freeway. Ascend the stream gully till a small vertical waterfall forces you to the right. Ascend the dirt and talus slopes to the right of the creek and aim for the upper saddle of Little Cougar, which is below Big Cougar.

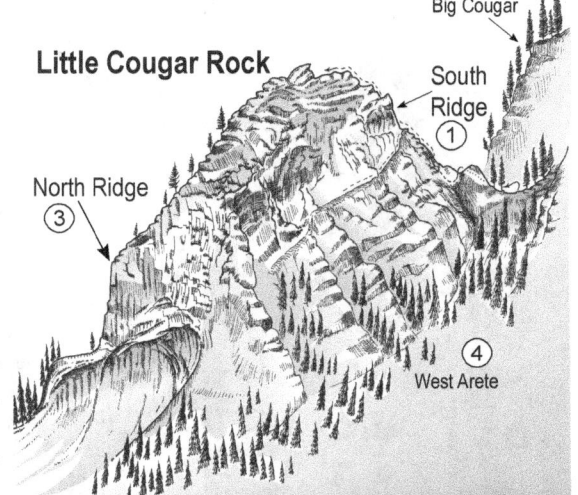

1. **South Ridge Lower 5th class**
   Multi-pitch climb, Pro: Minor gear to 2"
   This is the standard route. Ascend from the saddle out onto the South Ridge of Little Cougar over a minor hump. Traverse left and up loose scree, then back over to the right side of the ridge to a good corner crack. Ascend the short corner, then cross a jumble of blocks over to a notch for the final rather delicate balance move to get up onto the airy summit. Expect about 200' of technically easy but occasionally loose 4th and easy 5th class rock climbing.

2. **East Arête 5.4 R**
   Start near a prominent tree and ascend the crest until vertical rock forces you onto the north side. Climb a large tilted steep slab section on aid, then continue to the top on easier ground.

3. **North Arête 5.8 A2+**
   An unfinished climb that starts next to a tree on the east side of the north ridge, and ascends a leaning 5.4 crack system to a single 5.8 move onto a broad ledge and belay at 80'. Step over to the arête and aid climb the vertical face. This lead is about 80' long till it eases onto a ledge and continues up steep ledges to the summit. Incomplete ascent.

4. **West Arête Lower 5th class**
   This ascends the jumbled west face until it merges with the main wall. Traverse right on steep

St Peters Dome view from the west

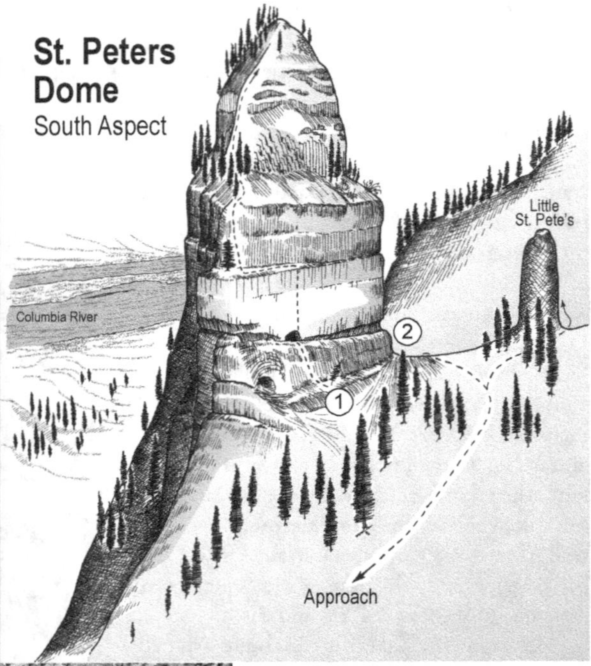

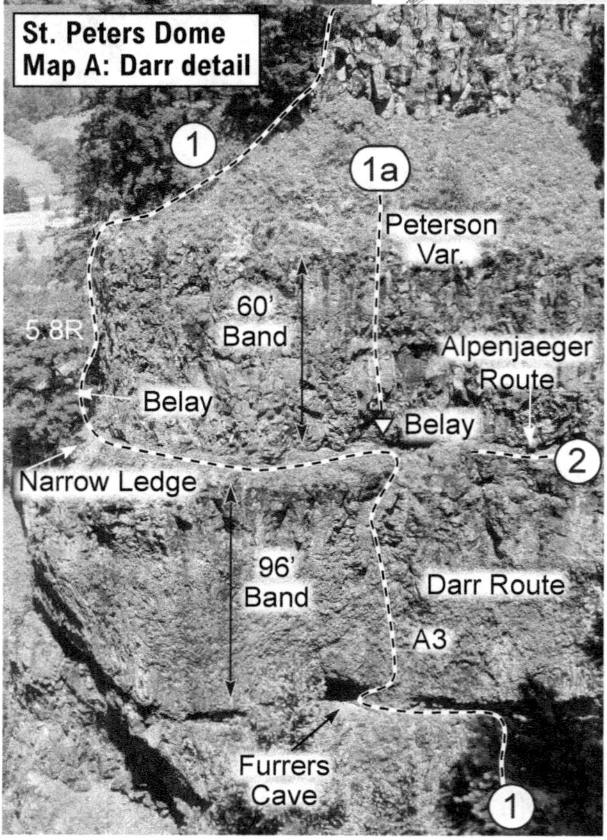

St. Peters Dome
South Aspect

Little St. Pete's

Columbia River

Approach

St. Peters Dome
Map A: Darr detail

5.8R

60' Band

Peterson Var.

Alpenjaeger Route

Belay

Belay

Narrow Ledge

96' Band

Darr Route

A3

Furrers Cave

rock and continue climbing diagonally upward until you can gain the south ridge.

ST. PETERS DOME

Southeast from Ainsworth State Park is a historical and prominent feature of the Columbia Gorge. St. Peters Dome (1525'), a decomposing monolith of volcanic rock that was fairly popular up till the 1960s but now relatively few climbers set their sights on this serious endeavor. An ascent of the Dome by *any* route is a very technical endeavor involving considerable risk. St. Peters Dome is a piton-required nailing aid climb on a vertical wall of cobblestone chunks of friable rock. It is the site of a fatal climbing accident so beware of the hazards.

This beta is included for historical purposes. For additional information on the Dome ascents reference the article by Don Baars & Jeff Thomas called *Dodging Peter:*

A Climbing History of St. Peters Dome, **Mazama Annual Vol. LXXX-IX, No. 13,** year 2007. For additional analysis browse the website www.summitpost.com for Rakek Chalupa's early 2008 ascent of the Dome, which will provide you with a strong taste of the characteristic nature of the Dome's friable rock quality.

At I-84 freeway exit #35 park along the shoulder of the secondary road, and hike up the creek drainage described for the Mystery Pillars. Walk up the creek drainage ½ mile south, but angle up left at the beginning of a deep ravine and scramble up a steep boulder field slope to the Dome. If the main dome is too wild for your taste ascend **Little St. Pete's pinnacle** which is a great alternative backwoods tiny summit that provides a nice view of its immediate big brother.

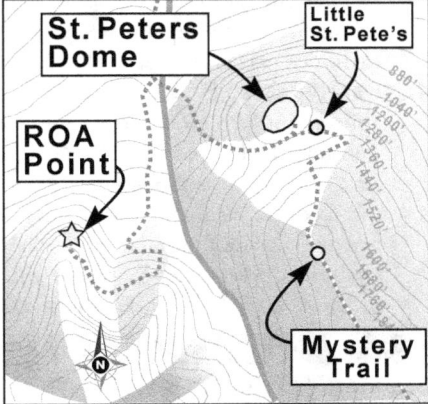

1. **Darr Route (the south face) III 5.6 A3**
   Length: 250', Pro to 1", KB and LA pitons
   Involves some risk climbing on friable rock. Distance to the Dome from the road is 1¼ miles with an elevation gain of 1525'. Expect 1½ hours to reach the south side of the rock dome.
   How to find the Darr Route: From the main saddle between big St. Peter massif and Little St. Peter contour west on a ledge system then proceed up a short loose 5th class rotten rock section directly to Furrer's Cave. From the east end of the cave nail straight up about 76' of aid, then traverse left slightly to a point just below a crack corner. Ascend the corner about 20' (5.8) to the steep dirt ledge above the 96-foot band and set a belay. From a belay move left to a tree on the outer corner of the Dome. Find a weakness in the wall on the prow, then ascend 60' up loose rock (5.8) to the top of the 60-foot band. Regain the ridge crest and continue up a steep slope of dangerous loose stacked moss-covered rock (low 5th class) to the top. Use considerable caution on this climb. Long thin KB & LA pitons are recommended for this ascent.

2. **Alpenjaeger Route (from the saddle) III A3**
   Length: 250', Pro: KB & LA pitons and nuts
   The Alpenjaeger route ascends on aid from the main saddle up bad rock to 8' of 5.6 moves near

a bolt belay just below the 96-foot band. Aid up left and then traverse left along the narrow 96-foot band west to join with the Darr Route where it must ascend the 60-foot band on the prow near the trees.

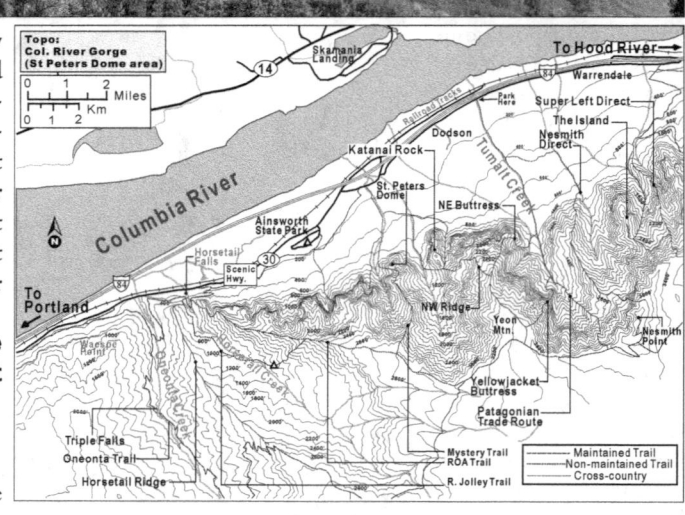

3. **Kirkpatrick Route (from the saddle direct to top) III A3**

Length: 250', Pro: KB & LA pitons and nuts

The Kirkpatrick Route ascends the Alpenjaeger route, but at the top of the 96-foot band it continues directly up the 60-foot band to a 5.6 exit mantle onto steep dirt slopes. The climb proceeds across the steep moss slopes westward to the last part of the upper Darr Route.

4. **Pearly Gates Route III A3**

Length: 250', Pro: KB & LA pitons and nuts

To climb the Pearly Gates Route, traverse from the saddle along exposed grassy ledges right (east side) to a rock shoulder, and then continue traversing to a point directly below the northeast face cave. Ascend a short distance up a fourth class section to the cave. Traverse east on a narrow ledge for fifteen feet, then climb up ninety feet vertically to a sloping grassy ledge and establish a belay. Then continue right 50'+ on a grass ledges, then continue up 80' on steep rock and moss. Another 80' will bring you to the trees near the summit.

LITTLE ST. PETE'S

Standard Route 5.7 R

Length: 60', Pro to 2" and a few thin pitons

Little St. Pete's pinnacle is a great objective. This 60' tall pinnacle composed of cobblestone-like basalt rock yields a commanding view of the Dome and the surrounding area, while offering a somewhat more pleasant summit experience. Rappel from anchor.

KATANAI ROCK

Katanai Rock (1500') is located ¼ mile directly east of St. Peters Dome. Katanai is connected by a saddle to the northwest ridge of Yeon Mountain. The top of Katanai Rock is a series of tiered basalt cliff faces capped by a forested summit that requires exposed scrambling along narrow ledges and steep gullies.

1. **North Couloir**

Pro: Pitons and minor gear to 1"

This is a cross-country endeavor with route finding challenges. The approach distance from the old Dodson school is 1¼ miles, 3 hours of hiking one-way, and mostly exposed 3rd class scrambling. Start this adventure by located some limited parking near the old Dodson school property at the tiny community of Dodson. Hike on an approximate bearing of 180° directly south through open forest to access a prominent couloir located immediately *east* of Katanai Rock and *west* of Yeon. Ascend the coulior, and before you arrive at the saddle scramble right along a narrow ledge to access a gully that ascends to a notch between the two summits of Katanai. Ascend north from the saddle up 60' of low 5th class dirt covered rock steps (pitons fixed) to a knoll. Descend 200' to the very northern tip of Katanai to the summit register. A rare place indeed that was first climbed by early 20th century photographers.

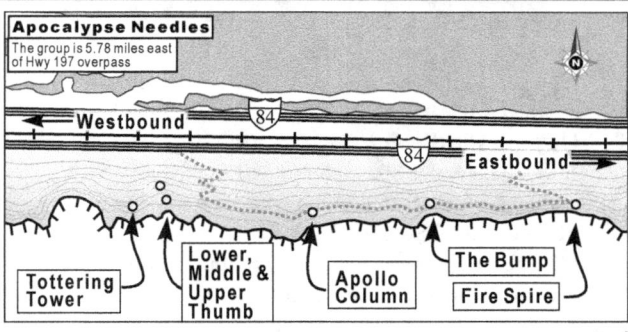

APOCALYPSE NEEDLES

This cluster of small spires is located on the south side of I-84 about 5¾ miles east of Highway 197 overpass (east end of The Dalles). The Apocalypse Needles are difficult to see because they tend to blend into the band of cliffs behind them. These pinnacles are quite challenging due in part to the friable nature of the rock. Best to climb here during cool weather (such as winter) because it is generally free of ticks and rattlesnakes at that time of year. Historically, this area has attracted climbers since the 1950s and possibly earlier. Park on the south shoulder of the freeway at a railroad access pullout ½ mile prior to the Tottering Tower, or at another pullout ½ mile beyond Firespire. Hike up the steep sandy slope to the pinnacle of your choice. The pinnacles are described from west to east. Some likely gear you may need for an ascent of these pinnacles will be a rope, pitons (KB, LA), nuts, cams to 3" and a helmet.

1. Tottering Tower

The western most pinnacle is the Tottering Tower, a thin pencil of rock that swayed when the first party of climbers Tyrolean traversed across on a rope tied to the wall above. It probably still sways

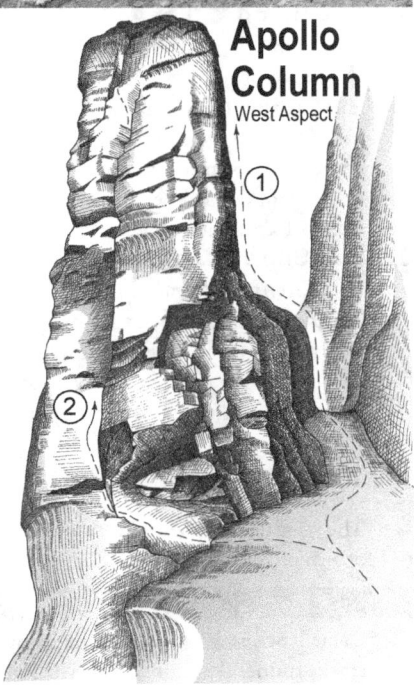

even today. Best to leave this absurd thin finger of rock to the credit of the very bold first ascent party (Eugene Dod & Bob Martin) who climbed it in 1963.

2. **Upper, Middle & Lower Sore Thumb**
   Immediately east of a well scoured rocky gully and west of Apollo Column is the Upper, Middle and Lower Sore Thumbs. These rock piles offer generally lower 5th class climbing (minor pro to 3" on the lower thumb). The Upper Sore Thumb is accessed from the top of the bluff. The Middle Sore Thumb (5.2R) can be accessed by rappelling to the notch from above, but may be accessed via a very steep ravine east of the pinnacle. The Lower Sore Thumb (5.4R) is readily accessed from the east to the notch where a short steep crux awaits.

3. **Apollo Column 5.4 R A2+ (or 5.9 X)**
   Pro: LA, KB, thin nuts and cams to 1½"
   First climbed in 1963 Apollo Column this large pinnacle is vertical on all sides and is generally ascended by nailing the south side crack from the notch. Located immediately east of the Sore Thumbs, this pinnacle is approximately 70' tall on the shorter side. The route is generally aided due to the moss and detachable holds. The west face **Schmitz Route** (II A2) is a prominent crack on the west side of the column.

4. **The Bump 5.8 or A1**
   This pinnacle is located east of Apollo Column on a flat rocky promontory. There are several climbs available on this 60' pinnacle. The **Golden Spike** route (5.8) on the north side is a good thin crack and ledge climb. The **South Crack** (5.8) climbs a short steep crack from the saddle to a stance, then up a short section of face climbing (bolts) to the top.

5. **Fire Spire 5.7 or A1**
   Pro: Pitons, nuts and cams to 2"
   Located ¼ mile east of the Bump is this unique 50' precariously pointed pinnacle. There are two routes, both of which start near the saddle behind the spire. One route is a left facing corner, and the other is a steep crack on the far right side. Both merge near the top again. Approach the pinnacle using the open slopes immediately west of the spire.

Fire Spire
South Aspect

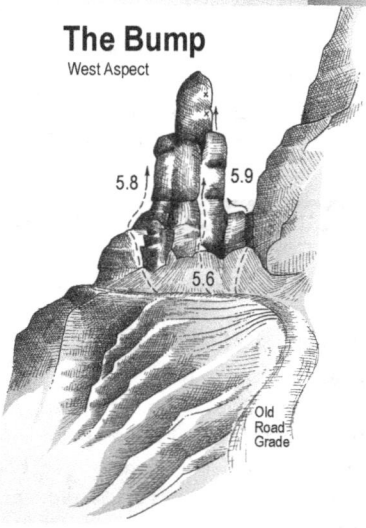

The Bump
West Aspect

NORTH SIDE OF THE COLUMBIA GORGE

The north section provides an historical analysis of climbing sites from Cape Horn eastward to Horsethief Butte.

CAPE HORN

Cigar Rock is a seldom touched small pinnacle located near the east entrance of the railroad tracks tunnel on Cape Horn. The pillar is composed of friable cobblestone sized basalt chunks of rock that tend to make an ascent quite difficult. Yet for those hardy individuals here are the logistics.

A possible access point is by using the Cape Horn Trail. Drive east on State Route 14 and park at mile post 24½ where the Cape Horn trail crosses the road. Follow the trail as it zigzags down below the initial scarp and then follows the precipice eastward. You can see the pinnacle from a viewpoint along the trail so do get a specific bearing on it if you are planning to rappel into the saddle. The trail continues to descend to the Cape Horn Road, but local land owners in the area do not appreciate people parking along the road, even though the road is county owned and maintained. The pinnacle protrudes from the southeasterly facing main wall on a wide rocky beach at river level about 500' west of the east entrance railroad tunnel.

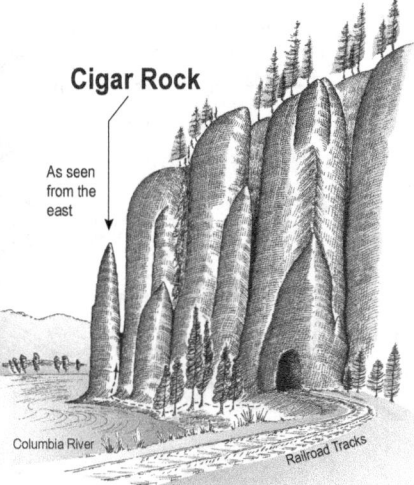

1. **East Couloir II 5.3 A2+ (5.7 X)**
The East Couloir is accessed from the rocky shoreline by climbing a short chimney and then scrambling up a debris gully to a fixed belay at the notch that separates Cigar Rock from the main massif. Climb up a short corner to an airy stance then ascend very rotten rock 30' to the top. Beware of friable rock. Pitons required.

2. **North Face Direct II 5.3 A2**
Climb the 50' friable crack on the inside wall starting near the notch.

Another generally avoided summit along this scarp is the **Tyrolean Spire** (II 5.4 A1), a 230' high pinnacle that is approached using the escarpment above the cliff. Original party rapped to the notch between the parent cliff and the spire, then proceeded to climb the north face directly to the summit using direct piton aid.

RABBIT EARS

Pro: A few LA, KB pitons, minor gear to 3", helmet

Deep in the heart of the scenic Columbia River Gorge, and north of Bridge of the Gods is a unique hike leading to the summit of Table Mountain. Low along the southern exposure of this mountain is the Rabbit Ears. The local Indians called the place Ka'nax and To'iha, while other residents refer to it as Sacajawea and Papoose. An afternoon sun will sometimes rivet these two small ears against an ethereal blue sky.

Rabbit Ears involves cross-country forested terrain of about 2½ miles one way, with an elevation gain of 1600'. Expect about 2 hours to approach and 1 hour to climb the pinnacle.

Least you might think this to be a casual tour hold onto your camel. For those who wish to proceed do so with the enthusiasm of a hunt, because the Rabbit Ears are indeed a remarkable summit for the adventurer. The quality may be less than desirable so don't expect great rock, but rather a challenging climb with a captivating view.

Turn off Washington State 14 at Bonneville, and drive north through the small community to the Bonneville Hot Springs resort. Continue driving 1½ miles west of the resort till you cross

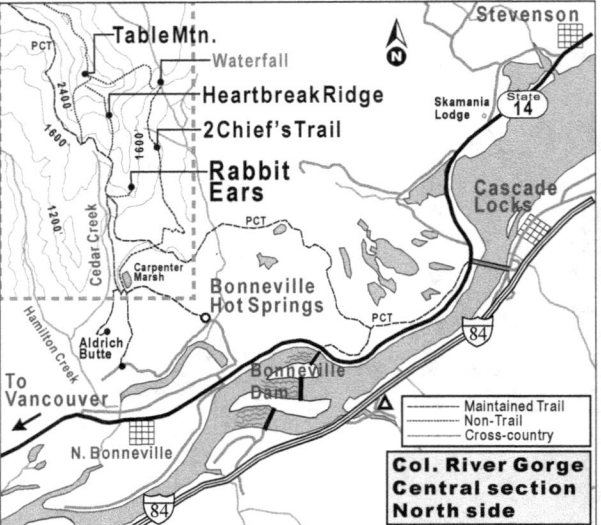

South side of Rabbit Ears

a small bridge at the end of the paved road. Park nearby and hike an old logging road directly north to Carpenter Marsh. The old logging road splits at the marsh. The left road branch leads to Table Mtn., and the right branch leads to Two Chief's Trail. Go left and as you turn the initial bend in the old road another left branch leads up to Aldrich Butte. Walk up the main road northward along Cedar creek and when you intersect with PCT #2000 at 1200' proceed eastward cross-country through an alder tree forest and ascend a very steep dirt gully on the SW side of the pinnacle.

Rope up on a narrow spit of soil separating two cataclysmic gullies (one of them you just came up). Eighty-five feet of 4th class scrambling leads to a belay anchor on a narrow point. Traverse right 30' on a small ledge around a corner, and then aim up toward (5.4) the notch between the ears. Belay at the notch or continue to the summit anchor. From the top of the ears the entire beauty of the Gorge can be seen and photographed.

Alternative access: Start at the Bonneville Hot Springs resort parking lot and walk southwest uphill to a trail (past a sign nailed on a tree) that enters the woods just beyond. Ascend trail to the southeast edge of Carpenter Marsh to junction with the old logging road at that marsh.

JIMMY CLIFF (TWILIGHT ZONE)

Route beta compiled by Bill Coe

This south facing crag might just be the place for your next adventure. Discovered by Jim O. and friends they quickly established a small selection of rock climbs on this wall. The southern exposure lends well to multi-season climbing potential, though due to the 2800' elevation can be snow covered at various times in the winter months (N 45.67926 / W 122.05244).

The andesite bluff formation likely formed by block slippage releasing along its base when softer terrain slid downhill exposing the cliff structure. Its less than vertical cliff face makes route cleaning a vigorous task. Wear a helmet while belaying and climbing here. Beware of yellow jacket bees that may nest on the wall. Be mindful of hunters in the fall out searching for the next deer or bear dinner. A year-round pure spring exists on the east end of the boulder field near the third clump of maple trees. Though the site lacks poison oak, scorpions are quite prevalent under rocks (just like the scorpions at Beacon Rock). Expect friable rock so beware what you are climbing on, whether an established route or a new project.

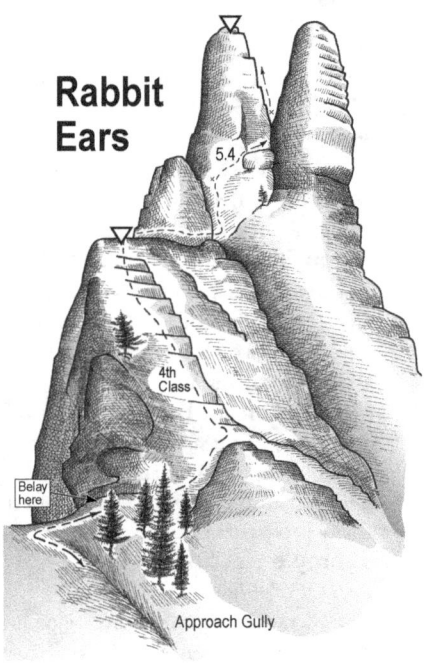

Directions: From State 14 highway at Beacon Rock State Park, drive north on Kueffler road. Set your odometer and drive exactly 5.1 miles. This road goes past the equestrian trail head, then at 2 miles turns to gravel on FS CG-1400 road. Stay on the main gravel road. At 5.1 miles the road veers left abruptly, but you will turn right into a small pullout onto an old logging skid road. Park here or drive a short distance along the skid road and park at its end.

The trail initially drops down to the east but becomes very apparent on a nice path that walks mostly horizontally east to the bluff in ¼ mile. The climbing routes are listed left to right, the first route being on the western end of the bluff. The routes start out at about 50' and increase to 300' tall by the center of the wall.

1. **The Short Bus 5.10b/5.10c**
   Pro (in sequence): long sling for fir tree root, several small/med nuts, .75-1" cams, medium cams, some Aliens, #7 or #8 Hex, 3" cam
   Scramble leftward up a steep slope from the trail to a big dead snag, passing it, then cut over right on a minor ledge to the route. This route is the left crack and when cleaner may be 5.10b. Climb to the Fixe carabiner style rappel station.

2. **Bride of Wyde 5.10a**
   This is a wide crack which leans to the right and appears steeper up close than from afar. Climb the ever widening feature as it goes from #4 cam to #6 cam size then for a short section

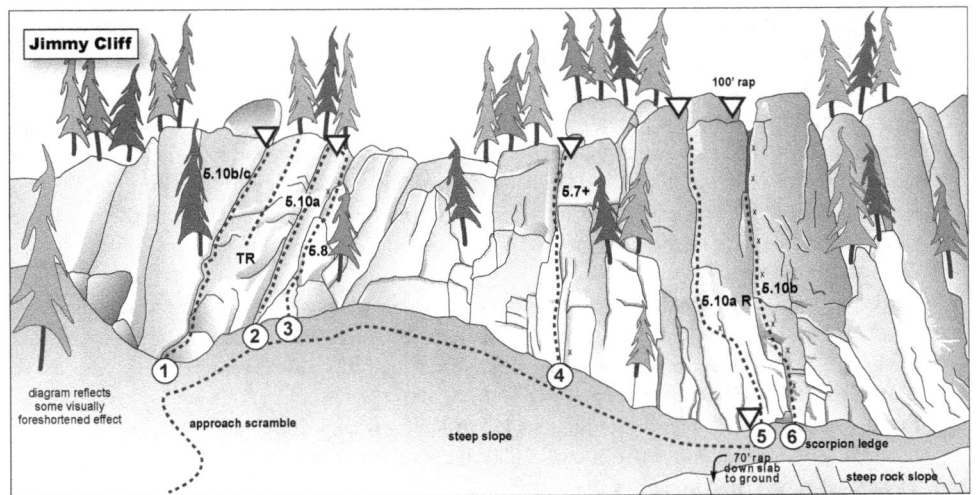

at the top to near body width size. Two Valley Giant cams (#9 and #12) were used but not critical. The climb involves adroit use of laybacking and arm bars with an odd face smear. A single bolt at the base for belayer. Shares rap anchor with The Move.

3. **The Move 5.8**
   Pro: _____
   Just right of 'The Short Bus' is a small pinnacle and a short route. Starting from the shared belay bolt of 'Bride of Wyde' ease up and right of the pinnacle, clip the bolt at the ¾ way point and make 'The Move' with the bolt right near your chest.

4. **Kyles Big Adventure Gear 5.7+**
   Pro: small selection of nuts up to 3" cams
   Climb pitch one of Mr Denton to Scorpion Ledge and traverse to the left 25' to a shallow dihedral above a rotting tree stump. Clip a lone bolt which can be backed up with a nut behind a flake for the belay.

5. **Mr. Denton on Doomsday 5.9 R (or 5.10a R)**
   Pro: small HB brass nuts, a screamer, 3", 3-½", 4" and/or 5" cams for upper crack
   Scramble up 4th-5th class above and right of the big dead snag to a 2-bolt belay on Scorpion Ledge. Climb up 15' and left about 10' to a bolt, then straight up following thin cracks and tricky pro past a small tree to a larger crack ending at a 2-bolt anchor on top.

6. **Jimmy's Favorite 5.10a**
   Pro: QD's only
   Completed and name in honor of Jim (who was unavailable). Climb easy low angle 4th - 5th class to the Mr Denton belay on Scorpion Ledge. Step right 8' and climb up (9 bolts) the face just right of (and then inside) the obvious shallow chimney to a belay anchor stance 8' from the cliff top. A single 60m rope rappel back to Scorpion Ledge.

7. **Beekeeper Magic**
   Project unfinished as Bill was stung 200+ times while on an inspection rappel of the line.

Rumba Ridge

The next climbs are on a 300' long ridge buttress on the far eastern end of the cliff scarp wrapped in a cluster of trees. Walk along the base of the bluff eastward, then up a 3rd class narrow low angle bedrock ravine scoured by water runoff. Walk east on a grassy tier covered with trees to the base of the ridge. The ground up routes are still raw; climb diligently; expect friable rock. Avoid leaving excrement here as the pure water spring is directly below.

8. **Conga Line 5.7**
   Pro: nuts, small cams, 1", 2" and opt 3" cam, 9-10 full length slings
   Likely five-star route eventually once clean. From east side of a buttress move up a gully to the first break in a rock wall. P1: Climb up a crack and face holds 15'-20' to the crux (bolt) then step left onto the ridge proper. Dance up the ridge on easier terrain using various trees that offer monkey hangs (the highlight of the route). Belay at a 9' long ledge at 110'. P2: traverse leftward up 15' to the base of a hidden rock pitch (a wide shallow gully). P3: aim up 100' and leftward, over a short final bouldery move, and past another 25' of spruce trees to the top of the ridge. Use a tree with rappel runners and ring to descend. Single 60m gets you down.

9. **Conga Variation**
   At the end of Conga line P1 instead of using the leftward traverse on P2, head straight up a thin crack and some face holds. Avoid the obvious loose flake in the corner. Move left across the buttress past a tree, and up trending rightward till Conga Line is rejoined.

10. **Couchmaster Shuffle 5.10+ (X-rated for now)**
    Pro: set of cams to 2", ¾" nut, doubles on ½" to 1" cams, long slings
    Starts directly at the foot of the buttress. Climb up a few feet, step left to a small ledge, and up an easy 12' ramp, then up left to the aesthetic Couchmaster Shuffle crack. Aim straight up the

obvious crack in a shallow dihedral for 70' until forced to wander out right on the face. Ascend up past a fir tree on easy ground to gain the ridge and belay at a tree. Finish via the standard P2 of Rumba Ridge.

ROCK CREEK CRAG

This small yet quality west-facing climbing crag (aka Clif's Crag) is great for afternoon warm sunny climbing in early Spring or late Fall seasons. Though limited in scope this site is an idyllic example of back woods cragging on a 40' to 65' tall cliff that has both trad and sport climbs.

Directions

Drive north from Stevenson, WA on Red Bluff Road at the upper west end of town. It quickly turns to gravel. Shortly ahead the road splits (go right) on CG-2000 forest road. This road follows alongside the Rock Creek stream. Cross a small bridge at six miles with a pretty waterfall on the left. At 8½ miles the road turns sharply left to cross another small bridge. Instead you will go right just before the bridge on road CG-2060 and park in a wide area below the crag. Way uphill perched like a castle overlooking the valley is this tiny little west facing andesitic crag. A steep narrow path starts just past the flat open area and angles up right into the forest to the right of the landslide. The steep climbers path ascends directly uphill till it is even with the upper tier of rock and then walks leftward to the base of the upper tier.

1. **Northern Pearl 5.8 R** ★

   Pro to 4"; length 45'

   A continuous crack that varies in size from fingers to fist. The crux is near the top; don't be tempted to bail left into the easy but loose blocks.

2. **Pearl's Jam 5.9 R** ★

   Pro to 4"; length 45'

   Start on the same

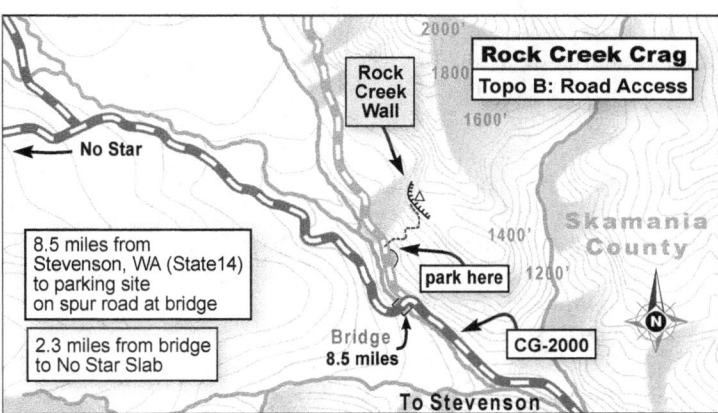

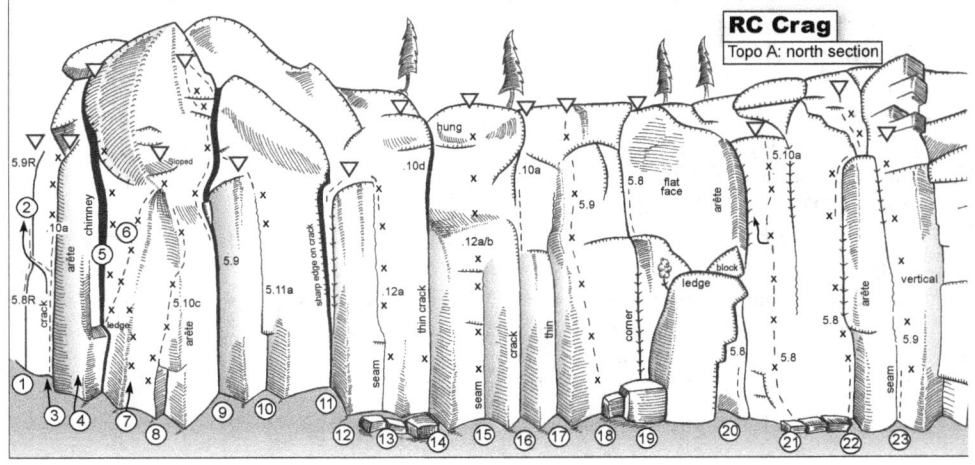

Chad Ellers leading *The Watchman*

jam crack as Slow Dance. When the crack ends, traverse left four feet and finish via the top half of Northern Pearl. Detached, but seemingly stable blocks form the left side of the crack on the top half of this and the following climb; because of this, all gear placements through this section are suspect. SS chain/ring anchor.

3. **Slow Dance 5.10a** ★★★
   Pro: 3 QD's & #1, #2, #3 Cam
   Jam up the sweet hand-crack located in a shallow dihedral. A small pedestal allows for a rest once the crack ends. Angling slightly right onto the face via a sequential blend of side-pulls, smearing, and crimps will get you near the top. If you've made it this far, a mantel move below the anchor won't throw you for a loop.

4. **Bearhug 5.11-**
   Pro: QD's
   A "double arête bearhug" climb with problematic stance positions. Falls are going to be *de rigueur* on lead. Ends at an anchor with Metolius rap hangers (shared by **Slow Dance**).

5. **Inner Sanctum 5.10c** ★★
   Pro: 5 QD's and a #2 Camalot for the beginning; length 60'
   The obvious off-width/chimney with several lead bolts lining the right side. Start by scrambling up a couple small ledges to the start of the off-width. Employ whatever trickery necessary to work your way up to several rests in the widening crack. Wiggle up the final 15' fully immersed in the bowels of the climb. SS chain/ring anchor. Could use some more cleaning.

6. **Bottle Rocket 5.10c** ★★
   Pro: 4 QD's and a #2 Camalot for the beginning
   This climb shares the start and first bolt with Inner Sanctum but avoids the off-width by

angling right onto a fun and exciting face. A final perplexing move will put you at the anchor which is shared by The Watchman.

7. **Mists of Time 5.12a**
   Pro: 6 QD's
   A face with a thin seam running up it. A stout direct start that merges into the Bottle Rocket route. Shares the anchor with The Watchman.

8. **The Watchman 5.10c ★★★**
   Pro: 6 QD's
   A stellar arête climb. This is the first route encountered immediately after turning the corner on the north end of the cliff. Look for the first bolt under a light-brown mini-roof on the left side of the arête. A deceptive and tricky climb that won't let you off the hook until rounding the arête near the top. After you finesse the balancy crux switch to the right side of the arête then finish with a sloped mantle to the anchor Perhaps the best, moderate sport climb on the cliff. Carabiners installed at anchor.

9. **Motional Turmoil 5.9 ★★★**
   Pro: 4 QD's, nuts to 1", cams to 5" (4" feasible); length 60'
   The standard and classic warmup at the crag with a bit of ye ol' punch to it. Place good pro in the initial moves then power through the steep crux till it eases at a large wedged block. The remainder of the crack widens to 18' (and fatter) but is pre-fixed with several bolts on the upper part for your convenience and pleasure.

10. **Butterfinger 5.10d ★★**
    Pro: 2 QD's and pro to 1", and small TCU's recommended; length 45'
    Quality climb that starts vertical and packs a healthy punch to it. Start climbing up a narrowing crack until it disappears. Continue on up the face making use of the arête to the left. A finishing mantel brings you to a sloped ledge where the climb moves left and continues up the final moves of Motional Turmoil. A variant exists on the upper right face has been lead.

11. **Wyde Syde 5.10a ★**
    Pro to 2" including two C3 #00. A 12" Valley Giant is optional
    A wonderful off-width that is a great introduction to the world of wide. The seam to the right takes small TCU's. SS chain/ring anchor.

12. **Electric Blue 5.12a ★★★**
    Pro: 5 QD's
    An arête to the right of the off-width that offers tricky sidepulls and crimper holds. Shares the same anchor with the next & previous route.

13. **Sands of Time 5.11d ★★**
    Pro: 5 QD's
    Unusual opening moves lead to a very powerful crux section. This is the clean face with the seam in the center. Shares the same anchor as Electric Blue.

14. **Naked 5.10d ★★★**
    Pro: Thin nuts and TCU's, and cams to 4"
    A stellar crack climb with powerful opening moves on a steep relentless thin corner seam that lands on a sloped slab at midway. A few moves up a fat crack ends with a wild ride up a sharp edged layback overhang crux to finish. This is a proud test of endurance and ingenuity. Stays wet longer than most of the climbs at Rock Creek because the crack corner faces left on the lower portion of the climb.

15. **Blue Highway 5.12a**
    Pro: 6 QD's
    Powerful line with several technical bulges to surmount.

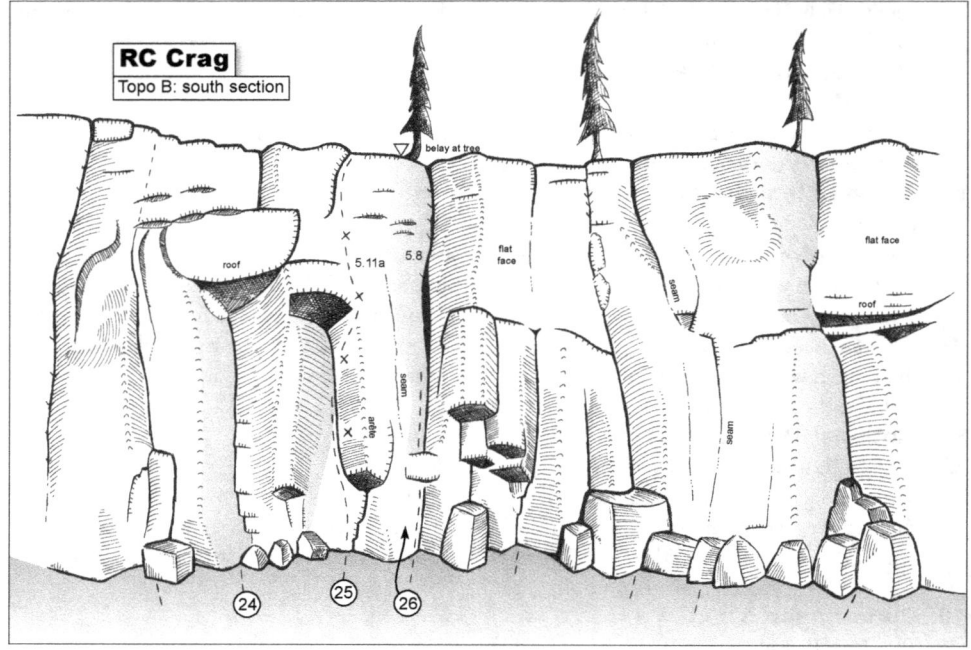

16. Mighty Mite 5.10a ★
Pro to 2" including small TCU's, doubles on #0.4, #0.5, & #0.75 Camalots optional
Begin in a small dihedral directly in front of the large fir tree. A tricky starting sequence is harder yet for those on the short side. After a good rest at the mid-point, the top half keeps you working right up to the (tree) anchor. Could use some more cleaning.

17. _____

18. Airtime 5.9
Pro: 6 QD's
The buttress on the right side of a blunt arête with numerous edges. A quality climb with tricky crux and a surprise crux ending.

19. Niceline 5.8 ★
Pro to 2"
This crack is never too difficult and consistently fun. Start by climbing up several large steps to get into the corner. SS carabiner anchor. Could use some more cleaning.

20. Plaidtastic 5.8 ★
Pro to 3"
Start in a blocky alcove with numerous edges. Halfway up, a small roof needs to be negotiated before gaining a pleasant crack that will take you to the anchor.

21. Committed Convenience 5.8 (crack finish) ★★
Pro for crack finish: 4 QD's, nuts and cams to 2"
Rating is 5.9 if staying on the face and using just the 6 bolts
Tricky opening moves combine pzazz with punch to make a worthy climb. Fairly fun but the face needs to cleaned better. Anchor is shared by this climb and the Plaidtastic crack.

22. Progressive Climax 5.8 ★★★
Pro: 7 QD's, length 55'
Awesome climb that ascends a large dihedral sporting numerous small horizontal edges. At the fifth bolt, step right (or move up to the jug then right) onto the airy arête and finish on easy

jugs. Great warm-up. Webbing anchor. A high quality steep face climb that seems to put a smile of satisfaction on the face of every climber.

23. Scorpio 5.8+ ★★
Pro: 5 QD's

A fun romp up an open book loaded with edges. The difficulty starts early but quickly gives way to easier climbing. There are two possible ways to finish Scorpio: The harder option is going straight up to the obvious ring anchor. Alternately, one can clip the last bolt on Scorpio with a runner and step left of the rock fin to finish on Progressive Climax (two more bolts).

Note: Approximately 100 feet separate the previous two climbs from the next climbs.

24. _____

25. Black Ribbon 5.11a ★★
Pro: 4 QD's and a #3 Camalot for the finish, length 40'

Directly in front of a leaning snag is a clean dihedral with a large roof at mid-height. After two intense cruxes, moving up the dihedral and clearing the roof, scamper up the relatively easy face to the tree anchor (shared with Bungee's Crack). Consider clipping the 2nd bolt with a single carabiner.

Chad Ellers leading *Bottle Rocket*

26. Bungee's Crack 5.8 ★★
Pro to 3", length 40'

The southern most climb at Rock Creek is this enjoyable well protected crack climb. Stemming on the numerous edges allows for several rests and casual gear placements. A crux near the top needs to be surmounted before reaching the (tree/chain) anchor. Could use some more cleaning.

NO STAR SLAB

A boorish tilted pocketed landscape straight from the moon this little steep*ish* angled friction slab with dimpled hand holds just might entertain you for an hour. The formation is a rotting siltstone erosional remnant from pyroclastic flows. Drive over the small bridge on Rock Creek road (CG-2000) at 8½ miles, then continue another 2¼ miles further up the main gravel Rock Creek road. GPS coordinates for this slab are 45°45.341'N by 122°02.833'W. Located on the immediate shoulder of the gravel road a short distance east of the pass. The slab presently has only one fixed route with room for 2-3 more easy climbs.

1. Lunar Dreams 5.9 ★
Pro: 7 QD's

A little example of friction slab climbing on mere rounded dimples. Probably not worth the drive up here just for this, but if you happen to be in the area.

SKOOKUM PINNACLE

A minor plug of steep rock tucked below another rotten plug of rock on a steep hill slope overlooking the upper Rock Creek valley above a clearcut logged area in the upper valley. The pinnacle is about 60'+ tall on the uphill side and is quite elusive, hidden from view except in a few places along the gravel road.

The route is 5.7 and fixed (8 bolts), but expect some hollow flaky, loose rock in places. Rap anchor in place. Typical gorge rock climb with plenty of off-trail adventure thrashing and route finding skills. Not a destination site, but an odd-ball plug vertical on all sides. A climb not for the weak minded due to the need for off-trail navigational skills and semi-dubious nature of the friable

150 CHAPTER 3

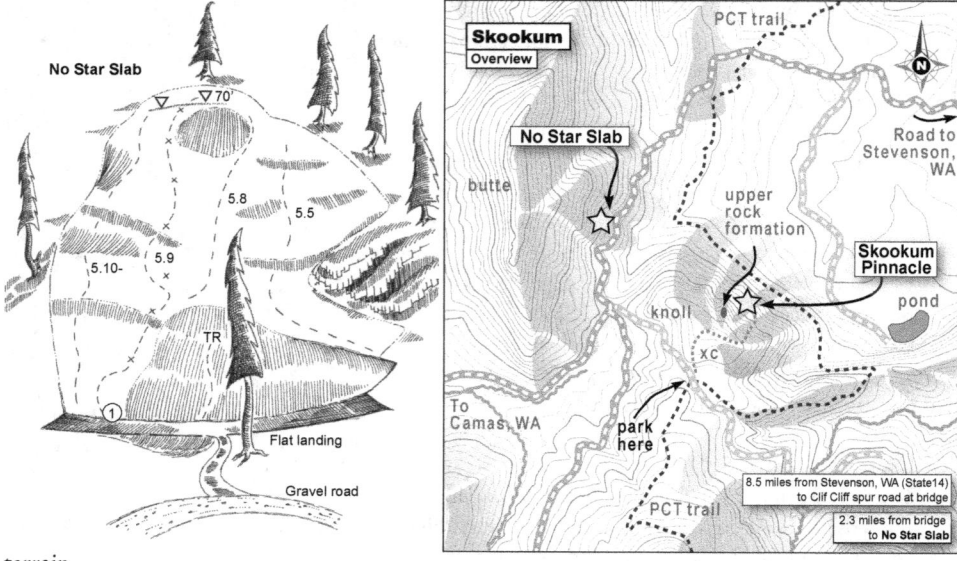

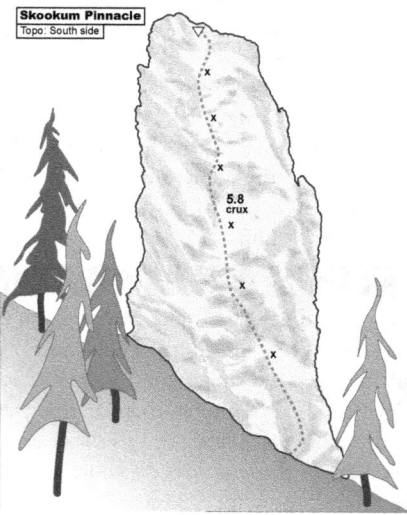

terrain.

Directions: Drive north from Stevenson, WA on Red Bluff Road at the upper west end of town. It quickly turns to gravel. Shortly ahead the road splits (go right) on CG-2000 forest road. Continue on CG-2000 all the way up to the pass to a 4-way intersection. Take CG-2090 uphill for about ¾ mile to where the PCT trail crosses. Park here.

Approach: Walk north on an old skid road (well obscured) to a wooded knoll, then descend a mild sloped ridge east, then down very steep slippery slope (ice axe) in forest about 300'. You will pass the Rotte Plug, the upper rotten plug of rock with a 5.7x minor boulder move to get to its top, so skip this garbage pile by descending down below it, angling left under its base till you see the Skookum Pinnacle. Car to pinnacle time is about 20 minutes, but the destination is instinct-based since neither rock outcrop is visible in the thick forest when approaching them. To depart, continue descending down the forested slope for another 400' to land on the PCT trail. From there just walk back up the PCT trail to the vehicle. Otherwise retrace your path uphill to the car on the steep slopes past the upper rotten plug.

WIND MOUNTAIN

The 500' tall west face of Wind Mountain is a rather imposing massif located ¾ mile east of Home Valley, Washington. This west facing aspect is certainly a visually appealing objective when viewed from the highway. The cliff scarp has notable sections of friable rock with challenging exposed leads. If you are considering climbing here expect difficult route finding assessment, friable rock, exposed scrambling, ticks, and dirt covered ledges. Bring a sixth sense of knowledge for route finding because each prospective climb is tough with no sharp distinction between 'R' and 'X' climb ratings. Wear a helmet. Definitely not a place to have a climbing accident. Park on the shoulder of State Route 14 at the west side of Wind Mountain and ascend the boulder talus field to the base of the main wall.

Both images: Matt Carter climbing on *Wind Mtn*

1. **West Face Crack 5.9 R/X**
   Pro: Pitons, nuts and cams to 3"
   This route is one reason why climbers might choke up the energy to venture up Wind Mtn. But don't be lulled into thinking its a breeze. There is considerable friable rock on the approach gully, as well as friable rock on several of the lead pitches that will tend to keep most climber's away. The route is the prominent crack system that faces south into the main amphitheater. The top portion of the climb becomes a left leaning, west facing ramp. The west side boulder field ends at a short cliff. Lead up this (5.4) into the main long exposed 4th class approach gully. There are several belay anchors in this gully on the right face, the upper one being at the upper most platform in the gully on the main wall. Step across the main gully and climb up the left face on 5th class rock aiming for the crack system above, avoiding the other huge loose deep chimney corner system to the right. Belay at a stance. Lead past the crux vertical rock corner crack system till it eases onto the left facing corner and ascend this till you can exit to the trees near the top. Descend by walking off to the north slightly through steep forests and cliff bands using game trails.

2. **Utopia 5.8 R/X**
   Pro: Pitons, nuts and cams to 3"
   This is the deep corner system immediately right of West Face Crack climbed by Jim Nieland. Climb a very short cliff (5.4) into a long steep exposed 4th class gully. Belay at the upper most platform in the gully at the main wall. Climb up into a low angle deep corner system (friable rock) that gradually steepens and aims up right. Expect some short sections of chimney, but otherwise 3-pitches of mostly variable sized cracks and wide sections.

3. **Lost Wages 5.8 R**
   Pro: Pitons, nuts and cams to 3"
   A prominent corner system on the west face that starts up a steep, brush filled 5.8 corner system. Belay at 80' on a small ledge at the bolt and piton. Continue up left in the 5.6 brushy corner 80' till it eases onto a scree slope where you will find a large fir tree (WC merges here). Belay. This huge fir tree is at the base of the prominent west side gully and is visible from the road. Scramble up the broad gully 100' and belay near an oak tree. Step up to the main steep corner system and climb on the right face on small holds (fixed pitons) until forced to stem the vertical corner past a 5.5 crux (piton). Scramble up a loose scree gully and belay at the large sling festooned block. Scramble into the prominent 3' wide vertical sided corner system and step up into a cavernous ledge to belay. This ledge is capped by a large overhang. Free climb

(5.8 or A0) by stemming or aiding the main wall and mantle out the top past the overhang. Scramble up left for 30' to a fixed belay. The next pitch is unfinished. Rappel the route.

4. **Workman's Comp 5.4 R**
Pro: Pitons, nuts and cams to 3"
This is perhaps slightly easier to get to the giant fir tree belay. It will still tweak your tail feathers, but the lower two-thirds of the first lead is on large relative steps in a wide corner system. From behind a large tree angle up left into a steep but easy series of steps in a corner. At about 120' the climbing abruptly veers directly upward crossing some friable rock. The lead is 180' long to reach the large fir tree mentioned in Lost Wages. Follow the remainder of Lost Wages from the huge fir tree at the base of the prominent gully. Rappeling down LW is feasible with a single 60m rope.

5. **Termination 5.6 X**
Pro: Pitons, nuts and cams to 3"
This route takes on the main lower west face directly, but does involve some meandering sections that provide a ton of rope drag. Beware of substantial friable rock on the final lead along the exposed x-rated ridgecrest just before the route merges with the main gully of Lost Wages/Workmans Comp.

WINDY SLAB

This crag is located along State Route 14 at the base of the south side of Wind Mountain. Windy Slab is a south-facing low angle 40' tall slab. The rock is reminiscent to granite friction climbing and is a perfect late Spring, Summer and Fall place to visit while traveling east to other objectives. Routes range from 5.4 to 5.10+. The crag was originally developed by the late Jeff Walker of Willard, Washington. He and friends climbed many of the original routes, but today most of the climbs have fixed gear.

Drive east of Home Valley 1 mile and park on the north side of the road in a large gravel pullout west of the Borrow Pit at milepost 51¼. Scramble up the scree slope for 200' to a comfortable, sunny platform at the base of the crag.

Windy Slab is a unique little site that attracts a small selection of rock climbers who are interested in low angle slab climbing.

Mike climbing at *Windy Slab*

Stop by and enjoy the simple beauty of this delightful small rock slab, so be considerate of others and use the site wisely.

1. **The Steppes 5.3**
   Pro: Minor gear to 2"
2. **Dare 5.5**
   Pro: Minor gear to 2"
3. **Night Music 5.6** ★★★
   Pro: 5 QD's
   The most popular climbing route here and it is usually the first route everyone leads.
4. **Icon 5.7** ★★★
   Pro: 4 QD's
   This great route has two variations at the small roof. Break left to #3 route, or stay right of the roof and finish on easy ground to an anchor.
5. **East Wind 5.10a** ★★★
   Pro: 5 QD's
   A stellar line with great smears and balance, but not in an extreme sense. Tenuous opening cruxy moves, balancy mid-section and a reasonable ending on jug holds. Quite possibly the best rock climb at Windy Slab. Go for it!
6. **Dark Apron 5.10a TR** ★★
   A top-rope problem that kisses the left corner of the dark apron. Technical balance smears and odd counter pulls to hold the friction. The route stays left of the bolt line of #7 and right of #5 on the upper prow clear to the anchor.
7. **Apron 5.10a** ★★
   Pro: 4 QD's and minor 1" gear for the crack
   A great line that rides on thin smears up the dark apron to the large roof, then follows the splitter finger crack to the anchor.
8. **Heatwave 5.10d TR** ★
   Squeezes between the two routes but has a combination of powerful moves with dicey smears

Don G. climbing at *Windy Slab*

up high. Exit right under the large roof to the anchor.

9. **Braille 5.10a** ★
   Pro: 3 QD's
   A quality climb that acsends the right most part of the dark apron. Start at a small outcrop rib of rock. The crux is between the second and third bolt.

10. **West Wind 5.9**
    Pro: Nuts and cams to 2"
    A typical natural pro climb that pumps through a series of small overhanging roofs, then finishes up a steeply angled crack to a stance.

DOG SPINE

On the southern flank of the famous Dog Mountain there is a super classic jagged backbone arête of rotten rock rising for 1900' directly from the roadside. Worthy? Absolutely—in fact for those who are looking for a daring alpine-like challenge totally in a league of its own, then this is the one for you! The highly exposed ravines and ridges along this backbone arête and the deep forest scramble for another 1000' to the summit of Dog Mountain is an extraordinary and historic Gorge classic.

The Dog Spine arête route is mostly 3rd class scrambling with some highly exposed 5th class sections. Depending on which variation you will be taking park in a pullout ¼ mile to the east or west of the 'toe' of a long rocky buttress along SR 14. This buttress is located ¾ mile east of the regular hikers trail head for Dog and Augspurger Mountain.

There are several different standard start variations: the **West Direct**, and the **Traditional** approach. Scrambling variations are practically unlimited on this mountain scarp. The Dog Spine spur can be ascended through out the year, but it is more difficult and serious when covered with snow and when the Gorge winds are blowing heavily across the Spine. Beware of ticks and loose rock. Average time one way approximately 2½ to 3 hours to the 1900' level. Gear might include an ice axe, 9mm rope, a few carabiners, slings, and several nuts or pitons to 1".

Winter snow ascent of the Dog Spine

The **Traditional Approach** ascends the long scree slope on the east side of the Dog Spine Arête near the forest edge. Then, angle up leftward through a sparsely tree covered slope into a large gully (elev. 640') immediately east of Dog Rock. This gully leads directly to the east side of the saddle next to Dog Rock (elev. 1100').

The best start is the West Direct, which is accessed up the slope to the west side of the main buttress. This will allow you to bypass the gully difficulties so you can proceed quickly up the ridges and ravines leading to the 'dead deer traverse'.

Scramble up leftward, and then rightward around a prominent buttress until you come to the base of a 100' vertical wall that covers the full breadth of the arête. Step right (east) over the ridge, and gingerly cross an exposed 4th class 30' long catwalk known as 'dead deer traverse'. The traverse is thin and loose and a belay rope is recommended. Wander up slope past a wide groove to a deceptive cul-de-sac. From here step left on small edges then continue up a steep leftward leaning 5th class ramp onto easier terrain above. Belay at a tree 120' up from the cul-de-sac. Either exit right to join the Traditional Route in the main gully, or...wander up left, then up a very steep 4th class moss

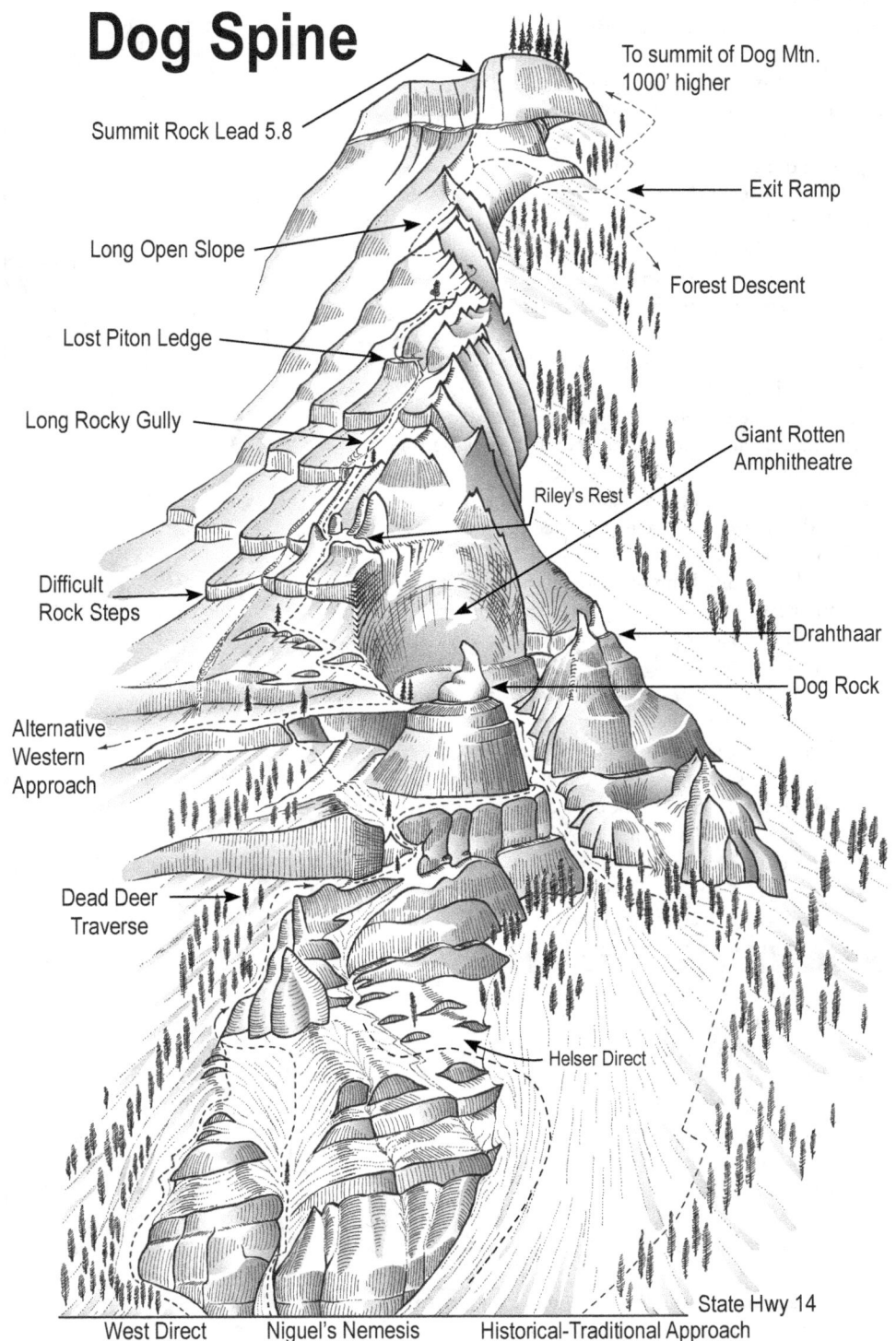

corner onto the main deer track immediately west of the obvious pinnacle, which is Dog Rock.

The **Helser Direct** ascends the long scree slope immediately right of the toe of the buttress and merges on the immediate right side of the Dead Deer Traverse.

To climb the 5th class 40' high Dog Rock Pinnacle you need a rope and pro to 1", otherwise the climb is mostly fixed. Just across the ravine is a flaky point of rock called Drahthaar. Both the **Direct Variation** and the **Traditional Variation** meet here at this saddle next to Dog Rock.

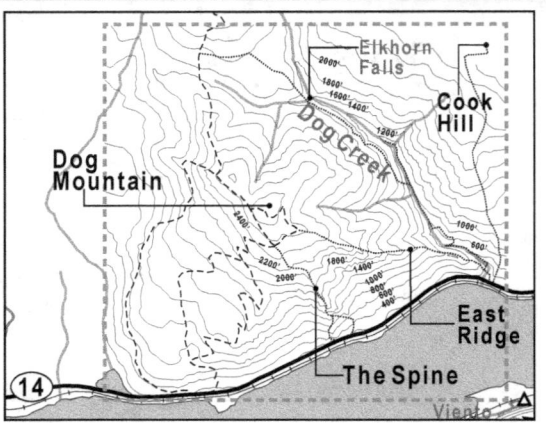

From the saddle at the Dog Rock pinnacle angle up left steeply to a small tree. Keep to the left of the massive amphitheater directly behind Dog Rock and right of a smaller westward sloping ravine. From the tree belay go up through an exposed 5th class place (fixed pitons) that allows passage to a terrace above. Belay at a fixed anchor at 160' on a terrace called Riley's Rest. Step left, and then scramble up some 4th class terrain for 150' to another tree belay. Waltz up an easy scree ravine for several hundred feet, then grunt up to the left by a short step onto Lost Piton Ledge (elev. 1400'). Move left (4th class) around the corner then up the slopes till you are on the very crest of the spine.

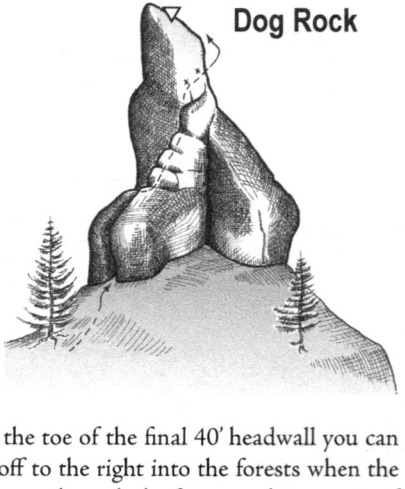

Continue to follow the spine directly or on either side where necessary for approximately the next 300'. At the toe of the final 40' headwall you can either climb the 5th class crack or take the standard exit off to the right into the forests when the spine ends at 1900' elevation. At this point either continue up through the forest to the summit of Dog Mountain for the supreme finale, or descend down forested slopes to the east while staying clear of the cliffs.

THE BYPASS

A little site that sports a surprisingly stout string of hard routes. When you're done climbing all the short pumpy sport routes, toss your dog a bone. The climbing is ultra short but a viable spot to get a summer evening fix after work. Indians and fisherman have been wandering across this land for a thousand years.

1. Old Geezer Teaser 5.8
Pro: 4 QD's

The standard line aims up right to the anchor. Another variation

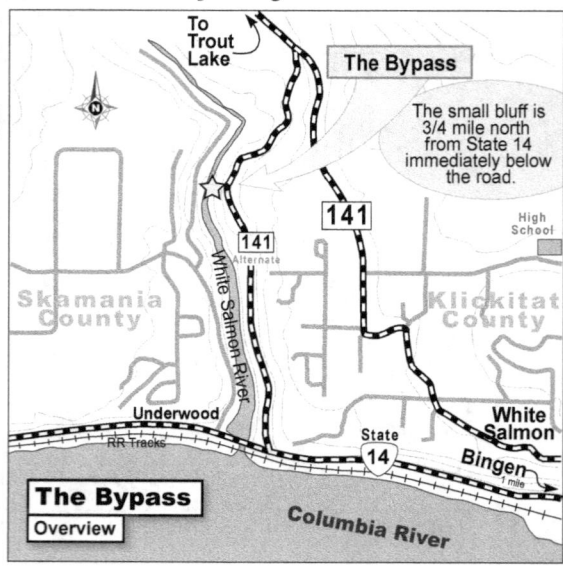

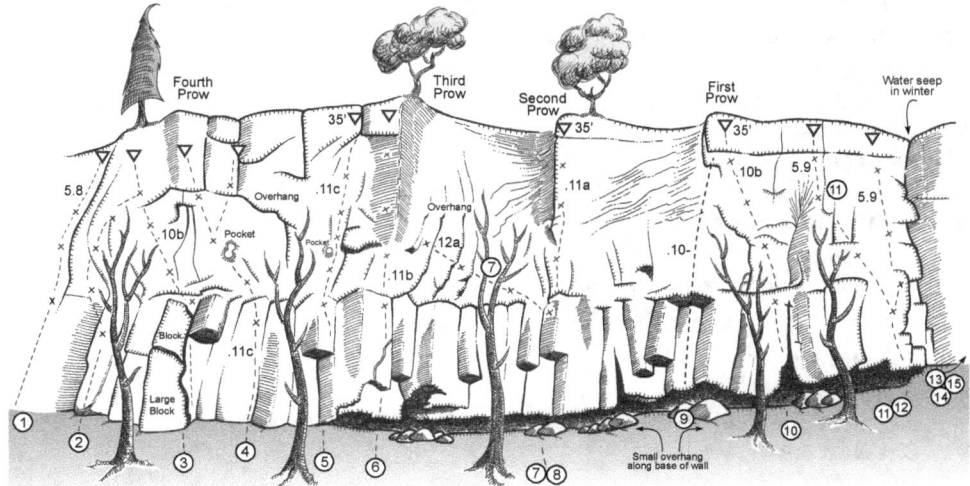

angles up left to join the same easy route.

2. **Barnyard Boogie 5.10b/c** ★
   Pro: 5 QD's
   Jaunts up hard right and merges at last bolt of next climb.

3. **Haiku 5.10b** ★
   Pro: 3 QD's
   This route starts off a stack of two large blocks and angles up left to a bolt anchor.

4. **Conundrum 5.11c** ★
   Pro: 4 QD's
   This face route ascends up slightly overhanging terrain past an obvious pocket.

5. **Yellow Bellied Sap Sucker 5.11b/c** ★★
   Pro: 5 QD's
   Excellent route and much harder than it looks from the ground. Power your way up overhanging terrain up to a hidden anchor on the left. An alternate exists: Climb first 2 bolts, then cruise a crack to the left.

6. **Aesthetic Anesthetic 5.11b** ★★★
   Pro: 4 QD's
   A quality power climb that does not give you anything easy. Starts up a minor corner utilizing face hold and pockets. The route aims up right to the small prow. Bolt anchor is visible at the lip, but take a small carabiner to get it through the link.

7. **Smirk 5.12a** ★
   Pro: 6 QD's
   This is a long pumpy left-ward angling traverse that ends at the previous routes belay anchor.

8. **Girlilla Pillar 5.10+** ★★
   Pro: 4 QD's
   A great powerful face climb that aims for a prow near the top. The 5.11+ traverse route starts here also.

9. **Stealhead 5.10-** ★★★
   Pro: 4 QD's
   Some holds are long reaches which make it possibly harder for short people. If you can stick with the final prow to the

anchor...great. Otherwise most step off right slightly near the belay anchor.

10. **Coho 5.10b/c**
    Pro: _ QD's
    A variation just left of Stealhead using the same belay.
11. **Daft Dogs 5.9**
    Pro: 4 QD's
    Nice basic route for starters. Both #9 and #10 routes start at the same initial point.
12. **Fish from a Friend 5.9**
    Pro: 4 QD's
    This is the dark colored water groove.

To the right of a groove are these extra shorty's at south end of crag.

13. **Cat Nip 5.10+**
    Pro: 3 QD's
    Just left of 'The Shark'. Tricky route seldom climbed. Same belay as Cat Nap.
14. **Cat Nap 5.9**
    Pro: 3 QD's
    Easier route sharing belay with Cat Nip.
15. **The Shark 5.6**
    Pro: 2 QD's
    The farthest route at the south end. An easy route put up for kids to climb.

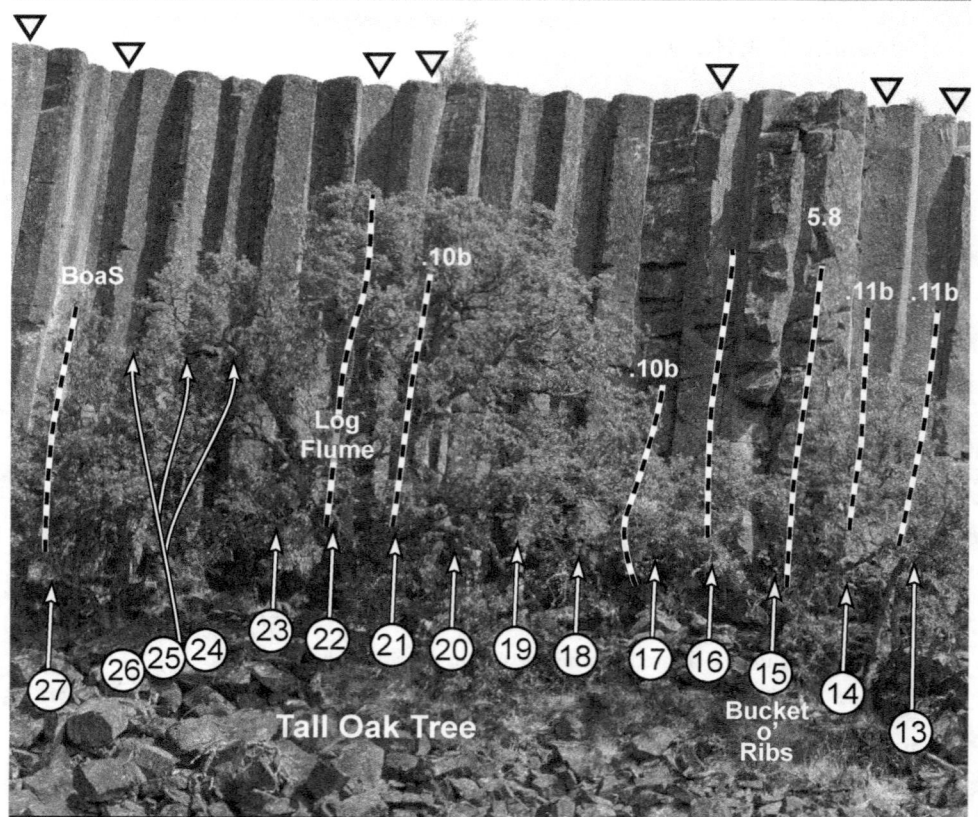

WANKERS COLUMN

This quality 50' tall basalt bluff is situated on a prominent south facing syncline immediately west of Rowland Lake. This syncline (aka Syncline Wall) overlooking the Columbia River is a scenic region to visit whether you are rock climbing, biking or hiking.

Wankers Column offers distinctively steep columnar crack climbing opportunities good for Fall, Winter, or Spring climbing, especially when the west side of the state is too rainy. The columns have a southwesterly facing orientation which takes advantage of the sunshine on wintery days.

Fixed anchors exist along the rimtop above most of the popular climbs making it well suited for setting up a quick top-rope although some routes are leadable. The easiest climb is a stout 5.7 so the site may not be conducive to beginner climbing. The routes are seldom lead, although the classic 5.7 Hanz Crack on the far left is definitely worth the blast either as a top-rope or lead.

Certain rock climbs start easy and then steepen to roughly 80°. In some cases, the routes start surprisingly easy on the lower half only to end ridiculously thin on the upper half. The basalt bluff has a right leaning two-directional tilt with slightly weathered cracks.

Flora & Pests

Ticks are active in the Spring season. Anticipate rattlesnakes during the warm season. If you are susceptible to getting the itch from poison oak it's best to avoid climbing here. Consider bringing a ground cloth to protect your rope.

Directions

Drive east from Bingen, Washington on State 14 for three miles. Convenient roadside parking is available at the old Highway 8 turnoff next to Rowland Lake, or at a popular mountain bik-

ing trail next to Locke Lake alongside Courtney Road. The approach will take about 20 minutes. Follow the narrow hiker/biking trail uphill as it follows alongside a small stream. When the trail crosses the stream, a prominent rock bluff is located directly uphill on the east slope of the stream.

South End (Rattler Area)

Common zone to begin climbing. Where the rough climbers path first meets the cliff.

1. _____ 5.12- [?]
Three very closely spaced narrow columns yield one difficult route. Hard TR on steep thin narrow columns. Starts just north of an oak tree.

2. _____
Tall box corner dirty chimney system (potential).

3. **Seven Eleven 5.11+**
A thin jam crack that starts easy but closes tight on the upper part of the route increasing the difficulty the higher you go.

4. _____ 5.__ [?]
Potential corner system.

5. _____ 5.12- [?]
The infamous detached column chimney is gone. Now its a powerful thin seam cruising up an orange colored face of a slight boxed corner. Top-rope.

6. **Rattler 5.11+ [?]**
Climb the initial corner system (of the above route), then move fully into a vertical left seam about 12' up the route.

GORGE ROCK   161

7. **Measure of Pleasure 5.8 ★★★**
   Located on the outside of the buttress immediately left of the detached chimney column. Clamber up past a stubby tree at the start, and cruise up a long steep crack corner. This long consistent hand jam crack is a stellar little climb.
8. **Wendell's Big Mistake TR 5.10+**
   Near the middle of the crag, about 15' left of Measure of Pleasure.
9. **_____   5.9+ (?)**
   A tall boxed corner system.
10. **Nuggets 5.7 ★**
    Climb a low angle slab and edges, then at mid-height, step left and continue up an obvious crack to top up. Use Sluice Box belay.
11. **Sluice Box 5.9 ★★**
    Climb low angle steps, and when the crack steepens stay in the crack corner. Tight opposition stemming smears to finish the upper crux part.
12. **_____ 5.10 c/d**
    Lower slabby climbing to upper tricky balancy face climbing. If you can't figure out the upper part don't be surprised.
13. **_____   5.11b**
    A thin seam in a slight corner.
14. **_____   5.11b ★**
    Stay in the thin seam in a tight corner the entire way using an occasional left jug.
15. **Bucket o' Ribs 5.8**
    A dirty rib with jug holds and edges on the outside of a column. Avoid the crack on left.

Tall Oak Tree Area

This section has a large oak tree at the base of the wall next to the popular Log Flume route.

16. **_____ 5.8 ★★**
    Quality crack corner system (2-bolts). Gear to 3").
17. **_____ 5.10b**
    Starts up a steep slightly mossy face, then punch past a tiny lip midway up the route.
18. **_____ 5.__ [?]**
19. **_____ 5.__ [?]**
20. **_____ 5.__ [?]**
21. **_____ 5.10b**
    Climb a corner system immediately right of Log Flume (which ends at same belay anchor).
22. **Log Flume 5.10a ★★**
    Start in a steep double corner behind the large oak tree. At the mid-point small edges launch into a series of tight oppositions stemming smears to finish the upper crux part.

North End

23. _____ 5.11-
    The upper half is a thin clean corner-*ish* seam.
24. _____ 5.__
25. _____ 5.__
26. _____ 5.__
27. **Birds on a Shelf 5.10+ (TR)**
    A wide stem box corner above a mossy shelf.
28. ___ 5.11+
    A very thin crack with a slight right lean to it.
29. **Thin Edge of Reality 5.11+ ★★**
    A top-rope that uses a combination of two tight seams on a steep face. Merges into Hanz crack for the last move.
30. **Hanz Crack 5.7 ★★★**
    A stellar jam crack worth leading or top-rope.
31. _____ 5.11
    Immediately left of Hanz Crack are three thin cracks on a steep face. This is the right and shortest corner seam.
32. **Ptero 5.11 ★**
    Middle thin corner seam.
33. **Latent Genes 5.11+ ★**
    The leftmost of three thin seam crack corner.
34. **Mouse in a Microwave 5.10a**
    Climb easy crack to a stance capped by a small lip. Surmount lip and climb a jam crack to top.
35. _____ 5.11- (?) ★
    Long thin tips crack corner with quality climbing.
36. _____ 5.__ (?)
37. _____ 5.__ (?)
38. _____ 5.__ (?)

OH8

Beta written by Kay Kucera and Paul Cousar

OH8 is a minor but conveniently situated road side crag along old highway 8 on the northeast side of Rowland Lake located at the extreme west end of the Catherine Creek syncline. Though easy to drive right past the fractured cliff, upon closer inspection you will find an interesting little treasure of rock climbs scattered along this fairly lengthy flood basalt rock formation. The crag faces west making maximum use of the afternoon sunshine suitable for a fast workout in the early Spring and Fall seasons. The basalt is a slightly grainy textured surface to which rock shoes readily stick, but the routes are deceptive; what appears easy and lower angled is actually surprisingly steep and difficult.

Accessibility and Concerns

Virtually all the rock climbs require some trad gear. Don't climb here if you don't have various cams, stoppers or hex's. The rock is a bit chossy so a helmet is advisable. Avoid walking along the rimtop as this will damage various ecological plants. The Barretts Penstemon is an endemic cliff-dwelling wildflower of colorful purple clustered blooms that makes its home here. Removing cliff dwelling plants and moving talus is prohibited. Most fixed belay anchors are not accessible from above so you must be a competent lead climber to use this place. Owners should keep their dogs leashed or leave them at home. Expect ticks, rattlesnakes, wasps, friable rock and plenty of poison oak along the cliff base. If you are susceptible to poison oak it is best to avoid this site. The rock climbs are listed from right to left as you are walking uphill.

1. **Blind Ambition 5.10b** ★★★
   Pro: 6 QD's, two ½" cams, one each 2" cam, ½" nut
   Thin cracks lead to a pumpy face.
2. **Buckwheat 5.10c** ★
   Pro: 9 QD's
   Same start as above. Two bolts to ledge, (runout) then left up smooth face. Contrived finish left over roof.
3. **Just a Freakin' Rock Climber 5.11a** ★★
   Pro: 7 QD's and one each 1", 1½" cam
   Two roofs, one low and one high with a crack.
4. **Ron Love Verly 5.10a** ★
   Pro: 6 QD's
   Technical move in corner, easier climbing above. A 2-bolt extension (5.12b) to second belay.
5. **Hostile Old Hikers 5.9+**
   Pro: 3 QD's, and two each 1", 2", 2 ½", 3 ½" cams
   Follows beautiful hand crack in corner onto ledge; finish up slabby ramp to crack in corner.
6. **Rattlesnake 5.9** ★★★
   Pro: 6 QD's, two 1", one each 1 ½", 3", & 4" cams
   Wide crack start, hard past first bolt then easier above.
7. **Sasquatch 5.11c** ★★★
   Pro: 8 QD's, and one each ½", 1", 1 ½" cams
   Technical, long, and pumpy. Lots of fun!
8. **Tidewater 5.9** ★★
   Pro: 8 QD's, and one each ½", 1" cam
   Cruise past small roof to ledge, then up and right.
9. **Wind Dummy 5.9** ★★
   Pro: 8 QD's and one 1" cam
   Same start as Tidewater but climb straight up off ledge.
10. **[Decomm]**

11. **OCD 5.11d**
    Pro: 4 QD's, and one each ¾", 2", 3" cams
    Same start as Grass Widow then left up bulging arête.
12. **Desert Dreaming 5.10d** ★★★
    Pro: 4 QD's, one ¾", and two 1" cams
    Gray slab at start morphs into faux sandstone at finish. Easier if you traverse right before the last bolt, and then up to the anchor.
13. **Penstemon 5.9+** ★★
    Pro: 5 QD's
    Start on gray face, do

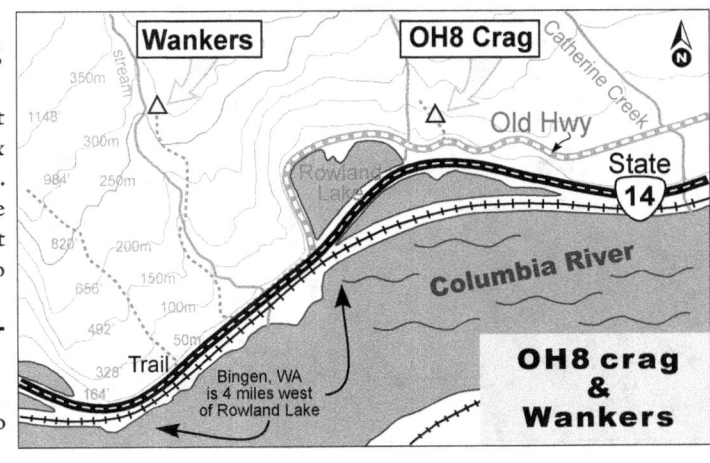

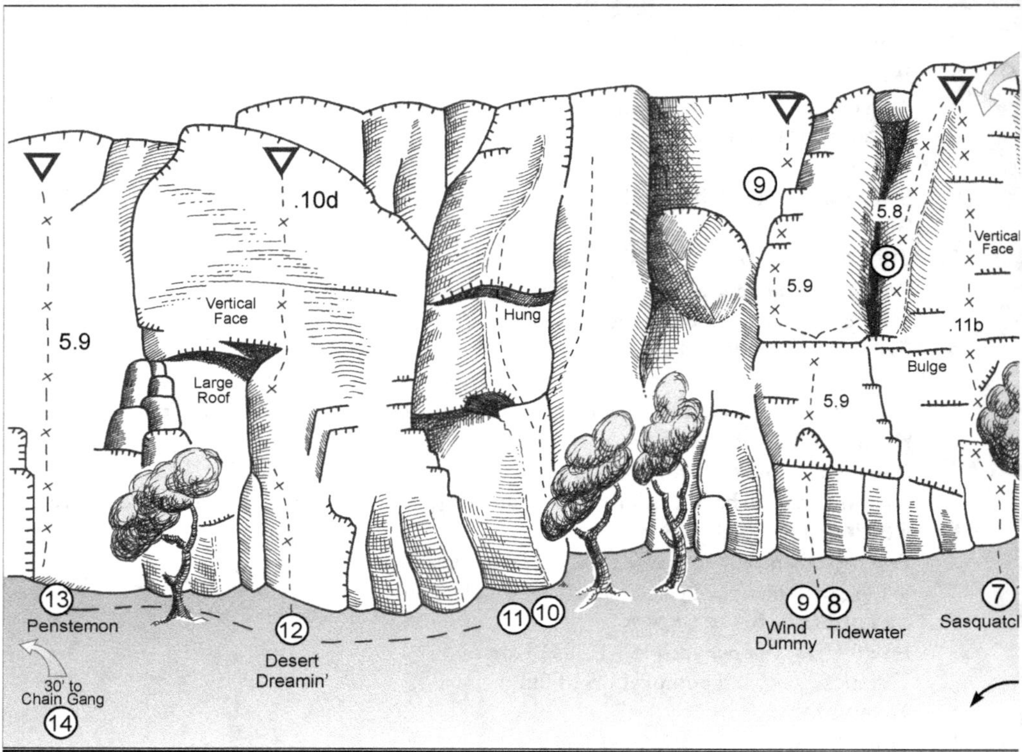
.10d
5.9
Vertical
Face
Large
Roof
Hung
9
5.8
8
Vertical
Face
5.9
.11b
5.9
Bulge
13
Penstemon
12
Desert
Dreamin'
11
10
9
8
Wind
Dummy
Tidewater
7
30' to
Chain Gang
14

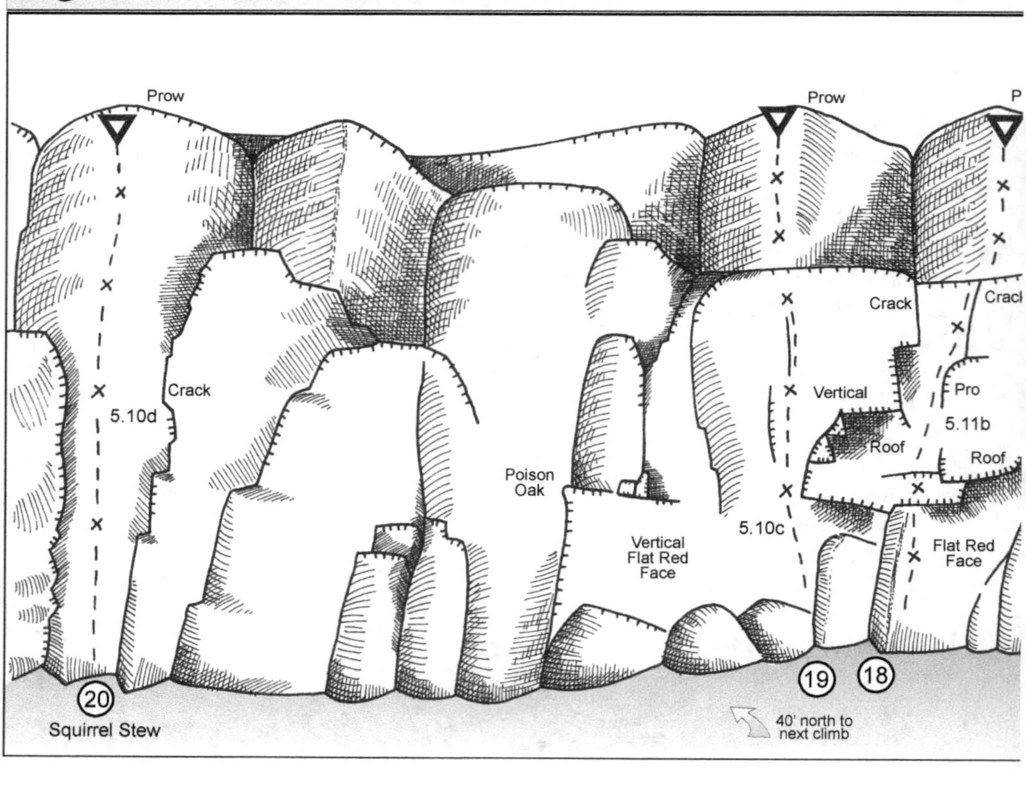
Prow
Prow
Crack
5.10d
Poison
Oak
Vertical
Flat Red
Face
Crack
Vertical
Roof
5.10c
Pro
5.11b
Roof
Flat Red
Face
20
Squirrel Stew
19
18
40' north to
next climb

GORGE ROCK

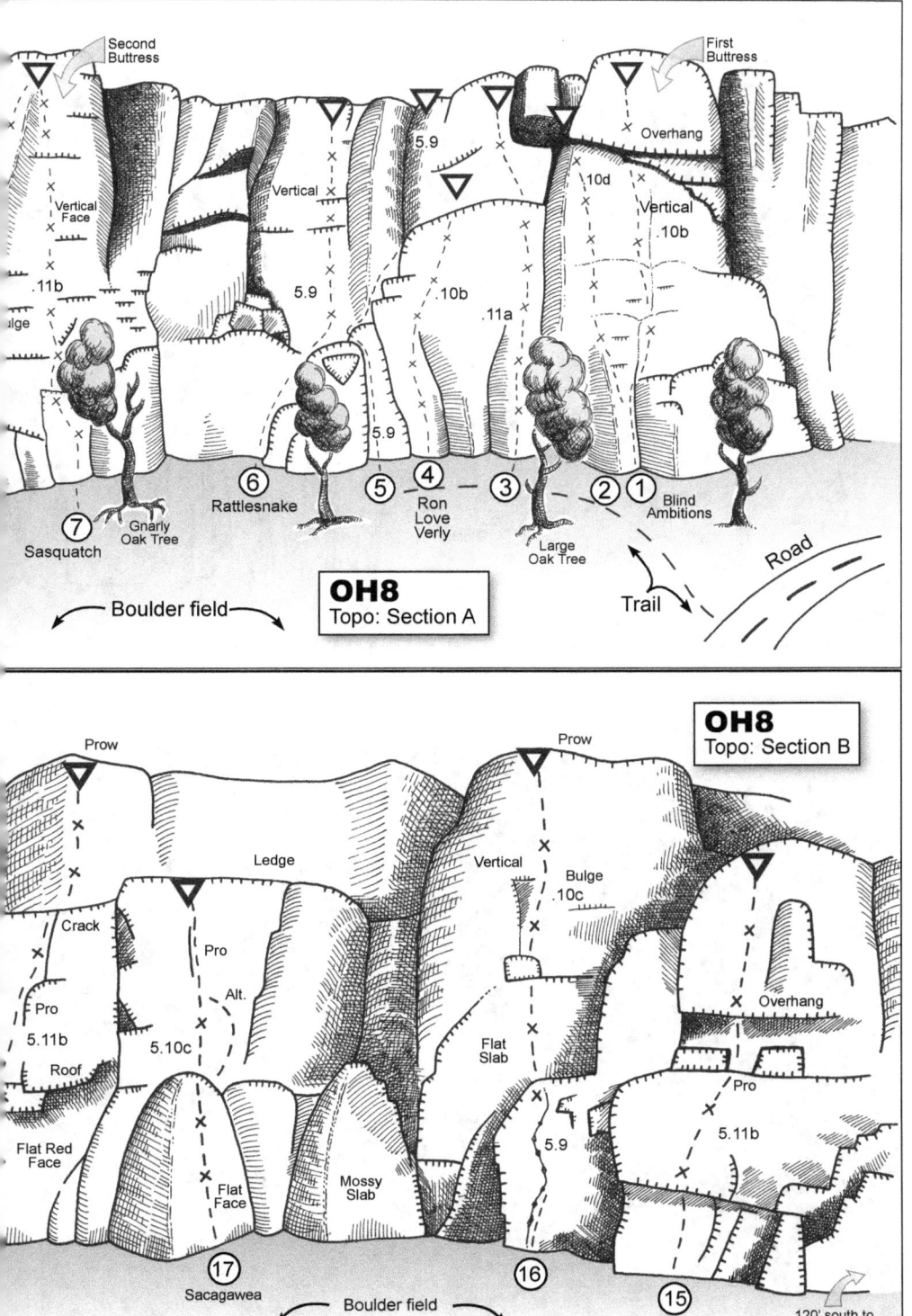

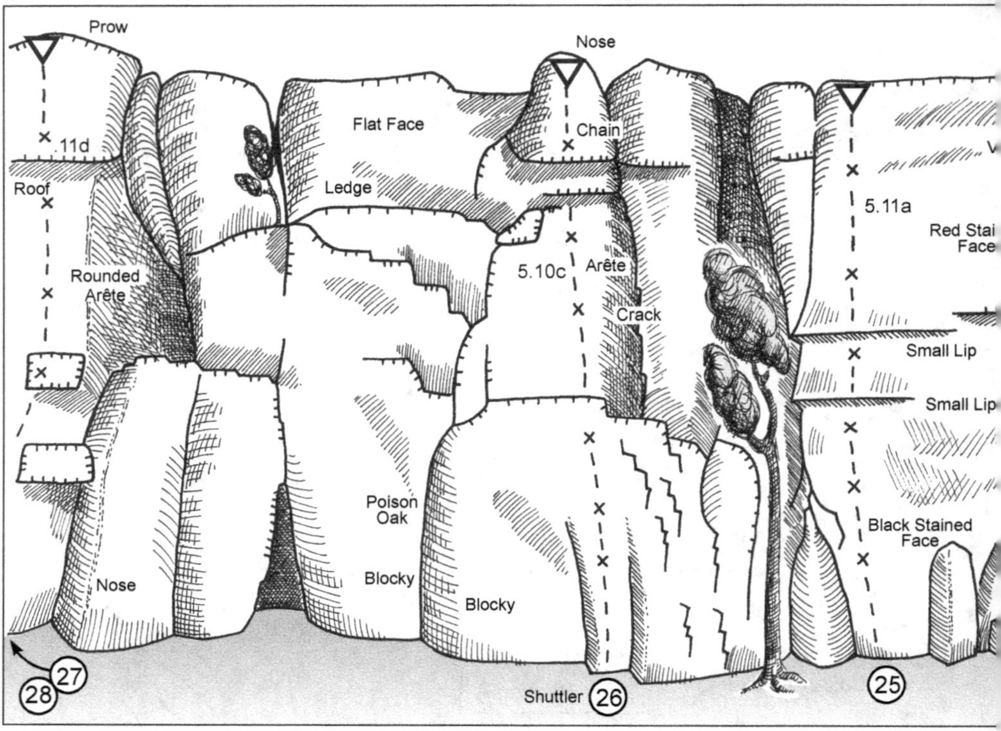

166 CHAPTER 3

Topo labels (upper diagram)

- Prow
- 11d
- Roof
- Rounded Arête
- Nose
- Flat Face
- Ledge
- 5.10c
- Arête
- Crack
- Poison Oak
- Blocky
- Blocky
- Nose
- Nose
- Chain
- 5.11a
- Red Stain Face
- Small Lip
- Small Lip
- Black Stained Face
- Shuttler (26)
- (25)
- (27)
- (28)

OH8 Crag Map 1

- Large Roof
- Vertical Face
- 5.10
- Climb face next to corner
- (12)

OH8 Crag Map 2

- Left side of bolts .10b
- Right side of bolts 5.11a
- Vertical
- (14)

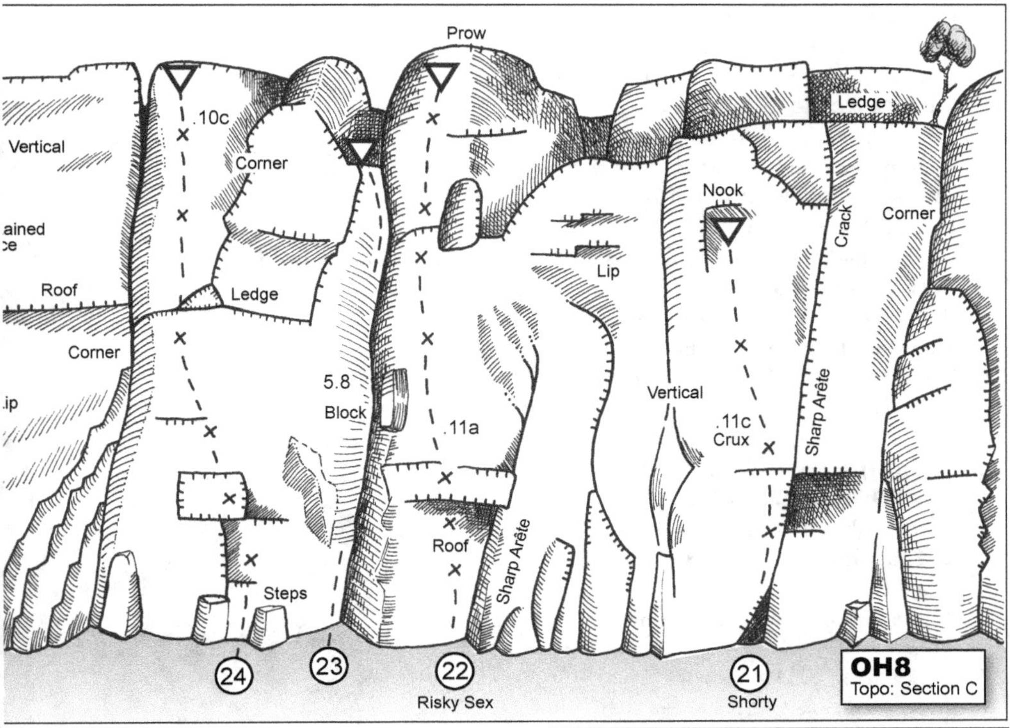

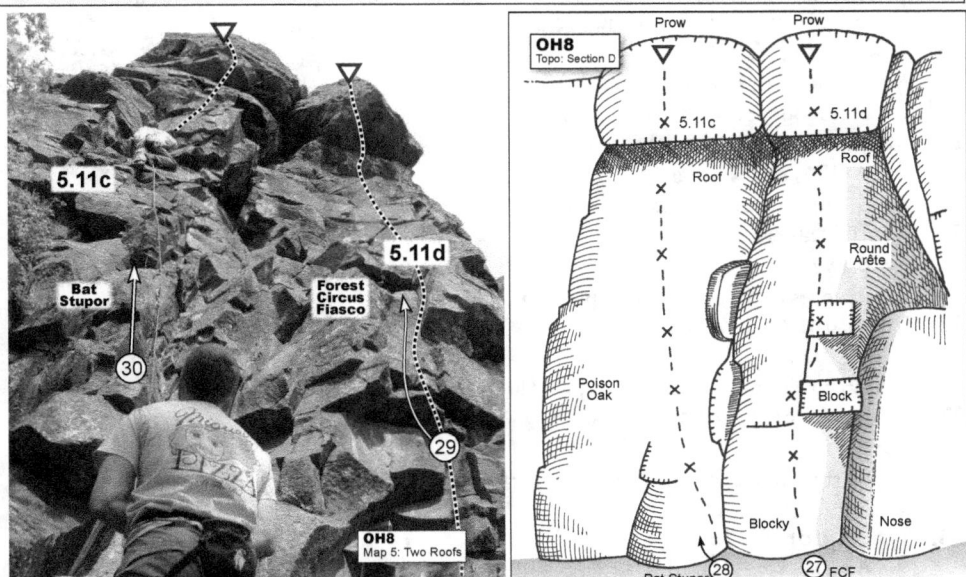

a tricky mantle, then climb past the penstemon at mid-height to more red rock.

14. The Chain Gang 5.10c ★
Pro: 4 QD's, one each 1", 2", 3" cams
Chain on second bolt at roof; super fun.

15. **Carl's Route 5.11b ★★**
    Pro: 5 QD's and cams to 1"
    Start up the left half of a flat gold face, then surmount steep bulge above.
16. **Molly's Route 5.10b ★★**
    Pro: 4 QD's and gear to 1"
    Start up crack on front face to a ledge, then up a slab to a bulging crux face.
17. **Sacagawea's Route 5.10b ★**
    Pro: 3 QD's, one each 2", 3" cams
    Start on smooth protruding face with fractures. Avoiding flowers, romp to top.
18. **Paul's Route 5.11b**
    Pro: 4 QD's, one each 1", 1 ½" cams
    Thin crack to bulge, finish high on prominent prow.
19. **Reed's Route 5.10c ★★★**
    Pro: 6 QD's
    Unusual movement on angular terrain.
20. **Squirrel's Stew 5.10c ★★**
    Pro: 4 QD's, one each ¾", 1", 1½" cams
    Increasingly difficult to bulgy prow.
21. **Get It, Shorty 5.11a ★★**
    Pro: 3 QD's
    A crux for each bolt, excellent movement on this tiny testpiece.
22. **Risky Sex 5.11a ★★★**
    Pro: 7 QD's, one ½" cam or nut
    Two bolts to roof; crux is the final bulge.
23. **Butt Shiner 5.8**
    Pro: lots of cams, some small nuts
    Discontinuous cracks in a dirty corner.
24. **Itchy & Scratchy 5.10c ★★**
    Pro: 6 QD's, one ¾" cam
    Wander up and left to bolted arête finish.
25. **Open Space Plan 5.11a ★**
    Pro: 6 QD's
    Initial moves on black rock, pumpfest above in red.
26. **The Shuttler 5.10b ★★★**
    Pro: 6 QD's
    Shattered columns to smooth face, wild arête finish.
27. **Forest Circus Fiasco 5.11d ★**
    Pro: 6 QD's
    Thoughtful moves below, footless mantle to gain right hand roof.
28. **Bat Stupor 5.11c ★**
    Pro: 6 QD's
    Easy climbing past questionable blocks, crimpy crux guards anchor above the left hand roof.
29. **Spring Breezes 5.10d ★**
    Pro: ___ QD's
    About 50' left of Bat Stupor. Initial bulge with crimps, then eases to 5.6 climbing.

Sam Elmore leading *Molly's Route*
Dave leading *Carl's Route 5.11b*

30. **The Gap 5.11d**
    Pro: 3 QD's
    Short face, surmount large steep faceted block to anchor.
31. **Columbina 5.10a**
    Pro: __ QD's
    About 10' left of The Gap is this short face line.
32. **End of the Line 5.9**
    Pro: __ QD's (optional gear to 1")
    Very short climb just left of Columbina; last route at crag.

LYLE WEST CRAG

This crag is located about ⅓ mile east of the state highway rest facility near Lyle. This miniature site offers road side access to some brief rock climbs on a small 40' tall bluff of vertical basalt.

Park at a small dirt pullout on the north side of State 14 at the west end of a small enclosed pond called Chamberlain Lake. Most of the rock climbs are bolted and have good fixed belay anchors although several are mixed traditional crack leads. Though the site was infrequently used in the past with several newer fixed routes it provides a viable stop over site while you are en route eastward to greater destinations.

West Section

1. _____ **5.9**
   Pro: 7 QD's
   Climb west arête passing a roof on the left then finish on a flat face.
2. _____ **5.10-**
   Pro: 7 QD's
   Climb face to a roof, then exit left and up left to merge with previous route.
3. _____ **5.10-**
   Pro: 6 QD's
   Climb a corner crack to a ledge, then bust up left onto a flat face to finish.
4. **Prow 5.9** ★
   Pro: 4 QD's
   Climbs the outside of the basalt column then angles off right to route #2 anchor.
5. **Corner / face 5.8** ★★
   Pro: 5 QD's
   A quality face climb utilizing the thin inside corner seam.
6. **Winter Roast 5.10+** ★★
   Pro: 4 QD's
   A powerful thin face climb with positive incut crimper face edges.
7. _____ **5.11- (TR)**
   Climb up to a ledge, then up to a roof, and surmount it leftward finishing on face crimps.

The Middle Section

8. **Half Seed 5.10- (TR)**
   A TR starting as a thin crack and face edges on upper part.
9. **Wide Crack 5.9** ★
   Pro to 4" (3 bolts on upper part of wide crack)
   Ascend the crack corner that quickly widens. Great route, and when the off-width size of the crack gets too big for casual pro several bolts ease your trip to the anchor.
10. _____ **5.9 to 5.10+ (TR)**
    Climb a crack to a ledge, then a short crack, then climb past a roof.

East Section

11. ____ 5.__ (?)
    Pro: _ QD's
    Thin seam passing a roof, to finish on face crimps to a belay. Project.

12. ____ 5.11 (?)
    Pro: 6 QD's
    Climb up passing two small lips, then crimps on face to the top.

13. ____ 5.11 (?)
    Pro: 4 QD's
    An outer column and arête, then face crimps to the top.

14. **Crack 5.9**
    Pro to 3"
    A crack climb on the right end of this small crag.

LYLE TUNNEL CRAG

The LTC is a minor rock formation viable as a climbing stop over if you are on your way to greater destinations for the day or if you are on a Gorge marathon climbing tour. An hour or two and you can ascend virtually all the rock climbs at this crag. LTC is a quaint tiny slice of bluff situated immediately west of the State 14 highway tunnel at the east end of the small community of Lyle, WA. The bluff faces directly south and tends to be a warm sunny site from mid-morning onward and is conducive to year-round climbing. The small 40' tall rock bluff is a vesiculated (pockets) old flood basalt formation. The well featured pockets provide good hand and foot holds as well as pro placements. Typical lead gear ranges from nuts and cams to 4". All routes have fixed belay anchors at the top. A history of rock climbing has taken place here and access is encompassed by WSDOT right-of-way.

1. ____ 5.6 ★★
   Pro to 3"
   Common initial foray that starts

vertical to a ledge with plenty of holds/edges to the top.

2. **Arête 5.7 TR**
The right arête.

3. **_____ 5.7+ ★★★**
Pro to 4"
Climb the deep double-duty crack corner system. A stellar fun and steep route.

4. **Arête 5.7+ TR ★**
This climbs the left arête.

5. **_____ 5.8 ★★**
Pro to 2" and QD's
Climb up the deep corner (bolts) and launch out right at the roof and up a thin crack.

6. **Roof Left Exit 5.9-**
Pro to 2" and cams
A boorish awkward left exit steals the quality of the show.

7. **_____ 5.8 TR**
A road show that would be nice to see it fixed for leading.

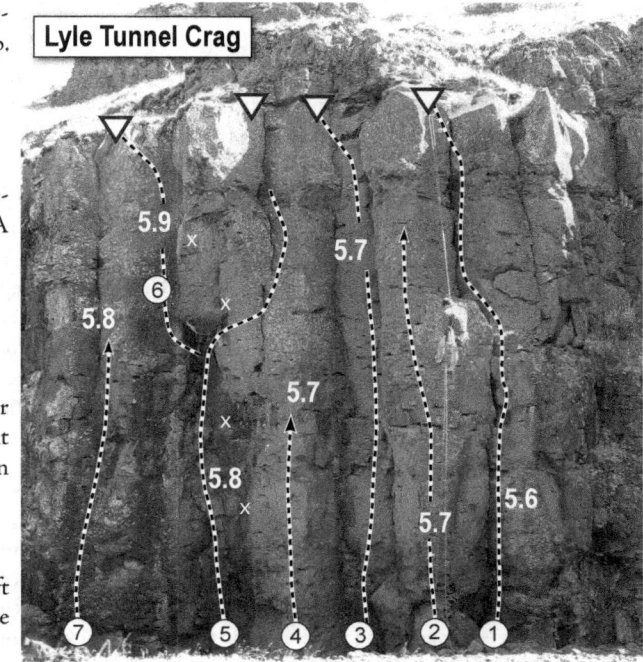

Lyle Tunnel Crag

HORSETHIEF BUTTE

The popular Horsethief Butte offers an ideal respite from the liberal amounts of western Oregon rain where you can often find sunny weather crag climbing by the Columbia River.

For rock climbers it offers a tremendous variety of short boulder problems within a series of corridors in the inner portion of the butte. This site offers an effective means to practice and enhance the basic concepts of rock climbing and rappeling. The natural open atmosphere of the inner butte offers easy communication from instructor to climber.

Brief History of the Area

The Butte is a prominent feature within the Columbia Hills State Park and is a popular site for climbing as well as hiking. The nearby lake was formed when The Dalles Dam was built.

For centuries local American Indians lived near the Butte. The ease of access to the river also provided excellent opportunity for them to catch some of the seasonal migration of salmon for food and for barter. Celilo Falls was the heart of a long established trading region that sustained a thriving community of native Indians from the Wisham, Cloud and Lishkam tribes. The Lewis and Clark expedition camped at a village during their journey west in 1805-1806. Salmon caught near the Celilo Falls provided an important source for trade and barter with other indigenous native tribes of the region. Excellent remnants of native Indian petroglyphs such as *'she who watches'* provide visitors with archeological insight of ancient tribal customs.

Visitor considerations and state park regulations

- Horsethief Butte has several areas signed as 'no climbing' for cultural resource protection. Columbia Hills State Park has archeological sites including Horsethief Butte which are protected by State and Federal laws. Disturbance and/or removal of any artifact, pictograph, or petroglyph is prohibited.
- Expect windy conditions.

- Beware of the occasional rattlesnake. Frequent visitor foot traffic tends to keep most rattlesnakes at a distance.
- Poison Oak grows along the base of several walls. This thick short shrub has seasonal glossy leaves which grow in groups of three per branch and have small white berries.
- Ticks are common in the Spring and Fall seasons. Ticks are quite small so be certain to inspect frequently for ticks if you visit here. There is a plethora of bouldering problems far beyond what this section could possibly convey, but this in-depth treatise strives to detail the greater portion of the well traveled climbs found at the Butte.

Directions

Directions from Oregon: From exit #87 at The Dalles drive north across the Columbia River bridge on U.S. 197 for 3½ miles, then east on Washington State 14 for 2¾ miles to Columbia Hills State Park. The Butte is located east of the lake at Mile Post 85. Hike on the path south to the butte and enter either via the west side trail or at the 'Entrance Cracks' gap in the wall. Camping (closed from Nov. thru March) is available at the developed facility on the west side of the 90-acre Horsethief lake. Climb safely and enjoy your visit!

ENTRANCE CRACKS

1. **OW & Hand Crack 5.9** ★★
   Left of the left prow are several climbs in the shaded portion of the bluff. Both begin up the same crack using edges and steps. From the midway stance, embark up *left* in a wide offwidth crack using a small hidden edge in the offwidth which leads to better edges at the top. The *right* jam crack is closer to the arête. Ascend the lower crack to the midway stance, then embark up right into a jam crack which forces you to use the arête more than the crack. There are several more thin optional climbs just to the left of these two climbs that are fairly difficult.

2. **Jam Crack 5.9** ★★
   Great hand and fist jam climb. Start initially in the Left Entrance Crack and punch out left to a short vertical jam crack.

3. **Left Entrance Crack 5.10c/d** ★★★
   This is the left major corner system. Ascend the steep tricky corner by smearing delicately on smooth sloped holds using the thin crack where possible. No such thing as a free lunch.

4. **Arête 5.12**
   Between the two Entrance Crack routes is a technical minor arête top-rope.

5. **Right Entrance Crack 5.10b** ★★★
   This is the right most (and best) of two classic corner systems known as the Entrance Cracks. Involves long reaches, technical smears, and powerful layback moves using a jam crack. On the right face of this entrance crack is another minor seam that branches up right at about 5.9.

THE PASSAGEWAY

These two under-age minors are together on the east wall of the Passageway just as it opens into the First Amphitheater.

6. **Face V0**
   A short smooth face ending on a ledge.

7. **Arête V1**
   Another short problem.

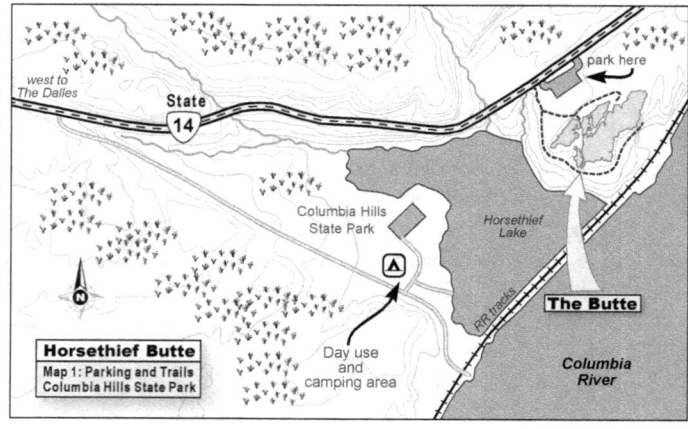

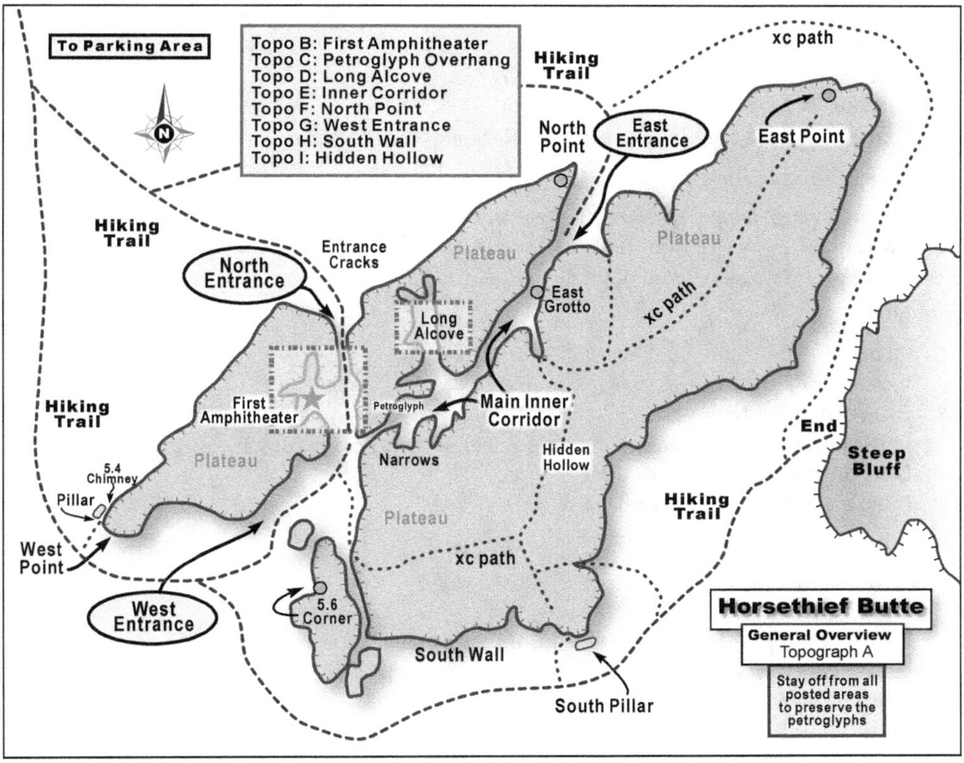

◆ GORGE ROCK 173

To Parking Area

Topo B: First Amphitheater
Topo C: Petroglyph Overhang
Topo D: Long Alcove
Topo E: Inner Corridor
Topo F: North Point
Topo G: West Entrance
Topo H: South Wall
Topo I: Hidden Hollow

Hiking Trail

North Point — East Entrance — East Point

xc path

Hiking Trail

Entrance Cracks

Plateau

Plateau

North Entrance

Long Alcove

East Grotto

xc path

Hiking Trail

First Amphitheater

Petroglyph

Main Inner Corridor

Hidden Hollow

End

Plateau

Narrows

Plateau

Steep Bluff

5.4 Chimney
Pillar
West Point

West Entrance

5.6 Corner

xc path

South Wall

Hiking Trail

South Pillar

Horsethief Butte
General Overview
Topograph A
Stay off from all posted areas to preserve the petroglyphs

5.9   5.9

5.9

5.12 Arête

5.10c

VB ②
       5.8

Var.

VB

①   ③   ④ ⑤
VB   VB   V5 V1

North entrance to first amphitheater

Horsethief
Map 1:
Entrance Cracks

This section faces northwest

The next two steep lines are found on the west wall of The Passageway.

8. Corner 5.8 ★
Layback up the pillar and then stem the corner.

9. Corner 5.7 ★
Climb up a crack to finish in a corner with a long reach to finish.

FIRST AMPHITHEATER

The following string begins on the west side of the Passageway and curls around the initial buttress counter-clockwise into the First Main Amphitheater. Two nooks (north tree nook and west nook) provide a great series of problems.

Wide Buttress

10. Groove V0
Right side of the buttress.

11. Smooth Dihedral 5.7
In the middle of the buttress climb up a dihedral corner using jams and stemming.

12. Discontinuous Cracks V0
Broken cracks on left most side of buttress.

Tree Nook

A tiny nook with a small tree tucked in the corner.

13. Face 5.9 ★
Deep in the Tree Nook on the left side before the small tree is a tall face. Climb up the well-featured and cracked patina face to a tricky finish.

14. Crack-Prow V1
In the same Tree Nook left of the tall face is a crack/prow. You can jam or bear hug this.

Half Nook

15. Thin Crack V1
A stubby. Use the right diagonal crack on a smooth slab.

16. Green Slab VB
This is the outermost nose of a low angle slab.

17. Prow V1
Climb the left side of the prow to a mantle.

18. Overhang V1
Start on a left trending seam. Climb up to a jug and mantle.

West Nook - routes on the right

West Nook offers a great punchy thin traverse all the way to Half Nook.

19. Flake VB
A great warm up flake climb.

20. Crack Seam V1 ★ ★ ★
This classic line (and the next one) are the central feature of the West Nook. They offer complexity, steepness, and quality great for bouldering

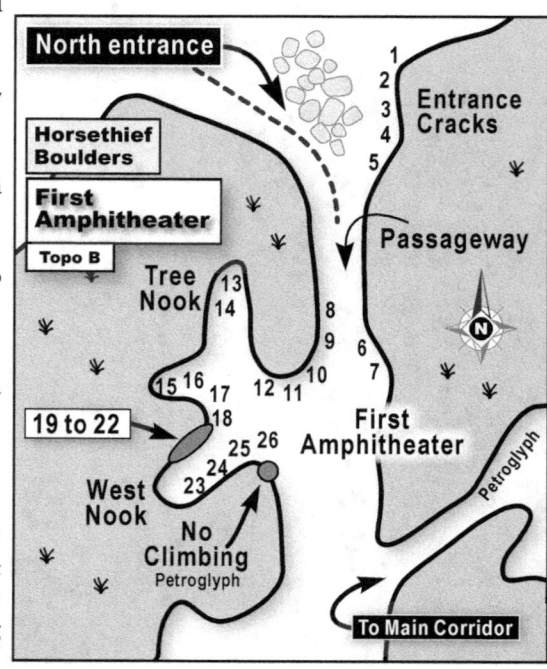

or for a top-rope.

21. **Corner V2-4** ★★★
A stellar V2 thin crack corner that is much harder than it looks. Using rules staying in the crack will make it V3. Traversing in from the far left then up the central corner crack is V4.

22. **Face V7**
Climb the thin face left of the corner using just the small holds on the face.

West Nook - Left routes

23. **Low Angle Face VB**
This is on the south side of the West Nook. Climb up on jug holds.

24. **Face V0**
Climb up through the missing block.

25. **Crack System V2**
Start on the jug and climb up the shallow crack to a flake.

26. **Arête (CLOSED)**
This is the outer buttress with posted off-limits signs informing visitors of the aboriginal petroglyph graffiti.

INNER CORRIDOR

From the First Main Amphitheater walk through a small opening in the cliff scarp (The Narrows). This quickly opens up into the Main Inner Corridor or Grotto. On your immediate left is the Petroglyph Overhang and just beyond (also on the left) is the Sunny Patina. A smidge beyond on the left is the Long Alcove. If you continue walking directly east all the way through this Main Inner Corridor you will pass the Long Wall and exit out the East Entrance to the North Point.

THE NARROWS & PETROGLYPH OVERHANG (TOPO C)

The first five problems are located on the right (south) wall in The Narrows just as you are entering the Main Corridor across from the 'off-limits' sign on the opposite side of the corridor.

27. **Thin Crack V1**
Jam the crack in the corner.

28. **Steep Face V0**
Climb up on fractured jugs.

29. **Bulging Prow V2**
A minor prow.

30. **Tall Face V3** ★
A very committing tall boulder problem.

31. **Tall Arête V4** ★★
A difficult line with tenuous pinches and smears on the lower half of a tall arête. Lock into each sequence, hold the balance, then slap for the rounded sloper.

Traverse Challenge

32. Narrows Traverse V3

Traverse from before #27 passing the tall arête #31.

Petroglyph Overhang (CLOSED)

This is an overhanging inner scoop on the north side of the inner corridor at the narrows. There are posted off-limits signs informing visitors of the aboriginal petroglyphs.

SUNNY PATINA

After you admire the off-limits petroglyphs wander a few yards east to a great little sunny kink where this fine selection of favorites can be found. Definitely fire up the triangular shaped pocket climb called Arrow

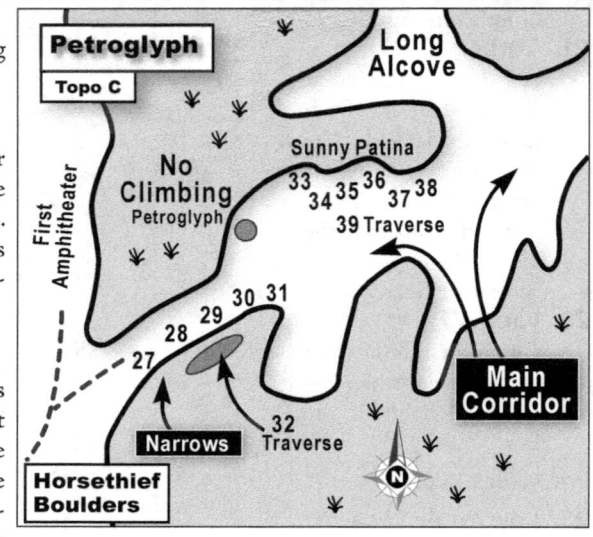

Point. In the distant past this line had a small block wedged in the triangle pocket with two ¼" bolts and a slice of metal holding it in place. Now days we all just enjoy the nature of the line without all that old hardware.

33. Arête VB

Short and juggy and a little loose on top.

34. Face V1 ★

A bump problem over a slight hang on a nose. A bit loose at top.

35. Arrowhead V2 ★★★

Certainly one of the best line face climbs at the Butte. Start left of the corner and balance up using the triangular arrow-like feature with your left hand. Power through a series of wild face crimper moves past the triangle, and to slightly loose jug holds at the top. Eliminates are possible also.

36. Cool Corner V0 ★★★

A classic stemming problem in the corner.

37. Thin Crack V1-V2 ★

Two thin cracks power up away from the corner. Using both thin cracks work up rightward and trick your way carefully onto the slopers above. Eliminates possible.

38. Arête V3

Sit start at hidden undercling and ends with a mantle finish.

The **Triangle of Pain V5** rules on this same arête: sit start to jug undercling, left crimp, triangle crimp in middle of face, left arête, mono-pocket right of the arête, and top to a mantle.

Traverse Challenge

39. Low Traverse V7
Start on #33 and traverse right staying low to finish on top block 6' right of route #38. It is about V4 if you start and end high, and V7 if you start and end low.

THE LONG ALCOVE (TOPO D)
Walking east along the Main Inner Corridor (or Grotto) past the Petroglyph Overhang you will find a Long Alcove running left (north). This long alcove splits into two directions; the longer portion continuing north while the Veranda cuts back hard west to a very popular cul-de-sac.

Veranda
The Veranda is a stellar slice on the immediate left in the Long Alcove. This north facing and very flat smooth face has become one of the most popular spots to power up. The tick-list of problems here and the quality of the rock (smooth and slippery) combine to provide a string of favorites that will keep you jumping. The first problem starts on the very nose while the remainder is on the flat, steep, north-facing shaded aspect.

40. Outer Buttress V1 ★
Crimps and stemming lead to jugs and a nice finish. Variations (V2-V3) exist.

41. Arête to Corner V1 ★
Smear up ramp using a seam, palm the minor arête onto a tiny perch, then finish up a small inside corner.

Jerad working a V4 in the *Narrows*

Low Traverse at the *Sunny Patina*

42. **Thin Crack V2** ★★★
Classic boulder problem, and polished from plenty of use. One of the most well-known Horsethief problems.
43. **Thin Face V3** ★★★
Start on the lowest holds 5' up for V3. Horsethief test-piece.
44. **Face V3** ★
Avoid the good jug on the right or it will be easier still.
45. **Face V0**
Right most very short problem. The finishing block seems kind of sketchy.

Traverse Challenge

46. **Long Traverse V6+**
Start on Arête (#41) and traverse low for the full length of wall, ending on the top of down climb rocks after Face (#45) and ends at the bush.
47. **Short Traverse V6**
Start on Thin Crack (#41) and traverse right to Face (#43) and finish up to the top on that route.

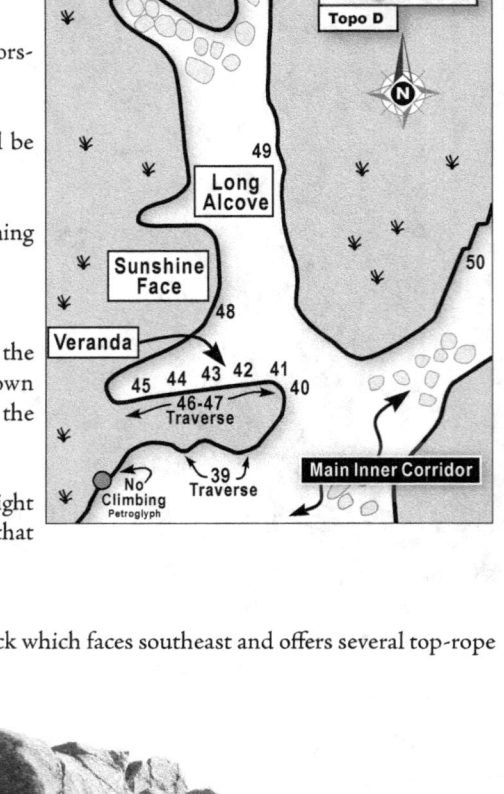

Sunshine Face on left side of Long Alcove

In the Long Alcove is this sunny slice of rock which faces southeast and offers several top-rope problems of moderate difficulty on a nice wide and tall section of wall.

48. Main Face 5.6 to 5.9 ★

Plenty of variables on a steep face quite suitable for top-rope climbing. Even has a few V2-V4 eliminate problems if it catches your eye just right.

Horsethief
Sunshine Face
Map 6

East Face of Long Alcove

Walk deeper into this Long Alcove until you are surrounded by poison oak bushes. On your left (west) side of the long alcove is a viable narrow minor arête with a thin left crack and edge-like features. On the right (east) side of the long alcove several fine long lead or top-rope climbs are available with plenty of variations, so do not feel limited to the only overaged hillbilly listed below.

49. Crack Corner 5.7 ★

The obvious tall crack and corner climb (multiple exits) on east wall of the Long Alcove.

EAST HALF OF INNER CORRIDOR

Walk further east along the Main Corridor beyond the Long Alcove. The Classic Arête is located on the sunny north side at a kink, while the ever popular Long Wall is on the shaded south side of the Corridor. At the far east end of the Main Corridor you will see the East Grotto Face, while beyond is the East Exit/entrance that quickly leads over to the North Point.

The Classic Arête

The next three problems are on a stellar sunny steep flat face with a prominent crisp short arête. Working the arête is one of the finest problems at the Butte. I never knew that V1 could be so fun till I tried this one. Nice sandy landing.

50. Dull Prow V1

A minor round prow as a left exit.

51. Sharp Arête V1 ★★★

Use the sharp arête and gingerly slide up left into the inside corner, and then dance up on intricate small edges to the large incut hold at the top. Classic Horsethief boulder problem.

52. Seam Only V3 ★★

Avoid arête on the left at this grade. Involves a long lock-off to a mono-pocket, and then to a jug hold (wobbles but still there).

LONG WALL (TOPO E)

The Long Wall is one of the most popular sections of wall at the Butte for top-rope climbing. This portion of wall faces north and on hot days stays shaded while offering a plethora of fine problems, including one of the best traverses at the Butte.

Many of the rock climbs along the Long Wall offer numerous variables, so rather than attempting to solve every idiosyncratic nuance, just get the rope out and set up a TR and have at it.

53. **Face to Mantle V2**
Immediately south of the Long Alcove on the shaded Long Wall. Down climb off right immediately after the mantle.

54. **Thin Crack 5.8** ★
The striking thin crack with good pure jamming, but is short lived.

55. **Green Slab 5.6 - 5.9**
A long green slab with many variations; some are harder while some are easier.

56. **Short Overhang V2-3**
Start sitting and end on ledge…or stand and make it V1 fun.

57. **Corner to Ledge 5.7** ★
Climb the shallow inside corner to an awkward move getting on the big flat ledge, then waltz up the right face to top out.

58. **Face to Groove 5.8** ★★
Great line! Climb the steep face on good holds to finish up a lower angled groove.

59. **Steep Face 5.10-** ★★★
Super classic line. Start at the thin crack and climb up an awkward face past missing blocks.

60. **Face to Groove 5.7** ★★
Climb up the enjoyable well-feature face that has lots of cracks and holds until it eases in difficulty in the groove to the top. Beware of a loose thin flake up high.

61. **Face 5.8** ★
Steep face with sequential holds.

62. **Thin Block 5.7** ★
Grab the thin block and climb up to a big edge and finish on the lower angle rock.

63. **Groove 5.5**
A moderate groove on good rock at the far left end of Long Wall prior to the uphill scramble.

Traverse Challenge

64. **Long Wall Traverse V3-V4** ★★★
A totally stellar boulder traverse can be done along the Long Wall in either direction. Start just west of Corner to Ledge #57 and continue to Groove #63. Likely V6 if staying low for the entire traverse.

East Grotto Face

A good location for top-rope climbing. The rounded slab formation is less than vertical and has many cracks and seams crisscrossing the face at an-

Dave leading *North Point Arête*

GORGE ROCK 181

gles.

65. Face 5.7 to 5.10- ★
Nice blocky climbing on a wide rounded face with a corner in the middle of the wall.

NORTH POINT (TOPO F)
The following routes are quite tall and are on the North Point which is a sharp prow of rock facing out over the East Entrance. Most climbers reach this locale by walking through the entire inner main corridor. A large boulder field is located at this East Entrance.

66. Old Bolt 5.10
Cruises up a smooth vertical face (several old ¼" bolts studs) past an upside down triangle roof feature on a flat patina face. Once you power past the triangle into the thin jam crack to a stance, continue

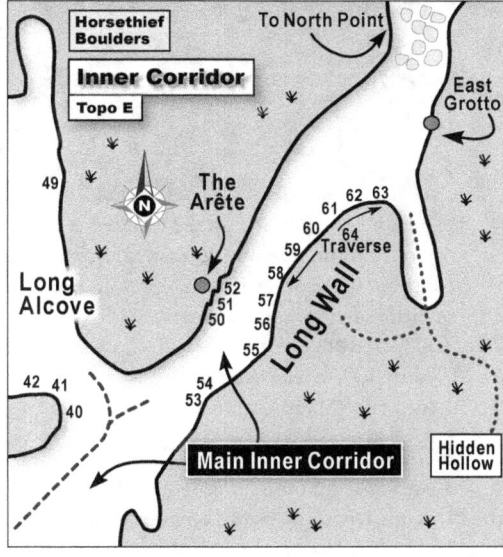

up easy steps in a corner to the top. Somewhat loose at the top. About 30' left of this line is a nice short VB (5.9) jug haul boulder problem on a flat face.

67. North Point Crack 5.10b ★
Climb a steep crack to a stance, and then climb a smear move into a corner system immediately left of the arête.

68. North Point Arête 5.11c ★
Start at the North Crack and launch up right (2 bolts) on a smooth face, and then power out (3 bolts) the severely overhung arête to the top.

WEST ENTRANCE (TOPO G)
There are several options near the West Entrance that are good for learning technique.

69. West Chimney 5.4
The West Chimney is found at the very tip of the West Point, and is a nice chimney smack between the main wall and a large obvious isolated pillar. Stem the chimney to the top of the

pillar, and then launch up the nice series of steps and ledges to the tip of West Point. Once you top out on the tip you can easily descend southward down a boulder field slope. Or you can continue up another short steep step onto the main upper plateau and walk east to descend into the First Amphitheater.

70. Tall Corner 5.6
A fairly well-used corner climb is available to your immediate south as you are hiking up the slope of the West Entrance.

SOUTH WALL (TOPO H)
To reach the South Wall river face hike past the Western Entrance south eastward around the Butte until you can see an obvious isolated pillar separate from the main massif. Scramble up a boulder slope to the base of the west-facing slot formed by this isolated pillar. These two climbs are on the main wall just to the left of the slot.

To set up a top-rope anchor walk east past the pillar to a steep ravine that accesses the top of this bluff. Or walk south across the plateau from the Main Inner Corridor to the top of the formation above the isolated Pillar.

71. Corner and Roof 5.10a
A good long climb and best done as a top-rope. Climb a steep corner and power out the overhang directly to the top.

72. Face and Prow 5.9
Begin by powering up left using the prow and nearby features and continue to the top.

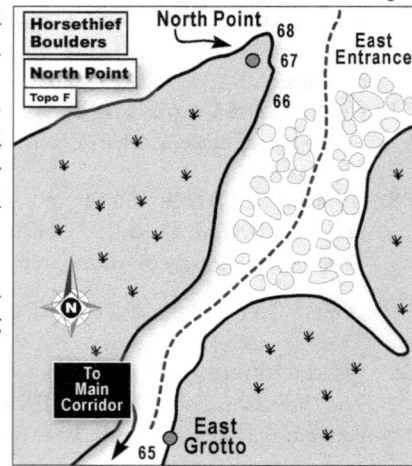

HIDDEN HOLLOW (TOPO I, J, K)

A quality string of short problems on a rock plateau south of the inner corridor. To reach it, ascend up a big stepped slot from the Inner Corridor at the Long Wall that land on a scenic plateau, then drop down into another low grassy dell.

North side of Hidden Hollow

The beta details for the north side problems, L to R (West to East).

VBss High Nose
Begin on low horizontal, then power up over high nose.

V0ss Crack
Climb crack

VBss OW Arête
Climb the face with right hand on the arête. The arête has a deep offwidth crack behind it.

V4ss Outer Point
Climb outer point.

V6ss Arête
A slightly overhung tall flat-face with a sharp outer edge on the lower left. Sit start on crimps with left initially low on outer edge. Crimps mid-face, yet hs better exits holds up high. A V4 exists to its immediate right.

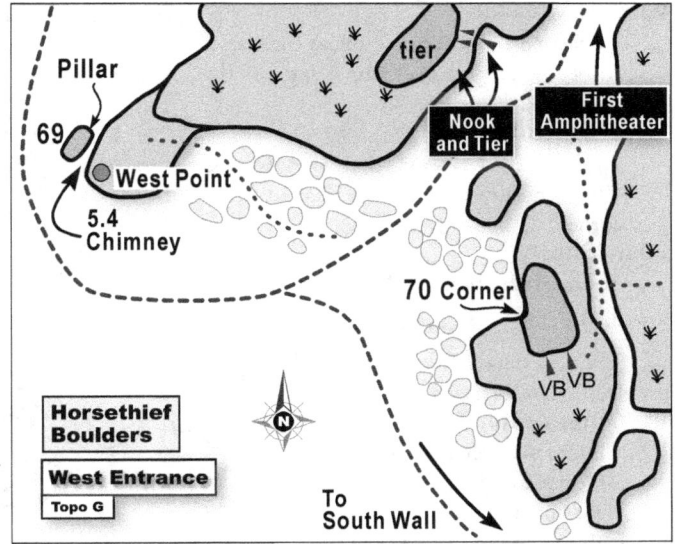

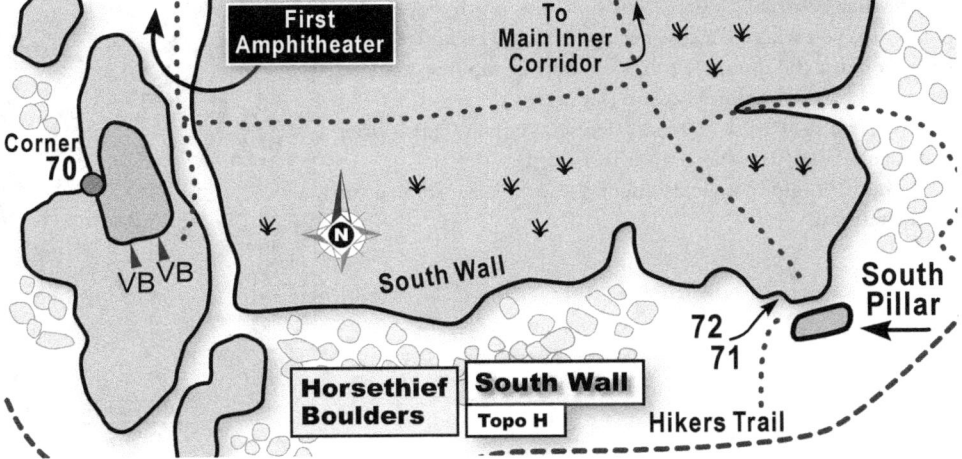

V3ss Low Bulge
At east end of Hidden Hollow. Sit start a short low bulging overhang using just the round arête.

V2ss Crack/Face
A short crack corner that is overhung. Climb mostly the deep V-shaped crack corner.

V0ss Shorty
Shorty round bulge with crimps.

South side - Hidden Hollow:

The beta details for the south side problems, L to R (East to West).

V1 Outer Arête
Climb the left-leaning arête of wide flat face. Left hand is on arête, right on crimps.

V0 Face
Numerous thin cracks and edges crisscross at angles on a nice wide flat face.

V0ss Jugs
Jugs on a short face.

A gap of about 30' exists to reach the next set of problems.

VBss Jugs
Jugs on a short flat face.

V2ss Crimps
Short low 'ss' using crimps and left prow, but marginal smears for feet.

HH PLUS

This is an extension of the Hidden Hollow (Part 1 & Part 2). This "plus more" zone extends as a northward deep long trough that eventually dumps out onto the north slope talus field. Here you will find a select string of unique boulder problems to spark the quest. A series of short crimp lines and/or juggy highball power lines beckon (*see topo*).

The HH+ Part 1 first deep low grassy zone has a brief pack of six VB-V0 problems (one is V-hard).

The HH+ Part 2 yields about 3-4 problems, some a bit on the tall side.

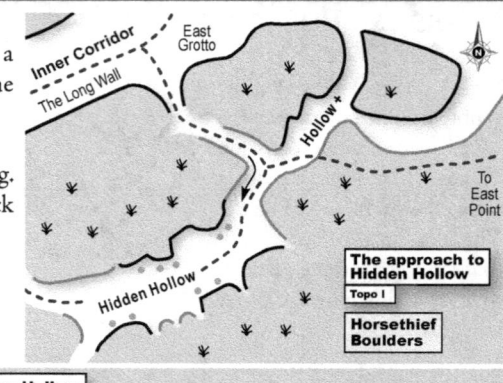

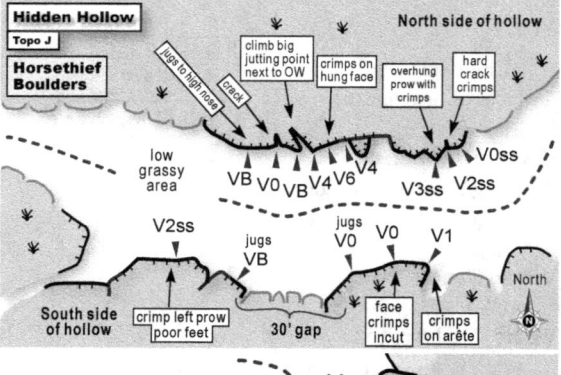

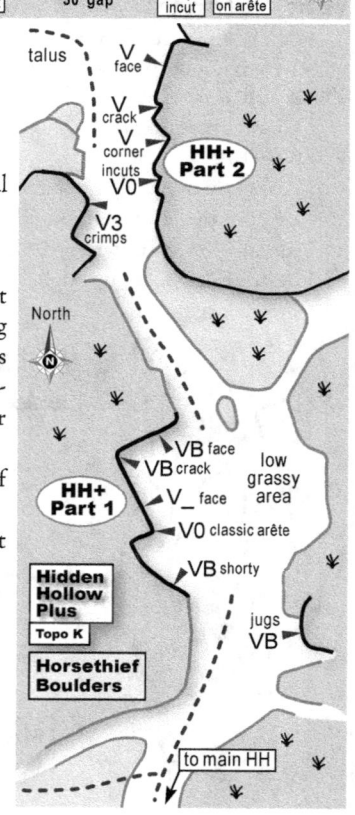

MONTE CRISTO SLAB

The MCS is an impressive diorite slab tucked along the west slope of a minor forested ridge crest overlooking a broad sweeping panoramic plateau of the fir tree covered South Prairie region near Trout Lake. The rock slab is a good example of the kind of granitic slab rock climbing you typically find at places like Leavenworth, Washington, but this crag is just a few hours from Portland.

Though not nearly as steep as you typically find at most major granite climbing sites, the MCS none-the-less is a quality destination for locals who relish low angle slab climbing. The steeper sections of the slab vary from 40°-55° overall angle (with a few near vertical steps). Considering its mid-Cascades Range locale, as expected the crag does have some minor moss and lichen, yet the slab does gets thoroughly scoured each winter by the snow pack buildup as it avalanches off the low angle slab. The west-facing aspect of the slab receives considerable hot summer sunshine, while the dioritic rock structure lacks micro-sized pockets between the crystalline matrix, thus tending to minimize moss growth. The crag is encapsulated in a forest of Douglas fir, cottonwood, alder, and willow brush thickets, yet the slab offers broad sweeping scenic view of the entire region to the west from the top of the wall.

The core emphasis for route grade ratings on this slab commonly range from 5.3 to 5.9 (the fun range), though a few short sections of several routes have slightly higher ratings.

One of the prime benefits about the MCS is to start warm-up leading on the short 100' climbs, then bust into a series of long 200' leads on the main wall of the South Dome. These long routes provide lead climbers with a distinctly unique opportunity to hone calf-burner sharp-end of the rope long slab leading skills, sending you home at the end of the day with a smile of satisfaction.

MCS is suitable for a certain general skill level of rock climber. Considering all factors, from the 4th class descent runnels, to good rappel stations, to the 9'-25' runout sections between lead bolts, to the large array of entry level routes, the MCS is quite suitable as a beginner to moderate climbing area. Most of the beginner routes (5.2-5.6) are well bolted. The youngest person to climb here was 3 years of age (little Davey). The site is especially well suited to the old-timer (and the young) generation climber who have no desire to climb much beyond the 5.9 range. The slab is <u>not</u> a hardman climbing site for dedicated 5.11/.12 (and higher) climbers pushing the 'number' game. Thus, a .12+ climber here is like a fish out of water burdened by a subtle incongruency [like an intentional under achiever].

Hugh leading *Superchron*

In addition, the crags numerative square-foot usability factor is quite small, yielding about sixty rock climbs maximum (considerably less than Broughton Bluff), while 50% of the visible slab is simply too low angle for any 5th class climbing purposes. The MCS distance from the city, its general isolated locale on back-country gravel roads may naturally limit overall user interest.

Road Directions

From Portland, Oregon drive east on I-84 freeway to Cascade Locks. Cross the Bridge of the Gods bridge. Continue east of Washington State Route 14 (through Stevenson, WA) for 14.5 miles (passing Dog Mtn Trailhead). Turn north onto Cook-Underwood Road (CR86) and drive 5.1 miles (through Mill A community). Turn left (north) onto Willard Road and drive 2.1 miles (passing through Willard). Willard Road becomes Oklahoma Road at Willard. Just north of the community of Willard turn left onto NF 66 road (South Prairie Rd). Drive north on paved road NF 66 for 12.7 miles (becomes gravel), then east on gravel road NF 6610 for 2.2 miles. Turn right on NF 6610-030 and drive 1/10 mile, then left on NF 717 a narrow old logging grade for 2/10 mile. Park at a circular loop turn-around sizable enough to hold perhaps 6-8 cars. Driving time from east Portland is about 1¾ hours (from Hood River about 50 minutes).

Several alternate driving directions to MCS for non-AWD vehicles.

From South Prairie Pond (for 2WD vehicles): Continue north on NF 66 past South Prairie Pond for several miles, then cut east on a rough road NF 8820 for 1.5 miles, then south on NF 070 for 1 mile, then west on NF 6610 for .5 mile, then south on NF 030 for .1 mile, then on final narrow decomm road NF 717 for .2 miles to loop parking spot.

From White Salmon (for 2WD vehicles): At highway SR14 at the White Salmon River (where it meets the Columbia River) drive north on SR 141 (the Bypass) 2.1 miles to a junction. Continue north on SR 141 for 19 miles to Trout Lake, then go through town and west on SR 141 for 4 miles, then turn left (southwest) on NF 86 (gravel) and drive 1.8 miles. At a 'Y' go right on NF 8620 (Cave Creek Road) and drive 4.9 miles west uphill to a 'T' intersection. Drive south from the T on NF 070 for .5 mile to a 'Y', then drive west on NF 6610 for .5 miles. Turn left (south) on NF 030 for .1 mile, then on final narrow decomm road NF 717 for .2 miles to loop parking spot.

Path Info

Two paths exist to reach the crag (the north path and the main path). Both start the same, but split in about 40' from the parking spot.

North Path: At the northeast end of the parking spot the primary foot path cuts northward. In about 60' you will reach a dry creek drainage. Cross the dry creek drainage, then gently gain elevation for several hundred feet, then cut directly sideways along the base of a minor rock outcrop to reach the North Nook Landing, a nice sunny gravel landing with a fat string of quality climbs. From the north nook walk south a few yards along the base of the 2nd rock lobe, then up onto a wooded minor ridge crest. Follow up this wooded ridge crest for about 200' (at 100' a brief short path cuts over to the base of the 1st rock lobe to access a string of rock climbs there) to reach the Middle Landing. This landing has a plethora of easier routes conducive for basic and beginner type rock climbing on a low angle slab environment. You can reach this section of the crag easily by taking either the north path or the main path.

Main Path: At the northeast end of the parking spot the primary foot path cuts northward. In about 40' just **before** reaching the dry creek drainage, the main path cuts directly eastward and cruises uphill to the cliff, landing just below the main south dome headwall section. A connector path exists along the entire base of the wall from the south end to the north end.

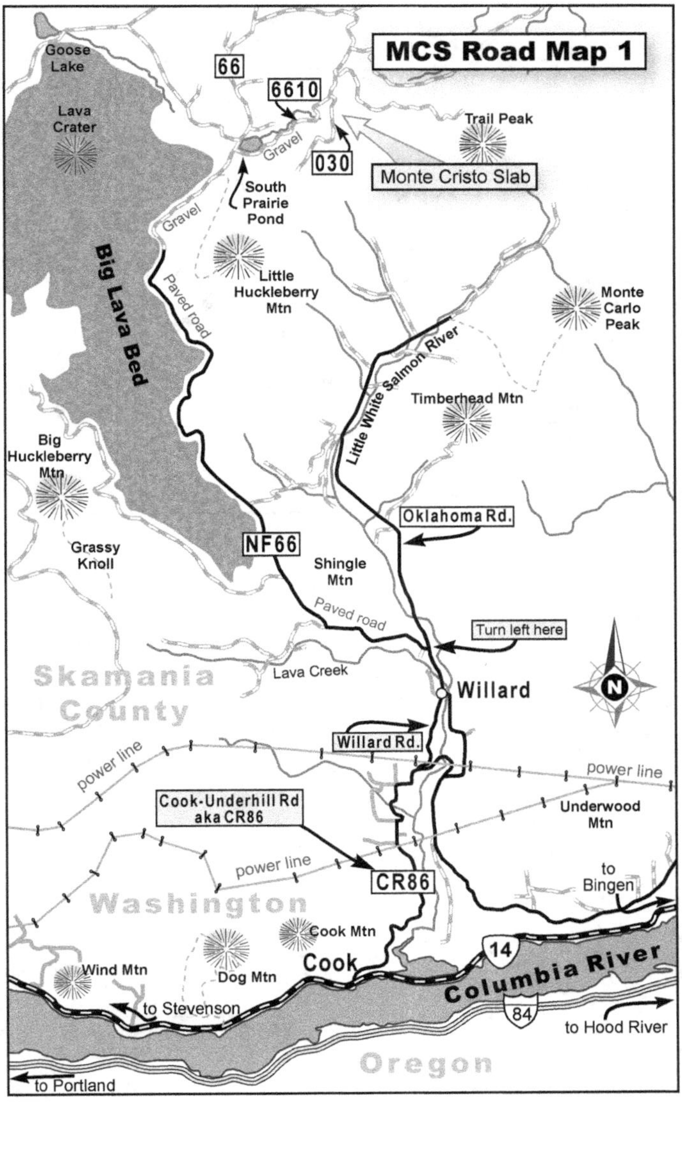

Rock Surface Nuances

Textural nuances of the rock vary from low angle to moderate angle slab, mostly flared rounded pockets (1"-5"), various water grooved runnels, delicate techy smears, and lots of undulating wave-like terrain offering rounded palm friction surfaces. The site is basically un-like any other Northwest Oregon or southwest Washington climbing site, so be prepared to relearn your footwork technique, especially if you are not accustomed to a slab climbing environment. The crystalline mineral surface friction is excellent (light to medium grade sandpaper) giving an ease for smearing on all surfaces.

Descent Options

About 80% of the routes are setup as 90'-100' lead climbs and all those routes are frequently ascended on lead or top-rope, and rappeled.

The steep solo descent runnels are mostly 3rd or 4th class, but you still may not like solo descending a steep slope of rock. Alongside the Dark Water Streak at the south end is a series of assistance or emergency rappel (ER) stations that you are welcome to use for rapping down that runnel. If you are really hard pressed, its possible to walk into the forest at the north end of the crag and descend a midst the trees.

South Dome Main Wall: Avoid rappelling down the long 200' routes on the steep main south

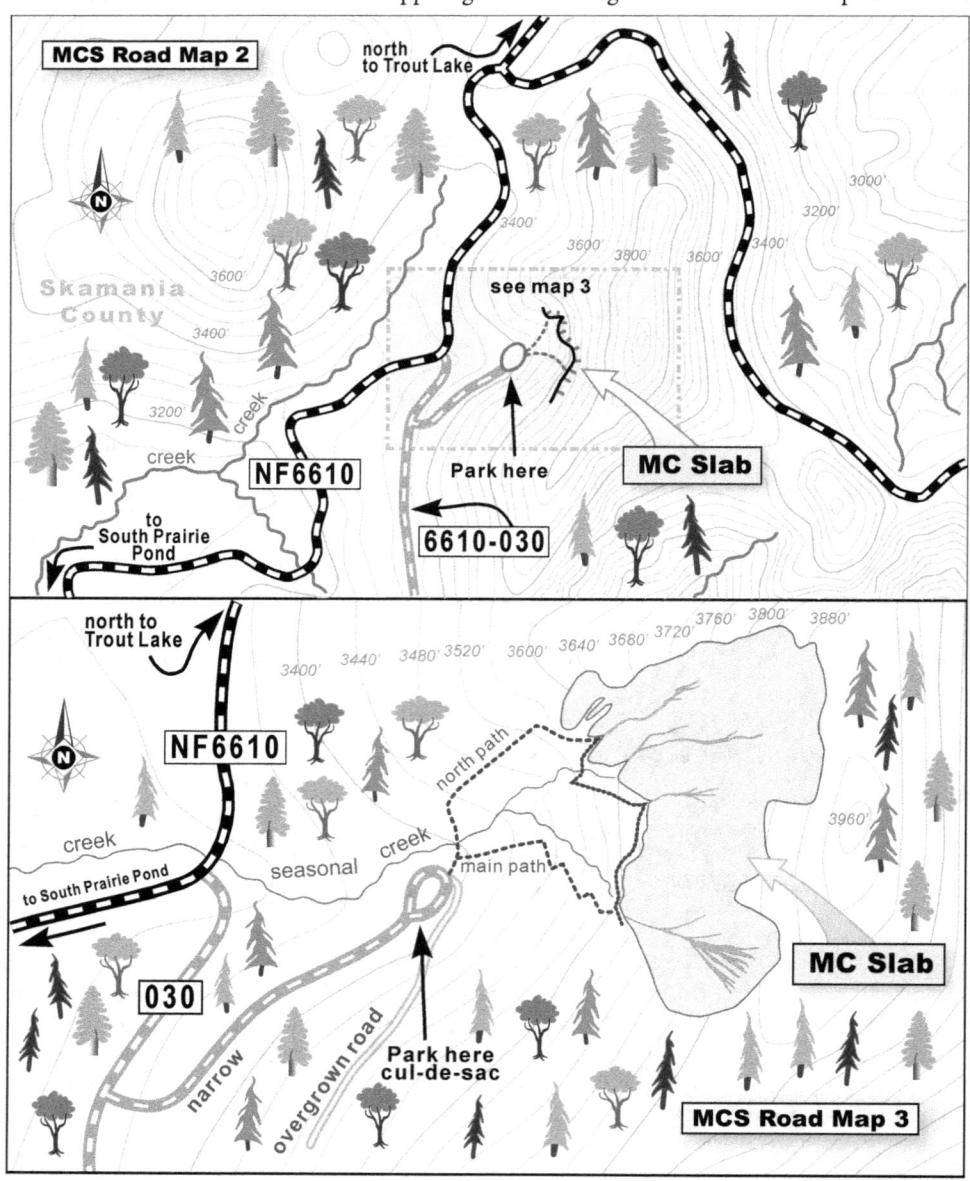

dome headwall. Why not? **1.)** Because other climbers will likely be climbing on a route directly below or next to you, or perhaps even starting on the route you just finished (you cannot see them from above). **2.)** When you rappel your knot will get snagged on a bolt hanger on the upper part of the wall and you will have a hernia trying to unsnag it. **3.)** To pull down 200' of rope on a rounded slab lets the rope snag every little pebble. **4.)** The rope may get entangled with another nearby climber and cause an incident. **5.)** Its very difficult to pull two ropes across 200' of rounded slab. **6.)** Its much faster to walk off.

So, coil up your rope and walk off south (or north) to the 4th class descent water runnels. Both walk-off options are steep yet fairly basic (provided you don't slide). Or, use one of the specifically arranged 100' rappel stations descent methods explained in the beta section.

Gear Needs, and Other Site Awareness Factors

Bring just quick-draws (or expandable loop quick-draws) because there are no cracks on the entire wall (leave all your stoppers and cam devices at home).

A 60-meter rope works for most routes, but the lead length of two routes require a 70-meter rope. A few routes are a bit over 60-meters in length (about 204' long), but can still be done with a 60-m rope provided the leader knows that when reaching the belay anchor they should tie in with a sling or daisy chain. The first six routes on the South Dome area are best ascended with a 70-meter rope.

If it begins to rain heavily while you are rock climbing, stop immediately and lower off from the nearest bolt hanger (or from the nearest belay station). The diorite slab can become slick very quickly during rainstorms, and the common 4th class walk-off descent methods may not be an option, so when need use the ER's near the Dark Streak.

If you are unfamiliar with slab climbing technique and its your first 1-3 visits, try not to get too bold on lead. Learn some foot smearing methodology on high-angle friction first before tackling a bold lead. If we all lived in the land of granite this would not be a lesson to relearn.

If you skate or grease off a slab while on lead you will slide and scrape your way down below your previously clipped bolt so perhaps long pants might be beneficial in this instance. Since bolts are 9' to 25' apart its best to build up your smear leading confidence gradually.

Technically speaking, there are no R/X rated lead climbs at MCS, though this parameter is based entirely on logical anticipatory preparation factors and skill level in dealing with slab climbing technique, which is all foot technique and not finger crimping. Some routes may still feel bold, but most crux sections are well protected. When the terrain angle eases on the upper portions of many longer routes, the bolt spacing increases to usually 15'-25' apart as the grade difficulty eases.

There are several sections (see diagram) at the top of the slab with some square-ish flat stones (2"-6") in diameter lay scattered along the edge of the forest. Do not drag the rope through these areas. A helmet may be beneficial when leading or belaying. If you accidentally dislodge any rocks while at the top of the crag, let us know you did something dumb, and yell loudly to any persons at the base of the slab. Due to the rounded curvature of the steep slab a tumbling stone may take perhaps 3-5 seconds to reach the bottom of the cliff, hopefully enough time for others to react quickly. Much of the slab is

Lisa Rust climbing Uluru

generally void of loose material, though the slab has some loose 1" flat rock chips that exfoliate a bit seasonally (typical of granitic rock).

The black lichen (mostly at the top of the slab) and the minor areas of moss can become very slick during rainstorms, and on cold October days (when the humidity is high), so use caution.

Etiquette

Friendly climber social interaction is indispensable here at MCS, primarily because communication helps each climbing team to coordinate its next climbing route goal, especially if a plethora of teams are actively climbing on the same day.

There is no poison oak, no ticks, no nearby water source (the ravine dries out quickly), and no cell phone reception. Car camping exists along NF 66 road at several fee based campgrounds with water and toilets. There are plenty of pullouts along various nearby gravel roads for free overnight car camping. Avoid car camping at the turn-around loop (limited space for vehicles). Refrain from setting up campfires at this site, because it's a fire risk with no nearby emergency water to put it out.

Parking space is limited, so plan to carpool. Park your vehicle so as to allow enough space for other vehicles to use the turn-around loop, too. There is minimal space for about 7-9 vehicles at the turn-around loop. Consider limiting your total group team size to 1-15 persons. Instructional guiding, commercial, clubs, and organization activities in this Forest Service district are permit regulated. Some advisory recommendations within the stewardship framework promote effectual continuity goals.

At present, the open square footage maneuvering space along the cliff base is narrow due to the encroaching brush thicket. There are 3-4 common spots along the cliff base where climber's tend to congregate and most of those are quite small (its more like rubbing shoulders in an escalator). The entire length of the cliff base is mostly a thicket of dense brush which makes it difficult for human or dog to step off the path to go potty pooh. So, the answer should be obvious (i.e. not on the path). Walk away from the cliff base a fair distance if you need to find a pooh spot. Consider leaving your pet at home. If you bring it here keep it fully controlled (e.g. leashed). Do not leave non-degradable trash strewn along the base of the crag.

Seasonal Factors

The MCS is generally accessible from late-May through late-October. Hot mid-summer temperatures can be a challenge, especially when the temperature reaches 90°F (or higher) in Portland, which is about 80°F at MCS. During July and August, when

Laila climbing *Bronze Whale*

there is little or no breeze, its best to get there early and climb until it gets too hot. On hot summer days (1-4pm) when the afternoon sun is directly facing the slab it can be unbearably sultry along the base of the crag. Some tall trees and minor shrubs grow along various parts of the slab base providing some shade (not at the North Landing or Middle Landing). During the summer months most west side rain systems forecasting 40% rain simply do not effect the crag much, primarily because of its slightly easterly locale in the high Cascades Range.

In early May and late October the slab can be damp with morning dew, or it may be damp with narrow water seeps all day, especially when the weather remains cool and cloudy, or had recent rainfall, or is well below 60°F at the slab. Shaded portions of the rock slab tend to remain damp during this part of the season making certain routes unclimbable. In summation, heavy rains in Spring or Fall season, excessive dew, and high humidity will effect the climbing options.

Limitations

Leave the power drill at home; all the hard work is done, and all the routes are developed. Do not strive to 'squeeze job' climbs between the existing climbs. The present routes are identifiable as lead routes, because of the slight separation (a factor lost through further condensing).

Though some of the routes may start a bit wider at the base of the slab, when a set of climbs reach the top of the slab they tend to get much closer together, primarily because the climbable portions of the slab have a dome-shaped aspect (like the top of an egg). Even smaller portions of the slab have additional mini dome-shaped curvatures, such as the first ½ dozen routes at the south end, and the string of routes on the 2nd, 3rd and 4th rock lobe at the north end. Some routes meet at the same belay station (varies from 1-4 routes per belay).

Most of the routes follow some form of natural nuance, be it a series of natural pockets, a fat rib, or a skinny water runnel. These characteristics give the route its sense of natural flow and intrinsic value. This goal enhances the leading experience without a potential tangle of grid pattern bolt lines that loose the essence of each routes characteristic qualities.

Stewardship at MCS

The view from atop the slab provides a stellar

Steve, Hugh, and friends climbing at MCS

captivating scene of distant Lemei Rock in Indian Heaven, the South Prairie Pond, the Big Lava Bed, Huckleberry Mtn., and (on a lucky day) very compelling peaceful silence, all wrapped in an extensive fir forest. Its thoroughly rewarding just to rock climb up to the top of the slab to sit and partake of the vast scenic beauty. Visit and enjoy the rock climbing here and experience the unique qualities and value of this Washington state natural resource.

Stewardship ideals emphasize user group diversification options, site maintenance needs through organized efforts, anchor program, and other practical site recreation goals.

MCS site stewardship ethical continuity ideals are coordinated through an advisory committee that works with various regional entities. MCS primary development phase is through the efforts of Mr O & Mr B (plus positive effort by friends). See the MCS CCA page for stewardship and general climbing info. Ethically based stewardship brings value, incentive and inherent harmonious quality toward use of this crag. Enjoy the serene experience and enjoy the climbing.

Rock Structural Characteristics

MCS is geologically known as Miocene Intrusive Diorite (Mid) of a granitic stock family with medium-grained dark minerals (1-5mm), lacking quartz minerals, roughly a porphyritic pyroxene diorite. The entire structure is likely the top exposed portion of intrusive diorite stock, formed originally as a subsurface congealed marginal portion of magma stock from a larger, deeper diorite mass. The west-facing exposure of the slab likely reached its present visibility when the upper layers of softer detritus materials eroded away, or possibly when the surrounding slopes abrupt-

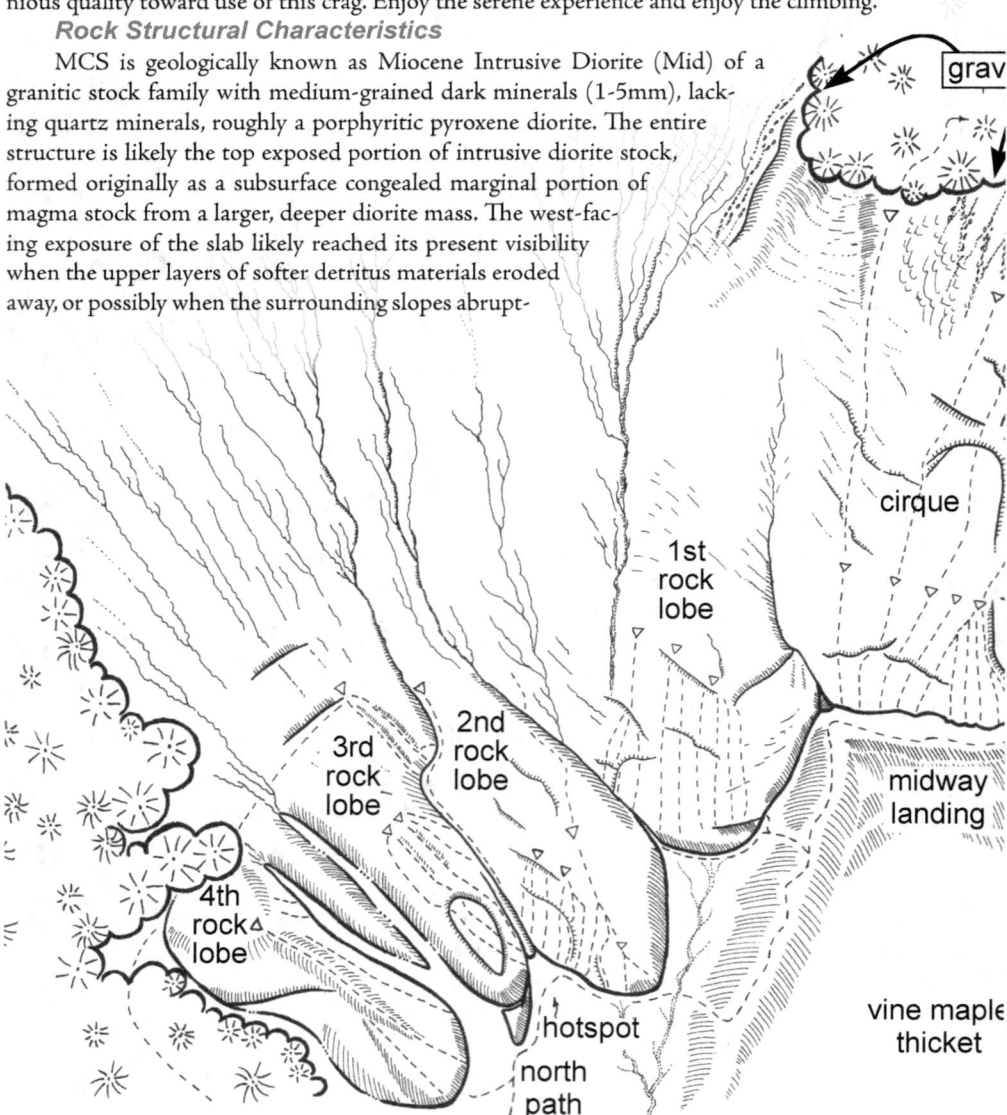

ly sloughed off downhill westward sometime in the past millennium.

The northern portion (with the lowest angle) of MCS shows very distinct heavy snow loading and avalanche impaction features, mainly long scratch lines (top down), a total lack of moss, and sections of unusually smooth surface rock where the natural rock curves were partially scoured for 200'+ down the slab. These factors match similar characteristics as those found on worn rock surfaces below various glaciers.

Several basic geographical observations for the MCS site are: elevation at the lowest point (3rd

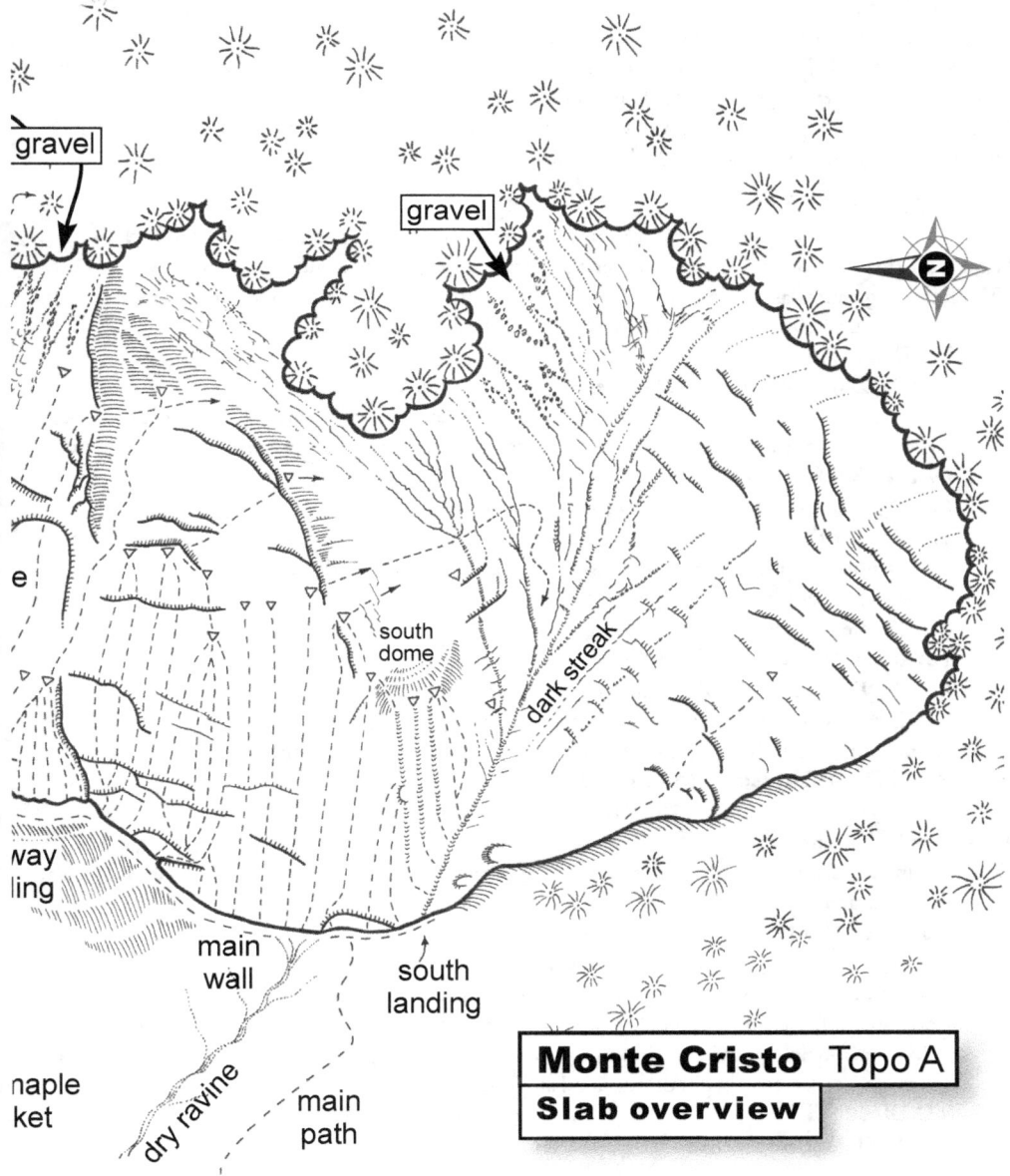

lobe) 3518'; elevation at the highest point (upper northeast end) 3818'; vertical height of slab: 300'; length (south to north): 815'; width at angle (top to bottom): about 510'.

The GPS (via GE [*see Introduction*]) geographical quadrangle coordinates are: UTM 10T 603653 5086444.

MC SLAB BETA

Beta is described from right (South End) to left (North End).

Dark Water Streak 4th class, descent groove, length: 250'

The standard 4th class descent route. This is a dark water stained runnel at the south end of the slab. This water stained groove can be quite slick in early or late season, and after rainstorms. At those times it may be unnegotiable or tricky to descend. A series of three 100' long assistance or emergency rappel (ER) stations exist on the immediate left side of this dark stained water streak, just in case you get caught up topside in a rain shower, or if you are uncomfortable with steep 4th class down smearing descents. To the far right of the Dark Water Streak is a basic **Beginner's Route** on a very low angle slab (5.0-*ish*) that has one 100' lead.

SOUTH DOME

To the left of the Dark Water Streak is a subtle yet broadly rounded dome shaped rock formation with three subtle and slightly darkened water streak grooves trending down its west aspect. The following routes ascend this rounded dome formation. A 70-meter rope is recommended for these routes, but a 60-meter rope is feasible in a pinch if you tie an end knot.

1. **My DNA 5.4**
   Pro: 9 QD's, Length: 110' (70-meter rope recommended)'
   A fun variation next to the dark water streak. Start up the initial part of Outback BBQ, then angle up right at the third bolt to climb up a set of giant steps (6 more bolts) to a belay station.

2. **Outback BBQ 5.4**
   Pro: 8 QD's, Length: 105' (70-meter rope recommended)
   This route is the first primary route left of the Dark Streak. It is a low angle smear run that steepens on its upper portion as it ascends a set of large rounded steps.

   Three Narrow Water Streak Grooves
   Each of the next three routes cruise up a set of three narrow water streak grooves all in a row.

3. **Tor the Hairy One 5.5 ★★**
   Pro: 9 QD's, Length: 105' (70-meter rope recommended)
   This is the right thin water groove. Initially ascend a low angle slab that steepens for its upper portion, generally utilizing the right edge of the groove. Mostly rounded sloping edges.

4. **Blind Deaf Old Goat (aka BDOG) 5.5 ★★**
   Pro: 9 QD's, Length: 105' (70-meter rope recommended)
   This is the center thin water groove. From a big fat natural bowl smear up low angle terrain passing a minor crux on the steeper upper portion. Mostly rounded sloping edges, but with good characteristics and quality.

5. **Count of Monte Cristo 5.6 ★★**
   Pro: 8 QD's, Length: 110' (70-meter rope recommended)
   A good quality climb ascending the leftmost of three water grooves. From a big fat natural scoop step left to a bolt, then climb directly up on low angle smears. A large round natural bowl at mid-height is the transition point where the low angle smears end and the high angle dancing smears (crux) begin on rounded slopers.

6. **MC Direct 5.7**
   Pro: 10 QD's, Length: 135'
   A brief tricky direct start initial crux move using steeply sloped rounded pockets and smears.

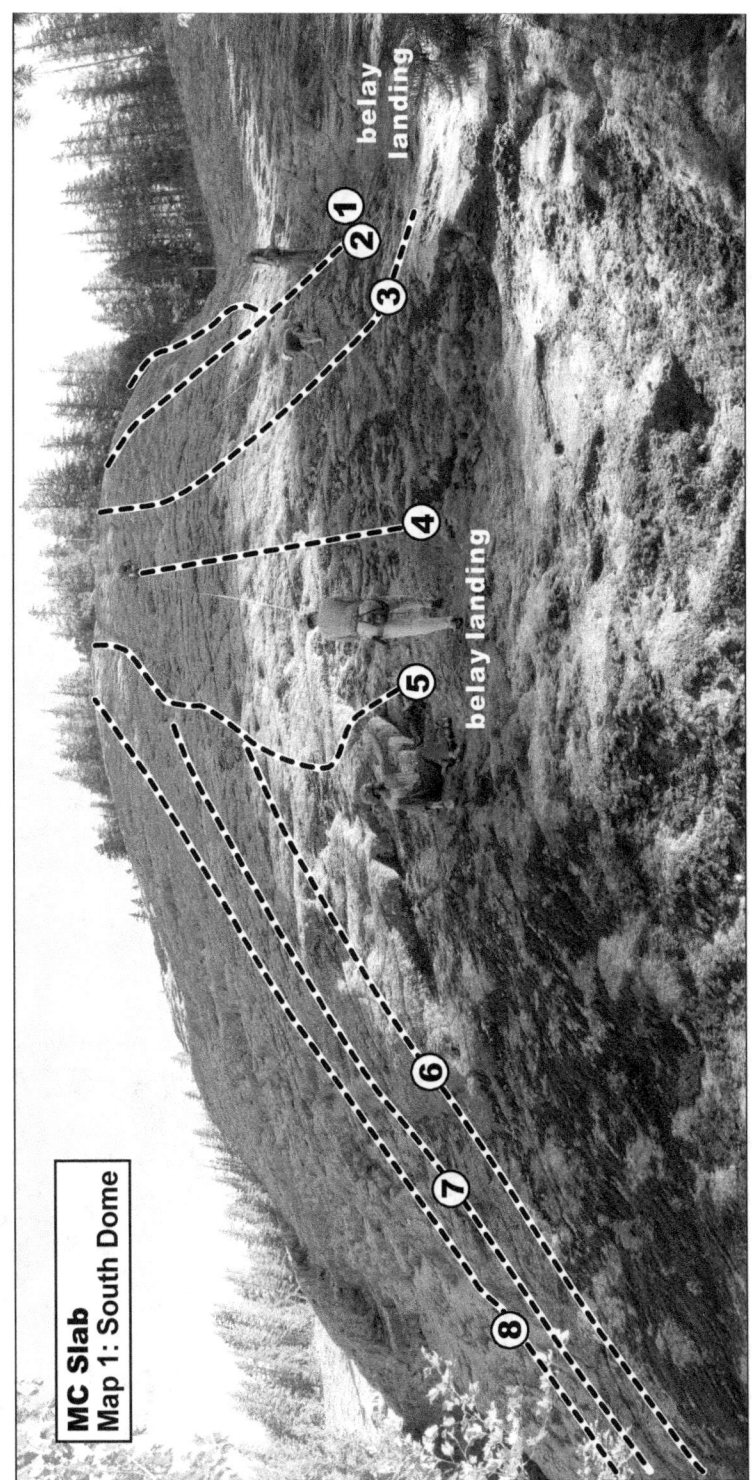

A high step puts you onto a round stance, then dash up easier terrain following a string of bolts. This direct start route merges at the large round natural bowl at mid-height into the Count of Monte Cristo.

MAIN WALL OF SOUTH DOME

From the little nook northward is a 40' wide, near vertical sweep of slab that offers a good string of powerful direct starts to all the long routes on the headwall.

Little Nook

A slightly overhung section of rock creates a minor 15' wide nook with a narrow gravel landing. The left side has a sloped step start (Uluru), and the overhung bulge to the right is the route Iceberg In A Sauna. The main climber's path from the parking spot to the crag lands here, too.

7. **Iceberg in a Sauna 5.8 ★**
Pro: 11 QD's, Length: 145'
Surmount up out of the little nook over a slightly hung odd crux bulge, then dance up a low angle slab. The route merges rightward into Monte Cristo at mid-height.

8. **Uluru 5.6 ★★★**
Pro: 14 QD's, Length: 145'
A superb climb. Though it has no specific crux move, the climb is a long series of sloping smears lacking prominent jugs. Begin at the left side of the overhung nook by stepping up a sloped step (bolt), reach over the lip to a jug, then from the second bolt continue straight up, past another minor rounded step, then up a long long flat face with thin techy sloped smears (160' to first belay). **Pitch 2:** Climb up (5.0) another 30' to another belay station then walk off south to the 4th class Dark Streak descent water runnel to descend.

9. **Silence the Serenity 5.10a [5.6] ★★★**
Specs: 5.10a (crux start), max 5.6 on upper ¾ route
Pro: 17 QD's, Length: 200'
Immediately left of the small nook a few feet is a very steep slab. The start dances up thin crux (5.10a) smears past a rounded bulge before easing at the 3rd bolt. The remainder of the route is a great little fun run traveling directly up the wall. Climbs various prominent ramps, scoops, small dishes, a brief thin smear-fest, then as the terrain eases it travels up easy 5.0 terrain to a belay anchor. Walk southward to the Dark Streak to descend.

10. **Sunday's Best 5.11a [5.6] ★★**
Specs: 5.11a (crux start) and max 5.6 upper ¾ route
Pro: 16 QD's, Length 200'
A thin tricky crux start smear problem that eases to a sloped ramp. Continue past a series of four closely spaced bolts, then cruise on high angle terrain using smears and rounded pockets. The terrain eases as you reach the upper belay anchor at a rounded low angle crest. Though a mid-belay exists on this particular route it is far more enjoyable to do the entire climb in one very long lead. Walk south to the Dark Streak to descend.

11. **Eternity 5.11a [5.8] ★**
Specs: 5.11a (crux start), max

Bob Murphy leading *Uluru*

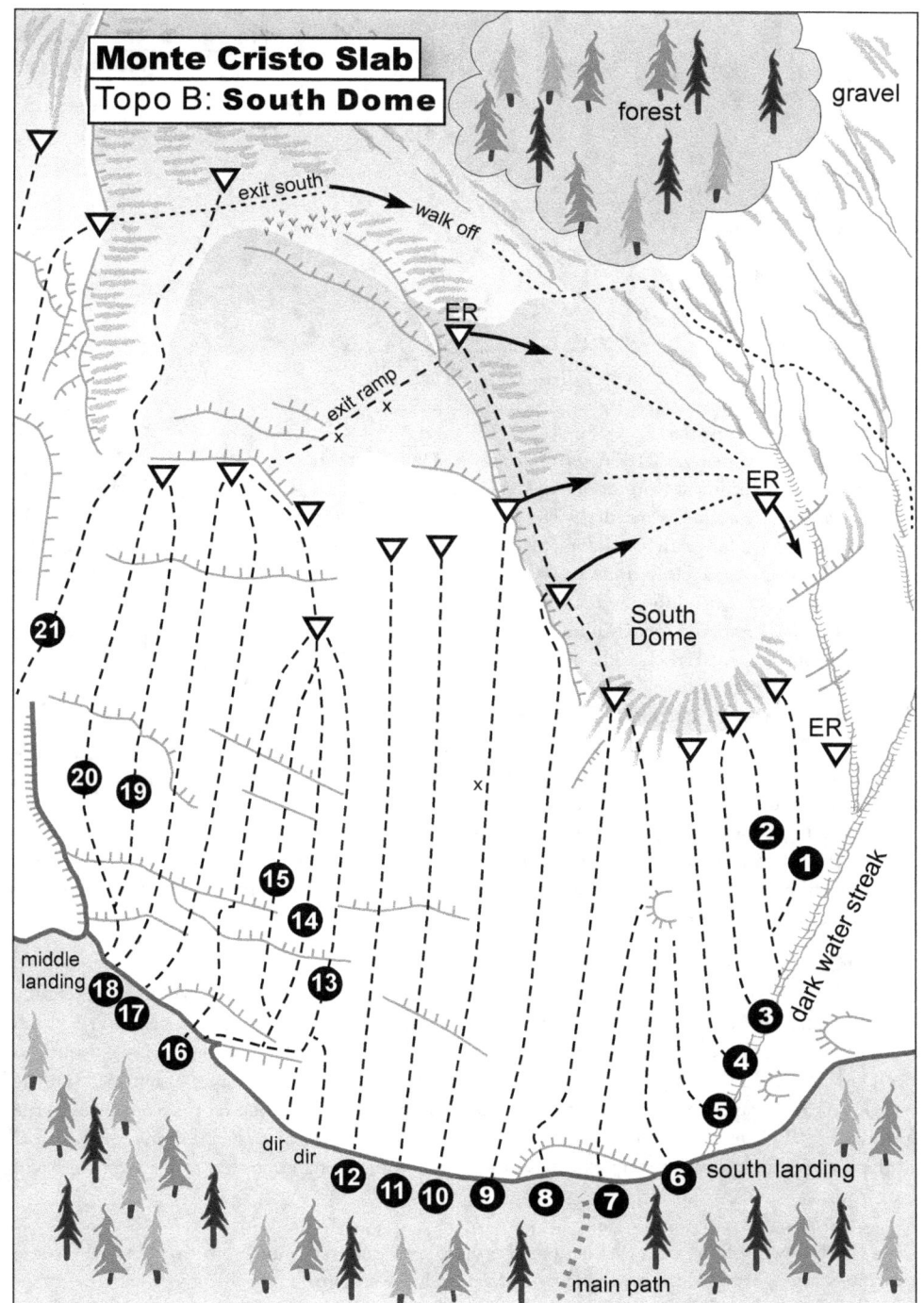

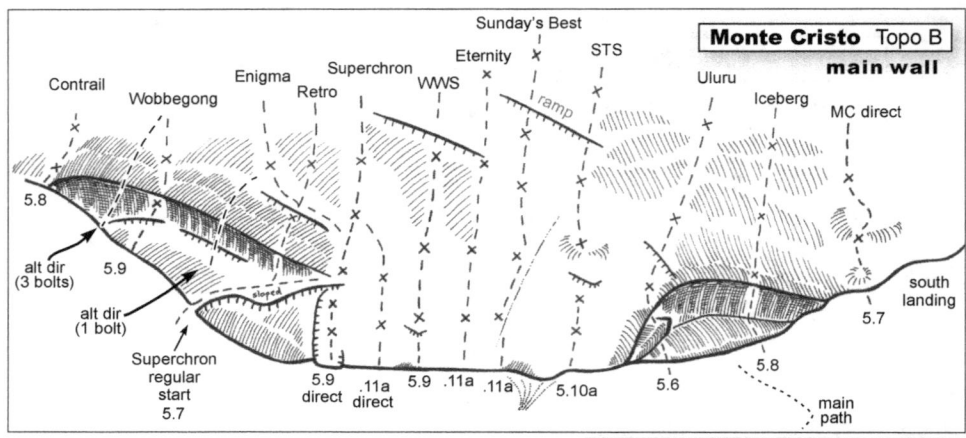

5.8 on upper ¾ route
Pro: 17 QD's, Length: 210' (70m rope required)
Power up a technical thin face (crux). As the terrain eases, dash up a short ways till the face steepens again. Continue up a long run of moderate (5.7-ish) smears, small scoops, and face climbing. When the terrain eases, dash up to an independent belay station. Belay here, then climb rightward to another belay anchor on a rounded crest, then walk off south to the Dark Streak water runnel.

12. Walk on the Wild Side 5.9 ★★★
Pro: 17 QD's, Length 210' (70m rope required)
A fun initial steep crux start using an incut crimp, then the angle eases briefly. When it steepens again continue up a long steep portion (5.7-ish) using smears and edges. The upper part of the route eases and ends at an independent belay station (at same level as Eternity belay). Belay here, then climb rightward to another belay anchor on a rounded crest, then walk off south to the Dark Streak water runnel.

TRIPLE BELAY STATION LEDGE SYSTEM
Several options for topping out from the broad triple belay ledge system. **1.**) Exit horizontally right (2 bolts, 5.0, 30') to another belay station, then walk south down Dark Water Streak. **2.**) Or... from the leftmost belay, ascend 50' uphill (5.0 terrain) to another belay anchor, then walk south to the Dark Water Streak. **3.**) Or...rappel from the leftmost belay station, down exactly 95' (tie the ends) to another rappel station (next to the Midway Landing belays), then rappel from there to the ground (95'). See introduction notes for why its best not to rappel down the 200' long routes. Most of the routes that land at the triple belay stations are a rope stretcher, in that a 60-meter rope will barely work.

Multiple Route Belay
The following four routes all land at the same 190' belay station. From this belay the route continues briefly upward to the Triple Belay Station ledge system.

13. Superchron 5.7 ★★★
Pro: 13 QD's standard sloped ramp start, Length: 190'
A very good route. **Pitch 1:** Begin by traversing rightward out a sloped ramp for 15' to a nar-

row stance (bolt), then make a delicate crux smear move and dash up easier slab smears till the wall steepens, then ascend a series of steep wavy undulations. As the terrain eases on the last part of the lead expect healthy runout on 5.0-*ish* terrain till you reach a multi-route belay station. **Pitch 2:** From this belay continue up leftward on low angle 5.0-*ish* terrain (1 bolt) till you reach a flat broad ledge system with three belay stations.

Superchron Direct Start #1: Minor 2-bolt 5.9 direct start exists for this climb which powers up a brief round nose of rock merging into the standard route at a small stance. You will need 2 extra QD's for this variation.

Superchron Direct Start #2: A minor 2-bolt 5.11a direct start exists for this same route. Initial technical crux moves that quickly morphs left into the standard route at the small stance. You will need 2 extra QD's for this variation.

14. Retro Cognition 5.7 ★★★
Pro: 11 QD's, Length: 190'
A superb route! Begin at a sloped ramp (same as Superchron). Surmount a vertical crux step (thin flake crimp), then smear up easy slab. The route steepens again as it travels up various sloped edges and holds. As the route eases to a lower angle, it surmounts one last short step, then eases to 5.0-*ish* terrain (spaced out bolts) ending at a multi-route belay station. **Pitch 2:** continue up left (1 bolt) on easy 5.0-*ish* terrain 30' to another belay anchor. This is the triple belay anchor ledge system.

15. Enigma 5.9 ★
Pro: 11 QD's, Length: 190'
The starting point is the same as the previous route. After the initial flake move, smear left, then up easy slab smear terrain to a near vertical face. Climb this near vertical face and at the upper lip (5.9 crux) slide sideways to the right (odd moves). Once past that continue up easier terrain till you dance up a long smooth slab (5.8). A final 3' high rounded lip is surmounted, then continue up easier runout sections till you reach a belay station at 190' (multi-route belay station). **Pitch 2:** continue up left (1 bolt) till you reach the triple belay anchors on a broad ledge system.

16. Wobbegong 5.9 ★★★
Pro: 13 QD's: Length: 190'
One of the classic routes at the crag with variety and techy movement. Commence the journey by surmounting an initial vertical 5' tall step (5.6), then dash up a long low angle slab to a steep near vertical cliff face. Ascend a crux section of technical movement using various rounded crimps, slopers and thin rounded finger pockets. Move right under a big lip, and surmount this at a big fat rounded pocket (crux). Then smear up a long flat steep face (5.8) till this eases to lower angle terrain. Dash up rightward slightly on healthy runout easy terrain to a multi-route belay station. **Pitch 2:** continue up left (1 bolt) till you reach the triple belay anchors on a broad ledge system.

17. Contrail Conspiracy 5.8 ★★★
Pro: 14 QD's, Length: 202'
A superb classic route with plenty of unique variety, certainly one of the best routes here. Start at an initial steep move (or skip the first bolt) then

Family day at *MCS South Dome*

dash up an easy low angle slab till the cliff steepens to near vertical. Ascend steep delicate movement (crux section) passing a brief lip landing on a stance. Then up a long steep smooth smear slab (crux) which eases quickly when you get past the next minor rounded lip. Continue to dash up considerable low angle slab terrain till you reach the triple belay station on a broad flat ledge system.

18. Indian Summer 5.8 ★★

Pro: 11 QD's, Length: 202' (a stretch for 60m)

Cruise up a low angle slab, surmount a step, then ascend a tall crux section utilizing various sloped edges. At about 100' the terrain eases to low 5th class ending at the triple belay station ledge system.

19. Sky's the Limit 5.10b

Pro: 11 QD's, Length: 202' (a stretch for 60m)

This climb is located where the base trail levels off just below a prominent ravine system. Two climbs utilize the same initial crux bolt at a short lip bulge. Dash up low angle terrain, surmount a minor lip bulge, and dash up more low angle terrain to the rightmost set of bolts on a vertical section of rock. Surmount this dicey vertical crux lip, then ascend a fun steep slab section to a second dicey vertical foot smear lip crux. The slab terrain eases for many meters eventually landing at the triple belay station on a broad flat ledge system.

20. Griddle Cakes 5.7 ★

Pro: 11 QD's, Length: 202' (a stretch for 60m)

Same starting point as the previous route. Commence up low angle terrain, surmount a minor lip bulge, and dash up more low angle terrain to the leftmost set of bolts on a vertical section of rock. Surmount the vertical crux, then continue up a fun run slab to a second easier rock step. The slab terrain eases for many meters eventually landing at the triple belay station on a broad flat ledge system.

Center Ravine Rappel

A prominent 100' tall deeply cut stepped ravine (rated 5.3) slices the central portion of this wall. To the right of it lay the steep main wall of the south dome. To the left of this ravine is an initial nose-shaped prow, then a long swath of friendly easy low angle slab climbs all situated at the flat sunny Middle Landing.

It is fairly common to rappel from the left belay anchor on the triple belay station ledge system, down 100' to another specifically setup rappel station on a terrace (next to the five other belays that serve the Middle Landing lower routes). From there, rappel again down the ravine 100' to the ground. Beware of climber's below. The rightmost rappel is designed to send you conveniently down the ravine system. Use the rightmost specific rappel whenever the other popular belays to the left are being used.

MIDDLE LANDING (AKA PLAY PALACE)

This wide flat terraced area offers qualitative variety, plenty of 90'-100' leads at a low angle slab with ratings ranging from 5.3 to 5.8 difficulty with some long second pitch leads. This section has some fine thrills that fit a virtual novice lead or top-rope repertoire. Even the old guys enjoy these climbs. There are five belay stations at the 90' mark to allow convenient top-roping for beginner level climbers.

21. Cosmic Journey 5.3 ★★

Pro/length: P1 6 QD's (100' 5.3), P2 9 QD's (140' 5.3)

A prominent quality prow route. **Pitch 1:** Commence up an obvious steep prow using various steps and edges. The prow rounds off to an easier angle for the last 25' to the belay station. **Pitch 2:** Let the fun continue by climbing directly above the belay on a subtle rounded buttress (20' runouts) for 180' (passing by the famous triple belay station on your right). The last

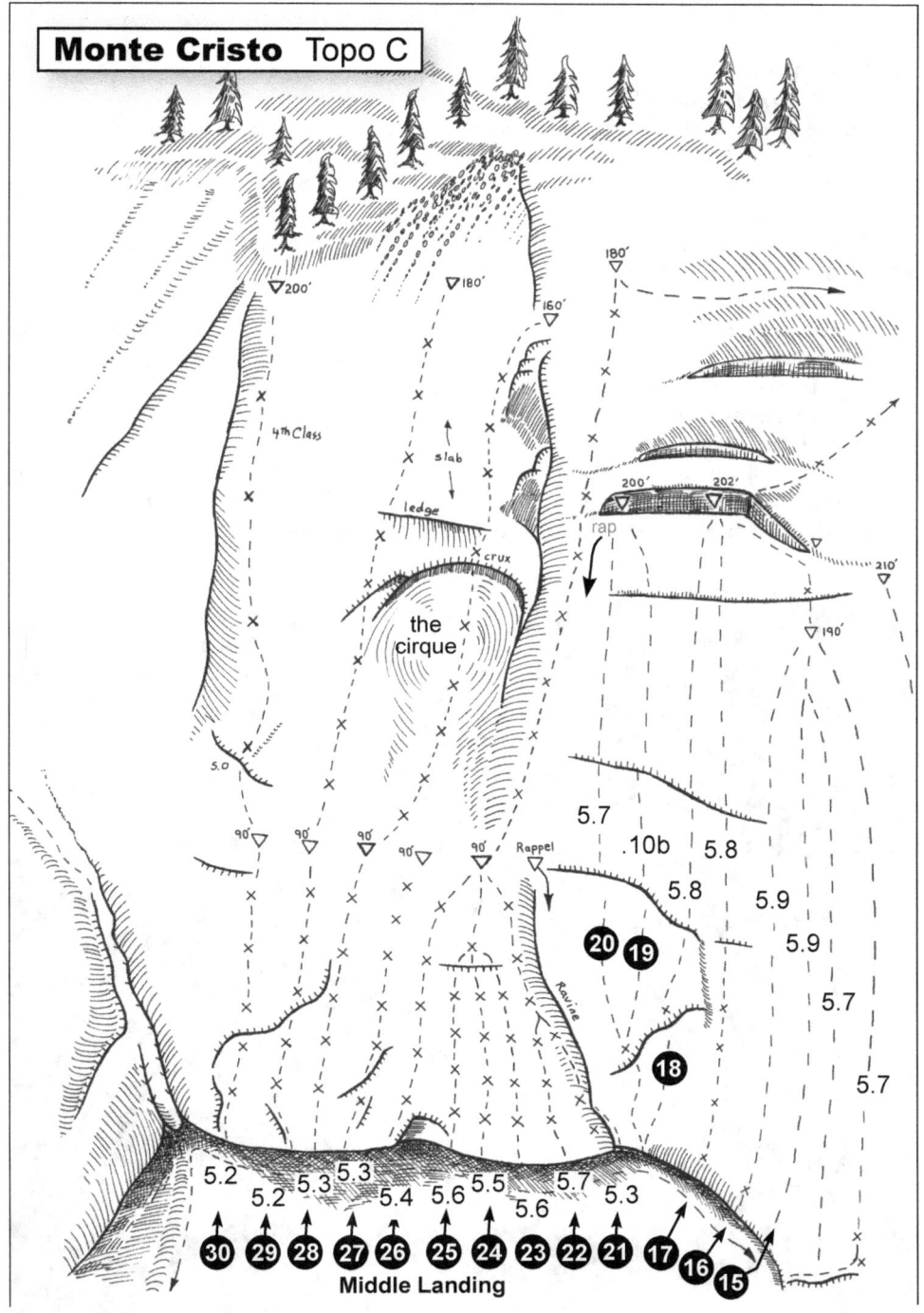

40' crosses easy 4th class terrain. From the last belay anchor, walk south and descend the Dark Streak water runnel.

22. Inukshuk 5.7
Pro: 7 QD's, Length: 95'
The opening move is the crux, then some minor smears up near vertical terrain till it merges onto the prow. Finish dancing up the arête to the belay station (same as the previous route).

23. Global Warming 5.6
Pro: 6 QD's, 95'
A nice moderately steep slab route that eases onto flat terrain near the belay station.

24. Raging Sea 5.5 ★
Pro: 6 QD's, Length: 95'
Climb steep steps on a slab passing a crux section (easier on the right side of crux bolt). The fifth bolt is shared with the route to the left. After passing that bolt you land on a wide low angle ledge system (bolt). Continue 30' more to a belay station used by the previous route.

25. Hammerhead Shark 5.6 ★★
Pro: 6 QD's, Length: 90'
A great climb. Start on a steep section of face, smear past a brief crux section, continue up moderate angled slopers till it merges at the fifth bolt, then lands on a wide ledge system (bolt). Continue 30' more to a belay station used by the previous route.

MC Slab
Map 2: Midway Landing

26. Bronze Whale 5.4 ★★★
Pro: 5 QD's, Length: 90'
A superb easy climb. Start at a slight vertical nook using smears on the left. Continue up a long series of sloped smears till the route eases onto the wide ledge system (bolt). Continue 30' more to a belay station used by the previous route.

27. Black Raven 5.3 ★★
Pro: 6 QD's, Length: 90'
Start up a minor left facing corner on a very low angle slab, then up a series of steep giant steps. When it eases onto a fat wide ledge system, continue up easier slab (bolt) terrain to a belay station.

28. Crooked Finger 5.3 (P2 5.7) ★
Pro/length: P1 5 QD's (90'), P2 9 QD's (160')
A fun run for beginner climbers on the first pitch. The unique second pitch ascends up into a broad rounded scooped out vertical sided rock cirque, but that lead is best for a climber who can deal with an odd crux lip bulge mantle.
Pitch 1: Begin up a very low angle slab, power through a brief steeper section (crux), then up easier low angle terrain to a belay station. **Pitch 2:** Continue up slightly right (bolts) aiming into the center of the rock cirque. When you reach the center bulge in the cirque, surmount the stout lip (5.7 crux) and move up to a flat landing. Continue up a nice low angle clean slab and when the terrain becomes a series of steps angle right to a belay station. Walk off south to the Dark Streak descent runnel.

29. Broken Hand 5.2 (P2 5.1) ★
Pro/length: P1 5 QD's (90'), P2 9 QD's (180')
A fun basic climb reasonable for virtual beginners. **Pitch 1:** Climb up a short very low angle slab until it steepens (crux), moving up slightly right, then continue directly up to a belay station at 90'. **Pitch 2:** Continue up from the belay on a low angle slab until you reach the left edge of the broad scooped out rock cirque. Continue up past its left edge to a brief flat landing, then dance up a nice smooth slab till the terrain eases near a belay station just below the forest. *Note:* Scattered gravel lay just above this upper belay station so its best not to climb up beyond this anchor station, but to either exit directly right south onto the rounded crest, and continue south to the Dark Streak Streak runnel to descend.

30. Tour de France 5.2 (P2 5.0)
Pro/length: P1 5 QD's (90'), P2 4 QD's (200')
A good beginner climb for the first pitch. The second pitch involves 25' runout sections. **Pitch 1:** Dance up the initial low angle slab to a minor vertical step (crux), then continue up more low angle slab to a belay station. **Pitch 2:** Continue up over a minor small step, and up easier terrain with well spaced 40' runout bolts on 4th class terrain. The final belay station exists just below a prominent single tree on a small black flat ledge. The upper portion of this climb follows a subtle slightly rounded rock knoll.

Note: There are several brief clusters of rock debris scattered along the cliff top (see diagram) just below the forest. Avoid disturbing both clusters of debris if possible. If there are other persons climbing at the Middle Landing it might help to communicate to each other in advance.

FOUR ROCK LOBES
Looking to the north from the end of the Middle Landing you will see four rock prominence's

or rounded rock lobes. This entire remaining northern end of MCS abruptly drops downhill for about 200'. Each rock lobe has a steeper aspect at the lower end of each lobe. Its these steeper aspects that yield a small selection of worthy rock climbs. From the Middle Landing zone walk the forested ridge crest path down hill to reach the next climbable sections. The lobes are described from south to north; the first lobe, the second, a third and then a fourth rock lobe.

FIRST ROCK LOBE

To access the climbs located at the base of the First Rock Lobe descend the trail about 100' then cut in along the base of the lobe. The last three climbs are tucked in a small rock ravine on the left steeper side of the rock lobe. This slab has numerous basic fun routes great for beginner's. Described from right to left:

31. Conscious Haze 5.5 ★★
Pro: 6 QD's, Length: 90'
A quality low angle friction slab ending with a series of large edges in a right-facing corner groove.

32. American Eagle 5.4
Pro: 7 QD's, Length: 90'
A low angle friction slab to a ledge, then delicate smears followed by easier terrain.

33. September Morn 5.3 ★
Pro: 7 QD's, Length: 90'
A series of thin smear moves up into a left-facing corner, then step up right onto easier terrain.

34. Raven's of Odin 5.4 ★★
Pro: 8 QD's, Length: 90'
A nice brief string of thin techy smears on a flat smooth section of the face.

35. Don't Tread On Me 5.2
Pro: 9 QD's, Length: 90'
A fun string of smears and sloped edges, then a steep rounded bulge crux section, which quickly eases as you near the anchor.

Bob M. leading *Seasonal Anxiety*

GORGE ROCK 205

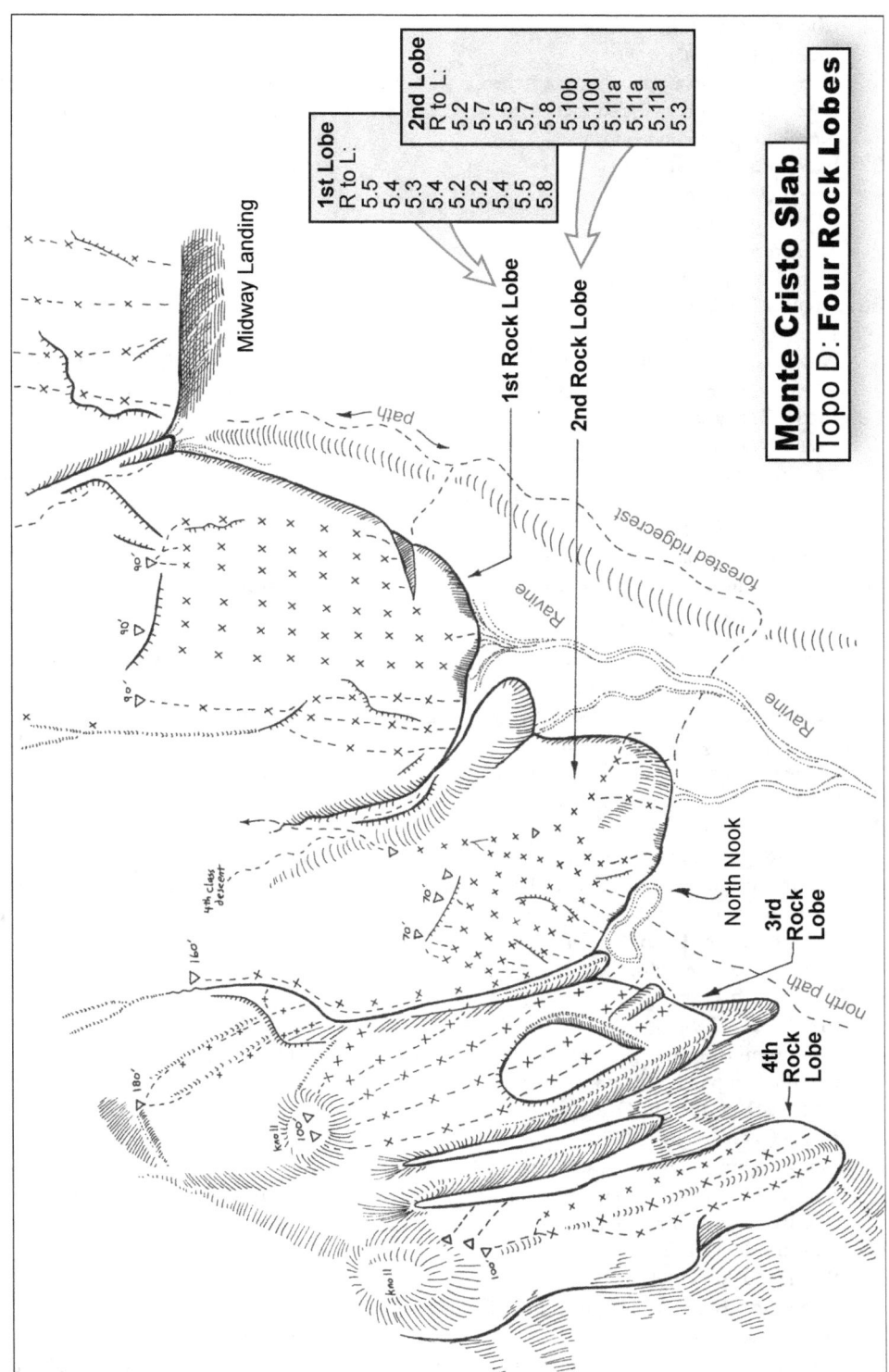

Monte Cristo Slab
Topo D: **Four Rock Lobes**

36. **Live Free or Die 5.2** ★
    Pro: 9 QD's, Length: 90'
    A few moves up a slab, a big step, then a brief smooth section, and a series of nice rounded edges on a minor rounded rock nose formation that eases near the belay anchor. Title is the New Hampshire state motto.

37. **Raven's Revolt 5.4**
    Pro: 5 QD's, Length: 90'
    Climb up a minor slab with smears and small edges, then surmount a 4' tall lip, and cruise easier terrain to a flat stance. Then continue up a narrow dark water stained groove another 25' to a belay station. Rappel.

38. **Crows Feet 5.5** ★
    Pro: 5 QD's, Length: 90'
    Ascend smears and friction along a minor rock rib, then up easier terrain to a flat landing. Then continue up a narrow dark water stained groove another 25' to a belay station. Rappel.

39. **Little Crow 5.8**
    Pro: 4 QD's, Length: 90'
    The crux is a briefly entertaining three pocket smear challenge. After the crux it merges into the route to the right at the flat landing and continues up a steep slab to the belay.

    4TH Class Runnel Descent
    Between the First Rock Lobe and the Second Rock Lobe a low angled 4th class rock groove provides an optional down scramble method to walk down off from certain nearby rock climbs.

SECOND ROCK LOBE

This lobe is the next prominence which juts down slope another 100' lower than the First Lobe and lands in an alder thicket. At the base of the lobes steeper aspect is a nice sandy alcove called the Hotspot or North Nook. A fascinating string of high quality power climbs exist here. Walk a forested ridge crest downhill to the base of this lobe and over to the Hotspot landing. This landing area is often sunny and warm, beneficial on cold October days, but a bit extreme if you are there on a sultry hot day in July. The routes are described from right to left for this lobe.

40. **Beginner's Route 5.2** ★
    Pro: 7-8 QD's (max per lead), Length: about 90' to each belay (multi-pitch)
    A viable beginner's first time lead route. Well bolted, and provides a grand tour of the wall for a beginner. Literally starts at the lowest point at the crag, and ends at the top. For **Pitch 1** (5QD's) 5.3, for **Pitch 2** (5 QD's) 5.0, etc. A very brief 12' long 5.5 direct start is feasible via a smear move to reach the standard 5.2 start.

41. **Quasar 5.7** ★
    Pro: 5 QD's, Length: 90'
    Two prominent small pockets on a steep flat face offer a brief technical climb. The route joins into the first pitch of Beginner's Route.

42. **Redneck Knuckle Draggers 5.5**
    Pro: 5 QD's, Length: 90'
    Waltz up a very low angle left trending groove, then dance up rightward on various shaped small edges and sloped pockets, dance through a thin crux smear move, then join into Beginner's Route at its first belay.

43. **Bullah Bullah 5.7** ★
    Pro: 10 QD's, Length: 100'
    A long slab route utilizing one obvious initial large rounded pocket at the start. Get to the pocket, then move up right to a stance, then up left to a sloped stance and make a skinny crux sequence move. A few more thin easier moves lands you at a nice step. Then continue directly

up the face using a variety of smears and sloped stances till it merges with the 3rd bolt on P2 of the Beginner's Route. Bullah Bullah is Australian the aboriginal name for Butterfly.

44. Silk Road 5.8 ★★
Pro: 4 QD's, Length: 60'
Superb route. Smear past several scoops, then smear holdless terrain using slight nuances, then at the final crux make a tricky move up right (or up left) to merge into either next route.

45. Autumn Gold 5.10b ★★★
Pro: 4 QD's, Length: 60'
This is a superb quality friction smear climb with some sequential techy movement. Commence up into a minor left-facing sickle shaped corner. At the top end of the corner the holds disappear, and the technical smear kicks in (crux) on high angled terrain. Dance your way through the tight moves until you reach easier terrain ending at a belay station.

46. Seasonal Anxiety 5.10d ★★★
Pro: 5 QD's, Length: 60'
The ultra classic gem at the north end of the MCS. High angle friction smears, lacking holds, sustained, mentally energetic, with fascinating yet committing sequential movement.

47. Autumn Joy 5.11a ★★
Pro: 4 QD's, Length: 60'
Another uniquely difficult high angle smear climb. Smear up a brief subtle corner 10', then commit to several very sequential moves. Exit the locked in crux moves carefully.

48. Manic Madness 5.11a ★
Pro: 4 QD's, Length: 60'
A shorter smear climb that begins a few yards up the great white dihedral.

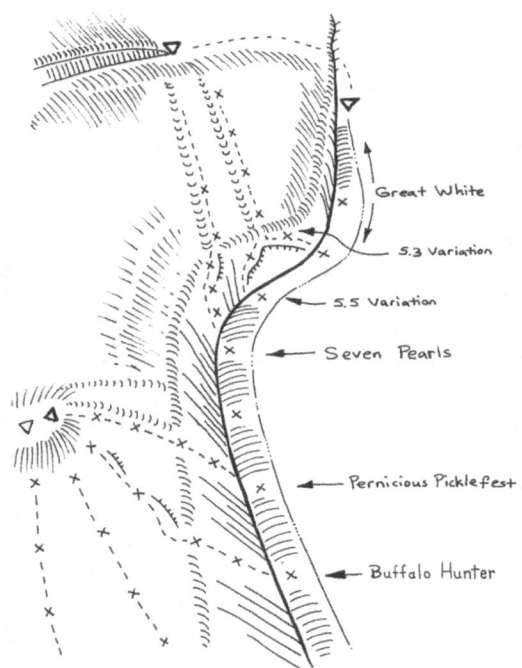

A busy day on *Seasonal Anxiety*

49. **Altered State 5.11a**
   Pro: 3 QD's, Length: 60'
   A brief technical smear-fest on steep terrain.
50. **Great White Book 5.3 ★★★**
   Pro: 8-9 QD's, Length: 160'
   A very prominent, light toned, deep cut corner ramp system that launches upward from a sandy landing zone. Ascend the dihedral passing a minor crumbly section at mid-height. When the left wall of the dihedral meets a steep cove, it angles up right and becomes a nice light colored fat clean ramp system. To descend: **1.**) climb up leftward to another belay station 30' and walk off around the 3rd lobe in the forest; or... **2.**) rappel (single rope) down to one of several anchors near the top of Autumn Joy.

Chuck on Contrail Conspiracy

THIRD ROCK LOBE
The third lobe is a large rounded buttress immediately north of the deeply cut great white dihedral system. The sunny south aspect of this lobe offers steep techy starts that land on a rounded upper slab. A surprisingly extensive string of superb climbs exist on this lobe (some being way up in the main dihedral). The following routes are described from LEFT to RIGHT (lowest to highest) going up the dihedral as if you are facing this lobe while standing at the sandy landing zone.

51. **Forest Fright 5.7 ★**
   Pro: 7 QD's, Length: 100'
   Start on the far left next to a large tree trunk. Step up onto a brief steep face (crux) with sloped holds. You quickly land on a narrow flat ledge facing a big circular donut-shaped amphitheater. Smear up the low angled face to a vertical rock step, surmount the 4' tall step onto a flat landing. Then smear up easier low angled slab to a belay station.
52. **Squatch's Travesty 5.8 ★★★**
   Pro: 7 QD's, Length 100'
   An entertaining climb. Ascend a briefly steep face next to a minor rock column. You will land on a narrow flat ledge facing a big circular donut-shaped amphitheater. Smear up the right portion of the slab, angling rightward. Surmount a minor vertical 4' step onto a flat landing. Smear up a holdless long dark water stained groove to a belay station.
53. **Barramundi in a Billabong 5.9 ★★★**
   Pro: 8 QD's (9 QD's if doing the direct), Length: 100'
   An ultra quality gem. The great dihedral is initially divided into two grooves at the base in the North Nook. This route has 2 starts (the left direct start is 5.9-*ish* while the right start is a tad easier). *Option 1:* The direct variation start climbs a vertical flat face then merges into the regular route at the 4th bolt. *Option 2:* Climb up the left groove past a brief odd move. Just before a bush step up left onto a steep vertical face, and make a high step exit left onto a stance. Two rounded bulges create two crux friction smear sections. After these bulges proceed up a long dark stained subtle water runnel on a steep holdless friction slab. The route ends on a broad rounded clean rock knoll with several belay stations.
54. **Buffalo Hunter 5.10c**
   Pro: 7 QD's, Length: 100'
   Not your casual affair, certainly bizarre, but if you like this kind of stuff, get 'er done. Climb up the dihedral about 30', then step left to the vertical face (bolt). A vertical face has a minor left leaning rail 1" wide. Use a vertical outer fin of a column, layback up, grab an incut (and clip the chain 'biner). Then, a delicate smear kissing moving to stand fully up (use a locking

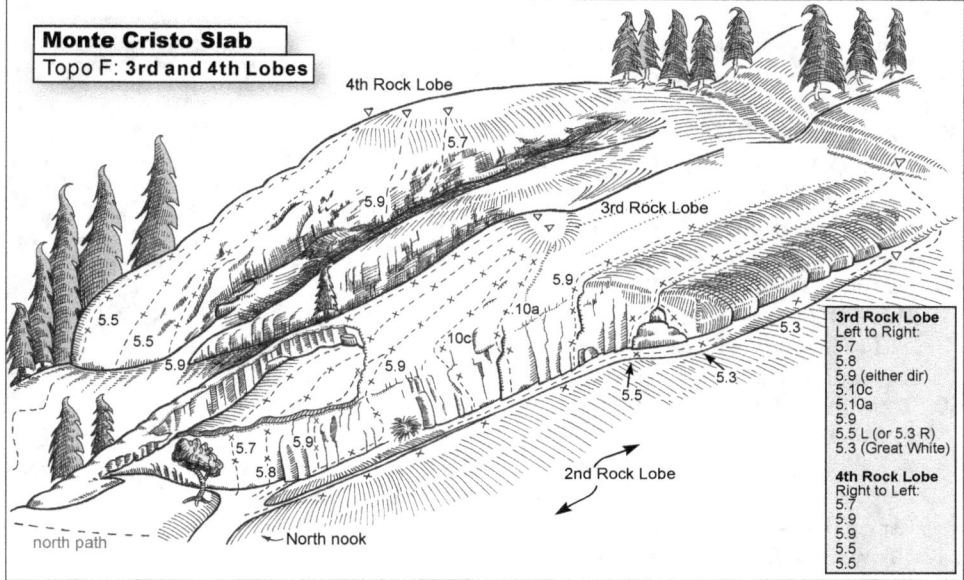

carabiner here). Move left, make the technical crux exit move up onto a steeply sloped stance. Gingerly ascend a series of steeply sloped steps to the belay station on the rounded rock knoll. *Note:* use a locking carabiner on the crux bolt hanger (not on the chain), and don't blow the clip (or you might kiss the slab).

55. Pernicious Picklefest 5.10a
Pro: 8 QD's, Length: 100'
Another odd climb. Dash up the easy dihedral about 40', then step left to the vertical face (bolt). You will be standing below a vertical dark corner system. Layback up to catch an incut, muscle onto a tight stance in the corner, then exit up right to catch an incut wedged block (quite hollow). Another very steep cruxy move to a stance, then more steep, sloped terrain that keeps you focused all the way to the rounded rock knoll belay station. Rappel. (Note: pull downward, not outward on the hollow block).

56. Seven Pearls 5.9 ★
Pro: 11 QD's, Length: 180'
An intriguing climb situated at the dark vertical headwall about ⅔ way up the dihedral. Dash up the dihedral to the ⅔ point, then layback up the incut angled ledges (crux) till the angle rounds off into a long low angle water channel. Dash up this runnel (bolts) to a shared belay station. Rappel with two ropes, or just walk off to the northwest, or to the south (see diagram). *Note:* Be sure to have available 5 QD's for the brief vertical section and beyond, using about six QD's for the lower dihedral. Shares belay with next route.

57. Bookmark 5.5 [L] 5.3 [R]
Pro: 9 QD's, Length: 180'
This route jumps up left out of the dihedral at about ⅔ way up the great white dihedral. Two ways to start this variation (5.5 Left & 5.3 Right) at the crux steep section; both merge after a few moves, then continue up a low angle water runnel (bolts). Rappel over to Great White Book belay, then rappel again. Or walk off to the northwest.

FOURTH ROCK LOBE
This is the final large rounded rock buttress at the far north end of MCS. There are several

entertaining climbs on this rock lobe. To reach this fourth lobe, you need to walk along the North Path for about 50' then cut uphill to the base of this lobe. The routes are described right to left.

58. Slim Pickins 5.7 ★
Pro: 3 QD's, Length: 35'
Unique route. Can be climbed on either the left or right side of the bolts. Just steep enough to keep you feeling on the dicey edge all the way.

59. Norwegian Queen 5.9 ★★
Pro: 4 QD's, Length: 35'
Techy movement with gently sloped holds yet uniquely beautiful in its own special way.

60. Toveline's Travesty 5.9
Pro: 8 QD's, Length: 90'
An odd diagonal traverse climb where most of the holds are steeply sloped to yield a tenuous experience. Start on the right side of lobe. Climb a right trending string of bolts (skipping the last bolt if desired) to a belay station. Rap or walk off.

61. Crowds of Solitude 5.5 ★★
Pro: 5 QD's, Length: 90'
This is the commonly climbed route on the fourth lobe. It starts near the toe of the buttress but on the sunnier aspect, and climbs fairly steep, sloped smears and edges, gradually easing to a long rounded low angle ridge ending at a belay station. Rappel or walk off.

62. Lonely Climax 5.5
Pro: 7 QD's, Length: 90'
The uttermost northern leftmost climb and a variation with a fair amount of moss on it. This starts at the utter lower leftmost portion of the buttress toe. It merges with the previous route on the final 30' of terrain (near the second to last bolt) to the belay station. Rappel or walk off.

A classic tour of the finest Gorge ice climbs

CHAPTER 4
GORGE ICE

The Columbia Gorge provides a fascinating opportunity for ice climbers to experience stellar waterfall ice climbing opportunities in northwest Oregon.

The elusive nature of Gorge ice can be bewildering at times when combined with the question, "Where is it?" Even though Gorge ice may be in an elusive league of its own by any standard the waterfall ice found here is of a caliber very comparable to some of the finest ice climbs throughout the upper western states.

Yet even with these limitations Gorge ice does form with a certain degree of regularity. By watching closely for specific weather pattern cycles, ice climbers can attain a reasonable edge of preparedness for its arrival. When extreme winter cold encases the Gorge in a frozen world of cascading ice, vertical ice pillars and ribbon-like ice smears, climbers discover a new dimension amongst the giant rock walls of the Gorge.

Wayne Wallace climbing *Black Dagger*

The northern US west coast environs are typically a wet marine climate impacted by onshore Pacific Ocean weather systems that are either warm 'pineapple-express' southwesterly oriented cycles or cold winter northwesterly storm cycles from a polar air mass.

Most Gorge waterfall ice is formed from groundwater flow, usually small or medium-sized creeks. Some ice formations are primarily from moisture saturated slopes that drip abundantly over a steep cliff, but do not normally have stream flow activity. Some examples are the classic Snazzic, Life Shavings, Bent Screw and Pumphauz.

The quality of waterfall ice varies considerably from one climb to the next. Some consist of thin delicate smears, or even brittle dinner plate ice on dry (non-seeping) routes. More likely you will encounter dripping wet plastic ice, a condition so common on many Gorge ice climbs that even a tossed brick can stick to it.

Some Gorge ice climbs are extreme dreams, often composed of huge ice umbrellas with wicked fingery chandeliers reaching out to snag the first climber who dares to climb it. Other climbs produce notorious cauliflower heads capped like white popcorn crowns that shatter to pieces if you strike the head directly with your ice tool. Diligently planting the ice tools between the solid cauliflower cores solves this riddle. Continued moisture from dripping water will help level off the cauliflowers and build step-like ice tiers (most noticeable at Mist Falls).

A greater water volume generally limits the scope of ice climbing to the peripheral edges (like Horsetail Falls), whereas a small seep often creates a beautiful thin delicate smear. Mist Falls and Crown Point flow liberally with water, but are well positioned in the primary wind zone for wind-sprayed ice buildup.

The greatest concentration of ice routes in the Gorge exists from Crown Point to Dodson along scenic U.S. highway 30, which traverses parallel with I-84 through the central portion of the Gorge.

One advantage Portland ice climbers enjoy is immediate access to stellar ice (when it forms) in the Gorge via well-traveled highway corridors. The I-84 freeway on the south side of the Columbia River and Washington State Route 14 on the north side provides an efficient conduit for fast access to all the Gorge ice climbs. Hiking approach time to most ice climbs range from one minute to one hour maximum, and this converts to more time climbing on the ice – and not sitting on your rear.

Marcus at *The Deer Hunter*

When ice is lacking in the Gorge you can compliment your ice climbing career with visits to other major areas such as Banks Lake, Leavenworth, Mazama, Colorado, or Canada, and still have time to catch a bit of the ice 'wave' as it rolls through the Gorge.

The Gorge ice climbing wave should be on your addicted ice climbers list. If your level is extreme WI4-5 then aim for one of the really big beasts like Ainsworth Left, or get a simpler taste of stylish sites like Bent Screw or Mist Falls for a quick roundup.

In the interim, while the rain pours ice-climbers-in-waiting can be found pulling down on tiny crimper's at the local sports gyms. Indoor gyms provide great training opportunity for climbing in this insane Gorge ice arena.

Detailed information found in this chapter is centered on this arena and its plethora of waterfall ice climbing opportunities. A Columbia Gorge winter ice climbing analysis was originally started at the tail-end pages of the 1993 edition of PRC and it is our primary focus in NWOR to provide an ongoing full spectrum treatise melding photo imagery and specific details about all the Gorge ice climbs in a concise reference format.

So...when the

Rappeling down *Blackjack*

Bill Price on *Salmon Run*

Gorge beast is in, it is really in, and you can get right to it fast.

Since time is of the essence in this crazy sport, and roadside access is ridiculously convenient, there is never a better reason not to take on some of these wild waterfall ice routes in the Columbia Gorge, especially if you are addicted to the adventure.

GORGE ICE HISTORY

The 1970s brought several seasons of intense lengthy cold spells which provided great opportunity for numerous historical ventures onto a vast arena of ice where climbers were able to conquer some of the obvious great Gorge ice classics.

Like the cold winter wind their conquests still stand true. People such as Jay Carroll, Mark Cartier, Ken Currens, Alan Kearney, Monty Mayko, Jim Mayers, Robert McGown, Mike O'Brien, Jim Olson, Ed Newville, Jeff Thomas, Scott Woolums, Ian Wade and others practically shook the earth when they delved into the sport during these early years. Popular Gorge ice routes like Crown Jewel, Bent Screw, Gathering Storm, and Shady Creek are several of the great ice climbs ascended during those early years of Gorge ice exploration.

Years later, during several cold spells in the early 1990s, and with high-tech ice-climbing hardware in hand a new generation of climbers approached the ice. The result is a new degree of modern ice climbing that has continued to forge a new frontier in the Gorge. Bold test pieces like Life Shavings, Post Nasal Drip, Brave New World, and Dodson were completed during those years. More recently, in 2005 successful ascents on both Ainsworth Left and Black Dagger have reopened the

Tara at Mist Falls

Photo credit: Steve Elder

Steve Elder on the stellar crux fourth pitch of *Ainsworth Left*

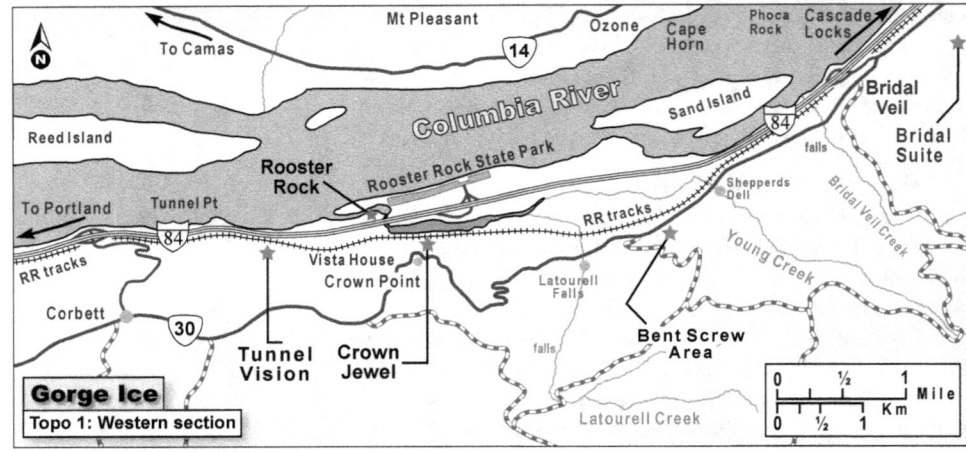

eyes of ice climbers to a new concept of endurance taken to the edge and well beyond currently known trends.

CLIMATIC NATURE OF GORGE ICE

We live in a wet maritime climate blessed with ample supplies of heat, rain and snowfall that loop through the region in rapidly changing atmospheric pressure cycles of upper level warm ridges or cold troughs associated with winter storm fronts. Onshore weather systems from the southwest and from the west tend to bring an abundance of rainfall to the region which results in high freezing levels. A northwesterly jet stream flow is more common in winter and adds to the regional snow pack, while an upper air mass flow that curls down from the north (out of Canada) brings very low temperatures.

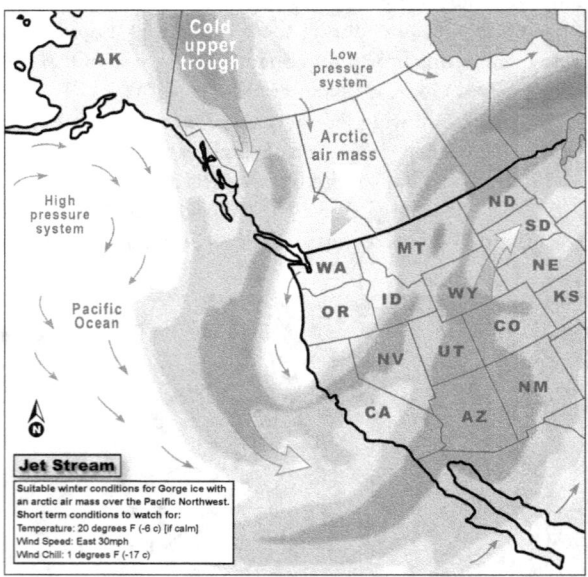

WEATHER PATTERN CYCLE

The temperate climate cycle in northwest Oregon has predicable patterns which help to clue ice climbers in to an upcoming surge of polar air in the Gorge.

The polar jet stream gradually descends southward each month in the Fall and Winter; Ketchikan Alaska in October, near Vancouver, British Columbia in November, Astoria-Newport in December, and Eureka, California in January.

The jet stream (upper air) impacts the regional weather around Portland most heavily from November 26th through the end of the month of February. During this three-month window ice climbers can keep a prospective eye open for possible Arctic or polar air mass cycles to sweep through the region.

When the jet stream develops a sharp southward swing over the mid-continent some of this Arctic cold air mass will pour over the Cascades from the east (and through the Columbia Gorge).

GORGE ICE

Wayne leading Tunnel Vision

Initially the weather system produces a mixture of snow or freezing rain. When the polar air mass pushes southward it brings very cold weather to the region. If the Arctic air remains in the region (with a strong enough flow) it can provide an extended period of very cold, but otherwise clear weather in the northern Willamette Valley.

These cycles vary considerably from year to year. In poor years expect little (1-4 days) or no ice to form in the Gorge. Good years will bring a polar air mass that sends a strong cold surge of weather into the region for 1-2 week duration and occasionally longer.

WATCH FOR THREE EVENTS

Three crucial patterns to specifically watch for in the Columbia Gorge: polar air mass bringing consistent low end temperatures, limited precipitation, and strong east winds.

Watch for the initial phase of an upper air jet stream from the Alaska-Canadian continental landmass to curl sharply down from the north into the northwestern U.S. this strong southward swing of the jet stream will provide the necessary surge of cold polar air deep into Washington and Oregon. The advancing cold front slides in under the warmer marine air producing an additional favorable condition - extreme Gorge winds in excess of 35 mph. These strong winds buffet the water flow by distributing smaller water droplet particles onto the cliff scarp. This crucial combination of events encourages rapid formation of waterfall ice in as little as three to four days.

Night time low temperatures should reach the upper 10° Fahrenheit with the day time highs in the upper 20° Fahrenheit for premium ice forming conditions. The south side of the Gorge is of greatest value to ice climbers simply because the north facing shaded environs helps keep average Gorge temperatures lower.

WATER ICE RATINGS

This explanation of commonly used ice grading systems serves to enhance your awareness of Gorge ice climbing variables from pure water ice to mixed terrain climbing. The book Mountaineering: The Freedom of

The Hills details common rating systems used in America that are modified from the Scottish system to achieve a comprehensive and useful Americanized grading system. The two main elements worth expanding upon are the seriousness/commitment grade, and the technical grade.

The length or vertical relief (whether 60' or 600') conveys a picture of general route height or elevation. The commitment difficulty grade (I to VII) indicates the approximate time necessary for such an ascent, including hazards, and remoteness. The technical open-ended grade WI (water ice) 1-8 will prepare you for the most difficult pitch and other associated problems encountered on the climb such as chandelier or mushroom ice, overhanging bulges, or thickness of ice.

WI1 ◆ Walking up low angle ice with crampons, such as the approach to an ice climb.

WI2 ◆ 60°-70° consistent ice pitch with good protection and belays with a few short steep ice steps.

WI3 ◆ 70°-80° ice pitch usually thick and solid. The ice may contain short, steep sections, but will have good resting places, good protection and belays.

WI4 ◆ Near vertical 75°-85° sustained ice, reasonable protection, fewer rests but with good belays on generally quality ice.

WI5 ◆ Generally vertical 85°-90° ice requiring considerable endurance on a strenuous pitch of quality ice.

WI6 ◆ Expect full pitch of vertical ice with considerable strenuous technical sections, few rests, and exposed belays. Ice quality and protection may be suspect.

WI7 ◆ Vertical or near vertical thin, poor quality ice where protection is marginal or non-existent and physical endurance is critical for success.

An open-ended mixed rating (M1 - M14) scale is used to define the difficulty of climbing rock and ice using ice tools and crampons. The first eight mixed ratings are as follows.

Mixed ratings are defined loosely as follows (adapted from AlaskaIceClimbing.com):

M1 ◆ similar to 5.5 climbing or occasional dry tool move

M2 ◆ similar to 5.6 climbing or a few dry tool moves

M3 ◆ similar to 5.7 climbing or 3-4 meters of easy dry tooling

M4 ◆ similar to 5.8 climbing or some technical dry tooling

M5 ◆ similar to 5.9 climbing or dry tool moves that require effort

M6 ◆ similar to 5.10 climbing or 8-10m of technical dry tooling; requires effort

M7 ◆ similar to 5.11 climbing or 10-15m of technical dry tooling

M8 ◆ similar to 5.12 climbing or 8-10m with some overhanging & technical dry tooling

For example the final rating may look like this:

Black Dagger 600' Grade IV WI 5+ M4

The ice climbs of the Gorge create a rare and quickly changing medium. A rating should never be considered absolute, but used only as a constructive physical reference point or an average estimate of potential challenges.

EQUIPMENT

Virtually any ice climbing gear will work fine whether old or new, yet modern high-tech equipment and good technique will certainly help improve efficiency considerably.

Two 60-meter twin ropes are useful if you have them. A standard single 60-meter 9-10mm rope is fine for nearly all short ice climbs, but a second rope is useful for longer grade IV routes. Since many routes remain quite moist from dripping water it is beneficial to use water-resistant ropes which limit saturation problems.

Reverse curved ice tools and rigid crampons are pretty much de facto standard hardware these days for ice climbing. A selection of aluminum or titanium ice screws, a small selection of long quick-draws, a few extra carabiners, extra webbing for slinging trees or bushes, and you're set to go. You might consider bringing a few LA or KB pitons, especially on routes where you desire a fixed belay at a rock wall, or if you are climbing an unknown or infrequently traveled ice route with limited beta.

Ice climbing entails focus, commitment and proficiency with a balance of analytical skills and good equipment. Prior to leading an ice route in the Gorge analyze your descent options. Does the climb offer a walk-off descent? If rappelling, look for trees or large bushes for possible rappel anchors. Cutting an ice bouillard works great but takes considerable effort and time, while V-Thread (Abalakov Sandwich) requires additional material (thin webbing & a hooked piece of coat hanger) and practical skill. Calculate the length of additional time necessary to safely descend, especially from long ice routes which usually require an early morning start or late evening descent.

The Columbia Gorge, due to its east-west axis allows cold polar air to funnel rapidly through to the north Willamette Valley. This open-door gateway does create a very strong wind-tunnel effect, particularly during the winter months when ice is most likely to form.

First time visitors may find the extreme winds to be brutally bone-chilling, but with an adequate selection of warm clothing to suit your comfort level you can quickly adjust to the unusual temperature extremes. For your survival you should dress well, and consider bringing some extra warm clothes just in case. There is a thin line between feeling the cold temperature and being seriously chilled.

The *Crown Jewel* on Crown Point

Most ice climbers will climb one or two routes in a day and be fully satisfied. But for the hard core climber who likes extreme climbs, an early start time will allow you to climb three-to-five 1-pitch ice routes in a day. The grade IV ice routes in the Gorge will generally need a full day to succeed. Very long ice routes (such as Ainsworth Left or Dodson) often require an early sunrise start or a rappel descent that may end near sunset. Always keep your friends or family informed of your plans. Let's go ice climbing before it all melts and crashes down!

NEARBY ICE CLIMBING OPPORTUNITIES

Other multi-season winter ice climbing options do exist. There is innumerable mixed rock/rime ice climbs on the upper slopes of Mt. Hood such as Steel Cliff, Devil's Kitchen, Black Spider, and Illumination Rock during the winter months.

Additional limited ice climbing opportunities exist at or near the Pete's Pile cliff formation south of Hood River. During extended Arctic cold spells this site will yield some 80-100' long, difficult ice climbs. This cliff formation is located one mile south of the junction of Hwy 35 and Cooper Spur road 3511.

A small rock bluff aptly referred to as 'Danger Cliff' is located immediately west of the lower bowl ski lift at Multorpor's West Lodge (Government Camp). This north-facing bluff forms a few short ice smears when weather conditions remain sufficiently cold to allow ice accumulation. The hike to Danger Cliff is a quick 40-minute approach from the vehicle.

During the summer season Portland based climbers usually suffice by visiting Eliot Glacier on the northern scarp of Mt. Hood to hone skills. The glacier offers good and accessible crevasse or serac climbing. For the hard core enthusiast seeking the edge of adventure, visit the glacier from mid-September thru October. Superb ice conditions can be found throughout the Eliot and Coe Glacier region.

Stellar extreme mixed black ice conditions are available on the Eliot Glacier Headwall. This Headwall provides six-to-seven pitches (IV AI3) of classic 60° high altitude alpine ice.

When it is extremely cold there was rumored to be a small selection of ice smears on a steep bluff immediately south the I-84 freeway 6-10 miles east of The Dalles, Oregon. Search and you will find.

Internet weather related websites provide meteorological short-range weather ensemble forecasting and are able to give reasonably accurate data on weather patterns 0-48 hours lead time, with general broad-range forecasting up to seven days in advance. Weather websites display very localized weather information in real-time. These websites also have links to satellite photographic images showing current and past weather conditions.

NOAA - National Oceanic and Aeronautic Administration (www.weather.gov).

SOUTH SIDE OF THE GORGE

The ice climbing beta begins with Tunnel Vision, at the west end of the Gorge along the south side of I-84 freeway. This initial ice climb of interest is located on an east-facing bluff immediately east of a prominent outcrop of rock where a short railroad track tunnel slices through the scarp. A minor roadside viewpoint is located here for the west-bound freeway tourists who stop to take in a scenic view the Gorge. This promontory is commonly referred to as Tunnel Point. Both Rooster Rock and Crown Point are visible to the east of this site.

Matt climbing *Bent Screw*

Forrest Kaye on *Organic Mist*

Tunnel Vision
Length: 120' WI 3
Park on the south side of I-84 approximately ¼ mile east of Tunnel Point where the railroad tracks cut through an outcrop of rock along the freeway. Walk east until you see the ice smear on an east facing bluff. Left of Tunnel Vision in the forest is an easier ice climb called **Wind Tunnel** WI 2 which was also climbed by the same adventurers.

CROWN JEWEL AREA

Crown Point is one of the great visual capstones of the Columbia Gorge with a nearby stream that forms the most prominent ice route in the western Gorge.

Crown Jewel (aka Crown Point)

Length: 300' II WI 3

A super classic ice climb in the Columbia Gorge. This popular and moderately difficult ice face is quite obvious from the highway and holds a spectacular position for all to see. Because of numerous parties ascending this route, it is wise to make an early start. Even though it takes a bit longer it is best to park your vehicle at Rooster Rock state park (exit #25) and walk over to the ice climb. There are several 'No Parking' signs on the freeway exit ramp shoulder so beware of the risk if you consider parking along the roadside shoulder. The approach takes about 15 minutes.

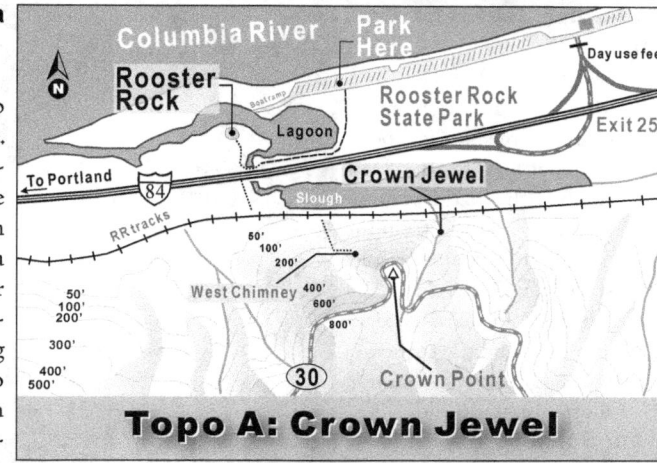

This two-pitch climb has a fair bit of moisture dripping through the ice so prepare to get a bit wet. The ice face is wide enough for several climbing parties to utilize the smear at the same time without problem. After the second pitch the ice climb eases to a large amphitheater where you can either rappel or continue up the easy gully to the scenic highway and the overlook, and then descend down a steep dirt ravine west of the Vista House parking lot.

Latourrell Falls area

Length: 35' WI 2

Some minor but limited ice bouldering left of the main waterfall.

Wayne leading the stellar Life Shavings

WEST BRIDAL VEIL AREA

The ice formations west of Bridal Veil develop at a wind sheltered site that offer multiple ice routes at one central location. From I-84 Bridal Veil exit #28 drive west on scenic U.S. 30 for approximately two miles passing the Bridal Veil Falls state park site. Park at a large dirt pullout on the north side of the road just before a residential ranch home. The climbs here often remain climbable days after other ice smears have collapsed. The ice climbs are as follows from right to left (west to east).

Cruiser

Length: 100' WI 2 (WI3+ on 2nd half)

Facing west-*ish* Cruiser is a nice little hidden ice lead offering a very thick low angle formation on the lower half. The second half is usually running with plenty of water which makes leading it far more challenging (WI3+).

Waterpipe (aka The Column)

Length: 90' WI 3+

This is the right-most route immediately above the road. A short, steep climb with a large volume of water. The Column needs an extended cold spell to fully develop. Another ice formation exists uphill around the corner to the right, but it is a minor short strenuous lead.

Bent Screw

Length: 150' WI 3

One of the first to form and one of the last to fall apart, because the water source is from seeps and not stream flow. Bent Screw provides very good steep plastic ice. Near the top of the lead it is usually a bit moist or slightly muddy.

Bill Price leading *Waterheater*

Adam on *Waterpipe*

Considering the minor drawbacks Bent Screw is still the *pièce-de-résistance* ice smear in this part of the Gorge so get an early start and anticipate plenty of tourists with cameras. Rappel from a convenient tree at the top of the cliff. A great climb you are sure to enjoy!

Organic Mist

Length: 150' WI 5+

A stellar and very difficult vertical ice curtain that is frequently top-roped, and occasionally

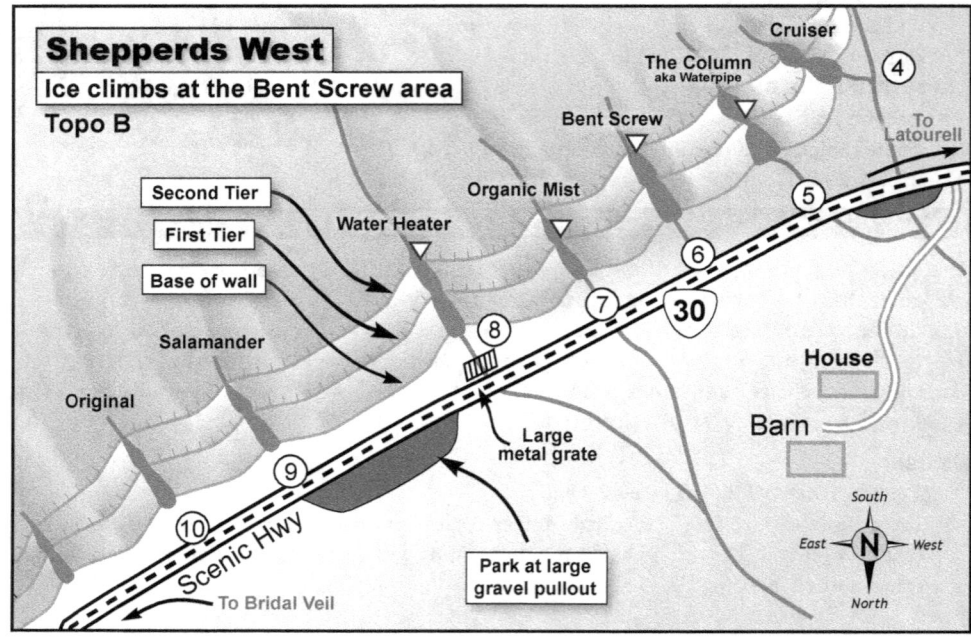

done as a lead when the ice is thick. Perfect conditions combined with a hard freeze build beautiful ice cauliflowers which make outrageous hooking opportunities for 60% of the climb. If you have the time do set a rope on this wild one!

Water Heater
Length: 160' WI 3

From the large pullout walk a few yards west to a large metal grate that protects the roadway from loose debris. Uphill from this metal grate is Water Heater. This ice route has plenty of stream flow to help build up the ice, and once a thick enough layer is established it can be a surprisingly technical sustained lead for those who dare. An old water tank is still at the base.

Salamander
Length: 140' WI 2+

At the very east end of the gravel pullout (see map) and across the road is Salamander. Infrequently climbed but in a sustained freeze forms a nice ice shield.

Original
Length: 60' WI 2

This is the left-most ice route in the Shepperd West area. It is located a few hundred feet east of the gravel pullout (see map). Though infrequently climbed is forms a nice shield of ice and often surprisingly quickly. A short ice climb leading to easy slopes above. Rappel from vine maples.

Shepperds Smear
Length: 60' WI 2-3

To the *east* of the Shepperds Dell is a single vehicle pullout on the south side of the road at a culvert. Uphill in the forest a short distance is a wide low-angle smear that is suitable for beginner climbing if the formation is fully developed with a thick layer of ice.

EAST BRIDAL VEIL AREA

Take eastbound exit #28 at Bridal Veil to access the scenic U.S. Hwy 30. The following sites are located along U.S. 30 traveling east from the small community of Bridal Veil toward Multnomah Falls.

Shark Attack
Length: 100' WI4

The following two climbs (SA & DH) are lo-

Climbing on the fabulous *Organic Mist*

cated beneath and slightly east of the Angel's Rest viewpoint, and can be accessed by hiking cross-country for 25 minutes uphill east of the houses along US Hwy 30. Shark Attack is a hanging icicle in the left portion of a small ravine.

The route involves mixed climbing using tricky gear (stubbies, Spectres, KB) and ice climbing over delicate features. Thin turf mixed top out, then rappel from a tree.

Dog House
Length: 100' WI3

This is the other cruiser ice route in this small ravine. Involves sustained climbing on typically very fat and fun moderate ice. Rappel from V-threads at top of route. The Dog House route is visible from the road.

Bridal Suite
Length: 150' WI ?

Bridal Suite is a good one pitch climb nestled in a bowl high above the road and below the trail leading to Angel's Rest. Long approach but other potential does exist nearby.

Pumphauz
Length: 150' WI 2+

The Pumphauz Bleuz route is an easy climb with a crux at the first move. Take I-84 exit #28 and drive east 1¾ miles and park in a very small dirt pullout immediately to the right of a chain-link fenced small brick building. Pumphauz is the obvious thin smear on the left that ascends to the top of this minor bluff. Expect some minor brush along this ice route.

Other routes: Directly south of this pullout are two upper-tier ice smears that occasionally develop; one is called Tatras and the other is Terminal Dysfunction. Access the upper tier by scrambling around to the right edge of the cliff.

Slippery Dolphin
Length: 160' WI 4 or 5

A steep and sustained ice climb that rarely forms in its entirety. Park at a large gravel pullout immediately across from a small landlocked lake typically used by fishermen approximately 1¾ miles east of the tiny community of Bridal Veil on U.S. 30. Located at the same gravel pullout as Gathering Storm. The ice route (if it forms) is on the 160' tall vertical rock bluff immediately south of the pullout. This particular ice route requires long term polar weather conditions to stay in the Gorge for it to develop fully down to the ground. Located at MP31 on U.S. 30.

Gathering Storm
Length: 500' (160m) III WI 4

Approximately 1¾ miles east of the tiny community of Bridal Veil on U.S. 30 you will find the staggering Thomas-Kearney route called Gathering Storm. Park at the same large gravel pullout as Slippery Dolphin near a vertical 160' rock bluff. The ice route immediately south of the road on this bluff is Slippery Dolphin. Gathering Storm is the multi-pitch ice climb on the major upper tier wall. From the pullout hike up left to bypass the initial bluff and continue up a steep brushy scree slope to the next large cliff (expect one hour to approach).

P1 165' (50m): Dance up an initial low angle ice apron to a vertical WI4 pillar.

P2 (130') 40m: Aim up a short WI3 pillar; follow easy

Photo credit: Marcus Donaldson

The *Gathering Storm*

Topo C: Mist Falls to Multnomah Falls

steps to the upper main bowl.

P3 (230') 70m: Climb very steep steps up to a dramatic, sweeping wing of crux ice (WI4), and up another long section of ice flow above to easy terrain. Rappel route.

MIST FALLS AREA

Mist Fall area is certainly one of the most heavily used ice climbing sites in the Gorge and for good reason. Convenient access and a fairly reasonable single-pitch ice smear lead on the lower apron make this site a worthy destination. The ice at this site consolidates well, even when the polar front is short lived.

Mist Falls

Length: 200' WI 2

From I-84 exit #28 drive east 1¾ miles and park on the south side of U.S. Hwy 30 at a large signpost just before Wahkeena Falls parking lot. Hike directly uphill on a faint climbers path near a small stream to a wide flat landing at the base of the main lower ice slab.

The main lower ice amphitheater is very wide (250'+) and about 160' tall. There is plenty of room for multiple climbing parties to visit this site and climb.

The section just left of center is the riskiest due to a large wet dripping hanging ice chandelier (Sword of Damocles) which can cut loose if it gets too heavy or the temperatures warm up. It is wise to avoid most of the wind-whipped spray from the stream of water pouring off the ice chandelier by climbing on the right side of the large main alcove.

You will need to design your own rappel anchor (bollard or v-thread, etc.) as there are no trees from which to descend. If the east wind is actively throwing the stream of water from the chandelier around the amphitheater, you will likely get a crackly suit of ice armor! Variations on the lower apron ice smear will provide a variety of levels from WI2 to WI3.

The Pillar

An impressive free standing pillar (when it forms dur-

Crux pitch of *Gathering Storm*

Photo credit: Marcus Donaldson

ing a mega-freeze) infrequently develops up left around the corner from Mist Falls. This rare Gorge free-standing ice pillar requires a long-term polar Arctic freeze for it to connect.

The Deer Hunter
Multi-pitch II WI5 M7

The new piece-de-resistance for Gorge ice climbers. Uphill left of the Pillar are two stunning curtains of ice that form from liberal amounts of dripping water trickling down a steep face. Once the ice extends down to the overhang, wind whips and curls the ice like flowing blond hair on a windy day. If the Arctic air mass is long-term this formation can reach the ground. But you no longer need to wait for it to touch down.

P1 50' M7: Climb an overhanging crack corner system to a bolt anchor.

P2 160' WI5: Step right and surmount the free hanging chandelier curtain, and then continue up relentless steep and technical ice to the top.

Sweetest Taboo
Length: 100' WI 3

Park at Wahkeena Falls and take the right side trail. After a zigzag off-trail scramble directly uphill a short distance in the open forest you will see two ice gullies. The right one has not seen an ascent (100') while the left is the combo Smooth Operator/Sweetest Taboo. Climb the ice for 100' until it fades into a dirt ravine. Scramble further up this ravine to another hidden ice lead called Sweetest Taboo.

An ice party at *Mist Falls*

Wahkeena Falls
Popular tourist trap for photography.

BENSON ICE AREA

The following six ice routes are located immediately across from Benson Lake at a very small dirt shoulder. This site is located between Wahkeena Falls and Multnomah Falls parking sites.

Benson Ice
Length: 165' WI 2 to WI 3

A very popular ice smear, but requires a long-term polar air mass to allow the smear to fully develop. This *'practice area'* has served the local ice climbers since the 1970s. The sites is located approximately ½ mile west of Multnomah Falls (¼ mile east of Wahkeena) and immediately across from Benson Lake. A steady drip of water tends to saturate the central portion of this smear, but the since the

Tracy Harton at Mist Falls

smear is wide it provides good low angle climbing on the right side or left side with numerous trees for belays. Topping out though, can be quite technical especially when the stream is flowing at the top.

Chillin' out
Length: 160' WI 3+

Approximately 150' left of Benson Ice smear are two minor vertical smears that ease back at 30'. Both smears have been climbed. This is the right and longer variation that continues up on ice steps ending with a vertical, hollow chandelier that fades to dirt slopes at the top.

Snazzic
Length: 100' WI 2

About 200' left of Benson Ice smear is an excellent and popular low angle ice lead that is simply a 'Must Do' for all beginners to the sport of Gorge Ice climbing. Start up a 12' wide ice base which narrows higher up. The ice route is liberally protected with trees and bushes for anchors, and it is best to rappel from one of the trees about 100' up the route. For the tech-

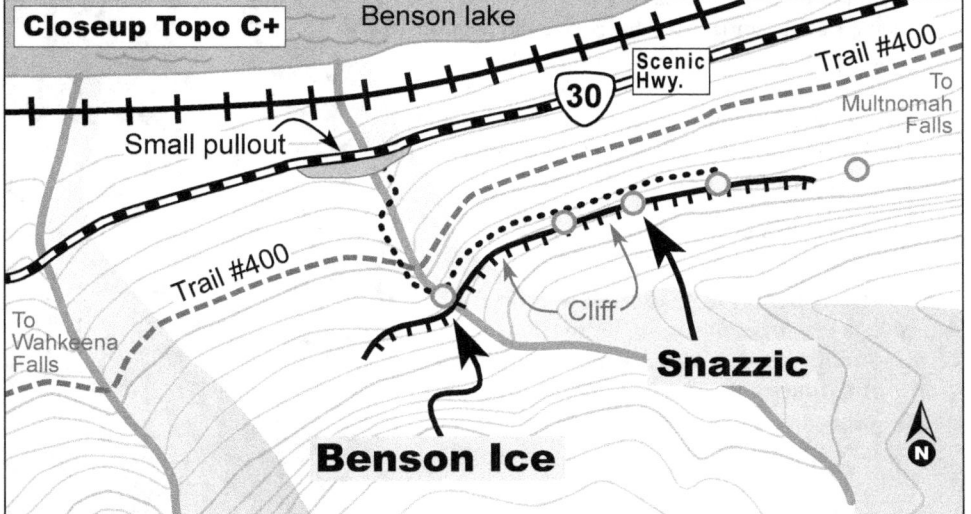

nically savvy, the top-out section is usually wet and abruptly ends in a steep dirt boulder move (WI 3).

Fractal Energy
Length: 40' WI 2+
Walk left of Benson Ice smear for 350' till you find a short ice route that ascends past a small tree and abruptly ends on dirt slopes above. Wander up left on easy grass steps. A rappel anchor does exist although it can be difficult to find.

Ice Cooler
Length: 40' WI 3
A minor ice smear located further left around corner from the previous route.

Multnomah Falls Area

Shady Creek
Length: 200' II WI 3
Located up and right behind the lodge at Multnomah Falls but is not accessible. Steady water flow keeps the ice smear moist at the top. Ascends steep ice to a vertical ice bulge to finish.

Climber on *Thick Enough To Screw*

Multnomah Falls
Always terrific to see, especially when the falls are encased in ghostly curtains of ice. In Jan. 1979 Jeff Thomas and Ed Newville climbed the right side approximately 200'. At present the Multnomah Falls amphitheater has Forest Service climbing restrictions prohibiting access.

Life Shavings
Length: 80' WI 4+
Stellar route of the highest standard. Located just east of Multnomah Creek road bridge in a tight corner across from the eastern parking area. Ascends an improbable partially formed thin seep in a tight corner which ends at a maple tree.

Fame and Fortune
Length: 200' WI 3
Premium quality climb and readily accessible, but requires a substantial polar freeze to build up properly. Top out to the woods above, then hike down to the east. The crux is the initial vertical start and the last section as it turns to frozen moss and bush pulling. Located east of Multnomah Creek across from the eastern parking area.

NEW WORLD AMPHITHEATER

The following three ice routes are accessed at the same dirt parking site located at milepost 21. A small steep frozen stream immediately west of the pullout is the access point for Brave New World and Black Dagger. The Gorge #400 trail heading up west is the access point for Blackjack.

Wayne on *Unfinished Business*

Blackjack

Length: 500'+ IV WI 3

A very exciting and challenging route with many pitches of moderate climbing. Park at a large dirt pullout immediately east of milepost 21 on U.S. 30. Hike up west on Gorge trail #400 a few hundred yards, then directly up steep forested slopes directly to the base of a detached pillar (base will connect only after a mega-freeze). To begin the frozen moss start walk right 100' until you can angle up to a mossy arête on the right side of another gully system. Use bushes for pro and belays. Cross the ice gully and angle up left till you can rappel into the main Blackjack ice climb ravine from a small tree. Ascend three main ice tiers, the last tier may be a little wet from stream flow near the top.

Access to Blackjack using the frozen moss variation is typical for Gorge ice climb approaches, but may be a bit unnerving for those not quite prepared for the concept.

Leading *Post Nasal Drip*

New World Amphitheater

Black Dagger

Length: 600' approx. IV WI 5+ (or 6) M4

Located ¼ mile east of mile post 21 at the dirt pullout next to a small bridge. **Brave New World** is the left route and **Black Dagger** is the right one in the large west facing amphitheater. Note: The central portion of this highly exposed vertical ice pillar can be done in one 60-meter pitch, except due to rope drag around the ice umbrellas, it is best in two shorter leads.

Three 60-meter raps off 'v' threads bring you back down to the ground. The **Black Dagger** would be slightly easier if it were not for the exposure on the pillar. This ice climb is considered to be one of the finest water ice leads in Oregon.

P1: The first pitch (M4) begins near a tree and moves up mixed mossy rock corners to the right of the main ice fall. At 100' traverse diligently left on steep terrain to a ledge on the ice. This places you above the lower detached section that normally

does not connect fully to the ground.

P2: Climb WI5 on very steep ice to a belay at a small protected cave.

P3: Climb WI5+ on more steep ice but avoid the ice umbrellas by climbing on the right side.

P4: The fourth pitch starts up a steep ramp of ice, then steepens again to a drippy WI5+ crux, a slightly hung 40' lead of ice which allows no stemming or place to hide. The last lead is a very difficult sting in the tail.

Brave New World
Length: 500' IV WI 5+

A bold venture of the extreme kind that set a new standard for the Gorge. This stellar classic is located immediately left of the Black Dagger. Formed by wind spraying the stream flow leftward onto the vertical wall, creating a fragile and technically extreme chandelier crux section half way up the ice route.

P1: Ascend a 25' vertical curtain of dripping wet detached ice, then scamper up easier terrain for 150' to a belay under the main ice curtain.

P2: Step up left and surmount (crux) the ice curtain and continue up steep a ice slope 160' to a bush belay.

P3: Either rappel with two ropes from here...Or traverse rightward into main ice gully. Exit this gully on the left to forested slopes and walk up west over to the Cougar Rock creek drainage to descend.

Unfinished Business
Length: 200' approx.

A colorful climb with several tiers. No known complete ascent beyond the first 80' pitch. Park to the west of Oneonta Gorge at the trailhead. Hike up westward to the base (20 min.) of this ice climb. The first pitch is gently angled 65° ice to a bush belay, followed by a vertical ice pillar ending in forested slope on the second pitch.

Oneonta Gorge
A good photographic stop, but yields

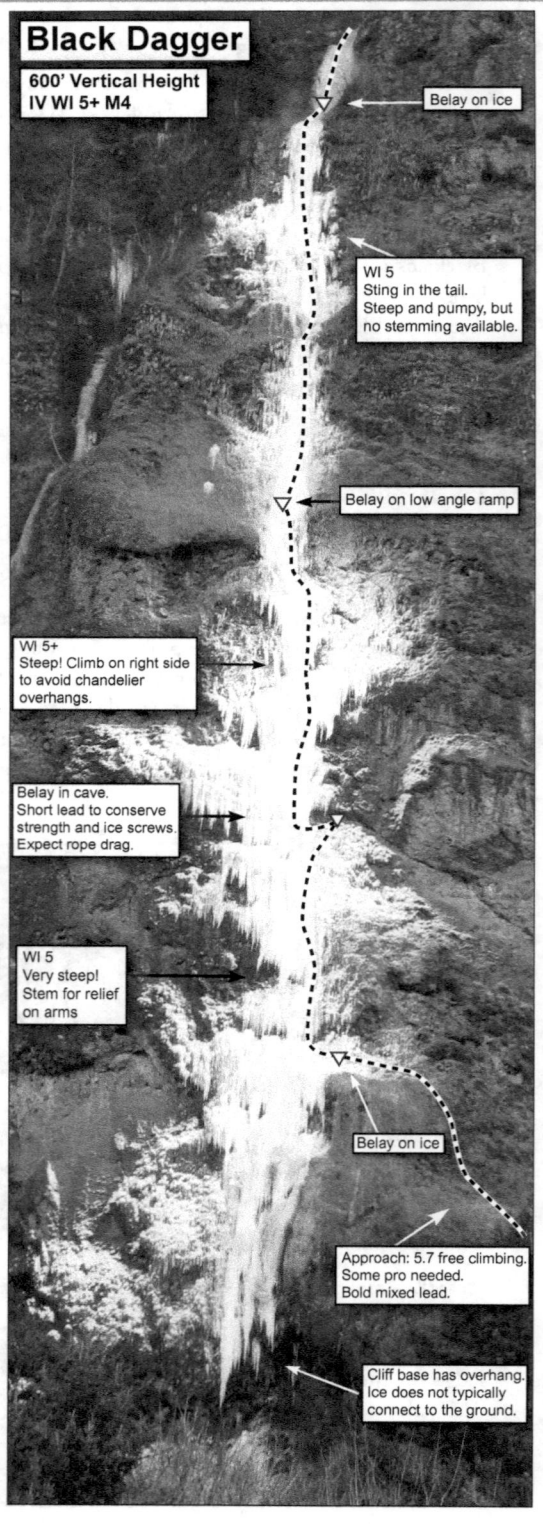

no ice climbing interest.
Post Nasal Drip
Length: 200' II WI 3
A terrific, enjoyable route. Located east of Oneonta Gorge ¼ mile at a small dirt pullout. Easily visible just uphill through the trees. The right and larger icefall is 20' wide, and is separated into two vertical sections. Both are sustained, while the second pitch fades near the top. Possible to exit left after the first pitch and rappel from trees (95 ft.).

Thick Enough to Screw
Length: 95' WI 4
To the left of the previous ice climb is a fabulous vertical ice smear. A local test-piece.

HORSETAIL FALLS AREA

The following four ice routes are accessed by parking at the popular Horsetail Creek parking area. Horsetail Falls is immediately south of the road. Pencil Pusher and Peter Piper are located uphill to the right, while Ponytail ice is located up on the left slope. Use the hiker trail to access the Ponytail ice smear.

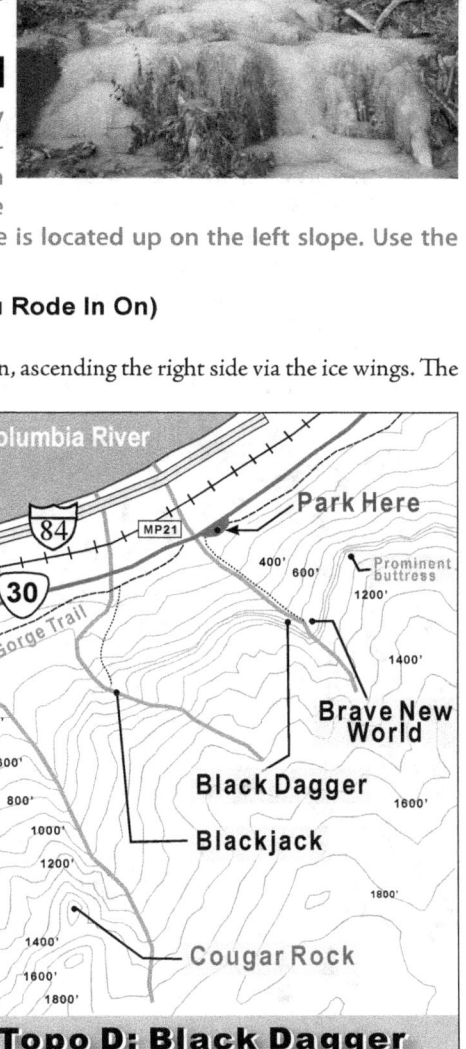

The stellar *Brave New World*

Horsetail Falls (aka ...And The Horse You Rode In On)
200' III WI 5
A modern test-piece of phenomenal proportion, ascending the right side via the ice wings. The route breaks with tradition by climbing on unusual terrain consisting of a very thin ice wing that separates the climber from the waterfall. Start on the right side and climb next to the waterfall on a short section vertical ice to easier terrain. Belay under an overhang next to the main waterfall. Climb the vertical ice window pane (2"-3" thick) separating you from the waterfall by poking your ice tools through it and diligently hook your way upward through the crux moves. As the terrain lessens gingerly dance up the right side on very thin ice wings passing bushes and a small tree. You can exit up right in the forest to the hiking trail or cross the stream to the same hiking trail. Walk down eastward on the hikers trail back to the vehicle.

Pencil Pusher
Length: 180' II WI 3
Uphill to the right of Horsetail Falls is

Topo D: Black Dagger

Pencil Pusher, which is a thin smear with a minor vertical ice pedestal at the top. The first part is a beautiful 70° ice smear to a steep slab, then finishes up the right side of a vertical ice step ending in brush. Step right to rappel 80' from a tree down near the cliff edge. Both Pencil Pusher and Peter Piper usually need sufficient moisture in the top soil in order to set up properly.

Peter Piper
Length: 90' WI 2+
To the right of Pencil Pusher is a short, fun ice climb. An easy lead on mostly slabby ice. Fades into the brushy hillside near top. Angle left to the rappel tree.

Ponytail
Length: 80' WI 2+
A great little 70° ice smear that protects well for the first 80' only. Located approx. 200' left of Horsetail Falls with convenient trail side access. Rappel from small tree above first bluff. The second pitch is WI4 but offers no protection at all.

Ainsworth Left
Length: 700'+ IV WI 5
This is THE ultimate Columbia Gorge classic ice route. The ice climb has been approached and attempted repeatedly by numerous strong climbers over many years, but was finally conquered in 2005. Take I-84 exit #35 and drive west ½ mile on U.S. 30. Park near the entrance to the Ainsworth State Park overnight camp area and hike south via a trail and creek drainage to the Ainsworth Creek amphitheater. On the left face of the major alcove is this stellar super classic. Expect very wet ice near the top of the ice route and variable ice on other portions.

P1 100' WI3+: Ascend ice steps to a short but difficult vertical section, then move up to a fixed piton belay anchor on the left.

P2 80' WI3: Continue up another difficult vertical ice step to the next tier and set ice screws for a belay.

P3 160' WI4: Scramble up an initial low angle ice step, then launch up a long difficult crux

Horsetail Falls, photo courtesy of Jim Apilado

Horsetail Falls, photo courtesy of Jim Apilado

pitch. Expect steep vertical ice (may have a huge ice umbrella buildup from sustained updrafts of wind) before you reach the very lower edge of the large upper amphitheater.

P4 200' WI5: From the upper amphitheater climb a long vertical sustained crux pitch of WI5. Expect lots of cauliflowers mixed with short chandelier sections on most of this pitch. The final part of this crux lead can be very wet soft ice due to stream flow. As the terrain eases back set up a belay on the left at a tree. Rappel with two ropes.

Note: If using 60-meter ropes you can connect the entire climb into three very long leads, but you may want to shorten certain leads due to the technical nature of the ice. The upper alcove is quite large so dividing P4 into two leads (40'+160') is an option as well.

As with other stellar ice routes in the Gorge (i.e. Mist Falls), Ainsworth Left also may create a large 'Sword of Damocles' near the crux pitch which may terrify some ice climbers.

Dodson

Length: 700'+ IV WI 4+ (to ice pillar at base of P6)

South of the tiny community of Dodson and east of Katanai Rock is the huge vertical face of Yeon Mountain. The ice route is located near the left arête and is visible from I-84. Dodson has been climbed in its entirety except for the large hanging ice chandelier on P6.

P1: Ascend a steep WI3 lead 80' to an anchor on the left side of a small ledge.

P2: Step right and ascend a 20' vertical 90° WI4+ crux section which eases to 85° ice for a full 160' lead. Belay on a small ledge at a tree on the left.

P3: Step up into the long ramp (200'+) and re-establish another belay at the base of the next long ice smear.

P4: A very sustained lead of WI3+ for 190' with no ledges.

P5: Continue up a full lead on minor ice steps till you enter the final alcove with an overhung

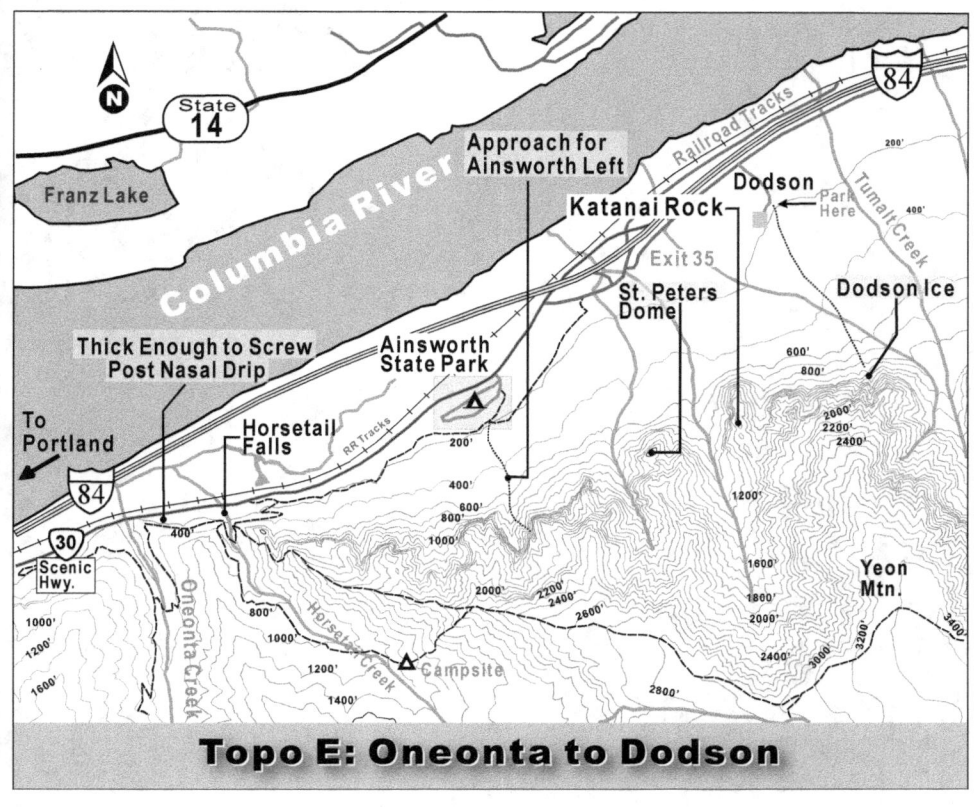

Topo E: Oneonta to Dodson

Steve Elder on the first pitch of *Ainsworth Left*

◆ GORGE ICE 233

Multi-pitch *Dodson Ice*

Ice Umbrella on P3

Wayne on P4

Ainsworth Left
IV WI5

Final belay

200' crux lead

WI 5

Upper amphitheater

Ice screw belay

WI 4+

160' lead technical and steep

Sloping ledge
Ice screw belay

WI 3

80' lead

Sloping ledge
Piton belay

WI 3+

80' lead

One hour approach time from road to base of Ainsworth Left

chandelier of ice connected to a wide ice base.

P6: Yet to see an ascent, but if the overhanging ice pillar is connected...climb it!

Tanner One (aka The Footbridge)
Length: P1 80' WI 2

At the Bonneville Dam I-84 exit #40 turn south into the Tanner Creek hiker's parking lot. Park here and walk south a few minutes along Tanner Creek to a footbridge that crosses a short low angle frozen ice smear that is well protected from the wind. The ice formation is wide and offers three distinct tiers (two tiers not visible) that you can climb if so inclined.

Tanner Two
Length: P1 150' WI 3

About 10 minutes walk south from the parking site on the Tanner Creek trail is another ice climb. Said to be a cool climb this 150' tall offers a scary mixed traverse (piton placement) rightward to the high tree. Rappel. Above is a vertical pillar that may be 50' WI4+ continuing up to who knows where.

Cascade Curtain
Multi-pitch II WI 3 [possibly harder]; approach time 45 minutes approx.

Cascade Curtain is certainly one of the great hidden gems of the Gorge and considering it is on a scale easily comparable to the size of Crown Jewel perhaps climbers will ascend this ice route a bit more often. The ice formation sets up quickly forming a dripping ice smear about 60' across at the base. The total height is estimated to be about 300' high, but offers numerous trees along the side to belay and rappel from if you choose not to climb the entire route. The ice formation is broken into numerous stair-stepped tiers with sections of 85°-90° ice in places. The stream flow at the very top part of the formation limits top-out options. The ice route is situated at the 1600' level near the lower portion of the old Rudolph Spur trail. To access this sweet gem of the forest: from the town of Cascade Locks drive south on Benson road and turn left on Ruckel road. Turn right onto a gravel access road called Dry Creek Falls road which follows Dry Creek uphill. A 4-wheel vehicle is recommended

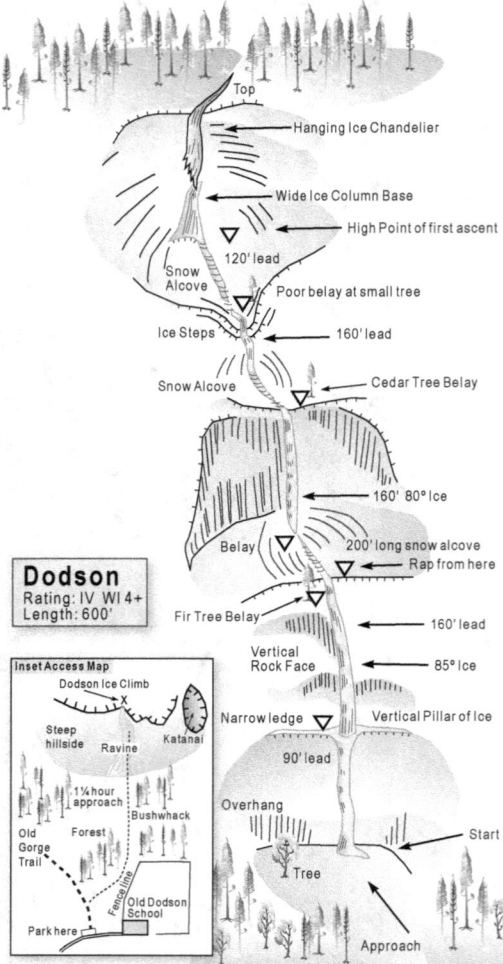

Steven Demsky on *Tanner Creek Ice*

Photo credit: Bill Price

Third pitch of *Dodson*   The elusive & stellar multi-pitch *Cascade Curtain*

as it is quite rough in places, otherwise you can park at a large clearing and walk (add 15 minutes) the remainder of the distance. Park the vehicle where the Pacific Crest trail crosses the gravel road which is about ¼ mile before the real Dry Creek falls.

Walk twenty-five feet (25'), stop, turn left (south) onto the old Rudolph Spur trail and walk 15 minutes up a gentle incline in a minor draw. As the trail tops the draw you will see a large open moss-covered boulder field on the left (south). A quick jaunt up the steep boulder field for 15 minutes more brings you directly to the base of this classic multi-pitch ice smear.

STARVATION CREEK AREA

The following climbs can be accessed at the Starvation Creek rest facility east-bound freeway exit. To reach these ice smears hike west on the unmarked roadside trail #413 at the west end of the rest facility parking area passing Cabin Falls.

In a short distance you will cross Warren Creek, a tunnel diverted falls. Tunnel Falls is also called Hole-in-the-Wall Falls. The dry portion of the old waterfalls is in an alcove on the left while the present waterfall tumbles out of the mouth of the diversion tunnel on the right of the rock buttress. It is possible to ice climb on portions of the Warren Creek falls when the ice forms sufficiently well.

After crossing the Warren Creek foot bridge continue hiking up west to a trail junction. The trail to the left leads to Starvation Ridge trail, and right leads to Defiance trail. Walk west on the Defiance trail a very short distance to a frozen waterfall called Lancaster Falls.

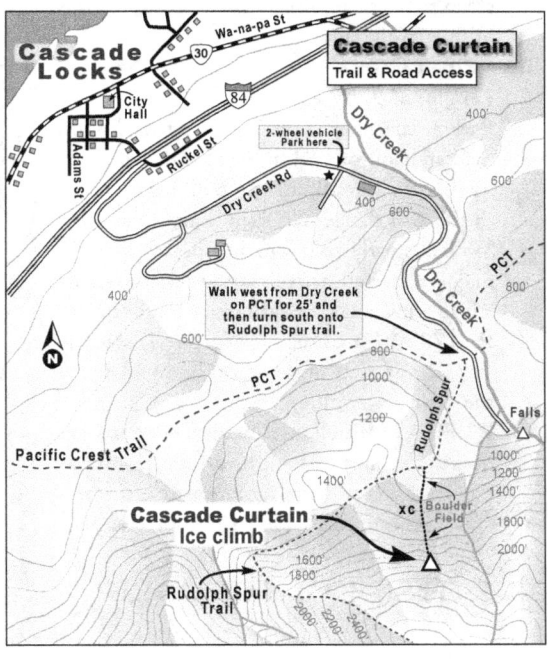

Lancaster Falls

Multi-pitch' II WI 3 on lower portion

This multi-tiered waterfall is readily visible from the freeway at the truck weight station. Park at the Starvation Creek rest facility and walk west on trail #413 passing Cabin Creek falls and passing Warren Creek falls. At the trail junction walk west a few yards to Lancaster Falls.

P1: An initial short vertical step (WI3) leads to easier terrain. About 90' total.

P2: Scramble up easy low angle steps of ice for 250'-300' to the next steep ice face.

P3: An 80' spray formed ice smear (WI3) to the left of the stream.

P4: Crux [WI 4-5?] lead on vertical ice to pass the waterfall. P4 rating not known.

Descent: Walk down in the forest to the east or rappel.

Melissa Demsky climbing *Tanner One*
Photo by Chris Means

Cabin Falls
Multi-pitch' WI [?]

Park at the Starvation Creek rest facility and walk west on the roadside trail that leads to Mt. Defiance. This obvious trail side waterfall at Cabin Falls can be an exhilarating and technical two-pitch ice route when it forms well.

Starvin' Marvin'
Length: 200' WI 3+

Park at the Starvation Creek rest facility located approximately eight miles east of Cascade Locks. This ice smear is the technical savvy route that faces north overlooking I-84 on a flat but steep rock scarp 200' uphill and slightly west of the parking lot.

Starvation Creek
Length: 250' II WI 3+

Park at the Starvation Creek rest facility immediately off of I-84. Hike past the rest facility then walk south into a small side canyon to the base of this ice climb in Starvation Creek. With a steady cold weather polar front this major waterfall actively sprays water to the left to allow a large swath of ice buildup.

P1 170' WI3: Climb on deceptively steep ice steps composed of giant cauliflowers left of the main waterfall.

P2 80' WI4: Follow a natural recessed section under an overhang and then climb past the overhang and aim for a tree near the crest of the promontory near the stream. Rappel.

Doug Hutchinson on *Tanner Two*
Photo: *David Keltner*

NORTH SIDE OF THE GORGE

Starvation Creek ice   Leading P2 on *Starvation Creek ice*

The north side of the Columbia River and can be accessed by using State Route 14 east of Camas, Washington.

CAPE HORN AREA

Cape Horn is one of the most impressive sights to see from across the river. The numerous ice routes on this long steep bluff readily capture the imagination. All the ice routes on Cape Horn are highly technical, unrelenting and long, while many are serious ice leads and often 200'+ in length. There are three vertical basalt tiers formed by multiple formations of old Columbia basalt lava flows. The Lower Tier is available by hiking along the railroad tracks westward 15 minutes from a county access road (or by descending the Cape Horn Trail). The Central Tier has some unexplored long potential leads.

The Upper Tier ice routes (see overview map) are located along State Route 14. Drive a very short distance east past a prominent Cape Horn roadside viewpoint. A steep bluff with a retainment fence is on the uphill side of the road. The first rock scree ravine immediately east of the retainment fence accesses the ice route Hanging Curtain which is a short vertical bluff at the upper portion of the ravine. The upper smear offers several possible ice climbing options.

Several hundred yards further east along State 14 is the second ravine which has a small chain link barrier to catch loose rocks that roll down the steep ravine. This ravine is Phantom Gully which has a short steep bluff higher up the gully. Immediately east is a tiny third ravine (Silver Streak) which has a short steep rock step partway up the ravine. Just past this last ravine is a wide flat rock face with a highly visible ice smear called Salmon Run which forms on a small near vertical bluff. Most ice routes on the Upper Tier will form quickly. Beta is left to right (for upper and middle tiers).

Cape Horn • Upper Tier

Hanging Curtain
Length: 80' WI 3+
Up a rock ravine is a short steep cliff that can be climbed when there is substantial ice forming.

Starvin' Marvin' at Starvation Rest Area

Phantom Gully
Length: 80' WI 3

This is an active stream flowing down a minor ravine above a metal protection grate. The stream splits higher up the slope and can provide several minor ice smears to climb.

Silver Streak
Length: 80' WI 3+

A short steep pumpy ice smear that is tucked in the trees just above the road.

Salmon Run
Length: 200' II WI 4

The classic test piece for the Upper Tier ice routes, and it's the most obvious ice route located in plain sight immediately above the road. It has two steep sections separated by a narrow ledge system in between. The difficulty varies depending upon the thickness of the flow.

Cape Horn • Central Tier

Climbing on the classic *Organic Mist*

Unknown

Wide ice smear located west of the stream along the Cape Horn Trail.

Cape Horn Falls
Length: ___', P1 WI2 and P2 WI3

The stream and waterfall. This falls has a trail side viewpoint at its top.

Jet Stream
Length: 135' (40m), WI4

The next frozen water ice climb located to the east of Cape Horn Falls.

Good Hearted Woman (aka Sid's Slot) WI3-4
Length: multi-pitch, P1 WI3 100', P2 WI4 50', P3 ___.

The first flow immediately left of Nancy's Run. P1 long lead, P2 short crux, P3 minor to reach the brush and belay.

Nancy's Run
Length: 250' WI4

This long smear is broken into two by a midway belay bench. P1 135' WI3-4, and P2 115' WI2+. The initial 30' start is a steep section which gradually eases to the midway bench. The second lead has exquisite giant ice feathers around the top of the seep. Low water seep that allows an excellent buildup of ice fairly quickly, although the site is known more for its gale force winds.

Unknown

Potential, steep, and hung for the initial lead.

Lower Tier, Cape Horn, photo by Nate Farr   *Catch of the Day*, Cape Horn, photo N.F.

Junk Yard
Length: 70m, WI3
Located in a very broad ampthitheater alcove.

Half Bridge
Length: multi-pitch, WI __ [?]
Multi-tier ice ravine directly under a half bridge on the highway.

Cape Horn • Lower Tier (beta right to left)

The known routes for the **Lower Tier** (beta is listed right to left). The approach to the river tier is from the east, so this list details the ice routes as if you are facing the cliff. Included are the two known rock spires along the river shoreline for a reference bearing point. Beware that some of the extreme ice leads have little or no protection available.

Wind Walker
Length: 150' (50m), WI 3+
Approximately 100 yards east of the railroad tunnel, then about 50 yards uphill on a cliffband above the railroad. First 10-meters is angled, then sustained WI3+ for remainder. Fades into frozen brush when you get near a tree belay.

Tyrolean Spire 5.7X A1
Exfoliating basalt rock spire that is rarely climbed.

Tyrolean Tear
Length: 230', WI5
Long ice smear that is tucked in behind the Tyrolean Spire.

Unknown
Potential tall vertical ice smear to the immediate right of Catch of the Day.

Catch of the Day
Length: 230' (70m) WI3+
This is the standard classic for the lower river tier and is often the first ice climb you will ascend in your initial foray along the lower Cape Horn tier. The ice flow offers reasonably fat ice for most of the climb (may be thin on the first portion) with the crux being the initial vertical

240 CHAPTER 4

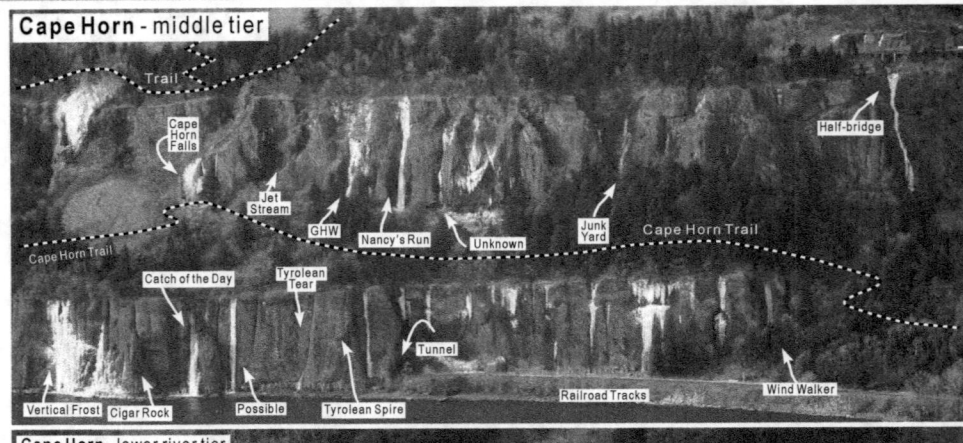

45'. This ice route is the prominent smear located to the right of Cigar Rock.

Cigar Rock 5.7X
Prominent friable rock spire; not recommended.

Unknown
Potential to the left of Cigar Rock tucked in a very wet creek corner.

Vertical Frost
Length: 230' (70m) WI 5

When an arctic blast rips through the Gorge a frenzy of wind-whipped spray creates a stellar technical ice climb on a tall vertical wall littered with cauliflower-like knobs of ice. Very steep and technical. This route is left of the flowing waterfall which is left of Cigar Rock.

Rivers Edge
Length: 230' (70m) WI 5

An extreme ice route that provides a wide swath of wind-whipped ice. Expect some stream flow near the top of the route.

Frozen Embers
Length: 230' (70m) WI 5

Rumored to have also been solo climbed by Jim and partner using ice screws for the belays only. The upper part of this extreme route flows with plenty of water.

Hamilton Mountain • The Strand

The Strand
This is one of several long multi-pitch smears on the prominent south face of Hamilton which form from water seeps. The obvious problem encountered on this face is due to the short time the cold polar Arctic air lingers in the Gorge. A sustained cold snap and overcast cloudy weather would make the ice route more feasible. No known complete ascent yet.

The Strand has seen attempts over the years by several strong climbing teams. McGown and Simpson explored it in the early 1980s, but more recent forays have also been done by others.

GORGE ICE

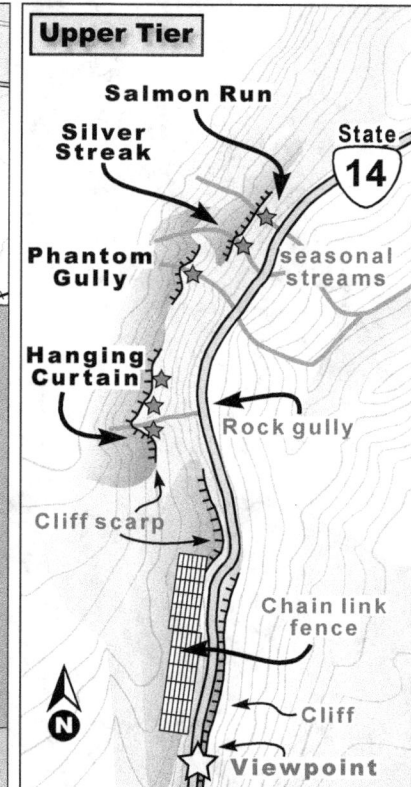

Cape Horn Upper Tier closeup analysis

Topo F: Cape Horn

Upper Tier on Road
1. Hanging Curtain
2. Phantom Gully
3. Silver Streak
4. Salmon Run

Salmon Run on upper Cape Horn

There are three possible smears on the main face (see photo). The middle smear is the typical candidate which these parties have chosen to explore. Recent climbers have been able to reach the midway point on the middle smear before turning back.

The Strand looks awesome because it forms as a very narrow multi-tiered smear with several vertical sections of ice with several exit options on the upper face.

The Strand can be accessed by driving on Forest Service road 4270, a steep narrow rough gravel road leading up to an abandoned gravel quarry. A quick one hour hike on an open slope boulder field leads directly uphill to the south face of Hamilton Mtn.

The bluff formation is a multi-tiered composition of welded cobblestone-sized basalt from old lava flow that tend to be quite friable. The south facing ice smear should only be explored on overcast cloudy days so the ice remains attached. When the Strand forms sufficiently you should anticipate extreme route technicalities up to WI6. Don't start dreamin' about the Strand or you will want to be the first do it.

The Strand on Hamilton Mtn

GORGE ICE CLIMBING

Unique SW Washington climbs

CHAPTER

SW WASHINGTON

In a region known for its great hiking trails beside swift flowing streams that carve canyons through lush forested hills, you might not think southwest Washington has much to offer for rock climbing. Yet climbing sites in close proximity to the metro area have been explored such as the well known granitic formations of Chimney Rocks, and more recently quality bouldering opportunities at Larch Mtn.

Though some destinations are isolated from the convenience of mainstream rock climbing, places like Chimney Rock offer adventurous sub-alpine rock climbing opportunities on a variety of spires both large and small. Avid rock climbers will relish the unmatched beauty and photographic grandeur while climbing at some of these places.

CHIMNEY ROCKS

Chimney Rocks is a semi-isolated, inspiring cluster of pinnacles scattered along a sub-ridge extending southeast from Silver Star Mountain. If the crag were located in Portland it would surely be a very popular climbing area. The outcrop though, is nicely situated on a wind swept ridge with breathtaking views of nearby mountains and the Columbia Gorge.

The crag is an intrusive (plutonic) lava formation part of the Silver Star dike and is composed of Aplite mantled diorite, which is granitic related stock that became exposed along the ridge crest after the surrounding terrain had eroded away. The spire offers great quality rock climbing. Numerous crack climbing opportunities exist ranging in difficulty from 5.6 to 5.11 and involve mostly natural gear protected leads. You could not ask for a better alpine environment near Portland than this. Never overrun with crowds, crisp mountain air, plenty of sun, plenty of climbing, easy two-mile hiking access along a gated road, and superb scenery. All we need is better access via a shorter hike in to the Chimney Rock spires.

Directions

To explore this climbing area drive east on State Route 14 to Washougal, Washington. Take the 15th street exit which is State Route 140 for 6½ miles and turn left onto NE Hughes Road (Vernon Road Bridge is just beyond on the right). Follow this winding uphill road for 3¼ miles up onto Bear Prairie to its junction with the Skamania Mines Road (412th street & Skye road). Follow this road 1½ miles downhill to the bridge at the West Fork of the Washougal River. Continue one mile uphill past the river to the 3-way intersection at W-1200 road. Drive north (left) for a few hundred feet then take the right branching dirt road. The left split leads to Yacolt/Silver Star Mountain. Continue on the right fork road for 1¼ miles and park at gated road #1250. Walk up this road 1 mile to

Brian on lead at *Chimney Rocks*

the 2600' level, then walk north on another heavily rutted and brushy dirt road for 1½ miles to the pinnacles. Access to this pinnacle crosses private land. Hiking is the standard accepted method of approach to access this outcrop of rock so please park your vehicle at the bottom of the hill and hike to the crag.

The following routes are described clockwise around Chimney Rocks, starting with the standard summit scramble. Most of the common routes have been lead or top-roped.

1. **Summit Scramble 5.0**
★★★

    Scramble 100' up the east side along a ridge crest to the top of Chimney Rocks.

2. **SE Arête 5.10b TR** ★

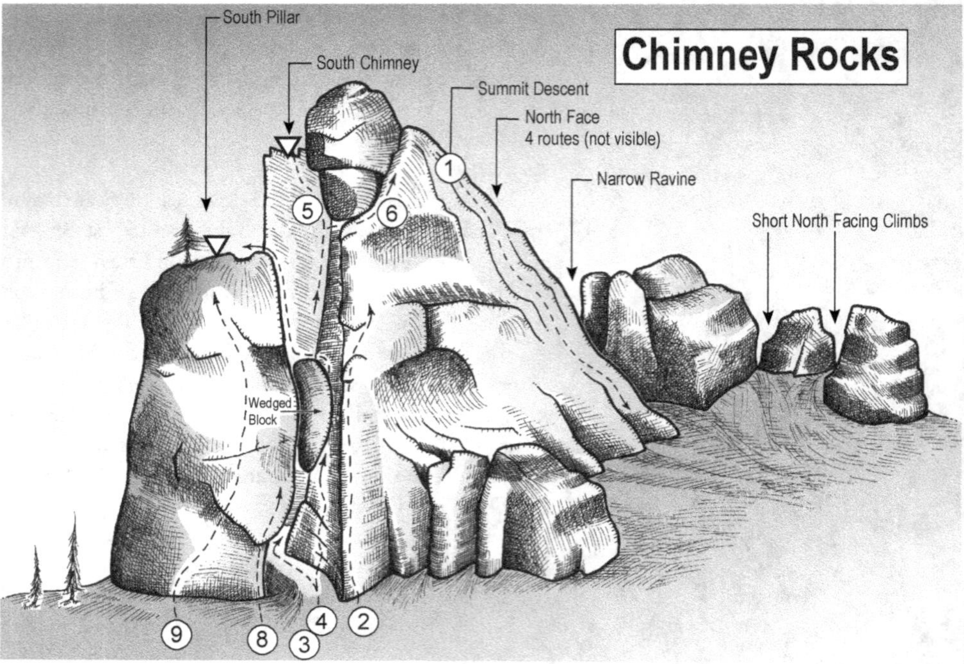

    A huge cavernous slot separates the main massif from the South Pillar. This cavernous slot has several large jammed blocks perched

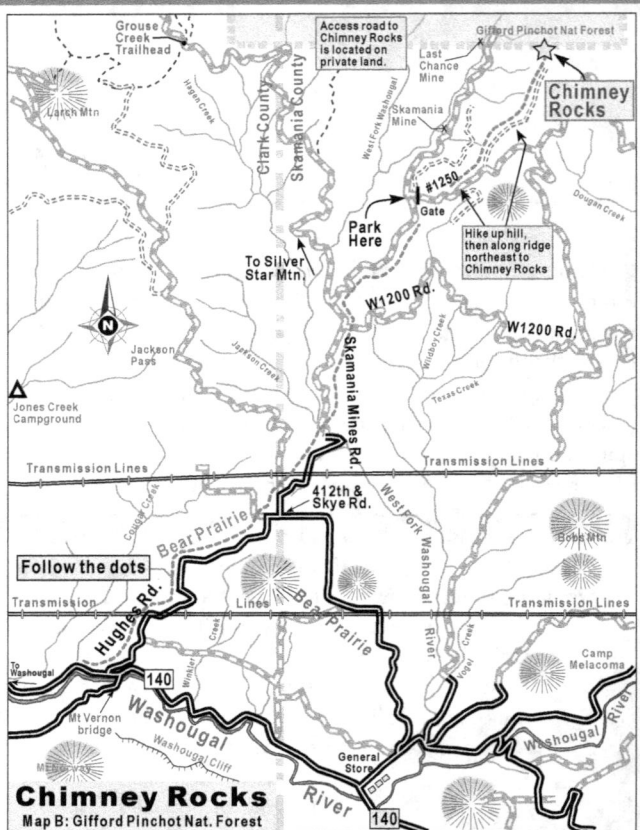

partway up the wall. A convenient walkway leads through this slot to the popular South Face Chimney.

At the east end of this slot on the immediate right is an arête. The arête is a fine top-rope, but a bit challenging to set up protection at the top for a belay.

3. **Wedged Block 5.4 R** ★

This is an alternative means for getting onto the summit of the South Pillar. Climb up the main wall on the right side under the massive block and squeeze around the block. Wander across the top of the massive block over to the South Pillar. Rappel from a horn with a sling or rap from the tree.

4. **Wedged Block Right Exit 5.4 R**
Climb the right same again passing the massive block. From the top of the block continue up onto the main Chimney Rock and aim for the summit. Descend down the standard scramble

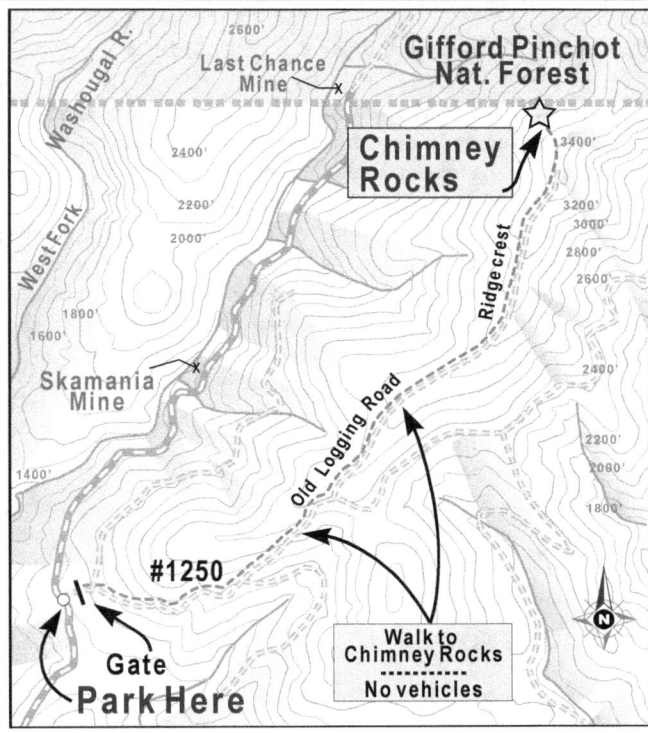

route.

5. **South Chimney 5.8 (or 5.9 direct start)** ★ ★ ★
   Pro to 4"
   The standard climb everyone aims for when visiting this site because the prominent dihedral chimney system is readily visible on the hike in. Walk through the cavernous slot. The high trail bypasses the 5.9 crux start. The lower trail lets you tackle the friable 5.9 crux start. The remainder of the climb is 5.8. Start by climbing the obvious wide chimney corner system. As you near the capstone, angle up left into another crack which also steepens to a small roof. Before you reach the small roof (at a bush) traverse right on face holds and exit through a notch to a large fat ledge to belay. Scramble 25' to the summit and descend route #1.

6. **Right Roof Exit 5.8**
   Pro to 4"
   Climb the South Face Chimney, but aim for the capstone, then traverse *right* under the roof and exit around the far end of it. Scramble to the top and belay, but be mindful of rope drag.

SOUTH TOWER

Brian on East Face of South Pillar

This is the 80' tall pillar on the immediate left side of the cavernous slot that stands separate from the main massif.

7. _____ **5.12- TR**

An extreme top-rope exists on the overhanging northeast side of the South Pillar next to the bivi site.

8. **East Face South Tower 5.6**

Pro: Mostly slings for rock horns

A nice method to attain the top of the South Tower. Fun climbing using mostly natural horns for sling protection. This starts just a few feet left of the bivi site.

9. **South Face South Tower 5.7**

Pro: Nuts and cams to 2"

Start a few feet left of the East Face route on steep terrain where you can power up to a central scoop on the face, then traverse up left using edges and dance gingerly up to the top.

WEST FACE OF CHIMNEY ROCKS

The west side of this spire has a very long 200' scarp.

10. Southwest Crack 5.9 R
Pro to 3"

A cool looking line, but very steep in places. Don't be lulled into thinking its a cruise. Located immediately left of the South Face Dihedral is a very tall noble fir tree. A few feet left of the tree you can access the mid point of this route on some easy steps, and then get right to it at the vertical crux. This method will shorten the overall lead.

If you want the full blown deal, descend down slope to the top of a massive block. An overhanging wide crack (crux) starts up the wall then eases to steps. It walks up right (mid-point merges here) then launches into the vertical 5.9 thin jam and finger crack.

11. West Arete 5.10b ★★★
Pro is 14 QD's, length 170' (some longer sling draws, and a few small cams)

A quality steep arête with plenty of exposure. Descend thru the slot downhill to Tree Frog, then climb a fat 15' tall slot between a monster block on the lower west face.

Climb past a crux and several bolts continuing on 5.8 terrain on the left side of the buttress. Move up an easy broken slab, then step around to the right side of prow, for some vertical exposed (crux) climbing, and finish with another 40' or so of easy climbing to attain a belay anchor

near the summit.

12. Tree Frog 5.8 R
Pro to 3" and may need pitons, length 170'

On the immediate lower west side of Chimney Rocks is another fir tree. From the top of a large block immediately right of the fir tree diligently dance 60' up small edges (5.8R) to easier ground. Wander up steps and ledges leftward to the north side till you merge with the north face crack system. The upper west side has a slightly overhanging section which commits to angle up left. Limited pro options.

NORTH FACE OF CHIMNEY ROCKS

There are three prominent crack corner climbs on the north face, as well as one bolt route. The crack climbs are nearly 200' long leads and are popular challenging climbs for visitors. The north side has a narrow squeeze slot for convenient access to all these routes.

13. Southern Cross 5.9 ★★
Pro to 5" if you have it

This is the lower of three major crack climbs on the north side. Start a few feet left of the west side fir tree and climb a consistently steep and dark stained wide crack corner. When you encounter a small capstone bust up right onto easy ground. Climb up left 30' and merge with the next crack system. This climb is best when broken into two pitches.

14. Orions Belt 5.8+ ★★★
Pro to 5" if you have it

A well-traveled route because it has small stances and it is not quite as sustained. But it has a 'poison pill' crux move mid-way up the route where you move past a large wedged chockstone that leans out at you. Still a cool route and worth the venture. A 200' lead.

15. Northern Lights 5.9 ★★★
Pro to 3½"

The upper left most route, but it is a stellar crack line as well. The climb is shorter than the other two, but has a definite overhanging crux bulge to surmount past. The climb eases significantly the remainder of the way to the top.

16. _____ 5.11+ ★
Pro: __ QD's

The north side has a narrow squeeze slot for convenient access. This route is on the vertical face uphill of the previous three routes. An extreme face climb. No fixed belay anchor.

17. The Point 5.11+
On the opposite side of the squeeze slot is well overhung overhang to put it lightly. The Point powers up a bolt line on the upside down chin of this pointless point.

NORTH BLUFF

Immediately northeast of Chimney Rocks is a north facing bluff about 40' tall. It can be accessed through the narrow squeeze slot that leads down to the north face. After you get thru the slot, walk around the bluff end to this short steep flat wall. Most of the routes have been lead although most visitors these days generally just top-rope the climbs. To set up a top-rope (see diagram) aim to either notch at the top of the northeast bluff. Plenty of horns and cracks allow easy anchor placements.

18. First Crack 5.7
Starts as slightly overhung moves, angling up leftward using a crack.
19. Second Crack 5.7 ★
Starts as overhung move, then a straight forward jam crack to top.
20. Corner Crack 5.6
A nice basic corner crack climb.
21. Left Arête 5.9 TR ★
The outside arête is a quality bit of arête pinching and face climbing.

You can also top-rope face sections between some of these routes if desired.

NW SPIRE

Climbing the north side cracks at *Chimney Rocks*   Brian leading the *South Chimney*

The large inobvious pinnacle downhill on the northwest side of Chimney Rocks. To get there, descend through the slot, and cut downhill across the talus to it.

NW Buttress 5.8+

Pro: cams to 4", nuts to 1", Length 200'+ (2-pitches)

Begin just right of the toe of the lower northwest end of the pinnacle.
P1 (120', 5.8): Climb 5.5 face (2-bolts) past a short crux diagonal finger crack to a large ledge. Climb sustained 5.8 dihedral above, then up a series of easy ledges to large belay ledge (with a belay tree). **P2 (80', 5.8+):** Climb up a short left-facing OW corner (protects with #4 cam) and trend to the right. Angle eases, then trend up left via an easy section till you reach several large chockstones. Traverse right (bolt) on 5.6 terrain to gain a ledge, then up left to a tree belay (near a bolt).

SW Buttress 5.9

Pro: cams to 3", nuts to 1", Length 220'+ (2-pitches)

Begin at the toe of the southwest end of this pinnacle. Mostly 5.6 climbing with a minor section of 5.9.
P1 (110', 5.9): Climb a crack to a small roof (bolt), do crux 5.9 move, then continue up crest of ridge, using thin cracks for gear, and utilizing various ledges to reach a large belay ledge (bolt belay). **P2 (110' 5.6):** Continue up past some small trees, then aim generally up to the left, making some exposed moves around a corner to attain a large ledge. Several final summit block cracks provide the last bit of entertainment. Belay at the summit belay at a minor notch.

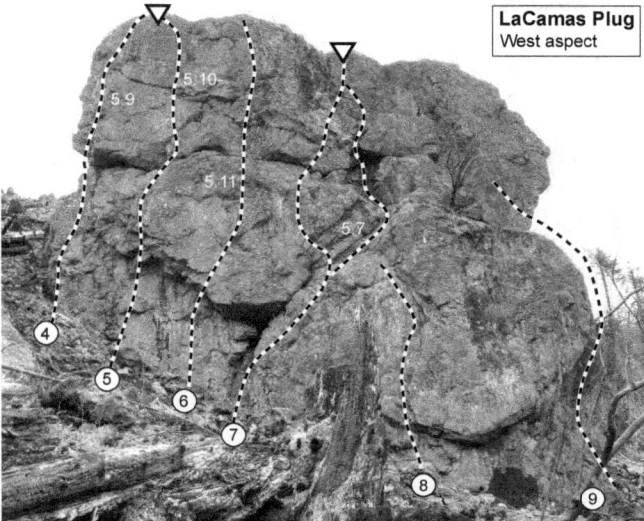

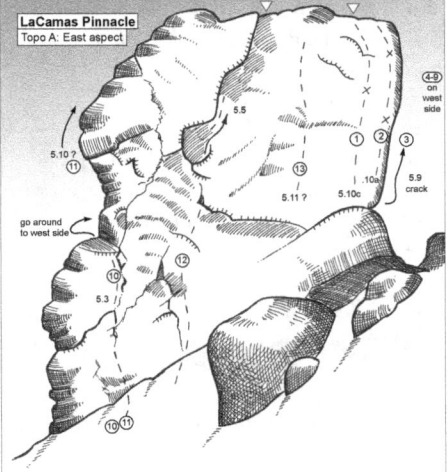

LACAMAS PLUG

A rather minor plug-*ish* stump of rock in outer suburbia northeast of Camas, Wa. Though partially developed, once it is well refined it may yield about 15 routes ranging from 5.5 to 5.11 (see diagram) for 360° around the plug, the shortest being 15' and the longest about 40' tall.

The short two-minute walk to the outcrop may make it viable for group climbing. The rock plug has a circumference width of about 40' max and is suitable for lower grades climbing (5.7 to 5.10+) and TR practice with a wide, flat summit. Maintain good etiquette here; the land is a mix of state DNR and timber company domain. The Lacamas Plug is granodiorite rock that is good for climbing on...even though this plug is desperately small. GPS 45°41.000'N / 122°16.000'W.

There are 3 possible country roads that will get you to the outcrop, and the following is one option. From I-205 bridge drive east on State 14 highway to Camas, WA. At the main light in front of the Safeway store, drive northeast of Camas of state 500 road passed Lacamas Lake. Turn right at NE 19th at Fern Prairie store and drive east 1 mile, and take a left at the "Y" and drive north uphill on 272nd. This winds north and east for 2 miles to a 3-way stop intersection. Turn north (left) on 292nd and drive one-half mile. Turn right on Ireland road, then 'Y' left onto Lessard road. Follow the signs to Jones Creek motocross parking area. The L-1610 gravel road continues past this parking

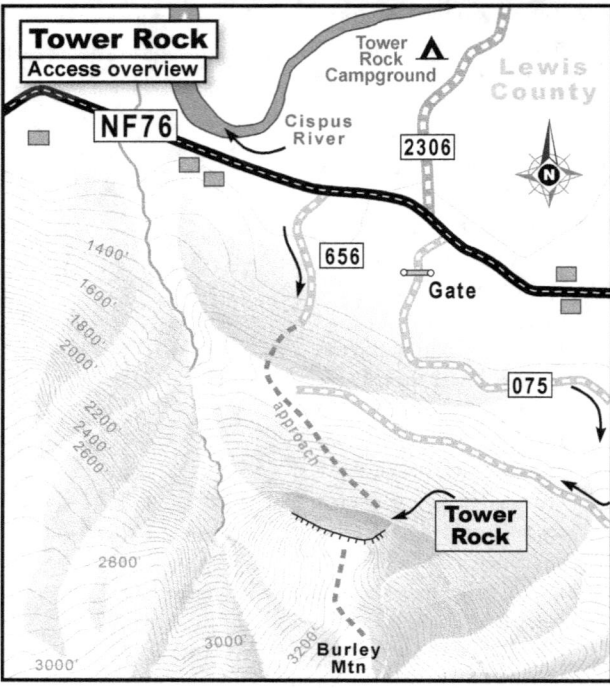

site and winds its way uphill to junction with L-1510 road. Go left (uphill) on L-1500 for ¾ mile, then take a left onto an unmarked well graveled road, and follow this downhill for about ¾ mile. The LaCamas Plug is apparent on the uphill side of the road in a logged zone. The last 4 miles are on forest gravel roads but this particularly gravel road is better maintained. Distance from I-205 bridge is 50 minutes on gravel roads (23 miles).

TOWER ROCK

Tower Rock is an imposing 1100' tall north facing diorite massif with vertical and slightly hung sections of wall. Though the impressive cliff scarp size might beckon you here to climb it, the combination of low altitude rainy climate, and northern mossy aspect seem to create ideal exfoliating conditions that frequently send voluminous quantities of stone tumbling down its steep face. Even the FA party found the stacked rubble piles en route to be a bit intimidating and yearned for a happy ending to their multi-day rock climb with an unanticipated bivouac due to a late start.

To reach Tower Rock, drive north on I-5, then take exit #68 and drive east 46½ miles on US 12 to Randle, Washington. Go south from Randle and cross the Cowlitz River. Drive south one mile, then turn east on NF 23 and continue southeast for 8 miles. Turn right (south) onto NF 28 and drive 9/10 mile (crossing the Cispus River). Turn west on Cispus River Road (aka NF 76) and drive for 1¾ miles. Park near an old closed dirt road NF 075 which can be used to access the lower slopes of Tower Rock. Walk up this old dirt road about 45 minutes to reach the base of the wall.

This north facing cliff scarp is located immediately north of Burley Mtn. overlooking the Cispus River valley. The wall is vertical, north facing, and at a fairly low elevation so anticipate gravel, loose rock, and moss on ledges. The GPS coordinates is N 46.432000, W -121.869000 with a high point at 3,160'.

Camping Options:

The Tower Rock U-fish RV campground is an ideal place to stay when planning to climb this

SOUTHWEST WASHINGTON 253

Tower Rock
Map 1: North Face

rock wall. When you turn onto Cispus River Road drive a total of 2.6 miles to reach this campground. This locale also has a excellent farmland open zone to view and photograph the wall.

NW Face (Nieland-Valenzuela route)
Pro: nuts, hexes, and pitons

Begin left of a large cleft on the left side of this broad cliff scarp (see photo), and 4th class up a ramp to a sloping ledge. Climb up right for 3 pitches (5.7) (some loose rock and some mixed aid). P4 acsends up for 60' and rightward for 30' landing at a large central nook on the wall with overhung cliff above. P5 and P6 ascend up right along a series of ledges on a steep ramp system. P7 moves up right and ascends a corner system (5.6) landing on a big ledge on the west ridge. P8 continues up a steep face (5.6) on the crest for one lead till you reach the final headwall. P9 move directly right onto the west side and face climb (5.8) upward on low angled small mossy ledges to the top of the cliff. Per Jim Nieland: expect some poorly protected sections, considerable moss, grassy sections, and loose rock. Descend down the ravine on the west side.

Rapunzel's Back in Rehab   Grade V, 5.9 C1, 1100' tall
FA: 7-2017, Eric Linthwaite, Bill Coe, Geoff Silverman.

Gear suggestions: Up to 30+ trad-style draws (if clipping all bolts) which is full length slings, 2 bathooks, 60'-meter rope (2 if you plan on rapping down), cheater stick perhaps, lower off webbing or quick-links/biners (for the follower when traversing), helmet. A hand drill is suggested (and a few bolts). A 70-m rope is optional.

Note: the above is not a free rating—but an aid rating. Rumor is some free sections are a bit difficult (aka 5.9+ -ish).

Note: the tower exfoliates random rockfall at times, but the route itself is generally cleaned up.

Note: the P1 first bolt is about 5' above the ground near a clump of trees about 50' above a huge lounge-like boulder (viable safe observation spot). The mid-pitches [P4-P5] and the upper pitches are tricky reverse rappels (be prepared for that challenge). The entire route is fixed with a ton of bolts/hangers, and numerous bolt holes for hooking. It's possible this route will eventually be free climbed.

The Rapunzel's route is 14-pitches total.

Lower Wall

P1 (35m long): "P1 (35-m long): Low angle moss lead fest straight up and then ease left where it changes from aid to free 5/8 of the way up"

P2 (40m): This a steeper tier of mossy rock to the next prominent ledge. Many hooks.

P3 (55m): The very steep vertical lower wall begins. Many hooks.

P4: Climb leftward under a huge corner roof system under a massive hanging detached block. One hook used.

P5 (55m): Continues up vertical mossless rock angling up left slightly. Many hooks.

P6 (20m): Fixed rope. Start up on the left side of the ledge you are standing on.

P7 (30m): lower angled mossy rock where the terrain eases as you reach the edge of 'the fault', a broad ramp system to the base of the upper wall.

Upper Wall

P8 (25m long): Move across 'the fault' which is a lesser angled mossy ramp system between the lower vertical wall and the upper vertical wall. This is also where the Nieland-Valenzuela route criss-crosses the Rapunzel route.

P9 (25m): The infamous 'Dances with Death' pitch which looks terrifying but is more solid than it appears. Long reaches, have the tall climber (if you have one) lead this pitch.

P10 (35m): Combining P10-11 together suggested. Takes off out of a cozy notch, and goes up just left of a vertical corner system. The first bolt is a long reach high.

P11 (25m): Belay from an uncomfortable corner position, free moves off the belay gets you the

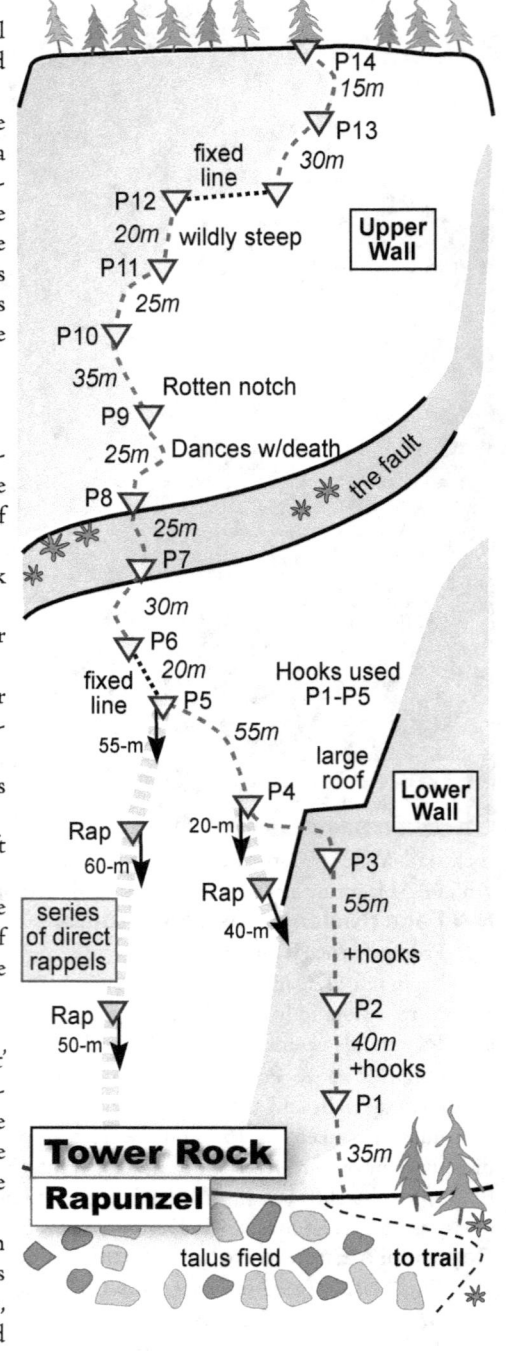

bolts which are to the right of the major corner.
P12 (30m): Climb the radically overhanging headwall above.
Belay on the small stance or use a fixed line traverse right about 25' to a better belay.
P13 (30m) goes up and then rightward up mossy corners and steep ramps.
P14 (15m): climb some 50' approximately to reach the summit saddle flop. Belay off of the trees. Success!

Descent:
Three options. A 2-car shuttle walk off is easiest (may scout in advance in case you top out in the dark).

Option #1: walk trail on top to the east, then down to a saddle. Then go right and bushwack down straight down a steep forest to the base where you started.

Option #2: follow the flagged hiking trail back ¼ mile as it turns right, then descends on a nice trail downhill to the trailhead. Parking spot is N 46.43017 W 121.87833 for that shuttle.

Option #3: follow hiking trail south, then uphill to intersect with Burley Mtn trail to your shuttle car N 46.42227 W 121.87108 for that shuttle.

SUNSET BLUFF

Deep along a forested backcountry gravel road about 30 minutes from Yacolt, WA are several tiny roadside rock formations that provide minor entertainment for beer swillin' gun shooting Yacolter's who have made the most of limited stone in their valley. The group of 3 sites are known as Sunset Bluffs. So, if you're not driven by selfish ideological perfection then these tiny crags may beckon. Each site is well situated with a WSW facing aspect to catch the early Spring and late Fall sunshine (sometimes even T-shirt climbing in Dec-Feb).

The first site is **Dalle de Cristal (Crystallin Slab)** at 1900' elevation. It's a slightly fractured rather puggish short 35' tall basaltic bluff which offers some fun slab climbs and some moderately desparate leads (including a smattering of TR's and projects).

The **Thunder Wall** (the second minor roadside site) is just a mere roadcut (made totally by machinery) composed of granite rock (the elusive stuff that keeps its little munchsky hidden around Silver Star Mtn).

The **Top O' The Bluff** (the third minor roadside outcrop) is a low angle outcrop of granodioritic peripheral complexity, but showing signs of metamorphic crystallin adjustment. It is loaded with edges, pockets (1" - 12"), and several cracks, and plenty of crimps (and 4 fixed TR belays).

Season:
Seasonal access is from May through mid-November typically, but often accessible even in the winter (at the first and second site). The NF41 road south of Sunset Campground is gravelled and generally maintained every 1-4 years. From there the road is occasionally maintained (when USFS has logging goals in the area). The latest road re-grade was in 2018.

History:
Mr M and Mr O were the primary route developers (cleaning, bolting, naming, leading) of the first two sites (while Mr M developed the third site). General development phase occurred from about 2011-2016.

Directions:
From Battleground, WA drive north on SR500, then east on Lucia Falls Road. When you reach Moulton Falls county park, turn east on Sunset Fall road and drive 7¼ miles. When you reach the campground called Sunset Falls Campground, turn south and cross a bridge. The Sunset Hemlock Road (aka NF Rd 41) is gravel and continues uphill from the bridge. Drive a total of 4 miles and park in a wide spot near an old gate (used by a dead-end road that descends to some mining claims along the creek). Walk the main gravel road uphill south about 100', then cut up a long

talus field slope for 550' to reach the rock climbing slab (Crystallin Slab).

DALLE DE CRISTAL (CRYSTALLIN SLAB)

The Crystallin Slab is a nice but minor little crag situated at about 1900' elevation (lowest of the three Sunset Bluffs). The main slab is the prime objective and it hosts several fine quality routes. Beta is described right to left (south to north).

1. **Dreamcatcher 5.11a** ★
   Pro: 4 QD's, 30' tall
   Very short uniquely stout route with closely space bolts; cruxy crimps on a flat face.
2. **_____ 5.11+ (TR)**
   Untested but possible, yet desperately short.
3. **Double Trouble 5.9**
   Gear to 3", 30' tall
   Double jam crack in a corner. Crux is getting off the ground.
4. **_____ 5.11+ TR**
   35' tall
   Tall flat slightly hung gold face with thin crimps power climbing potential. This is the right side of the tall prow.
5. **Viper's Nest 5.11b (TR)** ★
   35' tall
   This route is on the left side of the tall prow. Crux is first 15', then eases to 5.8. Not bolted.

A gap of about 20' to the next climbs which are on the main west facing slab.

Main Slab

6. **Coucher du Soleil (aka Sunset) 5.10a** ★★★
   7 QD's, 40' in length
   A superb route with steep, techy unique quality movement (smears and small edges), then up a brief prominent jam crack on the prow, then move left, clip main anchor and lower down.
7. **Le' Premie're (aka The First) 5.7** ★★★
   7 QD's, , 40' in length
   The classic route. Start at the toe of the slab and dance up a long series of enjoyable face crimps, edges, and

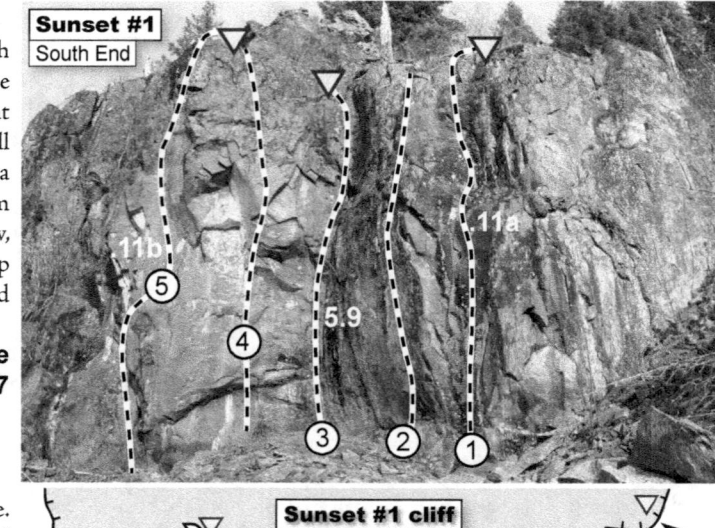

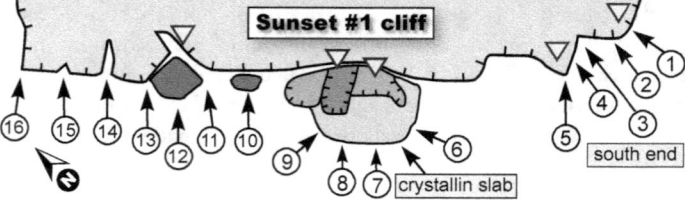

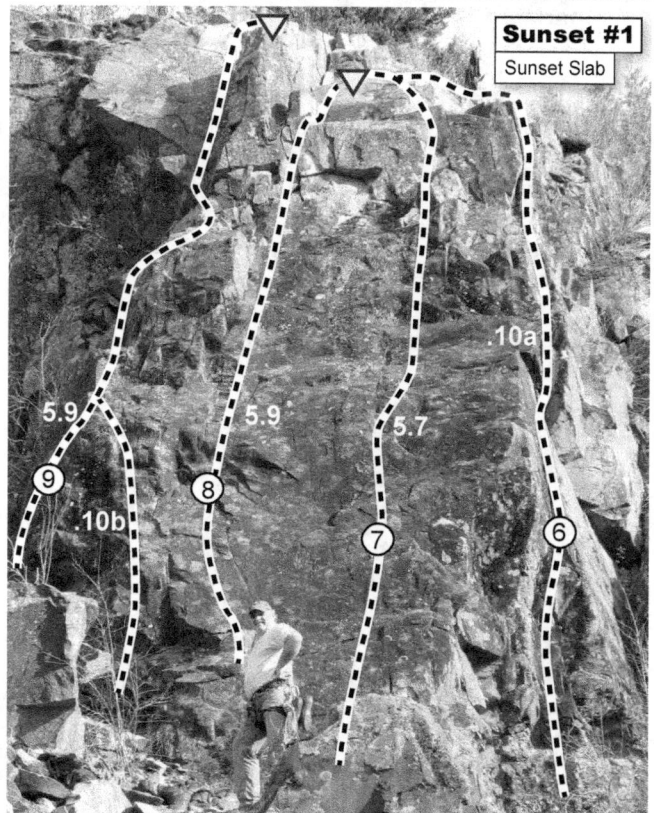

Sunset #1
Sunset Slab

smears passing a crux, then onto a pedestal and a final step. At last bolt move left and use the belay anchor on the route to the left.

8. Zabo's Enchanteur (aka Zabo's Delight) 5.9 ★★

7 QD's, 35' in length
Start as low as possible on low left part of the slab, move up left past a thin crux, then easy terrain to midway stance. Surmount the final vertical step to the nice belay anchor (merely clip and lower down).

9. Choix des Dames 5.10b ★★

7 QD's, 35' in length
On left part of Crystallin Slab. Closely spaced initial bolts set you up for the initial tricky crux. A set of easier edges, then a second steep face section (can bypass on big left ledges). Then finish up left facing crack corner. **Note:** lowest start yields crux variant at 5.10b while the upper left step-in yields 5.9.

Most of the following are mere short TR's and are on the left portion of the crag ending at a short prow.

10. _____ 5.11- (TR)
Potential short vertical face.

11. Double Eagle 5.8
Fat 18" wide chimney with odd fat movement. Belay anchor is used for this and the next two routes.

12. Lousy Putter 5.10- (TR)
Awkward face between both cracks.

12. Reckless Rookie 5.8 (TR)
Crack cruising up then right onto same landing for previous two routes.

13. _____ 5.10- (TR)
A short groove slot-ish weakness.

14. _____ 5.10+ (TR)
Minor short face.

Leslie at *Crystallin Slab*

15. **Charlatan Salesman 5.11+ (TR)**
The north end short prow. Awkward crux makes it a candidate for early retirement.

THUNDER WALL

Thunder Wall is a minor granite roadside roadcut phenomenon with a series of ultra short rock climbs on steeply angled rock. Definitely not a destination crag, but if you happen to live in the general area.... The site holds the rare distinction of being the closest developed rock climbing real granite crag to Portland. Some people refuse to climb here; after all its just a literal roadcut—they're convinced its not 'real' climbing (yet they'll go practice at a bloody indoor sport gym and somehow call that 'climbing'!?).

1. _____ **5.8 [?]**
Left Crack Corner system. A mixture of ledge, face, crack and corners. Needs extensive leverage yet.

2. _____ **5.10+ [?]**
A possible minor flat face with some thin holds that might yield a tricky hard line.

3. **Twister 5.10c** ★★
Pro: 9 QD's, Length 40'
Steep slightly leftward leaning prominent face route with a provocking leg-wrap block crux.

4. **Typhoon 5.10b** ★★★
Pro 9 QD's, Length 40'
See a large obvious drilled blast hole high on the face. Climb up the first part of #3 route, split up right but stay left of drilled hole on thin crimp holds. Classic? (well...its got quality).

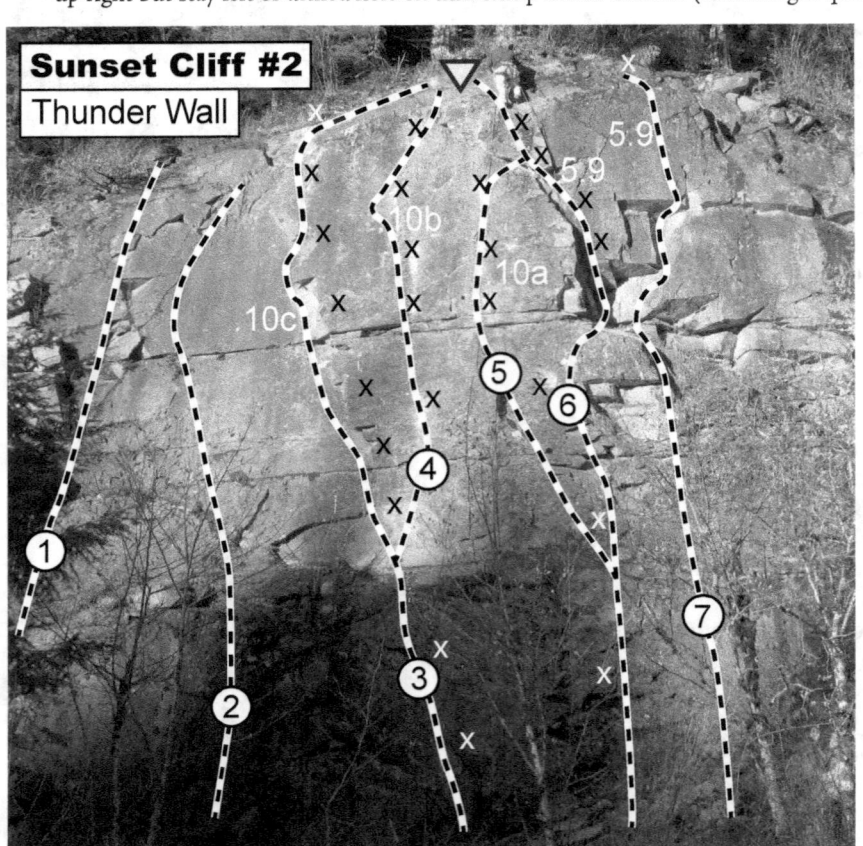

5. **Tsunami 5.10a** ★★★
   Pro: 8 QD's, Length 40'
   Dance up easy terrain to mid ledge. At the drilled mega blast-hole, climb a steep face just to the right of it on small crimps. At a thin stance, move right merging onto the ramp of the Squall route. Or....make a tricky left-*ish* maneuver up into the previous route (5.10b).

6. **Squall 5.9** ★★
   Pro: 7 QD's, Length 40'
   Numerous steep steps and ledges, then left up a nice steep ramp, then a few tricky face moves to finish. An enjoyable route.

7. **Tornado 5.9 (TR)**
   Pro: ___ QD's (just a top directional bolt)
   Climb a dirty face just right of "the squall" route, then at mid stance, smear up into a vertical slot, past a lip onto a flat thin face. Nice quality face but the best part is very short.

TOP O' THE BLUFF

The southernmost crag in this series along NF 41 road, is this roadside outcrop located where the road curls around the west end of a wooded ridge (see map). This site is generally used for top-roping purposes, and offers 4 fixed belay anchor stations to easily setup your sunny afternoon climbing session. Mr M was the primary route developer. This site is infrequently utilized by the Yacolt Search & Rescue team.

Beta is described north to south:

1. **North Face 5.9 (TR)**
   The north facing aspect, though mossy, yields several vertical face TR's.
2. **The Prow 5.8**
   A long steep arete that separates the vertical mossy north aspect from the easier west aspect.

The next climbs are on the tall sunny west facing aspect.

3. **The Roof 5.8**
   From a ledge surmount a roof then finish up an easy face.
4. **Luck of the Irish 5.7**
   On the main west face slab are TWO obvious cracks. This is the left one (facing the bluff) that surmounts a small roof above a ledge. Fixed anchor at the top of this climb.
5. **River Dance 5.6**
   The rightmost and easier of the two cracks in the middle (below a fixed anchor).
6. **Four Leaf Clover 5.5**
   Pro: 6 bolts, 35' tall
   Climb the lower part of the arete initially then mostly the face on the upper part.
7. **Blarney Stone 5.8**
   Climb immediately on the vertical south face next to the arete.

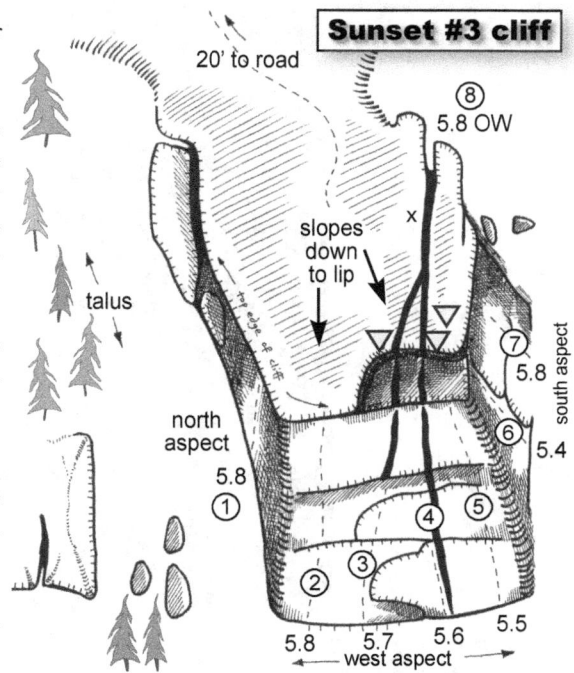

8. **One Half Shilling 5.4**
   Around on the shorter southern aspect and uphill is this short steep face climb.
9. **Pick Pocket 5.6**
   A very short face uphill of previous route.
10. **_____ 5.9**
    Way uphill on the south side of the outcrop is a short but 18" wide upside down off-width.

Climbs on the Clackamas & Molalla

CHAPTER 6

CLACKAMAS & MOLALLA

The watershed of the lower Clackamas River is composed of geologic rock type structures different from the trend commonly found elsewhere - it tends to be well-aged broken basaltic lava flows or tuffaceous conglomerate stock.

The resulting rock types found at some key low to moderate elevation zones produces several crags with notable challenging characteristics conducive to the skills of articulate well-honed adventure climbers who relish a bit of bold climbing.

Yet hidden on the upper reaches of both the Clackamas and Molalla River valleys there are much better quality rock outcrop structures relevant to the desired goals of skilled rock climbers. This brief chapter takes that big step to detail some of these unique cragging options.

CLACKAMAS RIVER VALLEY

COETHEDRAL

Beta by Bill Coe

Unusual climbing on knobby rock welded in a black-gray igneous breccia matrix the Coethedral climbing site deep in the heart of the Clackamas River Recreation Area may be just the place for a wild climbing tour unlike the typical Oregon crag. Initially explored by Mr. Priestly he quickly teamed up with Mr. Coe and associates to establish a string of wild routes, some nearly 400' tall.

If your rock climbing skills are not superb it is best to climb elsewhere. The site has comprehensive factors that require diligence for both leader and belayer.

How to get there

From the I-205 Clackamas exit drive east on Hwy 224 to Estacada. From the stop light in Estacada continue 21.8 miles along the Clackamas River on Hwy 224 till you are just past MP45. Where the road turns left onto a green bridge, you will go right up past the Indian Henry Campground on paved road FS4620 (Sandstone Rd.) for 10.2 miles total (five miles on gravel). At the five mile point the road becomes FS4622 and continues five miles on gravel as it winds uphill then northward. Park at a dirt berm and old gate with a closed sign affixed to it. Walk northeast along the old spur log road as it slowly descends around a minor butte to a slash pile at a viewpoint. You can see the Coethedral formation from here. Descend northerly along the forested ridge on a deer path to a saddle. Descend several switchbacks

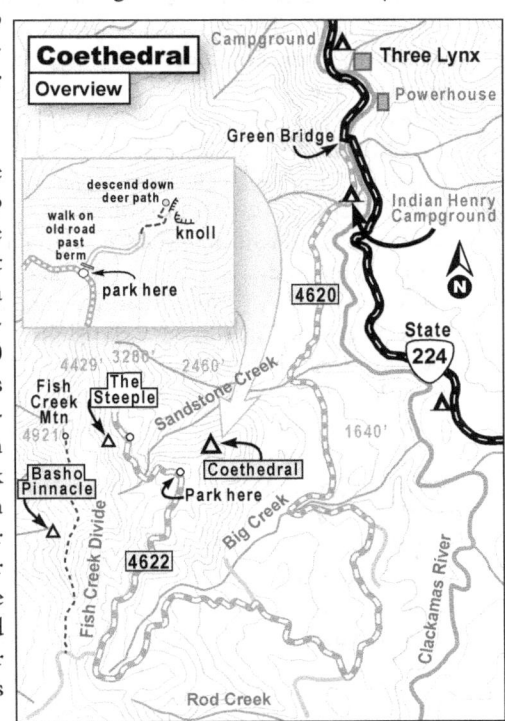

down the steep west side on the faint game trail to the base of the wall. Expect 15-20 minutes to walk to the site.

Requisite gear and site specifics

Wear a helmet, use thicker ropes such as a 10.5mm rope, QD's, and some gear. The rock is abrasive and can quickly abrade and ruin a climbing rope at this site.

Excessive hang dogging against the sandpaper like rock surface will affect the lifespan of your rope. Climb wisely as the site is an isolated area outside of cell phone range. Climb diligently because all the routes are serious, especially the easier routes even though they seem well bolted. When rappelling tie end knots for safety. Unless noted all routes are set so that a single 60m rope will get you down. Use longer slings where needed to reduce rope drag. Anticipate rock fall, particularly if you are at a hanging belay and your partner is climbing above you.

Coethedral is soft breccia matrix with larger stones of varying size (1"-5") welded into the gray groundmass. Lead bolts are typically ½" x 6½" stainless and provide the best long term usability margin. When adding another route or more bolts use similar type and standard. Consult local climbers who can assist you with recommendations for new additions, fixed gear spacing, or other hardware changes. The damp 3300' high altitude climate at Coethedral tends to aggravate lesser quality [non-stainless] fixed hardware. If considering traveling here, the weather should be reasonably stable one day prior to your visit as the site is west facing and can stay quite damp, especially after a rain shower in the spring or fall season. The Coethedral climbing season is generally limited to the months from June-October. The grades are relative and can change due to key rock holds popping off. Climbing routes that are infrequently traveled tend to be more friable. Rock hand holds may be less stable after heavy rains because the porous conglomerate groundmass is weakened. Routes are listed from left to right.

1. **Coe-Priestly 5.10+ R ★**
   Length: 300+', Pro: 15+ Quickdraws, some minor gear, and slings
   Originally done as two pitches but is better when broken into three pitches. Expect loose rock in middle of P1 which mars this otherwise reasonable route. Start 40' uphill from the reading room cave at a single anchor bolt. Aim up slightly right for 26m to a belay. Needs more bolts on the first pitch. Pitch two is a short 5.9 lead on great rock. Pitch three is 100' long. Rap the route with a single 60m rope.

2. **Bewitched 5.9 / 5.10a PG13 ★★**
   Length: 300'+, Pro: 19 Quickdraws [for longest lead] Pitch 1 is 100' (11 bolts) 5.9+ Pitch 2 160' (19 bolts) 5.10a [Bewitched Direct]
   This route ends on top of the Old Witch Pinnacle. Pitch 1 100' (11 bolts) at 5.9+. Crux move getting off the ground and delicate steep knob climbing up to a roof, then step right at the roof into a wide chimney (bolts are near the outer edge) and stem up this deep corner till you exit left to an anchor. Pitch 2 (Bewitched Direct 160' 5.10a 19 bolts) punches directly over the intimidating overhanging roof. Climb directly up above the anchor on a very steep sustained prow. Pitch 3 75' (9 bolts) is 5.6 climbing up steep knobby terrain till it eases onto the spire. Tie off a knob with a sling for the last few moves. The bolt anchor is on the back side of the Old Witch. Rappel down to the notch 40' to the belay at the top of Excalibur, then rappel down into Trench Warfare for a total of four raps.

3. **Upskirt 5.9**
   Length: 170' (52-meters), Pro: 17 Quickdraws (or full length slings) single 52-meter pitch
   Climb up the first short lead of Bewitched till it steps right under the roof into the chimney. Climb the chimney all the way up slinging knobs where possible. Exit through one of two holes on either side of a large unattached chockstone which used to be the belay stance for Trench Warfare. Belay at the Trench Warfare anchors.

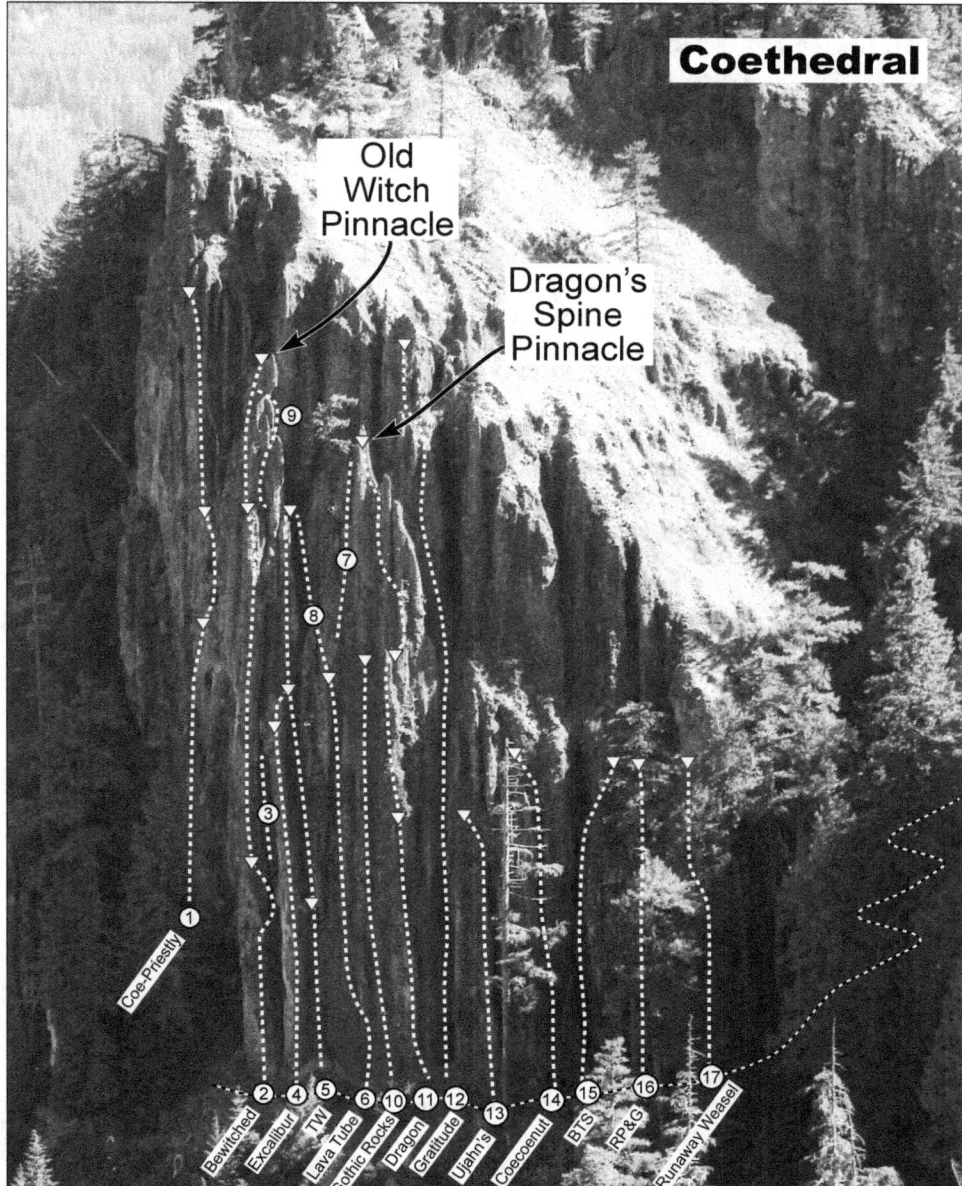

4. **Excalibur 5.10a** ★★
Length: 174' (53-meters), Pro: 28 Quickdraws
One of the better climbs at Coethedral with a prominent position on a steep knobby prow that offers sustained climbing with good rest points along the route. The first very long lead can be split by belaying at the Trench Warfare belay mid-route. The first full long lead ends on a rock point belay. Step over to a saddle, move up past the Trench Warfare second belay, and climb a 12 bolt knob face on the south side of the Old Witch to a small stance belay. Rappel down Trench Warfare in three rappels.

5. **Trench Warfare 5.10b R**
   Length: 166' (54-meters), Pro: 15 Quickdraws
   Climb the obvious deep rounded groove up vertical terrain past a bulge crux (optional belay point at 30m), and onward up an easier gully (sling knobs) till you land at a belay where Upskirt and Excalibur merge at a small ledge stance belay. The second pitch continues above the belay for 90' (12 bolts) to a small belay stance at the base of Salathe Highway. Rappel the route.

6. **Lava Flow 5.8 R ★**
   Length: multi-pitch, Pro: 24-26 Quickdraws
   Lava Flow is the easiest way to the top of the old Witch by combining the Gingerbread Shortcut to the Salathe Highway. Start slightly right of the arête and trend left to follow the gully straight up for 55m pitch (21 bolts). Tie knobs with slings to enhance margins. Pitch 2 (9 bolts) aims straight up to a rappel point at a large fir tree between the pinnacles. Rappel via Trench Warfare.

7. **Grey Ghost 5.7**
   Length: 50', Pro: 6 Quickdraws (more QD's for initial pitch from ground)
   Starts at top of second pitch of Lava Flow and steps right and up into a tough slot cleft (6 bolts) to the top of the Dragon's Spine Pinnacle. Sling some knobs.

8. **The Gingerbread Shortcut 5.7**
   Length: 50-60', Pro: 9 Quickdraws (more QD's for initial pitch from ground)
   From the P2 belay on Lava Flow aim left 10' to a large flake point, turn the corner and step into the gully, then race up the gully (9 bolts total) to a belay at the base of the Old Witch.

9. **Salathe Highway 5.7 X ★★**
   Length: multi-pitch, Pro: nuts ¼" to 1", and cams to 2", but has no fixed bolts
   This is the original route to the top of the Old Witch with zero bolts.
   From the high point belay of Excalibur or Trench Warfare, this route squeezes up left through a gap between the two pinnacles, and then chimney up to the top where the lesser pinnacle ends (use slings on knobs). Step left then up around to the north side of the Old Witch following a minor break in the rock and onto the crest to a belay anchor at the top. Rappel down to the notch belay, then rappel Trench Warfare.

10. **Gothic Rocks 5.9**
    Length: multi-pitch, Pro: about 28-29 Quickdraws
    Start on the ground between Lava Tube and Dragons Spine and follow the 28+ bolts a full pitch to the anchors. The mid-point rap anchors are visible 6' to the right of the route.

11. **The Dragons Spine 5.8 ★★★**
    Length: multi-pitch, Pro: 24 Quickdraws
    Some say it is 5.8 and others say 5.10. Pitch 1 ascends an arête (24 bolts) straight up and near a spine, but wandering a bit (intermediate rap anchor on left at midway point) on knobs to a belay at 56m. Pitch 2 steps up right then up 15 bolts aiming slightly left to the top of Dragons Spine Pinnacle. Rappel either of three ways: this route, Grey Ghost from the top of the pinnacle off the north side, or aim down Gratitude in the gully behind the pinnacle.

12. **Gratitude 5.8**
    Length: multi-pitch, Pro: 20 Quickdraws
    The deep gully right of Dragons Spine route. Pitch 1 climbs a gully (15 bolts) 40m and steps right onto a small belay stance on a buttress. Pitch 2 aims up a gully tending up left (20 bolts) to a steeper headwall to a belay anchor. Descend from four single rope rappels down past Ujahns Delight.

13. **Ujahns Delight 5.7** ★★
    Length: 100', Pro: 15 Quickdraws (well protected)
    Dance up the well bolted (15) face on numerous rock knobs on the right side of the buttress (right of Gratitude) to a single bolt rap anchor.

14. **Coecoenut Bridge 5.6** ★★
    Length: 100', Pro: 11 Quickdraws
    Bridge and stem (11 bolts) on lumpy coconuts in a deep 3' wide chimney to where you duck under a natural bridge 90' up in the buttress. Single rope rappel to ground.

15. **Better than Sex P1 5.7**
    Length: 100', Pro: 15 Quickdraws (well protected)
    Ascend plentiful rock knobs on well bolted (15 bolts) face up a nice low angle buttress where it merges with a knobalicious chimney up to the right. Single rope rappel.

16. **Rad, Plaid and Glad 5.9** ★★
    Length: 100', Pro: 14 Quickdraws
    This is the 14-bolt radical buttress immediately to the right of Better than Sex. Is it better than sex. Single rope rappel to ground.

17. **Runaway Weasel 5.8** ★★
    Length: 100', Pro: 14 Quickdraws
    In the center of a buttress to the right of RP&G is this 14 bolt interesting route. Single rope rappel to ground.

The Steeple

Length: multi-pitch, Pro: tie-off slings

Route was coined because of its similarity to other classic Beckey spire routes. From the parking site at the closed gate and berm you can visibly see several spire-like formations on the east slope of Fish Creek Mtn. The Steeple is the northern most formation (see map). To reach the Steeple continue driving on the gravel NF4622 road past the

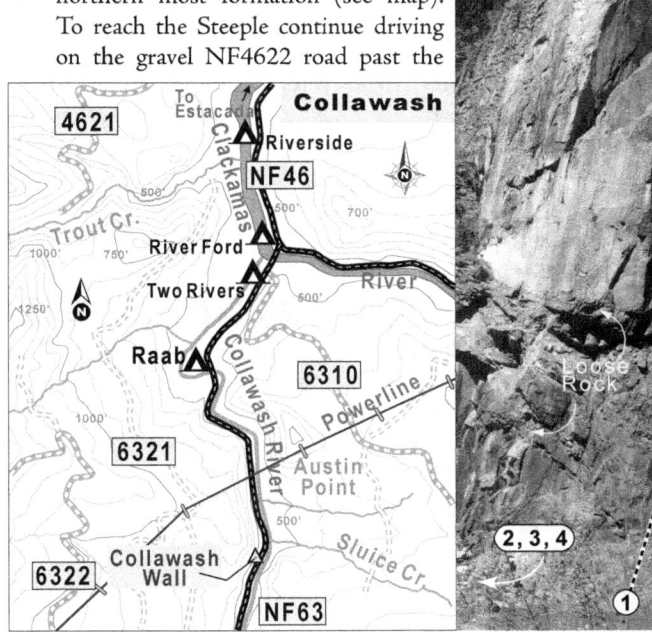

berm parking site till you are past a narrow spot that provides a view of Coethedral in the distance. Park at a minor spur, and scramble up brushy steep forested slopes to the upper side of the Steeple. Walk 400' along road, and aim uphill into the woods, staying left of a drainage till you encounter some small cliffs. Skirt the cliffs to the left till you reach the northwest side of the Steeple.

From the west side ascend 4th class 70m up a narrow gully to the notch and sling a big boulder and belay. The route aims straight up the big solid knobs (bring 20 slings) directly to the summit. Presently requires two ropes to rappel down west from the summit bolts, then rappel north from slings on a fir tree to ground. Alternate: rappel the "Brother Mike" route with one single rope.

Brother Mike 5.10- ★★★

Length: 400' (4 pitches long), 22 Quickdraws (some long ones are helpful), a single 60-meter rope

Located on the outer east facing aspect of The Steeple. The approach is the same as for regular route, but when you get near the cliff base traverse left to the east side aspect of this outcrop to reach the base of the route. A single 60-meter rope will suffice for both leading and rappeling. The climb is well bolted (1/2" x 5.5" stainless), not runout, and requires some minor natural protection for the first 60' (5.7) of the climb. The rock nuances are a characteristic mix between welded tuff and cobblestone (yet this particular outcrop is a slightly more solid form of breccia than the nearby Coethedral crag).

Basho Pinnacle

A minor 55' high summit on the southwest side of Fish Creek Mtn. that can be approached by the south side hiking trail and is visible about 300' below the trail in a forested ravine. The regular route (**Canine Conflict**) is about 5.7 and uses a minor choice of nuts and cams.

COLLAWASH CLIFF

The Clackamas River watershed region seems like one of the last places you would go to climb. But, even here along the Collawash River you can find challenging roadside "roadcut" climbs. There is not much there but if you happen to be in the area that day check it out.

When climbing at this crag wear a helmet and be wary of friable rock and tread carefully when using the steep, mossy slopes above the road. Just left of the main section of wall is a smooth near vertical 50' road cut which has one 5.10+ (TR), and two 5.11+ (TR). The favorite here is the **Johnson-Watt route** (5.9), which ascends 130' of rock on the main wall and is virtually all fixed with bolts. Bring some gear to 2" just in case.

Drive southeast of Estacada along the Clackamas River on Highway 224 to Ripplebrook, then south on FS46. Take the Collawash River road toward Bagby Hot Springs. Look for an extensive roadcut several miles up river. Near the upper left end of the roadcut you will find a few minor climbs. After the climb, and if the weather is hot you can step across the road to swim or fish. See photo diagrams for beta.

MOLALLA RIVER VALLEY

ROOSTER HEN & CHICKS

A popular trail frequently visited by hikers, yet the minor rock outcrops and plugs are seldom climbed. The site is located on the Molalla River on the same high altitude ridge crest as Table Rock, but to the south 1.3 miles. The minor rocky promentory is known as Rooster Rock. Hikers stop near it at a scenic alpine flower meadow en route to the Table Rock summit.

The main Rooster Rock summit is a mere scramble from the SW side with no technical difficulties (about 3rd class). Yet just to the east of that large flat topped rocky outcrop, there is a series of smaller rock outcrops that actually do create a bit of unique and entertaining minor adventure rock climbing (if you're into PG/R/X bold style climbing). All the summits are very short, ranging from 35' to 40' max (slightly taller on the Fat Hen). The rocky points had been humorously coined long ago and are from the west going east: Rooster, Fat Hen, Chick #1, Chick #2, Chick #3, and Ugly Duckling (#4 the eastmost unit). The rock composition is andesitic, and some routes are fairly protectable climbs.

Directions:

Drive to the east end of Molla, Oregon on Hwy 211, and turn south on South Feyrer Park Road. Just past that County Park the road crosses a bridge and T's. Go south on Dickey Prairie Road to the bridge at Glen Avon. Cross the bridge and drive south 12 miles on South Molalla Road (scenic corridor) till you reach the end of the paved road (at a bridge). Drive east on #7-3E-14.2 for about ½ mile, then turn left uphill onto gravel road #7-3E-14.3 (called Rooster Rock Road), and drive for about 5.5 miles to its very end. Hike the Rooster Rock Trail for 1 mile uphill to the ridge crest trail junction. The east trail goes to Peachuck Lookout. You will hike west on High Ridge Trail for about ½ mile to a meadow. The series of ridgecrest rocky outcrops are located uphill immediately above the trail.

Rooster Rock outcrop

This summit is flat on top, and makes a nice place to sit and eat lunch and enjoy the views of the surrounding region. The vertical east face and parts of the south face may yield more entertainment.

1. East Ridge 4th class

Exposed hi-ball scrambling almost 5th class and quite tall (each aspect of the outcrop drops away very steeply).

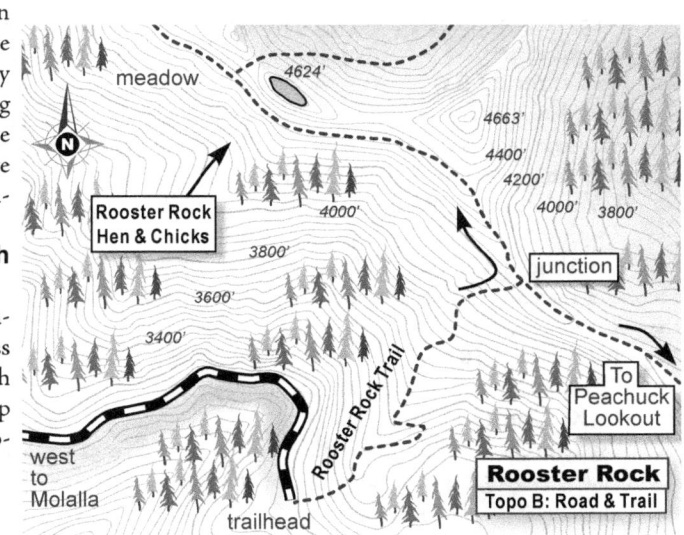

Rooster Rock
Topo B: Road & Trail

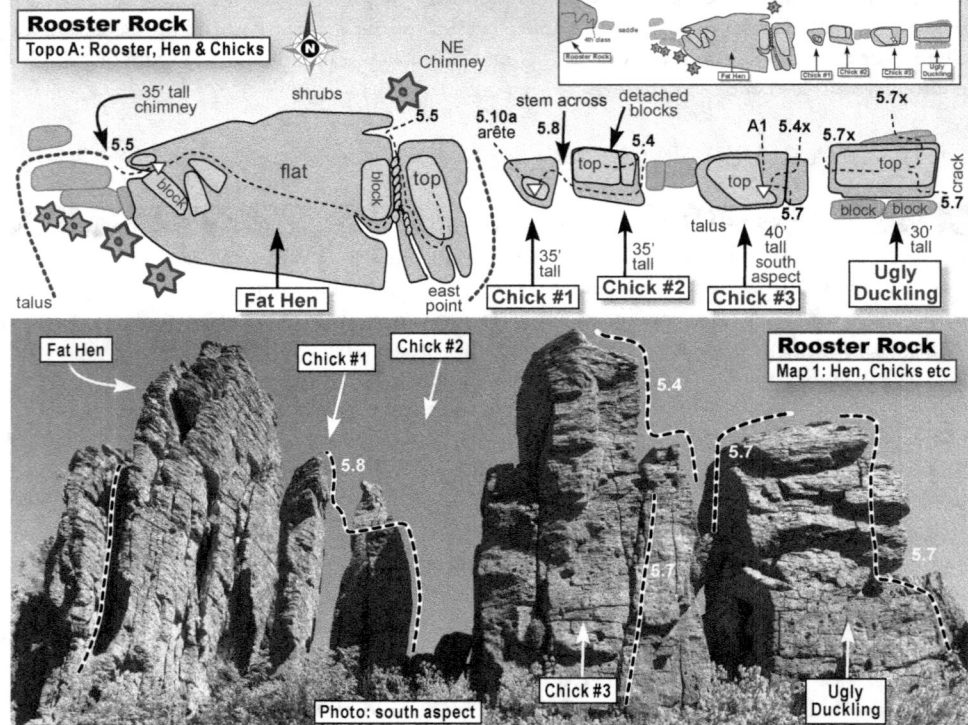

2. **SW approach**
   Rating: 3rd class
   The Fat Hen outcrop
   Smaller than the big Rooster, but has a large flat top to relax on. The common method to reach the top (and rappel) is the West Chimney.

1. **West Chimney 5.4**
   35' tall, Pro: minor wide gear
   Deep chimney system is a body sized slot. Initial opening move is the crux, then rest stance, and exit up left.

2. **NE Chimney 5.5**
   50' tall lead, Pro: minor gear
   Start next to a spruce tree, and climb into a large slot chimney cul-du-sac, then move left at a fixed piton over into the other wide slot crack system and climb it to the summit. Walk west to rappel down the West Chimney (it has a block to sling).

   Chick #1
   This is the first of a series of even smaller rock points, this one being the narrowest and most unique of the entire series, as well as fascinating to rock climb. This summit is the most stable of the entire 4-some group.

1. **NW Arête 5.10a**
   A cool quality crimps short arête worth doin'.

2. **Pesky Stepover 5.8**
   A spooky climb, but fun nonetheless. Start on the far east side of Chick #2, waltz around its sound side on a ledge, till you are at the gap between Chick #2 and #1. Be sure to place some gear nearby in Chick #2. Then gingerly step across the gap onto the Chick #1 and do a few moves to the

summit.

Chick #2
The second in the series, and well detached broken massif, and likely to tumble at some point in the future. Any way to the top is not pretty and not described (5.4x and 5.7x).

Chick #3
An OK summit, but not easily protectable; a plug of rock about 40' tall.

1. **North Seam A1**
   Pro: *a couple thin pitons and thin nuts.*
   Nail a seam on the north side.
2. **NE Steps 5.7x**
   Just solo climb the east side up steep steps with one tricky move.

Ugly Duckling (#4 outcrop)
The final outcrop with several options up, but no belay (rappel with your partner anchoring one end of the rope while you simo-rappel off the opposite side).

1. **North Side 5.7x**
   Solo the north side.
2. **West Side 5.7x**
   Solo the west side.
3. **SE Crack 5.7**
   Minor crack on the SE side that actually can be protected for what its worth.

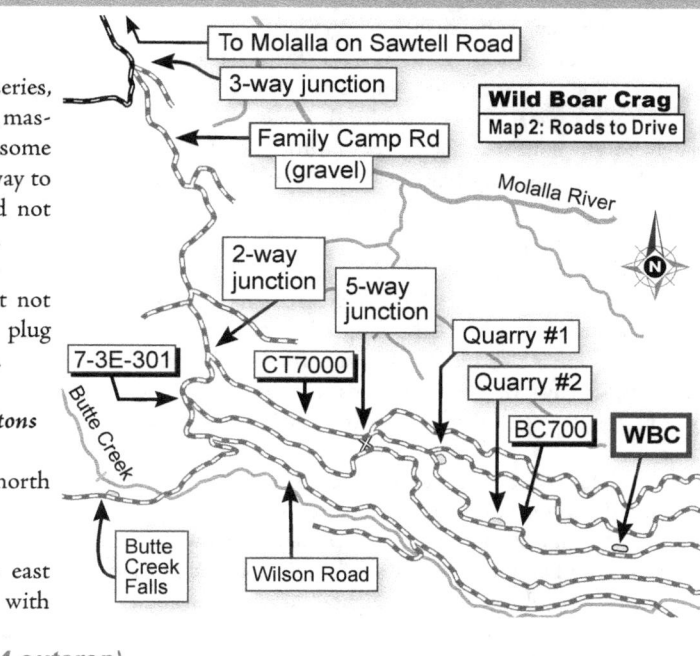

WILD BOAR CRAG

The WBC is a relatively small crag located along Gawley Ridge south of Molalla, Oregon (in a part of the state where nobody ever expects to find good rock climbing). WBC is an appealing forested south-facing little crag situated high above the Butte Creek valley, and it's packed with an unusually stout list of leads ranging from 5.9 to 5.12-. This quality crag is certainly a worthy con-

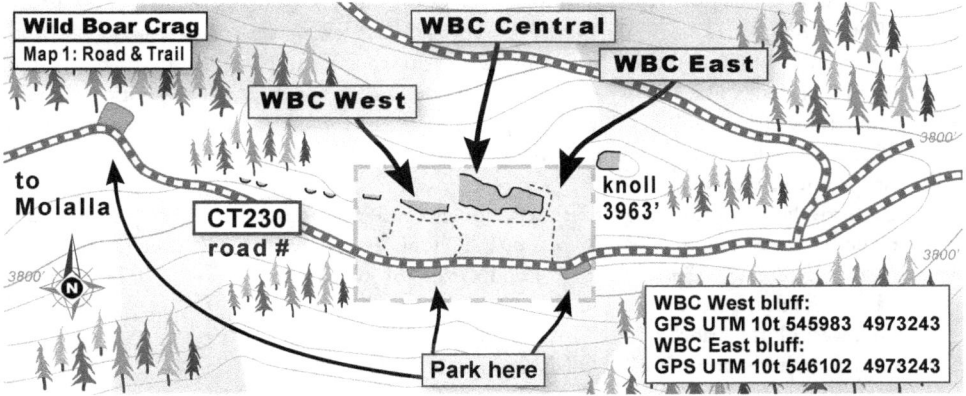

venient venue option for skilled mid-grade climbers who like short leads.

The rock quality at WBC is excellent with a textured surface like medium sandpaper with lots of (often sloped) horizontal crimps and grips. The core west bluff is vertical with a cool string of power routes. Most routes often hit the power button right out of the gate like a horse race. The height of this bluff is about 40' max (with some shorter lines). WBC is somewhat comparable to other back woods crags (such as Bulo Point) yet it's much closer to Portland. WBC is not a beginners crag. WBC is far more suitable to the power crimps rock climber accustomed to sending routes that involve a high degree of endurance and fingertip enduro. The unusual rock surface nuances kick into high gear in the 5.10+ range. WBC specifically caters to rock climbers who typically warmup on 5.9/5.10's, then aim for the jarringly stout 5.11's (and a few 5.12's).

The WBC West section is a mixed sun and shaded, flat-topped outcrop with a steep south-facing aspect that blends a lengthy list of rock climbs tightly packed into a compact zone barely 150' long. Walking eastward a path treads through a brief forested gap past a series of minor outcrops (with a smattering of rock climbs) to a final packed cluster of routes at the WBC East end of the crag.

Unique crag rock surface nuances exist at WBC, and most of it kicks into gear from 5.10+ upward. These may be a variety of the following: round open-palm holds, round downwards only slopers (that quickly burnout the forearms), a crux where you least expect it, power packed climbing the second you leave the ground, ridiculously short climbs packed with sustained climbing, numerous vertical routes, some slightly hung routes, some routes with a crux at the same height, unusual holds, inobvious crux, and techy foot smears. Yet each route tends to shuffle this deck of card tricks — just when you thought you were getting the crag style points all figured out.

The season for rock climbing is uniquely long climbing season from mid-May through the end of October (and even into November). The crag is situated at the 3900' elevation. Most primary gravel roads in this region are maintained regularly by ODF. If you have extra time at the end of the day go visit Butte Creek Falls, a nearby popular and scenic double waterfall.

History:

The WBC crag is entirely developed by Mr O and Mr A during the years 2017-2020. They prepped, bolted, and climbed the vast majority of the routes. All stewardship goals are coordinated through the CCA site steward program for this crag. *Note:* visiting climbers just focus on climbing; leave the power drill at home (the place is done).

Directions:

WBC is about 30-minutes drive from the city of Molalla (15-min of paved, and 15-min of gravel). The directions begin in Molalla (at the city center 4-way junction of Hwy 211 & Molalla Ave. Go south on Molalla Avenue, which becomes Sawtell Road. Drive the paved Sawtell Road south for 14 miles till you reach a 3-forked split (gravel-gravel-paved, L-to-R). Take the middle mainline Family Camp gravel road south for 3.1 miles till you reach a 'Y' junction. The right road goes to Butte Creek Falls (7-3E-301). These gravel roads have few signs so use a map.

Go left on CT7000 and drive for 1.6 miles till you reach a complex junction (5-road intersection). Note: it looks like a 3-way junction but if you look at the map you will notice its really a 5-way junction. Drive the BC700 mainline gravel road east for another .6 mile, then turn right onto CT230 road (quarry #1 is here). Drive this final gravel road for 2.5 miles (passing quarry #2 on left at the one mile point).

To effectively locate this crag site it's wise to have a GPS reading in your cell phone, a road map, and perhaps even a sixth sense. There is no cell phone reception at the crag (though certain cell networks can do texting). **Tip:** it's about 1¼ hours from the junction of I-84 and I-205 freeways in Portland (and it's much closer than Bulo Point).

WBC west bluff section: GPS UTM 10t 545983 4973243

WBC east bluff section: GPS UTM 10t 546102 4973243

Parking:

There is room for two cars to park immediately below the crags West End. If that's full, there is room for two cars to park along the road below the East End of the bluff. Be sure to get your car OFF the gravel road (otherwise you will create a substantial congestion problem for any large logging truck that may use the narrow gravel road). The parking spots are suitable for smaller compact cars.

Approach path options:

The crag is only about 80' from the gravel road (via any of three paths). A convenient forest path also traverses along the entire base of each outcrop from the crags West End to the East End of the WBC climbing area making it convenient to access any route goal.

West Path: Walk about 40' west on the gravel road from the main parking spot to a minor west path that ascends up slope to the crags west end.

Main Crag Path: Walk about 40' east on the gravel road from the main parking spot, then go up a nice switchback trail where it lands about 25' east of the route called Wild Boar.

East Path: a large boulder on the immediate south side of the road defines the start point of this path (the parking is just east of this roadside boulder). Directly across the road from the large boulder go uphill into the forest (past another large boulder) to the eastmost end of the crag.

Cliff Top Note: The top of the bluff has an abundance of stonecrop (blooms in June). Unless you have a specific need to be on the crag top, leading is the preferred method for sending the routes here. Virtually all belay stations are inaccessible from above.

WBC West Section (L to R):

The route beta begins at the utter west section and is numbered going eastward ending at the north side at the east section.

Cliff Section 1 (West End)

Short Pillar Face has three routes on a very short flat 30' tall section of outcrop.

1. **Double Eagle 5.10d** ★★
   Pro: 3 QD's, length 35'
   Quality vertical face with a slight lip crux bulge at mid-height. Ends at a large ledge belay anchor.

2. **Whipsaw 5.8**
   Pro: gear to 2", length 35'
   Fun crack system with plenty of grips and smears, and a high crux. Use same belay as previous route.

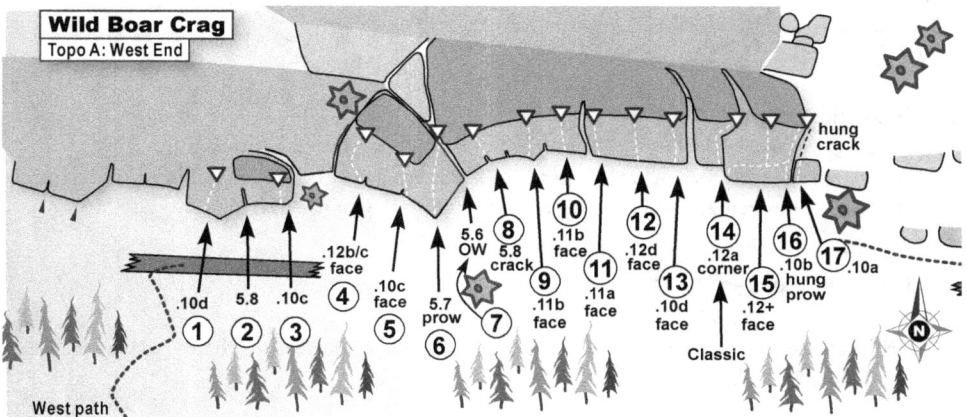

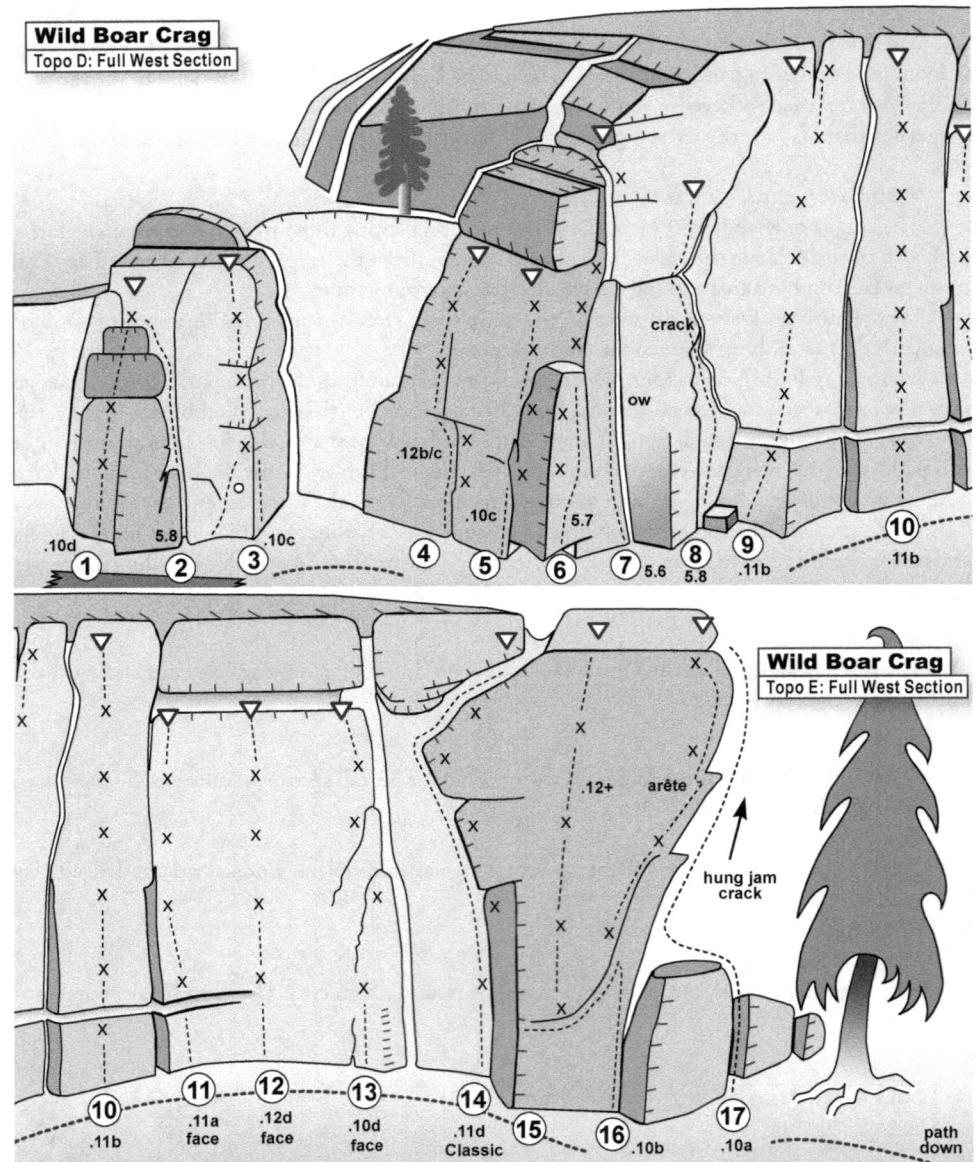

3. **Vitruvian Man 5.10c** ★★
   Pro: 3 QD's, length 35'
   Start at the 4" monster pocket, climb a quality rounded nose on sloped holds. A low left direct start yields momentary additional entertainment getting to the first bolt.

Cliff Section 2 (Main Core Pack)

4. **Infinite Regress 5.12b/c** ★
   Pro 4 QD's, length 35'
   Brilliant face climbing up a skinny flared seam, midway sloped stance, then a balancy tech crux just before the belay.

5. **Confucious Says 5.10c** ★★
   Pro 4 QD's, length 35'
   Climb a skinny seam (just left of the buttress) that land on a small ledge, then continues up a brief face section to a belay anchor below a giant overhung detached mega block. Rappel from belay.

6. **Pororoca 5.7** ★
   Pro: 5 QD's, length 40'
   Climb a prominent buttress to a small ledge, then continue up right merging into the offwidth (bolts) using various edges and ledges to reach a belay anchor above the mega block.

7. **Unobtainium 5.6**
   Pro: gear to 4", +QD's, length 40'
   A wide crack system that gets to OW status the higher you go. Merges in with previous route in the upper offwidth section.

8. **Boneyard 5.8** ★★★
   Pro: gear 3.5", length 38'
   Great crack route. Begin in a hung corner at two cracks. Cruise the left crack (both cracks merge 15' up). Continue up quality crack and edge climbing to a nook stance. Do a final fist move to the belay anchor. Route ends below the dirty stinky critter pod.

9. **Juju Warrior 5.11b** ★★★
   Pro: 6 QD's, length 40'
   Superb vertical crimps face climbing with techy slopers at a mid-way crux.

10. **Loco Moco 5.11b** ★★★
    Pro: 5 QD's, length 40'

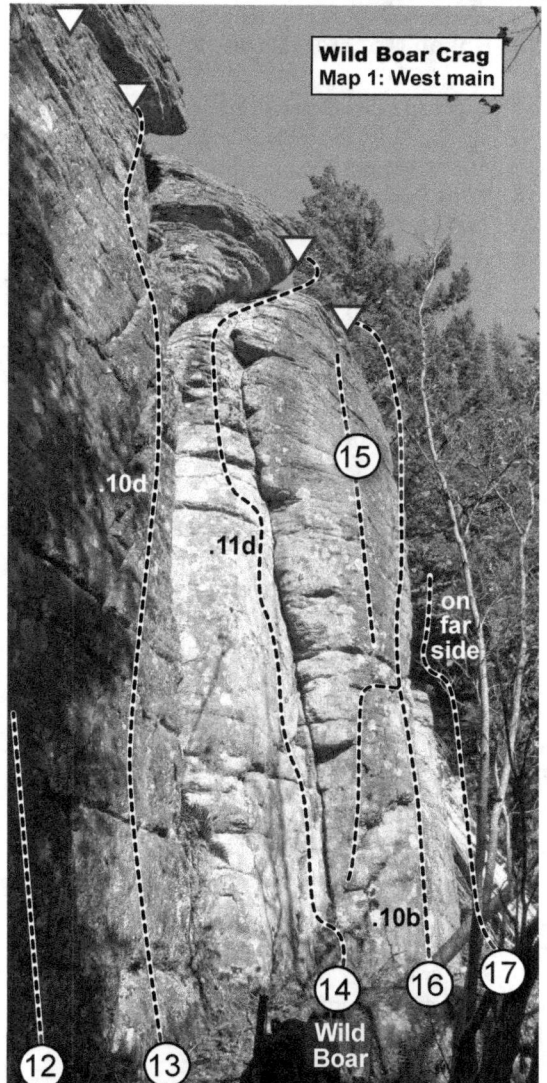

Superb quality vertical face climb. Begins at a pocket, and ascends a series of horizontal holds with techy moves between each section.
Note: Wide offwidth crack is partly used by the next climb.

11. **Extra-Virgin 5.11a** ★★★
    Pro: 4 QD's, length 38'
    Cool vertical crimp face route immediately right of the offwidth. Crux is at 1st bolt, followed by a long quality layback power fun run. Route ends just below the dirty stinky critter pod. The route utilizes some of the OW (near the belay anchor).

12. **Martini Rage 5.12c/d** ★★
    Pro: 5QD's, length 40'
    An extreme technical route. Power up vertical grooved seams and crimpy edges in the initial starting section, then a technical crux at mid-height, easing to a flat ledge belay. The jutting

overhang above is not climbed.

13. Bokeh Monster 5.10d ★
Pro: 4 QD's, length 40'
Begin up a thin face with grooved vertical seams and crimpy lips. Angles slightly leftward landing on a ledge at a belay. The jutting overhang above is not climbed.
Note: Offwidth is minor, dirty and avoided.

14. Wild Boar 5.11d ★★★
Pro: 5 QD's, length 40'
A superb quality overhung corner system with powerful climbing right out of the gate, leading up to a powerful crux section at the bulge. This is the classic best-of-the-best at this crag.

15. Age of Rage 5.12+
Pro: 5 QD's, length 40'
Start at Wild Boar crack corner, move horizontally right and then go directly up the face (clips first 2 bolts of Boar's Tusk) via a desperately thin face crux (3 more clips).

16. Boar's Tusk 5.10b ★★
Pro: 5 QD's, length 40'
Begin at Wild Boar and traverse hard right on horizontal crimps, then cruise up a series of face crimps/edges to a slight stance, make a crux reach, then several final top out moves. Great route. An alternate direct start yields same rating.

17. Xenophobia 5.10a ★
Pro: gear to 2", length 40'
Route faces east. Begins up a fat groove slot to a flat rock landing. Very short hung crack with flat jugs and a few jams intersparsed. Some of the left holds mingle with the previous route.

Cliff Section 3 - Forest section (beta from L to R):

Walking east you enter a brief forested zone (passing several isolated boulders) then reach two tall rock outcrops. Distance about 100'.

18. Yo Yo Draw 5.12a
Pro: 3 QD's, length 35'
Short face climb on leftmost part of this flat section of cliff. A powerful bouldery crux. Its the cello player.

19. Aquifer 5.9 ★★
Pro: gear to 2", length 35'
Cool quality vertical finger jam crack.

20. Ambient Noise 5.11- ★★★
Pro: 3 QD's, length 35'
Superb vertical face with powerful crimps, sidepulls and small edges, involving endurance. Ends just below a minor top block.

21. Supercalifragilistic 5.10a ★
Pro: 4 QD's, length 38'
Begin at a face that also has a wide slot. Utilize both face and slot till you reach a large stance at mid height. Then climb a series of fun crimps (crux) till you reach a final jug at the belay anchor. Rappel.

Note: Immediately right of the Supercalifragilistic route is a tall well-detached pillar. Walk eastward about 60' to reach the next climbs.

Cliff Section 4 (East End)

The entire next section is the East End of the crag where the last core pack of routes exist. This zone can also be accessed via the East Path (especially convenient by parking at the east pullout).

22. Never-neverland 5.11b/c ★
Pro: 3 QD's, length 35'
Short powerful crimpy vertical face climb with a mantle just before the belay. On the same brief outcrop as the next route.

23. Java Jive 5.10d
Pro: 4 QD's, length 35'
Short angled nose, cruxy lower section, ending on a small ledge below a round summit block. A cranky old thing with a nouveau twist.

The next two are on a slight high flat rock landing just above the trail. Both routes punch out a powerful short rounded bulge face.

24. Velociraptor 5.13- ★
Pro: 4 QD's, length 37'
Power climbing out the left round bulge using crimps and a left crimp rail. Eases onto a stance at 2/3 height, then a few minor face moves to the belay. The unexpected.

25. Vrooom 5.12c/d ★
Pro: 4 QD's, length 37'
Powerful short climb on an overhung bulge face using difficult crimps that angle up right

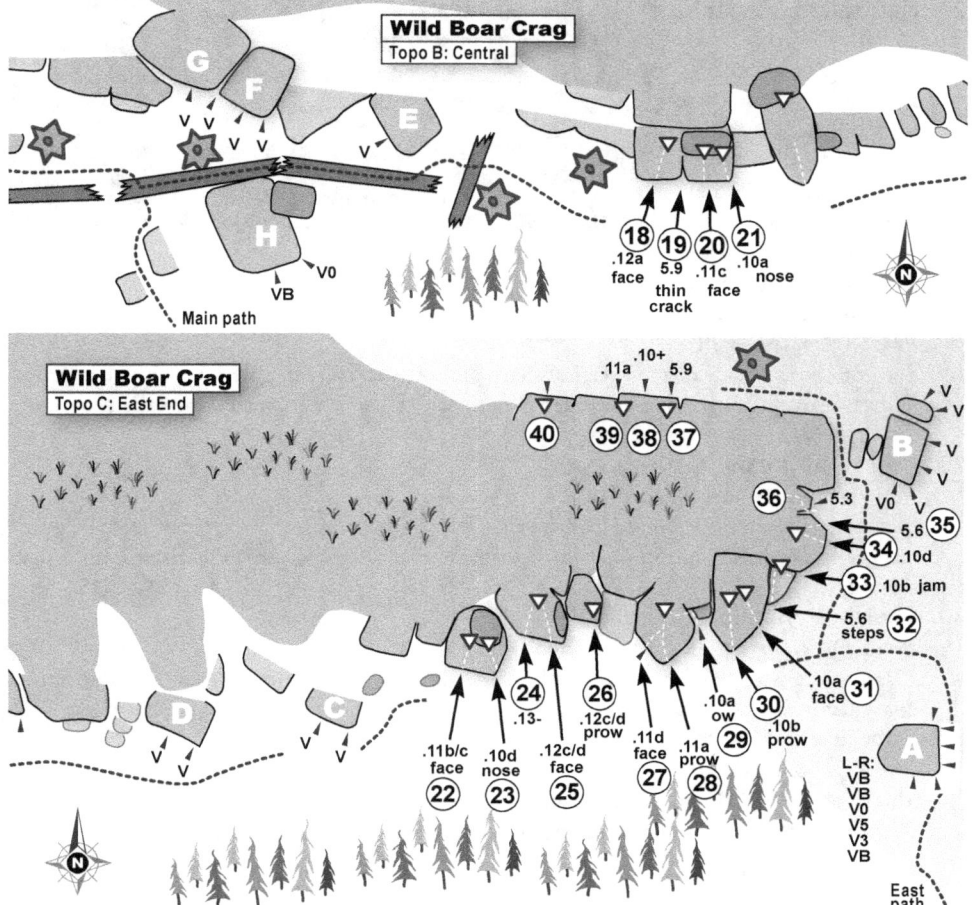

(crux) to a stance, then up easy slabby crimps to a belay (ends at same belay as previous route).

26. Algorithm   5.12d
★ ★

Pro: 4 QD's, length 40'
A very powerful series of boulder moves (V6) to the midway flat rail, then moderate climbing with larger holds to the top. Climbs a flat 1° overhung face with right hand on a round arete, then large horizontal holds midway, ending with nice crimps on right aspect of prow.

27. Neutralized   5.11c/d
★ ★

Pro: 5 QD's, length 40'
Powerful alternate start on the left side of a prominent tall sharp prow (merges with next route into its crux at 3rd bolt) involving trickier climbing on its lower half.

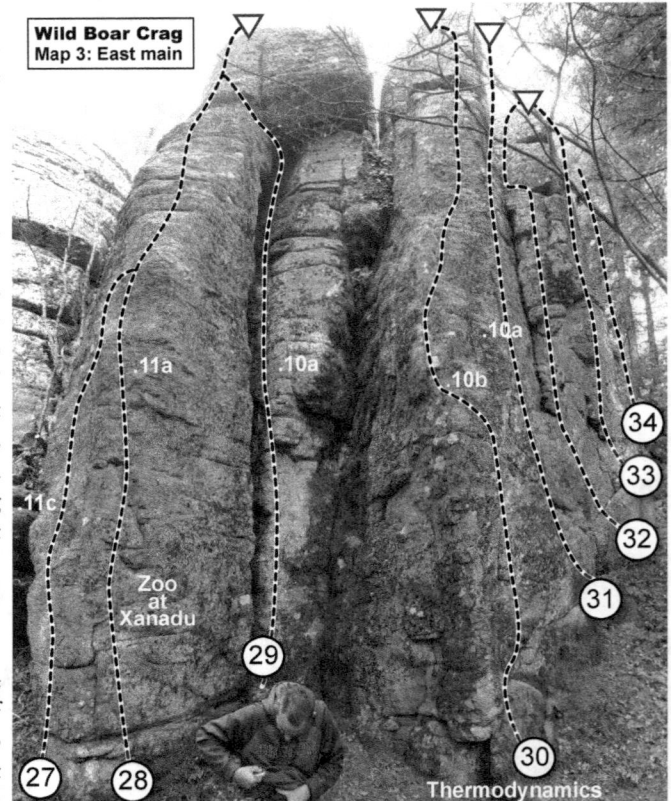

28. Zoo at Xanadu   5.11a   ★ ★ ★
Pro: 5 QD's, length 40'
Start on the right side of a tall vertical sharp prow. Climb basic initial moves up to a technical midway crux. Just beyond the rounded crux the climb lands on a small stance, then continues up edges and steepens at the belay.

29. Null Hypothesis   5.10a
Pro: gear from 6" to 12", length 40'
Very wide offwidth crack on immediate right side of the tall prow. Merges left into the previous prow route near the top. Usually top-roped (after all - who uses gear that big these days around here).

30. Thermodynamics   5.10b   ★ ★ ★
Pro: 5 QD's, length: 40'
Classic arete with crux at the first bolt. Cool climbing, tricky opening moves and dedicated finale just before the belay.

31. Ebb Tide   5.10a   ★ ★
Pro: 4 QD's, length: 40'
This is on the right aspect of the same tall prominent prow. Starts on a wide flat slab, then steepens to small reachy edge climbing all the way to the belay. Great little climb.

32. Makin' Moonshine 5.6 ★

Pro: nuts to 1", cams to 3"

Steps and edges in a prominent crack corner system that angles up right and lands on a final pedestal at a belay just below the top.

33. Propaganda 5.10b ★★

Pro: nuts to 1", cams to 3.5"

Begin up a crack through a small lip, then up a fat jam crack on a vertical face that ends on a stance at a belay just below the top.

34. Jade 5.10d ★★

Pro: 4 QD's, length 35'

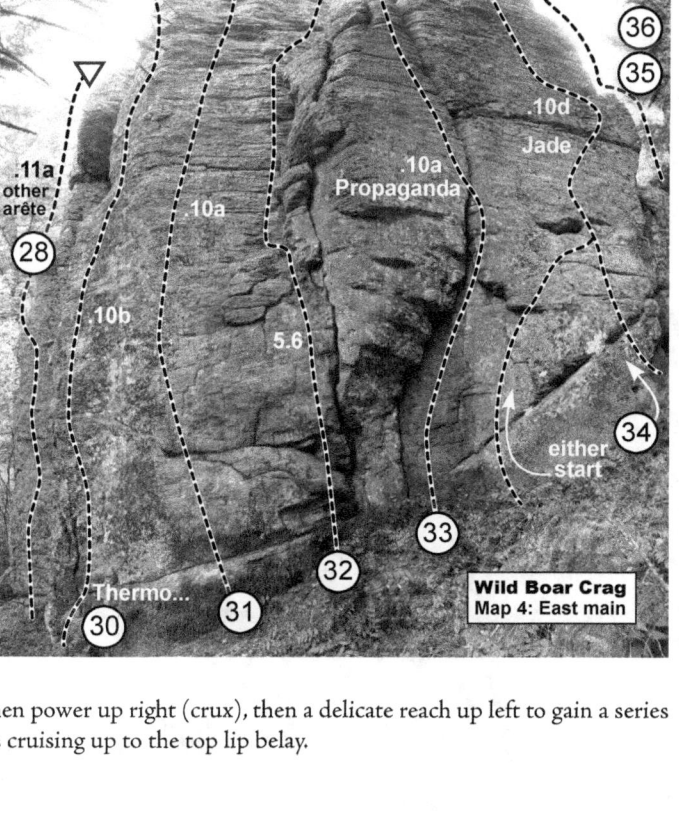

Start up a steep slab to a minor sloped stance, then power up right (crux), then a delicate reach up left to gain a series of quality vertical crimps cruising up to the top lip belay.

35. Bug Scum 5.6

Pro: 3 QD's

A minor low angle slab with ledges ending at the same belay station as the previous route.

36. Titanic Ego 5.3

Pro: gear to 4"

A minor 20' tall double slot crack corner system at the east end of the crag.

Cliff Section 5 (North Face Aspect)

A short walk around the east end of the bluff takes you to the shaded north-facing aspect of the crag where several overhung fun power routes exist. Shaded climbs for a hot day or just plain cool climbs anytime. The cluster is tucked in an open brushless area under the forested canopy of a huge mother Hemlock tree. The beta is described from left to right (east to west) for the north side routes.

37. RPM Overdrive 5.10a ★

Pro: 4 QD's, length 35'

Crux boulder move out of the gate, then jugs and 5.9 climbing on steep hung rock, exiting right into slot crack at top to belay.

38. RPM Riot 5.10c

Pro: 4 QD's, length 35'

Cool climb. Substantially overhung right out of the

Pesky Stepover on Chick #1

gate, involving a long series of powerful pulls on numerous jugs till it eases for the last few feet to the belay.

39. Turbocharged 5.11a ★
Pro: 3 QD's, length 35'
Initial power moves out of the gate, midway jugs, then finish with delicate face balance moves on the final flat face near the belay.

IN THE GREAT NORTHWEST

Santiam Summits - Stellar sub-alpine climbing

CHAPTER 7

SANTIAM SUMMITS

THERE ARE TWO GREAT RIVERS which gather the waters of the old Cascade range southeast of Salem — the North and South Santiam River. This region, known as the old or Western Cascades, are composed of older lava flows, tuffs and other intrusive rock formations. The hills surrounding these vast river drainages are characterized by steeply forested transition zones of vertical mountainous uplift. The crests of these rugged fog shrouded peaks, reach to an average height of 5,500', and hold many unusual gems of delightful beauty for avid adventurous climbers.

NORTH SANTIAM REGION

People have for generations come to these forests to experience the natural scenic wonders that abound here. There are natural rock arches, large caves with splendid views, deep blue-green lakes for fishing, and even pinnacles for rock climbing. This section will focus on the pinnacle and rock climbing destinations of the North Santiam River. The North Santiam River region is located east of Salem along U.S. 22, while the South Santiam River region is southeast of Albany on U.S. 20.

Tumble Lake Area

This area has a variety of wild pinnacles perched high along the ridge overlooking Tumble Lake. Steep forested slopes embellished in deep green, rugged rocky spires that stand like lone sentinels, and majestic views of Mt. Jefferson create a perfect place for exploring and photography.

The common destination is Needle Rock. To get there drive east from Salem on U.S. Hwy 22 to a left turn onto FS2223 just prior to the town of Detroit, Oregon. Follow French Creek road FS2223 till it splits left onto spur road FS520 and continue to Sardine Pass. Trail #3380 begins at Sardine Pass and traverses southeast past Dome Rock en route to Needle Rock, then descends down to Detroit Lake.

NEEDLE ROCK

This spire is the premier classic of the entire Tumble Lake region. To approach this elusive pinnacle overlooking Tumble Lake, park at the Tumble Lake trailhead #3379, and walk over the initial brief hill, then hike southeast on trail #3380 for 1¼ miles east passing Dome Rock knoll. You will see Needle Rock below the trail on your right in the forest. When adjacent to the spire descend through open forest a short distance to the classic 160' spire. Needle Rock has seen just a mere handful of ascents since it was first ascended by Eugene Dod and Jim Nieland.

The Tumble Lake hills are accentuated

Hugh on Spire Rock SE Rib

with a unique forested structure composed mostly of Mountain Hemlock, Spruce, Douglas Fir and low growing Vine Maple. Clumps of stout Bear Grass are plentiful on all the slopes, while tiny Rock Ferns, alumroot, and colorful penstemon can be found on vertical cliff scarps.

1. **Nieland Route 5.8 (or C1)**
   Pro: Nuts and cams to 3"; single 60m rope
   The Dod-Neiland (North Prow) route of Needle Rock is a stellar climb. Commence by scrambling up the initial 5th class mossy section 40' up to a good stance at a single fir tree belay. Step past the tree and free climb up a vertical blocky face (4 bolts) for 30' over a slight bulge overhang (5.8 crux) to a belay anchor located right at the lip. Traverse right along a sloping ledge system (1 bolt) that faces to the west to the base of a prominent wide corner system (1 bolt). Climb the wide corner (5.8 crux) by initially stemming and jamming the overhung crack corner till it eases near the top. Expect some friable rock (helmets!) and surprisingly technical climbing. One 60-meter rope will suffice for the rappel.

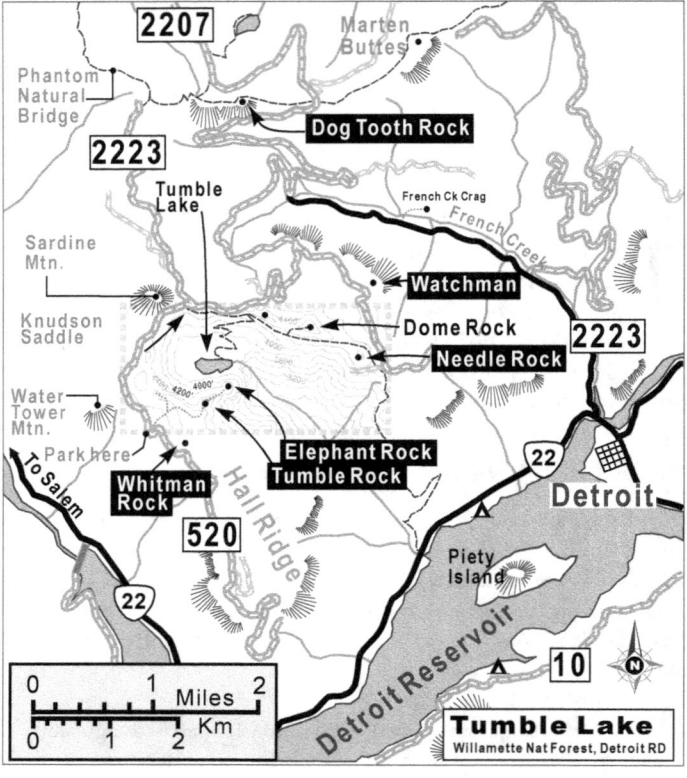

2. **The Direct 5.10a R**
   Pro: Nuts and cams to 2½"
   This route starts by clipping the first bolt on the Dod-Neiland, then embarks up and left on vertical ground to attain the summit at the notch. Definitely runout with limited protection, and has seen only one on-sight ground-up ascent mainly because the route is inobvious and loose.

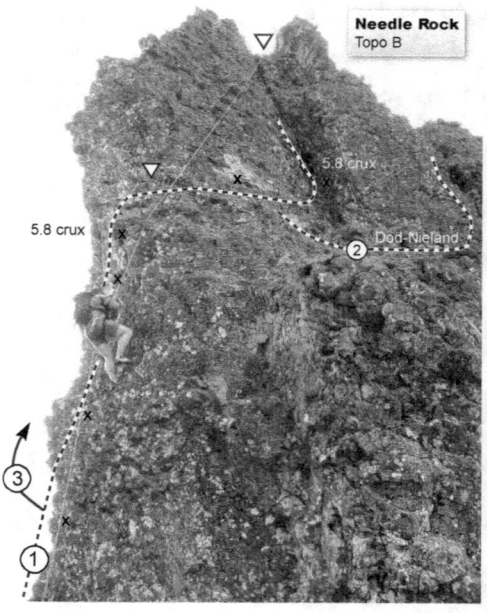

LITTLE NEEDLE ROCK

Yup, you gottr' right. There really is another pinnacle directly south of big Needle Rock.
This little pinnacle is invisible till you take

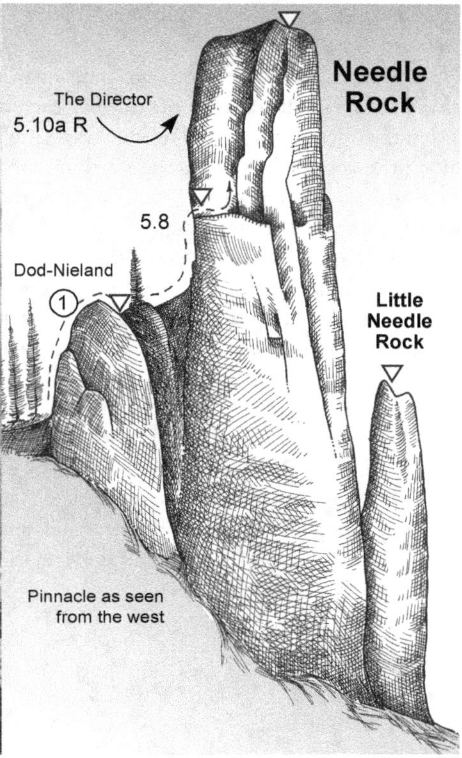

SANTIAM ROCK

Needle Rock

Standard Route
5.8 Crux

Original Dod-Nieland

The Director 5.10a R

5.8

Dod-Nieland

Little Needle Rock

Pinnacle as seen from the west

a tour down the slope on the east side of the main pinnacle. Then you realize there is actually something else here that is also a worthy objective.

Little Needle Rock is a 70' high crisp wafer thin spire that offers a well-protected (bolts) aid line from the saddle directly to the top. Though not free climbed at time of print it would likely go free at about 5.11-.

To aid the slightly overhung **Englund Direct** from the saddle follow the 5-bolt line (5.7 A0) using aiders, a few thin wires, cams, and perhaps a piton to gain access to the summit of this little forest gem. Here is the summit register up till June 2009: 1.) Brad solo 7-26-1997; 2.) Brad solo 8-1999; 3.) Brad solo 11-4-2002; 4.) Brad solo 7-19-2003; 5.) Brad solo 8-9-2003; 6.) Brad solo 7-30-2004. Yeowza! Way to go Brad. So...don't miss out on this Detroit favorite with great views in the wild outback.

ELEPHANT ROCK

To explore the next area, continue driving on the gravel road southwest (approximately 1¼ miles from Sardine Saddle) along spur road #520 past Knudson Saddle and park at a pullout. From this parking site

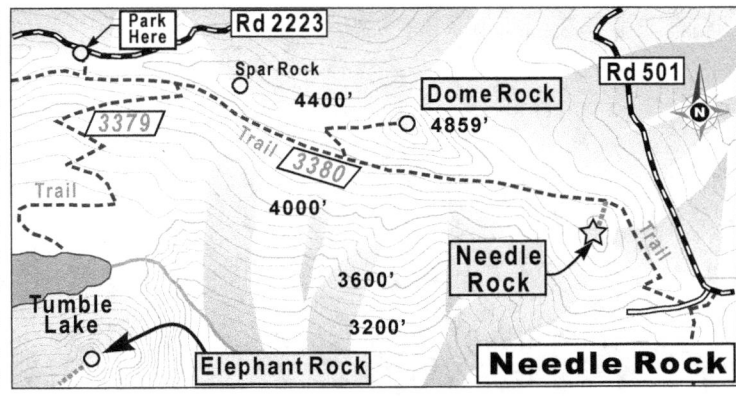

you can see the summit of **Whitman Rock** through the forest to the east above the road.

Hike uphill to the north on a minor ridge line through a thicket of rhododendron plants till you reach the main hill crest. From the open plateau knoll overlooking Tumble Lake walk east along the rounded ridge through a thick tangled forest southeastward till you are above a narrow ridge that descends down directly to the three summits.

The approximate distance from the vehicle to the spires is roughly ¾ mile. Descend the very steep ridge line directly down to **Tumble Rock**, **Split Spire** and **Elephant Rock**. The centerpiece of this high valley cirque is the deep and beautiful Tumble Lake.

Little Needle Rock

1. Tumble Rock 4th class

Pro: Rope, slings, and a few nuts

Tumble Rock is a fun but exposed 4th class summit scramble. From the south saddle scramble up left on gravelly ledges passing a short step, and then up left amongst the trees on ledges to the top. The forested slope on the north side allows for an easier ascent.

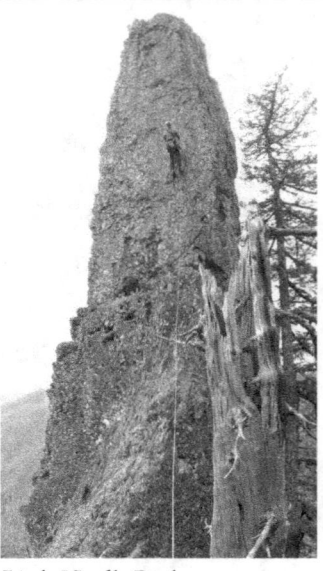

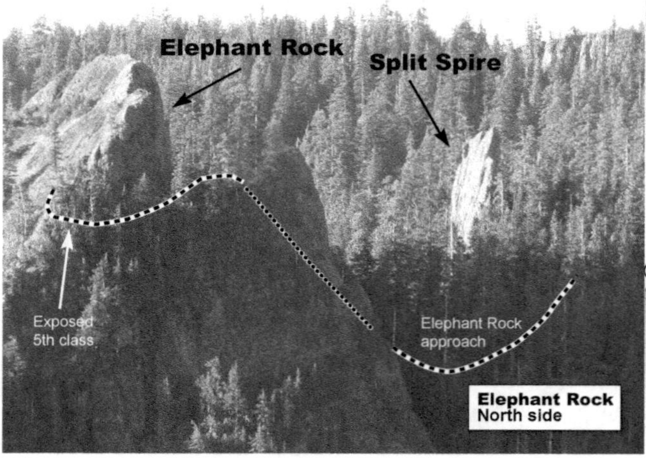

Elephant Rock
North side

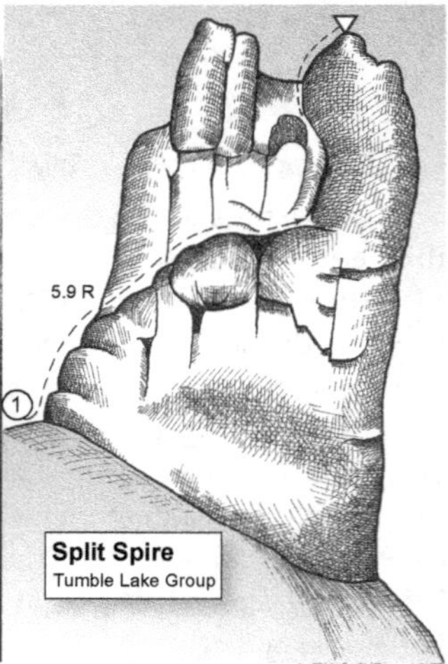

Split Spire
Tumble Lake Group

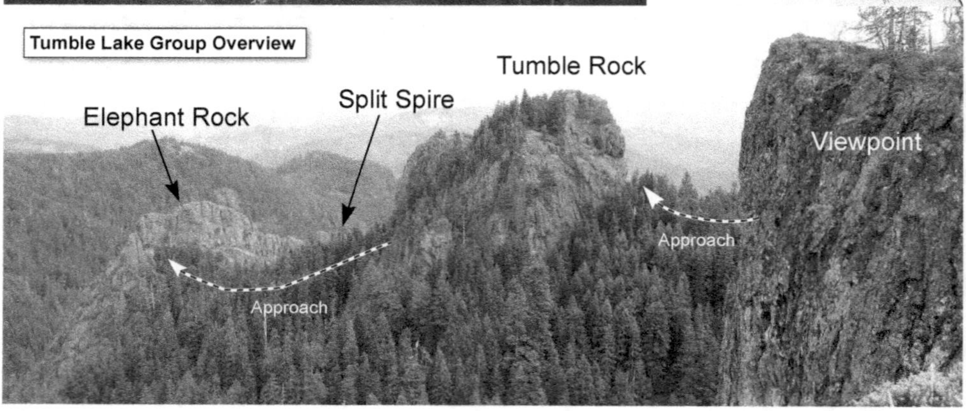

Tumble Lake Group Overview

Needle Rock

Nieland's Needle (aka Needle Rock)
Summit register as recorded. There were likely 1-5 additional ascent parties from 1995 through 2008 who did not write in the summit register or were unaware of it. The summit register contents were water damaged beyond readability by 2008. As you can gather from the registry Needle Rock climbing conquistadors have been quite minimal.

Nieland's Needle 7-28-68 (Sunday)
Jim Nieland, Eugene Dod, Gerald Bjorman
Climbed 5th class up 1st pitch on west then on up right gully to top. It looks like someone else has been here.

10-22-80 (Wednesday)
Greg Ham, Teddy Lovett
Ketchikan, Alaska
Climbed 'Nieland's Route' using 4 pitons that were in place on 1st pitch. Clear, sunny weather, high 55° Low 29° Note: The price of this spiral notebook is about 49¢ in 1980!!

7-21-84 (Saturday)
Paul Harken - Lakeview, OR.
Brian Boswell - Victoria, BC
Sunny 7:50pm Peaceful
[On the] 2nd pitch took left (east) crack. Gerry & Terry here's your runner back (we found a tattered piece of webbing stuffed in the summit box).

2. **Split Spire   5.6 A1 or 5.10-**
   Pro: Versatile rack of nuts and cams to 4" plus pitons
   The infamous double summited Split Spire is rarely climbed. Start up from the west onto a gravelly ledge then angle to the right till you are under the notch between the two spires. On the right ascend a wide groove corner that angles up left to the notch. The toughest section is the free climbing moves from the shaky piton onto the notch. Step from the notch up onto the summit and belay. Expect some friable rock on this strangely classic summit. The technical part of the climb is less than 80' and you can rappel with one rope to the gravel ledge and rappel again from the bush to the ground.

3. **Elephant Rock   5.3 R**
   Pro to 2" and slings
   Elephant Rock is the lowest pinnacle of rock along this steeply descending ridge line. The climbing route is an exposed meandering line with considerable scrambling. Scramble up a 4th class section on the south side till you can follow a ledge around left to access the north side. Ascend the obvious easy 5.3R rib leading directly up to the top. This summit is quite airy to attain yet yields exhilarating views once you are there.

DOG TOOTH ROCK

This minor wild jackal is a wild, friable adventurous endeavor on the French Creek Divide west of the pass just off FS2207 road. Take spur road FS2207 to the pass to access trail #3349. Hike west about ½ mile uphill to the eastern edge of the formation. Refer to the diagram and pick your weapon. This pinnacle actually has three minor knobs which can be gained by ascending a steep dirt and

moss gully on the north side between two of the summits.
GPS 44.78292° N / 122.22057° W Elev: 4490' / 1369m

1. **North Ravine 5.4 R**

    Pro: Minor nuts and cams to 1"

    Grovel up an exposed steep low 5th class dirty moss ramp (sling small cedars) 80' to access a notch separating the west horn from the middle knob. Drop down 15' on the south side, traverse east along a ramp, then scramble up (180' lead) rocky steps to the east summit. Rappel back to the same notch belay, then lead up to the west knob on easy sloping ledges. Rappel anchor on west knob takes you back down the north side ravine to your original starting point.

2. **Nasal Mozz 5.7 R/X**

    Pro to 1" and pitons

    This east ridge route is a mossy ledge climb that starts at a series of minor corners and steps landing on a ledge (70') covered with small cedar trees. P2 (70') punches past a crux move then eases to

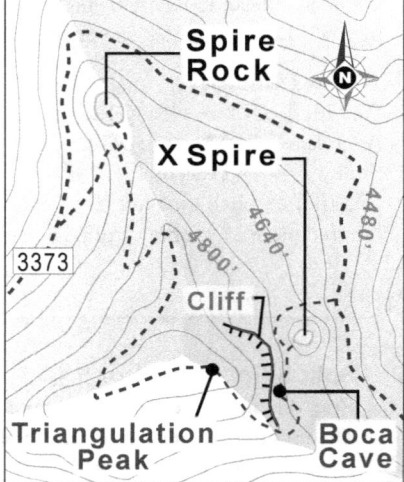

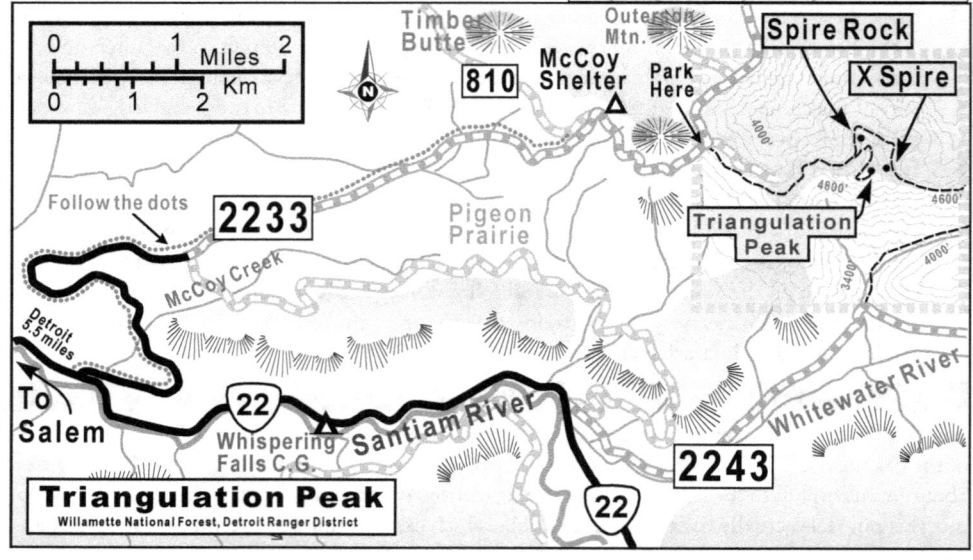

loose mossy edges, so escape up right to the notch, then up the last step to the summit anchor. Rap west to the notch belay. Rappel from the small cedar tree down the North Ravine.

TRIANGULATION PEAK - BOCA CAVE

Two great pinnacles in the Detroit region majestically crown a lightly forested ridge crest alongside the Triangulation Peak Trail #3373. This scenic 1½-mile hiking trail is a popular destination hike for people en route to the famous Boca Cave. For the adventure climber several enticing pinnacles sit along the crest of the ridge—Spire Rock and X-Spire. Great panoramic views of the Cascade Mountain range easily make these summits worth the visit. Spire Rock fits the typical northern Oregon pinnacle geological composition of weather-worn grainy-textured andesite adequate for friction but a little bit friable in places.

Directions

Drive east of Detroit on US Hwy 22 through Idahna and take road FS2233 left to the McCoy Creek shelter. Continue east from the shelter for another mile on gravel roads to the trailhead. Park and hike trail #3373 for 1½ miles east till it branches onto trail #3374. This trail zigzags uphill to Triangulation Peak.

SPIRE ROCK

1. **SE Rib 5.4**
   Length: 160', Pro to 2½" and slings
   The SE Rib of Spire Rock is the classic line on this pinnacle and the shortest climb. Spire Rock is the first pinnacle that the trail zigzags past on the way to

Hugh on SE Rib of Spire Rock

the summit of Triangulation Peak. Hike initially up the first zigzag on trail #3374, and then scramble along a minor ridg*elette* to access the notch on the rib. Rope up at a tree prior to reaching the notch at the base of the cliff face. Traverse to the notch and around the large block. Climb up large steps and corners (fixed pitons) to a small ledge, angle up left to a slot, then aim up right for a belay anchor at the base of a dead tree. Scramble to the summit and belay at a bush. One single 60m rope will get you off the spire.

2. **South Face 5.4 R**

Length: 230', Pro to 3" including cams

The south face is quite wide and offers a plethora of options for climbing on variable rock. Access is quick — just jump off the trail at the zigzag, rope up and start climbing. Pick a line that looks reasonably protectable. This is a fairly direct route to the summit although infrequently as-

cended and a bit friable in places.

3. **SW Buttress II 5.8 R**
Length: 500', Pro: Nuts and cams to 3" and several pitons

The **SW Buttress** holds the rare distinction for being the longest sub-alpine multi-pitch rock climbing route in the North Santiam Detroit region. Your first view of Spire Rock is the SW Buttress aspect. A serious climb involving difficult terrain navigation over friable rock and gravelly ledges suitable for the hard-core adventurer.

P1 120' 5.8R fixed gear: Start at the very toe of the buttress on the lower trail. Climb the initial steep slab, angle up right and surmount an odd vertical step (can be bypassed on right). Move up a groove

Hugh on Spire Rock *SE Rib*

and dance carefully up friable rock to a very steep vertical section of wall (crux). Balance up the crux section on small insecure sloping edges to easier terrain. Move up gravelly steps to a nice tree belay on a large ledge. Beware of friable rock.

P2 70' 5.4 pro to 3": Move up right on a sunny slope using steps and corners, move right under a large roof, then up a vertical corner to a tree belay on a ledge.

P3 100' 5.6 pro to 3": Start up an obvious crack using ample edges passing a small cedar tree. At a minor stance move up right into a crux offwidth slot crux. Place cams deep in the back and then surmount the slot carefully (best without a pack) and continue up to a belay anchor at a small stance.

P4 100' 5.4R pro to 2": From the belay ascend up right using a minor crack, then up steep steps (fixed pitons) and face moves onto the arête. Follow the arête (fixed pins) to a flat stance at a bolt where you can set a belay. Beware of friable rock.

P5 100' 5.4R pro to 2": Dance carefully along a tenuous narrow ridge crest then scramble along easy terrain to the summit. Expect 2-3 hours to ascend the entire buttress.

An alternative (Bypass Traverse 5.5PG) can be used to access the belay tree at the top of P2 and below the offwidth chimney on P3. It steps off the first switchback in the hikers trail and aims up along a rising traverse to a thin tree, then de-

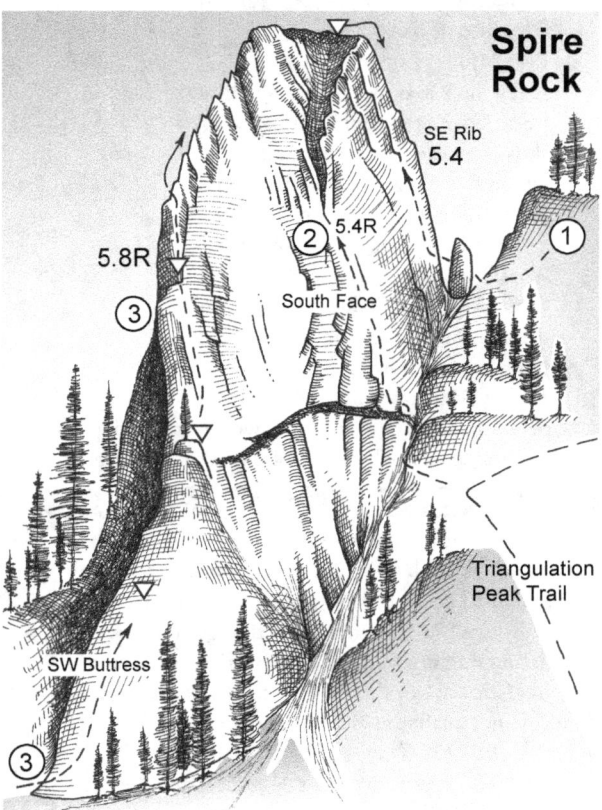

scends a bit to attain the belay tree at the top of P2.

Boca Cave

After climbing Spire Rock continue up trail #3374 to the top of Triangulation Peak, and then follow a rough descent trail eastward in a thick forest until the trail angles down steeply underneath a large vertical northeast facing rock promontory of Triangulation Peak. Tucked immediately under this promontory is the unique entrance to Boca Cave. Be sure to bring a camera so that you can take a picture of the rewarding view of Mt. Jefferson taken from inside the cave. For your next adventure look to the east, young man. On the far horizon you will see an elusive and barely visible pinnacle high up on the eastern slope of Olallie Butte.

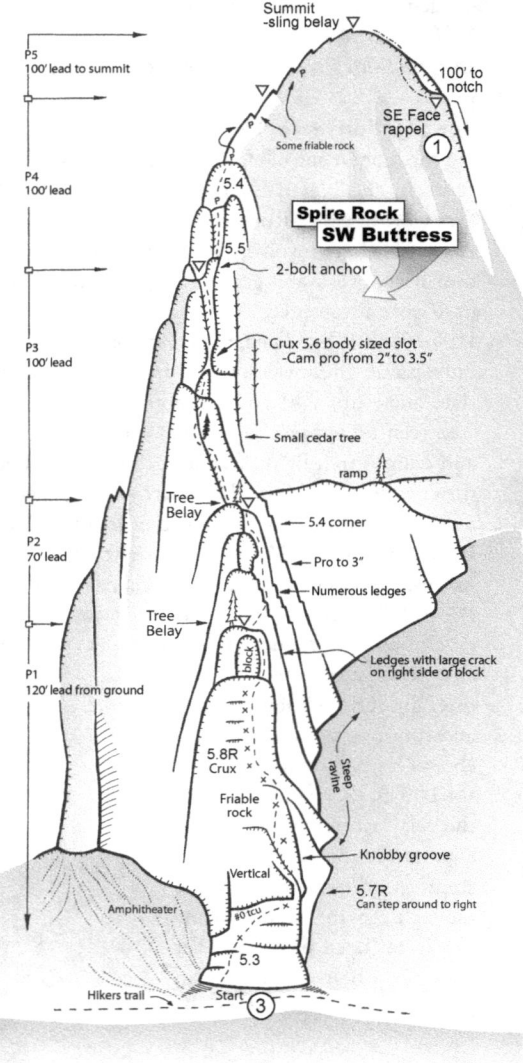

X-SPIRE

1. **Regular Route 5.1**
   Pro: Minor gear to 1"
   A few hundred feet to the north of Boca Cave is X-Spire, an easy 5th class pinnacle. From the saddle step up onto a ledge and walk around to the right to the east side. Climb a crack-like weakness (the pro is sparse) on the east face that offers good steps and ledges. Belay near the summit at a rock horn and fixed piton anchor. The lower trail is immediately below this spire and can be attained by descending down the scree slopes immediately west of the pinnacle. Walk to the west past the base of Spire Rock to complete this adventurous loop hike.

BREITENBUSH EARS

While you are having lunch at the top of Triangulation Peak look to the northeast to see two tiny sharp profiled 'ears' on a long forested ridge connected to Devils Peak. Breitenbush Ears, though not a typical destination might just spark your musical bandwagon.

Logistics to get there are not quite so easy (trail #3345 is not maintained). Best to approach it utilizing road FS2231 (hot springs), then road FS870. Park at 4000' elevation about ¼ mile after the final

Boca Cave

road switchback and immediately below the saddle along the ridge crest north of the ears. Bushwack cross-country uphill through taller growth forest to the saddle, then aim south along the ridge. Cut east along the eastern base of the north ear and aim for a saddle next to the South Ridge of the South Ear and belay here.

The climb is definitely 5.4R and requires thin pitons or bolts to rappel off from the pinnacle. Use minimal gear from small cams to 3", a few pitons, and a few nuts to 1".

South Face Climb: Clamber up a few big steps, traverse left along a main ledge till near a large tree. Aim uphill to a left facing corner system on steep terrain with ample edges to a small stance. The crux 5.4R is a short vertical slot that can be body jammed and stemmed. Immediately beyond is a large wide sloping ledge (100' lead). Set a belay here using thin pitons or bolts.

From this belay move onto the SW side along a narrow ramp, surmount a 5.4 crux, then follow a poor rock ridge a total of 60' to the highest point. This lead is mostly a horizontal traverse with some minor gain. High point has no anchor or pro. From the belay at 100' rappel back down the ascent route to the saddle.

THOR'S HAMMER

Thor's is located on an east facing aspect of a large steep foreboding cliff formation on the lower east side of Henline Mtn. If you are an off-trail aficionado who relishes climbing rare summit objectives, then Thor's Hammer is worth a visit. Thor is the sky god in Viking lore, and Odin is the Viking war god. Thor's is one of the North Santiam's rare rock climbing gems. Boasting a forested thrash scramble approach this wild summit offers good views of the Little North Santiam River valley. The summit can

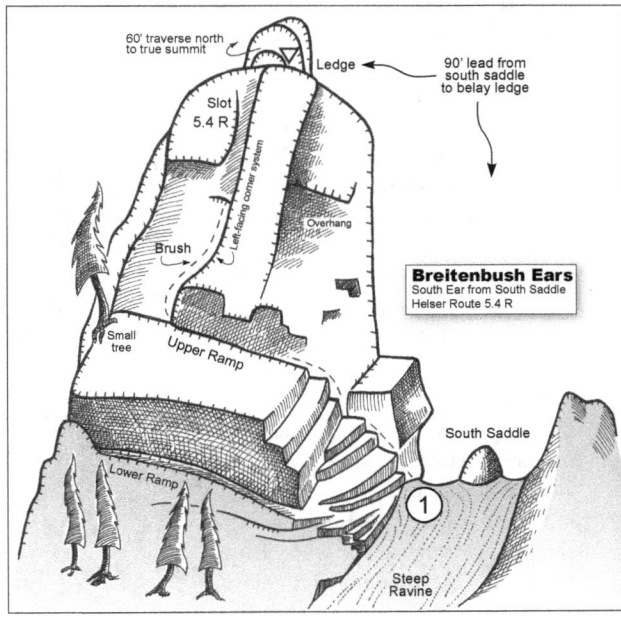

be climbed by either the north ravine or the south ravine.

Directions
From Salem drive 25 miles east on Hwy 22 and turn left (north) onto the North Fork Road SE which is one mile east of the small community of Mehama. Continue on FS2209. Park at MP 19 and step over the berm onto an old forest grade that meanders (see topo) up to a small knoll. Find an old miner's trace and follow this for about 200', then branch up onto a forested minor ridge crest heading due west following a game path. The uphill scramble gets steep as you draw nearer to the cliff base. **South Ravine:** bushwhack up left below the cliff to access the ravine. **North Ravine:** Angle rightward along the cliff base to a flat landing next to a mammoth fir tree.

1. North Ravine 5.7 R

P1: From the flat landing next to a large fir tree, rope up and lead up 5th class dirt and moss covered slopes 90' to a cluster of trees and set up a belay. This initial lead is not obvious so choose your path carefully as the terrain is very steep and trees to sling are limited.

P2: Continue up 5th class terrain for 70' to another belay.

P3: Angle left (south) up along a narrow 4th class dirt ramp for 70' to a third belay.

P4: From here you can easily scramble up 3rd class terrain for another 60' to the notch between the main wall and Thor's Anvil. Expect some loose rock in the approach gully. Set up a belay at a fixed anchor at the notch next to a large chock stone. Both the North Ravine route and the South Ravine route meet here at the notch.

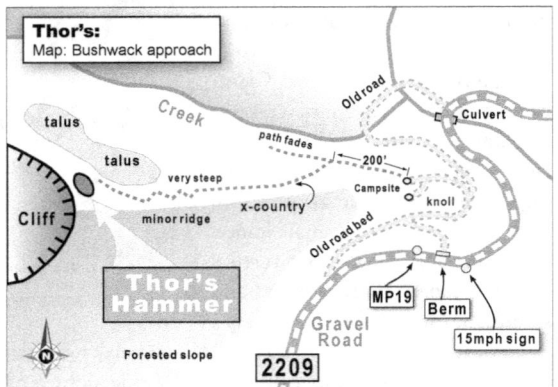

P5 from the notch: Stem off the large chock stone and the pinnacle, placing pro in a very wide slot (4" to 5" pro) and make a diligent 5.6 move onto a small stance. Climb a steep crux section (2" crack) to another stance, then step right (south) around to the sunny side of the pinnacle. Ascend the steps and corners until you are on top of a separate pedestal.

Gingerly step across the void and balance carefully up some nice hand and foot edges onto the main summit massif. This summit is a gently sloping flat fifteen-foot wide ledge perfect for eating lunch and enjoy-

ing the scenic views of the region.

2. **South Ravine 5.7**

When the deer trace meets the base of the cliff and begins to angle right, break left and up along the rounded ridge crest until you reach the base of the sunny South Ravine.

Scramble 200' up the 3rd class south side ravine to the notch between the main wall and the spire. Continue leading 100' to the summit by referencing Route #1 (North Ravine route) from the notch belay at the large chock stone.

3. **Vexation Variation 5.6**

Ascends part of the south side ravine, but after the first 100' step right at a large tree and ascend a series of rock steps into a deep boxed corner system. At a small tree on a small ledge the V-shaped corner becomes vertical. Behind the tree on the left face is a short 5" wide off-width crack. Ascend this (5.6 crux) for 20' to a stance, clip a fixed piton, then balance up onto the next large ledge where this route merges with the Standard Route in the middle of pitch 5.

Thor's Anvil rappel challenges: The rappel back to the chock stone notch (100') is tricky and should be done with care so your rope does not get stuck in the process. The rappel involves descending over and around several edges and warrants careful rope management by a skilled leader. **Pro:** Minor gear to 2" and cams (4" if you have it). Take minimal gear; the technical lead portion on the pinnacle is only about 100' long. Bring long slings to reduce rope drag. One 60-meter rope is sufficient for climbing and rappelling back to the notch if just a party of two climbers.

STACK ROCK

The volcanic landscape of the Santiam valley yields a broad history of remnant volcanic flow activity composed of basalt, olivine andesite, basaltic or oligolclase andesite which form summit caps on certain higher elevation ridges from

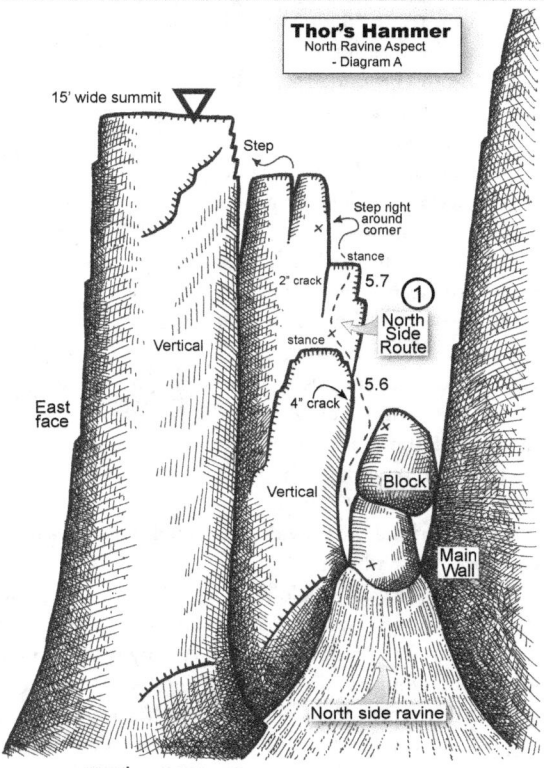

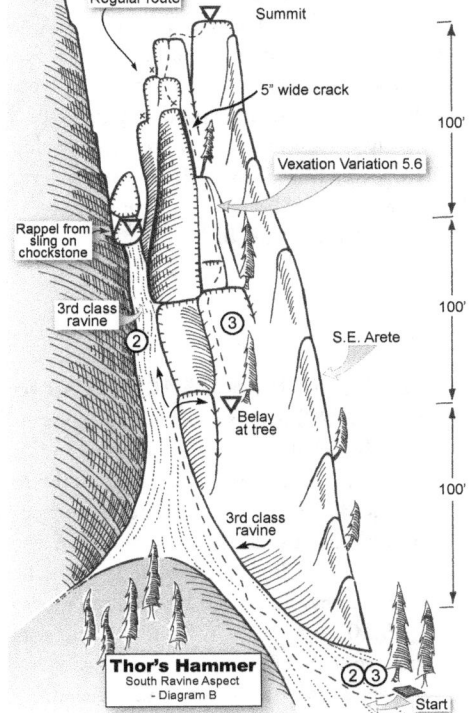

Martin Buttes to Mount Beachie west to the Henline Mountain ridge line and beyond. This volcanic cycle which ranges from about the middle to late Miocene epoch erupted mostly from a widespread series of dikes, plugs and related lava cones.

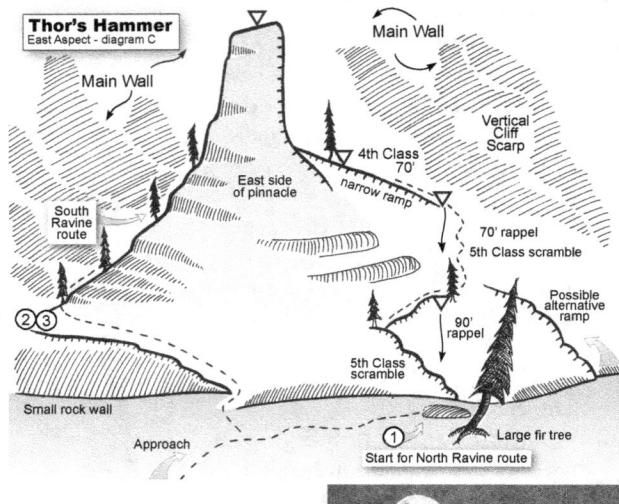

This cliff formation has infrequently seen a few ascents by hard-core climbers venturing here on the Little North Santiam River since the late 70s to experience big wall flavor. A friend mentioned the place to another friend who remarked, "Seen it, been there, done it!" Though seldom climbed the site provides sustained challenges for experienced climbers. Wear a helmet.

This wide valley region is filled with saturated colors of beautiful green, blue sky, and cold crystal clear streams rushing to the valley floor. The predominate tree canopy is composed of a dense growth of Douglas Fir, Western Hemlock, Western Red Cedar, and Vine Maple. The lower western region of valley has been logged and the forest you walk through to approach the wall is composed of second growth trees. Pacific Rhododendron dwells in the lightly shaded forest. Manzanita, Cascade Huckleberry, and Kinnikinnick thrive on certain slopes. A selection of vibrant floral colors dot the open slopes near the base of these crags. Indian Paintbrush and Mariposa Lily grow on open rocky slopes. The lightly wooded forest and steep rocky slopes provide a haven to saxifrage, alumroot, Mountain Parsley fern, Bear Grass, Salal, Twinflower, Sword Fern and Mahonia.

On the summit of *Thor's*

1. **Grand Alliance 5.9**
   Odd steps to a corner.
2. _____
3. _____
4. _____
5. **Steel and Stone II 5.10b PG A2 (or 5.12+)**
   Length: 220', Pro to 3" including cams, and KB, LA
   S&S is a challenging route that ascends steep cracks, seams and face climbing till it powers through a large overhanging roof on the third pitch.
   P1 5.8 55': Start up a flaky minor corner to a ledge (piton). Climb up a steep broken 5.8 face (piton) past a small bush to a belay on a small ledge.
   P2 5.9 60': Climb directly up past the hueco into a crux corner pod, or step right to a left-facing corner and ascend it 20', then move back left.
   P3 5.10b A2 100': Crank up the thin seam 15', smear up the infamous smooth slab under the great roof. Aid directly out the 12' roof to surmount the roof lip, then continue up 25' past the last small bulge to a belay on a nice ledge.

P4 5.7 20': Easier terrain quickly leads to the top.

6. **Monty Piton II 5.10c R**
   Length: 220', Pro to 3" and cams
   P1: Start at a lone thin fir tree at the lower left edge of the prominent central buttress. Angle up left (fixed) on steep but reasonably easy 5.7 run out terrain to belay just below the right edge of the great roof. **P2:** Step up and surmount the roof obstacle (5.10c R) and continue up (fixed) the obvious dark stained left-facing corner to the summit. The final exit moves near the end of the climb are highly exposed with considerable runout. Rappel the route.

7. **Eck-Rollings 5.8 A1**
   Length: 220', Pro to 3½" including cams and pitons
   Locate the main central headwall. To the immediate left is a crack corner system. The Eck-Rollings route is the next major corner system west of that. A lone fir tree stands at the base of the steep initial part of the first pitch. **P1 120':** Start at a belay stance and move left to a lone fir tree. Power directly up the crack system behind the fir tree, then move right and climb a wide (3-4") jam crack to a ledge. **P2 5.8 A1 140':** Aid up a slightly overhanging corner, step right and continue up low angle crack ramp system to the top of the wall.

8. **Adams Variant 5.8 A1**
   Pro to 3½" including pitons
   A direct variation joining onto Eck-Rollings route. **P1 5.8 A1 120'** to ledge where it merges with the above route.

9. **_____**
   This is the first major corner system immediately left of the main central buttress.

10. **Dead Grouse 5.9 A1**
    Length: 220', Pro: ?
    This route is the huge deep chimney system on the immediate right side of the prominent central buttress. **P1:** Starts in a deep chimney and power up through an overhanging slot. Once above the crux this corner broadens onto a wide open face. **P2:** Face climb on the right of the crack on small edges in this large scooped out face.

11. **Stone Scared 5.10a**
    Length: 250', Pro to 6"
    To the right of the prominent central buttress is a smooth slab on the upper cliff. Stone Scared takes a crack system up to this smooth slab. **P1 90' 5.9:** Ascend the obvious crack below the slab then step right to a 2-bolt belay on the bottom of the slab. **P2 160' 5.10a:** Head up and right from the belay into the wide flare, make a tricky move pulling off of the slab (crux). Traverse left to the bushes, and pull over a small budge. Start in the right crack, then as it difficulty increases traverse back left on the slab to another crack leading to the summit and a tree belay after 30' of 4th class. Two double rope rappels to the ground.

PIKA ROCK

ROCKY TOP MTN

A site seldom climbed at, but if you relish long drive time commitment, navigating AWD roads, helmet climbing, and rappel development at high al-

Climbing out of the giant roof on S & S

titude, this unusual yet scenic crag might be your ticket to adventure.

The crag is located on the north side of Rocky Top mountain (friends jestingly call the crag Pika Rock), which is a few miles east of Mill City (and east of Salem). That's the easy part - the difficult part is the uphill gravel road drive (which will consume an hour). The last mile of road retains snowpack through June, so July to October is the only viable season to go there. The crag faces northeast, yet it gets sunshine all morning, and cool shade in the afternoon hours. Hikers occassionally do park at the pass to hike the Rocky Top trail to the summit (fairly common). The last segment of road beyond the pass is in notoriously poor condition.

This site is helmet climbing, and (if your in to it) top-down only route development. Use caution if planning to do any form of route development here (do not be cavalier about it). Considerable loose rock (mostly off route) will limit future climber interest, so it's just a backcountry adventure climbers haven. The crag is an option in July on a boilerplate day when all the other places are too hot to climb at (this is at 5000' and it never gets hot there).

The cliff scarp is about 200' tall, very vertical, fairly decent rock (best after the loose stuff is removed), and capable of holding more new bolt routes, virtually no moss, parking is 2-minutes from the base (if the road is still drivable), scenic alpine environs, with some nearby bouldering potential. To access the summit is a 3rd class scramble up the back side. The outcrop is a volcanic vent of basaltic origins that plugged when the silica rich andesitic material congealed. The rock is composed of both dark and light plagioclase with minute quartzite minerals.

Directions:

Drive east of Salem on US Hwy 22 for about 36 miles total (till just before Niagara County Park). The gravel road turn off is about 3.9 miles east of the tiny community of Gates, Oregon. Turn north onto gravel road #2211 (part of the Santiam State Forest network of roads) which has a network of road branches (stay on the mainline #2211). Drive up this for 7.1 miles to the pass (en route you will pass the Natural Arch trailhead). At the pass the road splits again. Take the west road (#361) along the north slopes of Rocky Top for about 3/4 mile and park beneath the cliff scarp (or walk this last road segment).

Pika Rock (the beta is listed from left to right)

1. **Prima Donna 5.11c** ★★

    Pro: 7 QD's, 60' length

    Cool long crimpy face climb on stellar rock with a powerful crux sequence.

2. **Scorched Earth 5.8** ★★

    Pro: 6 QD's, 50' length

    Enjoyable face climb with thin crimp nuances that make the battle worth it.

3. **Radioactive Wolves 5.8**

    Pro: gear to 4" and

Rocky Top Map 1: Road Access

nuts to 1", 50' length

A short 50' lead the cruises directly up left toward the belay station. A minor hollow section where the crack breaks onto a small ledge with minor loose pebbles.

4. **Pikaville**   5.9
★★★

Pro: TCU's (#0) to 3" cams, and nuts to 1" (lite rack)

The reason to be. Pikaville is a multi-pitch 170' long unique power line that winds its way to the top of the cliff. P1 5.6: begin the climb up a right leaning seam (past several pitons & bolts), then angle up leftward along several small broken steps till you reach a belay station in a corner nook. P2 5.9: immediately above the belay climb a crux overhung slot to a stance, move abruptly right a few feet, then continue up a crimp and jug crux face section (bolts) to another belay. P3 5.8: climb up right in a deep slot (bolt) for about 15', then abruptly bust hard right into another crack corner system (bolt and pin). Climb up this final steep ramp crack corner (using gear) to the final belay. Rappel to the previous belay (via some backclipping), then directly to the ground from that mid belay. A single 60-meter rope will work.

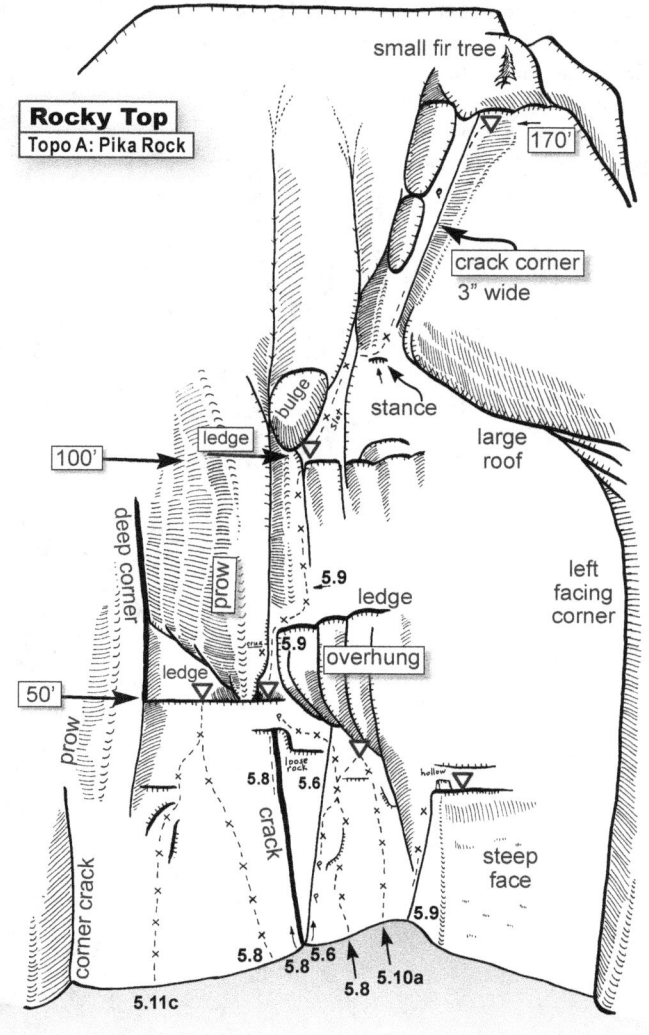

Rocky Top
Topo A: Pika Rock

5. **Cornucopia 5.8** ★

Pro: 4 QD's, 40' length

Crimps on a steep slab face make for a fun romp up to its own belay. Rappel.

6. **Never Neverland 5.10a** ★

Pro 4 QD's, 40' length

Stouter crimps on the same face landing at the same belay. Rappel.

7. **Acid Reflux 5.9**

Pro: gear to 2"

Minor corner (bolts) goes up right then abruptly moves right past a hollow block to a belay.

Beware of loose rock.

The cliff scarp has notable space for additional future mixed bolt'n gear adventure climbs for any route developer who lives in close proximity to this site.

CLIMBING ON THE EDGE

SOUTH SANTIAM REGION

The old Cascades east of Sweet Home offer a particularly complex diversity of natural beauty. Hidden in these hills is a wealth of treasure for everyone to enjoy. The few active mines and numerous old mine shafts testify to a history of busy gold and silver exploration. These days the area is frequented by hikers delving in deep old growth forests, or searching for quartz crystals, or fishing, and rock climbing on unique andesitic and tuff formations.

THE MENAGERIE

A Condensed Guide to The Menagerie

From a manuscript by Jim Anglin

Several miles east of Sweet Home, Oregon, and near the community of Upper Soda is the unique Menagerie Wilderness Area, a small wilderness region that contains a wealth of tuffaceous rock spires, arches and cliffs of unusual shapes and sizes, even some monstrous spires in excess of 350' high. The majority of summits and cliffs tend to be concentrated in the Keith Creek drainage, but a healthy selection of additional spires do exist in the Trout Creek drainage to the west, and Soda and Bear Creek to the east.

The Menagerie Wilderness is not a crowded destination climbing site, partly due to its distance from a major metro area. Other factors that tend to limit climber interest is the variable quality of rock, which can range from excellent quality at the Rooster Rock group, to less than ideal on some of the upper wilderness spires. Some pitches can be of poor quality rock, but the remainder of the climb may be reasonable. Each section will detail some of the pros and cons on certain routes where quality is an issue.

This brief analysis on the Menagerie rock climbing opportunities fulfills the desire of Jim Anglin who thought it beneficial for regional rock climbers to have access to a condensed version of his original detailed thesis. He believed that through a condensed version climbers would be enabled to quickly access the more popular and favorite rock climbing opportunities of the Menagerie Wilderness Area. This condensed version is dedicated to the memory of Mr. Anglin.

This brief study of the Menagerie is designed to provide route details for only the more commonly ascended rock routes. The focus of this section primarily points you toward spires and routes of greater value based on your likely time limitations, rock quality, technical difficulty and long-term user interest. Beware of dubious friable rock in the Menagerie, particularly the upper area. Numerous climbs, though not implied in the rating, are often R or X due to serious runout or lack of adequate pro options.

Directions

1.) From Sweet Home drive east on U.S. 20 for 22¼ miles and park near a state highway cinder yard. The 2.1 mile 2200' Rooster Rock Trail is an arduous hike from the parking lot on Highway 20, but if you can endure the steep approach hike the views from the top of the rock are beautiful.

2.) An alternative but longer 2½ mile trail starts at Trout Creek Campground and merges with the Rooster Rock Trail near the Rooster Rock pinnacle.

3.) To access the rock spires in the upper wilderness area, drive up FS2027, then park at the beginning of FS850 and walk along this overgrown road for ¾ mile (past a large landslide) to where the Rooster Rock Trail descends. The wilderness trail that descends from here to Rooster Rock is a bit faint in places, but is still reasonably easy to follow.

4) The common method to access the upper climbing sites is (see overview map) via FS2027 to FS850 which becomes FS857, then follow spur road FS856 to the landing, a nice overlook immediately above the wilderness. A short trail descends from the landing down to FS850 at the wilderness register sign.

At the registration sign your goal defines your direction: Go east along old FS850 to Turkey Monster, southeast to Rabbit Ears & Panorama Point, or south along the ridge crest trail to the Rooster Rock group. This upper approach to the Rooster Rock group is quite viable simply because the elevation and distance is considerably shorter than hiking 2200' from the highway in the valley.

Favorite climbs here are plentiful. The foremost is the Turkey Monster (III 5.6 A3 or 5.11a) is absolutely staggering, and has probably seen only a small handful of ascents since Eugene Dod, Dave Jensen and Bill Pratt completed it in 1966.

The most frequented pinnacles are Rooster Rock, Hen Rock, Rabbit Ears, Royal Arch, Turkey Monster and Panorama Point. A Peregrine Falcon seasonal closure is in effect for the upper portion of the wilderness which last until approximately August 1. Inquire at the Sweet Home Ranger Station about the status of the seasonal climbing closure concerning the upper wilderness access trails before driving to the Menagerie Wilderness.

ROOSTER ROCK

The Rooster Rock group is the most likely destination for visitors and climbers who come to

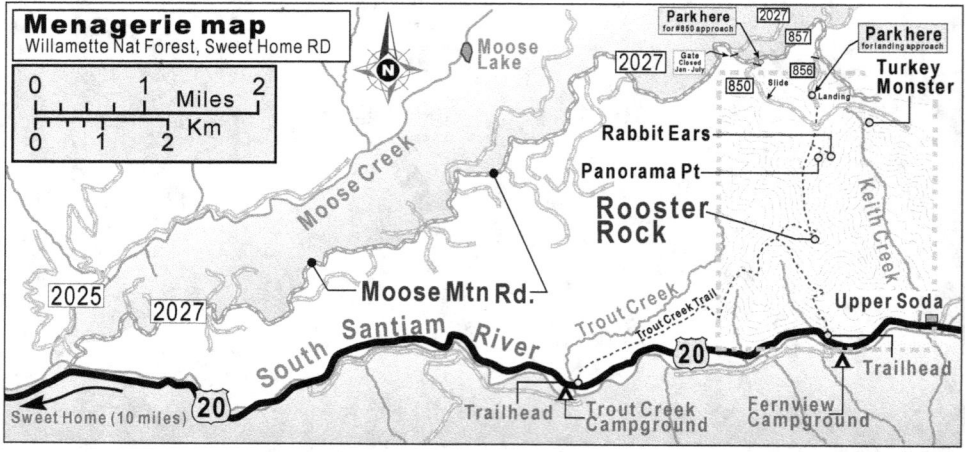

the region. The quality of the rock is good on all the spires in this group. The reasonable nature of the climbs provides climbers with a great venue of routes to choose from depending upon your skill level and time. Near the summit of Rooster Rock you will find a few remaining timbers and bits of rusted metal, which are the sole remnants of the small fire lookout that clung to the summit of Rooster Rock. There are a series of sturdy eye bolts still well-attached to the wall on the standard north side route which climbers usually clip into while climbing up this route to the summit. The first route on each pinnacle is the common line of ascent and descent unless other alternate descent options are noted. All the climbs generally require an assortment of gear to lead climb so bring a workable selection of wires and cams of various widths to suit your leading ability.

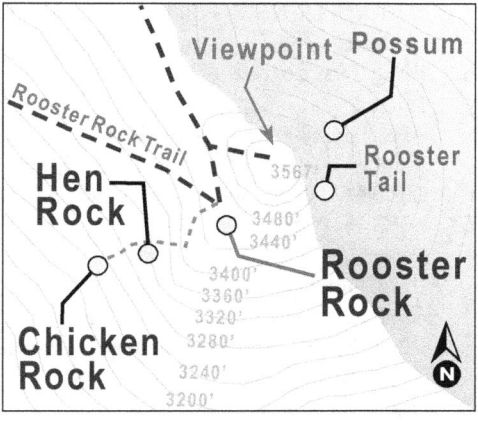

The Rooster Rock hikers trail encounters the north side of Rooster Rock at the 2200' level. This spire is the largest of a group of pinnacle in this area. From the trail step down right on a path for 30' and rope-up here for the regular North Face route.

1. **Standard North Face Route 5.4R**

    Minor pro to 3"

    The North Face route is the most frequently climbed route at the Menagerie and for good reason; conveniently reasonable climbing that quickly leads to a stellar summit view.

    Begin by stepping up past a mammoth eye-bolt to a short steep corner crack system. Use hand holds and friction smears on the right side of the crack until possible to move back left to the crack as you get near the notch. Clip another eye-bolt. Continue up easy large ledges past the old lookout timbers, and then angle right along the crest to the summit anchor. A single 60-meter rope will suffice for rappels off from Rooster Rock.

    The 5.6 variation is to simply use the corner crack directly for the entire way up to the notch. This is the better option provided you get good pro in the crack.

2. **North Face Jam Crack 5.8**

    Pro to 3"

    This climb starts a few feet to the right of the standard route, and begins upward from an obvious flake sticking out of the ground. Climb a crack corner to a rightward traverse and set a belay on the outer northwest point of the rock. Climb up right 30' on a moss covered ramp, and then up right to an obvious difficult overhanging jam crack. Carefully protect the upper section before committing to the moves.

3. **West Face Dihedral Direct 5.9+**

    Pro to 3"

    Considered to be the classic route at Rooster Rock this climb is a punchy hard route that in years past surprised the easier grade climbers because of its old underrated scale (5.8).

    Descend west down slope (along the north side) to a notch between the northwest face and a large rock spur. Set a belay at the notch.

    P1: Climb the west face via a steep crack which becomes an open chimney leading to a sloping ledge.

    P2: Climb a flake to an overhanging crack, and then traverse left 15' to the crux. Surmount the overhanging crux section to a stance, and then lead up to a nice open book crack corner 30' to the summit.

Note: On pitch two, a direct start leading up to the overhanging crux can be attacked directly (5.10a/b) by placing pro up right before firing into the direct start.

4. **Frog Traverse 5.5**
   Pro to 2"
   About thirty-five feet up pitch one of West Face Dihedral Direct break up left using a traverse friction slab (5.5) which joins the ledge on the outer northwest point of the rock spire. From this belay follow route #2 upper portion (5.8).

5. **NPG 5.11c**
   Pro to 2"
   P1: Climb approximately 30' of route #3 then aim up right onto a (bolted) hard steep face climb which leads to a crack and ends at a belay ledge.
   P2: Exit the right side of the ledge onto steep face climbing which leads to the summit.

6. **The Spur 5.11a**
   Pro to 1.5"
   A high quality route on the spur that forms the west end of Rooster Rock. Descend down to the west to a mossy ledge and a madrone tree. Climb a steep flake crack, clip a bolt and move left, then up (bolts) to a belay.

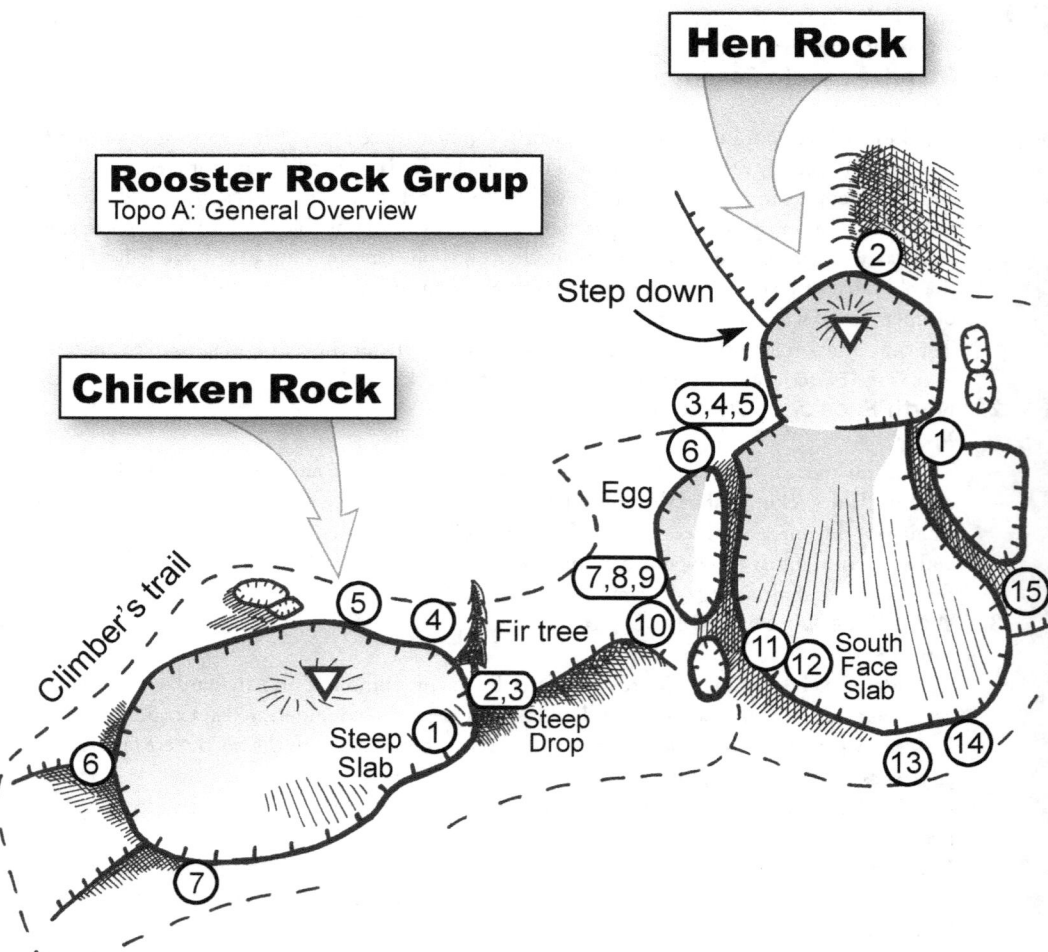

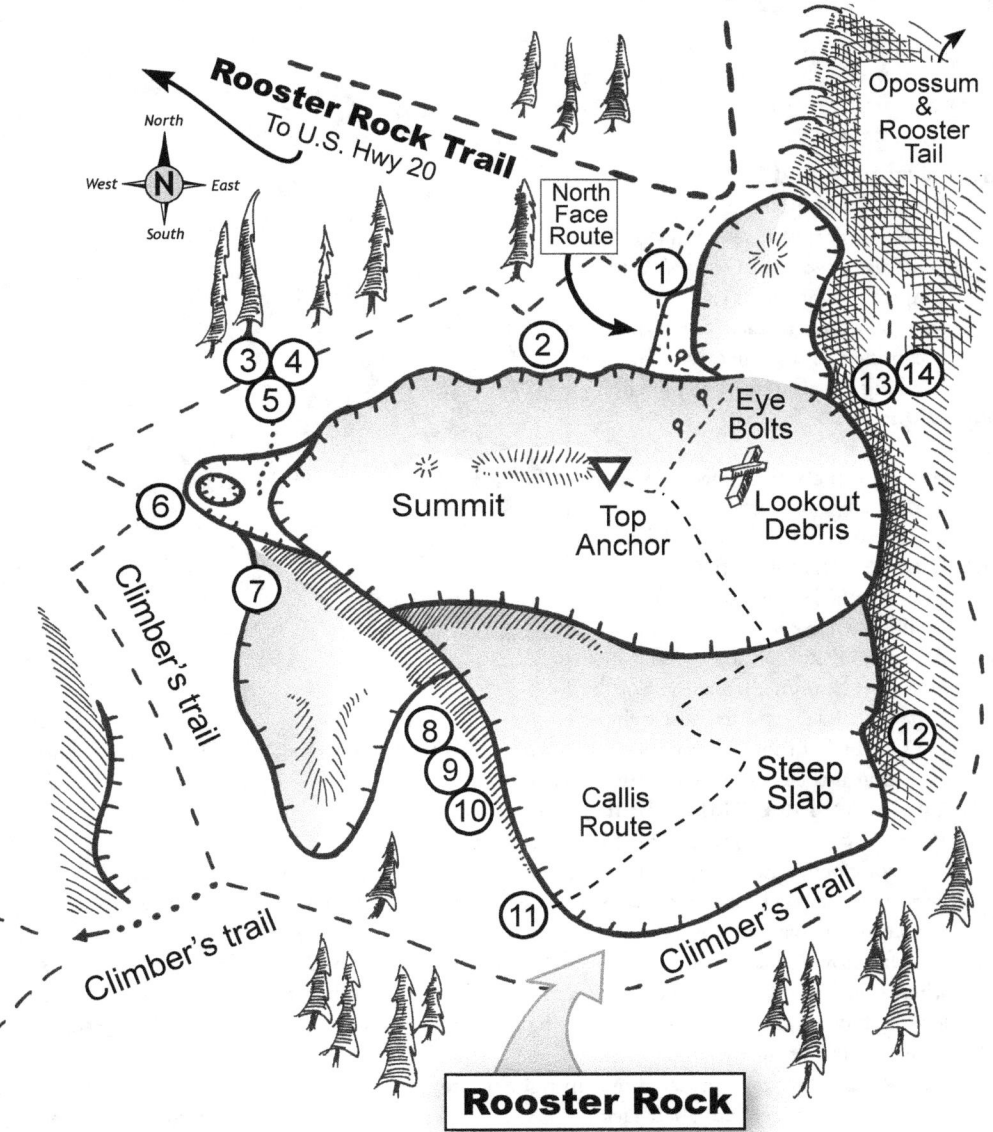

7. **South Face 5.9 A2**

   Pro to 1.5" including nailing gear

   Traverse above the large rock spur (mentioned in route #3) and angle around right onto the south face along a ledge above the large cave mentioned for the following routes. Belay.
   P1: Free and aid the crack above to a bolt ladder using more mixed climbing to a sloping belay ledge.
   P2: Move right around a corner onto a large south face sloping ledge (30') and then climb a rock step (5.5) continuing up a right diagonal crack 35' to another belay ledge.
   P3: Traverse right 25' and ascend a chimney to the site of the old lookout and finish to the summit.

A Large Cave is located on the lower southwest side of the Rooster Rock formation. The next three climbs are located in or start on the right side of this large cave.

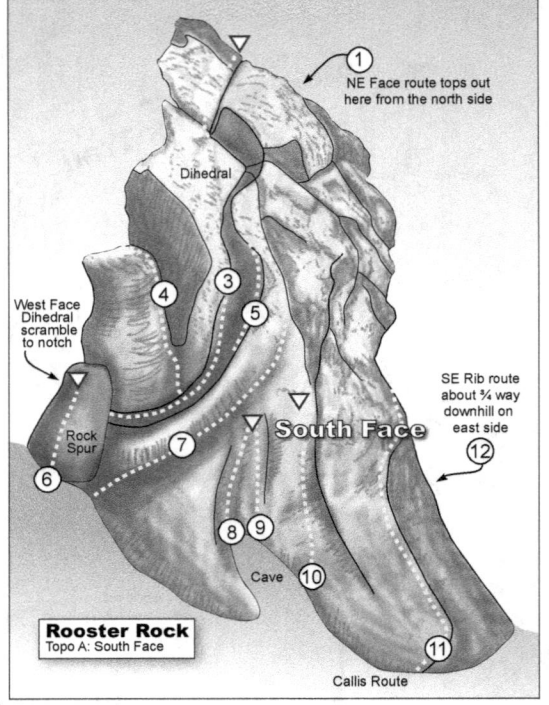

8. **Gizzard 5.10d**
   Pro to 2" and a cam to 4"
   In the deepest recesses of this prominent large cave is the Gizzard. Undercling out right (bolts) and up steep rock to a finger crack that becomes a chimney, and then escape by face climbing up left to the belay anchor.

9. **Old Flakes 5.10c**
   Pro to 1½"
   Power up the wall immediately right of the huge cave passing several bolts to a ramp. Rejoins the Gizzard route.

10. **Chicken Richard 5.11c/d**
    Pro: Mostly fixed but bring a few small nuts and cams
    A powerful line on a sweeping buttress of rock immediately right of the large cave. P1: Begin five feet right of the Old Flakes route. Climb a difficult and steep face to an easier slab which goes vertical to overhung at the crux. Rappel with 60m rope.

11. **Southeast Face (Callis Route) 5.7**
    Pro to 1" and minor gear to 3½" for the chimney
    A historic bench-mark route which established 5th class rock climbing at the Menagerie Wilderness and a good climbing route worth the adventure. If you have not done this yet, plan on it next time you are in the area.
    Descend down around the west side of Rooster Rock to the south face. The first large cave is where you will find routes like the Gizzard. Walk to the right a bit along the south face and look high up on the cliff for another cave halfway up on the south face. The Callis Route starts at the ground below this other cave.
    P1: Climb an initially mossy ramp up right passing several bolts. At the fourth bolt move left around a corner into a left facing dihedral and climb this crack (5.7) aiming toward the cave where you will find a bolt belay anchor just to the left. P2: Traverse rightward around a rock rib outcrop onto the southeast face (bolt), and ascend up a friction slab (bolts) to a wide chimney with several more bolts at its base. Ascend the chimney past a large fir tree and set up a belay.
    P3: Continue stemming up the chimney crack and merge with the standard route on the ridge crest. Anticipate partner communication difficulties on the second pitch.
    Options: An alternate variation exists starting at P2 by clipping the initial bolt to the right of the small cave, and then powers (5.9R) up and left to a small alcove, then to an exposed slab and upward to difficult face climbing to an undercling flake and jam crack leading to the summit.

12. Southeast Rib Direct 5.7
Pro to 3"

When descending about ²/₃ way down along the east side of Rooster Rock you will encounter an obvious 30' crack with an overhanging dihedral at its top.
P1: Climb 20' up the crack and exit left 15' (5.4) under the overhang and onto the main southeast face of Rooster Rock. Using smears friction climb up to the bolts at the base of the chimney on the Callis Route.
P2: Traverse left 15' onto a rock rib and climb the unprotected 5.7 rib for 40' which brings you to a jam crack (5.7) leading to the summit.
Note: You can skip the runout rock rib on pitch two by just climbing the upper Callis Route using the deep chimney.

13. Fred Hart Traverse 5.4
Pro to 1"

This is the other short viable alternate route on the north side of Rooster Rock that leads (nearly) directly to the summit. From the hikers trail step over onto the east side and follow a horizontal ledge system. When the ledge system ends, down climb a few feet and traverse left to a chimney. Climb the chimney 35' to the notch where it joins with the standard North Face Route #1 and continue another lead to the summit.

14. Fred Hart Lieback 5.9
Pro 1½"

This direct variation can be found by descending down the east side of Rooster Rock from the hikers trail 40' to a flake. Climb the steep flake (5.9) to where it meets with the Fred Hart Traverse ledge, and traverse left into a chimney and climb this for 35' to the notch, and continue another lead to the summit.

HEN ROCK

Hen Rock is a stellar rock formation and one of a cluster of spires forming the Rooster Rock group. It is located few hundred feet down west from Rooster Rock and can be approached by descending down a steep climber's path from the hikers trail next to Rooster Rock. Hen Rock has excellent rock and offers the highest concentration of sport routes in the Menagerie. If you plan to summit on Hen Rock rappel descend 75' down the vertical north side where route Eggs Overhard comes up.

1. Southeast Slab 5.9
Pro to 2"

A very popular and historic route way ahead of its time because it was first climbed in 1959.
Climb up a fun easy slab on the east side of Hen Rock left of a left facing corner that leads up to an airy stance. Smear up a deceptively hard and exposed steep slab (3 bolts) for 30' to the top. Rappel down the north side for

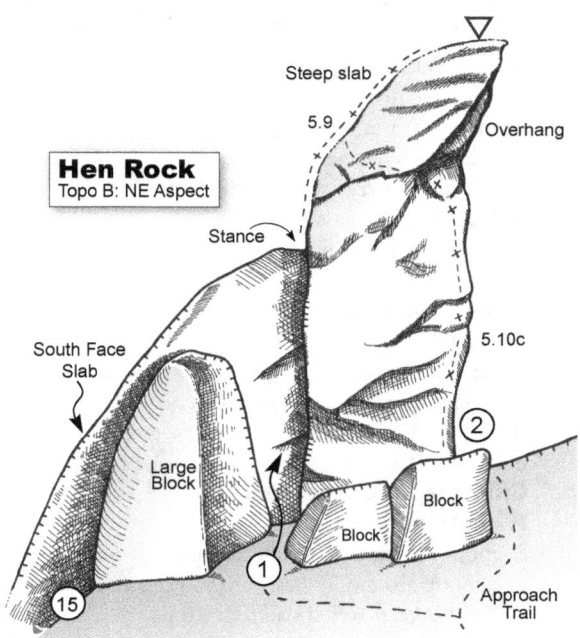

all summit-bound routes on Hen Rock.

2. **Eggs Overhard (North Face) 5.10c**

   Pro: QD's

   This is the north face route on Hen Rock. Although the original ascent traversed up rightward to the first bolt it is best to just 'stick-clip' it first and boulder directly up the hard crux initial moves to the bolt. Power up hard, tricky face climbing, and then at the third bolt move up left until you are under the large roof. Traverse left again around the roof bulge until the angle eases and you can friction climb up a steep slab to the summit.

3. **Eggs Overeasy (Northwest Face) 5.8**

   Pro to 2"

   Begin about 15' right of the previous route starting on a mossy boulder in a corner. Climb up thin cracks and flakes (20') to a bolt, and then continue another 35' to an easy hand traverse leading right to a small ledge on the west face. Follow an overhanging rib (bolt) to the top. Route is seldom climbed.

4. **Wild West 5.10d**

   Pro to 1½"

   Great route on excellent quality rock. Scramble down onto the west side of Hen Rock to a large left facing crack corner with a bolt 20' up the route. Climb this past the bolt until you are above a chinquapin tree, and then traverse left onto the overhanging west face climbing up past bolts and a few cam placements en route to the top.

5. **Chinquapin Corner 5.9**

   Pro to 1½"

   Begin in the same large left facing crack corner as the previous route, but continue to climb straight up around a block until you can join Southeast Slab (route #1) at the airy stance. Finish up the steep bolted slab to the top.

The following five routes are located on a minor formation called the Egg

6. Chimney 5.5
Pro to 1"
On the lower west side of Hen Rock is a large block called the Egg. The chimney ascends between Hen Rock and this 'Egg' and then steps across the void onto Hen Rock to end at a tree belay. Rappel or continue up Hen Rock to merge with route #1.

7. Sunnyside Up 5.11a
Pro to 1"
This face route ascends the southern sunny outside of the Egg.
P1: From the top of a pedestal slot a small nut, and then power up a series of bolt protected hard moves (crux). Place a cam and move left to a bolt, and then climb straight up to the top of the Egg. Step across the void onto the Hen and power up several hard moves to a large ledge.
P2: Exit off the left side of the ledge but stay on the rib until you join route #1 en route to the top.

8. South Crack 5.7
Pro to 4"
This route also ascends the southern sunny outside of the Egg. Immediately right of route #7 (Sunnyside Up) is a crack leading to the top of the Egg. Climb this while gradually working leftward up the Egg.

9. Poached 5.9
Pro: Mostly fixed with pins and bolts
This is a route immediately left of the south side chimney of the Egg. Climbs a steep clean buttress to the top of the Egg and merge with the Sunnyside Up and continue to the top of Hen Rock.

10. South Chimney 5.7
Pro to 4"
This is the other side of the same chimney as (#6) the Chimney route.

The following routes are located on the south side of Hen Rock. The original wandering route that zigzagged up the wide sunny south face was called Winter Sunshine. Jim Anglin realized that the entire south face could yield a finer string on directisimo lines if they went straight up the wall instead. Therefore several seasonal sounding names were applied to a fine selection of three additional new routes for this stellar site.

11. Autumn Reigns 5.10b
Pro: 10 QD's if going to the top
This is the first of four routes on the clean south face of Hen Rock. Begin with a belay at the base of the South Chimney. Climb the right side of the chimney wall on the southwest side of Hen Rock. Steep powerful climbing (bolts) leads to a tree. Rappel or continue to the top of Hen.

12. Rites of Spring 5.10a
Pro: 10+ QD's and a medium sized cam
From the south chimney which separates the Egg from the Hen step out right onto the top of a boulder. Step out from this boulder onto the south face of Hen, and climb upward (bolts) and aim up left. At the third bolt move right several feet, and then continue straight up passing two more bolts on the right of a small fir (place cam in horizontal crack). Continue upward past a large ledge which is on your left (bolt) to a lower angle slab, which you can move around using the left side of a block. Merge with route the Southeast Slab route #1 at the exposed airy stance and continue to the top.

13. **Summer Rules 5.10c**
    Pro to 1" including QD's
    This route begins immediately right of the lowest point of the sunny south face of the Hen Rock. Commence up left using a steep ramp (bolt). Climb straight up (bolt) and then past a difficult rightward move and over a small roof (cam placements). You will pass one of the old original ¼" bolts, but continue directly up the face to the next bolt and further up the face until you reach a crack. Pass a large loose looking block on the left and merge with route #1 at the airy stance and continue up the steep slab to the summit of Hen Rock.

14. **Winter Sunshine 5.9**
    Pro to 1" and QD's
    Winter Sunshine was the original zigzagging route on the south face of Hen Rock. It originally ascended crossing up left and back over to the right before joining into an upper route. Jim straightened the route to its present status as follows.
    Begin 15' right of the very toe of the south face and climb past three bolts to a shallow trough (fixed pin) and climb past a loose block on its right where you will shortly merge with route #1 (Southeast Slab) at the airy stance.

15. **Southeast Slab Direct 5.9**
    Pro to 1"
    Uphill a bit on the southeast side of Hen Rock is a large moss covered boulder. Begin by climbing two parallel sided cracks for 20' and then over a large loose block (mentioned in route #14) to merge with route #1 (Southeast Slab) en route to the summit.

Menagerie
Map 1: Chicken Rock
South Face

CHICKEN ROCK

Chicken Rock is located just a short spat downhill from Hen Rock. Though the standard 5.8 route is the easiest way to the top this pinnacle offers a selection of stout routes that will justifiably grab your attention. The rock spire is like a tall crooked finger with a broad flat south face. Several facets of the upper pinnacle tilt awkwardly to create difficult leading obstacles to pass over.

1. **Southeast Face Slab 5.8**
    Pro to 2"
    This is the original route and the easiest method to reach the summit of Chicken Rock. This route ascends this pinnacle in a clockwise fashion. Begin on the lower northeast side at a flat landing with an abrupt drop-off. Traverse out onto the exposed southeast face by diligently moving up leftward 40' to a large ledge on the south face. Move up 10' to a bolt, then a bit higher to a 2" jam crack and wander up right to a notch on the ridge crest. A final few moves of overhanging jugs on

the ridge crest brings you quickly to the summit bolt anchors.

Line of Descent
The common descent from Chicken Rock is via a 75' rappel on the north side back down to the ground.

2. Sticky Fingers 5.10c
Pro: QD's
Two sport routes exist on the east face of Chicken. Sticky Fingers is the left route while Free Bird is the right route. Traverse a few steps up leftward onto the southeast face from the landing. Ascend directly up the southeast face on easy rock steps (bolts) to a ledge. Power up a very steep (bolts) face leftward to the top.

3. Free Bird 5.11a
Pro to 1" and QD's
Start on the east side of the pinnacle at the landing. Climb on the southeast rib on very thin face holds past three bolts on the lower section. A combination of pro and bolts leads up steep terrain to a final leftward leaning layback near the top.

4. Chicken Legs 5.11a
Pro: QD's
A fine quality north side route on Chicken Rock that starts near a tall fir tree. The route is considered to be one of the best routes in the Rooster Rock group. Ascend a line of bolts directly up the shaded north side to a different set of bolt anchors on the summit. A 60m rope will suffice for rappel.

5. West Chimney 5.6
Pro to 1½"
This starts at the base of Chicken Legs, and traverses rightward on mossy ledge for about 30' to a shallow chimney.
Ascend the chimney to the ledge on the crest where it merges with the standard route #1 Southeast Face Slab. Finish up a series of very steep holds on the crest that quickly leads to the summit.

6. Crystal Ball 5.11a
Pro: QD's
Walk around to the west side of this pinnacle till you see a ramp. Climb the ramp to a bolt and then aim over a bulge onto the west face. Continue up left around several blocks (bolt) and aim up rightward to a ledge (bolt). Power up over a difficult mantle crux move and continue up steep rock (2 bolts) to the summit. The route has substantial runout. Note: A direct start variation exists from the first bolt by climbing directly up to the ledge below the crux.

7. Southern Exposure 5.11c
Pro to 1½"
Walk down around the west side of the spire to an obvious mossy rock rib that provides access to the south face. From the top of the rock rib climb up left following a steep left sloping ramp. At the end of the ramp ascend up to a large block and power around the left side of the block and traverse back right. A substantially overhung crux (3 bolts) leads to the large ledge of route #1. Finish up the crest on steep holds to the summit.

UPPER MENAGERIE WILDERNESS
The upper Menagerie Wilderness offers a wild se-

Bob McGown on *Turkey Monster*

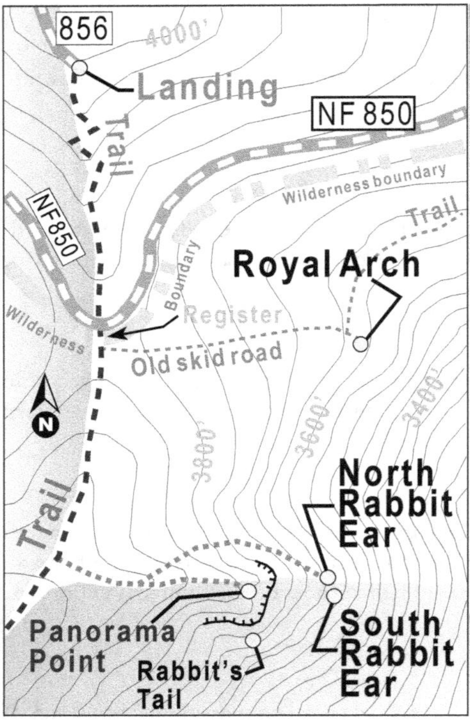

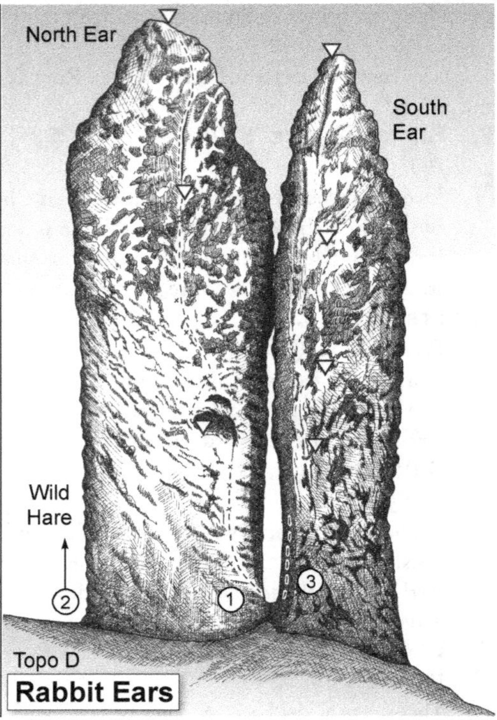

lection of spires of astounding shapes and sizes. The quality of the rock varies considerably in the upper area and may be a factor that limits user interest to some of these sites. But in all there is a stellar small selection of spires totally worthy of your attention if you are well skilled for the adventure. The following list of spires is best when approached from the upper entrance at the "landing" at the end of FS856. From that access point you can easily descend the hiker's access trail down to the registration sign at the wilderness boundary. Again, beware of dubious friable rock in the upper Menagerie. Numerous climbs, though not implied in the rating, should be R or X due to serious runout or lack of pro options.

The view from Panorama Point is absolutely stellar and provides an excellent visual bearing point for many of the spires in the upper Menagerie Wilderness. This panoramic viewpoint is such a superb site it is worth visiting even if you are out for a mere hiking trip.

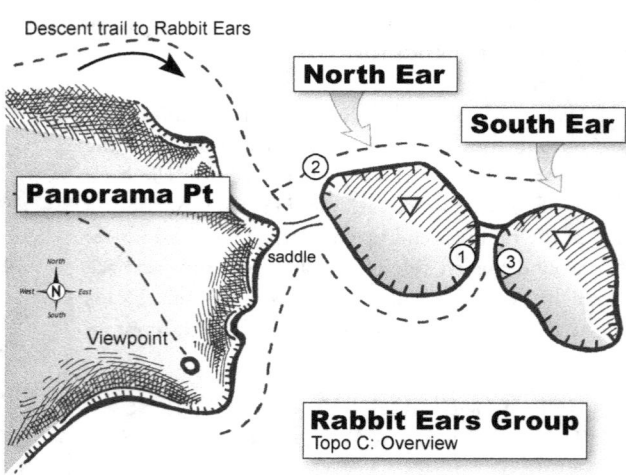

To reach Panorama Point: From the registration sign hike the Rooster Rock trail uphill for ¼ mile till it levels off. Aim left (east) through open forest and out onto an open ridge crest (a bit hard to spot initially because of the forest) that offers a nice path leading to the rocky topped knoll of Panorama Point. From this rocky knoll you will be overlooking the two massive towers of the Rabbit Ears. Several other spires are easily visible from this location as well such as Turkey Monster and The Spire.

To reach the Rabbit Ears: From the registration sign hike the Rooster Rock trail uphill for ¼ mile till it levels off. A narrow path will descend eastward down an old clear-cut logging grade around the north side of Panorama Point. The path leads directly to the lower east side of Panorama Point where you will find the twin 300-foot Rabbit Ears towers. The first ear you encounter is the North Ear. To access the notch between the ears descend around the right side of the North Ear.

To reach Turkey Monster: Walk east along FS850 to the campsite. Continue a few hundred yards further along the old road, and then descend off trail directly down to the Turkey Monster. The off trail portion is tricky especially for first timers. A very steep bluff (Turkey Point) and a tangle of brush can cause some approach frustration if you are too far to the west.

NORTH RABBIT EAR

1. The Cave Route 5.10a R/X
Pro to 2"and QD's

The Cave Route is usually the first climb of choice for climbers who are debating which route on the Ears to ascend. Beware, the 2nd pitch is serious R-rated, and the 3rd pitch is X-rated. The first Ear you encounter on the descent hike is the North Ear. Descend down to the right around the North Ear to access the notch between both Ears. The Cave Route begins left of the notch.

P1 5.10a: Climb up a few feet, and then traverse left to a bolt. Climb directly up 80' (5.10a) to the cave belay.

P2 5.10a R: Exit out the left side of the cave (bolt) to a ramp and tread carefully up and rightward to a dihedral (loose rock). From a high bolt traverse up left out the overhang face (bolts) to a notch, and then directly up jugs to a nice belay ledge. Two 50m ropes will reach the ground

Wayne Wallace on P2
Turkey Monster

from here.

P3 5.7X: Ascend a pro-less vertical groove system for a 90' past a bulge to an anchor, then cruise pro-less for 80' to the top of the Ear. Alternative: If you move left into route #2 you will find a tree ¾ way to the top.

Line of Descent:

A 90-foot rappel from the summit will bring you to the top of pitch 2. From there two 50-meter ropes will take you to the ground.

2. Wild Hare 5.10b

Pro to 2" including one 4" cam, otherwise mostly fixed

Wild Hare begins at the uphill saddle on the spires west face.

P1: Climb up and a bit left on steep face holds past six bolts to a short dihedral. Traverse left to the Piles belay ledge.

P2: Follow a wide crack up and right until it ends. Continue over a bulge and then move right on a ledge to another crack and punch over another bulge. Belay on a sizable ledge above the previous bulge.

P3: Easier terrain on good rock quickly

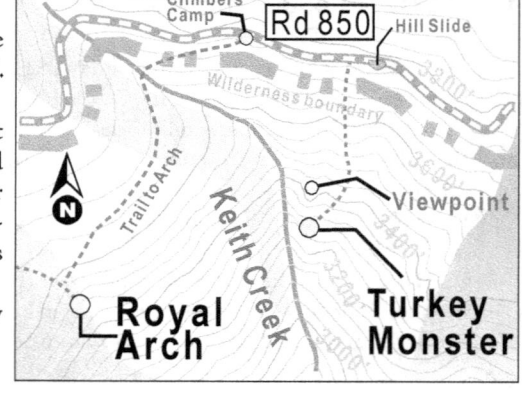

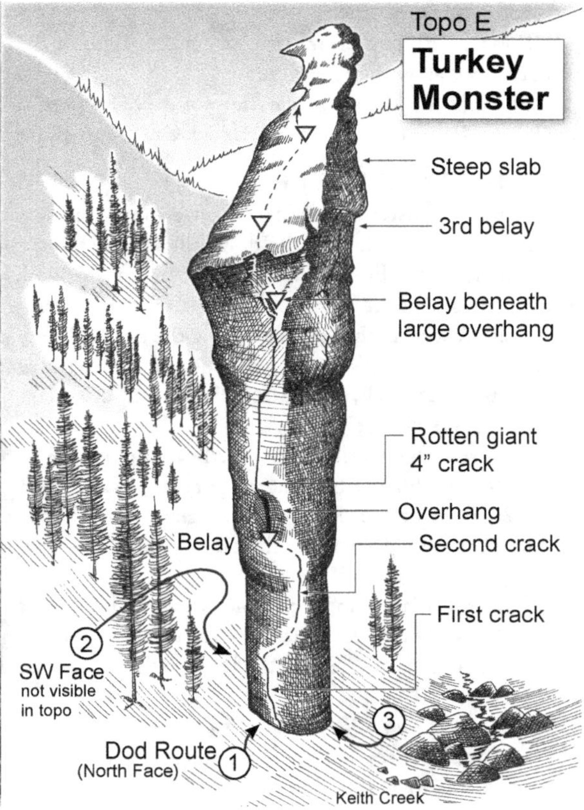

leads up to the summit of the North Ear.

SOUTH RABBIT EAR
Sure enough, the South Ear is right next to the North Ear.

3. West Face of South Ear 5.8 R
Pro to 4"

Considered to be a near classic route, but is marred by some poor (crumbly) rock on the lower part and a healthy runout section starting the 3rd pitch. Although a great route, it is definitely NOT a simple climb for a casual 5.8 climber.

P1: Begin at the notch between both Ears. Climb directly up for 25' on knobby rock to a ledge (bolt), and then traverse right 30'. Continue up 20' to a belay.

P2: Ascend the overhanging jam crack for 30' and belay at another small ledge.

P3: Traverse out right (5.7) for 30' and then straight up steep rock (5.8) to a chimney which leads up to a belay tree (bolts) at a ledge.

P4: Continue up this crack system 120' to the top of the Ear.

Line of Descent

Rappel with two 60-meter ropes from the summit down to the ledge with the tree. Rappel from the tree belay to the ground.

If you have only one single rope you will also need to rappel from the tree belay down to the small ledge belay at the top of pitch two. One more rappel will take you to the ground.

TURKEY MONSTER

Turkey Monster is certainly the most impressive tower in the Menagerie. An imposing sight standing nearly 400' tall on the downhill side it seems to defy the law of gravity with a summit larger than its base. First climbed in 1966 by Eugene Dod, Dave Jensen, and Bill Pratt this monster is definitely one of the more bold adventures to experience in the Menagerie.

Walk east from the campsite along the old FS850 road grade until you are directly above the monster. Descend brushy forested slopes slightly to the east of the tower.

1. **Dod Route (North Face) 5.11a (or 5.6 A3)**
   Pro to 3½"
   P1: From the uphill saddle (northeast side) move right a few feet, and then climb directly up (5.10a) for 80' to a belay at a small ledge in an alcove.
   P2: Power up the large overhang (giant rotten bong crack) 5.10c. The rock starts out horrible but improves partway up the pitch. Follow a long crack (5.8) to a double flake belay at a tiny perch.
   P3: Immediately above the anchor…muscle your way up and out the substantially overhung (5.11a and bolts) face surmounting this crux overhanging lip to another belay just beyond.
   P4: Waltz up easy terrain the leads to the summit of the Turkey's head.
   ### Line of Descent
   Must have two 60m ropes. The common line of descent is via the Dod Route. Be certain to test-pull your ropes as there is good risk in getting the ropes jammed on pitch 2 or pitch 3. An alternate rappel is to descend the Wild Turkey route.

2. **Southwest Face 5.10d A2**
   Pro to 3" including pitons
   From the uphill saddle drop down a little to the west.
   P1: Traverse out right past a bolt and around a corner 40' to a belay ledge.
   P2: Very difficult climbing (5.10d) up a long 120' crack ends at a large roof. Turn this 5-foot overhanging roof on the left and belay on a small ledge (2 bolts).
   P3: A 70' 5.8 crack leads to a belay on the left.
   P4: Strenuous nailing leads up to 3 bolts and a runner on a flake leading over right. Continue free climbing rightward around a corner then up left and then directly up to a belay ledge.
   P5: A short easy pitch leads to the top.

3. **Wild Turkey 5.8 A4**
   Pro to 4" including a selection of pitons, Rurps and KB's
   Begin this route just to the east of the uphill saddle.
   P1: Climb up a few feet to a bolt and traverse left (5.7) to a crack. A short section of aid (expanding A2) leads to free climbing (5.8) where the crack widens. Bolts lead left to a hanging belay left of an overhang.
   P2: Move right into a crack above the overhang. Mixed (5.8 A3) climbing leads to a belay ledge.
   P3: Difficult aid climbing (A4) leads rightward to a bolt. Climb up past more bolts and a runner to free climbing (5.8) that moves left and then up to a cave. Watch for rope drag.
   P4: A short section of aid (A1) starts on the left and leads up to a chimney. Follow the chimney (5.6) to a large ledge just below the top.

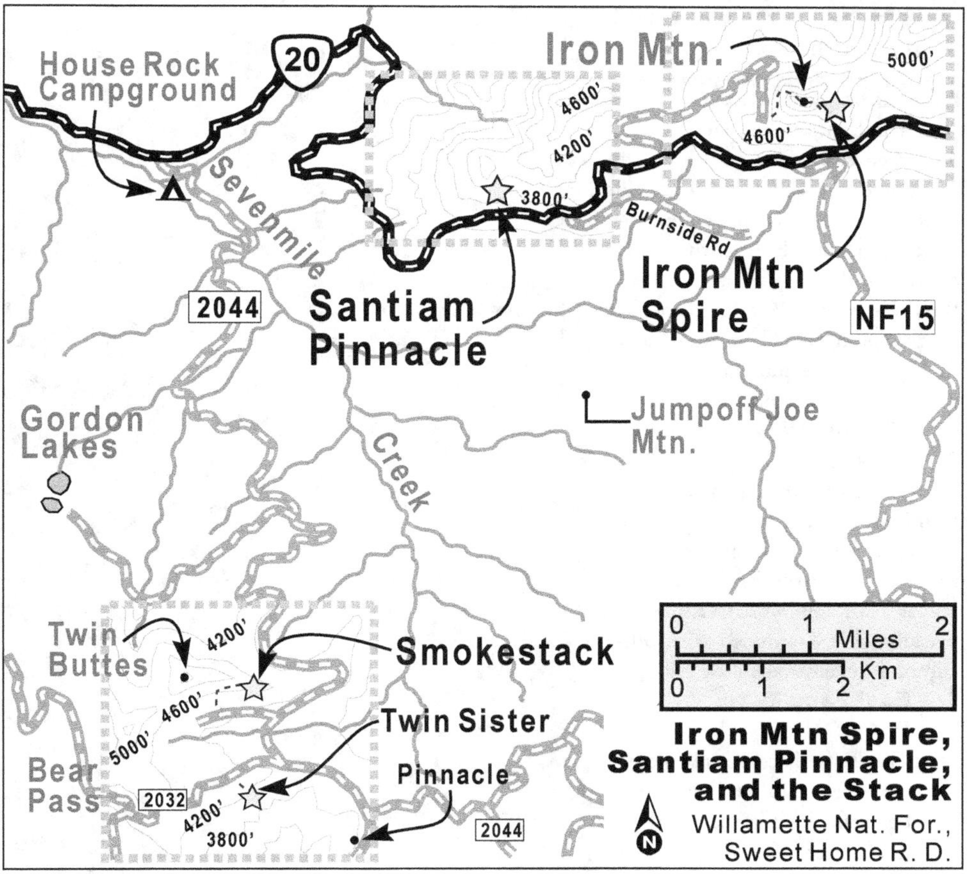
House Rock
Campground
20
Iron Mtn.
5000'
4600'
4200'
4600'
Sevenmile
3800'
Burnside Rd
Iron Mtn
Spire
2044
Santiam
Pinnacle
NF15
Jumpoff Joe
Mtn.
Gordon
Lakes
Creek
Twin
Buttes
4200'
Smokestack
4600'
5000'
Twin Sister
Bear
Pass
2032
4200'
3800'
Pinnacle
2044
0 1 2 Miles
0 1 2 Km
Iron Mtn Spire,
Santiam Pinnacle,
and the Stack
N
Willamette Nat. For.,
Sweet Home R. D.

Summit
Gonzo Pinnacle
North ridge
traverse
South
Face
Route
crux
Water
Buffalo
West
Face
Route
Santiam Pinnacle
Map 3: West Aspect

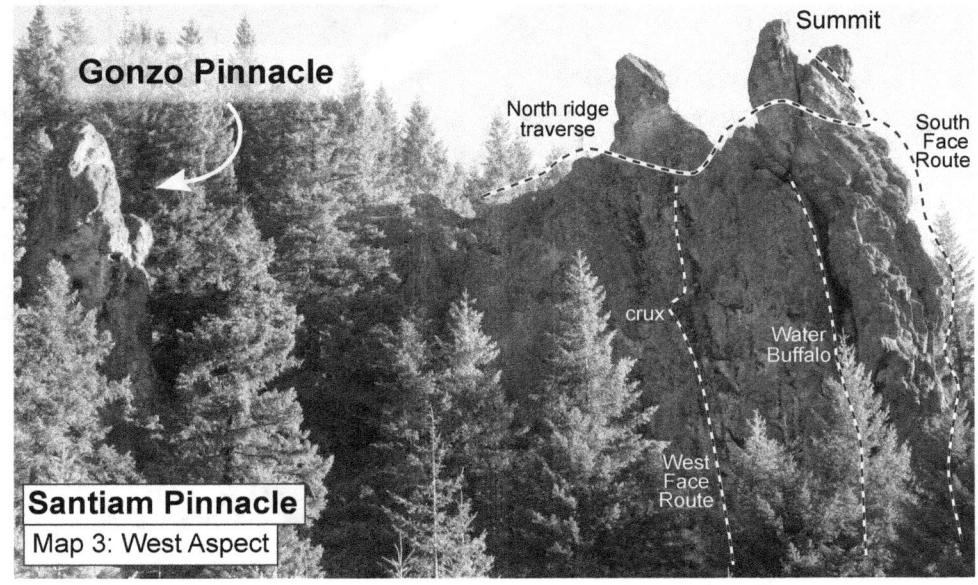

P5: A final short easy pitch leads to the top.

SANTIAM PINNACLE

The Santiam Pinnacle (3500') is located east of Sweet Home, directly above U.S. Hwy 20 at Mile Post 60½, which is about 2½ miles west of Civil (Iron Mtn.) Road on the north side of the highway. Burnside road is ½ mile to the east of the pinnacle. GPS coordinates for the roadside pullout at the pinnacle are Lat/Lon 44.23322°N / -122.11784°W at the altitude 3416'/1041m.

The Santiam Pinnacle is easy to miss because it is slightly hidden amongst the trees. The south face route is by far the best climb here and is definitely worth visiting, especially when combined with other climbing adventures in the region.

1. **East Face 5.6**
   Pro: _ [?]
   The East Face route ascends a friction slab, and then up a beautiful long crack to a belay nook. Exit left and up to summit.

2. **South Face 5.6** ★★★
   Multi-pitch, Pro to 2" and QD's
   The stellar South Face route is a quality rock climb on a fabulous broad steep nose with airy section on excellent rock.
   P1 80': Climb a chimney corner system on the lower west edge of the pinnacle. If the corner is too tough, step up left following the bolt line to a belay at the notch.
   P2 60': Climb the wide arête past a steep section and belay at a stance in a corner on the upper west side.
   P3 40': Continue up the outside face on knobs to the sum-

mit. Rappel from the summit toward the northeast to descend.

3. **West Face 5.6 R**
Pro: Nuts and cams to 2"
The West Face route ascends a crack to a delicate balance move right into a wide dihedral. Belay in the groove, then climb up left initially, to exit up right to a belay immediately below the summit. **Note:** There is a minor toprope route on the west face of Santiam Pinnacle. The **Water Buffalo** (5.11c) is to the right of the original West Face route on a vertical face below the summit.

4. **North Ridge 5.3**
Pro: Minor gear to 1"
From the upper saddle of the Santiam Pinnacle, traverse out onto the pinnacle using an exposed narrow ramp on the west side. Continue past the notch by walking along a ramp-slot on the west side just below the summit. Merge with the South Side route to top out.

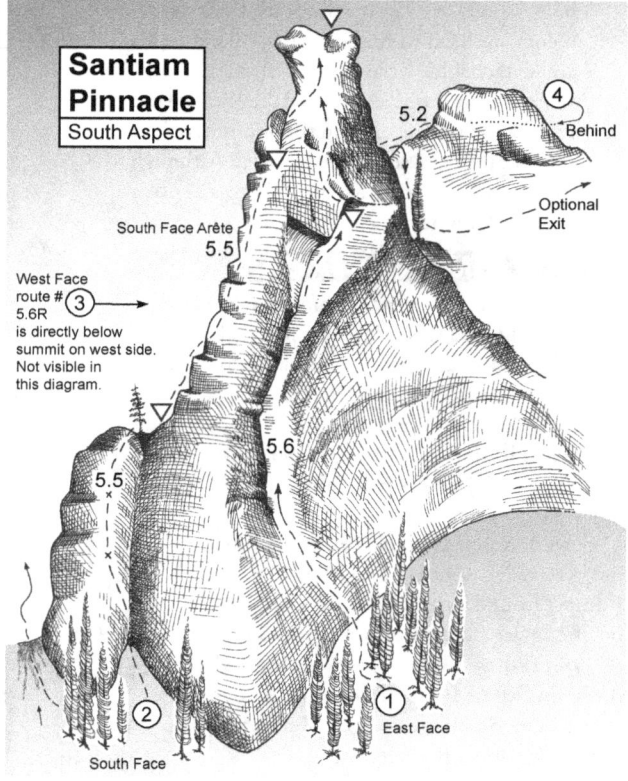

GONZO PINNACLE

Gonzo Pinnacle is a very minor plug immediately west 100' of the upper edge of Santiam Pinnacle. Virtually a boulder move from the upper side (5.4) you still might find this short (fixed) lead a worthy venture. A 4-bolt 5.7 sport route called **Archimedes** punches through an overhang on the east face of Gonzo Pinnacle.

IRON MOUNTAIN SPIRE

The Iron Mountain Spire is an exhilarating but rotten spire composed of welded tuff and crumbling basalt. The pinnacle is located several hundred feet south east from the top of Iron Mountain. The summit of this mountain has a lookout structure still in use by the Forest Service. Alpine forests, wildflowers, and superb scenic views of the Cascades create a beauty worth seeing from the top of Iron Mountain. The main south face was explored in 1971 by Joe Bierck, Paul Fry, and Dean Fry using a friable chimney system.

Directions
From Sweet Home drive 32 miles east on Highway 20 and turn left on Civil Road (FS035). Follow this gravel road for 2½ miles to the trailhead. Hike the 1½ mile trail to the summit of Iron Mountain and bushwack down the south east slope to the spire.

1. **Iron Mountain Spire 5.6 R/X**
Pro: Nuts to 2" and pitons
To ascend the spire requires a desperate instinct to survive and raw determination to summit on such a fine rotting massif. An 80' lead, then a 30' scramble to the top. The crux is a reddish

bulge about ½ way up the lead. Gear placements are hard to find, and most hand holds are detachable. Belay at the shoulder, then work left on the scree covered ledge up to the top. Two rope rappel from the summit, or one rope rappel from the shoulder belay. Although this is an easy rating for a climb, this is not a summit for a novice climber.

SMOKESTACK

What is it? A top hat...a smokestack? Few persons have climbed this ridge crest perched plug, but none-the-less it is a nice backcountry rock stack worthy of multiple routes. Though is has only one real climb, a mere 20 minute drive on gravel roads south of House Rock campground (east of Upper Soda) makes it a viable summit objective.

To access this smokestack like plug of rock drive south from House Rock Camp Ground on FS2044. It is located on the lower portion of a ridge line east of Twin Buttes. The smokestake plug and the Twin Sisters Pinnacle are short, enjoyable, and moderately easy rock climbs, and virtual neighbors to each other.

Park on a dead end side road south of the plug. The dense brushy thicket between the gravel road and the pinnacle is a bit too desperate to fight through. Instead, walk west 200' into a tall forest and hike cross-country up through the lightly wooded forest. When the slope steepens angle up right out of the forest onto the meadows. Walk along the sloping meadow east to the Smokestack.

1. **West Face 5.8**
   Pro: Nuts and cams to 1½"
   This enticing and totally overhanging 80' plug of rock is perched directly upon a prominent ridge one mile east of Twin Buttes. Hike to the left in the deep forests, then up to the right on an open south-facing meadow to access the Stack. The west face nose route presently is the only way up at 5.8.
   A 5.5 R variation (#2) bypasses the crux on steep moss covered rock

slope (cams to 3") by stepping left at the bolt crux move on the regular route. One 60m rope is sufficient to rappel.

TWIN SISTERS PINNACLE

Looking south from the summit of the Smokestack you will see the infamous Twin Sisters Pinnacle to the south ¾ mile in a clear-cut area along a ridge overlooking the Blue River basin. Though that pinnacle is not immediately visible from the place you park the vehicle along FS2032, a quick jaunt over a clear-cut slope leads to this spire.

1. Giant Steps 5.3 R
Pro: Minor gear to 3"

This spire looks impressive as you approach it, but the standard southwest facing Giant Steps route is actually quite short. Finding good protection placements is a challenge.

The **East Prow** is the only other known variation to the top. Scamper along sloping ledges around the southeast side till you can access the east ridge prow. Belay at a small tree then lead up friable unprotectable 4th class moves to the summit.

TWO GIRLS MTN

Rarely climbed raw adventure on double spires perched on a ridge crest overlooking the Two Girls creek valley on the upper eastern slope of Canyon Creek near Bear Pass. The pinnacles are composed of well-weathered crumbly Tertiary basalt with a variety of rock horns and rounded knobs (and occasional gear) for protection. The views from the top are great. There are two spires, the East Girl and the West Girl. The involved approach has a fair bit of cross country travel, some of it through rhododendron thickets, and very steep slopes. Expect loose rock (helmet country) and substantial runout sections on the 3rd and 4th class terrain.

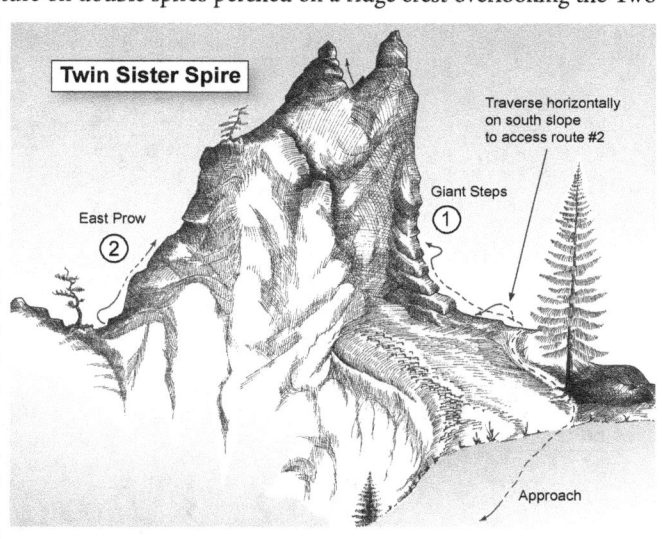

Directions:

Drive east of Sweet Home on US 20 past Cascadia for a total of about 11 miles. Drive southeast of FS2022 along Canyon Creek 6 miles, then up FS2024 to access FS2024-250, and then FS2024-251 and travel up this as far as possible in a vehicle or walk if the road is impassible. Where the NW ridge meets the road at 3700' cross-country up this forested ridge (800' approx.) to the main east-west ridge. Travel east to the Two Girls (¼ mile) to a meadow with a great view of the Two Girls. From here the adventure gets complex. Follow a deer trail that tra-

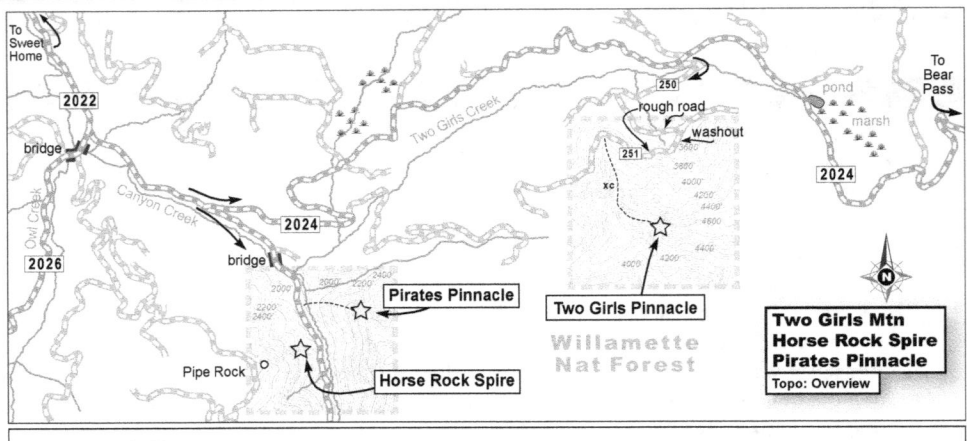

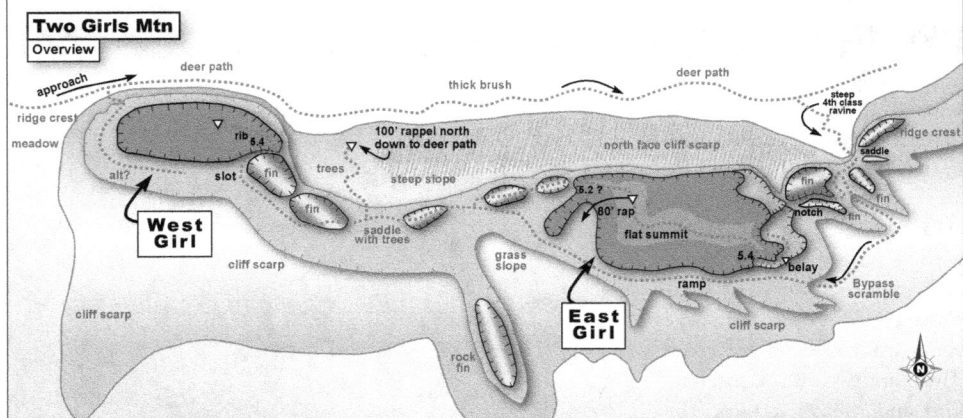

verses left along the well-vegetated north slope of the spires next to the vertical rock face. Scramble up a 5th class ravine (ice axe and rope?) to land on the east flank (see diagram). You can either climb the East Buttress or use the bypass scramble on the south side for quicker access to the West Girl. There may be other ways to access these pinnacles so good luck. GPS N 44.326793 N / -122.297296 W Elev 4656' / 1419m

East Girl

East Buttress of East Girl 5.4 R

Mostly 3rd-4th class terrain with a short crux that takes good pro. Bring a few pitons.

West Rib of East Girl 5.1 [?] very short (50') and likely climbed. Easiest way to the top.
West Girl
East Arête of West Girl 5.5
This is the standard route. Takes the obvious corner up to a notch, then up a short rib to the top (pitons help).
Descent:
If you have climbed both summits it is easier to descend down near the east edge of the West Girl. Make a short rappel from one fir down closer to the final large fir trees. Two ropes easily reach to the base of the wall where the deer path traverse is located. By carefully selecting one of the lowest trees on the steep slope one single 60m rope (100' rap) will suffice in getting you down to the deer trail on the north slope. Round trip about 7 hours.

PIRATES PINNACLE

Pirates Pinnacle 5.8 PG
Pro: minimal nuts and cams to 3", a few thin pins, and some TCU's

A minor pinnacle on the east slope of Canyon Creek about 8 miles southeast from US 20 on FS2022 road. This pinnacle is visible where the gravel road crosses the creek on a concrete bridge. Park just south of there and descend to the stream, cross it, then march up a long steep off trail scramble 1050' uphill to get to base of pinnacle. It was odd to find no evidence of previous ascent for such as prominent minor pinnacle in this valley. Anticipate 1½ hours up hill, 2-4 hours to climb pinnacle, and 1 hour to descend back to car. See diagram for initial route beta, although alternative methods of ascent are feasible. Canyon Creek

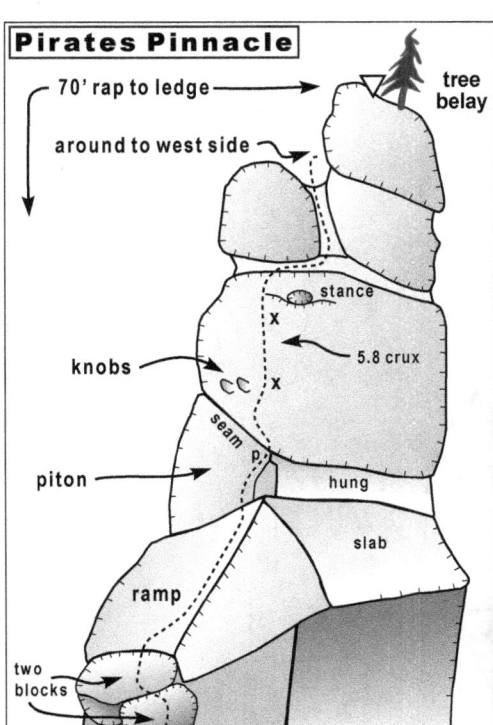

Horse Rock Pillar

valley offers 2-3 more possible wild minor pinnacle climbs for the savvy adventurous climber.

HORSE ROCK PILLAR

Horse Rock Pillar (250' approx.) has a multi-pitch route on a wild looking gnarly spire similar in character to the infamous Turkey Monster. Rock composition is rhyolite similar to the spires in the upper Menagerie which should give you an advance clue of the rock type. Drive east of Sweet Home, Oregon for 11.7 miles, then southeast on Canyon Creek Road for 9.3 miles. The spire is visible on the road as you get near it but obscured by trees when directly below it. GPS 44°19'00" N, 122°20'15" W. See diagram/photo for visual.

Regular Route   5.8 A2

Pro: a few medium sized nuts, cams .75" to 3", a set of QD's, two 60-meter ropes, a few pitons such as KB & LA, Rurp, a hook, and a selection of rivet hangers.

Pitch 1: 5.8, length 80'

Free climb on the left aspect (left of the saddle) using minor gear and clipping 6-bolts (a basic variable sized partly fixed wide crack).

P2 5.7R A2, length 130'

Pitch 2: 130' (20+ bolts) mostly mostly a fixed bolt ladder with some A2 aid climbing. Some bolts are missing the hangers (so bring rivet hangers). Runout free climbing terrain near the top. The rappel is 60-meters from summit using two ropes to reach the ground.

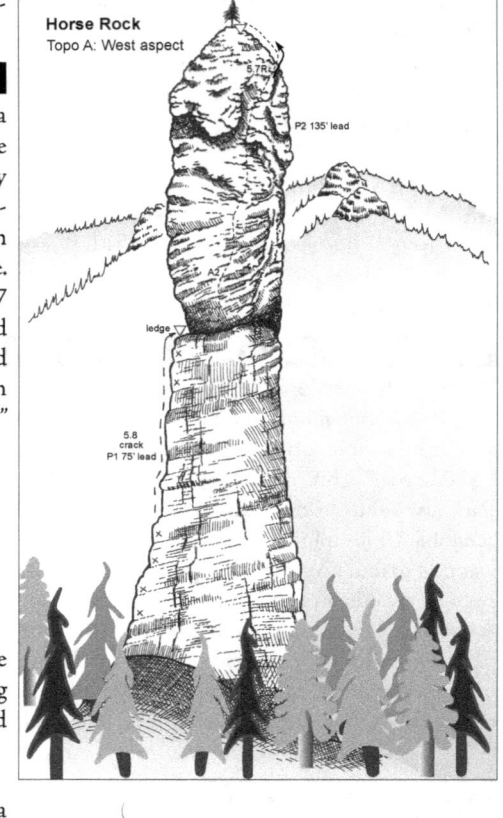

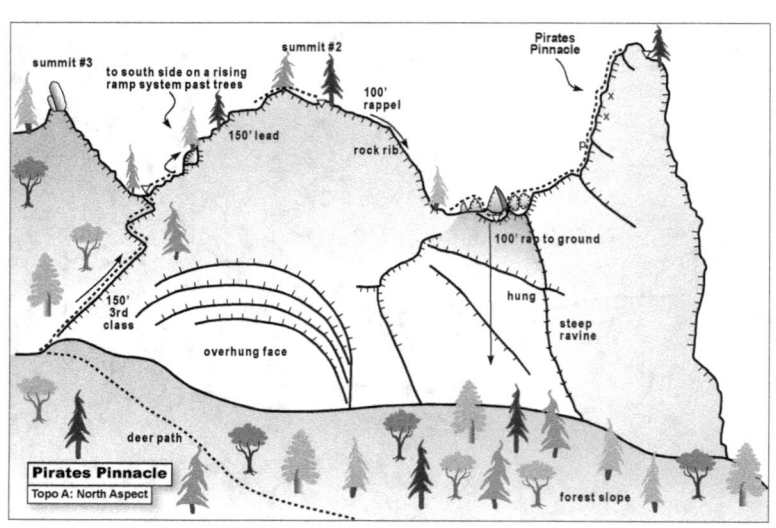

Climbing options near Eugene

CHAPTER 8

SOUTHERN WILLAMETTE

OREGON HAS MANY OTHER GREAT climbing destinations that involve a bit more driving time from Portland to visit but are well worth the venture when combined into an overnight climbing trip or a long fast day drive.

Make plans for an extended spring, summer or fall weekend journey around western Oregon state to experience some of these great climbing destinations. This chapter provides a selective analysis of rock climbing opportunities at several popular destination crags that continue to inspire and provide a great outdoor resource for everyone. Take the time and make the drive to the McKenzie region today.

SKINNER BUTTE COLUMNS

Written by Miles Noel

The Skinner Butte Columns are a group of relatively uniform high quality dark-colored columnar basalt which likely formed as a magma sill intrusion, then cooled to become gradually exposed through erosion, although a portion of the site was used for quarry material in the not-too-distant past. The bluff height is 45' tall and each column tends to lean leftward at a 70° degree angle. The cracks between the columns are excellent for various types of finger-to-hand-to-fist jams and present abundant opportunities to place rock gear protection while on lead.

The Columns at the butte have provided excellent training ground for rock climbers since the 1940s. Several near legendary climbers such as Wayne Arrington and Bob Ashworth used the site in the '70s, as well as other climbers like Gary Kirk, Ed Lovegren, Stu Rich and the Bauman brothers.

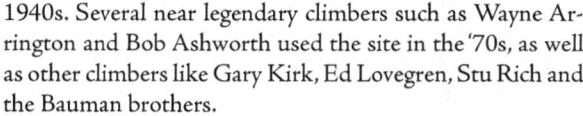

This climbing site is uniquely situated near the central core blocks of downtown Eugene, Oregon on the west slope of the Skinner Butte. With such convenient access this well-used crag offers climbers from beginner-to-expert good opportunity to refine their scope of rock climbing management technique. The University of Oregon Outdoor Program also instructs students here in the sport of rock climbing so expect the site to be busy on certain warm sunny weekdays and weekends, especially during the summer season.

The rock climb routes can be top-roped or lead on traditional gear. Many of the climbs are finger-size to hand crack-size and range in difficulty from 5.6 to 5.13a, while most are generally 5.8 to 5.10 in difficulty and include several face or arête climbs.

The Columns are available for year-round climbing and even though Oregon gets plenty of rain the small cliff does quickly dry because of the southwesterly orientation. Expect full sunlight on the rock face from about 10AM to sunset. You can usually climb 20-30 minutes past sunset with decent light. The site is not conducive to extensive

Climbing at *Wolf Rock*

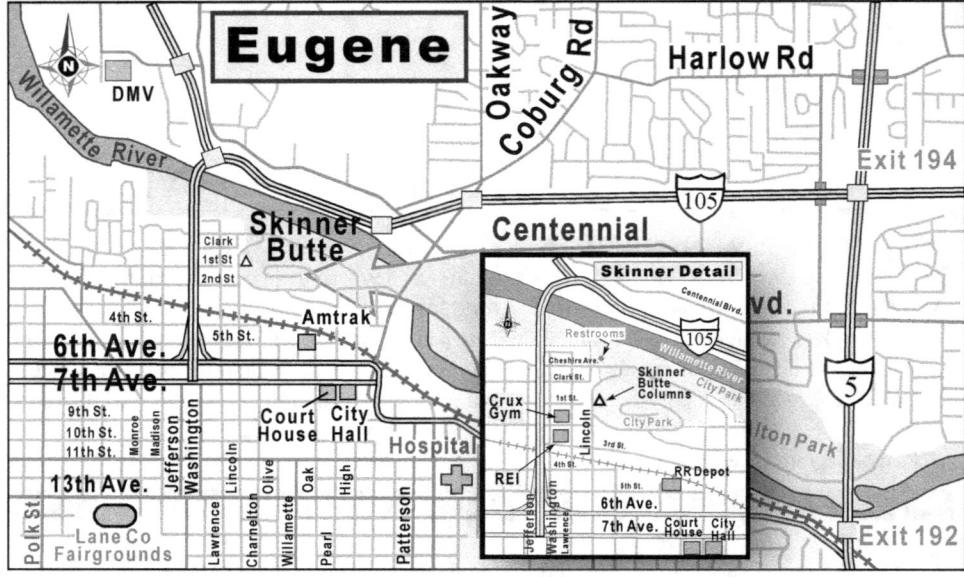

bouldering but the ease of setting up tope-rope belays alleviates this.

Beta in Brief

Due to the close proximity of cracks and edges the rock climbs tend to be contrived to varying degrees, making each climb just a narrow stripe of vertical rock. The route and rating beta described herein assumes a crack climb keeps hands and feet in the crack, and a face climb adheres to the face of just one column.

Convenience and Accessibility

The site is within the boundary of the Eugene city park and features basic site improvements such as steel chairs, a sign board, and wood chip ground cover. Local climbers also provide some care for the site.

There are a series of easily accessible fixed chain belay anchors along the top of the wall so tope-rope climbing is a standard practice. Bring sufficient lengths of long sling as some of the belay anchors are set back from the upper edge of the bluff. Use the stair step trail on the left of the bluff to access the top-rope belay anchors.

Restroom facilities and water can be found at the nearby river front park to the north, on the west side of the playground. Just follow Lincoln Street north as is curves to junction with Cheshire Avenue. Turn left (west) and park in a parking area. The restroom facilities are next to the children's playground.

For sporting equipment needs or a rain-free indoor practice site the Crux Rock Gym is two blocks away while REI is three blocks away on 3rd and Washington. A city police precinct sub-station is located a block away which tends to deter transient activity, but you may encounter broken glass near the cliff on occasion.

Wildlife

Ladybugs and other insects nest in the rocks, but deep enough in that you don't need to watch out for them. All are harmless, but the ladybugs emerge by the millions and are attracted to the salty perspiration left from sweaty climbers' hands. Hummingbirds, bald eagles, peregrine falcons, red tailed hawks and starlings frequently ride the updrafts above the Columns. There is poison oak nearby in the brush and also near the 'closed' off limits area.

Driving directions to the Columns

The columns are well-situated in the hub of downtown Eugene near the west slope of Skinner

Butte on Lincoln Street where 1st street would be if it came through to abut up against the west slope of the butte.

From the I-5 freeway at exit #194 drive west on I-105 taking the city center exit till it merges onto 7th Street. Turn left onto 7th Street, drive east three blocks and then turn left onto Lincoln Street. Drive north (cross the railroad tracks) five blocks to the Columns.

The climbing routes are listed from right to left.

1. **LD 5.10b**
   Use the crack and the column face to the left until left column ends, then finish as a face climb on the remaining column without using the top of the short column. This was a nice two star route until the top of the left column was removed in 2007. To top-rope this climb rappel down and over from chains above Hard Layback to the chains at the top of LD.

2. **Satisfaction 5.11a/.12a**
   Jam up the crack for a fingertip cranking 5.12a, or add the face holds for a 5.11a. Mostly just finger jams, but with a couple hand jams at the top.

3. **Hard layback 5.9+/.10b**
   Jam up the crack for a really nice 5.10b, or climb it as a layback for a (strenuous) 5.9+.

4. **Fat Crack (Outer Column Jam) 5.8 / 5.9**
   This very uniform crack is perfect for learning to jam. Finger jams leading to hand jams. Hands and feet in the crack for a 5.9, or add the face holds for a 5.8.

5. **Arête Layback 5.12a**
   Strenuous and slippery, the name says it all.

6. **Left Crack 5.12+**
   Extremely thin fingertips crack immediately left of the prominent outer column.

7. **Grass Crack 5.10b**
   The start can be awkward and many people use a left foot smear, but try to stay true to the crack and stay off the face holds.

8. **Right Ski Track 5.10a**
   The crack forks, but stay to the single clear line through it for a nice 5.10a. Lots of protection opportunities.

9. **Left Ski Track 5.10b**
   This is a tricky bouldery route without many good jams, so using the occasional nub to the immediate left is fair game.

10. Chimney Face 5.9

Face climb between Old Chimney and Left Ski-track until the holds peter out about 80% of the way up.

11. Old Chimney (Main Chimney) 5.7

Climb the chimney using classic chimney technique or by stemming. Great beginner route.

12. 1st Column Face 5.10a / 5.11a

Climb the 1st column in the buttress without the crack for a slippery 5.11a, or with the crack for a 5.10a.

13. 2nd Column Right Jam 5.10a

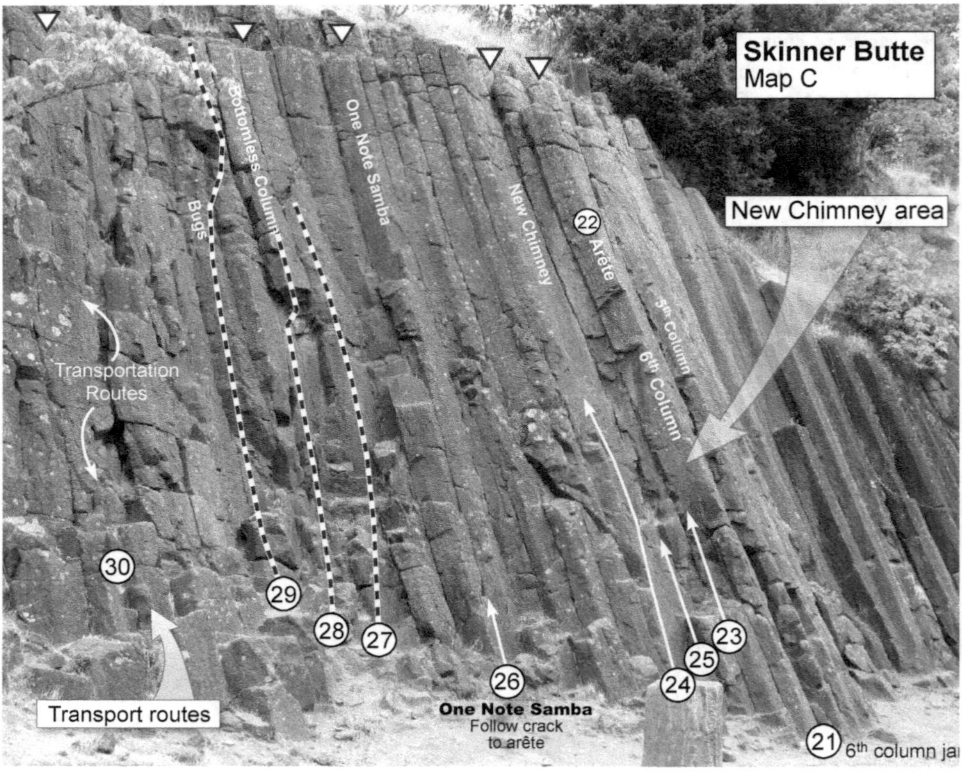

Jam up the crack with hand and finger jams. This crack just gobbles up passive gear, offering bomber placement opportunities every few inch-

es. Dyno past the thin, dirt-filled crack a third of the way up for style points.

14. **2nd Column Left Jam 5.9 / 5.10a**
    Jam up the crack with finger and hand jams. Keep hands and feet in the crack all the way up for a 5.10a, or let your left foot come out at the top for a 5.9.

15. **2nd Column Inclusive 5.7+**
    Climb using both cracks and the face holds on 2nd Column for a fun 5.7+. Great beginner route.

16. **3rd Column Face 5.8 / 5.10a**
    Face climb staying out of the cracks for a 5.8. The layback crux at the top can be height sensitive. Or climb it as a layback for the 5.10a barn-door layback variation.

17. **4th Column Right Jam (Forthright) 5.10a**
    Jam up the crack keeping hands and feet in the crack for a nice 5.10a. Finger and hand jams, and lots of gear placement opportunities for small to medium passive gear.

18. **4th Column Left Jam (Sign Crack) 5.10a / 5.12a**
    Variant contrivances can be attained by climbing all the crack using all the holds or using focused emphatic limitations.

19. **4th Column Inclusive 5.7**
    Climb using both cracks and the face holds on 4th Column for a fun 5.7. Great beginner route.

20. **5th Column (Sign Face) 5.10a / 5.12a**
    Climb the face with both edges, staying out of the cracks, for a 5.10a, or climb the face only without either edge for a 5.12a.

21. **6th Column Jam (Bat Crack) 5.7+**
    Climb this wide irregular crack with hands in crack and feet on the face of 6th Column for a tricky 5.7+, or feet in the crack to make it really awkward. This climb is sometimes wet or muddy deep in the crack, and frequently frustrates beginners.

22. **6th Column (Bat Face) 5.11a**
    Face climb staying out of the crack for a 5.11a.

23. **New Chimney Jam 5.10a**
    Jam up the crack in the right side of the chimney.

24. **New Chimney Column 5.9**
    Face climb with edges up the column in the left side of the chimney.

25. **New Chimney Standard 5.8**
    Climb the chimney using standard chimney techniques and face holds.

26. **One Note Samba 5.10a**
    Face climb with right side crack. Mantle crux.

27. **Un-named 5.8**
    Great face climb with a variety of holds. Immediately right of the bottomless column route.

28. **Bottomless Column 5.8**
    Fun little roof problem, using column and edges. Don't worry about using the cracks. This is the detached bottomless column.

29. **Bugs! 5.7**
    Climb this blocky 5.7 up past where the flying black bugs (flying ants maybe?) come out of the rocks. The bugs are totally harmless.

Ian Goss leading at *Wolf Rock*

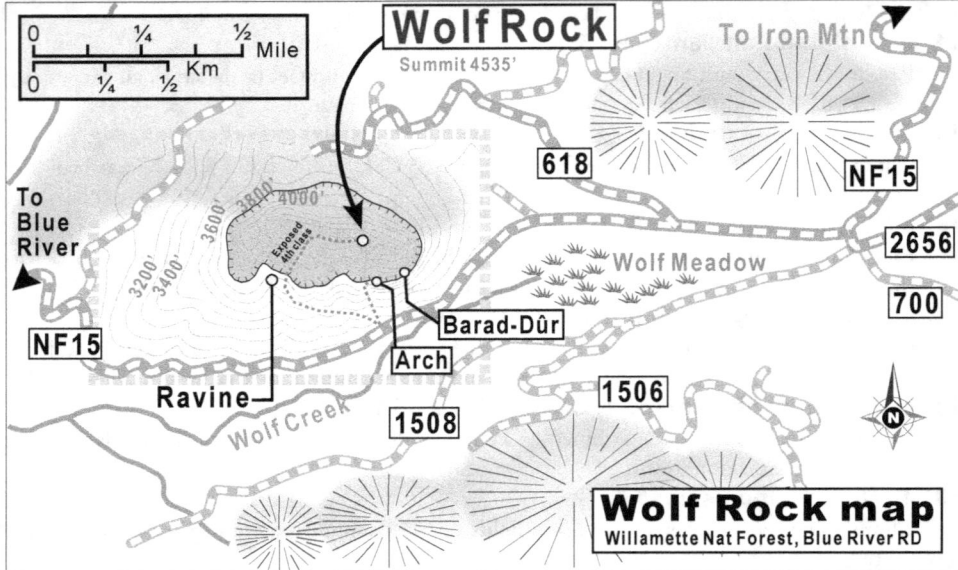

30. Transportation Routes 5.6

Blocky area that can get beginners moving, but not great climbing.

WOLF ROCK

Wolf Rock is an impressive 900' volcanic andesite (Ta3) massif that ranks as the largest monolith in Oregon with a summit perched at an elevation of 4535'. This virtual mountain is an old volcanic remnant plug that was exposed after surrounding softer soils eroded away.

Wolf Rock is home to one of Oregon's outstanding classic rock climbing routes pioneered in the early '70s. Wayne Arrington and Mike Seely in a multi-day effort they established the 8-pitch grade IV 5.9 A2 (III 5.11a/b) route Barad-Dûr (Dark Tower) on the main 900' south face headwall. The route ascends very steep terrain up to the awe-inspiring dark roofs, breaking past the improbable roofs a few hundred feet below the main summit.

Many of the long established rock climbs at the Rock are traditional ground-up affairs with typically runout, down-sloping round-edged rock holds, and often marginal or limited protection placements. The established longer routes on the south face and north face offer similar obstacles and challenges.

The old north face climbs are seldom visited these days, but if you do decide to venture over there expect overgrown logging roads and very thick bushwhack thrashing just to get to the base of the wall. Expect difficulty finding the known routes and anticipate loose rock with moss covered down-sloping holds and limited protection options.

Today, most climbers suffice with faster rewards by aiming

Mackenzie on *The Arête*, Wolf Rock

for the south side rock climbing opportunities. The standard scramble route to the summit (West Gully) is a great 1-2 hour uphill blast, but do expect several hundred feet of very exposed (3rd class) smooth rock slope terrain.

The Conspicuous Arch

For the sport minded climber a stellar selection of fixed bolt routes exists under the great Conspicuous Arch, a prominent feature on the sunny south side of Wolf Rock, just a mere 5-minute walk from your vehicle.

In all, Wolf Rock is a very fascinating place to visit whether just scrambling up the West Gully to the summit or climbing the classic Barad-Dûr. The Old Cascades are a delight to view and photograph from the top of this rock summit. The sheer bulk and magnitude of this rock, combined with lichen colored rock, dark-water stained ravines, vibrant green forest with vivid doses of yellow leafed Vine Maple provide a grand destination for everyone.

How To Get There

Directions from Eugene: Drive east 40 miles on Hwy 126 to the community of Blue River. Continue east another 2½ miles, then turn left on Blue River road (FS15). Follow this road up around the east side of Blue River Reservoir (paved along the reservoir) and past the Mona Campground. Turn right at the 'T' and follow this gravel road for a total of 12 miles to Wolf Rock. Park at a pullout below the Conspicuous Arch.

Trail Access

A very short 5-minute walk up a good trail leads up from the gravel pullout to the sport routes under the Conspicuous Arch. If you are aiming for Barad-Dûr continue up eastward along the base of the cliff from the Conspicuous Arch till you are beneath the great dark roofs. This route can be difficult to locate for first time visitors. Wear a helmet on any multi-pitch route.

West Gully summit bound scramblers can start near the same trailhead and aim up west through the forest below the cliff. See route beta below for full specs. Wolf Rock is accessible for climbing about 5 months of the year, typically from mid-June through October, but if the weather is perfect

Wolf Rock
Map 1: Southeast face
Barâd Dur

you might find the site climbable a bit earlier or later than that.

Climbing Routes

The Wolf Rock routes of greatest interest to climber these days are Barad-Dûr and the single-pitch sport routes under/near the great Conspicuous Arch.

Barad-Dûr is Oregon's great classic hardman route with long leads of moderate climbing up to the huge dark roofs which offer fierce exposure just to climb past. Hike a few hundred feet uphill east from the Conspicuous Arch to an open scree slope beneath a wide dark face. The routes Death March and Gigantor (upgraded bolt route) are located on this wide sweeping flat face starting from a large ledge just above the ground. Walk uphill east for another few hundred feet to find the start for Barad-Dûr. Look for a bolt about 5' above the ground. You should be standing directly beneath the great dark foreboding roofs high above.

1. **Barad-Dûr IV 5.9 A2 (III 5.11b)**
Length: 1000', Pro: wires to 2", cams to 3", double cams at 1" and long slings. Aiders, and a few thin pitons if planning to nail the roof.

Wayne on *Barad-Dûr, Wolf Rock*

P1 5.9+ 100': Climb directly up the face past five bolts using gear placements when you find it. Bolt belay anchor is at a little stance.
P2 5.9 90': Aim up and to the right (bolts), and up to a left-facing dihedral corner system. Climb the corner system to a bolt belay anchor on a ledge.
P3 5.8: Continue up and right (bolts) on lower angled slabs, and then up left (bolts) using gear when necessary (low 5th class) to a small belay nook on the far left.
P4 5.9+: Climb up to the right on lower 5th class corner ramp, and then up left under a left-leaning overhang. Continue leftward till you can surmount (crux) the small overhang just before a bolt belay anchor on a tiny perch.
Note: The fifth pitch involves launching into power climbing out a series of small bulge overhangs leading up to the final giant dark roof above.
P5 5.10d 60' (or C1): Take a photo of your partner as he starts this lead! Traverse right from the belay on a sloped edge where the wall leans out at you. Turn a blind corner and power your way straight up 50' to a hanging bolt belay anchor.
P6 5.11b 80' (or C2): Continue directly up an overhanging corner (bolts and KB) and power

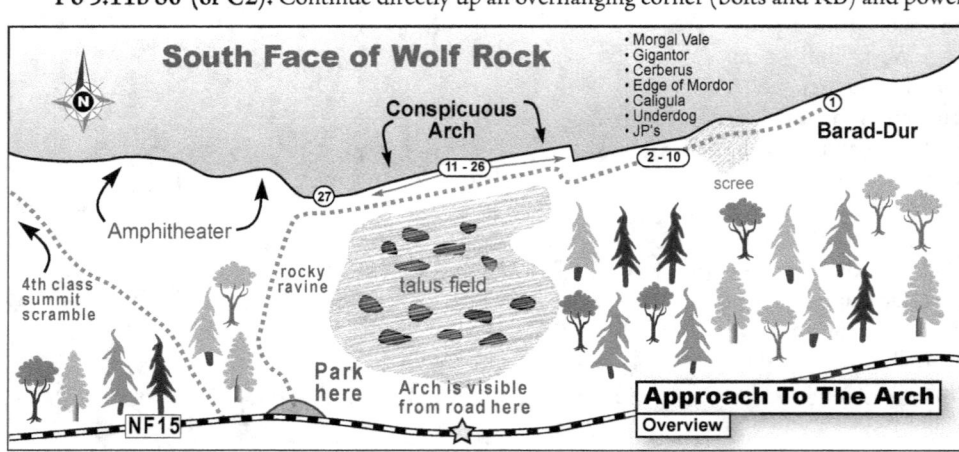

up over a small bulge crux. Begin a rightward traverse on a handrail under the final great roof. Turn the lip of the roof and waltz up to a bolt anchor belay on a large ledge.
Note: Pitch six overhangs nearly 15' from the belay. Be sure to place adequate protection for your partner to follow this safely.
Note: There is an A2-A3 variation which continues directly up the overhanging corner up leftward through the main roof from the pitch 6 belay anchor.
P7 5.4R: Climb up left (1 bolt) on steps with loose gravel making use of the natural features till you can reach a bolt belay anchor near the crest.
P8 Low 5th class: Continue up steps and corners along the ridge crest up west to the summit.
Line of Descent: Walk along the ridge crest for ¼ mile to descend the long smooth rock ravine called West Gully. Once at the treeline angle along the base of the cliff but in the forest gradually descending downward to the FS15 and the parking site. Expect at least 45-minutes to descend.

2. Ian's Route 5.10a
8-10 QD's, 2-pitch lead
A quality addition to the long face climb routes in this zone. P1 is a 5.10a face climbing, and P2 is a 5.5 lead. It merges with Morgal Vale (bring more gear for this).

3. Morgal Vale 5.9+
Pro to 1½", about 10 QD's, Multi-pitch
A long multi-pitch lead that is becoming fairly common route to climb these days. P1 is 5.8, P2 is 5.6, P3 is 5.9, P4 is 5.7, P5 is 5.7, P6 is 5.8, P7 is 5.4, P8 is 4th class for 400' to top. See topo.

4. Gigantor III 5.8 R
Length: approx. 1000'
Multi-pitch
Pro: __ QD's mostly, optional cams ½" to 1" and minor set of nuts.
Retro-bolted in 2010 so as to reduce the high risk runouts. The wide dark face has a series of steep sections broken with minor ramps and ledges. The base of this area (telltale lack of trees) is prone to volleys of loose rock so beware if climbing parties are above you.
P1: an easy lead up rock steps to a ledge system.
P2: where the face steepens, move right along easy

Wolf Rock
Map 1a: SE face

ramp steps. **P3:** at a small light colored section of rock is a left-facing minor corner capped by a lip. Climb next to this directly up the face (crux). **P4:** is a short lead. **P5:** moves up left of the great roofs. Quality deteriorates; expect loose rock. **P6:** uses numerous ledges, traversing up left across loose terrain. **P7:** unprotected 4th-5th class slabs/ramp till the terrain eases to a scramble.

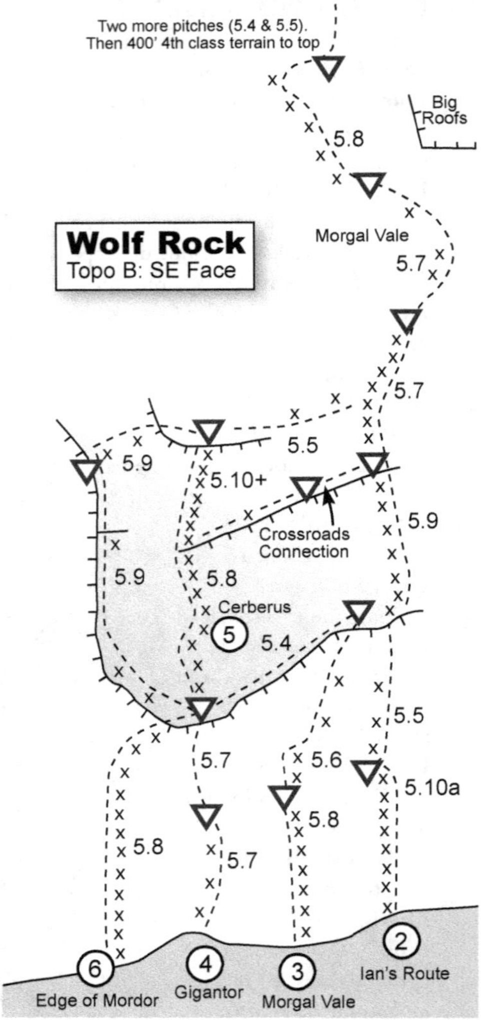

5. **Cerberus 5.10+**
   16 QD's
   A single pitch lead directly above the first pitch of Gigantor. Climb Gigantor to a ledge belay, then punch directly up this bolted face route.

6. **Edge of Mordor 5.9**
   Pro ___", and ___ QD's, Multi-pitch,
   This is a 3-pitch climb immediately left of Gigantor start. P1 is 5.8 face climb, P2 is 5.9 right facing corner. Belay, then do a short traverse moving rightward to another belay (used by Cerberus). Rappel. Or traverse further right to merge with Morgal Vale.
   Note: Crossroads Connection is a minor traverse on a ledge system between routes.

7. **Caligula III 5.7 R/X**
   Length: approx. 1000' Multi-pitch
   To the right of the Conspicuous Arch is a low angled face and corner system leading to a prominent ramp system on top of the Arch. Climb down-sloping rounded edges to a chimney. Ascend the chimney to a dirt ramp and belay at an anchor. Follow this ramp system up left until reaching an obvious ramp traverse that continues up left. Exposed easy friction leads straight left to another major corner system where it merges with Space Cowboy. Climb up friable terrain to the top. **P1-P2** 5.7r/x, **P3-P4** 5.6/5.7r/x, **P5-P6** 5th class to 4th class.
   Partial quote: *A Climbing Guide to Oregon, by Nick Dodge 1975*

CONSPICUOUS ARCH

The following are great quality face climbs located under the prominent south face arch. The climbs are listed from right to left (westward). All of the climbs are single pitch leads using a 60m rope. A 5.12 route powers into the roof and several lines on the far west end have difficult second pitch leads if you are so inclined to take them on.

8. **_____ 5.7**
   Length: P1 70', Pro: 5 QD's for 1st pitch, 10 QD's for entire lead
   Walk 100' uphill east from the arête Spine Buster. This fine route angles up left on steep ter-

rain with good holds till it merges at route #3 belay anchor. Continue up (5.7) a steep corner (5 bolts) till it merges with JP's Route and lands on a small stance at belay anchor. Rappel to previous anchor and then rap to ground.

9. **Underdog 5.10b/c**
Length: 70', Pro: 9 QD's
Just to the right of JP's Route is this quality steep face climb. Finesse up the initial moves, chill a second, then launch into the power moves at a slight bulge. Chill at the next tiny perch, then dance up small edges to the bolt belay anchor where it merges with route #2.

10. **JP's Route 5.10a**
Length: 150', Pro: 15 QD's
To the right around the corner (east) of the arch arête about 15' you will find a vertical bolted face climb. This route powers up a long steep face staying on the outside portion from the Arch. Rappel with two ropes or rappel to the mid-point belay on route #2.

11. **The Arête 5.8**
Length: 60', Pro: QD's
This is a classic arête climb that ascends the lower portion of the prow on great edges and quality rock. Good climb for everyone to lead.

12. **Arch Corner 5.8**
Length: 60', Pro to 4"
This is the inside crack corner of the lower right end of the Conspicuous Arch. Rappel from belay anchors on the The Arête.

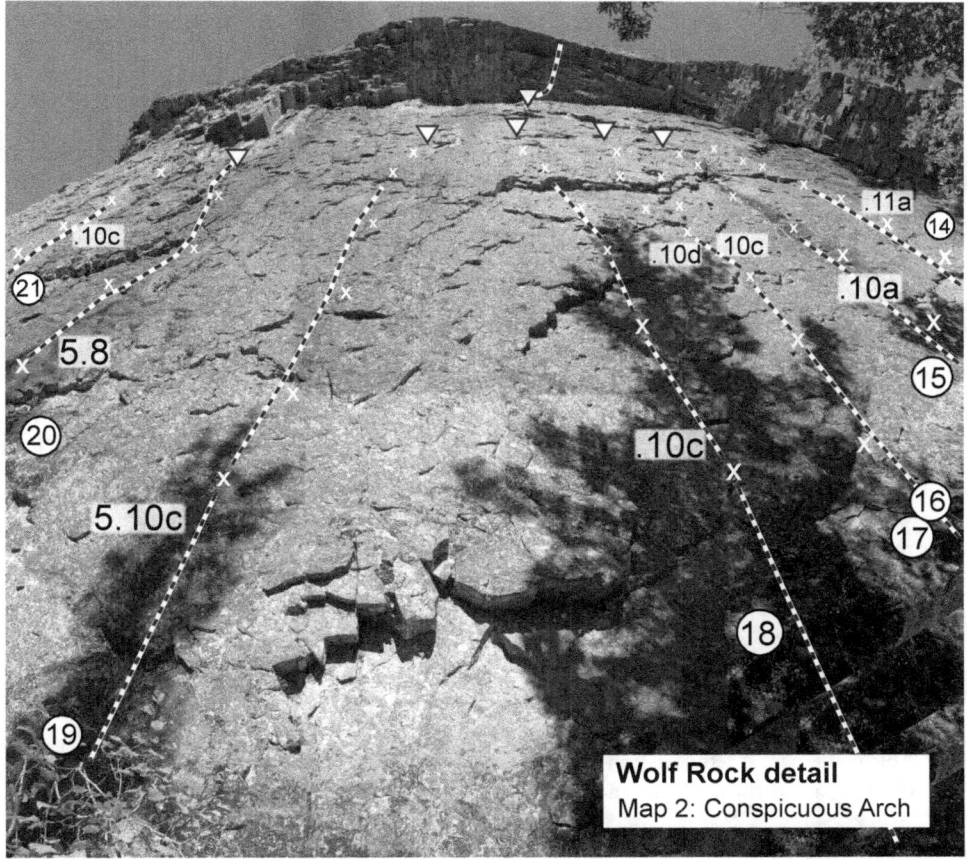

Wolf Rock detail
Map 2: Conspicuous Arch

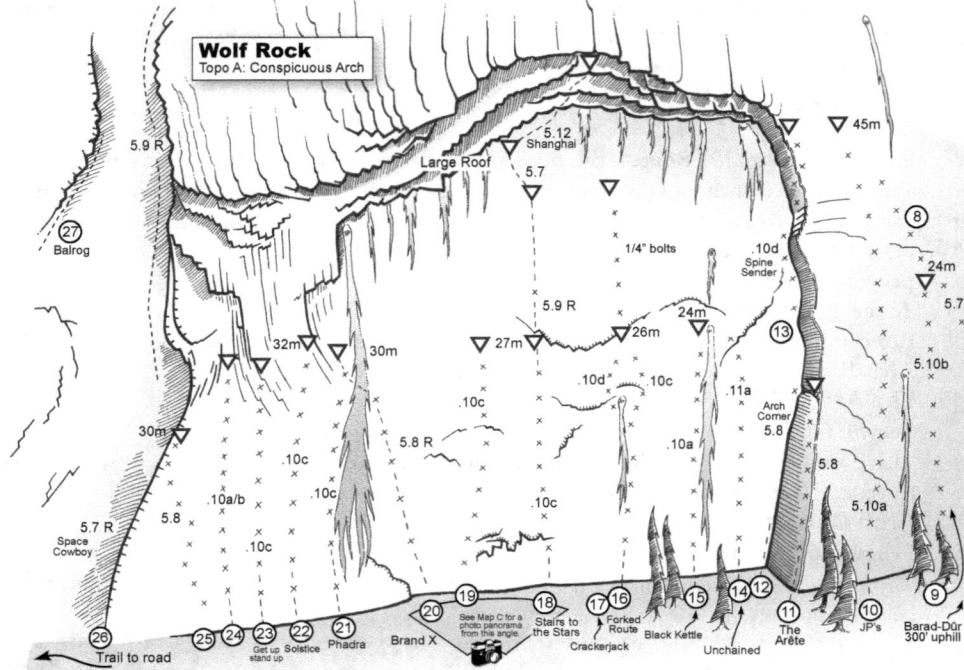

13. Spine Sender 5.10d R
Length: 150' from ground including The Arête
Pro: QD's and small pro to 2"

This is the upper portion of the inside of the Arch or spine. From the belay anchor at the top of **The Arête** (5.8) climb up left close to the inside crack corner placing small pro for protection. At 25' clip the first bolt and climb a vertical face (bolts) up and rightward to exit to the outer edge of the prow to the bolt belay anchor.

14. Unchained 5.11a
Length: 80', Pro: 8 QD's

The first long face climb on the flat smooth face under the main arch and immediately right of the dark-colored water streak. There are three no-hands rests on this route. The crux is near the last bolt. Angle up left to the anchor on Cold Shut to belay.

15. Black Kettle 5.10a
Length: 80', Pro: 7 QD's

A classic route on steep rock, and has numerous positive holds once you are past the little roof. This route is easily recognizable by the obvious dark water streak. A shoulder jam at the little roof provides a no-hands stance.

16. Forked Route 5.10c
Length: 85', Pro: 8 QD's

A pumpy climb with two variations a mid-height passing a small lip and then merges at the bolt belay anchor. Forked Route takes the right line of bolts at the overhang.

17. Crackerjack 5.10d
Length: 85', Pro: 8 QD's

This is the harder left variation of the Forked Route involving a crux lip move and sustained climbing above the lip to the anchor.

18. Stairs To The Stars
P1 5.10d, P2 5.9R, P3 5.7

Multi-pitch (P1 90'), Pro: 8 QD's 1st pitch

P1 5.10d 90': A nice first pitch with surprisingly demanding balancy start, and a crux at a small lip. Don't forget to use the no-hands rest at the crux lip.

P2 5.9R: An initial hard crux move, then clip the single bolt and dash up 5.5 terrain for 25' to the next anchor.

P3 5.7: Another short lead on large holds ending immediately under the giant roof.

P4 5.13a or C2 called **Shanghai.** A hardman route that pumps its way out the upside down giant roof of the Arch to an anchor. Use two ropes to rappel.

19. Captain Courageous 5.10c

Length: 95', Pro: 9 QD's

A reasonable route with some minor hollow hand holds just below the sloped ledge halfway up the route. Climb near a black water streak on the upper portion of the route to the bolt anchor.

20. Brand-X 5.8

Length: 100', Pro: 8 QD's

A stellar route and enjoyable to lead with a definite crux partway up. This route ascends the other dark colored water streak. Expect some hollow rock in places and well-spaced out bolts for the grade. Plenty of large steps and edge on the entire upper portion of the climb. This route was likely ascended using ground-up technique.

21. Phadra 5.10c/d

Length: 100', Pro: 8 QD's

A good climb with numerous small positive holds and a tight crux move on a short vertical section halfway up the wall. Shares same belay anchor as Brand-X.

22. Solstice Party 5.10c

Length: 105', Pro: 9 QD's

A steep power line ending at its own belay anchor slightly up left of the Brand-x anchor. Use two ropes

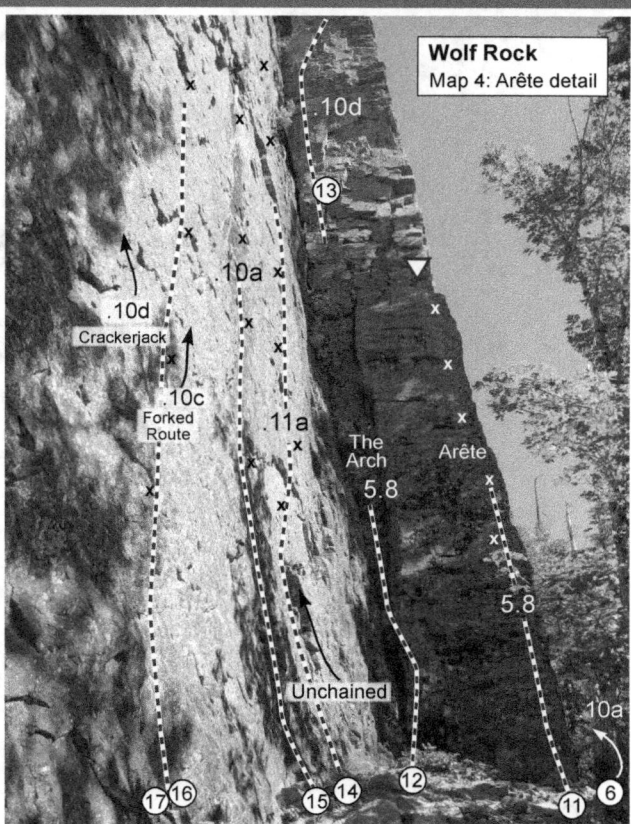

Mackenzie leading *The Arête 5.8*

to descend or jump over onto Brand-X to descend with one 60m rope.

23. Get Up and Stand Up 5.10c
Length: 100', Pro: 9 QD's

A cool sustained first pitch on numerous small edges. The **Big Bad Wolf** route continues from this belay anchor up through the roof above for an additional four pitches.

24. _____ 5.10a
Length: 100', Pro: 10-12 QD's

Another nice long face climb left of GUSU.

25. _____ 5.8+
Length: 100', Pro: 9 QD's

This route is lacking something, but at least it is easy-*ish*. Dance up mossy steps leftward, then up several steps rightward till the large edges end. Balance up left through a tricky section aiming to an easy right leaning ramp. Dash up the ramp to the belay anchor.

26. Space Cowboy 5.9 R/X
Multi-pitch

Bold climb for its time, with substantial runouts. P1 ascends a prominent left-facing stepped corner system. P2 continues up the left-facing corner. P3 powers past a steep section and dashes up a ramp. P4-P5 the angle eases but anticipate considerable runout terrain to the top.

27. Balrog 5.6 R/X
Multi-pitch

Located between Space Cowboy and Coriolis up high on the face is a right facing corner system. Balrog aims for this corner, then dances up right to another right-facing corner. Waltz along an exposed ramp up left to easier but loose terrain. Minimal pro options.

28. Coriolis Effect 5.9
Multi-pitch, Pro: 13 QD's & minor cams to 1½"
This is the first climb you encounter as you hike up the trail to the cliff scarp. Look for a right facing dirty corner at the ground with a bolt route 15' right of that. What the first pitch is lacking the second pitch makes up for it in stellar position and stellar quality. Rap with two ropes.
P1 5.8 120' 11 QD's: Climb a steep face with some hollow sections of rock till the terrain eases to large steps. Continue up another steep section to a belay anchor on a ledge.
P2 5.9 150' 13 QD's Cam/nuts to 1½": Move up right from anchor then dance up near vertical terrain on great hand edges and various small stances. A single hard move aims up to a crack then exits up right to a belay anchor. Pitch 3-5 has a few bolts, limited pro options, and is runout with friable rock. Best to rappel after the second pitch.

29. West Gully (to summit) 3rd class
This is the scramble gully to the summit of Wolf Rock. From the parking site at a culvert follow a faint trail up left to a large stone cirque. Carefully prance across this wide smooth rock amphitheater and continue leftward up a narrow dirt path. The path ends next to a deep ravine gully system to your immediate west. Above is a broad slope initially of dirt and gravel slopes and a very long steep (3rd class) rock ravine aiming up and slightly right. There are several very steep sections on this long rock slope so be cautious going up and down (rope suggested). As the upper portion of the smooth rock ravine eases near the ridge crest begin to angle eastward near the crest aiming for Wolf Rock's highest point to the east. Time up will vary from 1-2 hours depending on your endurance. An alternative is to take the West Ridge that is between the West Gully and the Amphitheater. In either case, the ascent technicalities are about the same. Bring water and snacks and enjoy the view.

The following four climbs are located on the north face of Wolf Rock. The common method of approach is to hike along the base of the south face past Barad-Dur and curl up around to the north side. These routes are seldom climbed and should be considered of dubious quality with substantial runouts on mossy, down-sloping holds.

30. North Face II 5.4 R
This route uses the second non-overhanging section east of the hogback and starts at the point where the vertical extent of the north face is greatest. Ascend for 100' and begin belaying. The first lead goes up and right for 130'. The next lead goes up for 20', then right for 130'. The next lead goes up for 20', then right to skirt an overhang, then up another 220' to a belay position on ledges

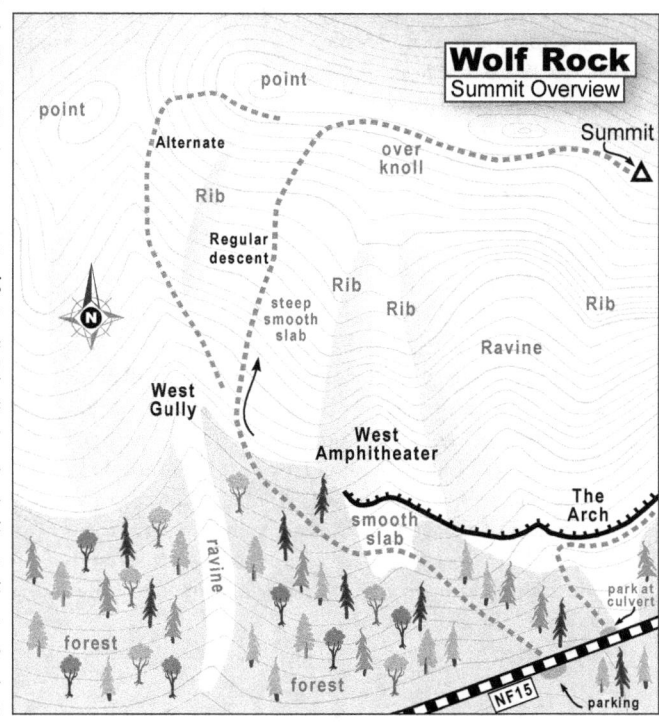

below an overhang (pitons). The fourth lead is directly up a small, easy gully. From the top traverse right on ledges to heather and scramble to the summit. Anticipate about 4 hours for the ascent (Dodge, *A Climbing Guide to Oregon* (1975), pg 61-62).

31. Barton's Gully II 5.5 R/X
Barton's Gully is the fourth gully on the north face when approached from the clearcut east of the rock. It is the most prominent of the four gullies. At a point east of the large overhanging bulge, climb sloping ledges and slabs to a belay point in a small Douglas fir 130' up in the gully. From here traverse left (east) 30', then climb straight up over mossy ledges to a poor piton belay 40'. Continue up 35' then traverse left 100' to a bush belay. From here continue straight up for 200' to the summit ridge. Anticipate about 6 hours (Dodge page 61-62).

32. Hogback Chimney II 5.5 R
This route utilizes the deep chimney splitting the north face directly above the hogback. Ascend the chimney (30') and come out of a hole on the face of the cliff. Climb the face up and slightly left to a sloping belay ledge to the left of a small gully. From here diagonal up toward a low notch in the summit ridge (Dodge page 61-62).

33. Hairy Tale II 5.7 R
Traverse the base of the north face beyond the hogback past a dip in the base of the face to the top of the next rise. The climb begins above and left 40' of a small point separating rock terraces to the right and mossy slopes to the left in a left facing open book. Climb the book through a roof (5.6) and belay 10' above. Continue up to the second roof and climb 60' (5.4) to an awkward belay below a wall. Diagonal left, then right to a flared jam crack behind a flake. Proceed up this (5.7) crack. Gear to 3" including cams, and pitons. Anticipate about 6 hours to climb (Dodge page 61-62).

Steve on *Coreolis*, Wolf Rock

A Rock Climbing Guide To

Thad Arnold climbing *X Marks the Spot*
Photo archive: *T. Arnold*

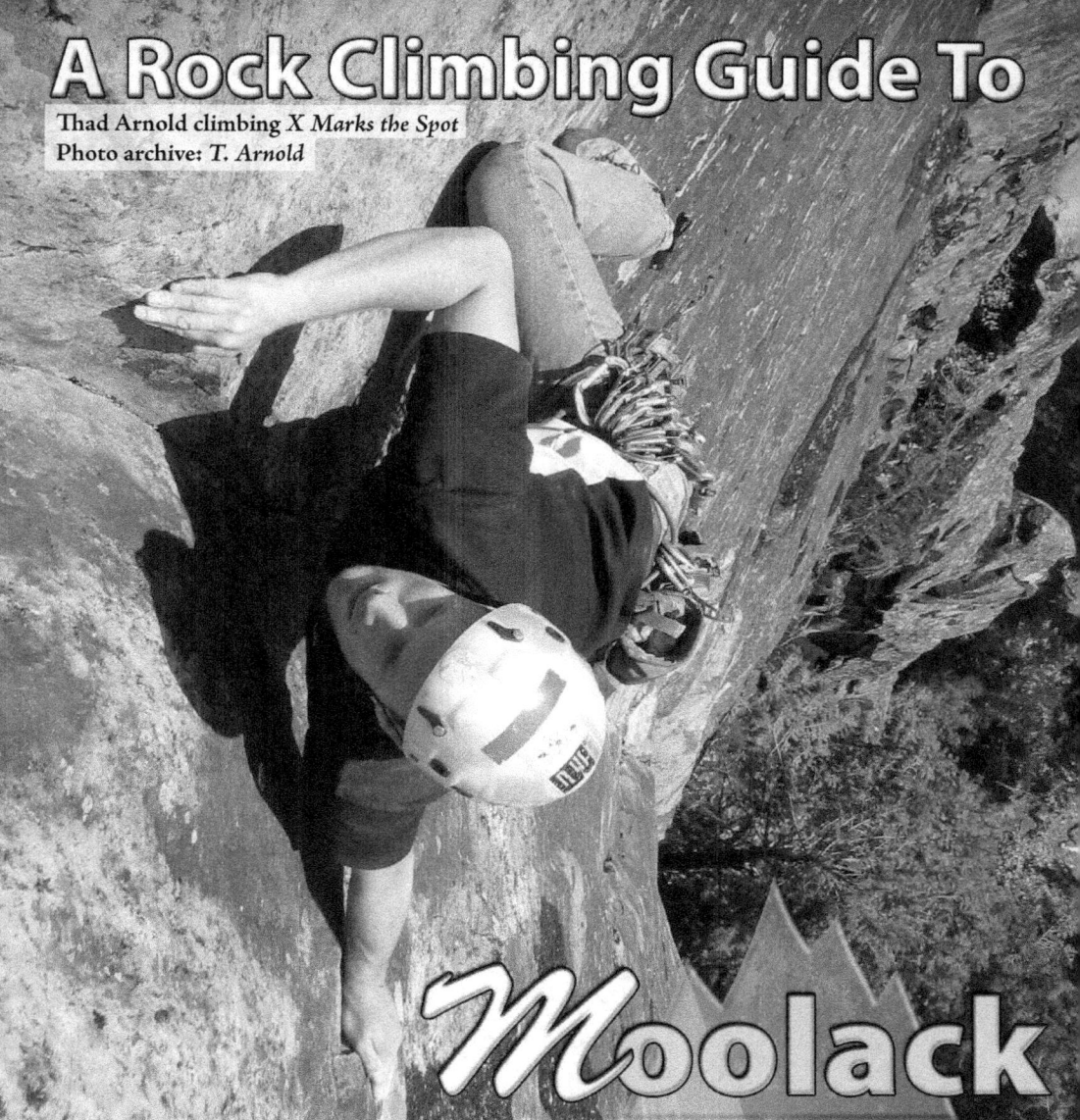

Moolack

Original manuscript written by Paul M. Waters and Jennifer M. Mower (and dedicated to their daughter Eva)

    Guidebooks have acted as the backbone to Oregon rock climbing for as long as the histories of ascents have been recorded. In 1968 Nick Dodge published *A Climbing Guide to Oregon* and since then a slew of guidebooks in Oregon have been printed ranging in quality. Great guidebooks have ascent information, discuss climbing history, and outline local practices (ethics, styles and tactics) of a particular crag in addition to providing readers with route descriptions. The traditional focus of the Moolack area creates a truly unique climbing experience, thus the traditional focus created a framework for this guide, from its first and second ascent information to its emphasis on a completely natural climbing experience. We aim to share the boltless standard and the uniqueness it has added to the experiences of those who have spent time at Moolack and those who will visit in the years to come. In summation, Moolack is an inescapable and inherent part of the grand guidebook

* All Moolack photos courtesy of Paul Waters except where noted

Bill Soule leading Gold 5.11b/c
Photo credit: Ari Denison

journey.

Moolack is for the moderate-to-experienced rock climber familiar with the concept of boltless climbing. Emphasis is placed on traditional on-sight, ground-up lead practices where feasible. Top-down new route development, including pre-practice to adequately prepare a route when needed (if the terrain has friable rock or has unknown difficulties or protection). Both methods are commonly practiced at Moolack. Even seasoned Moolack rock climbers still find it difficult to identify certain routes, so keep focused on the route you intend to climb and avoid uncleaned friable rock terrain. Moolack is a no-bolt crag, so categorizing established climbs and the individuals who developed a route necessitates information gathering usually in the form of a guide. Fixed gear implies provenance, so route development and first ascensionist establishment at a bolt-less climbing area would remain a mystery until written formulation is articulated.

For climbers less familiar with boltless climbing it is my hope to open your eyes to the thrill of traditional climbing in a pristine setting with zero visual interference from bolts. Finding crags with traits suitable for boltless climbing is rare, but rarer still if future generations of climbers have no awareness that zero-bolt standards do in fact exist. Sport and mixed-sport climbing that utilizes bolts as fixed gear is quite popular throughout Oregon, but Moolack's traditional style boltless climbing will continue to have appeal.

Bolts have historically been utilized at climbing areas of Oregon on land identified as protected wilderness areas, and in some cases appropriately so (e.g., Menagerie). At Moolack the boltless ethic exists primarily due to its geographic location in a "protected wilderness" region, making bolting here unlawful. But it is inappropriate to believe that making strides towards keeping Moolack boltless stops there. The Moolack climbing community has rallied around the boltless standard and it is not hard to see why. Moolack is completely conducive to non-bolted climbing because it has diverse cracks of all sizes with ample opportunity for ledges mid-climb for multi-pitch opportunities. Rarely has a hanging belay been implemented for even the longest of climbs. Finding unprotectable climbs is a greater task than finding readily protectable climbs. Those rare gems that haven't taken gear, are great top-rope problems. As for the cliff top, there are trees close enough to the cliff edge to provide quality top anchors, but far enough away to rarely encumber a lead climber when he tops out. Keeping Moolack boltless depends on stewardship abilities to express the Moolack standard, beyond merely localized community discussion.

Moolack is located in a quiet forested sanctuary. Climbing activity here is primarily due to its popularity and availability of route beta. In recent years evidence indicates that new climbers are being drawn to Moolack often with limited knowledge of the area. Not having a guide or a friend familiar with the area tends to limit the visiting climbers options resulting in crowding at the better known areas of the crag. A no-guidebook mentality to Moolack forces people to huddle around the same few rock climbs. I am promoting Moolack hoping that others are willing to be proactive in maintaining a user friendly environment on the climbing routes (moving some moss), and by being helpful to visiting climbers.

This book divides Moolack climbing into primary areas (e.g., Pedestal Area, Goldband Area) and within each area identifies routes in sequential order from right to left, east to west. Most climbs can be descended by rappelling or lowering from the top of the band, and some routes can be accessed by adjacent nearby routes. When top-

Max Tepfer leading *Sideways*
Photo: *T. Arnold*

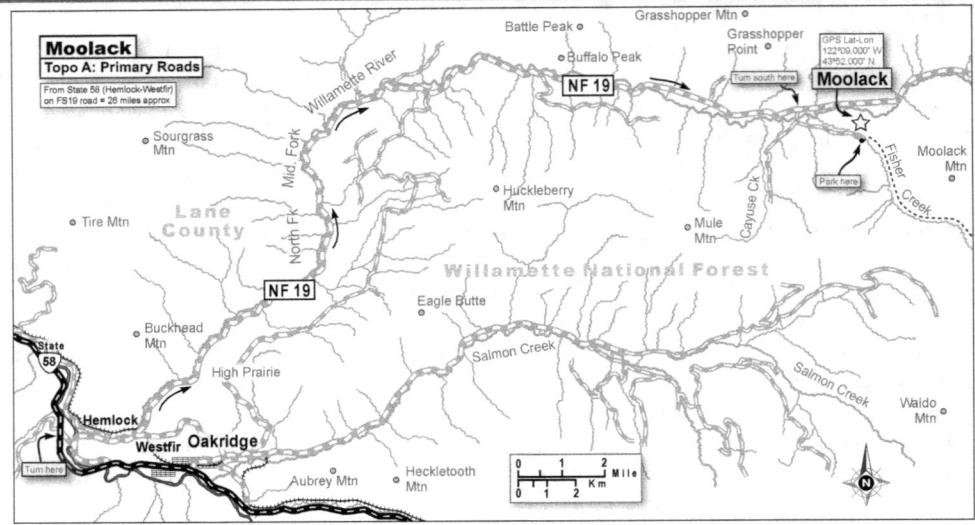

ping out on a climb you can walk east along the rim top to descend via the cliffs termination on the east flank instead of rappelling.

This guide emphasizes the traditional practice of placing nuts, cams, tri-cams, hexes, sliding nuts, and sliding chocks (Big Bro) on lead, from the ground-up. Developing skills with a qualified and proficient friend or guide can lead to safe and well managed climbing at Moolack. Make sure you have plenty of long solid anchoring material (i.e. cord, webbing, static-rope) and avoid climbing over your traditional leading skill level unless you understand the risks. In the Southern Willamette Valley there are academic rock climbing classes, private lessons, and other areas used for practice of placing gear and building anchors with relatively easy access (e.g. Skinner Butte, Marys Peak). For top-down route access prior familiarity is beneficial in order to safely locate a specific climb.

Some route descriptions have abbreviated wording when discussing a nearby route, for example UOAP is Up on a Pedestal, EE is E.T.A. Eva, and OC is Orange Crush.

Moolack Mountain (5,490') a prominent rock hill northwest of Waldo Lake was formerly known as Elk Mountain because of the local abundance of that animal. It was renamed due to an abundance of Elk Mountains throughout the state. The Oakridge-Moolack region receives a substantial quantity of rainfall each year, which encourages profuse tree growth, lush dense brushy green foliage and thick brightly colored carpets of reddish-brown moss.

Moolack History

Bill Soule came to Moolack in the mid-to-late 1990s and started developing the approach trail and the areas earliest routes. Mike South, a Willamette Valley native also frequented the area. In these initial years Soule and South developed Lost Art, Up On A Pedestal, X-Marks the Spot, Perverts in Paradise and Geek on A Leash to name a few. Soule and South applied a strict cleaning method that focused on retaining the natural wilderness aesthetic.

On-site, ground-up climbing was a primary focus for Soule-South from 1996 to 2000, but cleaning has always been a big part of safety. Around 2000 new parties made Moolack a regular climbing destination. Including Karsten Duncan, Jason Krueger, Paul Waters, John Brewer, Kimball Holloway, Dave Campbell, Cody Peterson and others began visiting Moolack. They replicated leads on established routes and began to clean and establish new routes. Other Willamette Valley climbers, many from the Eugene area began day-tripping the crag, but few climbers took to the gardening, the approach, the driving distance, and other unique aspects of Moolack. By 2003 there were over 14 known routes. During the winter 2005 season climbers/developers Lee Baker, Jeff Baldo, Criss Steiner and Brian Gilbert joined the process and by the end of spring 2006 known

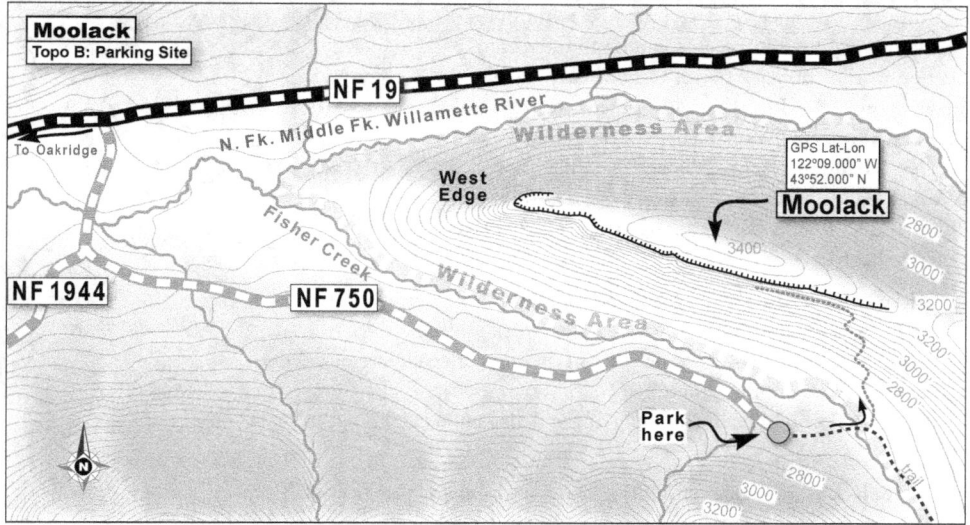

climbing routes from the eastern edge to beyond the Gold Band had increased to over 34. By the end of 2008 Moolack had attained 48 (30 single pitch and 18 multi-pitch climbs) developed routes, including an additional 12 incomplete project routes. By 2011 Moolack had 72 climbable routes; significant numbers considering the locale of wall.

The Climbers of Moolack

Bill Soule, considered to be the "Godfather" of Moolack, is an icon in the Oregon climbing community. Without Bill Soule there would be no Moolack. Beyond finding the area and committing tireless hours to its development, Bill had the foresight and experience to identify boltless climbing potential within Moolack. Bill Soule created a lasting legacy that endures with every climber that comes away from the area, with the understanding of the boundless opportunities within climbing and the satisfaction of climbing within a bolt-less climbing standard. In a time and place where Oregon rock-climbing was typified by bolting methods of various design on new routes, Moolack's progressive nature of not bolting at all broke the mold. The fortune of having all natural elements conducive to climbing top notch crack and face climbs, with a pure natural ethos, and zero application of bolts is rare. But to identify that these elements were in fact present at Moolack was truly visionary. Bill Soule's contributions to the climbing world are immeasurable; in the number of climbers he has inspired and the positive influence they in turn have on others.

To quote an article written by Dane Tornell in 'The Iceaxemen' (May 2009), a South Eugene High School climbing club, of which both Bill and Mike mentor, "Even if you are one of those that knows Bill or heard of him, you might not necessarily know the entire story. But, like Moolack with someone like Bill we'll never know all the secrets and mysteries."

Mike "Mr. Clean" South is a major steward to Moolack alongside Bill. Beyond setting the standard of relentless route-cleaning he has also set high route standards on ev-

**Max Tepfer leading *Full Circle*
Photo: *Thad Arnold***

erything from finger to fist climbs to wide body off-widths. Mike South gems can be found at any section of the Moolack band. Other heavy-weight players on the Moolack development scene are Karsten Duncan, Justin Kruger, Lee Baker, Max Tepfer, Thaddeus Arnold, Mark Koehler, Forest Weaver, Ball Oh, Kimball Holloway, Mike Holmes, Ryan Young, Evan Mikkelson, Matthew Jones, Dave Carr and others.

> "Although bolts are the lightning rods of ethical controversy, they are in fact only an emblem of the debate. Other problems, such as noise, litter, trail abuse, and graffiti, all threaten to creep into our climbing areas if we aren't vigilant."
> -- Don Mellor in Climbing in the Adirondacks, 1997

Moolack Ethics, Styles and Tactics

Moolack is a 'no-bolt' climbing area. Development practices at Moolack typically have two parts: (1) attempt the onsight after cleaning and (2) pass the route on to another in an effort to preserve a more pure onsight. If the route is not completed in its first attempt, most developers pursue subsequent top-down pre-practice of crux moves until a successful red-point. Moolacks' route grades are subjective, but if you are familiar with the 'old-school 5.9' concept a competent leader can stay safe in this 5.9-5.10 level.

Soule and South epitomize a cleaning standard marked by leaving routes in a state that the random hiker wouldn't know we'd been there. In other words leaving the bottom 20' with moss relatively intact and the cracks relatively un-cleaned. This aims to preserve a natural aesthetic for non-climbers to the area. Cleaning should be done from the top-down as the majority of the danger lies at the loose top 20 meters of rock. Avoid cleaning sections that are of no route value to help maintain the natural aesthetics of the area. If unsure how much to clean on a lower section attempt it on top-rope. The climbing routes direction may be revised over time when better protection or a greater esthetic quality is found. The issue over cleaning and what is considered too much cleaning was discussed in 2001 by Soule and Jason Krueger. Karsten Duncan and Krueger cleaned and developed new routes at Moolack with a "to-the-base" cleaning concept. Other developers have adopted similar cleaning concepts while many still adhere to leaving routes mossy through their opening moves which are typically easy-to-moderate terrain.

Boltless climbing is not for everyone, and if we expect to maintain a no-bolt ethic at Moolack, the climbing community needs to acknowledge an alternative way to access routes. With a moderate-level of climbing knowledge, plenty of rock climbing can be done by top-rope on shorter sections of the cliff band. Sporty arêtes and blank faces provide amazing top-rope problems, with more to still be discovered.

Nailing at Moolack is uncommon and most developers tend to leave a route un-pinned to avoid degradation to the route or the rock. Aid climbing has been implemented for rainy months, and for would-be route cleaning on lead. Pins have been utilized during would-be free ascents turned aid for initial on-site leads, then followed up with all later all free ascents. Sometimes the pin has stayed, sometimes it has been removed. Routes known to have utilized pins have been mentioned.

Moolack Geology

The Moolack cliff band is composed of Tertiary Basalt (Tb1) from the Pliocene Era (2-7 mil yrs) from an old volcanic vent source likely centered at a higher point about 1 mile southeast of the wall. Rock bluffs such as Moolack with a compositionally younger age structure tend to offer better

Thad Arnold leading *Orange Crush*
Opposite page photo: *T. Arnold*

quality climbing opportunities because weathering disintegration processes have had less impact on the feature, particularly if the cliff scarp has only recently sloughed into existence.

For climbers who know how to place protection and are familiar with a range of crack and face climbing techniques used at other columnar basalt or andesite crags, then you will be prepared for climbing the andesite here. Crack route systems at Moolack have an unrivaled number of protection opportunities that are unique for Oregon. Though Moolack is columnar it is a far cry from basaltic columns such as Skinner Butte or the Lower Gorge of Smith. Crack systems are non-uniform with rare reachable double-crack opportunities and minimal columnar structure, while the upper portion of the wall has horizontally layered fracturing. Each climb carries a style unto itself, like no other, again lending to the non-uniformity. Infrequent splitter cracks exist and do provide sustained finger to fist-size jam climbing. Most rock climbs blend a mixture of finger-to-hand-to-fist sized crack climbing with short sections of face climbing technique. Some visually prominent routes offer powerful wide cracks or burly off-widths certain to test your skill.

Oregon Rock Climbing in the 1990s

In the 1990s, during Moolack's earliest development, bolted routes outweighed traditional lines in Oregon. Smith Rock remained center-stage for not only Oregon, but nationally and internationally, as developers continued to push difficulty levels in sport climbing. Routes of all difficulty and ethos continued to be added throughout Oregon with an emphasis on bolted lines. Oregon sport-climbing crags of the 1990s included but were not limited to The Callahans, Rattlesnake Crag, Hills Creek Spires, Area 51, Ozone, and coastal areas. Despite the popularity of sport climbing traditional routes emerged in the nineties and early 2000's. "New" high quality trad routes included but was not limited to Half Moon Crack, Crazy Crack, and Magic Blocks. A number of new trad-ish routes were developed at the Menagerie. Areas like Trout Creek, Beacon Rock, Cougar, Williamson River Cliffs and other rock formations of yesteryear saw continued climbing or in some cases routes were rediscovered. The climbing scene in Oregon was experiencing a trad climbing renaissance of sorts with new trad areas and new trad development in old areas every year. Time will tell how Moolack routes fare against other traditional areas in Oregon. Location, time commitment, gear requirements, and mossy routes may deter repetitive climbers. The nature of crack-climbing is apples and oranges when compared to places like Trout Creek.

"Without ethics there would be more cliffs like the Sport Park, in Boulder Canyon, with chiseled holds everywhere....every crack on the planet would be bolted. We need climbing ethics, as we all have such pig-headed opinions."
    -- Bobbi Bensman

Driving Directions

From I-5 at the south end of Eugene, Oregon take exit 188-A. Drive on US Hwy 58 for 34 miles (passing Lookout Reservoir) until you reach the Willamette Fork Ranger Station just west of the small town of Oakridge. At the Willamette Fork Ranger Station take a left onto the Aufderheide Memorial National Forest Service Road 19. In less than a mile you will cross a bridge and take a left turn. After the community of Westfir the road becomes windy but scenic. Turn right on Forest Service 1944. After crossing the bridge take an unmarked left turn onto graveled Forest Service road NFSR 750. The

Paul W. working a Moolack boulder

Brian Gilbert on *Knife Fight*
Photo: *Paul Waters*

Moolack cliff band appears on your left high up on a hill. The road yields the best view of the cliff band. There is a single-car campground on the left side of the road with nearby river access. The road continues to a parking lot that also marks the beginning of the Fisher Creek Trail. The road ends just beyond the parking lot which accommodates about a half-dozen mid-size cars.

The NF19 corridor recreational drive is dedicated in memory of Bob Aufderheide, a past supervisor for the Willamette National Forest. Moolack Mountain (5490') is located in the Waldo Lake Wilderness. You can attain area maps, forest passes, and information at the Middle Fork Ranger Station on Highway 58 in Oakridge. The Fisher Creek Trail that takes you to Moolack also leads to the Waldo Lakes loop trail system.

Moolack distances from other points of interest:

Corvallis, OR	85 miles	Eugene, OR	44 miles
Portland, OR	150 miles	Seattle, WA	320 miles
Dunsmuir, CA	220 miles	Leavenworth, WA	430 miles
Almo, ID	620 miles	Squamish, BC	508 miles

Trail Approach

From the parking lot the Fischer Creek Trail immediately crosses a log bridge and drops into a campground. The Fischer Creek Trail heads away from the Moolack band just past this campground. A series of small paths connect camp sites to the left of the Fischer Creek Trail. These minor paths and downed logs intersect with an unmarked climber's trail that heads uphill past the Mane Boulder. This path skirts trees and brush and ascends up a steep scree field to a well-worn Z-path, then to a visible upper trail. The upper trail switch-backs up moderate terrain to a fork marked by a large flat rock. A right turn at the trail fork quickly leads up to the cliff band and ends at the cliff base trail under Lost Art. The left turn at the fork is an unfinished path that may eventually end at the cliffs mid-point. A secondary deer-path approach has been traveled from the Mane Boulder heading N-NW to the boulder field below the X-marks and Gold Bands.

This Guide To Moolack

With admirable commendability we recognize Alan Watts efforts to climbing 90% of the routes he describes in his Smith Rock guide. Other guidebooks with a "trad" focus like Red Rocks, the Adirondacks and the Squamish guide were written by authors who also climbed virtually all the routes in their books. However, I did not climb 90% of the routes in this guide. Route development and beta acquisition is a primary goal as well as enjoying rock climbing, though if time allows I may climb a greater number of routes at Moolack unfamiliar to me. This guide is a collaborative effort based upon the exploits and experiences of a group of climbers. This beta is based on first and second ascentist (and sometimes a third) knowledge, which may include anecdotes and physical characteristics associated with the route in question. Gear, though subjectively based on user preference is hopefully broad enough to meet your needs. With such details buried in the beta, some have expressed concern that I will take the "adventure aspect" out of Moolack. For the established routes no amount of beta can take away from the adventurous nature of Moolack's routes. If you want to know less, read less to attain your preferred spice level.

Cliff Top Access

Views from the top of the cliff make it one of the rare treats at Moolack, but accessing routes along the top of the cliff band can be challenging without prior understanding of start-to-end route configuration. Top-down route access methods usually require crag familiarity best learned with friends familiar with this crag. It is a poor place to learn anchor building, protection placement, or multi-pitch tactics.

Starting eastward along the base of the cliff from the end of the approach trail the initial opening rock climbs are Sophie and Gwenevere. Beyond, there is a 200'+ stretch of rock band that is shorter than the shortest route, yet too tall for safe bouldering. At the cliffs termination, there is a series of downed trees. Scramble up the slope, then walk westward along the cliff top till you see the madrone tree above Sophie and Gwenevere. This trail continues on to "The Hub", a popular tree anchor point usually slung with a bike tire tube or webbing wrapped 10.8 mm static rope with a simple chain rap ring. The Hub is the top anchor for Lost Art, Up on a Pedestal and other nearby routes. Tree anchors used for Zion Train and Sideways are visible from The Hub and are quite manageable with a 70-meter rope. Zion Train has a prominent outward leaning tree and obvious clean jug holds beyond the routes crux, visible from the top.

A large sun-baked column top after Pledge Crack marks the top of Fist-fighting Plumbers section, visible beyond a gap between the two columns. While Fist-Fight and Plumbers are easily defined and accessible, the top of Pledge crack is chocked with madrone trees. This section is usually climbed from the ground up due to difficult upper access points.

Looking past the very obvious Mushroom Band from the top of Fist-fighting Plumbers, the large black column split by Cleaned For Her Pleasure marks the end of the Fist-fighting Plumbers band. A small belay ledge tucked into a large tree marking the top of Fist Fight can be accessed past minor madrone trees, above the anchor tree via an easy but airy scramble down the columns top around negotiating the tree.

A large dead tree and nearby madrone's anchor mark the end of Where the Wild Things Are and Sasquatch (visible from Fist Fight top). A burnt-out old growth tree marks the top of One Flew Over the Cuckoo's Nest.

One very obvious single tree is the top anchor for all of the climbs for the Mushroom Band, but is down a slight slope below the cliff top trail. After Mushroom Band the trail continues extremely tight to the cliffs edge for a short distance. The locale for Mr. Clean and Pleasure Palace and nearby routes is difficult to gauge from above. There is a large dead old growth that marks the end of a 25 foot loose 5.3 section above the end of Mr. Clean. Leading Mr. Clean is a better way to familiarize access, rather than attempting to navigate it from above.

The cliff section beyond the Pleasure Palace slopes downward so the routes are best as lead climbs. They incorporate multi-pitch tactics, use mid-point belays which can be difficult to find other than bottom up, and many of the routes do not follow direct ground-to-top crack lines. The only other area that may be easily accessed top-down by first time visitor are routes on the Guillotine Band, because the tree anchor for Guillotine often has a webbing or cord wrapped in a tire tube at a clean ledge that looks out over the Guillotine double cracks and nearby tree also offers top belay stance for Pool Guy.

The anchor ledge for Dru's Cruise is visible from the trail. A dead tree marks the top of Age Before Beauty. This is a nice entry point to access some quality difficult routes. From Dru's Cruise to the Goldband it is best to lead the routes from ground up. Gold Gulley is just beyond Yay Climbing and before Sendero Sangre, and top-down access is feasible for routes like Sendero de Sangre

Max Tepfer leading *Sideways*   Photo: T. Arnold

and Slot Machine. Top-down access to Gold is possible, but not convenient. Most Goldband routes are best as ground up lead routes. Need more info...search Moolack Rock Climbing on the web.

> *"It's crucially important that climbers don't hasten the inevitable by chiseling tomorrow's 5.15s down to 5/12c."*
> *-- Alan Watts*

Pedestal Area (Classic Cracks Area)

The Approach Trail ends at the Pedestal Area (i.e. Classic Cracks). To the right are Scum Suckers, Bitch I Won, Gwenevere and Sophie. The routes are described right to left starting at Sophie. Continue on the trail past Sophie till the cliff band ends at a series of downed logs, then scramble uphill and back west along the top of the cliff to reach access points for various climbs. Lost Art is at the intersection of the Cliff Band Trail and the Approach Trail. Blood on the Cracks climbs the steep corner dihedral to the right of Lost Art. This area extends left to the routes Sideways, Zion Train and right with Radical Sabbatical and Thaddalic.

1. **Sophie 5.7**
   Pro: Size 5"+ cams for opening moves, then minimal fist-to-finger cams and nuts
   A right-facing 90-degree open-book dihedral with a tree at its base. The crack starts wide, but utilizes a secondary thin crack to the right mid-climb for pro and jams. Two lie-back moves gain easy hand-jams and face holds. The last section of the climb has foot ledges and a twin crack. Belay at a low hanging madrone tree shared with Gwenevere.

2. **Gwenevere 5.7**
   Pro: ¾" to 5"+ large cams off the deck (#4-6 BD), TCU's and nuts for double crack
   Gwenevere is accessed via a short scramble using a tree left of Sophie. From below the ledge two awkward off-width moves utilize a wide crack. Access a small face ledge with solid finger jams after initial moves, then easy hand-jams and foot ledges with good protection. The route ends on two ledges with a tree anchor hanging out over the second ledge, sharing the belay with Sophie. Can skip large pro if you're willing to stem across the initial belay ledge to the foot ledge and fist crack after the wide crack.

3. **Scum Suckers 5.10a** ★
   Pro: ½" to 5" cams, nuts, hexes and a Big Bro's for the top may ease top-out
   Start on a high saddle using a thin finger crack, foot-jams and ledge options on either side of a crack. It widens up higher from 3½" to 5"+, then after a gully finishes in a wide chimney. Beware of loose rock in the gully. The column separates from the cliff band when the crack ends; anchor to small trees at the top. *Originally called Hazeldell after the historic community now called Oakridge.*

4. **Bitch I Won 5.9** ★
   Pro: #00 to 5" cams, nuts, hexes and Big Bro for the top
   This route, parallel and immediately right of Scum Suckers, climbs a thin finger crack with delicate feet out on a face up to a dirty rock gully. Follow this to a dihedral with a small seam in back and a mini-roof at the top.

5. **Radical Sabbatical 5.10c** ★★★
   Pro: #00 to 4" cams, nuts, hexes, off-set TCU's
   This is a former 30' variation to Blood on the Cracks, but now with a new base direct. The new start is very steep off the ground with gear opportunities every foot or so, and horizontal jugs to grab the whole way. This 5.8 bottom section directly links into the steeper upper portion that makes for the 5.10c crux. The final layback is short, but stout, and pretty committing over the last 3" cam. This direct makes for a more quality first section than Blood on the Cracks.

SOUTHERN WILLAMETTE 347

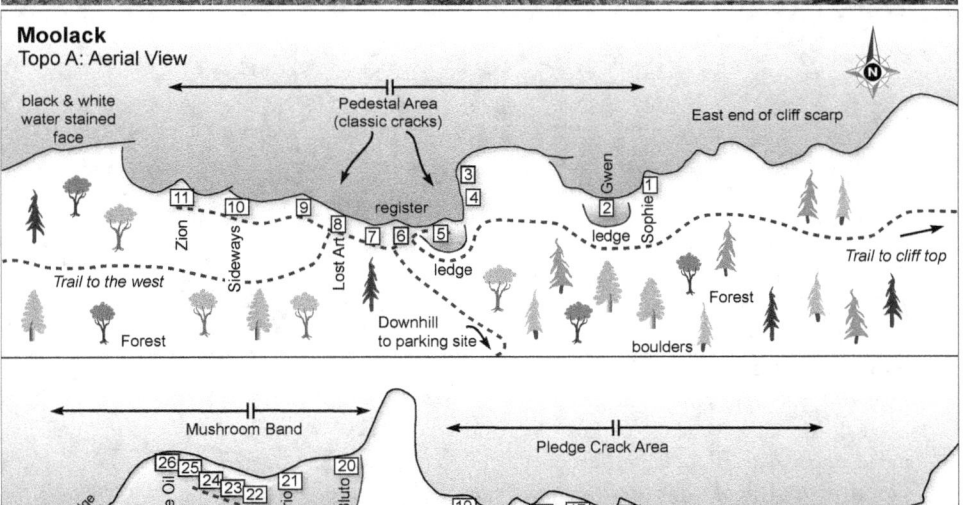

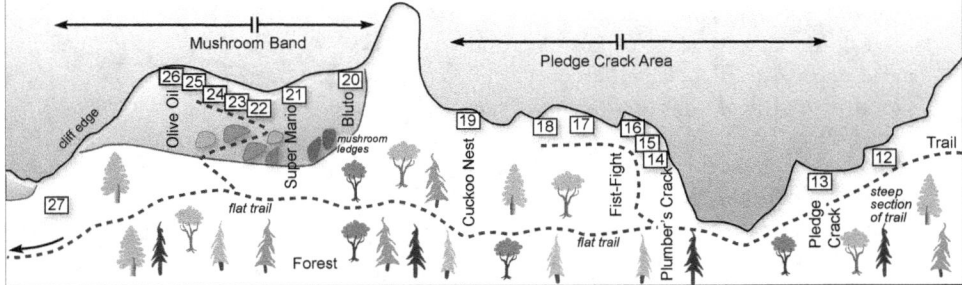

6. **Thadallic 5.10+** ★★★
Pro: #00 to 4" cams, nuts, hexes, off-set TCU's
Thadallic formerly shared a start with Blood on the Cracks, but a direct start was added to offer 5.8+ to 5.9- climbing. From the base trail move up to a distinctive dihedral past a crux marked by a short, steep roof to the right of the dihedral. This upper dihedral is identified with flaring cracks and odd gear. It climbs like a gym route...may be height dependant, may be with an R rating, but offset cams really help. *When Baker was establishing this line his would-be*

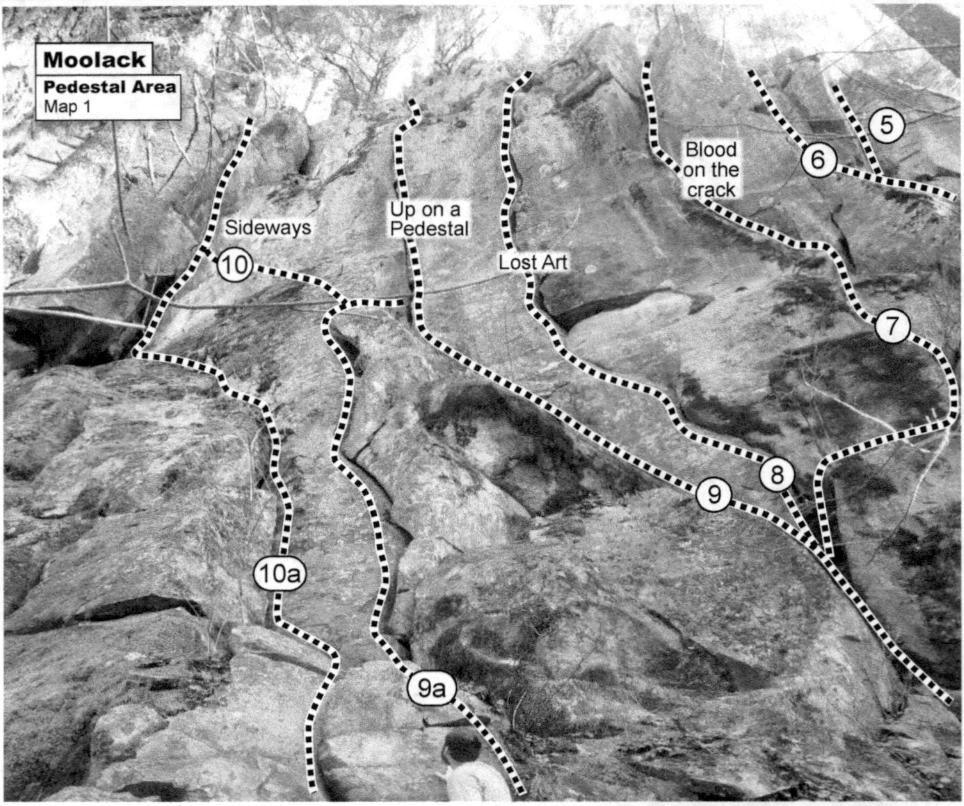
Moolack
Pedestal Area
Map 1
Sideways
10
Up on a Pedestal
Lost Art
Blood on the crack
5
6
7
8
9
10a
9a

belayer (Thad), overwhelmed by the areas potential missed the routes inception when scouting further along the band. On a chance occurrence Bill Soule, always willing to lend a belay, was available to help with the FA.

7. Blood on the Cracks 5.10c ★★★

Pro: #00 to 4" cams, nuts, and hexes

Start up the first 3-meters of Lost Art, and move right to a ledge. Climb moderate 5.8 past three more ledges to a steep dihedral corner where the crack widens to fist-size jams. A second crack picks up mid route, which eases the level of difficulty. Stemming and solid fist jamming on steep terrain leads to a jug hand hold that ends the short 5.10c crux section on the last 5-meters of the climb. Multi-purpose top anchor serves 3 routes (LA, UOAP, and BOTC with extra tree runner).

8. Lost Art 5.10c ★★★★

Pro: #00 to 3½" cams, nuts; optional TCU at mid-climb directs rope out of crack

Start with stiff 5.8 thin finger jams and minor

Scum suckers
Pedestal Area
Map 3
4

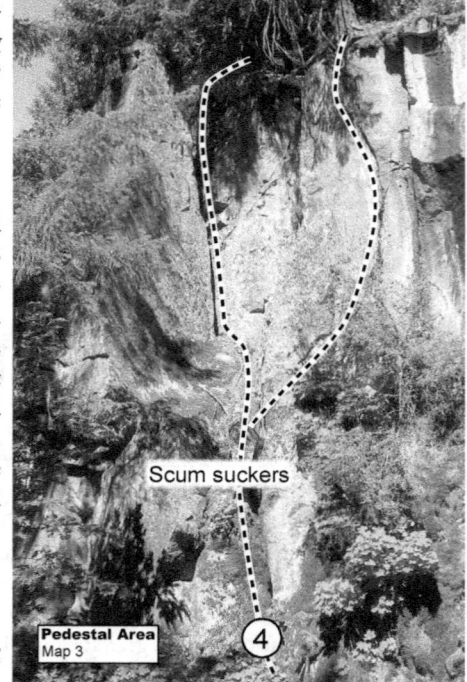

foot holds up a strenuous leftward arching crack with delicate feet (lower crux) to the routes mid-point roof and rest point. The upper crux section begins above the roof as the climb steepens using hand and finger jams. A fairly long, sustained crux section more so than UOAP. Multi-purpose top anchor serves 3 routes.

9. Up on a Pedestal 5.10a ★★★★
Pro: #00 to 4½" cams, nuts
The original line of UOAP shared the start with LA moving left to a dirty dihedral corner that leads to the 'Pedestal.' As the Pedestal Direct gained popularity in the mid-2000s the old start became overgrown and mossy. The direct starts up nice hand holds to a ledgy corner and up a wide 5.6 crack with hand and foot edges to a small stance below the Pedestal. From this small stance move up and connect to a short left arching splitter crack that ends on the Pedestal. From the Pedestal climb continuous crux 5.9 hand and finger jams till the route steepness eases, then finish on 5.6 pinches on a low angle slab to complete the route.

10. Sideways 5.10a ★★★
Pro: #00 to 4" cams; Pedestal Direct and Sideways Direct use 4"+ gear
This line shares the first half of UOAP. A less traveled direct is feasible using fists to wide crack that links to the Sideways upper dihedral. Typically, you will start on UOAP route to the Pedestal ledge, and then make an easy 5.6 traverse leftward to the Sideways dihedral. Stem and jam up the dihedral past where the crack disappears for 10' on varied face climbing. The top is steep with semi-positive jams/stems. Slightly more technical but less pumpy than nearby climbs. The crux is a lie-back move and a reach/jam near the top ending with easy climbing off the ledge to multiple tree anchors.

11. Zion Train 5.9 ★★★
Pro: #00 to 4½" cams, nuts, hexes
The stance for Zion Train and Sideways Direct are 10-yds uphill from the base of The Pedestal. Easy 5.6 ledge climbing leads into a steep 5.9- corner that requires full stems with large face and foot holds through a chimney. Physical stemming, hand jamming, and face climbing opportunities lead up to a higher ledge beyond the chimney. From an upper ledge a crux 5.9 thin finger jam move links to the final 5.6 moves to a tree anchor. This last crux reach is considerably easier if you are tall.

Pledge Crack Area

The Pledge Crack will stand out even during the arduous approach hike. As you walk west away from the Pedestal Area the trail starts downhill. A large distinctive trailside tree stands just opposite of Pledge Crack before a rough section of trail. The wide Plumbers Crack to the west is the opposite end of Pledge Crack. To the climbers right of Compromising Positions is a wide black and white drainage wall.

12. Compromising Positions 5.10d

★ ★ ★

Pro: #00 to 2" cams, nuts and hexes

One hundred feet in length, this route contains a blend of chimney-moves, stemming, and difficult finger locking through steep terrain. The crux is marked by a short roof with finger locks. The roof was infested by hornets before cleaning. Baker explains it like this: Gain a stance via a few easy moves then pull over some vertical terrain and move up the groove toward the overhanging chimney. The crack eats up gear as you humbly wiggle up being forced into a rather exposed position. The 180° stemming move to gain the block is as good as it gets, then one more mantle, and up a layback flake to the final steep corner. Up and over gets you to the belay.

13. Pledge Allegiance (aka Pledge Crack) 5.10d ★ ★ ★ ★

Pro: #00 to 4" cams, nuts, hexes, plus extra long slings for belay station

Climb 12' then move right through moderate (5.8/9) climbing up an often moist crack with odd flaring gear. Protect first portion before the traverse with long slings to avoid ropedrag beyond the tonsil later. After the start of the crux roof traverse, with low height jamming or lie-backing with an underling technique moving up to a downward facing tonsil-like feature where the crack arcs to vertical. Transition out right onto the tonsil and up past it using small edges (mental/physical crux). Place adequate gear before and through this section to avoid a ground fall. Continue up to the left jamming, right facing corner crack, bear-hugging the tonsil, with small feet to the right until a small ledge marks the end of difficult climbing. Some fun 5.7 stemming with positive jams and holds is used to access a lower ledge. A small tree can be used on this ledge to avoid rope drag issues of belaying or top-roping from the cliffs top. An exposed 5.7 section links this lower ledge to an overgrown tree anchor at the cliff top.

Fist-fighting Plumbers Area

After Pledge Allegiance the trail wraps around a large column. The first visible large crack is Plumbers Crack, followed by Knife-Fight and Fist-Fight, Sasquatch, Where the Wild Things Are and lastly One Flew Over the Cuckoos Nest. The Mushroom Band is to the climbers left from here. From the cliff band trail a short uphill scramble lands at a series of belay stances for all Fist-fighting Plumbers Area routes.

14. Plumber's Crack 5.10+/.11- ★ ★ ★

Pro: ¾" to #6 cams (#4, #5 & #6 for the top) and Big Bro's (doubles recom.)

Early sections of moderate 5.8 fingers to fist crack climbing leads to a large off-width crack. Use your small gear for the

John on *Where the Wild Thing Are*

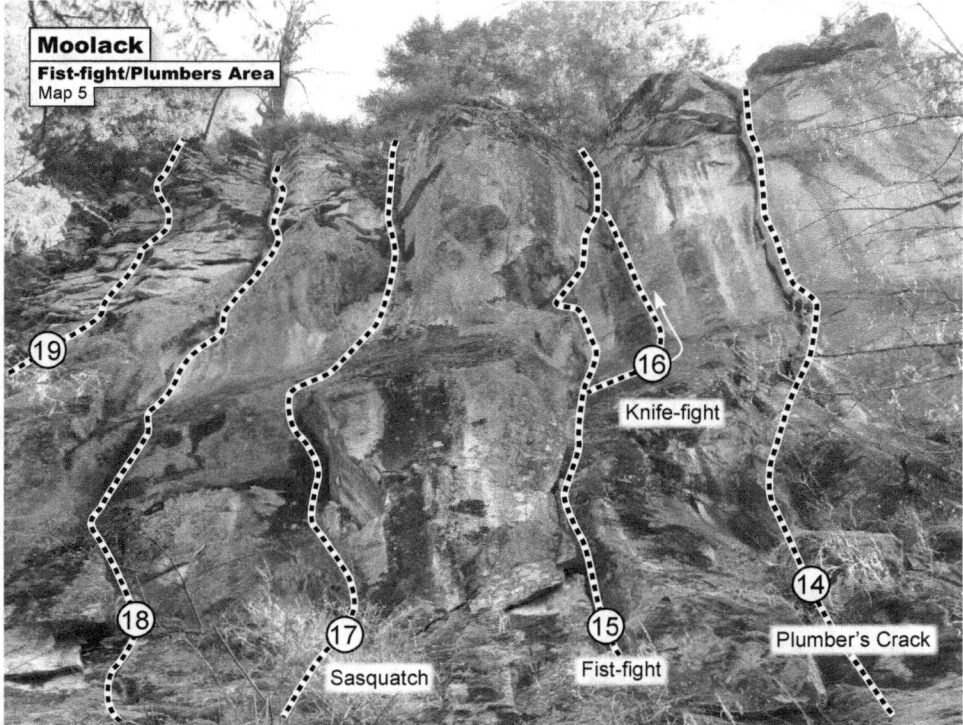

lower part. The large off-width section runs for 60% of the route and requires intensive off-width technique including knee-bars, chicken wings, and other unique off-width techniques. Protection like Big-Bros and over-sized cams may hinder crucial jams that are otherwise more negotiable on TR.

15. Fist-Fight 5.9 ★★★
Pro: #00 to 4½" cams and nuts
An often uncleaned 5.6 low section gains a clean 5.8 crack that requires lie-backs, stems and bomber finger-jams up a right facing dihedral corner. Move out onto a slab for a move, to a gain a great lie-back section leading to a rest point under a large roof. The climber is hidden from the belayer under this roof and through the crux. A bold exposed steep fist-sized crack traverse represents the routes crux. This crux can be jammed or lie-backed. The traverse ends on a small rest ledge before easily stemmed face holds and wide to the left, thin to the right crack climbing. The route ends with horizontal pro and tenuous stems to gain a small ledge with an encumbering large tree anchor.

16. Knife-Fight 5.10+ PG-13 ★★
Pro: #00 to 4½" cams and nuts, beaks, ball-nuts, and brass
An upper variation right of Fist-Fight. After the first lower crux of Fist-Fight (instead of following the crack left to the rest stance at the roof) move right to a short face slab leading to a thin ending crack. A hand-placed 'beak' protects a few sloping edges and tenuous balance moves. An essential finger slot represents the key hand match and protection through a set of bouldery moves to gain Fist-Fight's ledge above. 'Head-point' tactics, a TCU, and a hand-placed beak were adequate for FA.

17. Sasquatch 5.10+ ★★
Pro: #00 to 3" nuts and cams, sliding nuts and brass units for bottom, Big Bro's and 4", 4½"

and 5" cams for upper pitch

From the stance, start a quick traverse on unscrubbed terrain to an obvious thin finger crack (sometimes moist). This initial crack marks the routes crux and a fall will land the leader back on the belay ledge. The second can bring up Big Bro's and big cams for the 2nd pitch wide crack. OW moves and edges outside of the crack make for a much more manageable wide crack climb than other test-pieces in the area. Requires multiple fist-sized pro to properly protect top, but some alternative ½" to 1" size pro in horizontal cracks is feasible.

Brian Gilbert on *Eat Your Spinach*

18. Where the Wild Things Are 5.8 ★★★
Pro: #0 to 6" cams, Big Bro's size 4" and 6"

One of six climbs that start from a common base stance area. Easy climbing to access the inside of an arching, right-facing 5.7 finger jam corner. Before exiting the dihedral, physical chimney climbing with Big Bro's protect through the first crux. From incut jugs, mantle up to a rest ledge prior to the middle crux section. An arching finger crack (#0 or #1 TCU's) ends with a lie-back and a long reach to a jug crack, mantle and minor ledge stance. Lead past a less than protectable, airy second 5.9 crux, followed by a larger ledge by a wide, off-width crack with steep roof climbing offering alternating positive hand holds and body wedging rests outside of the crack at the last section. Non-cruxy ending. Use a curvy madrone tree for belay, prudently backed up to a larger tree 30' from the cliff's edge. *Formerly named 'Split Finger' after a split finger incident on the trail, postponing the free ascent a few weeks. The crux also has a short splitter crack.*

19. One Flew Over the Cuckoo's Nest 5.9 R ★★★
Pro: #00 to #6, and Big Bro's

Embark up a physical finger-to-fist flake crack to a large finger crack blocked by a small tree landing on a small slab. From the slab there is an 8" crack with fun 5.6 climbing and scary protection (Big Bro's), body jams and exposure. A large ledge at mid-climb is a poor location for a belay with big bros at your ankles and a crackless crux face section above. From the ledge a slab traverse using poor shallow thin gear protects exposed, risky moves to an exhilarating dead-point to an open finger jug (good pro) and a rest ledge. Bust through horizontal incut edges and multi-layered cracks up blocky steep roofy terrain for an amazing finish. Walk over to a large dead tree (directional), then over to the same madrone tree used for WTWTA. No redpoint to date because the crux section microplacements (and last available big-bro) involves a risky fall. *The infamous author Ken Kesey is intrinsically linked to the nearby city of Eugene, but beyond that his life was linked to Pleasant Hill, the last outpost for gas, food or coffee on the way to the Lack before Oakridge. The bus "Further" is still parked in the region and many in town acknowledge the man's huge influence there.*

Mushroom Band Area

The next seven climbs begin on the same stance ledge under a wide steep cliff face broken by a series of cracks, corners and face sections. Please use the winding, well trodden approach thru lower ledges and avoid cleaning alternate lines on lower scramble, for aesthetic preservation and ease.

20. Bluto 5.6
Pro: #0 to 3½" cams

From 8' below Super Mario's start veer hard right, ledge to ledge with easy protection through the path of least resistance. A short easy crack gives way to top. Less than stellar route. May be

an optional get-to-the-top quick means for accessing other top-roping goals.

21. Super Mario 5.10- ★★
Pro: #00 - 2½", Multiple thin pro TCUs, nuts, brass nuts, and cams
A steep finger-to-fist sized crack climb on the right side of the band with gray and black rock. From the shared ledge stance, aim up and right on easy climbing that becomes steeper and the finger jams get thin. Shift to hidden hand holds in a crack that takes good pro. After a short roof the upper section consists of stiff face climbing with thin pro (enduro crux). Holds are positive but well spread out with tricky to see, sometimes horizontal pro placements.

22. Eat Your Spinach 5.9 ★
Pro: #0 to 3" cams
A major crack splits the left middle section of the band marked by gray and white rock. Opens with jugs and ledges into fun finger jamming and great pro through the lower ledges. At the steeper first crux a series of thin jams offer either positive jams or positive protection (or place pro below your jams). Beyond moderate face climbing with occasional thin jam links to top section. The last bit of climbing is a shared roof finish with Stems and Caps.

23. Stems and Seeds 5.8 ★
Pro: #0 to 3½" cams, nuts, and brass nuts
Climb the lower easy portion of Eat Your Spinach, then before its crux you must move slightly left and climb an on-the-edge vertical minor seam with moderate movement on an incredible protectable face section immediately left of EYS. It merges with Stems and Caps at a small roof, then up right into EYS. Task intensive for the leader to protect yet remain on the vertical face and not move into the restful easier ramp nearby.

24. Stems and Caps 5.7 ★★
Pro: #00 to 4½" cams, nuts and micro nuts
A 40-meter climb on the left side of the Mushroom Band. From the shared base stance with Stems and Seeds and Super Mario veer hard left using large holds and ledges to a 4' by 4' ledge. Continue left a move or two utilizing a large 7" crack, then move out onto the face, with hand holds and foot smears through fracturing rock. Thin pro on easier terrain gains a low angle slab with hand jugs and a thin crack. Positive holds and foot edges gain easy stemming

that gets harder through a steep roof to reach a ledge 5-meters from the top (at stance place horizontal micro-cam at hip level). Traverse right several moves on an exposed arête protected by this cam, then gain a large double crack that takes fingers to fist sized cams and nuts. A set of steep but easy roofs with jugs share an ending with EYS, S&S and Super Mario.

25. Sweet Pea 5.5
Pro: #00 to 3" nuts and cams
This line offers early easy holds and ledges with large protection followed by a single exposed move to face holds and a ramp with more pro opportunities. Only a utility route to gain top for other routes.

26. Olive Oil 5.4
Pro: #0 to 2" cams
At extreme left side of the mushroom band is a large tree level with the base stance ledge of the Mushroom Band. This route of little resistance is an alternate means to reach the cliff top. Can be climbed in boots with backpack.

Pleasure Palace

Past the Mushroom Band the cliff height temporarily dips down, and then elevates again at a large black pillar indicating the top of the Pleasure Palace. The arching to horizontal hand crack of Sidewinder is unmistakable, and the top anchor tree of Hit and Run stands out at the cliffs edge.

27. Cleaned for Her Pleasure 5.10c ★★★
Pro: P1 1½" to 2½" cams & nuts; P2 is large fists to small OW gear and micro cams
The initial start of the climb is defined by a right-facing corner dihedral to the right of Sidewinder and includes jams of all sizes and a broad range of protection. From Olive Oil a ledge to ledge traverse right to left lands you on CFHP belay stance. This route and Sidewinder intersect ½ way under a large black and silver colored column at a ledge, followed by short moments of powerful climbing in the corner above.

28. Sidewinder 5.10c ★★★
Pro: #0 to 3" cams, nuts and hexes
A west facing and easily overlooked line, when focusing on a suffering trail. Sidewinder offers great short bouts of powerful climbing as it ascends a sideways arching, low angle crack wrapping around the large fractured column, left to right until the southeast flank is gained. Sidewinder is a half-pitch of great climbing before it traverses right under a large black and silver colored bulge of rock to intersect with CFHP at a rest ledge.

29. Mr. Clean 5.10c ★★★
Pro: #00 TCUs to 4" cams
Mr. Clean starts in an awkward finger jam corner. Climb to a C-shaped arch with a low crux move to access a small ledge. From this ledge unprotected 5.8 face climbing links to another group of ledges (pro) using a combination of arête moves and finger jamming. The ledges disappear as you enter the upper crux. A series of thin, awkward finger jams takes you to a thin ending flare crack. A hip-high foot crux move unlocks a difficult to reach jam. Fun 5.8 climbing ends at large tree anchor.

Chris Steiner leading *Mr. Clean*

30. Hit and Run 5.10a ★★★★
Pro: #00 to 3½" cams, nuts, brass nuts, and sliding nuts
A leaning column forms a small roof in the lower section. This route goes up the right side of this column. Easy to moderate climbing with frequent ledges, face holds, and a blend of off-width, stemming, chimney and crack climb-

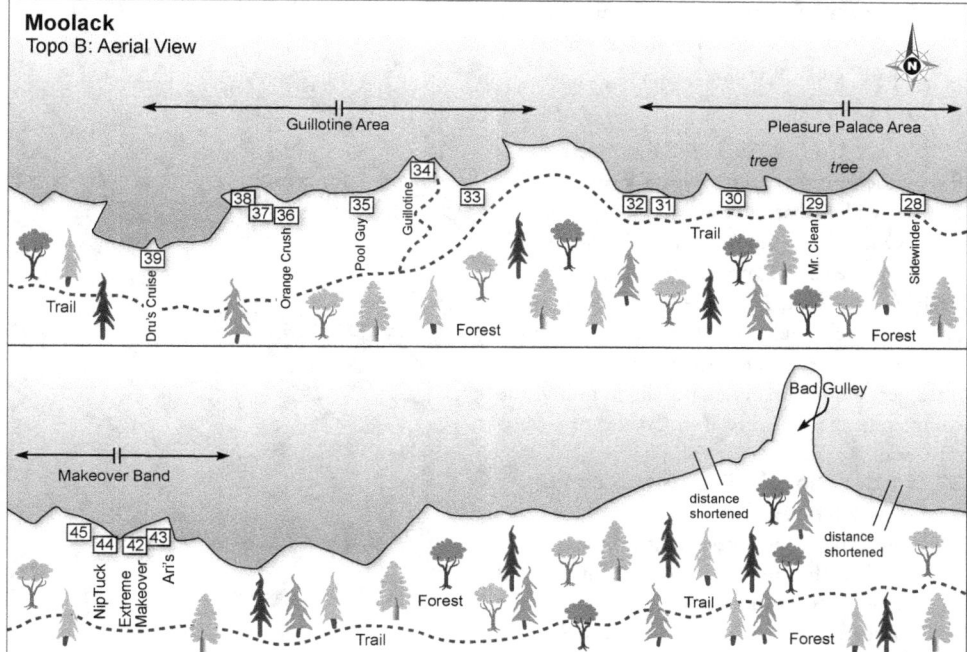

ing techniques access a ledge. From the midpoint unprotected but easy, fun lie-backing of a small free-standing fin accesses the upper portion of the crack system. The upper route, while having rest spots and positive jams, remains consistently difficult through the steep upper corner.

Variation on Hit and Run 5.10a ★★
Pro: #00 to 4½"
A linked roof variation through the middle crux of Hit and Run, avoiding M. South's original less than protected 5.8 fin slab that connects to the top 40-meter crack naturally. After the first crux, from a ledge veer slightly left to a steep chimney, climbing steep, juggy chockstones in larger protectable roofs.

31. Age Before Beauty 5.10b/c ★★★
Pro: #00 to 4½"
A left-facing book dihedral with an unknown first half that runs up a wide crack near the top.

P1 offers 5.8 climbing that remains heavily vegetated. Beta intensive movement makes for difficulty at crux.

Guillotine Area

While UTBT, ABB and Two Beers and a Baby hide in tight forest cover, a large visibility window will expose Guillotine and its namesake flake. Once the Guillotine flake is found it is easy to locate the neighboring Pool Guy with its slasher finger crux. The upper right side portion of Guillotine's double crack has regrown moss. Guillotine Area, though tucked in a cluster of trees gets some sunshine and shade unlike the completely shaded Mosserati Corner or Pedestal Area.

32. Under the Big Top 5.10b/c ★★
Pro: #00 to 4½"
The crux is an overhanging lie-back off-width with some enduring run out. Tucked between ABB and TBAB, this line actually shares a finish with Two Beers and A Baby.

33. Two Beers and a Baby 5.10- ★★★
Pro: #00 to 4½"
This quality two-pitch climb shares the first 10' of Guillotine, and then moves right to a dihedral crack system. A 5.10- face move crux with funky pro is presented mid first pitch. Finishes in a corner dihedral immediately left of Under the Big Top. One of the better 5.10's here.

34. Guillotine 5.10a ★★★
Pro: Multiple #00 to 3½" cams, nuts, and hexes
A long well protected climb. From the base good holds lead up to a 5.9 stem and jam section linking a mantle move to access the mid-point ledge. Pool Guy is accessible from this ledge. Easy climbing leads to a distinctive undercling flake (the Guillotine) with finger-sized jams and jugs. Stem and utilize both left and right cracks of the Guillotine. After a section of lie-backs and jams the left crack offers 5.10a single crack line. Avoid the overgrown trees blocking the last 20-meters of the right crack. Continue up the left crack using large featured face holds and ledges with ample cracks for gear and occasional jams. At the end of the pitch there is a large tree anchor and belay chair. *Named after the undercling flake at half height. Warning: the flake may break loose; avoid using it after the crux by moving up to better edges by stemming.*

Thad Arnold leading *Orange Crush*
Photo: T. Arnold

35. Pool Guy 5.11- ★★★★
Pro: #00 to 2½" cams and nuts

Pool Guy starts on the left side of Guillotine's mid-point ledge under a steep dihedral. Fun, moderate finger jams and toe edges offer classic climbing. As the bulge steepens foot holds disappear and the crack thins to just finger tips. A distinctive crux consists of a high reach fingertip jam off of thin toe jams, followed by more face hold options. Moderate climbing and protection to the tree anchor at the edge of the cliff band. A true classic for its relative grade. Hand size makes a definitive difference (small hands puts climb in .10+ range). *Possibly clean aided by Bobby Pool, a Eugene climber in early 2000s.*

36. Orange Crush 5.11 ★★★★
Pro: #00 to 2½" cams and nuts

Stellar climb marked by a distinctive Z-shaped crack. This route shares its first 20' with Wide-

spread Panic and has a large base stance. The shared start is a 5.9 flaring chimney. Where Orange Crush breaks right a 5.8 low angle crack leads to an overhung roof pod. A crucial rest is found before 25' of steep finger crack climbing (¾") ending at a large jug handhold. A 20' 5.9 finger crack in a ramp ends with a no hands rest. Move out left to 5.9 face climbing using widely spaced solid gear. The belay lies 30' beyond the cliff edge (static line suggested).

37. Widespread Panic (aka The Wave) 5.10c ★★★

Pro: #00 to 5" cams (1 small sliding nut, brass nuts, #5 RP at the crux)

Blends finger-to-fist size crack climbing with face climbing on minimal protection. From the base stance (also utilized for OC) the line starts with well spaced thin*ish* finger jams following the crack arching left. Some rest points with sustained climbing throughout. Pure face climbing technique is necessary as the crack becomes a seam (thin pro). When the crack widens the route steepens with awkward jams and stemming in a corner near the top. A tree belay marks the end of the line.

38. Full Circle 5.10b ★★★★

Pro: #00 to 3" cams, nuts, and hexes

Parallel and to the climber's right of Dru's Cruise, a large belay ledge 30-meters off the deck exposes a leaner left-facing dihedral above an exposed ledge. The slightly less than vertical slab is tackled by well spaced finger jams in a crack heading left with small foot edges. These initial ledges are riddled with prickly Oregon Grape plants. The crack heads to a left facing dihedral with a steep overhead roof. One steep bulge leads to the next, all surmounted with bomber finger and fist jams. The middle crux section is awkward stemming and foot jams in a steep crack with some positive jams. The last 40' of the climb diverts right (primary crack), or can use a thinner left splitter crack (multitude of face holds). This ends on a small ledge, and a few scramble moves to the top of the cliff marked with a huge decaying tree that can be used as an anchor point. Use longer webbing for other nearby trees.

39. Dru's Cruise 5.10a ★★★★
Pro: #00 to 5" cams, nuts, and hexes

Pre-2009 this climb started by gaining a large ledge system utilizing dirty blocky climbing either right of the large roof visible from the base, or extremely left up an easy dirty 5.7. Bill Soule established the stunning 5.9 first pitch heading directly at Dru's distinctive off-the-belay-ledge crux visible from the base of the band. From the initial base stance after Bill's Dru's Direct 7-meters of fun, easy climbing to a large ledge with a yellow flake sets up the routes overall crux. A 5.10- crux move utilizes thin finger jams leaving this flake at its apex, onto a steep face with small*ish* feet. A reach and mantle move leads to another ledge. The upper 30-meters are exposed with a mix of 5.6 face and fist jams with available body jams. Once past a short bulge at the top the difficulty eases. Tree belay at the cliffs

Mike South leading *Extreme Makeover* Photo: M. South

edge. *Name was coined after a student traveler cleaned the route in early 2000s, though he never attempted its lead.*

40. Dru's Direct 5.9 ★★★
Pro: ___

The new direct leading up to the midway ledge. Protection consistent with Dru's but an extra couple TCU's may help for direct.

41. Noodle Cracker 5.10a ★★
Pro: ___

A 2-pitch climb near where the trail goes into a shady area and right up next to the rock.

Bad Gulley

A trailside bright reddish-orange colored 40' pillar with a large trench below it (part of the trail) indicates end of Guillotine Area and its junction with Bad Gulley. The trail dips downhill into a shady brushy region beyond this pillar. Avoid using Bad Gulley (loose rock, dirt slopes). Subsequent Gulley's (e.g. Gold Gulley) have steep paths to the top of the cliff band. A second Gulley just after Mosserati is a bit more reasonable, but still a risky scramble with loose blocks, dirt and slippery leaves. The Gold Gulley is a feasible scramble with a minor trail that can be utilized to access the top. The east end walk-up is longer, but easiest and well traveled.

Makeover Band

There are routes (some not listed here) between Dru's Cruise and Extreme Makeover that are easy to miss because the trail runs flush to the cliff band with minimal visibility. As the trail dips away from the cliff next, the highly visible wide cracks of Extreme Makeover, Dangerous Toys, and Nip Tuck/Tic Talk along with a large boulder field below, make Makeover Band a difficult to miss

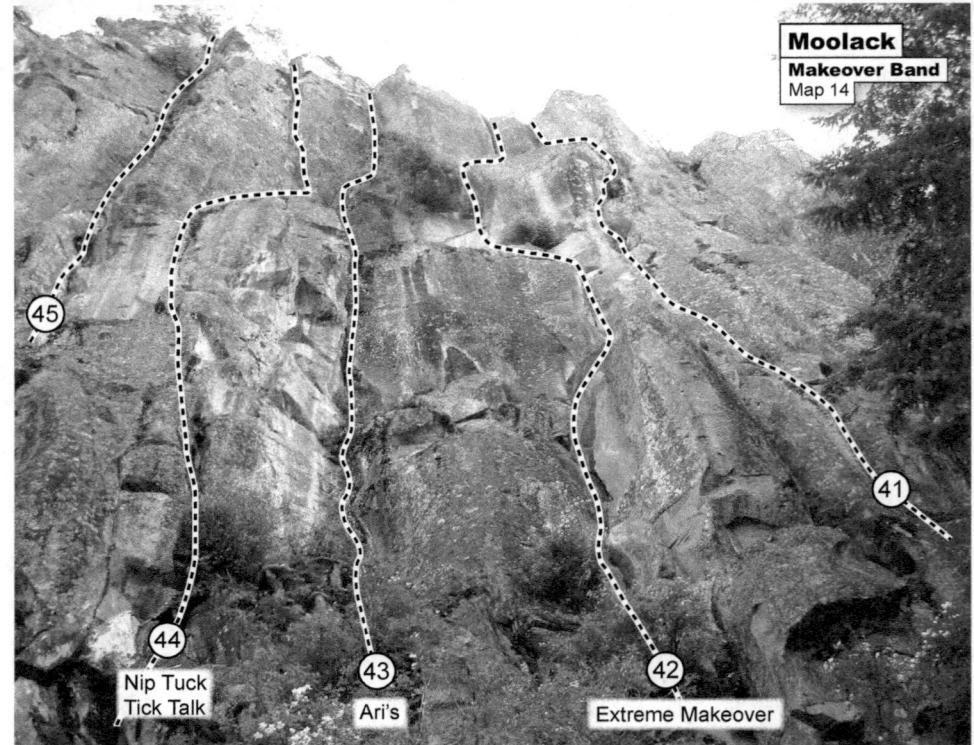

area. On a sunny day this area can be seen from road #750 campground.

42. Extreme Makeover 5.10+ ★★★★
Pro: ¼" to 6" cams, nuts, hexes, Big Bro's (70m rope needed)
A short uncleaned 5.6 section gains a small stance and the start of cleaned climbing. Easy finger jamming, alternating lie-back and stemming moves are used to access a ledge that breaks the continuous crack where the route splits in two directions. Continue left to access the ledge under a small tree (avoid going right into loose uncharted territory). Moderate climbing leads to a second ledge shared with a tree. This lower ledge sets up the 5.10- finger crux and mantle to a larger ledge. The upper pitch off-width should be set up with the belayer on this larger ledge. A chockstone breaks the off-width into two parts. The lower part of the crux is awkward and requires contorted leg jams. The mental crux involves nauseating exposure and awkward off-width movements in the upper pitch. Once the chockstone is gained the lead climber is prepared for the final crux off-width section. Anchoring at the top is best with big-bros or 4"+ cams or static line to bridge the distance from the tree to the edge of the band. *Before year 2000 this route was known as Dan's Chimney. Dan Crow, a Eugene guide had cleaned and TR'd the route.*

43. Ari's Dihedral 5.11 [?]
Gear: ¼" to 5" cams, nuts, hexes, and Big Bro's
Cleaned and likely TR'd in 2001 but never led. Access this upper thin finger crux from the same last ledge as Extreme Makeover's end crux. The upper pitch of Ari's is apparently more difficult, steeper than Extreme Makeover consisting of thin tips crack climbing. It is a micro thin crack in a 90° stem box. If people could get their fingers in it, it would have been lead by now. Tops out same as Extreme Makeover, with same anchoring considerations.

44. Nip Tuck / Tic Talk 5.10+, 5.11b/c ★★★

Pro: #00 to Size 6 cams, nuts, big bros

Mike South cleaned and climbed this route bottom to top in 2007. Karsten Duncan had formerly cleaned and rappelled into and led large portions of the route in the early 2000's. This route is located in a dihedral near MWAD. It has two short crux sections. It has mostly thin pro. Karsten said this is the best and hardest line that he put up at Moolack, by first rap cleaning and removing a wedged keg-sized block before freeing the climb.

45. Morning Wood Afternoon Delight 5.10b/c ★★★

Pro: ½" to 3" cams, nuts, and hexes, multiples of ¾" sized gear

A multi-pitch climb (depends on rope length and rope drag) that shares a first pitch with Extreme Makeover. Led ground-up for the full length of the cliff band. When an obvious tree is encountered a 2" cam placement marks where the route deviates from Extreme Makeover. An

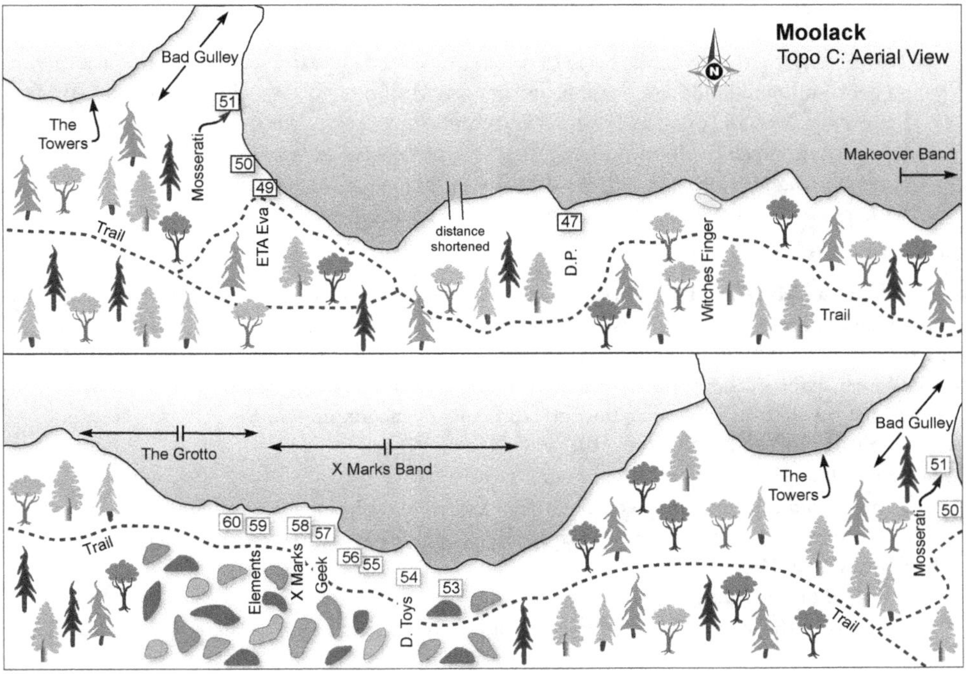

OW chimney section in the upper portion is eased by a thin finger crack.

46. _____ (project lines)

While a multitude of potential route exist between Witches Finger and D.P., currently D.P. sits alone, amongst a series of uncleaned gem lines and the minimally cleaned Witches Finger. A distinctive column dubbed by Karsten when developing Mosserati a stone's throw away splits away from the band with a wide crack route up the fingers backside.

47. D.P. 5.10c ★★★

Pro: #00 to 6" cams, nuts, hexes, Big Bro's, doubles in larger size

This three pitch route is located just after the Witches Finger. The first pitch is a shallow dihedral at 5.8. The second pitch is a short 50' long 5.10b to a ledge, and the last pitch is an off-width/chimney for about 50'. Beta in detail: P1 Climb a 5.8*ish* crack/corner system using the crack for hands and gear and the walls for feet/stemming (pro small/medium cams). The pitch ends at an obvious ledge/alcove where the crack widens and steepens quickly. The climbing is much cleaner from here onwards. P2 The crack starts overhanging and is a wide off-width most of the way. Lead out from the belay using medium cams (2", 3", 3½" etc.) with strenuous fist jamming (5.10b/c) and foot jamming, too. The crack straightens and gets dead vertical using fist jams, hand jams, and a few edges. Traverse right from a crack a bit to a big ledge with a large flake (nuts and small cams for belay). P3 Traverse back across from the belay to the crack. Ascend an easier section of the crack (5.9*ish*) on good jams and holds to a bulging, overhanging chimney (5.10a) using feet on the right face. Place a #6 Camalot (or other big gear) and shuffle up till you clear the lip of the overhang and mantle up to finish the hard climbing. Belay from the trees and rap down. *D.P. stands for Dave Patterson who was involved with the development of the route, but not its FA. Thank you Julian Buck for the amazing route section by section breakdown.*

Mosserati Corner

Where the Makeover Band tapers down to long single pitch lines (before The Towers formation) small quality corner lines exist in a southwest facing orientation. Mosserati was the original line here and other lines added after 2006. This area offers many of the best parts of the Classic Cracks area: shade in the summer, and quality single pitch lines. The second tier of the Mosserati Corner does make it slightly taller, but little difficulty is encountered in the extra top section.

48. Project Helter Skelter 5.10b ★★

Pro: #00 to 4½" cams, hexes, and nuts

Top-roped during the final working of Eta Eva and Deception Crack, this Project missed out on its final send. Protectable and fun to climb. A bit easier than other lines in the region.

49. Eta Eva 5.10b/c ★★

Pro: #00 to 4½" cams, hexes, and nuts

The crux of this route, like other nearby routes, comes in the first 30-meters. While seemingly

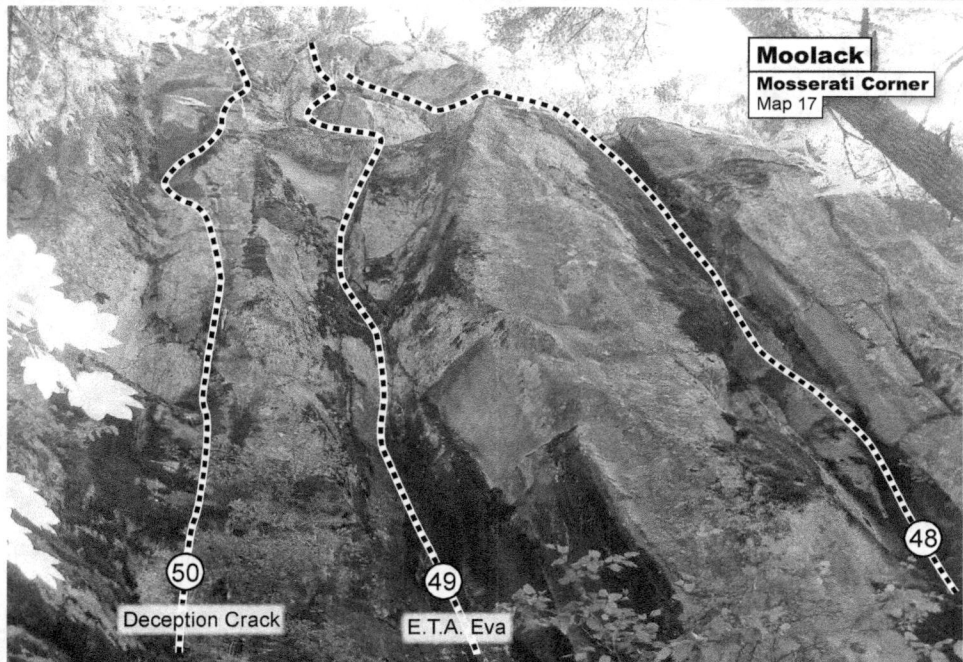

steeper than the neighboring Deception Crack, this line provides secure crux jams with viable pro. Low angle terrain gives way to a series of ledges. Belay here if tackling the remaining 5.8 section as a second pitch. This ledge may be accessed via the first portion of DeCr. Rope drag is an issue in the upper reaches of this route if done in one pitch due to the low angled nature of the second half. A blank section of face up high between EE and DeCr may make viable 5.11 lead terrain (TR so far).

50. Deception Crack 5.10c/d ★★
Pro: #00 to 3½" cams, hexes, and nuts

Climb up edges and thin cracks to a ledge stance a few meters off the deck. A tricky 5.9 crux mantle gains this rest ledge (place #00's, brass units below it). A 1"-1½" finger sized crack offers pro and jams while stemming through a 5.10c/d crux. Move left of an overhead column bottom through a bulge past the second crux and up to easy terrain at midway ledges (EE joins here on ledges). Deception Crack avoids the TR boulder problem (mentioned in ETA Eva) by wrapping around left (ETA Eva wraps right) up easy jams to low angle easier terrain to the top. All routes in the Mosserati Corner are done in two pitches even with a 70-meter rope (lengthy stretch of rock from cliff top to tree anchors). *Named after Deception Creek in Westfir, and its manageable grade despite appearances.*

51. Mosserati 5.10a ★★
Pro: #00 to 4½" cams, hexes, and nuts

Mosserati climbs the relatively low angled fist-sized

Mike South on *Perverts in Paradise*
Photo archive: Mike South

crack up to a horizontal break under a tree to the furthest left of the cliffband before a breach near The Towers. Move right into the corner that separates the pillar and main band. This route does not utilize the obvious tree as a mid-climb P1 belay point, but actually gains the second ledge staying left and avoiding the upper pitch of Deception Crack. P1 is a long first pitch and P2 is much shorter. This route offers high quality technique and movement. *Mike South mentioned that Slover had minimally cleaned and climbed this line. Originally minimally cleaned and climbed (unrecorded) by Shane "Parn" Slover. Duncan (inspired by this mossy line) re-cleaned and led the route. By 2008 the foliage and moss has returned. The start of Mosserati, though re-cleaned a third time in 2010 with the introduction of new lines in the area, retains a mossy start.*

The Towers

52. _____ (project lines)

This amorphous lump of towers and wall offers climbing, but may offer top-roping challenges and more than normal fracturing than other walls. It is a short section of wall, offering a half dozen to dozen routes at most. Topping out, you may have to down-scramble back to sturdy ground for anchoring.

X-Marks Band

The X-Marks Band begins just after The Towers. The trail under it is visible from Mosserati Corner (The Towers is not very large). The X-Marks Band hosts a large sun-soaked open expanse of face and crack climbing with a sparsely wooded talus/scree field below it. Its possible to walk right past Dangerous Toys (faces southwest) due to foliage along the trail. Where the trail dips downhill and flattens, views behind you of the band reveal a large ledge 15' off the deck that marks Dangerous Toys. Beyond both X-Marks The Spot and Elements of Style the trail reenters the woods limiting views of the Grotto. Routes at this part of the cliff band are very tall and can be difficult to distinguish one from another. An obvious 'X' is formed by two crack systems at a steep roof section acting as a guide to locate this and other routes in the area.

53. Project Happy Rapping 5.10+ ★★

Pro: #00 to 3" cams, nuts, and hexes (doubles in 1"+)

The face crack to the right of Dangerous Toys, and the common rappel for nearby routes. Happy Rapping has been TR'd, but not led free. A large ledge with a large tat wrapped tree parallel to Dru's Cruises' midpoint crux transition is the end of HR's first pitch.

54. Dangerous Toys 5.10+ ★★★★
Pro: #00 to 3" cams, nuts, and hexes

From a large ledge roughly 15' off the trail finger jam and stem in a left-facing corner dihedral till you gain a mid-point ledge where the crack bends slightly left at a steep bulge. A large tree at this ledge (utilized as a rappel) is part of the PHR top-rope finger to fist jam line. The route splits at this ¾ mark; the right variation is Scared Alive, while Dangerous Toys traverses horizontally left via stems and face holds into the next dihedral (use care to avoid dislodging any "dangerous toys" loose rock). *Name coined from the loose rock avoided by the FAists by utilizing alternative crack and face holds.*

55. Scared Alive (variation) 5.4 C1
Climb P1 of Dangerous Toys taking a right variation at the ¾ point roof bulge, before DT's left deviation. A step-off ledge will avoid the loose roofs; walk out onto a thin ramp to a body jam OW (5.4) and continue to the top. *Name coined during a wet winter day solo clean-aid ascent. Loose rocks along the traverse fell and sliced the climber's rope at the ground anchor, momentarily stranded him on a ledge just short of the cliff top. An easy, but loose chimney gained the top resulting in the aided start with a free finish variant.*

56. Bag Full of Hammers 5.10+/ 5.11- ★★★
Pro: #00 to 4½" cams, nuts, and hexes

A start-less gem that can be linked into from Dangerous Toys' start. A P2 variant to Dangerous Toys. This line is further left than the normal Scared Alive and Happy Rapping.

57. Geek on a Leash 5.12a ★★★★
Pro: #00 to 4½" cams, nuts, and hexes

A three-pitch climb with a 5.12- crux (starts at a nice base belay stance). Climb to a small mid-point belay ledge. From the left side of a small ledge move and climb past a steep crux roof that has steep hand jams. The climb eases to 5.10a where the crack arcs and pinches down to finger jamming in another left facing dihedral. A four star classic at its grade.

58. X-Marks the Spot 5.11+/5.12- or 5.10 C2 ★★★★
Pro: #00 to 2" including a #1 BD C4, lots of RP's, Ballnuts, Brass (or aid gear C2)

P1 consists of thin finger-climbing. Crux section is visible in the black roof where the crack system forms a distinctive 'X'. P2 is steep 5.9 climbing, then a short bit of overhung aid (wet black streak), then more 5.10

Moolack
X-marks Band
Map 19

(54) Dangerous Toys

Mike Holmes leading *Bold Deli Flavor*
Photo: *Thad Arnold*

climbing. P3 consists of steep crack climbing leading to an anchor 40' from the top. The route remained mixed free/aid till 2007/8, then true to good form Mike sent the route in free style, making quite a legendary story for Moolack. Can be done as a two pitch route (or one pitch using long runners). Less than suitable opportunities for belay before the routes ¾ mark. The crux consists of run-out difficulty past a #1 Ball-nut.

59. Elements of Style 5.11a ★★★★
Pro: #00 to 3" cams, hexes, nuts (Ball-nuts may help)

P1 has a low 5.11a crux in the first 30-meters. The line ends left of a log at the bands top edge between the two cracks. The route remains straight through P2 involving steep terrain with 5.10 crux followed by 5.9 jamming. Those who have climbed this route claim that, despite the appearance, the upper portion is manageable if you are capable of climbing the lower crux.

Mike South leading *Plumber's Crack*
Photo archive: *M. South*

The Grotto

All views of The Grotto are obscured by tree cover along the trail. It is an area just short of the Goldband developed between 2008 and 2010.

60. Case of the Blues 5.11 ★★★★
Pro: #00 to 2", ball-nuts, RPs, doubles in thin pro (TCU's helpful)

Start to the left of Elements of Style and wrap into The Grotto, this route divides the two

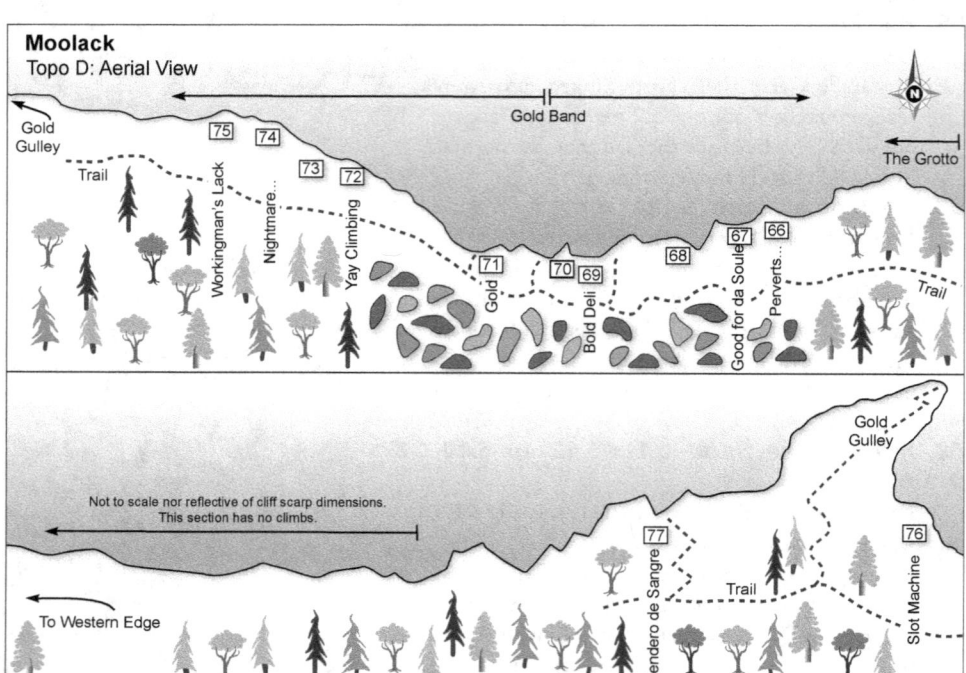

walls. While the top is often dirty, this route stands proudly with other classic lines of the region. One crux consists of 10 feet of thin hands.

61. Whiskey River 5.10+ / 5.11- ★★

Pro: ____

Located at the start of the Grotto where X-Marks Band ends, linking X-Marks to Goldband.

62. Jessie's Route, Wish That I Had 5.11+ ★★★★

Pro: #00 to 2" cams, nuts, RP's, brass nuts, and sliding nuts

An impressively proud two pitch line incorporating very thin pro on a thin crack line. The initial pitch is 5.11d and the top pitch is slightly easier at 5.11c. Located next to Whiskey River. From the bottom, this route is in between Case of the Blues and Perverts. Jessie's Route is two lines right of BKS.

63. Best Kept Secret 5.11a ★★

Pro: #00 to 5" nuts, cams, TCU's and Ballnuts

A new (2011) route with no beta other than its location and difficulty. A climber who's sent it rated it at ★★★ if it stays clean. Located two lines left of Jessie's Route.

64. Locked and Loaded 5. 11+/- ★★★

Pro: #00 to 3½" nuts, hexes, cams, RP's, and brass nuts

Lots of 5.10 climbing with an overhanging section of fingers, reminiscent to Pool Guy. Located 4 -5 cracks to the left of Jessie's Route.

65. False Alarmageddon 5.11b ★★★

Pro: #00 to 5" cams, nuts, hexes

Currently (as of 2012) the left most route in the Grotto. Belay from a small tree, or a small ledge 8' off the trail where medium cams suffice for an anchor. A bouldery start makes way to steep blocky moves that traverse right into a 5" crack. Jam and lie-back this crack to a minor stance with a roof over head. Exposed climbing out and around the roof leads to the next 20' of overhanging fingers. This finger crack ends with flaring hands when the steepness lets up. Another 20' beyond the cliffs edge finish the route at a tree anchor.

The Goldband

The most stunning swath of cliff band at Moolack, tall and loaded with plenty of stellar rock climbs. As unlikely as it may seem numerous untapped lines still exist here between completed routes and at the outer flanks of Goldband, before Perverts and after Gold. The upper cliff edge involves low angle technical (often unprotected) scrambling just to reach the forest above. Goldband has forged an energetic group of route developers into a commendable ground-up on-site movement involving risk, aid ascents, and free ascents, resulting in a historical legacy known far and wide, with plenty of room for more route lines. Average height of this section of wall is 240'.

66. Perverts in Paradise P1 5.10c, P2 5.10b ★★★★

Pro: ½" to 3" cams, nuts and hexes

Three pitches of flaring overhung crack climbing. A high quality climb. A friend proposed that it might be led as one single pitch, but this may require an 80-meter rope. Perverts In Paradise and Good For The Soule share the first 100' pitch with a slight leftward veer in a left-facing dihedral. The second pitch for both PIP and GFTS are within 10' of each other, GFTS on the left, PIP to the right, both finishing well right of the large obvious 2nd pitch pillar close to Southern Exposure. Perverts in Paradise is characterized as finger-to-hand-to-fist (mostly hands), while GFTS offers tight fingers.

67. Good for the Soule 5.10+ ★★★

Pro: ½" to 3" cams, nuts and hexes

This route shares the first pitch anchor with Perverts in Paradise. It has a low crux and a midroute crux. The crux is "tight fingers and more of a fitness crux" than PIP.

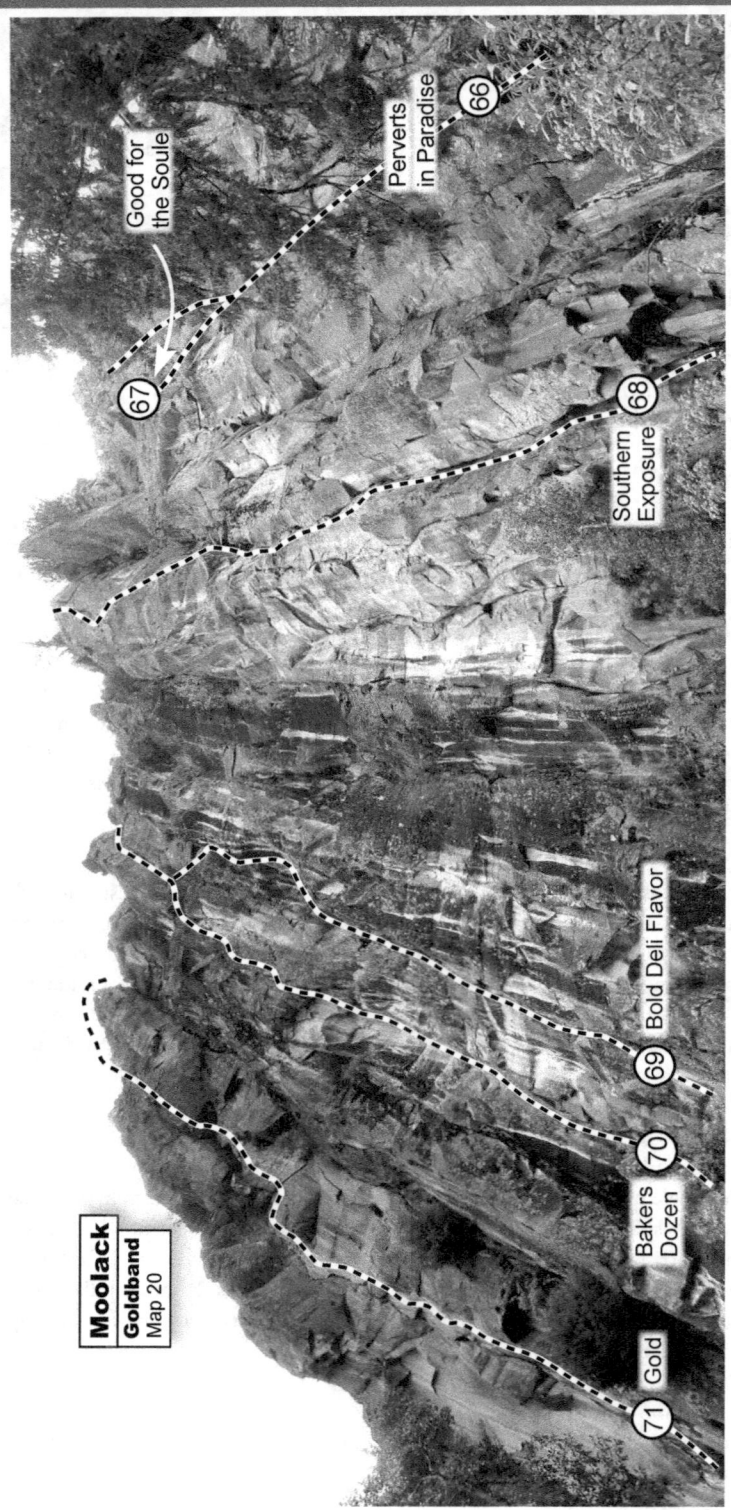

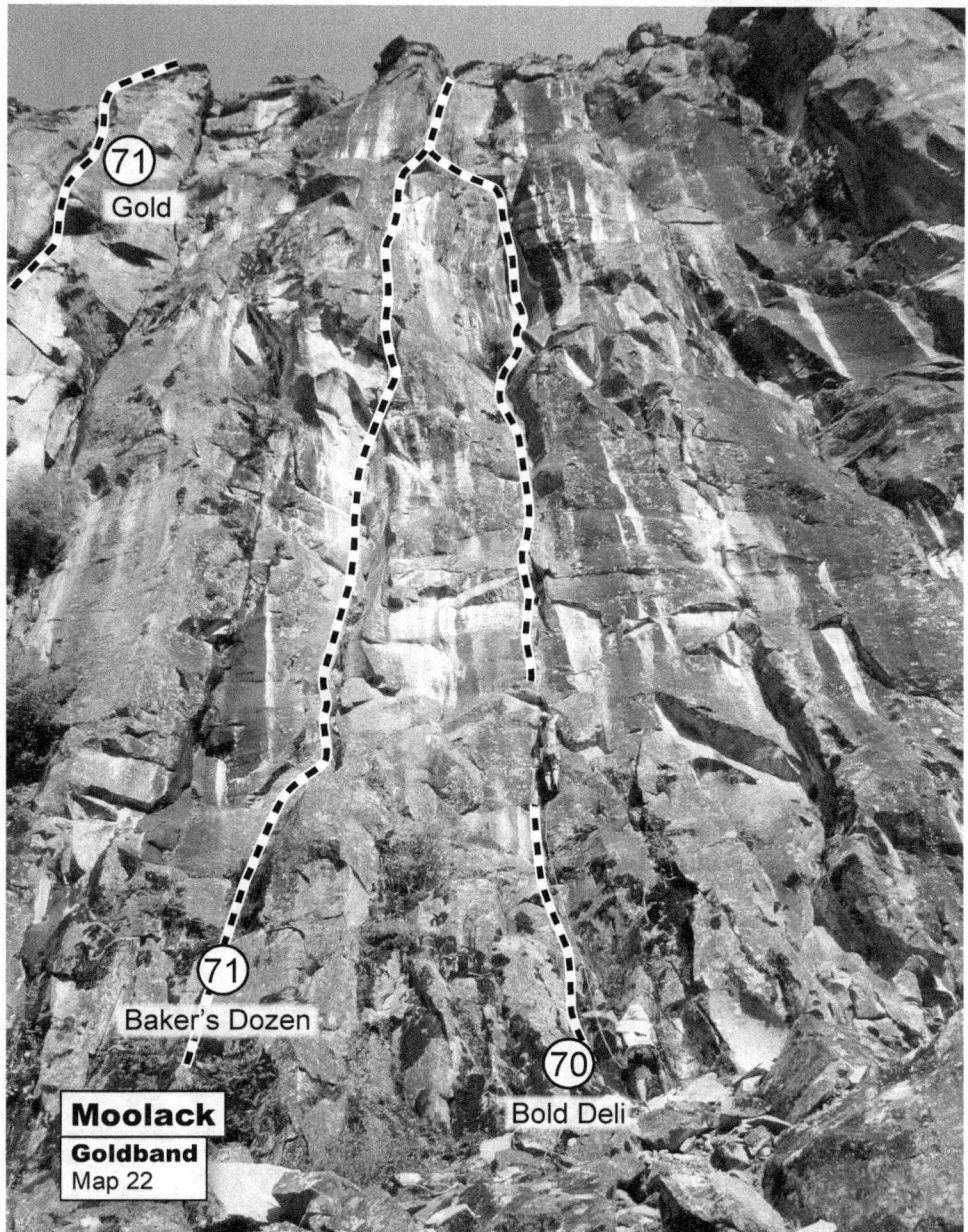

68. Southern Exposure 5.11+/ 5.12- ★★★★
Pro: #00 to 3½" cams, brass nuts, sliding nuts helpful
This two pitch climb (235' high) sends one of the left-of-center lines on the Goldband. P1 is 5.11+, and P2 is 5.11 with three well protected cruxes. Expect some sections of 5.10 and a short section of 5.8 in the middle, and the last pitch is reminiscent to Orange Crush with a slasher finger crack. Originally done in two pitches, but with some rope drag. Breaking it into three leads presents crux/belay challenges. This route climbs the path of least resistance using variable options for gear, weaving in and out of the crack system.

69. Bold Deli Flavor   P1 5.11-, P2 5.11
★★★★

Pro: #00 to 3½" nuts, cams, and hexes, doubles in 2-3", triples ¾"-1½"cams. RP's and sliding nuts as well. (Full pro notes from FA'ist: RP's, blue, red and yellow Ballnuts, doubles from grey (#00) Metolius to yellow (#2), triples of orange (#3) Metolius, doubles above that to 2", one 3" and 3½" piece).

This route was initially climbed by Max as a 5.10 C1 with hangs on gear throughout the crux sections. Max returned and red-pointed the climb identifying the first pitch as 5.11- and the upper pitch as 5.11/5.10+. It breaks cleanly in half in two pitches at an obvious ledge beneath a left-facing dihedral. Use small gear on P1, and big gear for P2.

70. Baker's Dozen 5.12+/- ★★★

Pro:#00 to 2.5", many ball-nuts, RP's

To the climber's left of Bold Deli Flavor is this fine hard-core route that punches out of the biggest roofs at Moolack (at mid-route). Heady climbing up a clean white dihedral capped by a massive roof. This leads to mind-bending crux section up high. Merges with the upper right-facing corner of Bold Deli Flavor.

71. Gold 5.11 ★★★★★

Pro: #00 to 3½" cams, nuts and hexes (sliding nuts are helpful)

This route starts above an open area at the far left end of Goldband before the cliff band trail wraps around the Gold Pillar. The climb starts with easy moves and ample protection, but after 15' the route steepens using finger and hand jams splitting a face. Gear gets thin where a distinctive protected lower crux unlocks some easy climbing up to a ledge rest. Upper pitch is considered to be easier, but is steep and retains its 5.10+ difficulty. The route is longer than it appears from the base due to an extension from the top of the band to the tree anchor. After the business is over a 5.*easy* scramble runs for a long distance making it necessary to climb with a 70+ meter rope or splitting the route into pitches. *This 5-star classic readily compares to other Oregon climbs such as The Sickle and Hammer at Broughton Bluff, Delirium Tremens at Smith Rock, Dod's Jam and Blownout of Beacon Rock, J.R. Token of Trout Creek, Blackberry and Blueberry Jam of Rocky Butte and Crazy Crack*

Moolack
Goldband
Map 21

at Medicine Rock, to name a few classics in Oregon. Even at Moolack, with a plethora of high quality routes, Gold endures as "the" area classic.

72. Yay Climbing P1 5.8, P2 5.11 ★★★

Pro: #00 to 6" cams, nuts, hexes and Big Bro's

Nightmare on Madrone St. is to the left of this route. The distinguishing characteristic of this route is P2, which starts on a huge ledge, works an OW crack, powering through a crux using large fists to get over a bulge (20' above belay) into a tight squeeze chimney that gets wider all the way to the top. About ¾ up the corner the crack splits; one crack goes straight up the headwall (11a? with sporty moves and loose blocks). Climb out left further and up blocks in another crack to a gigantic ledge belay under a large overhang with a 4-6" crack in it (20' lead approx). Ideally (per FA-ists), a 5.11a P2 through the upper headwall will be the better finish for this gem. Leader took two 30'-40' whipper falls trying to lead the 5.11 headwall, ripping out a few wrist-sized trees during each fall.

Moolack
Goldband
Map 23

73. Up an Alchemists' Sleeve 5.10+ ★★

Pro: #00 to 4" cams, nuts, hexes

Probably developed by Caleb at about the time that Workingman's Lack was completed. Another nearby route (Way of the Alchemist) also linked to the college student 'Caleb' indicate he set a few lines at Moolack. The route starts with 5.8- finger-sized crack climbing, bending to the right to access a large belay ledge marked by a gnarled tree. A consistent straight forward climb that ends at a brush choked pillar top (several yards from a tree anchor). *The Way of the Alchemist:* Rumored ascent by Karsten Duncan, but FAist likely named the line after Karsten's influence. Karsten moved to Las Vegas and began developing all natural boltless lines and bolted routes in the Red Rocks Canyon and surrounding region.

74. Nightmare on Madrone Street 5.10b ★★

Pro: ½" to 3½" cams, nuts, and hexes

Only P1 (80') has been established and was originally done ground up because the line looked inviting and naturally clean. P1 consists of fingers at the bottom, hand jams at the middle till the crack widens to wide hands at the top. Easy to identify with Workingman's Lack to the left of the dead tree, and NOMS to its right. Potential second pitch of overhanging OW.

75. Workingman's Lack 5.9 ★★

Pro: #1 TCU's to 3½" cams, nuts, hexes, sliding nuts (nice but not crucial)

Ground up first ascent that utilized the obvious dead tree at a mid-climb belay. From the base trail the route starts as a 5.8- finger-to-fist crack in a left leaning corner. The lower section ends on the ledge with the gnarled tree. Rather than heading right (NOMS) Workingman's Lack climbs behind the upper pillar, then aims slightly left in an arching crack with foot ledges and a large crack with flared sections. The top of the cliffband is choked with madrone and brush.

76. Slot Machine 5.10b ★★

Pro: #00 to 3½" cams, nuts and hexes

Slot Machine is the upper part of a single pitch wall with a convenient midway belay ledge. The route is located left of Gold on a short section of the cliff band. Begin up a 5.9 body slot chimney off the starting ledge to a two move mid-point crux (5.10b), then 5.9 jams to the end of the climb. A stellar line, but needs a base linkup as the climb has only been led via rappelling in from above. *Name coined after the 5.9 body-slot chimney off the starting ledge.*

Sendero Section

After the Gold route on the Goldband you enter an area obscured by low foliage, however the Gold Gulley is easy to find as it's the cliff bands next big break. The very obvious Sendero Tower is just beyond the Gold Gulley. Sendero De Sangre splits the center of the Sendero Tower. The non-existent trail wraps around Sendero Wall and heads slightly uphill. An unclimbed swath of route potential lay beyond. The Western Edge Turn-around and Shangri-La are all unclimbed "final" walls.

77. Sendero De Sangre 5.10d ★★★★

Pro: #00 to 3" cams, nuts, and hexes, doubles 1" to 1½"

The band height shortens but still has route potential clear to the Western Edge. To get to this route, scramble uphill from the non-trail to a small ledge at the base of this primary splitter crack (veers rightward). Thin finger/hand jamming with thin toe jams, but infrequent foot edges and smears. Viable pro opportunities in the horizontal features.

Western Edge Turn-Around / Shangri-La

The remaining cliff formation over to the Western Edge Turn-around, while never developed, has garnished visual interest. Some obvious gems will eventually see development here.

78. On the Road to Shangri-La 5.10c/d (TR) ★★

The climb is located on the north flank of a large pillar near the cliffs western point. The route starts in a protectable crack from a short ledge leading up to positive holds on a steep face with sporadic odd minor cracks. A quality climb, minimally cleaned, but viable pro options feasible if cleaned further. TR only to date.

Karsten leading Sendero de Sangre, Photo collection: K. Duncan

Select climbs in the land of Juniper trees

CHAPTER 9

CENTRAL OREGON

This region is primarily known to the rock climbing world through Smith Rock's popularity as the early roots of American sport climbing. Today, Central Oregon has a plethora of limitless rock climbing opportunities that a brief analysis of this sort taps only a small fragment of the entire beast.

This small chapter includes several wild adventures such as Twin Pillars, including a brief introduction to Trout Creek, the stellar crack climbing paradise near Madras. Though not an extremely common destination, the beta for Steins Pillar in the Ochoco mountains will hopefully spark your interest to climb there. The spire has seen increased climber activity in recent years, and a detailed historical study of the entire Steins Group is an quintessential part of the sport of rock climbing in Oregon.

STEINS PILLAR

Route information courtesy of Chip Miller, Kent Benesch, Gavin Ferguson

Steins Pillar is an impressive 350' tall tower with a steeply overhanging aspect on all sides. This light-colored rock tower with its dark red summit cap stands out well above the forested pine trees overlooking the idyllic ranches on the upper Mill Creek valley in the Ochoco mountains northeast of Prineville, Oregon.

The monolith is composed of moderately welded tuff from pyroclastic flows typical of dacitic or rhyolitic ash eruptions, a relatively soft light-colored rock, deposited in deep layers from a series of volcanic eruptions that were part of the John Day Formation. While still hot the soft ash compacted to form a solid layer of rock. Erosional processes gradually swept away the surrounding lesser resistant landscape, leaving this monolithic feature cresting the hillside. Soft welded tuff ash formations often lack the type of solid rock that climbers appreciate most. Putting quality aside, climbers still energetically opt to scale this impressive tower enduring the chossy nature of the scarp. The pillar was named in honor of an 1860s explorer Major Enoch Steen of the U.S. Army, and although misspelled the incorrect version eventually became official.

How To Get There

The pillar is located roughly 19 miles northeast of the town of Prineville, Oregon. From downtown Prineville drive east on U.S. 26 for 10 miles (MP 28) and turn left (north) onto the paved Mill Creek road. At 5.1 miles the pavement ends, but continue on Mill Creek road for another 1½ miles

Chris stylin' P4 on *Steins Pillar*

to the road junction for Steins Pillar trailhead.

From the junction to the Trailhead:
Turn right (east) at the road junction sign crossing a small bridge and continue uphill on FS500 for exactly 2 miles. The trailhead site is a small turnaround loop on the north side of the forest road with a USFS self-registration permit box where you can attain a free permit for hiking on the trail.

Hike north on a well-maintained trail for 1¾ miles to the pillar. The trail initially gains elevation and then gradually descends down to the pillar to land at the saddle. Anticipate a 45-minute approach with an elevation difference of 700' as the trail descends a bit down to Steins Pillar at 4377' (1334m) elevation.

From the junction to the roadside overlook: Continue north on Mill Creek road approximately another 2 miles from the junction and park at a signed parking area on your right. This overlook provides good photographic view of Steins Pillar from just north of a ranch house. It is best not to shortcut from here to the pillar.

Steins Pillar is best suited for three season (spring-summer-fall) climbing. The pillar is located just outside of the Mill Creek Wilderness in the Ochoco National Forest.

Historical Analysis

In 1920 a local settler made the first attempt to climb the rock, using what now seems to be an absurd collection of crude equipment: ropes, ladders, wooden pegs, and boards. Years later Don Baars, Leonard Rice, and Russell Johnson reached a point above the cave, leaving a rope ladder affixed to the wall about 50' above the first major ledge. Not until 1950 after three years of labor did [several] college students reach the summit. The party used hand-forged pitons, and hand-drilled 110 holes for $^5/_8$" shell bolts during the ascent, involving hours of hanging from ropes on vertical terrain. They also invented a modified "bosun's chair" attached with pulleys with which the leader could hoist himself up from bolt to bolt while in a sitting position, while belayers

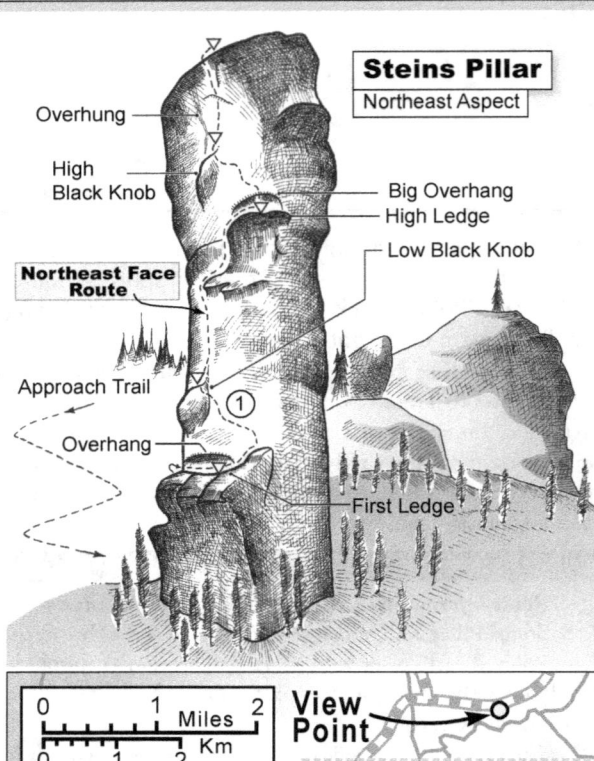

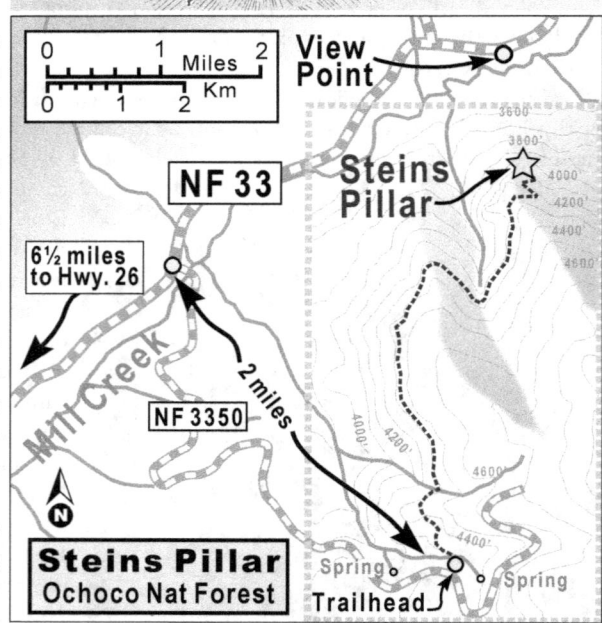

✦ CENTRAL OREGON 375

took the slack from below. On descending it was only necessary to sit back and have the belayers let him down; gravity did the work. There were frightening moments, too. At one point in the climb the constant wear on the rope caused two of the three strands of the pulley line to part. When they snapped the tension caused them to unravel for 10 feet in each direction, but somehow the remaining strand held together, while the leader was hastily lowered to the ground. Partial quote: '*A Climbing Guide To Oregon*' by Nicholas Dodge, published 1975, page 154

 Technically, only Don Baars and Floyd Richardson succeeded in reaching the summit in July 1950, but they received considerable help with drilling and belays up to the high ledge from Glenn

Richardson, Leonard Rice and R. Shay during their bold 4-day effort. The second and third ascents were completed by Fred Beckey and partners in 1963 and 1964.

1. Northeast Face   III 5.11a (or III 5.9 A2+ or C2+)

Length: 350'
Pro: mostly a small gear rack to 2" but include a 3" cam and a few pitons

The original aid rating was 5.7 A3, but newer fixed gear on the route limits some of the risk. Bring extra long webbing to alleviate the risk of getting a rope stuck on the summit rappel. Still, you should expect some loose 'chossy' rock.

P1 5.9 40': Crux boulder move to start out of the cave, and then a 5.4 jaunt up a short wide chimney to a bolt belay on a mighty big ledge.

P2 5.10c R (or 5.7 A2 or C2) 70': Walk to the far north (right) edge of the big ledge. Free climb up several feet to a leftward traversing crack, and then resort to aid (A2 or C2) for this long gradually ascending crack passing a loose block at the mid-point. As you near the belay anchor (lots of old fixed gear) you can launch into several free moves.

If you plan to free this entire pitch the technical crux (5.10d R) is just before the hollow block. The first half of this lead can be difficult to protect. The anchor bolts for top of P2 are located at right side of a nice ledge.

P3 5.10b (or 5.4 A1 or C1) 60': Begin by stepping to the left side of the ledge, and then climb up a shallow dihedral using trad gear then aim up right using mostly fixed gear past a bulge. Route wanders up left using cracks and face holds (bolts) then up right to surmount another bulge to land on a large split-level ledge. The belay anchor is located on the lower ledge.

P4 5.11a (or 5.8 A1 or C1) 60': Step up onto the upper tier of this double ledge system. The upper roomy ledge has an overhanging roof with a cool view looking out over the northwest face. This is the major halfway ledge on the monolith. To attack the next part of the climb, start on the upper ledge at a weakness in the overhang and reach up high to clip the first fixed piece.

Power past the overhang (5.11a) and follow a

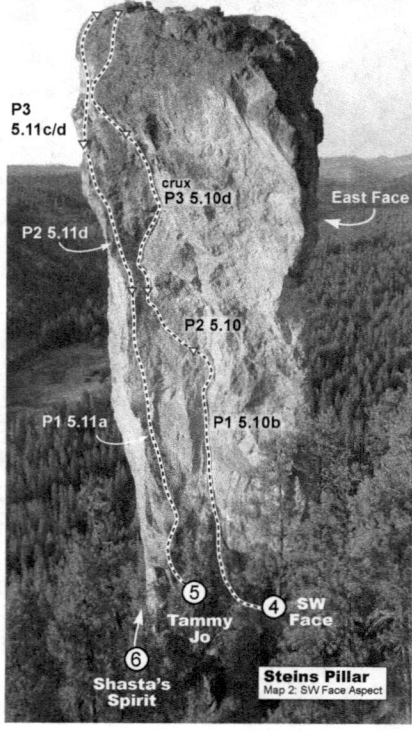

string of fixed gear directly up vertical cliff to a mantle onto a high black rock knob with a tiny ledge and bolt belay anchor.

P5 5.10d (or 5.8 A1 or C1) 60': The first fixed piece is very high and can be stick-clipped or just make a free move to it. Climb directly up a slightly overhanging wall using a ladder of fixed bolt ladder and mixed trad gear placements to a free move or two near the summit. This section can be free climbed, but beware of some of the ancient fixed gear.

Line of Descent
Rappel with two ropes from the summit anchor down to the belay anchor at the top of pitch three on the midway ledge. Rappel again with double ropes to the ground. Be sure to avoid getting your ropes stuck on the summit rappel. All the belay anchors have been upgraded to quality standards, but numerous route lead bolts and other various old fixed gear is still rather historically antiquated and should be treated with scrutiny and caution.

2. **Rocket Ride 5.9**
Length: 75', Pro: 8 QD's
Rocket Ride is a sport route variation to the big ledge on the Northeast Face route. Walk over to the right on the ground to find the start to this climb.

3. **Schmitz-Caldwell variation IV 5.7 A4**
Length: 350'
Pro: Nuts, cams, and pitons
This directisimo variation bypasses the first two pitches of the standard Northeast Face route by climbing 2 pitches of difficult rotten seam nailing. The Variation begins just to the left of the overhanging cave start at the ground. The grade IV rating covers the entire climb to the summit.

P1: Ascends vertically up a rotten seam to join at the second belay station on the standard route.

P2: Ascend another rotten crack above the belay until a tenuous nailing traverse forces you rightward to rejoin the stan-

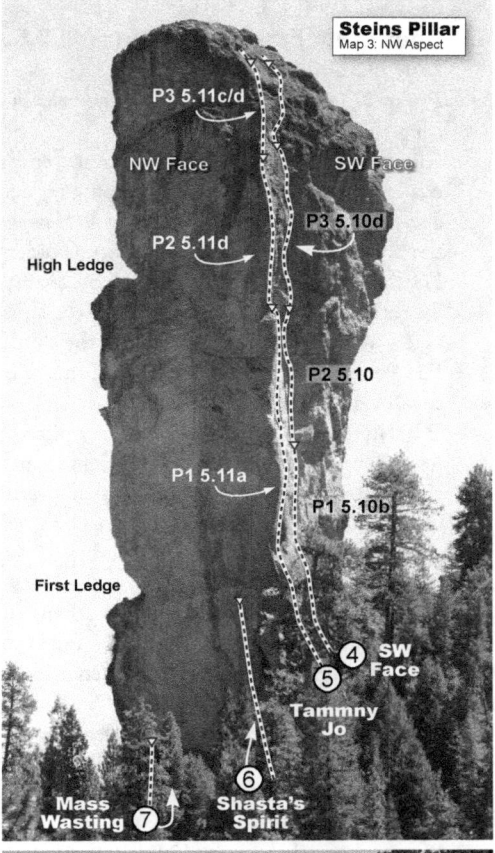

dard route at the 3rd belay.

4. **Southwest Face III 5.10d (or III 5.6 A3)**
Length: 350'
Pro to 2" including small cams and extras in the 1-1½" range

Climbers who venture up this climb tend to enjoy the challenge when done in free-climbing mode, but it probably makes a nice little aid line as well. Newer bolts exist at the belays, but still expect to find some older fixed pitons. For the most part it is a good climb on quality rock, except for rotten rock at the crux on pitch two. This route begins below an obvious corner system on the southwest face.
P1: Power your way up the crack corner dihedral system to a hanging bolt belay anchor.
P2: This lead is fixed with bolts and pitons, except for a few minor gear placements. Move left about 10' and then climb directly up a very steep face to an overhang and pass the roof on the left and move up to a bolt belay anchor at a comfortable stance.
P3: Climb over a bulge just above the belay and traverse right. Power through another overhang using bucket sized holds, and then muscle over a final crux bulge (expect about 15' of poor rock), and then march up a crack to a bolt belay anchor.
P4: Climb initially leftward up a leaning crack, move up right and then up left using long slings on your QD's. Finish up relatively easy face climbing to the top of the pillar.

Line of Descent
Rappel down the standard Northeast Face.

5. **Tammy Jo Memorial Route 5.11d**
Length: 350', Pro: 12 QD's

A difficult rock climb, and probably the best route when compared to the rock quality of the other routes that top out. My route is all bolts, so it can be climbed with quick draws only, then you can descend the north face Further left and downhill a bit is the start to this powerful line which takes on the west arête for three long leads of pure sanity to the very summit of Steins.
P1 5.11a, Pro 10 QD's: Start immediately left of the SW Face route and aim up onto a face just right of a blunt arête.
P2 5.11d, Pro 6 QD's: Power through a tough crux sequence that sends a few climbers into a bit of flight time. The climb eases to a small perch belay.
P3 5.11c/d, Pro 9 QD's: Continue up a hung section and finish to the top. Rappel route.

6. **Shasta's Spirit 5.11+**
Length: 100', Pro: 11 QD's
A powerful bolted face climb down slightly left of the Fi-

Pete G. & Chris A. on Northeast Face, Steins Pillar

nal Cut.

7. Mass Wasting 5.10a
Length: 40', Pro: 7 QD's
A bolted face climb on the lower north side of Stein's Pillar.

The Steins Pillar Group has three formations (Steins Pillar, Sideshow, & Ringside) that have existing rock climbs. The following two routes are located on the Ringside Formation.

8. Heatstroke 5.9
Multi-pitch, Pro: 10 QD's
A nice four-pitch climb on the southeast side of the Ringside formation. Descend off the trail down along the southeast side of the formation. If you see a nice thin crack with an old bolt you are a few feet too far.
P1 5.9, 3 QD's: Dance up a bolted face route up left onto steep terrain to a belay ledge.
P2 5.8, 5 QD's: Climb steep face up left to a nice large ledge and belay.
P3 5.8, 5 QD's: Climb a short steep face then dance along the ridge crest to another belay.
P4 5.9, 6 QD's: A short vertical crux on great holds ends at a belay on the summit of the east spire. From the summit of the east spire rappel directly down east 90' to a ledge. Rappel again 90' to the ground.
To get to **Money, Whiskey, Sexy** you can scramble northward along the crest of the for-

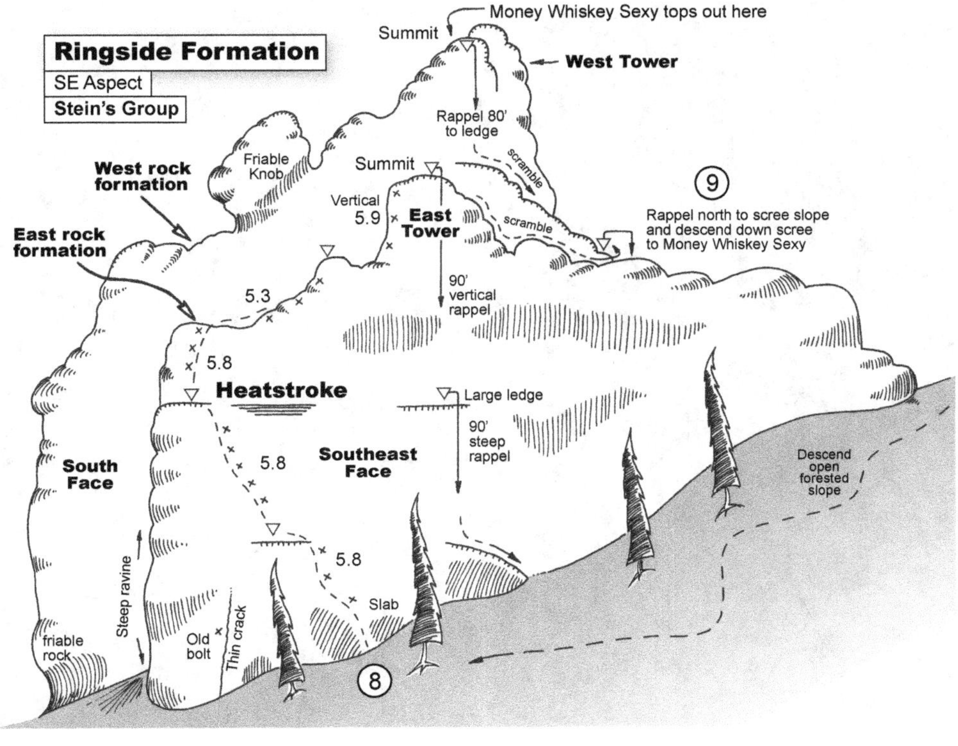

Brian on P3 *SW Face 5.10d*

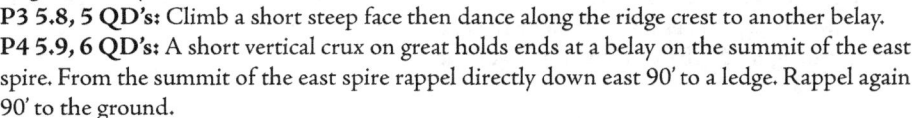

mation to the Mossy Ledges. Find a rappel anchor that allows a convenient descent down north to the scree slopes. Scramble down the scree slope to MWS.

9. **Money, Whiskey, Sexy** II 5.10a

Multi-pitch, Pro: 10 QD's, long slings, optional pro to 3", one 60m rope

Quality climb on good rock with plenty of bolts, this sport climb brings a bit of adventure into the game as it ascends a natural ridge crest with a touch of lichen, a dash of moss, and a quiet alpine feel. No frills and no waiting lines, but once you are on the route it is worth the ascent.

The best method to climb this route is to first ascend the 4-pitch **Heatstroke** route, then rap descend north off Mossy Ledges down the cliff scarp northward. Slide down the scree slope west to the start of Money-Whickey-Sexy near the base of the west face.

Or...stash your pack and gear along the upper north side of the Ringside formation. Scramble down a steep scree slope 150' along the edge of the formation. The route begins up left of the overhanging cliff base of Ringside's west face.

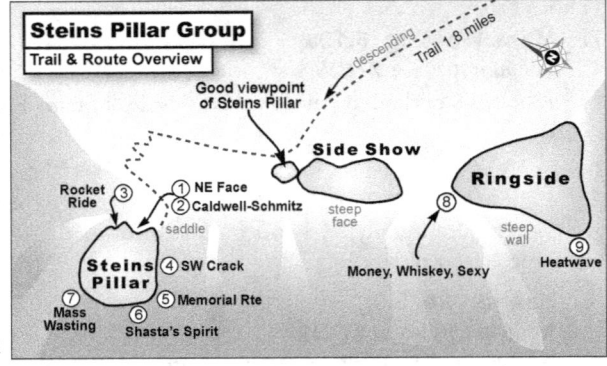

Stein's Pillar Group
Map 4: West aspect from road

P1 5.10a 7 QD's (optional gear) 100': Follow bolts up right on a steep face to a short vertical crux after the mossy ledge that continues to a flake crack with one bolt. Just beyond is a two bolt belay at an alcove.

P2 5.9 10 QD's 120': From the alcove surmount the bulge (crux) and continue up the ramp for another 80' of great 5.7 climbing (runout) to a ledge with a small tree. Belay anchor.

P3 5.6 3 QD's 50': Stay up left on arête. Clip the second bolt with long sling and traverse right 25' on the obvious sloped edges below the summit to a belay anchor. If desired, you can scramble to the 'official' summit from here.

Descent: From the P3 anchor step over the hump and look by your feet for a Metolius Rap station. This 65' rappel will put you on the top of Mossy Ledges. Once on the ledge, head due North down Mossy Ledges looking down and right 25' for another Metolius Rap station. This 65' rappel takes you down the final ledges to your pack.

TWIN PILLARS

The Twin Pillars are located northeast of Steins Pillar at the headwaters of the upper East Fork of Mill Creek. The upper main (north) pillar and the lower (south) pillar are of dubious friable quality (tuffaceous rhyolite), which tends to keep climber appeal to a bare minimum. Though lacking in seeming quality the pillars are quite massive in size (250' high) and surprisingly photogenic even with the lack of green trees. If you are so inclined to take the challenge to explore on Twin Pillars beware of the risk and always wear a helmet. Consider taking pitons, and perhaps even a hand drill. The routes are a combination of free climbing and direct aid, particularly in the loose areas.

Directions: The pillars can be accessed by a south or north trailhead entrance. For the *south trailhead* entrance...from Prineville, Oregon drive east 9¾ miles to the east end of Ochoco Reservoir, then north on Mill Creek Road (FS33) past the Steins Pil-

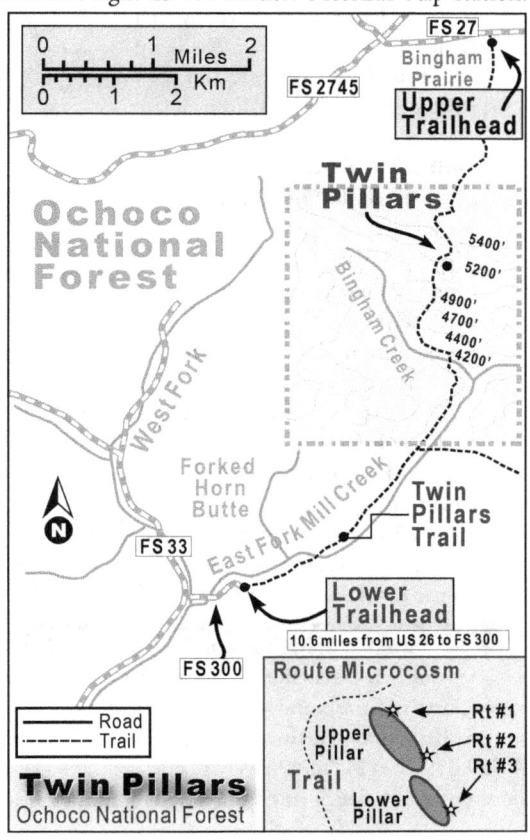

lar viewpoint for 10½ miles. Turn right at FS300 if you want the lower trailhead which is considerably longer and steeper (4¾ miles and 1600' elevation gain). For the *north trailhead* entrance...from Prineville, drive north on Main Street with becomes McKay Creek Road (FS27) and continue to a 4-way junction at 26¼ miles. Turn right at Bingham Prairie and drive 1 mile east to the trailhead at Bingham Spring on FS27 road. The north trail starts at Bingham Spring and is a 2½ mile hike that travels over a minor knoll and then descends 400' to pinnacles.

1. **Upper Pillar (North crack) II 5.8 R**
   Multi-pitch, Pro to 4"
   Start at the uphill saddle where the trail meets the spire. Climb up to a belay underneath an overhang in a right facing crack corner. Angle up left around the overhang and then back onto the face. Climb a jam crack that leads to the top.

2. **Campfire Route II 5.5 A3**
   Multi-pitch, Pro to 3" including pitons
   The Campfire Route starts at a camping spot part way down the slope to the east from the saddle in about the middle of the cliff face.

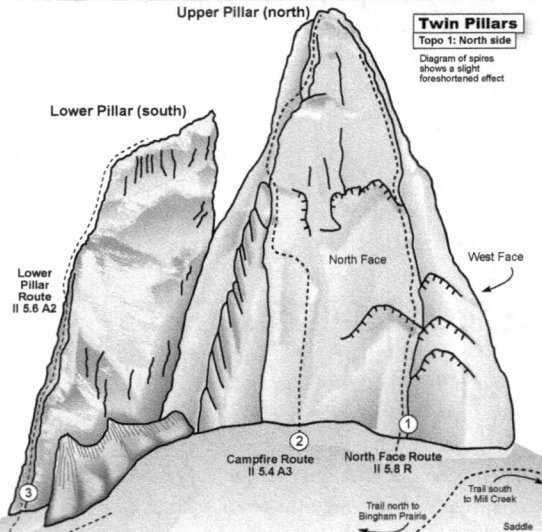

   The route has a distinct left-hand jog about half way up the first pitch as it steps into another crack system. From east corner of the upper pillar ascend overhangs (A3), steps and corners to the summit.

3. **Lower Pillar (East crack) II 5.6 A2**
   Multi-pitch, Pro to 3" including pitons
   This route starts at a flat spot and ascends the line of least resistance by means of a crack system. Climb the crack to a ledge on the ridge. Belay, then climb a system of grooves and corners on the east face to the summit of the Lower Pillar.

GOTHIC ROCK

Gothic Rock is cluster of 350' high towers located in the foothills of central Oregon near Grandview (north of Sisters and southwest of Lake Billy Chinook). This large tuffaceous complex of spires are perched on the northwest end of Green Ridge high above the Metolius River. GPS coordinates 44°39.039' N -121°34.406' W will place you at 4114' elevation about one mile north of Castle Rock outcrop near Adler Springs. Directions: From U.S. 20 at Indian Ford (north of Sisters) drive north around Black Butte, then northeast past Summit Spring and Thorn Spring along Fly Creek on Squaw Back Ridge Road. This road will gradually ascend up into Adler Spring Creek valley passing Adler Springs. Just prior to roads end park and walk up west ½ mile to the crest of Green Ridge just west of the northernmost high point 4665'. Expect about 32 miles total from U.S. 20.

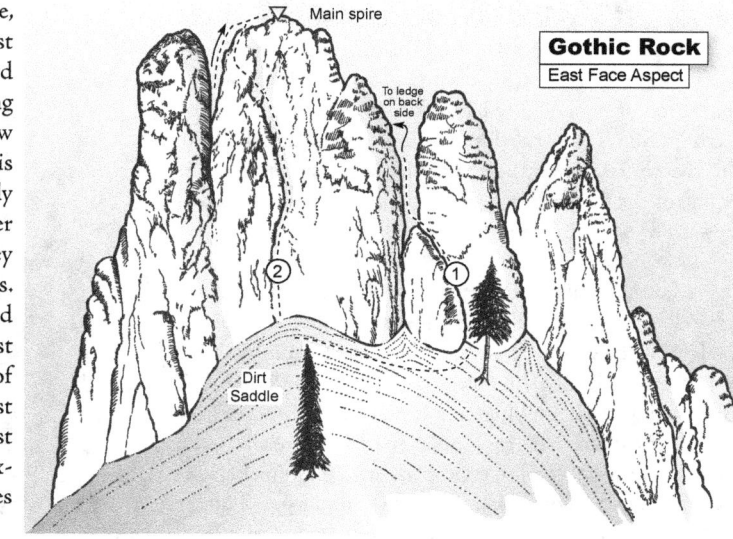

1. North Ravine 5.4
350' Multi-pitch
From the dirt saddle descend 100' down right to a ravine that separates the main Upper Tower from the Middle Tower. Proceed up this steep rock ravine for 200' and then angle to the left to a ledge that provides a good viewpoint on the west side. Continue counterclockwise to the SW side and climb the steep rock face to the summit. The rock is reasonably solid with minor loose material. Rappel.

2. East Face Direct 5.5
350' Multi-pitch
From the uphill dirt saddle the East Face of the Upper Tower (5.5) can be climbed by a depression in the face directly to the summit.

3. Middle Tower 5.4
Multi-pitch
The Middle Tower can be attained from a large rocky bowl at the ledge viewpoint on the west side of the Upper Tower.

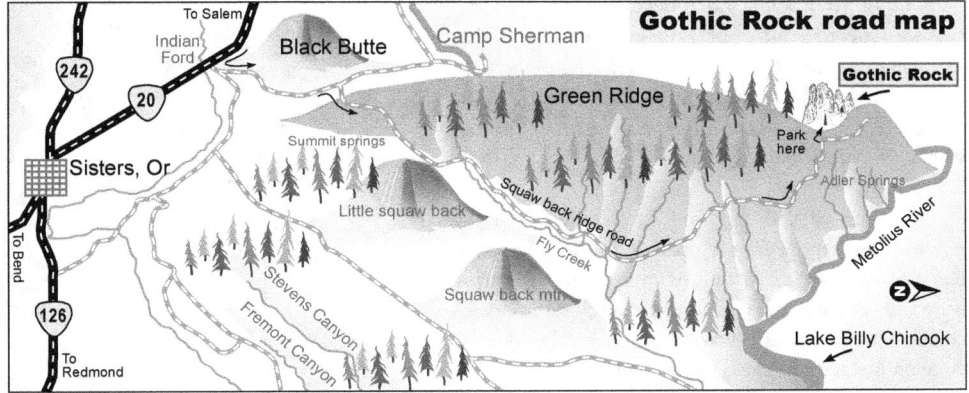

TROUT CREEK

Welcome to Trout Creek, Oregon's answer to desert crack climbing. Trout Creek is not a large area but the concentration of high quality natural lines is immense and the setting alone is well worth the hike. Positioned high above the Deschutes River the crag provides a sweeping panorama of the Central Oregon landscape and gorge framed viewing of Mt. Jefferson.

Access

Madras locals will tell you that Trout Creek is inaccurately named since the actual Trout Creek is nowhere in sight of the climbing. In fact, there is no running water near the cliff at all. The local name, Dry Island, is much more fitting. The climbing area is named Trout Creek for the campground where climbers park to approach the crag. To climb at Trout Creek, park at Trout Creek. Simple. Parking at spots other than the campground forces hikers over private land and could lead to access problems for us as a user group. The mesa above the cliff is a hunting preserve owned by the original homesteaders of Gateway who quite understandably do not want climbers walking or driving over their property.

Eugene Dod rapping *Gothic Rock*

Locate the Day Use Area in the upstream corner of the campground (and follow the directions posted at the end of this intro) to approach the climbing. Now if we want to get technical, Trout Creek campground doesn't sit next to Trout Creek either, instead the creek meets the Lower Deschutes downstream from the campground where it flows through private land. Private land is important to respect in this area, even if you are as far from the climbing at Trout Creek as Trout Creek itself. Much of the private land is not clearly posted so if in doubt, don't venture off the beaten path and please keep a friendly low profile. The hike from the campground to the cliff takes about 45 minutes at a normal pace. Don't forget to bring plenty of water; it's a dry island up there. For those interested in camping, while the campground has the Lower Deschutes running past, it offers no potable water.

Trout Creek will likely have a partial seasonal closure due to raptor nesting habitat. Check Jeff Wenger's website for additional details, or contact the regional BLM office for an update before driving out there, or browse one of several regional climber website forums for an update.

Dangers

Getting to the climbing site, rather than the climbs themselves, might present the biggest challenge of the day. Ticks can be an issue in the spring especially close to the river and rattlesnakes are commonly spotted in the warmer months. Every year cougars are seen in the Trout Creek area. Having a

Jeff Wenger stylin' on *JR Token*

Inset: Jesse leading *Fun Soup* 5.10

Trout Creek Wall

run-in with one of these predators could be a one time bad deal. If you see a mountain lion give it lots of space and assume it has been (and will be) watching you for some time. Fear not, you have a much greater chance of getting hurt slipping on the talus at the main wall than ever spotting a mountain lion, let alone getting attacked. Negotiating the super-sized blocks of fallen columns at the cliff's main area is an arduous mixture of boulder hopping and scrambling. As a result, the base adds another dimension to Trout Creek's already isolated position and can present the most risky aspect to be encountered during your visit. Several people and several dogs have had close calls. If you are planning on bringing canine pals make sure they are comfortable on talus before hiking them all the way to the crag.

The Climbing

Trout Creek is characterized by boulder hopping approaches to exceptionally clean inside corners and stem boxes. The protection is generally bomber and very straightforward. A double to triple set of cams works fine for many of the routes but some of the most sustained require five or more pieces of the same size for adequate protection. Similar in nature to Bill's Columns above Hwy 26 in Warm Springs, the climbing is on columnar basalt with a golden, high friction layer appearing on the sunnier aspects. The rock tends to be quite abrasive and most climbers tape their hands, especially for the wider cracks.

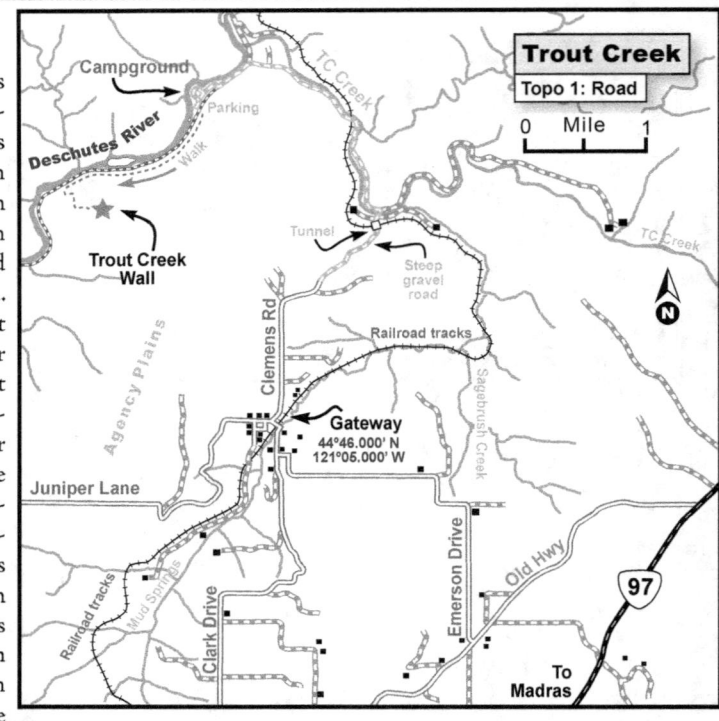

Anchors are situated well below the top of the cliff. If you plan on visiting, plan on leading… or talking someone else into it. Climbers that frequent the area tend to be very willing to combine efforts and share top ropes. Also, many of the areas 100+ routes have common anchors or can be connected to other lines with a little creativity. From fingers to chimneys, straight-in jamming to all out stem-fests, there's something to suit every crack fan's strength or weakness at Trout Creek.

The highest percentage of classics come in at 5.10 and above but the spaces between the lower angle columns produce many quality 5.7-5.9 routes. These climbs are shorter in length and wrap to the north providing good shady options in the warmer months. A separate north-facing wall, called the Cool Wall, provides a variety of shady classics in almost guaranteed solitude. Even so, most visiting climbers never venture further than Trout's crown jewel, the main west-facing wall. The main wall's westward orientation means you'll typically be seeking the shade (or more likely the river) by early afternoon in the summer and shivering until after 1:00pm in the winter. Spring and fall consistently offer the best conditions.

Stewardship

Despite increased attention, Trout has retained a small community feel. At the main staging area climbers maintain a community bucket containing a crag copy

Climber on *Gold Rush*

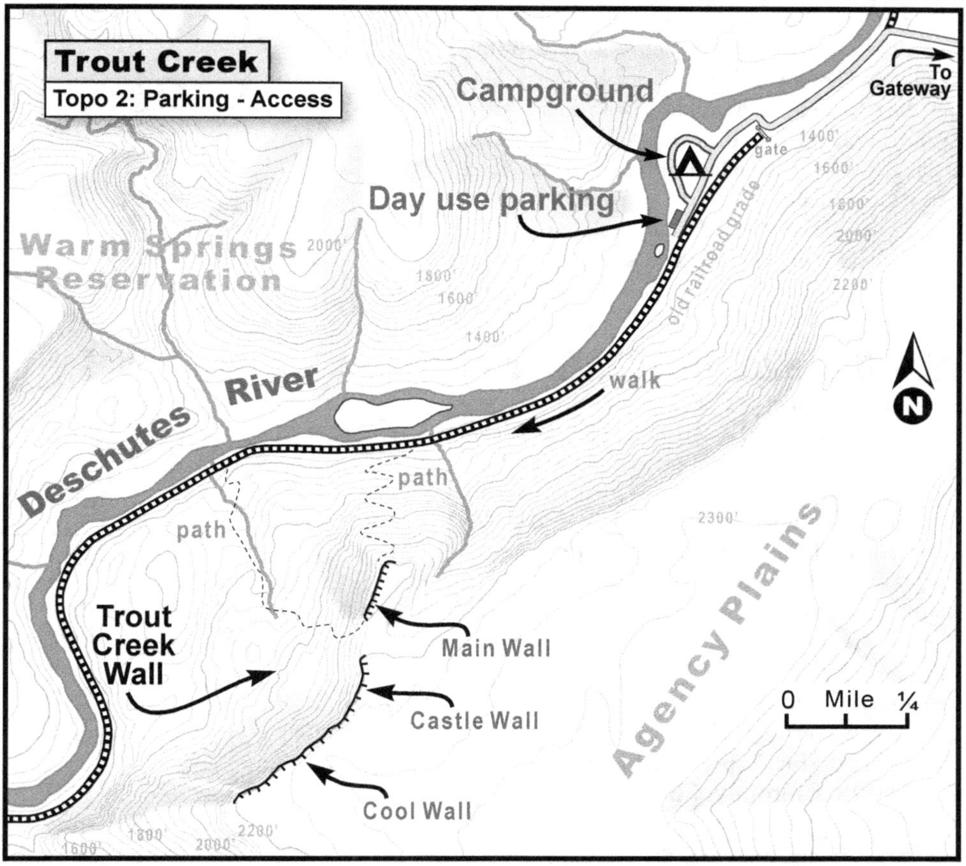

Trout Creek
Topo 2: Parking - Access

of the guidebook, a first aid kit and usually a few donated items. Thanks to this simple donation process the majority of Trout Creek's routes are now equipped with lowering carabiners on chains. The most popular routes have steel carabiners in place, the others have aluminum. Steel 'biner donations are greatly appreciated, just drop them off in the bucket and they'll get used. If you want to donate other items like chalk or tape, the bucket is a good spot. Please don't leave perishable food, glass containers or money in the bucket. On second thought, money is fine. Thanks to everyone that has generously given over the years to make this system fun and workable.

Directions

Want to go exploring? Find the tiny town of Gateway, Oregon, north of Madras. From there follow Clemens Dr. all the way to the Trout Creek Campground; the last few miles of the drive is on a dirt road that is sometimes in disrepair. Park at the Day Use Area at the SW (upstream) end of the campground and walk upstream to access the river road past a cattle guard. There are a couple different approaches off the river road; the main trail approach leading to the crag bucket is described here. Walk 20-25 minutes upstream and cross a second cattle guard. Continue two hundred yards along the river road to the first weakness

in the hillside. Leave the road here and follow the trail up the short rise to the left. The bulk of the climbing at Trout Creek will be clearly in view. Follow the trail another 20 minutes or so to the Main Wall. The crag copy of the guide will be at the main staging area, roughly in line with the obvious hand crack, Gold Rush.

For a complete guidebook, check out the free download or printable guides at: www.lulu.com (search for Trout Creek climbing, or Jeff Wenger).

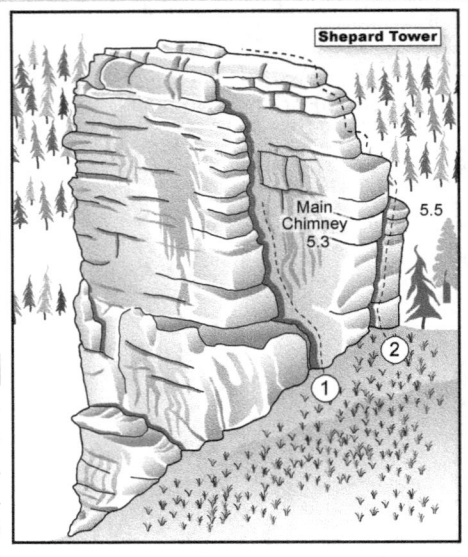

SHEPARD TOWER

Shepard Tower of the Metolius is a very minor block of rock on the northern leg of the Metolius River on a hill slope above the old river road. First climbed in 1961 by Gil and Vivian Staender. Directions: Drive east of Salem on US 22 to US 20 over Santiam Pass. From Suttle Lake drive northeast 4¾ miles to Camp Sherman, then north to Lower Bridge Campground. Park at a closed gate on the old Metolius River road that travels north. Walk or ride a mountain bike north along this bumpy road for 6¾ miles. The small minor pinnacle is ¼ mile uphill and can be difficult to see in the forest. GPS 44.64580° N / -121.6112° W.

1. **Main Chimney 5.3**
From the east uphill side climb up large steps to a ledge, then up a wide vertical south facing chimney to the top. Rappel from fixed anchor.
2. **Middle Chimney 5.3**
At the uphill saddle begin up a short steep wide crack to a stance. Climb up a short steep section and continue along the rib to the top.

There is another minor climb (5.2) on the northeast side. The steep south face and west face have likely been top-roped.

Climbing Out in the Great Wide Open

CHAPTER 10

NE OREGON ROCK

The Wallowa Mountains and the Anthony Lakes region have inspired several generations of alpine climbers willing to explore bold new lines on steep 300' to 1,000'+ tall buttresses on granite and limestone alpine peaks that are certainly a rarity for Oregon. In the early 1970s Dave Jensen, after years of prolific rock and alpine climbing with Eugene Dod and Jim Nieland, moved to the Enterprise area to continue his photography business. His move fit well with his outdoor goals, as he quickly became drawn to the abrupt alpine big-wall formations of the high Wallowa Mountain range.

West of North Powder in the Elkhorn Mtns at Anthony Lakes the Slab Route (5.7) on Lakes Lookout was ascended in August 1971 by Dave Nelson, John McCormick and Dick Pooley. While employed by Lute Jerstad's adventure school, Jensen made numerous multi-pitch forays on several nearby granite peaks. He soloed various routes on Lee's Peak and Lakes Lookout, but also teamed up with Mead Hargis or Dave Coughlin to climb various routes on the 50° ramps on Lookout, Lee's, and Angel Peaks. Certain first recorded ascents on Lookout Peak were accomplished by Steve and Stu Ryman, Richard Candeleria, and Mark Evey in the late '70s and early '80s. Some of the Hoffer Lakes granite slabs at Anthony Lakes were utilized in the early 1970s by instructors working for Lute Jerstad, who offered rock climbing seminars and adventure camps at his Total Adventure Company. In 1982 Allen Sanderson, who climbed in the region in the early 1980s, teaming with Tim Bailey to pioneer Gardener's Delight (5.6), a 400' 5.6 alpine route on Gunsight Mountain. Moderately difficult climbs (up to 5.11) do exist on rock ribs of Van Patten Butte, and on the steep faces of Gunsight and Lee's Peak.

In the Wallowa Mtns, Dave Jensen partnered with Coughlin to ascend the West Face Chimney of Matterhorn in 1973, a 1500' long IV 5.9 A1 mixed aid and free multi-pitch and multi-day

Anthony Baker at *Spring Mtn*

alpine climb on a steep friable limestone wall. In the following year, he and Coughlin also pioneered the West Face Wall (V 5.8 A3) on Matterhorn, another dicey multi-day effort involving several bivouacs en route. Some years later, local hardman Mark Hauter of La-Grande tried to free this line via a different start variation, but found the poor quality limestone difficult to negotiate. Jensen felt the 1973 WFC route offers exciting free climbing in cracks and chimneys, but also involves substantial sections of poor limestone rock and risky climbing, which may be a limiting factor for those interested in repeating one of these two lines.

Benthos Buttress (9,000 el.) is a unique set of long steep granite rock ribs in upper Scotch Creek cirque slightly east of Traverse Ridge point 9085'. The pillars on this abrupt north-facing aspect offer four known alpine climbs. The primary objective of interest to those few alpinists who choose to explore this cirque, is usually the main Benthos Buttress route (5.8 A1), a 600' mixed trad alpine climb pioneered in 1974 by Dave

Jensen, Dave Coughlin, and Ted Winchel. The climb may possibly be one of Oregon's best high-altitude granite alpine routes. Years later, in the '90s, Mark Hauter free climbed this entire buttress cruising the crux 5.10c section in the upper last ¼ of the route. Mark Hauter returned again to this cirque with Steve House and Elmo Hendrickson in 1989 to ascend a dihedral on same buttress, which they called the Kozjak Route (5.10). Benthos Pillar is 6 miles directly west of Joseph, Oregon at the headwaters of Scotch Creek, though the original method of approach had been via the Silver Creek trail, and cross-country to Murray Saddle and south up into the cirque.

High on the west slope of the Lostine River in Bowman Creek (near Laverty Lakes), a steep granite peak called Chimney Point, guards the entrance to Brownie Basin. The multi-pitch 400' alpine route Granite (5.7) was climbed by Mark Kerns and Dan Sherwood in the '80s. The same rock formation offers an enjoyable route called The Slab, a 5.10b granite friction slab on the west face of Chimney Point was climbed by Hauter and Hendrickson in 1989.

Though the high peaks certainly have great fascination, the lowly valley crags provide great value to rock climbers who need an easily accessible training ground for rock climbing purposes. The High Valley crag fits that bill as the original early era center of rock climbing activity in northeast Oregon. This roadside crag offers a great place to learn the ropes in a reasonable environment just a short distance from town. The Cliffhangers, a LaGrande high school climbing club spearheaded by Joe Sandoz and Steve Ryman, utilized the crag extensively since the 1970s. From this club several prominent hard-core climbers, alpinists, and a founding board members of the Access Fund began their climbing career at this crag. At High Valley trad gear crack leads were initially established in the late 1970s and early 80s. The late 1980s and 1990s brought another sweep of interest as locals began to bolt some of the faces and arêtes, besides adding several more crack leads. Some early players were Casciato, Kerns, Wilkins, Sanderson, and Brown, followed later by another core group composed of Steve Brown, Hauter, Hendrickson, Daniels, and Jason Shapp.

When Kevin Pogue moved to Walla Walla to teach at Whitman University, he became captivated with Spring Mtn crag, a site initially discovered by LaGrande climbers sometime in the '80s. After putting up "Welcome to Spring Mtn" all the locals in the region decided it was time to get busy, and development really took off, seeing a storm of quality new routes established from 1995 to 2005 by Pogue, Hauter, Brown Cunningham, Jones and others. Spring Mountain crags high elevation at 4,000' (considerably higher than High Valley) has not slowed its popularity, and today the site is generally considered to be the center-stage crag for quality rock climbing in northeast Oregon, and who would argue a point like that when you have 120 quality routes to choose from.

Geographical Considerations

This region is a highly diversified touchstone of rock and alpine climbing opportunities, though separated by considerable driving distances, does offer a surprising wealth of cliff scarps and mountain peaks that suitably meets the needs of a plethora of recreational climbers. Citizens who live in this region certainly can sense the beauty of this great region, and know the reason for its prosperity.

Northeast Oregon is climatically a midlatitude semiarid plateau region, punctuated by wide sweeping fertile valleys, and crowned with stunningly majestic granitic and sedimentary mountain peaks. The sagebrush covered Columbia River Plateau region on both sides of the Blue Mountains serves as a wide transition zone that separates the western Oregon temperate climate from the higher elevation subalpine and alpine zones of the Blue Mountain range. Though much of the lower plateau region is now cultivated for farm crops, originally the valleys were lush grassland biomes. These semiarid grasslands give way to rolling hills of wild perenial grasses, with limited rocky riparian zones where shrubs, bushes and stunted oak proliferate, and with further elevation gain, forests of widely distributed ponderosa pine trees that wrap around dry open sweeps of prairie.

Predominant floristic vegetation communities become established based on the effects of temperature and precipitational factors associated with vertical zonation and local ecosystem variables.

Low elevation plateau grasslands experience an abundance of sagebrush, balsamroot, buckwheat, yarrow, etc., and a prolific host of wild grasses and sedges. Prickly pear cactus cling to bluffs of the Hells Canyon. Mid-elevation ponderosa pine forests and alpine meadows yield wildflowers such as clarkia, Indian paintbrush, lily, larkspur, shooting star, and bluebell. Forests of variable stature such as spruce, mountain hemlock, subalpine fir and whitebark pine grow at higher elevations, and douglas fir, white fir, tamarack, and lodgepole pine exist in certain stands based on localized temperate variables. Birch, willow, and poplar are quite common along valley or canyon stream banks.

Dave S. at *Spring Mtn*

The northeastern Oregon grassland plateau and forest biomes support a extensive and adaptable wildlife fauna species. Elk, bighorn sheep, mountain goat, deer, black bear, wolf, cougar, "wiley" coyote, bobcat, and a variety of smaller mammals such as badger, beaver, chipmunk, hares and rabbits, mink, pika, marmot, pine marten, squirrel, and river otter. A diverse array of bird species include the bald and golden eagles, peregrine falcon, finch, hawks, owl, partridge, woodpecker, and water dipper. Pronghorn antelope dwell on the open, wind-swept plains of the plateau region, while jack rabbit, squirrel, and varieties of mice are common throughout the region from mid-altitudes to the semiarid juniper and sagebrush plateau grasslands.

The Blue Mountains

The Blue Mountains are considered to be one of Oregon's oldest mountain ranges originally formed as a series of mountains along a broad Klamath-Blue-Wallowa arc, though dramatically altered over a grand period of time. The extensive Blue Mountains chain includes the Ochoco, Strawberry, Greenhorn, Elkhorn, and Wallowa Mountain ranges. The tallest peaks in the Blue Mtns are: Elkhorn Mtn 9,108' (2,776'), Strawberry Mtn 9,038' (2,755m), and Mt Ireland 8,304' (2,531m). In the distant past this region began as a broad sedimentary oceanic shelf. Powerful events thrust up a large near surface intrusive magmatic pool, then experienced slow subsurface cooling that produced granite stock. Tremendous continental and oceanic plate tectonic forces folded and compressed the surrounding sedimentary layers, while thrusting the granite Wallowa Mountains upward to the 9800' level through faulting and crustal movement, creating a resillient slow weathering central core to the Wallowa mountain range. This Wallowa Mountains granite batholith uplift is directly related to the enormous Idaho batholith. The margins of this intrusive granite batholith produced limited quantities of gold mining in the Wallowa Mtns mainly from the mid-1800s up till about 1940s, but few mines in the region remain active today. The Martin Bridge bedrock formation at the headwaters of the Lostine River (and on the Imnaha River near Marble Mtn), is a prominent marbleized limestone escarpment on the east face of Matterhorn and Sacajawea Peaks along Hurricane Ridge. This formation is overlayed with the Hurwall rock formation, a mix of shale, slate, sandstone, and black marble beds. This grand mix of both granitic and sedimentary structures is a complex interlaced bedrock matrix of limestone, granite, dark-green blocky pyroxene greenstone andesite, gabbro, schist, slate, quartzite, and basalt strata formations. This bedrock strata variability lends credence to the incredible diversity of rock climbing opportunities of northeast Oregon.

The Columbia Gorge basalt flows were created by a multi-layered sequence of events triggered by the Grand Ronde volcanics quickly spreading from a series of vertical dikes that thrust voluminous quantities of molten black fluid lava out across the region, then congealed one layer at a time. These very fluid basalt flows ranging from 50-300'+ thick managed to travel quite far, even hundreds of miles along river channels as far away as Astoria, Oregon. These flows are evident in many places of the Columbia Gorge, eastward past Wallula Gap, and in much of the surrounding plateau region of the Columbia River basin. The flood basalt generally lacks olivene, but has distinct cleavage planes at a 90° angle to the vertical axis of the 5-6-or-8 sided octagonally shaped columns. A large number of prominent old vertically oriented basalt dikes can be seen in the Grand Ronde canyon and Joseph Canyon north of Enterprise and near Dayville, Oregon, and southeast of Dayton, Washington.

The easternmost edge of the Wallowa range abutts on the Hells Canyon carved by the Snake River. This deep canyon, the deepest in the USA, was cut when an ancient impounded lake upriver of the site released its natural force. The Snake River has continued its downward cutting process deep into the surrounding lava plateau bringing a vertical relief of several thousands of feet to its steeply sloped canyon walls. The upper bedrock terrain is basaltic rock, while the lower portion of the canyon is composed of noticably contorted limestone sedimentary layers.

The broad fertile synclinous sedimentary valley basins and rolling anticline plateaus around Walla Walla, John Day, LaGrande, and Baker City are ideal for a wide variety of crop farming. Agricultural farming is an economically important facet of life in this region, from the distinctive Walla Walla onions, to the burgeoning vineyards and wineries (known as the 'Napa of the north'), to the brilliant yellow canola fields near LaGrande. The diversity of farm production crops range from seed grass, mint, alfalfa, wheat, sugar beets, seed potatoes, corn, cherries, to strawberries.

Today, the Wallowa Mountains are known as the 'Alps of Oregon', cresting to its highest point at Sacajawea Peak 9,838' (2,999m), are encompassed within the Eagle Cap Wilderness. In the mid-1800s, the Blue Mountains were a formidable obstacle for pioneers traveling on the Oregon Trail route. In our recent historical past, various indigenous American indians dwelt in this haven of beauty. The foothill prairies on the northern flank of the Wallowas Mtns originally were the homeland of Chief Josephs' clan of the Nez Perce. The region was host to several other native tribes including the Cayuse, Umatilla, Walla Walla, and Shoshone who found the valleys around present-day LaGrande quite suitable for their needs. Today, the Eagle Cap Wilderness encompasses the entire high peak region of the Wallowa range. On its northern flank is the beautiful Wallowa Lake, a 4-mile long impounded morainal lake formed by multiple advancing Pliestocene glaciers that cut a deep trench, pushing debris 900' up into tall side hills next to the lake. Spectacular scenic views of this region are available if you ride up the Wallowa Lake tramway, an aerial cable gondola lift running from the valley floor (at the south end of the lake) up to the top of Mt Howard 8,000' (2,400m).

Season for climbing

Generally, the best seasons for rock climbing in northeastern Oregon are from early April through early November. Reasonable climbing temperatures (55°F and above) can be had at most rock climbing sites in this region. The summer months are dry and sultry, with an averge August high of 90°F, particularly on the grassy plateaus and valleys. Common daily high summer temperatures for cities like Pendleton, Walla Walla, Baker City, and LaGrande range from 90°F to 100°F (and sometimes a bit higher). The summer extremes of heat may force you to seek out shaded aspects of a crag, or send you swimming in a nearby river. The region sees minimal summer rain compared to western Oregon, though is accentuated by erratic precipitation in the form of thunderstorms actively traversing the region when two opposing thermal air masses collide. Approximate rainfall totals are 20" a year for Walla Walla, and 18" a year for La Grande; the months of greatest precipitation being November-to-June (roughly 1" to 2" a month).

Winter months around LaGrande-Baker City tend to be significantly cold. Winter snowstorms are common and snowpack accumulation tends to remain deep above 5,000' elevation during the colder months. Though some years only receive minimal snowpack, you should anticipate heavy winter snow loads to linger at most higher altitude climbing sites. Winter season daily high temperatures range from 30°F - 45°F and occasionally lower, while nighttime low temperatures can dip down to 10°F - 20°F. Winters cold extremes will limit climbing opportunities to the milder days and mainly at the lower elevation climbing sites. On certain warm winter days the weather is reasonable enough to climb at places like High Valley, or on that very rare day, when snowpack is minimal, at Spring Mountain crag.

Besides the popular climbing sites like Spring Mountain, High Valley, and Burnt River, there are plenty of other worthy destinations, such as the 500+ climbs on Hells Canyon's stellar limestone cliffs. Rock climbing opportunities at Hell's Canyon is feasible even in the depth of the coldest winter months, but mainly on the south-facing cliffs warmed by the rays of the sun. The high peaks of the Wallowa range offer a fine selection of wild and rather extreme alpine climbing on huge walls. Though the region is of closer proximity to Idaho-based climbers, the virtually infinite variety of rock climbing opportunities make for an ideal multi-day outing suitable for all road-bound rock climbers.

SPRING MOUNTAIN

Original route beta manuscript used for this section was loaned courtesy of Kevin Pogue

Out in the great wide open in the ponderosa pine forests of the Blue Mountain range is a stellar rock bluff painted in brilliant hues of reddish-orange, nestled in an idyllic back country setting. The Spring Mountain crag is a unique gem well suited for any traveling climber especially if you are en route to other quality sites in the region such as Burnt River or Hells Canyon. Characteristically similar to Ozone Wall and offering a quality of andesite seldom matched, the crag sees a steady core of local climbers who frequent this site each summer to experience the mystic and quality.

Spring Mtn crag is located in the northern Blue Mountains between Pendleton and LaGrande and is certainly one of the best climbing crags in the heart of northeast Oregon. The crag offers superb quality rock climbing opportunities on a ¼ mile long 100' high andesite cliff. Convenient access with open skies camping, and situated reasonably close to several major regional cities, the crag has long been a popular cragging destination for both locals and road-bound climbers.

The south-southeast orientation of the cliff scarp allows most routes to receive plenty of sunshine from early in the morning until mid-afternoon. Large trees provide shade for certain lower portions of the crag, particularly at the southern and northern end of the crag. A compact and smooth lower half of the bluff is countered by a fairly porous and knobby upper half due to the profusion of tiny vesicular gas pockets.

Rock climbing is usually possible from mid-April to late October depending on snow pack melt. The cliff is located at an elevation of 4600' so the temperature at least 15°F cooler than Pendleton, although it doesn't feel that way when climbing in direct sunlight. Mosquitos, horse flies, and deer flies can be a nuisance from late spring through mid summer, and in certain years aggressive yellowjackets can be nearly intolerable in late summer. There are plenty of open skies free camping sites in the grassland meadows along the Whitman Route Overlook road. The crag is situated in the Walla Walla Ranger District of the Umatilla National Forest.

Regional History

The Emigrant Trail passes near to the south of Spring Mountain. It carried a multitude of travelers who in the 1840s to 1880s were seeking a better new beginning out west in Oregon Country. The Marcus Whitman party came across in 1836 likely very near Spring Mountain, then descended into Meacham Creek. The Blue Mountains extend from the reaches of the Wallowas south past John Day valley. The tall 4000' mountain range is composed of vibrant stands of well distributed ponderosa pine trees and a mixture of grassland meadows quite colorful in Spring time. By late season the grass dries and the soil becomes brown and hard packed, yet a tinge of crisp

394 CHAPTER 10

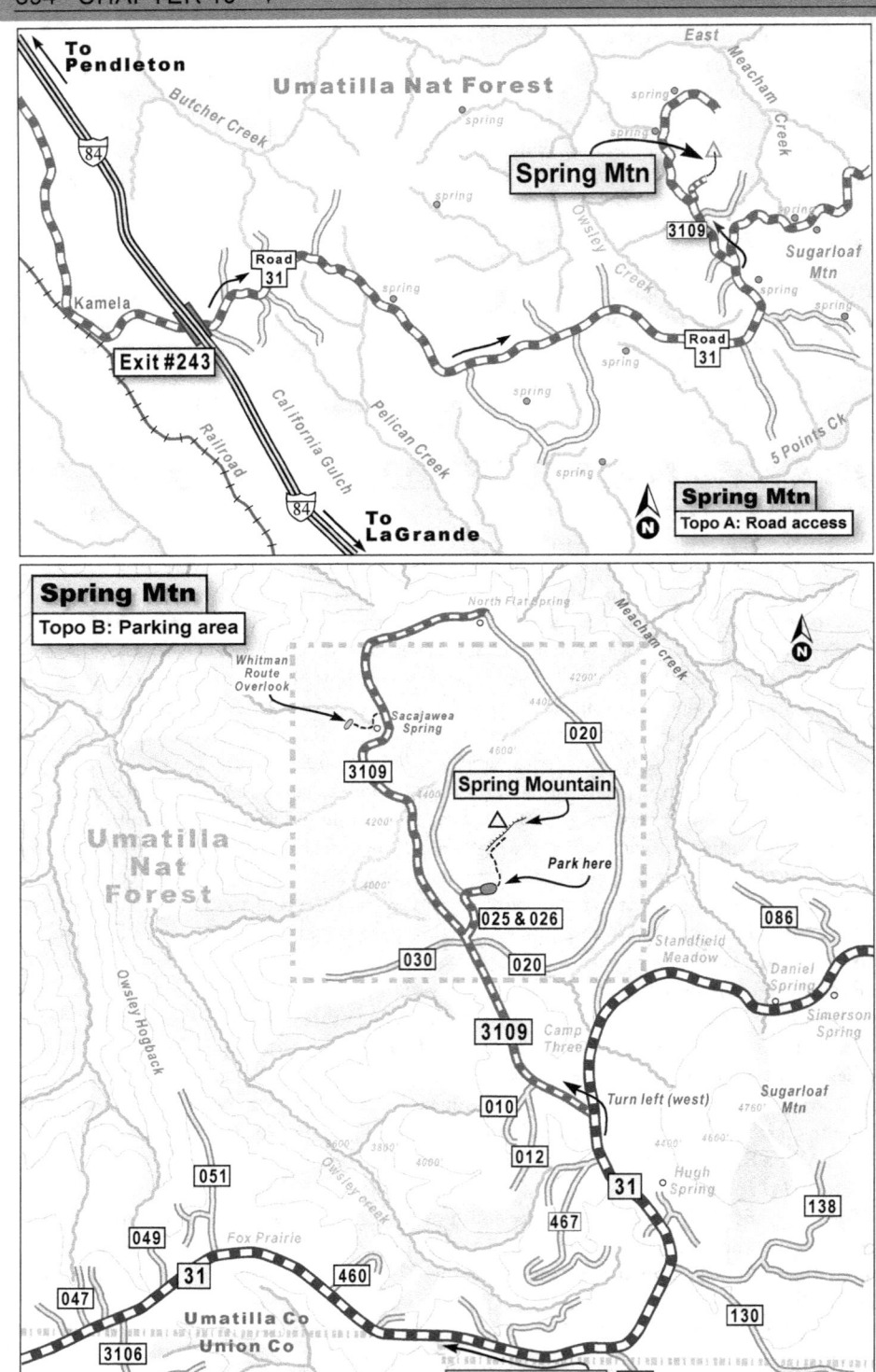

clear flavorful scent still resides in the mountain air. Reaching this climbing site in an automobile is quite reasonable today, but long ago this area seemed like such a difficult mountain crest to traverse over for families of settlers traveling in wooden wagons pulled by oxen.

Route Beta

The route descriptions are in the order that you first encounter the crag along the trail (west to east). The route developer (RD) listed is the person(s) most responsible for the creation of the route. Almost every route (sport and trad) at Spring Mountain required extensive moss, lichen, and loose rock removal. In most but not all cases, the RD is also the person responsible for the FA. Some long-term projects were almost certainly first climbed by someone who did not know they were making a first ascent, and some FA's were "gifted" by the route developer to other folks. The RD information also helps you to find or avoid routes based on that persons style. Some of the routes require a 60-meter rope in order to lower a climber to the ground from the belay anchor.

Directions

The crag is located in the northern Blue Mountains about 9 miles northeast of exit 243 on I-84 between Pendleton and LaGrande, Oregon.

Drive from Portland on I-84 for 209 miles to Pendleton. Continue east from Pendleton on the I-84 east for another 33 miles up to the pass (elevation 4193' east of Meacham). LaGrande is 17 miles east of Summit pass. Take "Summit Rd., Mt. Emily" exit 243 off I-84. Turn left (north) on Summit Road, cross over the interstate, and proceed approximately 8 miles on the well-maintained FS31 gravel road (Spring Mtn is visible in the distance from near Fox Prairie). When you see a sign on the right that says, "Whitman Route Overlook", turn left at the next road (FS3109) and drive about one mile, turn right (north) onto FS3109-025 at another grassy meadow. Drive FS3109-025/FS3109-026 for about ½ mile till it dead-ends at a turn-around blocked by several large boulders. Park here, and walk the trail past the boulders. The trail is a short 3 minutes uphill walk (300') to the south end of the crag. GPS 45°27'27.45"N 118°14'15.34"W

Camping and Amenities

This is back woods climbing with no nearby stores, so bring your own camping gear, flashlight, food, water, etc. There is a bathroom and a signed spring (must be treated) near the Whitman route overlook parking area (one mile past Spring Mountain), but otherwise no water is available. Camping options are plentiful and free by searching out any one of several spur roads for a nice secluded pullout. Nearest city large is LaGrande at 26 miles or Pendleton at 42 miles. A sheriff office is located west of Summit pass on the south side of the highway. No cell phone reception up here so bring your version of nightly entertainment.

Route developers (RD) are listed as the first ascentionist (FA) in abbreviated form in the beta list. MB = Mark Bergman, BB = Bob Branscomb, SB = Steve Brown, PC = Pete Cassidy, JC = Jim Cunningham, TD = Terry Dietrich, JD = Jesse Dwyer, JG = Jay Goodwin, MH = Mark Hauter, KH = Kevin Hibbert, JJ = Josh Jones, BL = Brent Lansing, KP = Kevin Pogue, JS = John Spatz, VS = Vern Stiefel, U = unknown.

The South Forest

The initial portion of the crag you encounter when the trail first meets the wall. A well forested section popular on hot days when shaded climbs are better than sunny backing hot rock climbs.

1. Gome Boy 5.11a ★
   Pro: (sport) 3 QD's, FA: KH
   The first bolted route at the crag on a very steep short face (stick clip first bolt). Crux is getting the 2nd clip and arete on right is off-route. Rap hangers.

2. Beginner's Route 5.4 TR ★★
   Pro: Top-rope, FA: U
   Low-angle slab around the corner to the right of Gome Boy. It is easy to set a top-rope by walking around to the left. Rap hangers.

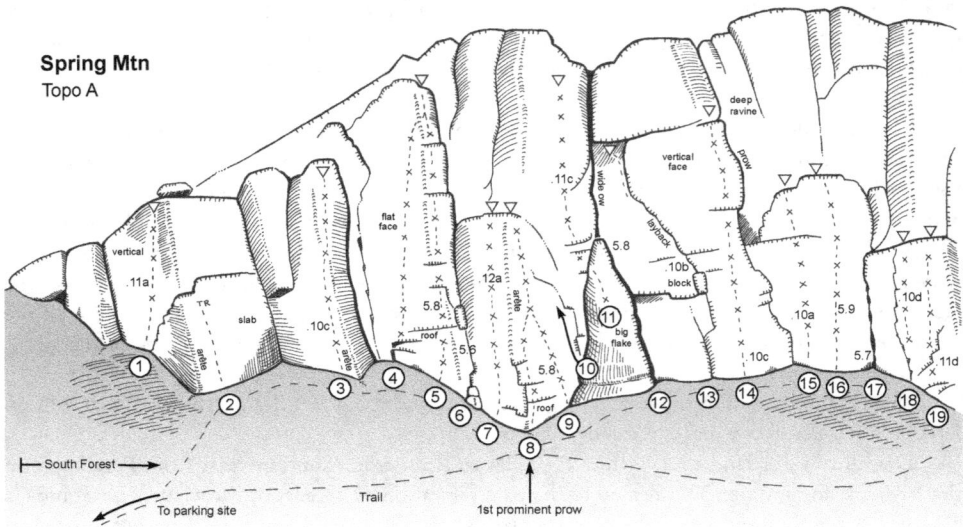

**Spring Mtn
Topo A**

3. **Jack and Jill 5.10c** ★★
   Pro: (sport) 4 QD's, FA: KH
   A difficult steep face climb using an arête. Difficulty varies depending on which side of the arete (.10a right side start or .10c left side start). Rap hangers.

4. **A Few Tense Moments 5.10b to 5.11-** ★★★
   Pro: (sport) 9 QD's, FA: KP
   Start at left edge of a small roof and pull a tricky boulder-problem move to thin face climbing above. The final moves surmount an exciting blocky overhang. The route is moderate 5.10b if the right arete is utilized for the middle portion (above the third bolt). A few more "tense moments" can be had by eschewing the arête and climbing straight up the thin crimpy face (5.11-). This route is unusual for Spring Mountain in that it is easy to set up for a top-rope from above (without leading). Has quick-clip rappel chains.

5. **Passing Lane 5.8** ★★
   Pro: (sport) 8 QD's, FA: KP
   Excellent long face climb. Climb steep smooth face using arete on right, pull through an overhang, move slightly left and then scamper up a blunt arête and around a big block. Shares anchors with A Few Tense Moments and is also easy to set up for a top-rope from above, although you might want a directional quick-draw lower down. Quick-clip rappel chains.

6. **Mountain Ears Route 5.6** ★★
   Pro: (trad) medium-large nuts and cams, FA: KP
   Left-facing dihedral crack system. Scramble up easy ledges, crank over a bulge (crux) and then cruise a ledgy face with good protection to a tunnel-like exit beneath a large chockstone. Good route for a beginning traditional lead climber. No fixed top anchors.

7. **Unnamed 5.12a** ★★★
   Pro: (sport) 12 QD's, FA: SB?
   A quality stout crimpy face route with few rest points that ascends straight up a steep face on the left side of the 2nd prominent arête prow. Rap hangers.

8. **Welcome to Spring Mtn (direct) 5.11a** ★★
   Pro: (sport) 3 QD's, FA: KH
   Begins under the overhang prominent arete prow below and left of the regular route and climbs past three bolts. Stick clip the first bolt.

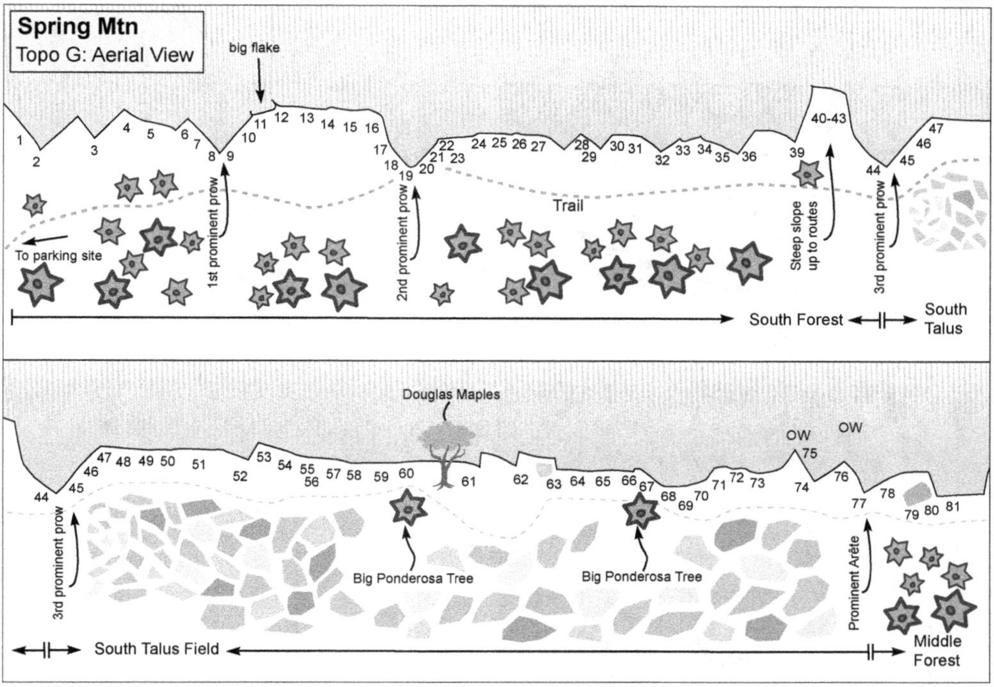
Spring Mtn
Topo G: Aerial View
big flake
1 2 3 4 5 6 7 8 9 10 11 12 13 14 15 16 17 18 19 20 21 22 23 24 25 26 27 28 29 30 31 32 33 34 35 36 39 40-43 44 45 46 47
Trail
To parking site
1st prominent prow
2nd prominent prow
Steep slope up to routes
3rd prominent prow
South Forest
South Talus
Douglas Maples
44 45 46 47 48 49 50 51 52 53 54 55 56 57 58 59 60 61 62 63 64 65 66 67 68 69 70 71 72 73 74 75 76 77 78 79 80 81
OW
OW
3rd prominent prow
Big Ponderosa Tree
Big Ponderosa Tree
Prominent Arête
South Talus Field
Middle Forest

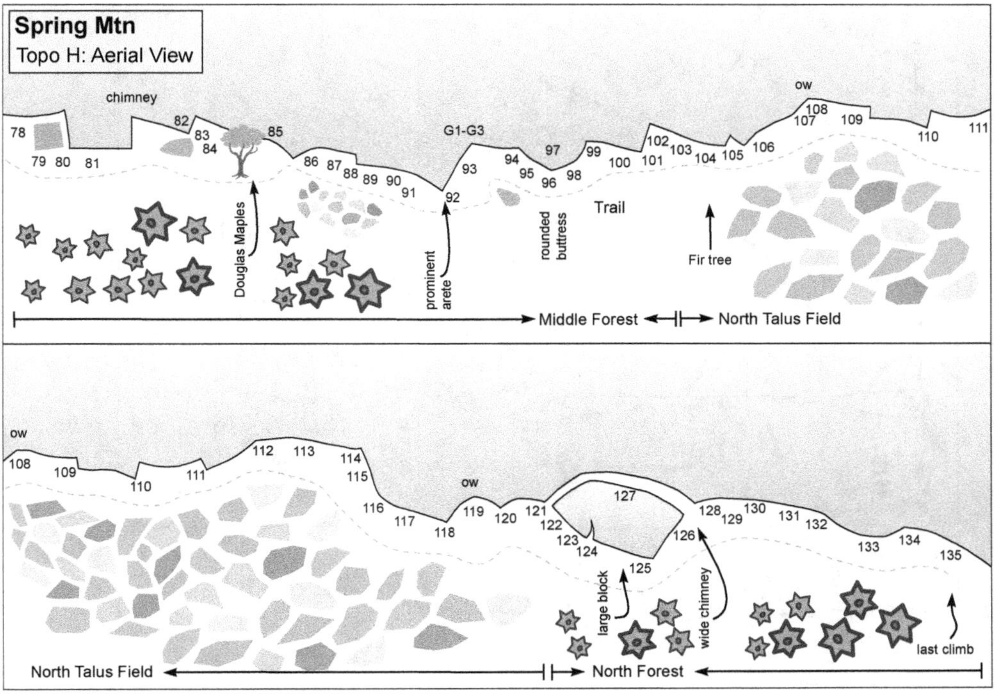
Spring Mtn
Topo H: Aerial View
chimney
78 79 80 81 82 83 84 85 86 87 88 89 90 91 92 93 94 95 96 97 98 99 100 101 102 103 104 105 106 107 108 109 110 111
G1-G3
ow
Trail
Douglas Maples
prominent arete
rounded buttress
Fir tree
Middle Forest
North Talus Field
ow
108 109 110 111 112 113 114 115 116 117 118 119 120 121 122 123 124 125 126 127 128 129 130 131 132 133 134 135
ow
large block
wide chimney
last climb
North Talus Field
North Forest

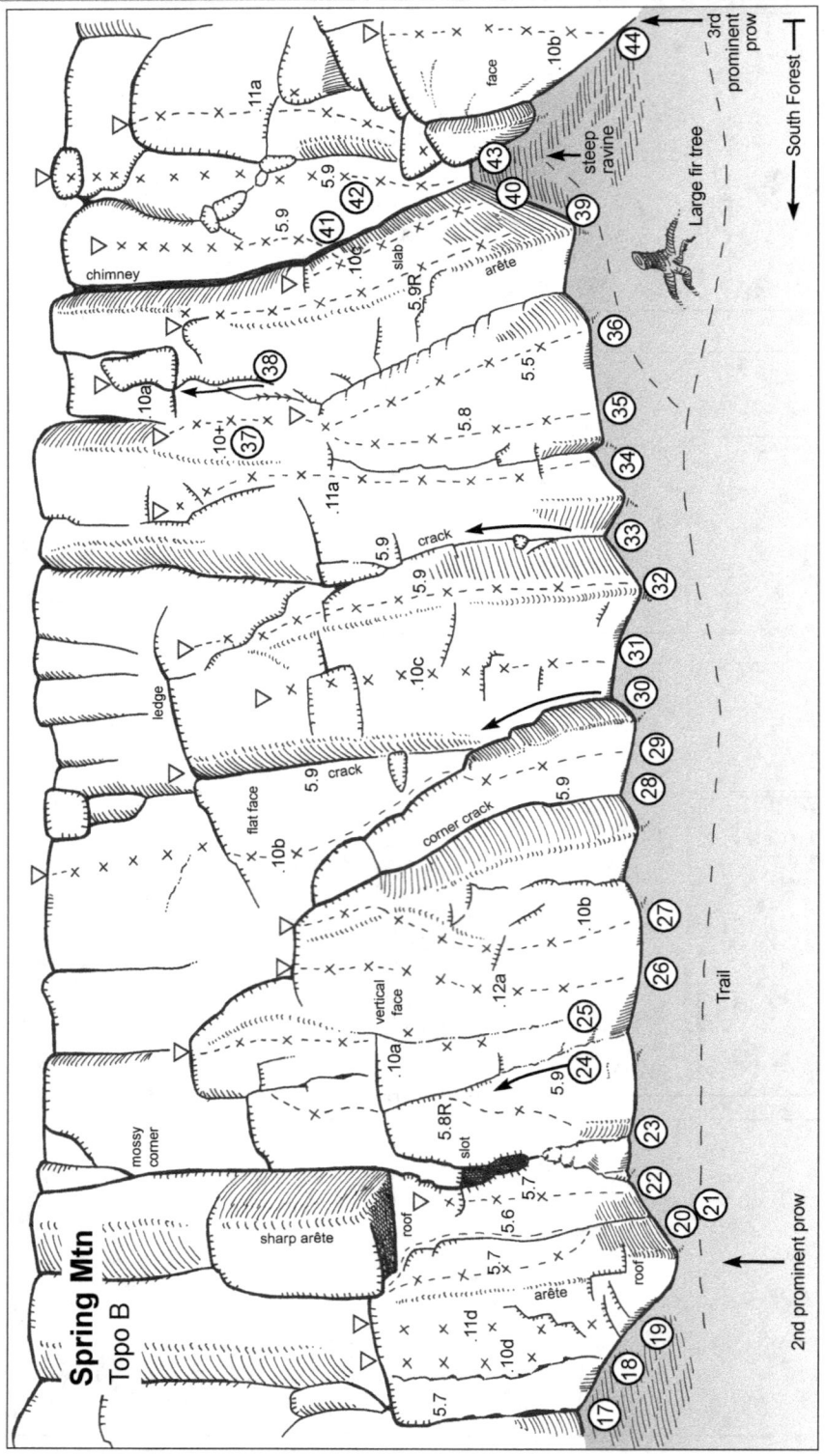

9. **Welcome to Spring Mtn (regular) 5.8** ★★★
   Pro: (sport) 8 QD's, FA: KP
   Face climb just past small overhang. Rap chains in place.
10. **The Diving Board 5.9** ★★
    Pro: (trad) up to 4 ½" cams for P2 offwidth, FA: JC
    The slightly mossy crack just to the right of Welcome to Spring Mountain. P1: Climb the crack and face to the belay for WTSM. P2: Climb the steep off-width to the top of the cliff.
11. **Spider 5.11c** ★★★
    Pro: (sport) 8 QD's, FA: SB
    Start up a fine quality slabby face, and continue up the steep crimpy and balancy headwall above. Rap hangers.
12. **Fish for the Future 5.8**
    Pro: (trad) _____, FA: BB
    Wide crack right of Spider. Rarely climbed, somewhat dirty. Shares chain anchor with Moving to Manhatten.
13. **Moving to Manhatten 5.10b**
    Pro: (trad) _____, FA: JC
    Somewhat narrower crack right of Fish for the Future. Pull a strenuous overhanging block and then undercling your way up left (sketchy feet) to chain anchors below another overhang.
14. **Nurse Ratchet 5.10c** ★★
    Pro: (sport) 12 QD's, FA: KP
    Slab to overhanging rounded arête. Step left around corner after pulling the overhang. When leading avoid clipping hanger on ledge above overhang (it's for directing rope for top-roping). Take a #3 friend to supplement bolts above overhang (optional). Rap chains.
15. **Mirage a' Trois 5.10a** ★★
    Pro: (sport) 11 QD's, FA: KP
    Climb the steep, apparently well-featured slab just past the wide dirty crack right of Nurse Ratchet. Most of those nice looking holds vanish into thin air on close approach. Rap hangers.
16. **Face the Facts 5.9** ★
    Pro: (sport) 5 QD's, FA: BB
    Climbs a gentler section of the same slab as Mirage a' Trois starting about 8' farther right. Crux is getting to the first clip. Stick-clip suggested. Rap hangers.
17. **Face the Crook 5.7** ★
    Pro: (trad) medium-large cams, FA: KP
    Stem and jam the crack in the dihedral between Face the Facts and By Hook or by Crook. After 40' traverse right to rap hangers.
18. **By Hook or by Crook 5.10d** ★★★
    Pro: (sport) 4 QD's, FA: MH
    A good route that asends a slightly overhung pumpy face. Rap hangers.
19. **Unnamed 5.11d/.12a** ★★★
    Pro: (sport) 5 QD's, FA: SB?
    A bouldery start crux powers up onto a steep face to the right of By Hook Or By Crook. Cold shut rap anchor.
20. **Exterminailer 5.7** ★★
    Pro: (sport) 7 QD's, FA: JS
    A fine quality face climb on a steep slab just above a large roof 15' right of By Hook or by Crook. Above the third bolt it is possible to traverse left to double cold shut anchors for "unnamed" or to anchors for By Hook Or By Crook. Exterminailer continues up and right above roof past 4 more clips to rap hangers near the top.

21. **Bat Crack 5.6** ★★
    Pro: (trad) small-medium nuts and cams, FA: BB
    A well-protected obvious crack in corner immediately right of Exterminailer.
22. **Feat Petite 5.7** ★★
    Pro: (sport) 4 QD's, FA: KP
    A sporty slab climb on a short face next to Bat Crack. Cold shut anchor.
23. **Captain Winkie 5.8R**
    Pro: (sport) 3 QD's, A: JS
    Runout mossy and slabby face right of Feat Petite. Rap hangers.
24. **Shafted 5.9**
    Pro: (trad) ___, FA: MB
    Start in left-leaning crack in ledgy slab just right of Captain Winkie. Angle back to the right above a wide mossy section of the crack to reach a steep finger crack. Climb this crack (crux) to the anchors for Captain Winkie.
25. **Skinny Hippie 5.10a** ★★★
    Pro: (sport) 8 QD's, FA: SB
    Slab to steep techy smooth face using some thin finger jams in a seam. Rap hangers.
26. **Dog Show 5.12a** ★★
    Pro: (sport) 9 QD's, FA: SB
    Steep slab to overhanging steep techy face just right of Skinny Hippie. Rap hangers.
27. **Eaten Alive 5.10b** ★★
    Pro: (sport) 6 QD's, FA: KP
    Climb a 20' vertical crack, then bust up right past bulge, and race up the left edge of an easy ramp. Rap chains.
28. **Clavical Crack 5.9** ★
    Pro: (trad) ___, FA: TD
    Stem a dirty awkward crack in the corner to the right of Eaten Alive that finishes at Eaten Alive anchors.
29. **Triple Threat 5.10b** ★★
    Pro: (sport) 12 QD's, FA: KP
    Start on a steep crimpy face 10' right of Eaten Alive (stick clip first bolt). Route continues straight up alternating between slabs and gently overhanging faces. Rap hangers.
30. **Cruisin' to a Bruisin' 5.9** ★★
    Pro: (trad) ___, FA: KP
    Climb a well protected crack past a layback crux near the top. Ends on a ledge with double cold shuts.
31. **Crimp or Wimp 5.10c** ★★★
    Pro: (sport) 8 QD's, FA: KP
    Climb the thin balancy slightly hung face 5' to the right of Triple Threat. Crux at third bolt. Rap hangers.
32. **Flaked Out 5.9** ★★★
    Pro: (sport) 10 QD's, FA: KP
    Climb a slab past a steep thin section to a flake, undercling flake up left to jam crack. Rap chains. The Flaky Wimp variation (5.10c) can be done by clipping the first few bolts on Crimp or Wimp, then move slightly right to join Flaked Out.
33. **Sfinks Crack 5.9** ★★
    Pro: (trad) ___, FA: JC
    An open book corner crack with tricky pro placements and a bulge crux about 20' up the route. Exit left at 60' up to double cold shuts.

34. Mojo Risin' 5.11a ★★★
Pro: (sport) 10 QD's, FA: KP
A long, vertical techy face climb involving some pump factor due to its steepness. Rap chains.

35. Aloha Direct 5.8 ★★
Pro: (sport) 6 QD's, FA: KP
Long steep steep face route (crux at 2nd bolt) that steps right at 30' and joins the next climb. Cold shut rap anchor.

36. Hawaiian Slab 5.5 ★★★
Pro: (sport) 5 QD's, FA: KP
A quality ramp face climb with a crux midway up route. Shares anchor with AD. Cold shut rap anchor.

37. Split Decision 5.10c/d ★★
Pro: (sport) 3 QD's, FA: KP
Continues above Hawaiian Slab into a dihedral above the belay. Creative stemming and power crimping permits a traverse left under overhang to anchors above a good ledge. Rap hangers.

38. Moufot's Woof 5.10a
Pro: (trad) medium cams and nuts, FA: JC
From the anchors for Hawaiian Slab, jam the crack on the right wall of the dihedral to below a roof. Pull through the roof using the magnificent hand crack provided. The route ends at chains 10' above the roof.

39. Funny Trumpets Arête 5.9R
Pro: (sport) 7 QD's, FA: BB
Runout mossy slabby ramp with an arête on the immediate left (has 2 fixed pins). Rap anchor.

40. Noble Slabbage 5.10c ★★
Pro: (sport) 4 QD's, FA: KP
Starts on same ramp as above by ascending straight up the middle of the slab, then veer right to gain the ledge above the 4th bolt (holds right of bolt line are off-route otherwise rating is a mere 5.9). Rap hangers.

41. Shagadelic Groove 5.9 ★★
Pro: (sport) 12 QD's, FA: KP
Shares first 4 bolts with Noble Slabbage. The next three climbs all start at the head of the steep eroding slope right of Noble Slabbage. This is the one on the left. Climb the slab staying just left of the wide crack. From the Noble Slabbage anchor ledge, step across a wide gully, up and right onto a steep face with a prominent flake. Continue up past 8 bolts to anchors near the top of the cliff. Rap hangers.

42. Deep Impact 5.9 ★★
Pro: (sport) 13 QD's, FA: KP
This is the middle route at the head of the steep eroding slope. Climb a ledgy face to a steep pull past a giant chockstone. Stem and/or chimney up a corner with two wide cracks clipping bolts on the face to the left. Make a delicate traverse move onto the face to the left of the corner and up to a good ledge. Finish with an airy step out to the right to reach the anchors. Rap hangers.

43. Mantle with Care 5.11a ★
Pro: (sport) 8 QD's, FA: BL
This is the right route at the head of the steep eroding slope. Climb a blunt arête with a strenuous mantle to an overhang surmounted with another difficult mantle. The slab above is equally challenging. Rap chains.

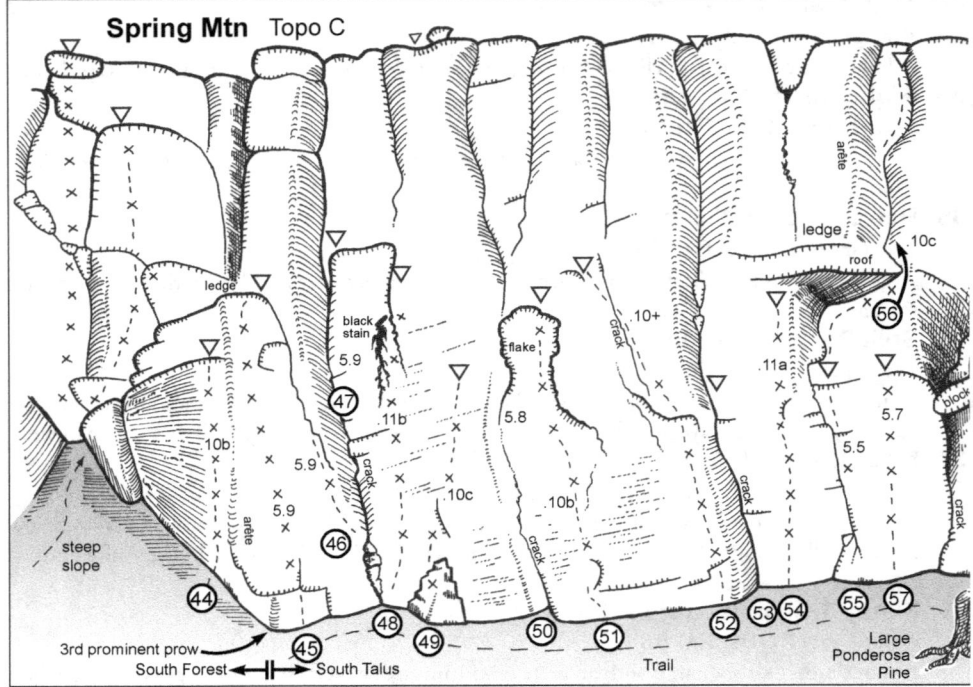

44. Breathe the Air 5.10b ★★★
Pro: (sport) 5 QD's, FA: SB
A sustained difficult face climb that starts low on the left side of the 3rd prominent prow (blunt arête) at the entrance to first talus field. Rap hangers.

South Talus Field

Just past the South Forest you will enter onto a sunny broad talus field with a brilliant reddish-orange hue colored section of wall lined with a great selection of routes. This popular section of wall but can be quite hot in the morning hours during the summer.

45. Fab Slab 5.9 ★★★
Pro: (sport) 9 QD's, FA: KP
Start at 3rd prominent prow/arête under a short overhang at left side of first talus field. Crank through the devious overhang (crux) and continue up a slab to short steep headwall. Stick clip first bolt. Rap hangers.

46. Red 5.9 ★★★
Pro: (mixed lead) gear to 3", FA: JJ
On the same steep slab as the previous route climb reachy crimpy face holds past 3 bolts to a crack, then climb the crack straight up through a bulge to Fab Slab rap anchors.

47. Triple Arthrodesis 5.9 ★
Pro: (trad) medium to large nuts and cams, FA: TD
High quality corner crack. Climb ledgy face left of crack in dihedral to rap hangers (5.5). Stop here, or crank through a steep lieback and fist crack (5.9) to ledge with rap hangers. The Dirty Dancing variation (trad 5.7): Traverse left at the lower anchors to upper crack of Red and climb through a short steep bulge to reach the anchors for Fab Slab.

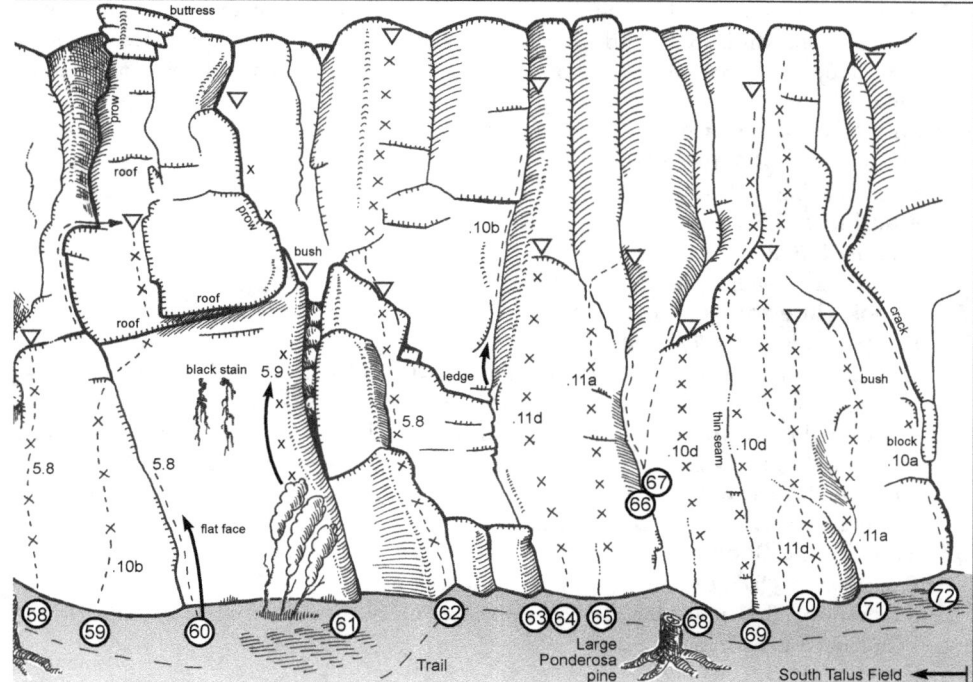

48. Blackout 5.11b ★★★
Pro: (sport) 7 QD's, FA: KH
Climb a steep face past a (black streak) techy overhanging crux to an anchor. Rap hangers.

49. Snapped it Off 5.10c ★★
Pro: (sport) 5 QD's, FA: SB
A steep face climb next to a minor arete. Rap hangers.

50. The pod of god 5.8 ★★★
Pro: (trad) medium, FA: JC
A corner crack climb with a tricky bulge crux near the flake. Prudent pro placements at flake section will limit risk. Joins at anchor for Rally Race.

51. Rally Race 5.10b ★★★
Pro: (sport) 6 QD's, FA: SB
A popular steep techy face climb (with a crux start) leading up to a seam then a crack on the right side of a prominent flake. Stick clip first bolt. Rap hangers.

52. TBA 5.10c/d ★★
Pro: (mixed lead) gear to 1", FA: MH
Starts at head of talus field at small overhang. Climbs past 4 bolts to crack (pro to 1"). Continues above rap hangers past three bolts to top (upper section is dirty, loose, and not recommended). Variation: Climb the first 25' of Geophysical then step left to join TBA at the last bolt. This lowers the rating to 5.10b.

53. Geophysical 5.6 to 5.10a ★★
Pro: (mixed lead) medium to large cams and nuts, FA: KP
Climbs crack system right of TBA to the top of the cliff. First 35' is fun, easy-to-protect crack climbing suitable for a beginning traditional leader. Quick clip anchors at the top of this section allow a speedy descent. Above the first anchors, the climbing is steeper and more physical with two strenuous wide-crack cruxes. There are single bolts at each of these difficult-to-pro-

tect spots. There are two bolts on the face near the top of the cliff that protect moves toward the top chains which are 10' to the right of where the crack intersects the rim (need 60-meter rope to top-rope, don't lower from top anchors with a 50-meter rope.). 4 bolts, intermediate and top anchors.

54. Initiation 5.11a ★★
Pro: (sport) 6 QD's, FA: KH
Steep face climb using sloper holds leading up to an arête below a large roof. Rap hangers.

55. Wanderer 5.5
Pro: (trad) medium, FA: BB
A minor crack with big ledges to rap hangers 25' up.

56. Snack Time for Kea 5.10c ★
Pro: (mixed lead) small to medium nuts and cams, FA: JC
Clip the anchors for Wanderer and continue straight up into a dihedral with fun liebacking (5.9). Clip the rap hangers and come down from underneath the big roof or make a sketchy traverse right past two bolts to reach another crack/dihedral system. Follow a tips crack straight up (soft rock and small gear) and then move right underneath another bulge (crux) staying to the right of a wider crack. Beware of rope drag after the roof. You'll need a 60-meter rope to top-rope. Rap from chain anchor.

57. Blue Suede Shoes 5.7 ★★
Pro: (sport) 5 QD's, FA: KP
Starts at large flake near a big ponderosa pine tree. Climbs a steep angular face to the right of Wanderer. Rap hangers.

58. Geophagy 5.8 ★
Pro: (sport) 4 QD's, FA: KP
Climbs slabby face to steep finish 20' right of Blue Suede Shoes. Rap chains.

The Middle Forest

A central section of cliff between two talus fields that has some minor brush, Douglas maples, and small fir trees near the base of this wall.

59. Epiphany 5.10b ★★★
Pro: (sport) 6 QD's, FA: KP
Starts on boulder 10' right of big ponderosa pine tree and climb up a ledgy slab angling right up to and over a large 4' roof. Don't clip the last bolt until you've cranked through the overhang or ignore it entirely. Rap hangers.

60. Trix 5.8
Pro: (trad) small to medium, FA: BB
Left slanting hand/finger crack 8' right of Epiphany. Ends on same ledge system as Epiphany. There are no anchors but it is possible to traverse right to the Epiphany anchors.

61. Something Else 5.9 ★★
Pro: (sport) 15 QD's, FA: KP
Climb steep face 20' right of Trix using sharp arête on right. Pull into dihedral and stem up to a good ledge with chains 45' up. Stop here or scramble up and left on some easy ground to more fun climbing on an exposed slab. Climb ends at chains near the top of the cliff. Rap chains.

62. Cornered 5.8 ★★
Pro: (mixed/sport-ish lead) gear 1-4", FA: KP
Stem up the arete/dihedral 10' right of Something Else. After 45' and 6 bolts (5.7) stop at chains on a big ledge, or continue straight up over big blocks past two more bolts to a fun crack system in a dihedral (gear, 1-4"). Ends at chains just below the top. Rap chains.

63. Dawg Daze 5.10b ★★★
Pro: (trad) small to large, FA: JC
Excellent steep crack climb 15' right of Cornered. Lower off from chains where crack deteriorates 20' below the top of the cliff.

64. Get a Grip 5.11d ★★
Pro: (sport) 7 QD's, FA: KH
Face climb up a techy face to a sustained red colored arête just right of DD crack. Rap chains.

65. Steppin' Out 5.11a ★★
Pro: (sport) 7 QD's, FA: MH
Ascend a steep face to a minor crack in a corner then back to the face and a left slanting crack. 10' right of Get a Grip. Rap chains.

66. Van Golden Brown 5.10d ★★
Pro: (trad) ___, FA: SB
A finger/hand crack system. Bail out left to rap hangers after 60' as upper part of crack has not been cleaned.

67. On My Face 5.10b ★
Pro: (trad) ___, FA: VS
Climb the first part of Van Golden Brown crack until it is possible to exit right to a thin crack about 20' up. Follow the thin crack straight up (somewhat difficult to protect) to the ledge

Spring Mtn
Map 1: South Talus

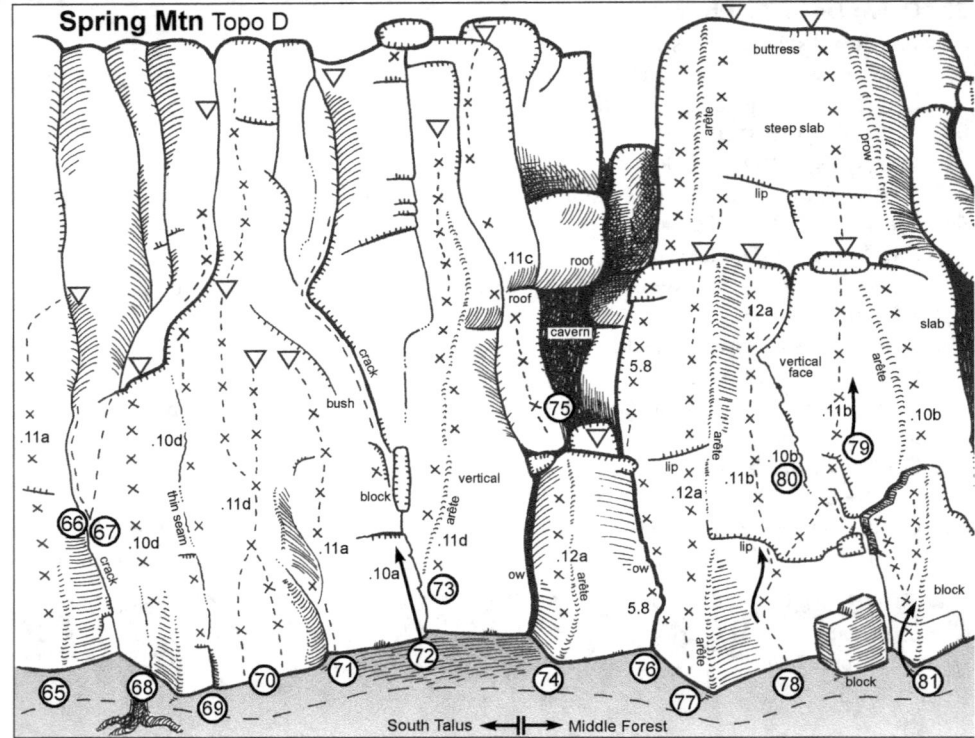

Spring Mtn Topo D

with anchors for Lorraine.

68. Lorraine 5.10d ★★★
Pro: (sport) 7 QD's, FA: KP
High quality face/seam climb on a steep discontinuous crack with pockets. Crux is at last bolt. Rap hangers.

69. Chicken Pox 5.10d ★
Pro: (sport) 8 QD's, FA: MH
Sustained steep face climb with three .10d crux sections. Seldom climbed, and upper part is dirty. Rap chains.

70. Mark's Route 5.11d ★★
Pro: (sport) 7 QD's, FA: MH
Steep, crimpy face climb just to the right of Chicken Pox. Stick clip first bolt. Rap chains.

71. Ticked 5.11a ★★
Pro: (sport) 5 QD's, FA: KP
Start in a shallow flared bolted dihedral and ascend up well featured section pulling through several short steep bulges to a sloping ledge with anchors. Rap hangers.

72. Inversion 5.10a
Pro: (mixed lead) medium to large, FA: KP
Start at a 2" wide crack 15' right of Ticked. When crack system widens and splits 20' up take the left fork. Climb past one bolt to a ledge and follow the crack system to the top. Five more bolts can be clipped (some placed for adjacent routes) between the ledge and the top, but be sure to take supplemental pro. Rap hangers.

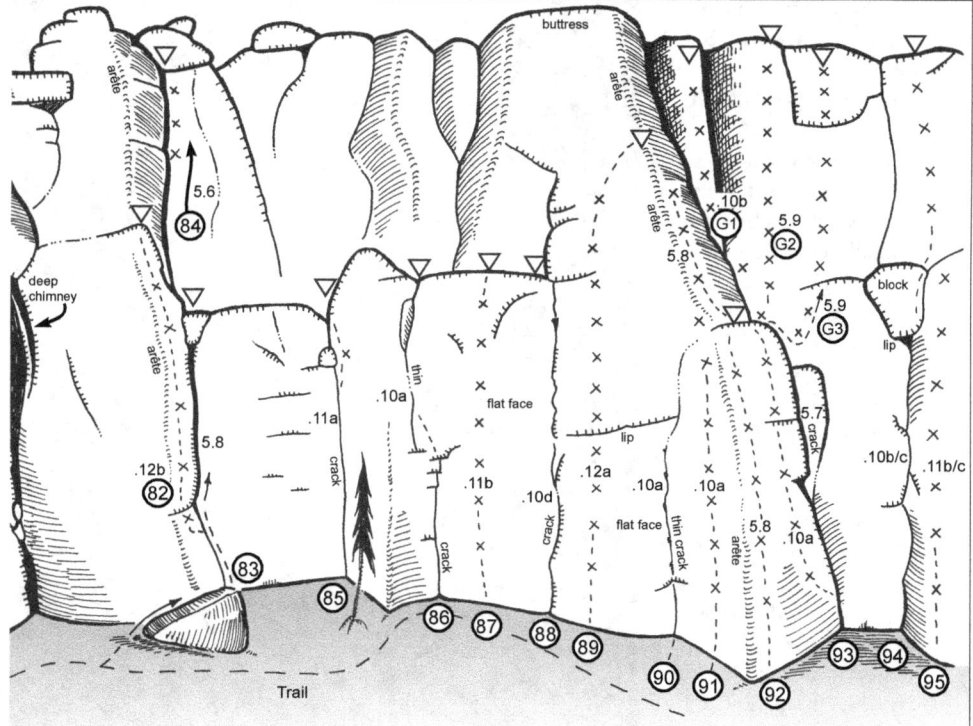

73. Tick Spray 5.11d ★★★
Pro: (sport) 12 QD's, FA: JD
Face climb up a sustained steep arête on lower half. Punch past a central overhang and continue up onto another long techy crux arete. Rap chains.

74. Smackdown 5.12a ★★★
Pro: (sport) 4 QD's, FA: JJ
A short 40' tall sharp profiled overhanging arête on a large block separated from main cliff. Rap chains.

75. Frogger 5.11c ★
Pro: (sport) 7 QD's, FA: JJ
Start on top of large block that hosts previous route and climbs through a crux bulge with small shallow dihedral. Continue up a rounded face above. Start is most easily reached via Chunky Monkey. Rap chains.

76. Chunky Monkey 5.8 ★★
Pro: (sport) 16 QD's, FA: KP
Lieback, arm-bar, and stem up wide steep offwidth in dihedral just left of Chubby Hubby. At the big ledge on top of the large block (best to belay here first), climb up onto a big boulder and make a delicate transitional step across to the right onto a buttress face. Continue up interesting featured steep face and slab to the summit anchor. Stay right of the bolt line for the last 5 clips to avoid potentially loose rock. This is one of the longer routes at Spring Mountain and requires a 60-meter rope to top-rope. Rap chains.

77. Chubby Hubby 5.12a ★★★
Pro: (sport) 9 QD's, FA: KH
Excellent quality climb on the left side of a prominent, sustained overhanging arête with a crux

at ⅔ height. Rap chains.

78. Freddy's Dead 5.11b (or .12a) ★★

Pro: (sport) 8 QD's, FA: MH

Follows right side of steep arête using horizontal pockets and knobs through a small roof. Continue up face using left hand holds on arête, then move up right to a crack (5.11b), or stay with the arête/face on the left (5.12a) for a punchier finish. Rap chains.

79. Hang 'em Higher 5.11b ★★

Pro: (sport) QD's, FA: KH

Clip first two bolts of Freddy's Dead and head up and right on steep thin face. Can also be climbed by clipping first two bolts on Doc Holiday then branching off to the left. Rap chains.

80. Block Party 5.10b

Pro: (trad) small to medium, FA: JC

Climb through the big scary, detached block (it's solid) and move out onto the finger crack in the face right of Freddy's Dead. Ends at Freddy's belay anchor.

81. Doc Holiday 5.10b ★★★

Pro: (sport) 15 QD's, FA: KP

Ascend steep face on left outside of buttress (just right of Freddy's Dead) to ledge below a blunt arête. Climb blunt arête via devious balance friction moves to a double cold shut anchor at ledge. End here or continue up knobby face past 5 more bolts to top of pinnacle ("Extended Holiday"). Need 60-meter rope to toprope from highest anchors. Unclip from cold shut anchor before continuing to top to lessen rope drag. Cold shut rap station with chains.

82. Unnamed 5.12b ★★

Pro: (sport) 6 QD's, FA: JJ?

Located near a large gray block about 30' right of Doc Holiday. Climb an easy ramp quickly busting out left onto the right side of a steep arête passing close to a big chimney en route to the belay anchor.

83. Cassidy's Crack 5.8

Pro: (trad) bring big pro!, FA: PC

Start at same place as previous route. Climb the wide crack system to a flared slot where you can muscle over a chockstone to belay chain anchor. Rappel or climb Spiral Stairs above.

84. Spiral Stairs 5.6 ★

Pro: (sport) 4 QD's, FA: KP

From the belay chain anchor on Cassidy's Crack, stem up the outside edge of a wide, wide chimney system directly (bolts) above to the top of the bluff. Rap chains.

85. Arthritis 5.11a ★★★
Pro: (trad) gear to 1", FA: SB
Steep high quality 40' tall thin finger crack located directly behind a tree. Chain rap anchor.

86. Longtime Coming 5.10a ★★
Pro: (trad) gear to 1", FA: MH
Steep thin crack just right of a minor arête. The good climb is mostly on delicate face edges with protection opportunities found in the crack. Chain rap anchor.

87. Drama Queen 5.11b
Pro: (sport) 7 QD's, FA: SB
Steep powerful thin face climb that may seem more like a 5.12- until you figure out the sequence. Rap chains.

88. Hospital Corner 5.10d ★★★
Pro: (trad) gear to 2" (including TCU's for crux), FA: SB
Awesome stemming and jamming up a steep corner. Ends after 60' at chain belay left of crack.

89. Puppets Without Strings 5.12a ★★★
Pro: (sport) 11 QD's, FA: SB
A very long steep techy and sustained face climb. Rap chains.

90. Nut Up 5.10a ★
Pro: (mixed lead) gear to 2", FA: SB
Ascend a surprisingly thin crack (tricky pro placements) on a steep face next to Puppets Without Strings. When the crack ends midway up the face, move right and follow four bolts to a belay anchor for Johnny Nowhere. Rap chains.

91. Johnny Nowhere 5.10a ★
Pro: (sport) 10 QD's, FA: JS
Climb a steep bolted face on the feft side of the arete just 10' right of a thin crack. This older style route may be a bit 'R' spicy for some. Rap chains.

92. Summertime Arête 5.8 ★★★
Pro: (sport) 10 QD's for full meal deal
FA: BB lower, KP upper portion called Endless Summer
Begin on the right side of the same arête used by Johnny Nowhere. Move up, then traverse out left onto the face, then climb the steep slabby face to a rap anchor on a ledge half-way up. Rappel...or climb "Endless Summer" to reach another set of rap hangers after 5 more bolts. Rap hangers.

93. Gidrah 5.9 to 5.10b ★★★
Pro: (sport) see paragraph below, FA: KP
Just like Godzilla's foe by the same name, this beast has three "heads". Begin in the dihedral right of Summertime Arête. Stick clip first bolt and climb the face (5.10a) or use the crack

Spring Mtn
Map 3: Middle Forest

(5.7). After the 6th or 7th bolt there are three ways to finish. For the middle or right head, down climb a bit and unclip the last bolt on the "torso" after you clip the first bolt on the "neck" to prevent rope drag. Left head [G1] (5.10b, 11 bolts): Continue straight up on a slab on the left side of the crack/chimney system and crimp up a steep rounded arête to a ledge with cold shuts. Middle head [G2] (5.9, 15 bolts): from friction slab above ledge, step right across a wide dirt-filled crack and climb a steep but juggy face to chain anchors at the top of the cliff. Right head [G3] (5.9, 15 bolts): from ledge with chains for Summertime Arête step right across crack to steep knobby face. Climb straight up to chains at the top of the cliff.

94. M.T.P. 5.10b/c ★★
Pro: (mixed lead) gear to ___, FA: JC
Climb the reasonable shallow open book crack in the corner via strenuous fist jams and surmount the obvious flake and crux roof on the right using the huge holds provided. Continue straight up to the top of the cliff clipping 4 bolts on the steep knobby face of the upper section of The Final Shred. Rap chains.

95. Unknown 5.11 [?]

Pro: ___ *(sport)*, *FA: [?]*
Climbs steep face just right of M.T.P.

96. The Final Shred 5.10d
★★★

Pro: (sport) 12 QD's, FA: MH
Excellent face climb on large rounded wide buttress. Climb a steep thin face, then use an arête continuing (six clips total) to rap anchor on ledge (5.10d). Quit here or move left and continue past 6 more bolts to anchors near the top of the cliff (5.10b). Intermediate and top belay anchors.

97. Junior Birdman 5.11a
★★

Pro: (sport) 4 QD's, FA: SB
Starts at mid-height belay anchor for The Final Shred, and continues straight up to top of cliff. Rap chains.

98. Mr. Flexible 5.11b ★★

Pro: (sport) 6 QD's, FA: SB
From the ground, climb next to a rounded arete on a steep face (right of The Final Shred). Avoiding the crack on right and arête on left gets you an .11b rating. Rap chains.

99. Chopper 5.8 ★★

Pro: (trad) gear to 3", FA: BB
Climb a dihedral crack system past a small crux roof and flake, then move up left to share belay chains with Mr. Flexible.

100. Etched in Stone 5.10a ★★

Pro: (sport) 15 QD's, FA: KP
Steep enjoyable face climb with pockets on left side of arete. Located behind a big dead tree. Clip the chains and rappel, or mantle over the lip to reach the anchors for Oot. Rap chains.

101. Oot and Aboot 5.10a ★★★

Pro: (sport) P1: 5 QD's, P2 10 QD's, FA: KP
Popular face climb on a prominent arete. P1: Five bolts lead to rap hangers at obvious ledge (Oot). P2: Continue past 10 more bolts to chains near the top of the cliff (Aboot). Rappel chains.

102. Stemulation 5.7 ★★

Pro: (trad) gear to ___, FA: KP
Slightly awkward crack in a corner. After 50' the crack deteriorates so step right to double cold shut anchors.

103. Digital Delight 5.10a ★★★
Pro: (trad) gear to 3", FA: JC
Steep thin crack right of Stemulation. Shares double cold shut anchor with Stemulation.

North Talus Field

This section has a broad rock talus field along the base of the wall. The cliff scarps sunny exposure can be a bit hot during summer morning hours but offers some stellar climbs including the hardest route at SM.

104. Johnny's Got a Gun 5.10a ★★
Pro: (sport) 10 QD's, FA: JS, MH
The lower pitch is a nice steep face climb that dances past a bulge (7 bolts) up to a belay anchor under a large roof. It is considerably harder if you avoid the arête on the right side. P2: Continue through the large roof above first belay passing 3 more bolts to another belay anchor. Intermediate and upper rap chains.

105. Blockhead 5.9 ★
Pro: (trad) gear to 4", FA: JC
Climb a variably featured crack offering jams, and face holds for 30', then bust right onto the other side of the arête and continue a few more feet to an anchor at a bush. Ends at same belay chains as Betaflash.

106. Betaflash 5.10b ★★
Pro: (sport) 5 QD's, FA: KP
Climbs the right side of the arête. Traverse in from boulders on the right to clip the first bolt. Start from the traverse or scramble back down and start at the base of the cliff to add more fun climbing. Rap hangers.

107. Crack Atowa 5.8 ★★
Pro: (mixed lead) P1 gear to 3", P2 6 QD's, FA: KP
The left crack in a broad open book corner system. P1: Jam the delightful hand crack, surmount the large flake (it's solid), and move up to a belay anchor. P2: continue past the quick-clip belay anchors to a delightful (six) bolt-protected chimney. Feel free to bail out at the first anchors if you are intimidated by the chimney. Rap chains.

108. Marley's Route 5.9 ★★
Pro: (trad) gear to ___, FA: JC
Climb the crack in the red colored corner 4' right of Crack Atowa. Ends below roof at rap hangers.

109. Indian Summer 5.9
Pro: (trad) gear to ___, FA: JC
Crack climb 10' right of Marley's Route.

110. Phoups 5.10b ★★
Pro: (trad) thin nuts and cams to a large 3½" cam, FA: JC
Thin finger crack in a shallow right facing dihedral at head of 2nd talus field. Lieback up a nice flake above dihedral and then traverse right past an awkward bulge to chain anchors 50' up. Large cam protects the traverse.

111. Phlogistomat 5.10d ★★
Pro: (sport) 8 QD's, FA: KP
Climbs face with small overhang 10' right of Phoups. Shares chains with Phoups. Usually TR after leading Phoups. Rap hangers.

112. Eighteen Wheeler 5.8
Pro: (trad) gear to ___, FA: JC
Climb crack in right-facing corner 10' right of Phlogistomat. Ends at rap hangers 45' up.

NORTHEAST OREGON 413

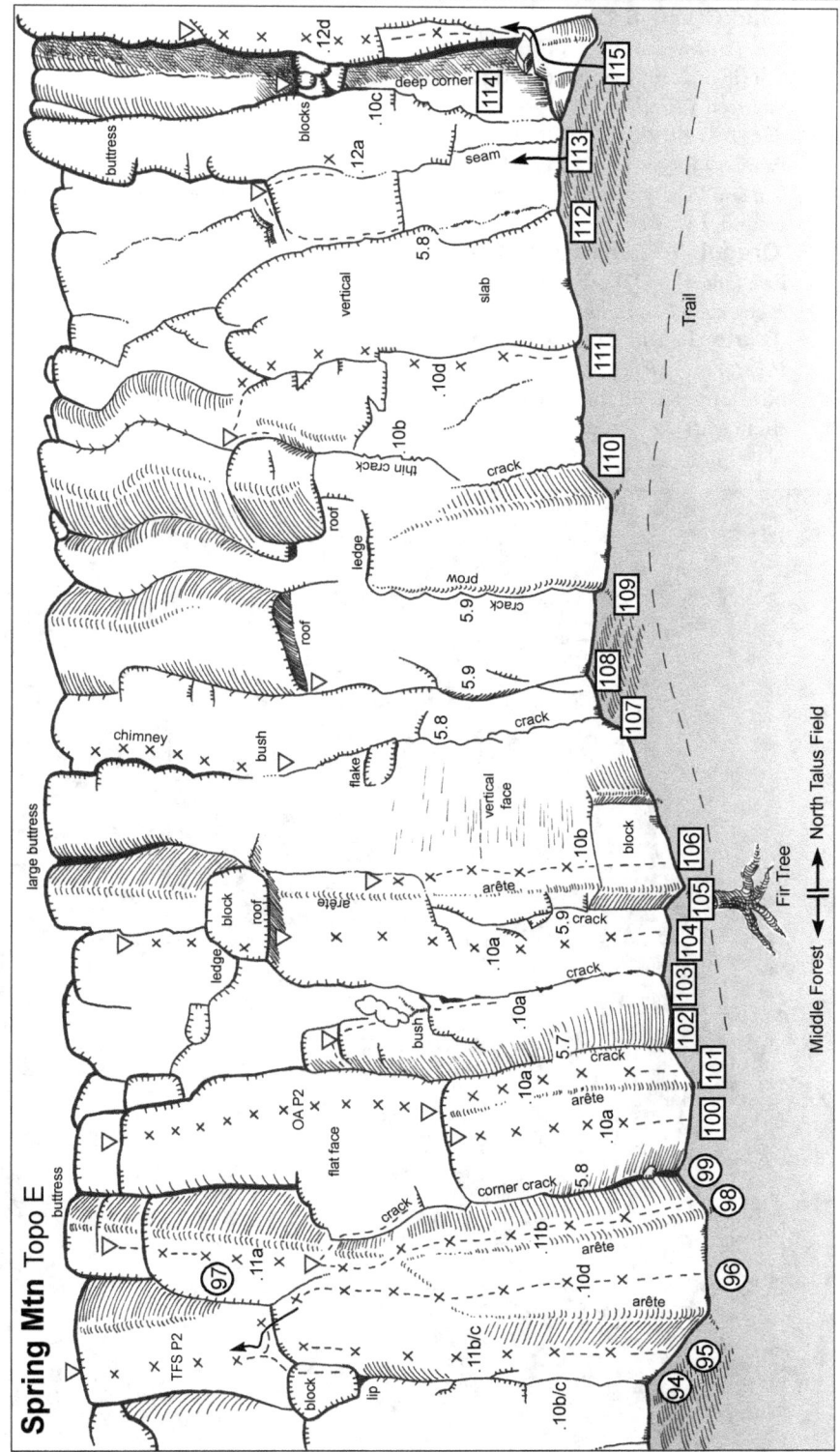

Spring Mtn Topo E

113. Mud Crack 5.12a
Pro: (trad) gear to ____, FA: JD
Jam (if you can) the very thin crack to the right of Eighteen Wheeler. Shares rap hangers with Eighteen Wheeler.

114. Gran Delusion 5.10c
Pro: (trad) gear to ____, FA: JC
Jam and lieback steep thin crack to the "Womb of Doom" below large chockstones. Stem out, around, and over chockstones to bouldery ledge with rap anchor belay.

115. Oregon Yosemite 5.12d ★
Pro: (sport) 6 QD's, FA: JD
A strenuous overhung face that ascends the right side of a large chimney system. Rap chains.

116. Blister in the Sun 5.12d ★★
Pro: (sport) 10 QD's, FA: JG
Nice long steep blunt arête with lime green lichen near center of second talus field. Strenuous climb with a techy crux on a blank slab 2 bolts below the belay anchor. Rap chains.

Spring Mtn
Map 6: North Talus

117. **Unknown 5.11d** ★★★
   Pro: (sport) 6 QD's, FA: KH?
   High quality steep arête and face climb on same formation as previous route with a thin crux up high.

118. **Final Exam 5.12c**
   Pro: (sport) 5 QD's, FA: JD
   Steep face just left of large crack system that hosts The Last Dance. Rap chains.

119. **The Last Dance 5.10b** ★★★
   Pro: (sport) 18 QD's, FA: KP
   A very long climb that starts at the base of an offwidth. Stem and chimney your way up the wide offwidth. Step right across the chimney to a ledge system then scamper up a beautiful exposed arete, moving left briefly two bolts from the top. Need a 60-m rope to lower from top anchors. Rap chains.

120. **Twister 5.10c** ★★★
   Pro: (sport) 5 QD's, FA: SB
   A short steep face route involving some delicate techy climbing. Rap chains.

121. **Eekwinocks 5.10c** ★★
   Pro: (trad) gear to ___, FA: JC
   The crack in the face between Twister and the obvious chimney. Ends at belay chains that are 5' above and right of chains for Twister.

122. **Phish Food 5.11c** ★★★
   Pro: (sport) 5 QD's, FA: KH
   A crimpy steep thin face route just right of a large chimney. Shares anchors with Plumber Boy. Rap chains.

North Forest

This section is popular on hot summer days because numerous tall fir and ponderosa trees shade much of this portion of the wall.

123. **Plumber Boy 5.10b** ★★★
   Pro: (sport) 6 QD's, FA: SB
   Face climb on south corner of large detached buttress just around the corner from Phish Food. Rap chains.

124. **M&M's 5.10a**
   Pro: (mixed) gear to ___, FA: MH
   Starts at large crack just right of Plumber Boy and takes right-leaning finger crack across steep face (3 bolts), intersecting Spring Cling about 20' up. Finish at belay anchors for Spring Cling. Rap chains.

125. **Spring Cling 5.10a** ★
   Pro: (sport) 6 QD's, FA: KP
   Start just right of crack on a thin steep face and climb up the outside of the large detached block formation. Can be finished directly (5.10b) via two bolts through overhang. Rap chains.

126. **Spring Fever 5.9** ★★★
   Pro: (sport) 11 QD's, FA: KP
   A very popular route that ascends the north end of a large detached block formation next to a 6' wide chimney/alcove. P1 (70') 11 QD's: Start on the east buttress of the large detached block formation (with wide chimney to the right) and climb a moderate angled blunt arête to the top of the formation. Belay chains. P2 (40') 5 QD's: Climb a steep knobby arête to a belay anchor near the upper cliff edge. Cold shut belay anchor.

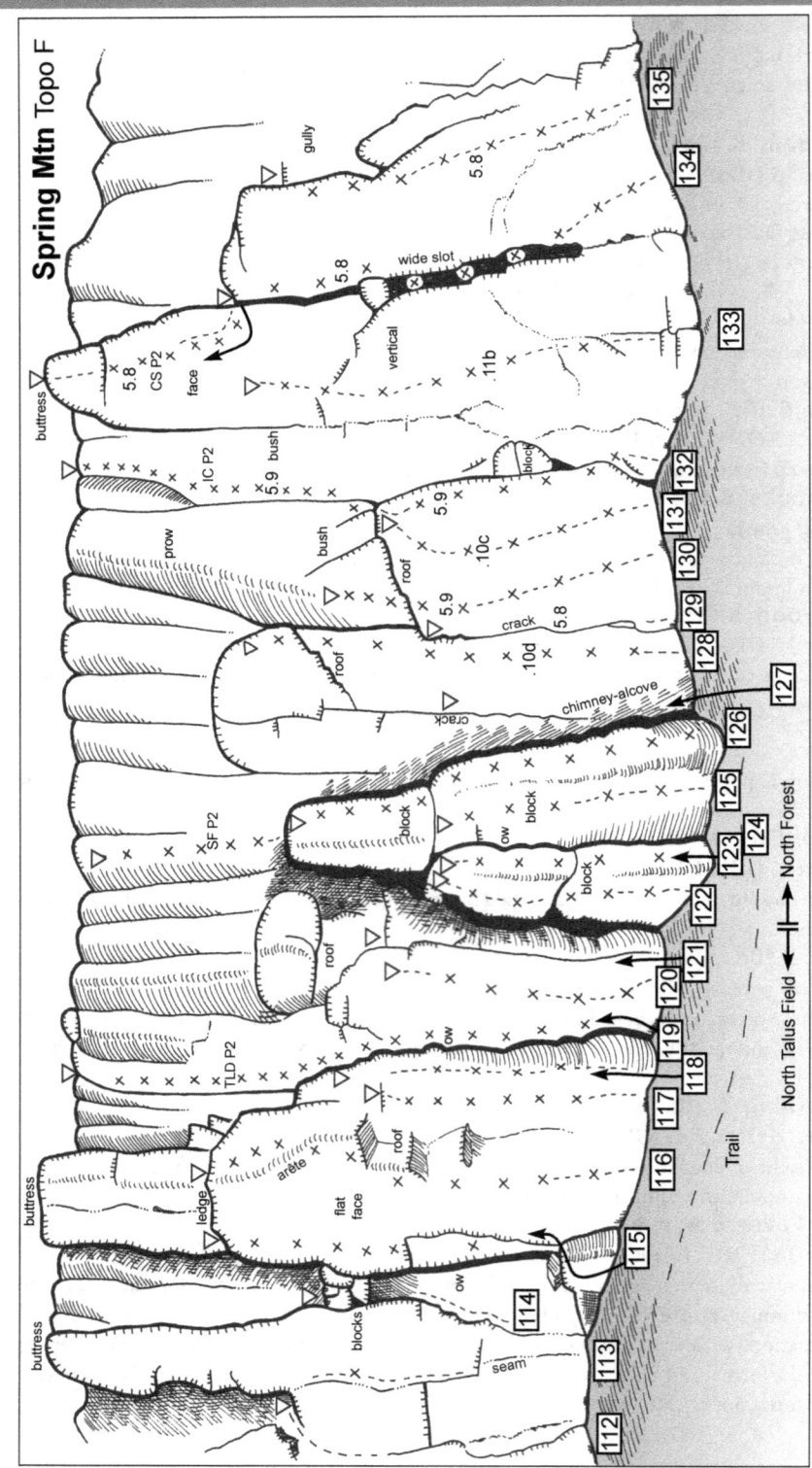

127. Maid in the Shade 5.9 ★★
Pro: (sport) 15 QD's, FA: KP
Scramble to the back of the large chimney/alcove right of Spring Fever and look for a hanger on the left wall. Chimney up about 15', cross a large chockstone, and climb a short face to a large ledge. Make a delicate traverse left (crux) to an exposed arête. Climb straight up the arête to an exciting mantle near the top. This is a good climb for a hot day. Rap hangers.

128. Learning to Fly 5.10d ★★
Pro: (sport) 9 QD's, FA: MH
A long steep face climb punching past two minor bulges. Located about 10' right of Spring Fever just past the chimney containing some large rotten logs. Rap chains.

129. Lively Up Yourself 5.8 ★★
Pro: (trad) gear to 3", FA: KP
The crack right of Learning to Fly. Ends at double cold shut anchor below dirty roof with trees.

130. Special Delivery 5.9 ★★
Pro: (sport) 9 QD's, FA: KP
Popular face climb that dances up left then up right for 30' (5 bolts), then punches past a small roof on large holds and continues up past 3 more bolts to an anchor. Rap chains.

131. Blue-Tailed Skink 5.10c
Pro: (sport) 5 QD's, FA: KP
Short face climb 10' right of Special Delivery on the same wide section of face. Steep climbing on big holds leads to a thin crux on slabbier section above. Rap hangers.

132. Iron Cross 5.9
Pro: (sport) 20 QD's, FA: KP
Start near crack 10' right of Blue-tailed Skink. Cross crack between 1st and 2nd bolts and climb face just left of crack to large ledge with Blue-Tailed Skink anchors. Scramble up more ledges, clipping two bolts, until large handholds make possible an exciting move right onto a slabby face. Climb this fun face to a corner with large blocks below an overhang. A series of exciting "iron cross" moves left and out around the overhang establishes you on a final short face just below the anchors. This is a long, fun climb with lots of bolts (60-m rope and 20 quick draws!). Rap chains.

133. Face Lift 5.11b ★★
Pro: (sport) 7 QD's, FA: MH
Just right of Iron Cross is a tall steep face. Climb the middle of the face aiming up left gradually passing a crux bulge section. Pumpy and sustained climbing. The 5.11b grade applies only to a line straight up the bolts. Most folks that lead this route make extensive use of a corner and crack system on the left, which lowers the grade to about 5.10c. Rap chains.

134. Clean Sweep 5.8 ★★
Pro: (sport) 15 QD's, FA: KP
This route, the longest at Spring Mountain, starts behind a tree 15' right of Face Lift. P1: Traverse up and left on ramp-like ledges to a steep slot. Stem through the slot and up a ledgy dihedral. Stop at belay chains at a big ledge above the dihedral. P2: work leftward above the Face Lift anchors and climb the outside of a blocky pillar past 6 more bolts to the top of the cliff. A 60-meter rope required. Rap chains.

135. Worth the Walk 5.8 ★★
Pro: (sport) 8 QD's, FA: KP
The last route on the cliff. This one lives up to its name if you enjoy steep rock with big holds. Start at the same place as Clean Sweep and climb straight up a system of fractures and blocks (they're solid) to a ledge. A few tricky slab moves get you to the top of the route. Rap chains.

THE DIKES

Original route beta manuscript (and portions of the intro) used for this section were loaned courtesy of Kevin Pogue

The Dikes are fin-like crags of basalt protruding from the steep eastern flank of Chase Mountain formed from intrusive igneous magma forced up through cracks in the landscape. These magma filled cracks were some of the conduits that supplied molten rock to the voluminous volcanic eruptions that produced the Columbia River flood basalts. After the eruptions ceased, the magma within the cracks slowly cooled and hardened into basalt more coarse-grained and less fractured than the contact zonal structure it intruded. The erosion resistant dikes decompose at a slower rate than the surrounding softer structure leaving behind large prominent fins of rock. The dike walls are vertical while the joints are horizontal, breaking the rock into horizontal columns resembling stacks of characteristic firewood-like "cordwood" jointing. For climbers, this pattern of jointing means that the climbing on the edges of a dike is very different from climbing on the sides.

The Dikes are bolted adventure climbing with limited user activity. Wear a helmet while climbing and belaying. Approaches are steep and trailless. Due to the nature of the horizontal fractures the dikes tend to be littered with easily detached loose chunks so anticipate loose rock (dirt and moss), especially if you are off route. On the plus side, the site offers sunny climbing when lower elevations are foggy and cold due to wintertime temperature inversions. The access road is plowed all winter (for ski area). Some areas remain shady and comfortably cool even when it's over 100°F in Walla Walla. If this type of wild 'choss' climbing is not your cup of tea, it is best to climb elsewhere.

Directions:

The Dikes are located in the Walla Walla Ranger District of the Umatilla National Forest in the East Fork Touchet River valley within a few miles of the Middle Point Ridge trailhead. From Walla Walla (1 hour drive) drive east on U.S. 12 to Dayton. Turn right (south) at Dayton just past the PDQ Chevron Mini-Mart where a sign points the way toward Bluewood ski area. The Touchet River valley gradually becomes steeper and narrower as you drive upstream. Between 16 and 17 miles from the turn at U.S. 12 you will reach the Middle Point Ridge trailhead parking on the left (east) side of the road. The directions to the parking spots for the various crags are referenced from this point so set your trip odometer to zero here. The Dikes area is 1.1 miles past the Middle Point Ridge Trailhead parking area at a pullout on the left (southeast) side of road. During winter ice forms just across the river. A trail leading to some of the routes on The Dikes begins on the other side of the road near a culvert.

Almost all of the climbs have been established on two closely spaced dikes that intersect the highway about 1½

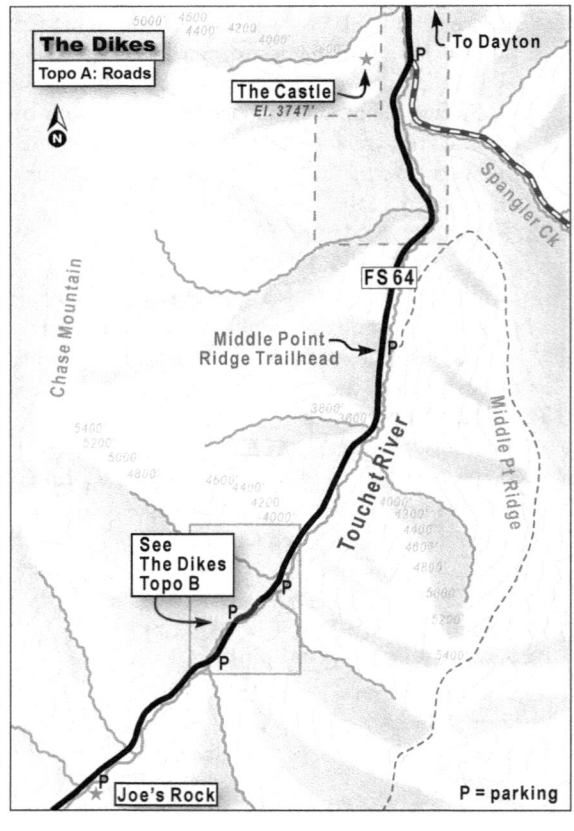

miles beyond the Middle Point Ridge trailhead. The eastern dike is called "Megadike" because it is the longest and thickest dike in the valley. The smaller western dike is "Minidike". Erosional breaching of the dikes creates discrete triangular fins like those on the back of a dragon.

The Approach:

1. To access the northern part of Megadike (The Dragon's Back and Cordwood Tower) park 1.1 miles past the Middle Point Ridge trailhead where a dirt road intersects the paved road on the left. Cross the paved road and look for the beginning of the approach trail (path A) where a culvert passes beneath the road.

2. To access the south part of Megadike drive 1¼ miles past the Middle Point Ridge trailhead and park on either side of the road near a bridge over the river. A faint path begins at a pile of rocks near the bridge abutment. Follow the trail (path C) uphill until it is possible to cross through the dike in a steep gully. Branch to the left early (path D) to reach Roadview wall. In early season, follow the more exposed (and snow-free) ridgeline to the east (path B) to reach the Febmar wall.

3. To reach the Minidike park 1½ miles past the Middle Point Ridge trailhead on the left side of the road just before a bridge over the river. Walk across the bridge, scramble down the embankment, and follow a trail (path E) downstream on the NW side. A steep uphill trail leading to the west side of Minidike branches off just before the Local Boy's wall comes into view.

Joe's Rock is a rather small boulder-like erosional remnant of a dike on the south bank of the East Fork Touchet River. The top of the rock is level with the road. Park in a wide pullout, scramble down and cross the river after snowmelt has dissipated. Presently only one route on Joe's Rock.

Weeping Wall is a 40' tall well fractured cliff formed by erosional undercutting of the basalt bedrock by the East Fork Touchet River. About 40' above the river a series of seeping springs issue from a ledge that marks the boundary between two basalt flows. In winters both cold and wet enough the seeps freeze to form ice thick enough to climb. Once formed, the ice persists for weeks due to its shaded location. A series of six an-

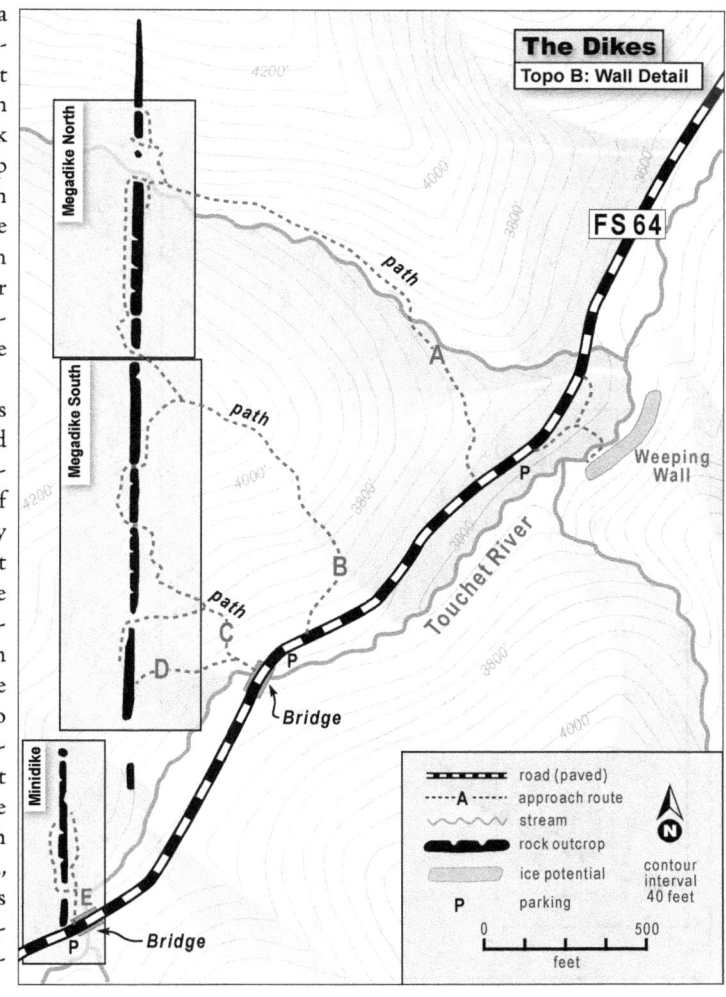

The Dikes
Topo C: Closeup and Beta

Minidike
Local Boys Wall
1. Firearms 5.10b
2. Cheap Beer 5.11c
3. Internal Combustion 5.10a
4. Just For Fun 5.5
5. Ahoot 5.8
6. Joe's Arete 5.8
7. Henpecked 5.7

Megadike South
Roadview Wall
8. Curly 5.10d
9. Moe 5.8
10. Larry 5.7
Black Tooth
11. Dirty Dog 5.8
12. project 5.9
13. Redtail Arete 5.7
14. Heinous Thing 5.10b
15. Way Up 5.0
Febmar Wall
16. Safety Dance 5.8
17. Czech It Out 5.10a

Megadike North
Dragon's Back
18. Sketchfest 5.3
19. Blown Away 5.8
20. project
21. Out There 5.9
22. Psychotic Interlude 5.8
23. Face Farce 5.8
24. Rad Zinger 5.7
25. Morning Thunder 5.9
26. Fathers and Sons 5.4
27. Stem-gem 5.9+
28. Chunky Scoop 5.9
29. project 5.11
30. project 5.9
31. Desperate Housewives 5.8
32. You're Not Worthy 5.9
33. Just Enough 5.8
34. Notta Slab 5.8
35. Lady Slipper 5.5
Cordwood Tower
36. Monkey on a Woodpile 5.5
37. Cordwood 5.8

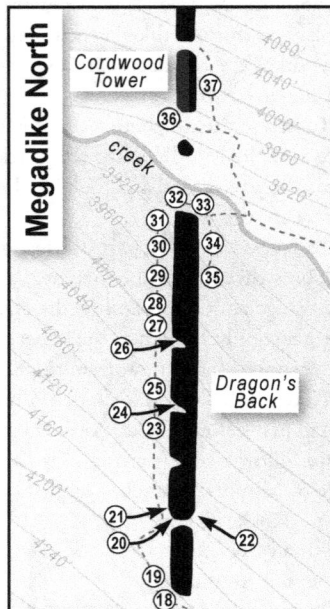

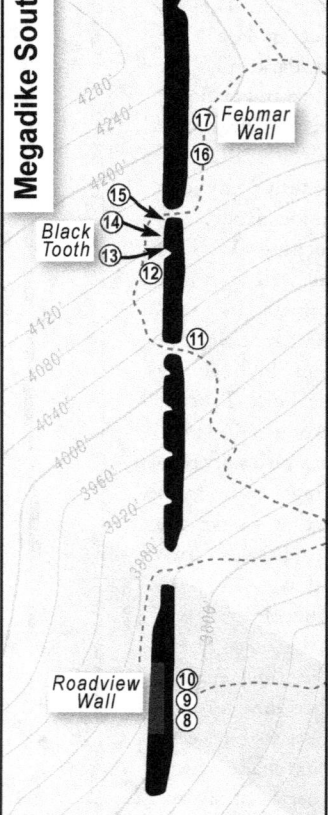

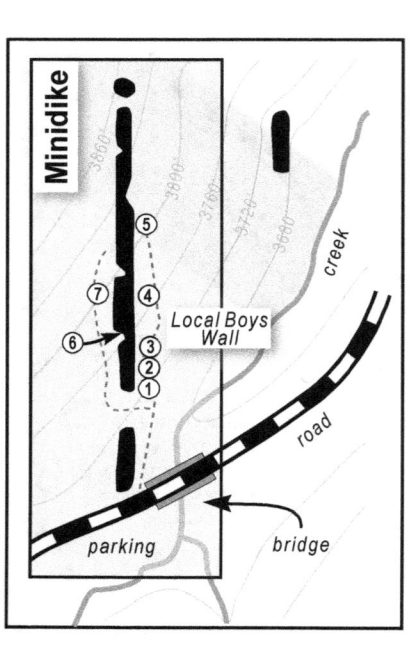

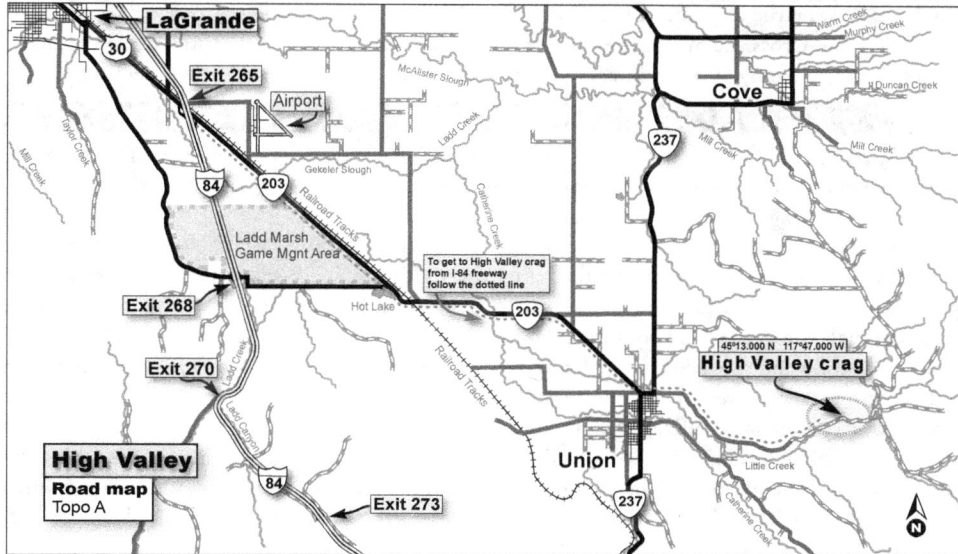

chor sets exist along the ledge, although it is sometimes necessary to chip through 6-8" of ice to reach the anchors. To set up top-ropes walk around the right side of the cliff and rappel down to the ledge from trees on the hillside above. Cliff steepness and rating difficulty increase leftward (WI2 to WI5). Weeping Wall is 1.1 miles past the MPR trailhead. Park on the left where a dirt road intersects the main road (also used to access parts of Megadike).

The Castle is a 45' tall rock outcrop situated on a ridgecrest just west of the confluence of Spangler Creek and East Fork Touchet River. The Castle is not eroded from a dike, but consists of parts of three lava flows of the Columbia River basalt. The short vertical columns at the base of the flows are compact, while the fractured upper flows offer small vesicles produced by gas bubbles in the lava. The nature of the outcrop or the stout uphill hike may dissuade you from venturing

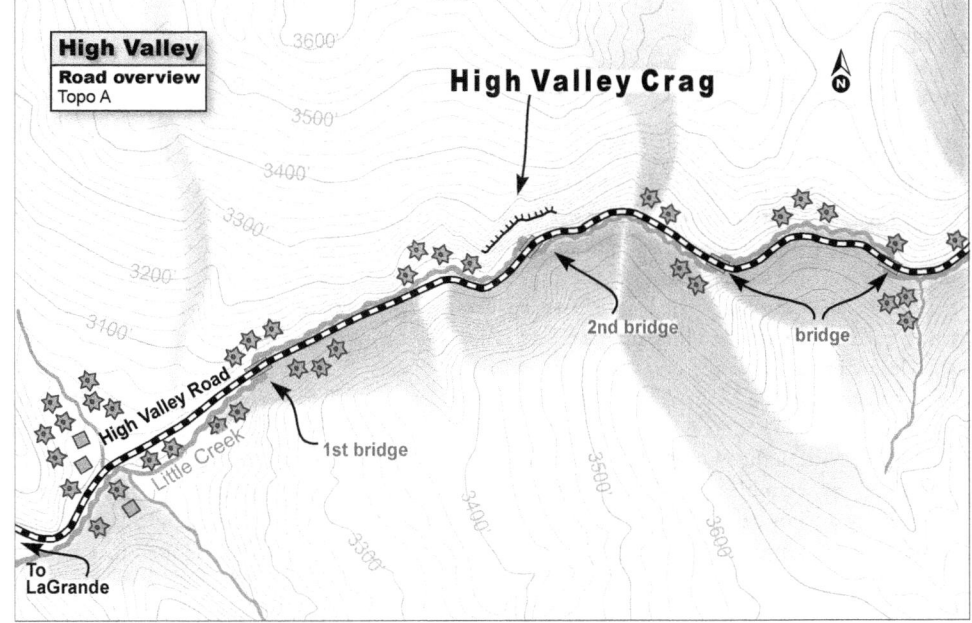

up there. Park on the east side of the road where a dirt road from Spangler Creek valley intersects the main road. Cross the main road and hike up a long steep hillside. All routes are south facing, established on a sunny 50°F+ winter day when Walla Walla was foggy and below freezing.

HIGH VALLEY

High Valley route beta written by and provided courtesy of Allen Sanderson. His reference sources were (Summit V33 N4 1987) (Sanderson and Ryman), Climbing N100 1987 (Sanderson and Ryman), and Climbing N119 1990 (M. Hauter).

High Valley is a small 25' to 60-foot tall rimrock basalt bluff that has conveniently served the interests of local LaGrande rock climbers since the 1970s. The crag offers single-pitch traditional gear leads and sport routes using various cracks, corners, and prows. The crag is nestled above the meandering Little Creek Canyon, surrounded by semi-arid grassland hills accentuated with occasional pine trees and creekside willows. High Valley (30 minutes from LaGrande) is popular from Fall to Spring, and on reasonably temperate Summer days. There is limited parking space, so the site is not recommended for large groups.

The well-known alpinist Steve House, began his climbing career at this crag in the 1980s. Allen Sanderson, one of the founding board members of the Access Fund, started climbing at High Valley during the late 1970s. Both were involved in the high school climbing club called the "Cliffhangers", an organization spearheaded by Joe Sandoz and Steve Ryman. The Cliffhangers often utilized High Valley as their rock climbing practical learning site.

High Valley was initially tapped into by Lin Casciato, Mark Kerns, and Richard Wilkins. They pioneered notable classics, including Do or Fly, a stout 5.10 overhanging jam crack. In the same decade Steve and Stu Ryman established the aptly named Pesky Rodent, a 5.7 offwidth crack. Allen Sanderson completed several ascents, Sausalito (5.7+) in 1981, and Unnamed Symphony (5.9) in the summer of 1983. In 1989 Mark Hauter established the technical La Siesta Tick Attack (5.11c) on mostly trad gear (bolts at crux). A slightly overhung blunt face/arête climb with long reaches named Wasp Roast (5.11b), also freed by Hauter, is now considered to be one of the better climbs at the crag. In the same year, Hauter established Elvis is Everywhere (5.12a), High Valley's hardest climb. Later this same year, Steve Brown freed the overhanging face right of Smokestack chimney, calling it Chimney Face (5.11b), while Brown and Hendrickson did an initial TR on the chimneys left face (5.10b), saving the lead for another date. For the bouldering enthusiest, a short distance north from the main crag is a 20' tall rock band that stretches for several hundred feet, offering a long powerful traverse, and numerous vert boulder problems. The lengthy traverse, rarely completed in a one-shot circuit, involves intricate moves, pendulums, overhangs and blind corners.

While High Valley crag is on private land. The owner has graciously allowed climbers access to the land for rock climbing purposes, but with limitations that depend on your courtesy and ability to show responsibility in how you care for the site (e.g. no littering, leave gates as you find them). Be respectful of the owners rights, and use the site with discretion. The property owner is NOT responsible for any injury, damages, theft, etc., so you assume all personal risks associated with visiting and climbing here. The land is used for livestock pastureland grazing purposes (you must cross a barbed wire fence to hike up the user trail) so beware of the organic bovine frisbees, as well as rattlesnakes and a healthy community of rodents.

Trail access: The Main Wall is located about 200' above the road on a southeast facing bluff that receive morning sunshine. From the bridge, step over the barbed wire fence, then hike up a steep zigzag path to the bluff. A short ravine on the right end of the wall offers scrambling access to the rim top (or scramble up on the far left). Most of the climbs require long slings and natural gear to set up top anchor belays. Bridge Rock is a minor short bluff formation located next to the parking spot near the bridge. This roadside bluff offers a convenient smattering of bolted rock climbs.

Do a few, then hustle upstairs to the greater rewards.

Driving directions: From LaGrande take exit #265 and drive southeast on State Route 203 for 11 miles to the small community of Union. Continue east on State Route 237 (Lower Cove Road), then at a Y branch off right onto High Valley Road. Drive this (turns to gravel in two miles) till the valley narrows into a rim rock canyon. Prior to a white bridge, park your vehicle on the right side of the road. The main (upper) wall is a double-tiered bluff system that is uphill about 300' on the north side of road. Be sure to park well off to the side of the narrow gravel road. Fee camping is available east of Cove, but free camping is feasible to the east of the climbing site a few miles, or east of Cove. Nearest major town with a full selection of amenities (and a hospital for emergencies) is LaGrande.

Main (upper) Wall

Routes are listed from right to left. Trilobites is just right of the approach trail on the east end of the bluff.

1. **Trilobites 5.8+**

    Pro: nuts and cams; length 25'
    FA: unknown

    Three short 25' tall climbs located within 10' of each other to the right of the approach trail. The left is a 5.8+ finger crack, the middle is a 5.6 off-width open book corner, and on the right is a 5.4 squeeze chimney.

2. **_____ 5.11a**

    A minor sport route a short distance east of Two Cheeks.

3. **_____ 5.10b**

    A TR located next to the above route.

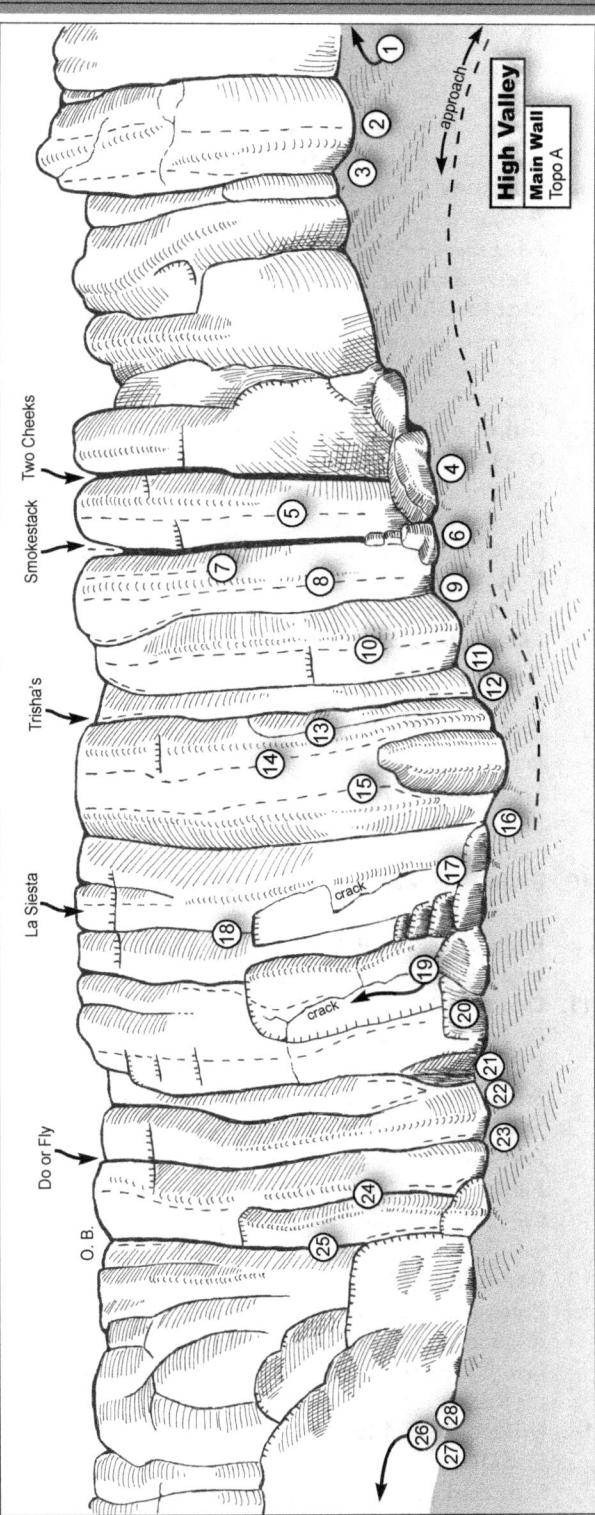

4. **Two Cheeks 5.6**
   Pro: nuts and cams; length 50'
   FA: unknown
   About 50' left of the top out scramble gully are two prominent rocks bulges with a crack separating them, known as the "cheeks".
5. **Chimney Face 5.11b**
   Pro: mostly QD's augmented with some nuts, length 50'
   FA: Brown 3-1989
   The overhanging face immediately right of Smoke Stack.
6. **Smoke Stack 5.4**
   Pro: nuts and cams, length 50'
   FA: Unknown
   About 10' left of "Two Cheeks" is a wide deep chimney.
7. **Chimney Face Left 5.10b**
   Pro: QD's, nuts and cams ½" to 1", length 50'
   FA: Brown, Hendrickson 3-1989
   The overhanging face immediately left of Smoke Stack on a prominent arête. Start in the crack, then branch up left onto the vertical arête.
8. **Fret Arête 5.9+**
   Pro: ½" to 1" cams, mostly QD's
   FA: Hauter, Daniels 1988
   A high quality top-rope on a prominent arête. Start in the crack, then branch up left onto the vertical arête.
9. **S#&t Eye 5.6**
   Pro: nuts and cams (large for top out); length 50'
   FA: Unknown
   Immediately left of Smoke Stack on a rock nose is a left leaning crack. Ascend the face, then continue up the jam crack and offwidth to the top.
10. **Elvis is Everywhere 5.12a ★★★**
    Pro: mostly QD's; length 50'
    FA: S. Brown 3-1989
    Elvis climbs a steep face just right of Classic Crack.
11. **Classic Crack 5.7 ★★**
    Pro: medium sized cams and nuts; length 50'
    FA: Casciato, Kerns, Wilkins in 1977
    Stem or layback a dihedral left of Smoke Stack avoiding the other nearby crack.
12. **Trisha's Dilemma 5.5 ★★**
    Pro: medium to large nuts and cams; length 50'
    FA: Casciato, Kerns, Wilkins 1977
    Climb the obvious crack and ledge system, then stem right around a semi-detached midway flake.
13. **Sausalito 5.7+ ★★**
    Pro: small nuts and cams; length 50'
    FA: Sanderson 1981 (TR), 1985 (FFA)
    Left of "Trisha's" ascend a ledge and crack system up to midway ledge, then move up left from the ledge using underclings, finishing on nubbins and air pockets.
14. **Unknown 5.10a**
    Pro: QD's
    Start on the right side of a pedestal up a crack. Face climb the outer aspect of a rounded but-

tress, then punch past a slight overhanging crux lip.

15. Spacy Face   5.8
Pro: nuts and cams; length 60'
FA: FA Unknown FFA J. Brown 1984
Climb an easy crack on the left side of a small pedestal to a ledge, then up the face (using the nose to the left if desired).

16. Dusty Devil   5.8   ★★
Pro: medium to large cams and nuts; length 60'
FA: Unknown
A great example of a challenging deep offwidth at HV, because of several slightly overhanging sections. Power up the crack past the first overhang to a small ledge, then up a similar crack where the rock is smooth.

17. La Siesta Tick Attack   5.11c   ★★
Pro: small nuts and cams, and several QD's for two bolts; length 60'
FA: Hauter 3-1989
A technical crimpy face climb using very thin pro, pass two bolts in the central portion, and use more thin natural gear on the final face to the top.

18. Pesky Rodent   5.7
Pro: medium to large nuts and cams; length 60'
FA: S. and S. Ryman 1978
Start by one of two methods, either directly up the main crack or up a thin crack that traverses up left into the main crack, both landing on a small ledge, then finishing up an offwidth crack to the top.

19. Afternoon Delight   5.7
Pro: Nuts and cams; length 60'
FA: Unknown
Climb a single crack up a small face, then up left (or directly up the face) to a ledge. From the ledge ascend an offwidth crack to the top.

20. Wasp Route   5.11b   ★★
Pro: mostly QD's; length 60'
FA: Hauter
This route ascends the face / arête between US and DOF and involves some long reach moves.

21. Last Hurrah   5.8+
Pro: medium to large nuts and cams; length 60'
FA TR: S. Ryman 1978, FFA Sanderson 1982
A long overhanging deep crack from bottom to top, that has a chockstone wedged at the top final moves.

22. Unnamed Symphony   5.9-
Pro: nuts and cams; length 60'
FA: Sanderson (TR) 1982, (FFA) 1985
Begin up Last Hurrah for 15', then bust up left using a jam crack. Climb a jam crack up under an overhang (Do or Fly overhang) then move right into the remaining part of Last Hurrah at the chockstone finish.

23. Do or Fly   5.10-   ★★★
Pro: medium to large nuts, cams (or hexes) up to 4"; length 60'
FA: Casciato, Kerns, Wilkins in 1977
THE classic route at High Valley. The climb ascends a beautiful hands to fist jam crack, where it leans to a slight crux overhang at the final upper moves where a nice exit jug awaits.

24. Amp'd 5.11a
Pro: QD's; length 60'
An electrifying sport climb just left of DOF ascending a ramp, then up a steep overhang.

25. Old Bologna 5.5
Pro: several nuts and cams; length 50'
FA: Ryman 1978
The last climb in this string; it offers an easy ascent up to a wide chimney.

Far to the left of Old Bologna next to the southern top out scramble are these three additional climbs.

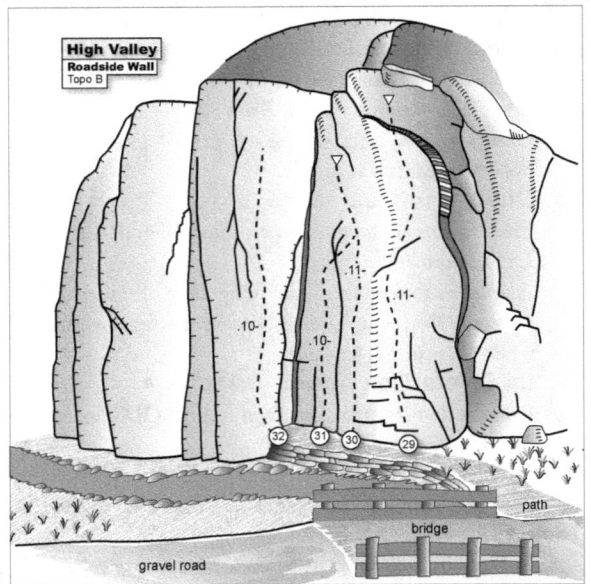

26. Can't Dance 5.7
Pro: Nuts and cams; length 40'
FA: S. and S. Ryman 5-1983
This climb begins under a roof and ascends a wide chimney to the roof, then traverses right onto a face, and continues up above the roof.

27. Too Fat to Fly 5.5
Pro: nuts and cams, length 35'
FA: S. and S. Ryman 5-1983
Ascend a finger crack with horizontal ledges immediately left of Can't Dance.

28. Too Wet to Plow 5.5
Pro: nuts and cams; length 30'
FA: S. and S. Ryman 5-1983
Climb a short finger crack to the left of Too Fat to Fly.

Bridge Rock
The routes for Bridge Rock are located at the parking site on the south side of the road, and are listed here from right to left:

29. _____ 5.11-
Ascends the face on the right side on the minor prow using thin crimpy holds.

30. _____ 5.11-
Steep and cruxy in the initial part utilizing the arête, then up small crimps on near vertical face to anchor.

31. _____ 5.10-
Variant start (3 bolts) that merges into SW.

32. Old Aid Route 5.10-
An old seldom climbed route.

"Going to the mountains is going home."
John Muir

A few more sparks

CHAPTER 11

MACROSCOPIC ANTHOLOGY

As a finale I have included a slice of select climbing sites of interest. The following snippets provide an additional glimpse of existing regional rock climbing sites, several bouldering locales, and potential climbing of which some is purely exploratory in scope. Check with locals to find out a bit more about certain sites.

Future books or editions will continue to incorporate more climbing sites throughout the northwest portion of the state. When the database and visual imagery of some of these sites is sufficiently refined it may be included. Some of these sites listed below are documented in other guides or on the web. Though an abbreviated description of the climbing site is mentioned below, it does not imply that the sites are ideal, nor that you should spend your time there (unless it is a well established climbing site). This is merely a 'teaser' section of generalized raw info, and some of the lesser sites are of relatively limited discussion and of unconfirmed scope.

Wishram Bluff might provide an hours worth of climbing if you are desperate. Drive east from Horsethief Butte park on State Route 14 and take a right turn south downhill to Wishram, WA alongside the Columbia River. At the west end town just past the water treatment plant is a minor south facing basalt rock bluff. Scramble up a short rocky slope to the cliff. From left to right:

1. **The Party** 5.8, Pro: Up to 4"
The easy standard left most climb that stems up twin cracks.
2. **Ugly Sister** 5.10a, Pro: Up to 3"
Reasonable climb with challenging ending moves.
3. **Relentless** 5.10b, Pro: cams and nuts to 2"
A hand and finger crack climb.
4. **Thin Pickin's** 5.11b (TR), Pro: [?]
Very thin twin cracks on the right. A TR if you move your anchor over from previous line.

Ice climbing at **Pete's Pile** has left a minor history of those who ventured there for a bit of the rare stuff (when it forms). In the 1970s McGown, Mayko, Casey, and later by Wallace, Brown and others. Some lines were TR's but other lines were actually climbed on lead by McGown, and Wallace. Exact beta is indeterminate, but include the drip near the route "Even" (e.g. *Life in the Fast Lane*), and the small waterfall ice curtain in the stream drainage to the south of the main bluff.

Government Camp Area: At the west end of Multorpor Mtn is **Multorpor Slab**, a small outcrop explored by locals, and by McGown who ascended a discontinuous crack (5.9) in the 1970s, though interest in the site is lacking even today. **Sand Canyon Wall** is located at the junction of Zigzag and Sand Canyon. Though of limited interest McGown did climb a route there (*In Search of a Jam* 5.8) in the 1980s. **Mirror Lake Cliffs** also known as Tom-Dick-Harry Mtn cliffs see exploratory climbing on occasion. Some of the snow/ice gullies have been climbed (B. Englund back-in-the-day solo, Babcock and McGown in the late 70s (*Surveyor Gully* WI3 and *Ice Nine* WI4), and likely others.

The **Danger Cliff** near Ski Bowl are infrequently used for rock climbing and ice climbing (when it forms). This small mossy bluff is easily reachable from the ski slope. Walk partway up alongside the ski slope, then west a very short distance to the first lower bluff.

In northern Oregon and southwest Washington various scarps and outcrops seem to intrigue adventurous climbers on occasion, but the rock quality may be varied or the site is isolated by distance, or other factors. Again, this list is not a promotion to send you out to these places, but if you happen to be in the area mushroom hunting or something, here is a sampling: Ramona Crag along the Sandy River; Sturgeon Rock on Silver Star Mtn has some short columns that have seen activity in the past; Pyramid Rock (south side of Silver Star) has a sizable cliff that may provide climbing if you're up to a way stout hike. The minor Saturday Rock outcrop (point 3,893') at the headwaters of Lewis River east of Yacolt; a minor 80' tall outcrop on the Washougal River near Dougan Falls may be useful (so far only *Wanderlust* 5.11a TR exists). The Mt Margaret backcountry (near Boot Lake northeast of Mt St. Helens) has a plethora of granite rock bluffs that are providing short alpine climbing opportunities for certain savvy locals who relish adventure.

North Santiam River Area

Detroit Lake Area: Like Brad said, this general area certainly is Rock City. Most of it though, does not make the quality scale, and approach factors limit interest. But of the few that do stand out we have detailed fully in the Santiam chapter, or here in short form to entice you to go out and explore this vast region of rock.

The Watchman is located ¼ mile east on spur road NF2223-501 and faced north overlooking the French Creek valley. Quite aptly named, this point overlooks the beautiful French Creek valley and watches you with a foreboding eye as you drive up the gravel road up into this area. The ascent is a very short easy 5th class move.

French Creek Bluff is a small south-facing bluff deep in the lower portion of French Creek has some vertical climbing opportunities in close proximity to Detroit. Located approximately 2½ miles up French Creek Road NF2223 at a small pullout. Walk down to the stream, and cross over near an electrical tower. The crag is on the immediate north side of the creek facing the road. Has several (2-4) climbs ranging from 5.8 to 5.10 and has potential for more.

The **501 Slivers** are one of Mr. Englund's wild rope-solo jaunts along a descending knifeblade ridge crest overlooking the French Creek valley near Detroit, Oregon. Drive up NF2223, then along NF501 (park when the brush thickens). Walk to the very end of NF503 and look down at a string of twisted thin rock slivers. See topo diagram for full beta tour.

On the south side of Mt Jefferson on **Sugar Pine Ridge** overlooking Jefferson Lake several long steep rock ribs, one of which was climbed (see old *AAJ*). Hunts Lake southeast of Pamelia Lake has a minor blocky pinnacle and a nearby thin rock rib that provides exploratory climbing.

South Santiam River Area

Various points of intrigue exist along the Quartzville Road northeast of Sweet Home, Oregon. From Sweet Home, Oregon drive east on Highway 20 a few miles, then turn north onto Quartzville Road and immediately cross a bridge over the reservoir. Continue past Sunnyside Campground. At 3½ miles you will pass **The Garden** bouldering site just prior to the GP dam. The **Highway Pillar** is located just before Mile Post 13 marker. The road winds around the west side of the Green Peter Reservoir. Along the northern arm of Green Peter a certain distance after Whitcomb Creek Park (closer to Dogwood Rec site?) you can catch a momentary view of Crown Rock (or whatever its called) from the roadside. Access to it uncertain. So, based on the potential in this region, plan your goals based on distance, time, your energy level, and gas cost, which may rule out distant obscure options. Below is a generic analysis of several common sites.

Highway Pillar is a minor dirty bump located along the north arm of the Green Peter Reservoir. From Sweet Home drive east on U.S. 20 and turn north onto Quartzville Road which

becomes NF11. Drive 13¾ miles from U.S. 20 (¼ mile prior to MP13) about 2 miles north of Whitcomb Creek Campground above a steep road cut bank.
1. South Side 5.6 Short sport climb on the south side. Anchor.
2. East Side 5.7x Four bolts on lower half of east face, but runout to the top.
3. NE Side 5.7 Short 3-bolt lead on the northeast side. Quick ride to the top. Anchor.
4. North Side 5.8 Steep pockety north side offers a minor (bolts) climb on mossy rock.

Quartzville Crag is a minor site with an exploratory climb or two that has steep corners and pillar systems on a little bluff east of Little Meadows several miles. QVC is on NF1133 road, a gravel road off of NF11 (Quartzville creek backcountry byway) northeast of Green Peter Reservoir at approx. Locale 44° 35.7400'N 122° 9.3700'W.

Upper Soda is a minor cluster of homes east of Sweet Home. The general region round Upper Soda has a surprisingly prolific quantity of rock spires and outcrops of various shapes and sizes scattered in the foothills (beside just the Menagerie) that might suit your adventurous needs. **House Rock, Shark Fin Rock**, the **Smokestack** (whatever its called), and **Iron Wall** are some of the minor contrivances just to name a few. House Rock (3,000' el) is visible high on the hill to the south of U.S. 20 just before you reach House Rock campground. Another large spire (3,400' el) exists directly south of Upper Soda on upper Stewart Creek.

Platypus Pinnacle is an elusive minor roadside pinnacle south of U.S. 20. Route ascends an corner-ish weakness on the north aspect. This minor pinnacle is immediately underneath the gravel road (the summit is about horizontal with the road). Twin Sisters Pinnacle is visible a mere mile to the northwest of this site. Access by driving the same USFS roads to reach Smokestack/Twin Sisters area, then continue southeast 1+ miles to this spot. GPS 44°19'01" N, 122°13'03" W, elevation 3400 approx locale. Rating: II 5.4 A2. Pro: nuts & cams ½" to 5", pitons (KB, angles).

South Willamette Area

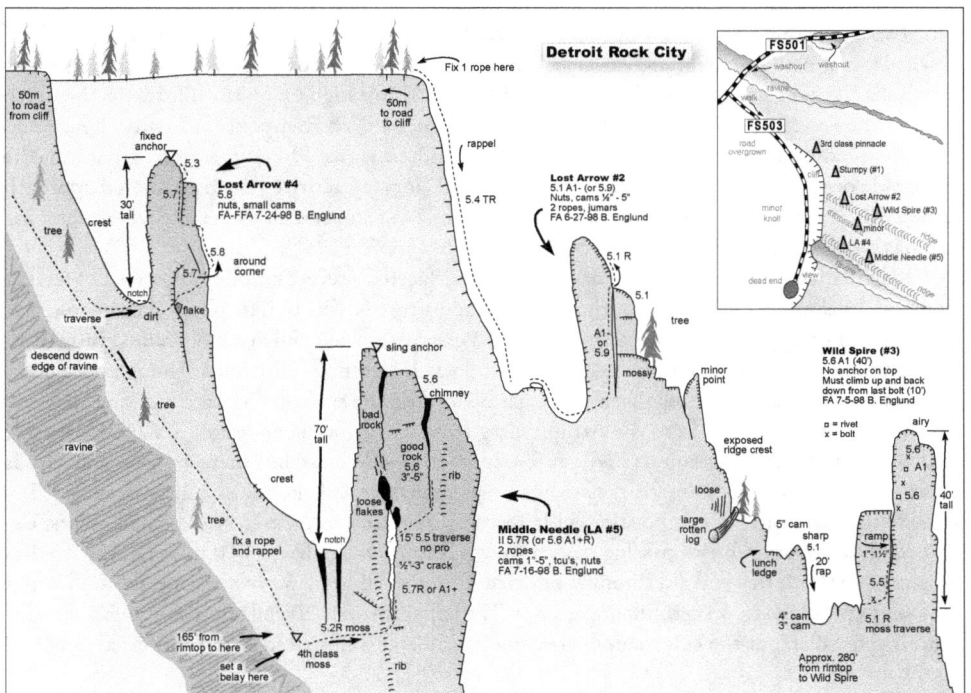

Hills Creek Spires is a series of minor pinnacles on the southern aspect of Kitson Ridge that provides a mixed gear-bolt climbing agenda on little volcanic tuff spires. Definitely adventurous climbing and not overrun with crowds. Drive south from Eugene on I-5 for 4 miles, then southeast on U.S. 58 to Oakridge. At the east end of town turn right (south) onto NF23 road. Drive 4¼ miles (you will pass a dam along the way) till you are at the eastern arm of the reservoir. About ⅛ mile past the junction of NF2118 (bridge on your right) you will turn left onto NF5875-565. Follow this gravel road for 4 miles uphill. Park at NF569. Walk down slope a short distance to the main climbing area.

Flagstone southeast of Eugene is this stellar andesitic rock formation perched in the forested hills at the 4100' level. The cliff generally has a 6-month (May-Oct) climbing site, and has three aspects (west-north-east) forming a single long bluff on the toe of a minor forested ridge crest. The extensive little crag offers many bolted face climbs on steep friction slabs. The routes are interspersed with dimples, grooves and edges, but the characteristic texture of the rock surface allows excellent friction opportunities. Initially explored in the 1980s the site is considered to be one of Eugene's premier climbing destinations.

Directions: Drive east of Eugene on U.S. 126 alongside the McKenzie River for 38 miles to the tiny community of Finn Rock. Turn right at Quartz Creek Road, cross a bridge, and drive south on this gradually ascending gravel road which becomes NF2618 road. Turn right at MP11, and then take a left turn at MP13. When you arrive at the junction of NF2618 and FS350 proceed right for about ¼ mile. Park at a minor pullout on the outer slope of the road. Expect about 1 hour drive from Eugene to the crag. The site is just above NF350 road immediately north of Sardine Butte, a total of 13½ miles from Finn Rock. The trail enters the forest here and meanders 200' up to the base of the wall at the north point area. If you walk left it will take you to the east side aspect which is great for hot summer days. If you walk to the right it travels uphill to the west aspect where you will find the stellar Hydrotube route. Climbers usually rappel from certain common routes with a 60' rope, but you can also walk off descend southward or eastward if desired.

Two sites along Lookout Point Reservoir (southeast of Eugene) may entice your rock climbing adventure instinct. The first (and closer) is **Little Machu Pichu** and the second site is the **Armpit Crag** (aka Dexter Crag). Little Machu Pichu (LMP) is visible high up on the hillside on the north flank of the reservoir a few hundred yards west of Landax Boat Ramp. From Landax boat ramp walk the road back towards Lowell (west) a few hundred yards. Hike up a logging road on the north side of the road that leads up to the small bluff (logging activity may have altered approach some). There are two formations with some climbs, a lower site and an upper site where climbing also has taken place.

Machu Pichu (tertiary miocene dacite) is a multi-faceted site, yet despite a brief spat of fervent climbing development it has only a few very short sport routes. The unique physical characteristics of this small tuffaceous crag blends gnarly cliff shapes with a colorful array of stained brownish-reds to yellowish-orange colors; an assortment of pocketed crimpy face climbs. Though once heavily shrouded in trees, recent logging activity has opened up the site somewhat to a greater degree.

The second site, known as the Armpit Crag (tertiary oligocene andesite) is a small roadside crag next to the same reservoir as LMP. A few sport routes do exist, but there are gear crack leads available as well, though many cracks are not frequently ascended and may be dirty or mossy. The small bluff is andesitic in composition with a variety of cracks, faces, arêtes, and small pillars. Expect road dust from vehicles passing near the crag. Ratings range from 5.10 to 5.11. The site has been used for both free and aid climbing practice. On most climbs a 60-meter rope will suffice, but midpoint anchors exist on certain longer lines. The left cliff end is 20' tall short columns but rightward it gets taller, but the crack corners become sparse and well spaced apart. The existing bolted routes (half dozen) are found at the apex of the cliff band.

Directions to both sites: drive 13 miles southeast on U.S. 58 past Dexter, then turn left on Pioneer Street and cross a bridge span into Lowell. Drive east of town on Main Street (or N. Shore Drive) which becomes North Boundary Road along the edge of the reservoir. Continue about 4 miles to Landax Boat Ramp. Park off the road near the boat ramp if you plan to access LMP crag (see initial paragraph for path). Continue east on Boundary Road to reach the Armpit Crag, which is about 10 miles total from Lowell and on the immediate north side of the gravel road opposite of the reservoir. This gravel road continues all the way to Westfir near Oakridge.

Roman Nose Mtn, though seldom used for rock climbing is a long cliff with potential climbing on a 30m tall columnar south-facing rock feature. Less than vertical, but steep enough terrain possibly suitable for 5.8 type climbing. The top of the hill has a communication tower complex so respect the site by not walking through the complex. Climbing has taken place here, but public access has not necessarily been granted. Located west of Eugene 48 miles. Drive state highway 126 past Walton, turn left (south) onto Siuslaw Road at Wildcat Bridge, and drive south about 11¾ miles and park near a gate (small pond nearby). Do NOT block the gate. Park off the road out of the way. Walk up the steep gravel road south past the communication tower complex to the bluff.

Central Oregon Area

The Steeple is a Prineville oddity typically avoided, but if you are gripped with adventurous savvy the Steeple might fit your caliber. The pillar is a seldom climbed steep, friable, poorly protected, exfoliating tuffaceous rhyolitic chossy climb. From Prineville, Oregon drive north on Main Street with becomes McKay Creek Road (NF27) for 12½ miles. Park at a pullout less than ½ mile past the Forest Service boundary sign. The 160' spire is uphill on the northwest side of the road. Scramble up the steep dirt slope to the uphill notch on the pinnacles north side between the spire and the upper cliff formation. *The Airy Traverse* 5.4R was first climbed in 1965 by Bill Cummins, Nick Dodge, and John Barton. From the saddle climb a steep crack, moving up left on small holds to a large ledge. Belay. Make an exposed traverse right onto the south face then climb up to the summit. Another line (*Bee Crack* 5.11c) is a top-rope on the southeast side of the pillar.

Eighteen miles east of Antelope, Oregon at the Clarno day use site near the John Day Fossil Beds, is a minor rock pinnacle readily visible on the slope above and west of the parking site. **Hancock Tower** II 5.3 A3 (5.11 free), FA 1963 Bob Martin, Kim Schmitz, Eugene Dod. From the uphill saddle climb an overhanging diagonal crack system to reach the summit.

Central Oregon has numerous other rock climbing and bouldering options besides merely Smith Rock. **Cougar Cliff** (Tumalo Rock) is good for some sport, trad, and multi-pitch climbing; Bend has a great selection of convenient bouldering and climbing sites such as Widgi Creek boulders, and Meadow Camp cliffs. **LaPine Wall** has basalt trad lead routes ranging from 5.8 to 5.12. **Bill's Columns** above U.S. 26 at the Deschutes River has trad climbs. Green Ridge north of Sisters has some minor roadside climbing.

The northern **Oregon Coast** has many coastal rocky outcrops but the often poor quality nature of the rock, which is commonly sandstone & mudstone, tends to limit user interest. Salty marine air and a healthy dose of rain makes a cookie crumble. The few coastal sites that may offer viable climbing options are typically located near exposed layers of old Miocene/Eocene basalt.

Rocky Creek has a small 30'-80' tall east facing conglomerate nubbin bluff formation with one single 5.9+ route that acsends a steep hueco bucket face. Drive on U.S. 101 south of Depoe Bay for about ½ mile south of the Rocky Creek State Park campground and park near the gated road #2800. Walk east 10 minutes and look for a minor bluff on the left. Route specifications: *Buckets of*

Rain 5.9+, height 80', pro: 12 QD's.

Some additional places that might (or might not) be of interest to climbers are as follows (check with friends first before launching out there into the blue). Kings Mtn area, Neahkanie Mtn area (intrusive volcanic breccia and pillow lava), the general region near Onion Peak (limited access and friable pillow lava), and perhaps Nestucca River Slab. And finally Saddle Mtn., situated about 15 miles southeast of Seaside, Oregon on the north side of U.S. Hwy 26, this peak offers a great hike amongst big steep cliff scarps. The rock is an uplift of subterranean pillow lava typically formed under water, yet the views from the top on a sunny day are excellent.

Where ever you choose to travel to climb, walk or hike, always enjoy the scenic adventure.

"The only true sports are bull fighting...and mountain climbing. All the rest are mere games."
Ernest Hemingway

NW OREGON ROCK CLIMBS

APPENDIX A

A FIRST ASCENT HISTORICAL SUMMARY OF ROCK CLIMBING AT NORTHWEST OREGON CRAGS

This appendix lists first ascent data for most of the climbs in this book. A special thanks to all who freely shared toward this analogy. This database has been gathered from well over a dozen climbers and all of those individuals are a valuable part in this compilation. Certain portions of first ascent route data could not be attained by the time this edition went to print.

This information base in no way represent a perfectly accurate specification list. For example, a person who cleans and fixes pitons or bolts on the new climbing route may or may not be the same person who attains the first ascent. Given the considerable time and effort that goes into the development phase of climbing routes your level of commitment is greatly appreciated by all of us.

A partial list of persons who provided data for this section are: Carl Neuberger, Nicholas Dodge, Jeff Thomas, Wayne Wallace, Robert McGown, Paul Cousar, Kay Kucera, Paul Waters, Tymun Abbott, Dave Sowerby, Marcus Donaldson, Dain Smoland, George Beilstein, Jim Scott, Brad Englund, Norm Watt, and many others.

The following brief definitions will help readers to interpret the first ascent data:

FA (First Ascent): Aid ascent, attempted free ascent, or an ascent.

FFA (First Free Ascent): Free ascent with NO tension, weighting of pro or falls. A prior ascent was made usually by FA.

FRA (First Recorded Ascent): It is likely that the climb was done previously, but no record exists as to who did it.

TR (Top-rope): Climbing a route with a rope that is anchored from above. The route may have been free climbed or aid climbed already, but is usually tope-roped.

GFA (Ground-up First Ascent): Without pre-inspection.

Mt. Hood Regional Climbs - Chapter 1

French's Dome
Rhoid Rage: FA Gollner [?]
Road Face: FA 1966 Phil Dean, Steve Heim, Jan Cummins
  FFA Vance Lemley, Hermann Gollner [?]
Road Rage: FA Gollner [?]
Road Kill: FA 7-13-2008 Dave Sowerby, Tymun Abbott
BSD: FA Dave Sowerby
Jackie Chan: FA 5-27-2007 Tymun Abbott, Dave Sowerby
China Man: FA Vance Lemley, Tom Kingsland, and ____
The Dark Side (aka The Seige): FFA either Dave Sowerby or Hermann Gollner
Pumporama: FA Hermann Gollner
Crankenstein: FA Vance Lemely, Tom Kingsland
Silver Streak (Dirty Deeds): FA late 1990s Patrick Purcell
Straw Man: FA 1970 Steve Strauch, Wayne Haack
Emerald City: FA John Rust
Alpha: FATR 8-30-1992 Olson, FFA 10-12-1992 Tim Olson, Bob McGown
Oz: FA John Rust
Tin Tangle: FA 1968 Jim Nieland rope-solo
Do It Again: FFA 1990s Bill Price, Tim Olson
Giant's Staircase: FA 1958 Ray Conkling, Leonard Conkling, Keith Petrie
Giant's Direct: FA Unknown
Static Cling: FA Bob McGown and partner
Low Voltage:

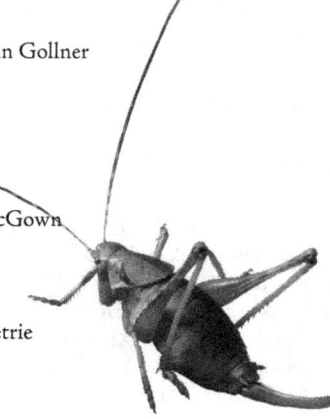

Psoriasis: FFA 7-1-2010 Phillip Hranicka
Yellow Brick Road: FA 1966 Bill Cummins, Steve Heim, Jan Cummins

ILLUMINATION ROCK
West Arête: 1913 Ray Conway
Southwest Ridge: GFA 10-18-98 Wayne Wallace, Richard Ernst
April Insanity: GFA 4-14-96 Wayne Wallace, Lane Brown
Iron Maiden: GFA 3-16-95 Wayne Wallace, Lane Brown
Rime Dog: 12-26-99 Wayne Wallace, Leesa Azaar
South Chamber: 1945 Bill Blanchard
East Ridge of South Chamber: 1938 Gary Leech, Bill Blanchard
Abracadabra: Wayne Wallace, Tim Olson
March Madness: GFA 3-28-96 Wayne Wallace, Lane Brown
Northeast Ridge: (aka Northeast Face): 1933 Gary Leech
North Face: 8-1938 Gary Leech, Bill Blanchard
Northern Skylight: 3-4-10 Daniel Harro, Nate Farr, Collin Bohannon
Southern Skylight Direct: 3-21-99 Wayne Wallace and partner.

RAZORBLADE
Gillette Arête: GFFA 9-29-1991 Tim Olson, Cindy Long
Machete: GFA 7-19-1997 Tim Olson, Mike Schoen
Leadhead: GFA 10-20-1991 Wayne Wallace, Tim Olson
Indirect East Arête: GFA 7-15-1995 Tim Olson, Harry King
East Arête: GFA 7-25-2001 Jim Tripp solo
Desert of Reason: GFA Sept 2nd & 3rd, 1995 Steve Elder, Tim Olson

ENOLA HILL
Tibbet Crack: FFA 8-2010 Dave Sowerby
Granny's Got A Gun: FFA 8-10-09 Tymun Abbott
Scorpion BBQ: FA 10-2009 Tymun Abbott, Dave Soswerby; FFA 12-6-09 Tymun Abbott
Fifty-Seven: FFA 9-2009 Dave Sowerby
Twenty year hangover: 8-10-09 Brian, Dave Sowerby, Tymun Abbott
Opal's Arete: FFA 2004 Orion and Sonya Kepler
Sea Hag Roof: FFA 2004 Orion and Sonya Kepler
Hillbilly Hot Tub: FFA 8-14-10 Tymun Abbott

KINZEL TOWER
Conkling's Pinnacle: FA as recorded in the register.
    2nd ascent 10-10-1951 Ray Conkling, Bud Frie
    3rd ascent 7-20-1958 Ray Conkling, Len Conkling
Squeaky Alibi: FFA 7-24-1994 Tim Olson, Don Gonthier
Butterfly: FA summer 1993 Tim Olson, Don Gonthier
Ripples: GFFA: 8-7-1993 Steve Elder, Tim Olson
North Rib: Unknown

CASTLE CANYON
First (Lower) Pinnacle: FA Jim Nieland and Libbly Kramm in 1969
Second Pinnacle: FA Bill Cummins, Janet Marshall and Jim Nieland in 1968
Third Pinnacle: FA Jim Nieland and Libbly Kramm in 1969

COETHEDRAL
Coe-Priestly: FA 10-10-2009 Ben Priestly, Bill Coe, Ujahn Davisson
Bewitched: FA 5-30-2010 Adam Winslow, Ujahn Davisson, Bill Coe
Bewitched Direct: FA 10-17-2010 Chad Ellers, Josh Gold
Upskirt: FA 7-31-2010 Adam Winslow, Bill Coe
Excalibur: FA 6-12-2010 Adam Winslow, Bill Coe
Trench Warfare: P1 8-1-2009 Bill Coe, Jeff Thomas, Ujahn Davisson, P2 11-1-2009 Bill Coe, J. Thomas
Lava Flow: FA P1 8-8-2009 Jeff Thomas, Bill Coe, FA P2 9-26-2009 A. Winslow, B. Coe, U. Davisson

Grey Ghost: FA 7-10-2010 (from the notch) Ben Priestly, Bill Coe, Scott Peterson
The Gingerbread Shortcut: FA 10-24-2009 Bill Coe, Jim Opdycke, Jeff Thomas
Salathe Highway: GFA solo from notch 9-26-2009 Bill Coe
Gothic Rocks: FA 7-20-2010 Bill Coe
The Dragons Spine: FA P1 8-15-2009, P2 7-14-2010 Bill Coe, Ujahn Davisson
Gratitude: FA P1 8-22-2009 Kyle Silverman, Bill Coe, P2 7-15-2010 Geoff Silverman
Ujahns Delight: FA 6-5-2010 Ujahn Davisson, Bill Coe
Coecoenut Bridge: FA 6-26-2010 Haydar Kutuk, Shaun Coe, Bill Coe
Better than Sex: FA 6-8-2010 Scott Peterson, Bill Coe
Rad, Plaid and Glad: FA Bill Coe, Plaidman, Shaun Coe
Runaway Weasel: FA Bill Coe, Shaun Coe
The Steeple: The Beckey Route FA 7-30-2010 Adam Winslow, Bill Coe
Basho Pinnacle: FA 9-2010 Schoen, Campbell, Carter, and Carter Jr.

COLLAWASH CLIFF
Watt-Johnson Route: GFA summer 1992 [?]

East Side Rock Climbs - Chapter 2

NEWTON PINNACLE
Wage Slave (aka Entropic Gravity): FA Tim Olson, FFA Robert McGown and partner early '90s likely
Poison Pill: TR Tim Olson and partner early '90s
Logisticon: TR Tim Olson and partner early '90s
Neophytes: TR Tim Olson and partner early '90s
Gravity Waves: FFA Robert McGown and partner early '90s

LAMBERSON BUTTE
Pig Newton: GFA 5-30-1992 Wayne Wallace, Tim Olson
Great Pig Iron Dihedral: GFA 5-30-1992 Wayne Wallace, Tim Olson; FFA 9-29-1993 Steve Elder
Headhunters: FA 8-15-1992 Tim Olson, Bob McGown, FFA 7-4-1993 Steve Elder, Tim Olson
Panorama: GFFA 5-2-1992 Tim Olson, Cindy Olson
Trafficosis: GFA 8-9-1992 Tim Olson, Cindy Olson
Mytosis: GFA 8-9-1992 Tim Olson, Cindy Olson
Thirty-Six Light Years: GFA summer 1993 Tim Olson, Steve Elder
Catch me if I fall: GFFA 9-27-1992 Steve Elder, Tim Olson
Fever: GFFA 8-8-1993 Tim Olson, Don Gonthier
Poultry Picnic: GFFA 5-2-1992 Tim Olson, Cindy Olson
Crash of the Titans: FFA 1992 [?] Wayne Wallace, Tim Olson
Bag of Tricks: 7-3-1992 Wayne Wallace, Tim Olson
Upper Prow: Unknown
Trafalgar: FFA 7-19-1992 Wayne Wallace, Tim Olson
Arête: TR 7-19-1992 Wayne Wallace, Tim Olson
Test Tube: GFA 5-16-1992 Tim Olson, Cindy Olson
Quantum Gravity: GFFA 5-31-1992 Tim Olson, Wayne Wallace
Pushover: GFA 5-31-1992 Wayne Wallace, Tim Olson
Sunset Bowl: FA 7-19-1992 Wayne Wallace, Tim Olson
Momma Bo Jamma: FFA 5-31-1992 Wayne Wallace, Tim Olson after pre-cleaning
World is Collapsing: GFFA 9-27-1992 Steve Elder, Tim Olson
Sanctum: FFA summer 1992 [?] Steve Elder, Tim Olson

BULO POINT
Line Dancer: pre-90s climbers
Bulo Dancer: pre-90s climbers
Power & Politics: pre-90s climbers
Cattle Guard: pre-90s climbers
Nuked: FA 1997 Dain Smoland, Dan Arnold
Cattle Trough: pre-90s climbers

Climbs with a Fist: FA 1996 Ron Hampton, Don Cossel
Silence of the Cams: FA 1996 Don Cossel, Joyce Cossel
Inversion Excursion: FA 1997 Mike Richey, Don Cossel
Awesome Possum: FFA Kay Kucera
Separated at Birth: FA 1997 Mike Richey, Don Cossel
Atomic Dust Buster: FA 1996 Mike Richey
Barking Spider: FA 1997 Don Cossel, Ron Hampton
Slice of Pie: pre-90s climbers
Alice: FA 1996 Mike Richey, Matt Stevens
JRat Crack: FA 1996 Don Cossel, Joyce Cossel
Raiders of the Lost Rock: FA 1996 Don Cossel
Fat Rabbit: Paul Couser
Plumbers Crack: pre-90s climbers
Return of Yoda:
Nook and Cranny: pre-90s climbers
Jet Stream: FA 1996 Matt Stevens, Mike Richey
Streamlined (aka Jet Wind): FA John Rust
Black Market: FA 1996 Matt Stevens, Don Cossel
Don't Call Me Ishmael: FA 1996 Dain Smoland
Scene of the Crime: FA 1996 Mike Richey
DaKind: FA 1996 Mike Richey
Who's The Choss:
Big Al:
Rock Thugs: pre-90s climbers

HELIOTROPE PINNACLE
GFA 7-23-1995 Tim Olson, Mike Schoen

AREA 51
Young Jedi: FA Year 2000 Dave Boltz
Dreamland: FA Year 2003 Jai Dev
War of the Worlds: FA Year 2005 Jai Dev
Men in Black: FA Year 2004 Jai Dev
Crash Landing: FA Kay Kucera & Paul Cousar
Earth First: FA Year 2004 Kay Kucera
Shape Shifter: FA Year 2000 Dave Boltz
Alien Lunacy: FA Year 2004 Paul Cousar
Luna: FA Year 2004 Jim Anglin
Take Me To Your Leader: FA Year 2004 Jim Anglin
Cattle Mutilation: FA Year 2003 Kay Kucera & Jim Anglin
The Eagle Has Landed: FA Year 2003 Jim Anglin
Erased Memory: FA Year 2004 Jim Anglin
ET (Extra Trad): FA Year 2005 Jim Anglin
Phone Home: FA Year 2003 Kay Kucera, Jim Anglin, Paul Cousar
Little Gray Men: FA Year 2005 Kay Kucera
Mars: FA Year 2003 Jim Anglin
Crop Circles: FA Zach Plank; FFA Year 2004 Matt Spohn, Adam McKinley 2004
Friend or Alien: FA Year 2004 Jim Anglin
Trouble With Tribbles: FA [?]
The Cover Up: FA Year 2004 Kay Kucera, Paul Cousar
Out Of This World: FA Year 2005 Jim Anglin, Kay Kucera, Paul Cousar
Rocketman: FA Year 2003 Jim Anglin
Major Tom: FA unfinished
First Contact: FA Year 2003 Kay Kucera, Jim Anglin
UFO: FA Year 2004 Kay Kucera
Roswell: FA Year 2003 Kay Kucera, Jim Anglin

Uranus Has Rings: FA Year 2003 Jim Anglin
It Taint Human: FA Year 2005 Kay Kucera
Journey To The Sun: FA Year 2003 Elmo Mecsko
Solar Flair: FA Year 2004 Kay Kucera, Paul Cousar
Sunspot: FA Year 2004 Jim Anglin
Vulcan Mind Meld: FA Year 2005 Kay Kucera
To Boldy Bolt Where No Man Has Bolted Before: FA Year 2005 Jim Anglin
Live Long and Prosper: FA Year 2005 Kay Kucera
Captain Jim: FA Year 2005 Jim Anglin
Alien Autopsy: FA Year 2001 Paul Cousar
Close Encounters: FA Year 2004 Kay Kucera, Jim Anglin, Paul Cousar
Black Ops: FA Year 2004 Kay Kucera, Paul Cousar, Kent Benesch
Open the Pod Bay Door HAL: FA Year 2004 Reed Fee
The Truth Is Out There: FA Year 2004 Paul Cousar
Death Star: FA Steve Mrazeck
Mothership: FA Steve Mrazeck
Even Horizon: FA Year 2004 Kay Kucera, Paul Cousar
The Wormhole: FA Year 2005 Kay Kucera, Jim Anglin
Stargate: FA Year 2004 Paul Cousar
Lies and Deception: FA Year 2004 Paul Cousar
Full Denial: FA Year 2004 Paul Cousar
Alien Observer: FA [?]
Probe: FA Year 2003 Jim Anglin
Dilithium Crystals: FA Year 2004 Kay Kucera
Alien Invasion: FA Year 2004 Jim Anglin
Abducted: FA Year 2003 Jim Anglin
Taken: FA Year 2003 Jim Anglin, Paul Cousar
Glue Me Up Scotty: FA Year 2004 Kay Kucera, Jim Anglin
We Are Not Alone: FA Year 2004 Jim Anglin
The Borg: FA [?]
Lights Over Phoenix: FA [?]
Resistance Is Futile: FA Year 2005 Kay Kucera
Covert Research: FA Year 2005 Kay Kucera
Groom Lake: (top-rope): FA [?]
Conspiracy Theory: FA Year 2005 Kay Kucera, Paul Cousar
Conspiracy Lake: FA Year 2005 Kay Kucera, Paul Cousar
Ben Cartwright: FA Year 2005 Kay Kucera, Paul Cousar
Ponderosa: FA Year 2005 Kay Kucera, Paul Cousar
Adam: FA Year 2004 Jim Anglin
Hoss: FA Year 2004 Jim Anglin
Men Are From Mars: FA Year 2005 Kay Kucera
Alien Encounter: FA Year 2005 Jim Anglin
Starship: FA Year 2004 Kay Kucera, Paul Cousar
Event Gate: FA Year 2004 Kay Kucera, Paul Cousar

Gorge Rock - Chapter 3

ROOSTER ROCK
South Face: FA 4-11-1915 Ray Conway, William Clark, R.L. McLeod, Lester Miller, J.N. Walker
East Face: FA 3-16-1958 Jim Fraser and Charles Carpenter
North Face: [?]
Southwest Face: FA 1960 Dave Bohn and partner

CROWN POINT
Zucchini Route: FA 1964 Bill Cummins, Allen Smith and Gerry

Schilt
Jewel In The Crown: FFA 8-21-1993 Steve Elder
RURP Traverse: GFA 6-26-1993 Steve Elder, Tim Olson
West Chimney: FA 5-28-1950 Don Comer, Don Richardson

PILLARS OF HERCULES
East Route: Unknown
South Face Route: FA 1952 Don Comer, Vivian Wright
West Arete: FA 1963 Bill Cummins, Gerry Schilt
North Face: FA of this pillar 11-3-1940 Bob Wallace, Bill Nelson, *Mountaineering Notes, Vol. XXII Mazama Annual*
North Face Traverse: FA John Ohrenschall

THE RAT CAVE
Project:
Pissfire: FA Eric Brown
Project:
Burrito: FA 10-2003 Dave Sowerby
Chicken Burrito: FA 9-2004 Dave Sowerby
Dorkboat: FA Hans Kroesen
Held Down: FA Gary Rall
Conquistador: FA 6-22-2008 Tymun Abbott
Super Burrito: FA 9-2002 Dave Sowerby
The Stiffler: FA Tom Scales
Tuffnerd: FA Tom Scales
Warmnerd: FA 12-10-2007 Ryan Palo
Freakshow: FFA 10-2009 Ryan Palo
S#@t Fire: FA Tom Scales
Enchilada ala Carte: FA 10-25-2003 Sam Elmore
The Maverick: FA Ryan Palo
Getting Rich Watching Porn: FA 5-30-09 Ryan Palo
Boxcar: FA 4-24-2009 Ryan Palo
Horizontal Delight: FA 6-7-2005 with blocks Dave Sowerby; No blocks Tymun Abbott 1-24-2010
Fully Horizontal: FA 7-1-2008 Dave Sowerby
Project:
Project:
Push to Close: FA 2-2009 Jeffrey Hyman & Andy Davis
Spared No Expense: FA Andy Davis

LITTLE COUGAR ROCK
South Ridge: unknown
East Arête: FA 1952 Art Maki, Frank Tarver, Vivian Staender
North Arête: 6-17-2000 Tim Olson solo to high point
West Arête: FA 1952 Carl Neuberger

ST. PETERS DOME
Darr Route: 6-23-1940 Glen Asher, Everett Darr, Ida Darr, Joe Leuthold, Eldon Metzker, Jim Mount, Vol. XXII 1940 Mazama Annual
Alpenjaegar Route: FA 6-18-1947 Don Baars, Floyd Richardson, John Morris
Kirkpatrick Route: FA 8-28-1968 Glen and Don Kirkpatrick
Pearly Gates Route: FA 5-4-1958 Dave Bohn, Dave Nelson, Art Maki. The route was named in memory of Joe Quigley and Don McKay.

LITTLE ST. PETE'S
Standard route: Jim Mount summited 4-22-1934. Any earlier ascent?

KATANAI ROCK
North Couloir: Climbed by turn of the century photographers. In 1932 L.G. Darling summited on

Katanai Rock. Don Onthank explored the north couloir route in 1934.

Apocalypse Needles
Tottering Tower: 3-1963 Eugene Dod and Bob Martin
Upper, Middle and Lower Sore Thumb: Possibly as early as 1923.
Apollo Column
   South Crack: FA 3-1963 Eugene Dod and Bob Martin
   Schmitz Route: Kim Schmitz and partner
The Bump
   South Crack: [?]
   Golden Spike: FA late 1990s Tim Olson, Mike Schoen
Fire Spire
   South side: Climbed on 5-4-1956 Jim Prichard and Klindt Vielbig. Probable earlier undated ascent.
   East Face: FA Willi Wyland made an FA via the East Face Route on Fire Spire.

Chimney Rocks
1953 Jack Zimmerman and Al Schmitz initially explored the site, but prospector's and miner's likely summited on the basic pinnacles at an earlier date.

Cigar Rock
East Couloir: [?] Bill Cummins climbed the pinnacle in the '60s but was not likely a first ascent.
North Face Direct: [?]
West Crack: 1953 Jack Zimmerman

Jimmy Cliff
The Short Bus: FA: Ujahn Davisson and Bill Coe 8-26-07
Bride of Wyde: GFA: Bill Coe, Ujahn Davisson, Kyle Silverman 9-13-0
The Move: FA Bill Coe, Kyle Silverman, Geoff Silverman 9-1-07
Kyles Big Adventure Gear: FA Kyle Silverman, Bill Coe, Geoff Silverman 10-27-07
Mr. Denton on Doomsday: FA 9-19-07 Geoff Silverman, Kyle Silverman, Bill Coe
Jimmy's Favorite: FA Bill Coe and Kyle Silverman 9-7-2008
Conga Line: GFA Bill Coe and Kyle Silverman 6-29-08
Conga Variation: FA 7-19-09 Ujahn Davisson, Jeff Thomas and Bill Coe
Couchmaster Shuffle: GFA Bill Coe and Jim Opdycke 7-26-08

Rabbit Ears
Standard Route: GFA 1941 Mazamas Climbing Committee lead by Randall Kester

Clif Cliff
Northern Pearl: FFA 6-19-2011 Chad Ellars
Pearl's Jam: FFA 5-28-2011 Chad Ellars, Bill Coe, Tim Olson
Slow Dance: FFA 6-4-2011 Chad Ellars, Kyle Silverman, Bill Coe, Tim Olson
Bearhug: FA TR 6-4-2011 Chad Ellars
Inner Sanctum: FFA 5-21-2011 Bill Coe, Chad Ellars
Bottle Rocket: FFA 7-4-2011 Chad Ellars, Bill Coe
_____ **5.12-:** FA TR 5-29-2011 Tymun Abbott
The Watchman: FFA 7-31-2010 Tim Olson
Motional Turmoil: FFA 7-31-2010 Hugh Brown, Tim Olson
Butterfinger: FFA 4-30-2011 Chad Ellars
Wyde Syde: FFA 6-4-2011 Bill Coe, Ujahn Davisson, Chad Ellars, Kyle Silverman
His 5.12a project: FA 5-29-2011 Tymun Abbott
Stark Raging Naked: FA 8-2010 Jyllan Grütten, FFA 6-9-2011 Tim Olson
Mighty Mite: FA 6-4-2011 Ujahn Davisson, Bill Coe
   FFA 6-4-2011 Chad Ellars, Ujahn Davisson, Bill Coe, Kyle Silverman
Airtime: FA TR 6-9-2011 Hugh Brown
Niceline: FFA 6-11-2011 Bill Coe, Chad Ellars, Scott Peterson
Plaidtastic: FFA 6-11-2011 Chad Ellars, Bill Coe, Scott Peterson
Committed Convenience: FFA 11-6-2010 Hugh Brown, Chris Alexander, Tim Olson

FFA via face only 2011 Tymun Abbott
Progressive Climax: FFA 7-31-2010 Hugh Brown, Tim Olson
Scorpio: FFA 6-11-2011 Chad Ellars, Bill Coe, Scott Peterson
Black Ribbon: FFA 6-25-2011 Chad Ellars
Bungee's Crack: FFA 6-25-2011 Mark Johnson, Chad Ellars

Five Star Slab:
Lunar Dreams: FFA 8-11-2010 Hugh Brown, Tim Olson

Skookum Pinnacle:
FA 6-24-2011 Olson (FFA also), Schoen, Brown

Wind Mountain
West Face Route: An early attempt by Jim Davis and Wayne Haack in summer 1975, leaving fixed pins and a bolt. Jim returned a year or two later for another attempt with Charlie Priest and John Tyerman but backed off due to objective hazard. Wallace and Olson attempted it in the summer 1994. Steve Elder did the complete FFA in September 1994 by rope-soloing the route.
Nieland-Valenzuela (Utopia): summer 1984 Jim Nieland, Francisco Valenzuela. Jim noted seeing a fixed piton on the first technical lead.
Lost Wages: 4-1997 Olson and Schoen
Workman's Comp: 8-28-2004 Schoen and Keith Campbell
Termination: 4-2009 Schoen, Olson and Hugh Brown

Windy Slab
The late Jeff Walker of Willard, WA climbed many of these routes prior to 1996. Most routes have been retro-bolted for safety and enjoyment.
The Steppes: FA unknown
Dare: FA unknown
Night Music: FA Jeff Walker and partner probably
Icon: FA Jeff Walker and partner probably
East Wind: FA Jeff Walker and partner probably
Dark Apron: TR early 1990s Wayne Wallace, Tim Olson
Apron: FA Jeff Walker and partner probably
Heat Wave: TR Tim Olson
Braille: FA Tim Olson
West Wind: FA early 1990s Wayne Wallace, Tim Olson

Gorge Ice - Chapter 4

Tunnel Vision: FA 1-9-1993 Wayne Wallace, Tim Olson, Dennis Harmon
Wind Tunnel: FA 1-9-1993 Wayne Wallace, Tim Olson, Dennis Harmon
Crown Jewel: FA: 1-1979 Alan Kearney and Chuck Sink
Cruiser: FA 11-28-1993 Bill Price, Tim Olson, Don Gonthier, Steve Elder
Waterpipe: FA 1-1979 Alan Kearney and Sheri Nelson
Bent Screw: FA 2-1979 Ed Newville, Jeff Thomas
Organic Mist: FA in the '80s
Waterheater: FA 1-1979 Jeff Thomas, Dave Jay
Salamander: FA 2-1979 Jeff Thomas, Ed Newville
Original: FA 1-1974 Phil Jones, Tim Carpenter, & partner
Shark Attack: FA 12-2005 Marcus Donaldson, Mike Layton
Dog House: FA 12-2005 Marcus Donaldson, Mike Layton
Bridal Suite: FA 12-1985 Jeff Thomas, Bill Thomas
Pumphauz: FA 1-4-1995 Tim Olson
Slippery Dolphin: FA 12-1983 Mark Cartier, Monty Mayko
Gathering Storm: FA 2-1979 Jeff Thomas, Alan Kearney
Mist Falls: FA unknown
The Deer Hunter: FA 12-8-2009 Marcus Donaldson and Bill Amos
Sweetest Taboo: FA 12-1990 Wayne Wallace, Tim Olson; Complete: 2-1996 Lane Brown and Blake

Benson Ice: FA Unknown
Chillin' Out: FA 1-10-1993 Tim Olson, Cindy Olson
Snazzic: FA unknown
Fractal Energy: FA 1-10-1993 Tim Olson, Cindy Olson
Ice Cooler: FA 1-16-1993 Tim Olson, Cindy Olson
Shady Creek: FA 1979 Ken Currens, Monty Mayko
Life Shavings: FA 12-1990 Wayne Wallace, Tim Olson
Fame and Fortune: FA 12-1990 Tim Olson, Chuck Buzzard
Blackjack: FA 12-1990 Wayne Wallace, Tim Olson
Black Dagger: FA 12-17-2005 Wayne Wallace, Lane Brown
Brave New World: FA 1-1996 Wayne Wallace, Tim Olson
Unfinished Business: incomplete
Post Nasal Drip: FA: 1-9-1993 Wayne Wallace, Tim Olson, Dennis Harmon
Thick Enough To Screw: FA 12-1990 T. Olson, W. Wallace
Horsetail Falls (...and the horse you road in on): FA: 1-17-1993 Bill Price, Tim Olson
Pencil Pusher: FA 12-1990 Wayne Wallace, Tim Olson
Peter Piper: FA 12-1990 Tim Olson, Jay Green
Ponytail: FA Unknown; FRA complete: Wallace & Olson
Ainsworth Left: 12-16-2008 FA complete, Marcus Donaldson and partner
Dodson: FA to high point: 2-1993 Bill Price, Tim Olson
Tanner Creek: unknown
Cascade Curtain: FA left side: Lewis & Larson; FA right side: Bauman & Jeff Thomas 2-9-8_ [?]
Lancaster Falls: FA unknown
Cabin Falls: FA Steve Buchan and Ron Houck 12-30-85
Starvin' Marvin':
Starvation Creek: FRA 12-1985 Scott Woolums, Terry Yates
Nancy's Run: FA (top-rope) 2010 Bill Price, Rachel French
Hanging Curtain: FA 1979 Ian Wade, Scott Woolums
Phantom Gully: FA 1979 Monty Mayko, Robert McGown
Silver Streak: FA 1979 Monty Mayko, Robert McGown
Salmon Run: FA 12-1980 Jim Olson, Robert McGown
Nancy's Line: TR 1-2011 Bill Price, Rachel French
Tyrolean Spire:
Catch of the Day: FA: 1980s Jim Scott and partner
Cigar Rock:
Vertical Frost: FA: 1980s Jim Scott and partner
Rivers Edge:
Frozen Embers: FA: 1980s Jim Scott and partner
The Strand:

Southwest Washington - Chapter 5

Tower Rock
NW Face: FA 6-20-1982 Jim Nieland, Francisco Valenzuela

Dark Divide Area
Kirk Rock: RA Fall 1990 Jim Nieland, Bob Baker
Shark Rock:

Santiam region - Chapter 6

Split Spire
FA Unknown

Spire Rock
SE Rib (standard route): FA Unknown
South Face: FA Unknown
SW Buttress: FFA 8-29-2009 Jyllan Grütten, Thor Svenssen, Olaf Jansgaard

Breitenbush Ears
GFA 7-9-2009 Karl Helser, Brian Jenkins, Mike Schoen, Tim Olson

Needle Rock
Dod-Nieland Route: FA 7-28-1968 Jim Nieland, Eugene Dod, Gerald Bjorlman (per register) (additional member probably Dave Jensen as per email)
The Direct: GFA 7-16-1995 Steve Elder, Tim Olson
Little Needle Rock: FA 7-26-1997 Brad Englund

Menagerie
Rooster Rock:
Hen Rock: FA 1959 Pat Callis, Willi Unsoeld, Art Johnson, Norm Lee
Chicken Rock: FA 1959 Pat Callis, Tom Taylor
North Rabbit Ear: FA 1960 Pat Callis, Soren Norman by the Cave Route
South Rabbit Ear: FA 1966 Tom and Bob Bauman by the West Face Route
Turkey Monster: FA 1966 Eugene Dod, Dave Jensen, Bill Pratt

Santiam Pinnacle
East Face: FA 1972 Dean Fry, Joe Bierck
South Face: FA 1964 R. Steve Knudson, Skip King
West Face: FA 1968 Scott and Keith Schmidt
North Ridge: Unknown

Two Girls
East Girl:
West Rib: Unknown
East Buttress V1: FA 8-7-11 Tim Olson, Keith Campbell
West Girl:
East Rib: FA Unknown

Southern Willamette region - Chapter 7

Wolf Rock
Barad Dûr: FA 1972 Wayne Arrington, Mike Seely
Gigantor: FA
Caligula: FA 1972 Wayne Arrington solo
Various Arch routes established by: Chris Fralick, Jim Anglin, Kent Benesch, Tyler Adams, Joe Crawford, Doug Phillips, John Barrar, Dean Fry, Bret Hall, Jeff Thomas, Jay Peterson, and others.
North Face: FA 1963 R. Steve Knutson, Don Housley, Roger Korn, Lucy Pratt
Barton's Gully: FA 1971 John Barton, Nick Dodge
Hogback Chimney: FA 1960 Gil and Vivian Staender
Hairy Tale: FA 1971 Keith Edwards, Bill Zeller, Brian Olson

Moolack
Sophie: FA Jason Krueger 2003; SA [Second Ascent]: Karsten Duncan 2003
Gwenevere: FA Paul Waters 12-2005; SA: Bryan Schmitz 4-2006
Scum Suckers: FA Mark Koehler 2008; SA: Ryan Young approx. same time
Bitch I Won: FA Ryan Young 2008 SA: Mark Koehler approx. same time
Radical Sabbatical: FA Lee Baker 5-2007
Thadallic: FA Lee Baker, Bill Soule 5-2007
Blood on the Cracks: FA Paul Waters 12-23-2005; SA: Bryan Schmitz 5-19-2006
Lost Art: FA Bill Soule in late 1990s; SA: Mike South in late 1990s
Up on a Pedestal: FA Bill Soule in late 1990's; SA: Mike South in late 1990s
Sideways: FA Mike South 6-15-2006; SA: Paul Waters 7-2-2006
Zion Train: FA Paul Waters 6-7-2006; SA: Mike South 6-2006
Compromising Positions: FA Lee Baker 10-28-2006 SA: Evan Mikkelson
Pledge Allegiance (aka Pledge Crack): FA Mike South on-sight 2001; SA: Karsten Duncan 2002 or '03
Plumber's Crack: FA Mike South 9-18-2008 SA: Bill Soule approx. same time
Fist-Fight: FA Mike South in late 1990s; SA: Bill Soule approx. same time

Knife-Fight: FA Paul Waters 1-2006; SA: Dylan Bygny same day
Sasquatch: FA Paul Waters 2009
Where the Wild Things Are: FA Paul Waters 6-25-2006; SA: Brian Gilbert 6-2006
One Flew Over the Cuckoo's Nest: FA (Led with pre-placed cam protection where unprotectable)
Bluto: FA Paul Waters 2009
Super Mario: FA Paul Waters in late 2009
Eat Your Spinach: FA Paul Waters 8-2006
Stems and Seeds: FA Paul Waters 6-2006
Stems and Caps: FA Brian Gilbert 5-2006; SA: Paul Waters 5-2006
Sweet Pea: FA Paul Waters 2009
Olive Oil: FA Paul Waters 2009
Cleaned for Her Pleasure: FA Karsten Duncan in early 2000s; SA: Jason Krueger in early 2000s
Sidewinder: FA Karsten Duncan in early 2000s; SA: Jason Krueger in early 2000s
Mr. Clean: FA Mike South 7-2006 SA: An ascent (Maybe 2nd Paul 2009)
Hit and Run: FA Mike South 7-2006; SA: Jeff Baldo and Paul Waters 8-2006
Variation on Hit and Run: FA Brian Gilbert 7-12-2006
Age Before Beauty: FA Bill Soule Summer '07; SA: Mike South 9-2007
Under the Big Top: FA Mike South Summer 2007
Two Beers and a Baby: FA Mike South Summer '07 An Ascent: (May be 2nd) Max Tepfer 2011
Guillotine: FA Bill Soule in late 1990s; SA: Mike South in late 1990s
Pool Guy: FA Bill Soule in late 1990s SA: An ascent by Ball Oh 2009/2010 (maybe 2nd)
Orange Crush: FA Mike South 4-15-2007 SA: Max Tepfer 2008, 09
Widespread Panic (Aka The Wave): FA Mike South 10-2006 SA: Bill Soule approx. same time
Full Circle: FA Thad Arnold 2008; SA: Max Tepfer 10/17/2008
Dru's Cruise: FA Bill Soule in early 2000s; SA: Mike South in early 2000s
Dru's Direct: FA Bill Soule w/ Dave Carr 2009/2010; SA: Lee Baker approx. same time
Noodle Cracker: FA Mike South in Summer 2007
Extreme Makeover: FA Mike South late 1990s / early 2000s; SA: Bill Soule approx. same time
Ari's Dihedral: FA TBD
Nip Tuck/ Tic Talk: FA (¾ route): Karsten Duncan in early 2000s ; SA (First Full Route): Mike South, 2007
Morning Wood Afternoon Delight: FA Lee Baker 2009
D.P.: FA Forest Weaver 2009; SA: Ball Oh 2009
Project Helter Skelter: FA (Open)
Eta Eva: FA Paul Waters 9-2009
Deception Crack: FA Paul Waters end of 2009
Mosserati: FA Shane Slover in early 2000s; SA: Karsten Duncan in early 2000s
Dangerous Toys: FA Bill Soule SA: Mike South
Scared Alive (variation): FA Paul Waters 2003 rope solo aided and free
Bag Full of Hammers: FA Mike South 2008 or '09; SA: Bill Soule w/ Dave Carr 2009
Geek on a Leash: FA Bill Soule in late '90s to early 2000s SA: Mike South approx. same time
X-Marks the Spot: FA M. South early 2000s aided; FFA: M. South late 2000s; SA Max Tepfer 1-13-2012
Elements of Style: FA Bill Soule in late 1990s to early 2000s; SA: Mike South approx. same time
Case of the Blues: FA Mike South beyond 2008 SA: Open
Whiskey River: FA Mike South SA: Open
Jessie's Route, Wish That I Had: FA Jessie [? 2008-2010 (PP ascent) SA: Max Tepfer 2011 (2nd pitch redpoint)
Best Kept Secret: FA Max Tepfer, Lead 2010 No RP to date SA: Open
Locked and Loaded: FA TBD
False Alarmageddon: FA Lee Baker SA: Open
Perverts in Paradise: FA Bill Soule, Mike South in early 2000s
Good for the Soule: FA Lee Baker 2008-2009
Southern Exposure: FA Lee Baker 7-17-09
Bold Deli Flavor: FFA Mike Holmes 2009, FA & SFA: Max Tepfer

Baker's Dozen: FA Mike Holmes; SA: (Open)
Gold: FA Bill Soule in late '90s to early 2000 SA: Mike South approx. same time
Yay Climbing: FA Mark Koehler
Up an Alchemists' Sleeve: FA Likely Caleb in 2004 or '05
Nightmare on Madrone Street: FA Lee Baker 7-29-2009
Workingman's Lack: FA Paul Waters in 2005
Slot Machine: FA Bill Soule 5-2007
Sendero De Sangre: FA Karsten Duncan in 2003; SA: Leif Karlstrom in 2003
On the Road to Shangri-La: FA Open

MOOLACK BOULDERS
The Mane Boulder: FA Paul Waters, Spring 2005; SA: Criss Steiner, Summer 2006
Iron Lion Zion: FA Paul Waters, Spring 2005; SA: Brian Gilbert, Spring 2005
Boo to Trustafarians: FA Paul Waters, Spring 2005; SA: Jeff Baldo, Fall 2005
Quick Burn: FA Paul Waters, Fall 2005; SA: TBD
Get a Job: FA Paul Waters, Spring 2005; SA: Brian Gilbert, Spring 2005
Less Than Maney: FA Paul Waters, Spring 2005; SA: Brian Gilbert, Spring 2005

Get Your Slice Boulder
Scorpion King: FA Brian Gilbert 2006; SA: Criss Steiner 2006
Beer and Pizza: FA Paul Waters, Summer 2006; SA: Brian Gilbert, Summer 2006
Cold Pizza: FA Paul Waters Summer 2006; SA: Criss Steiner, Summer 2006
Get Your Slice: FA Paul Waters, Summer 2006; SA: Brian Gilbert, Summer 2006

Central Oregon - Chapter 8

STEINS PILLAR
Northeast Face: FA 7-1950 Don Baars, Floyd Richardson, Glenn Richardson after various attempts spread out over several years.
    FFA (Northeast Face) 7-1979 Jeff Thomas, Bill Ramsey, Alan Watts
Rocket Ride: FA 5-2003 Chip Miller, Brian Mulvihill
Schmitz-Caldwell Variation: FA 7-1965 Kim Schmitz, Dean Caldwell
Southwest Face: FA 10-1967 Jim Nieland, Eugene Dod
    FFA 7-1977 Bob McGown, Jeff Thomas
Tammy Jo Memorial Route: FA 2004 Kent Benesch and partner
Shasta's Spirit: FA Gavin Ferguson and partner
Mass Wasting: FA Gavin Ferguson and partner
Heatstroke: FA approx. 2003 Chip Miller, Jim Ablao
Money, Whiskey, Sexy: FA 6-2003 Chip Miller, Brian Mullvihill

TWIN PILLARS
Upper Pillar: FA Fall 1967 Jim Nieland, Eugene Dod, Bill Cummins, Janet Marshall
Campfire Route: FA Fall 1967 Bill Cummins, Jim Nieland
Lower Pillar: FA Fall 1967 Jim Nieland, Eugene Dod

GOTHIC ROCK
West Ledge: FA 1964 Gill and Vivian Staender
East Face Direct: FA 9-1968 Eugene Dod, Dave Jensen, Jim Nieland
Middle Spire: FA Jerry Ramsey, Jim Ramsey

HANCOCK TOWER
Diagonal Crack: FA 1963 Bob Martin, Kim Schmitz, Eugene Dod

Index

SYMBOLS
1st Column Face 324
2nd Column Inclusive 325
2nd Column Left Jam 325
2nd Column Right Jam 324
3rd Column Face 325
4th Column Inclusive 325
4th Column Left Jam 325
4th Column Right Jam 325
5th Column 325
6th Column 325
6th Column Jam 325

A
Abby Normal 40
Abducted 117
Abracadabra 33
Achilles 43
Acid Reflux 295
Acoustic Kitty 87
Adam 118
Adams Variant 293
A Few Tense Moments 396
Afternoon Delight 425
Age Before Beauty 355
Age of Rage 274
Ahoot 420
Ainsworth Left 230
Airtime 148
Alice 103
Alien Autopsy 115
Alien Encounter 119
Alien Invasion 117
Alien Lunacy 110
Alien Observer 116
Aloha Direct 401
Alpenjaeger Route 137
Alpenjager 128, 129
Alpha 25
Altered State 208
Ambient Noise 274
American Eagle 204
Amp'd 426
And The Horse You Rode In On 229

Apocalypse Needles 139
Apollo Column 140
April Insanity 32
Apron 153
Aquifer 274
Arch Corner 331
Archdeacon 42
Archimedes 315
Area 51 107
Ari's Dihedral 360
Armpit Crag 430
Arthritis 409
Atomic Dust Buster 103
Atomic Garbage Can 124
Autumn Gold 207
Autumn Joy 207
Autumn Reigns 305
Awesome Possum 102
Axe with a Passion 40

B
Bad Gulley 359
Bag Full of Hammers 365
Bag of Tricks 72
Baker's Dozen 370
Balloon Knot 27
Balrog 334
Barad-Dûr 328
Barking Spider 103
Barramundi in a Billabong 208
Barton's Gully 336
Basho Pinnacle 266
Bat Crack 325, 400
Bat Face 325
Bat Stupor 168
Bear Claw 94
Bearhug 146
Beekeeper Magic 144
Beginner's Route 206, 395
Belly of the Beast 96
Benson Ice 225
Bent Screw 220
Best Kept Secret 367
Betaflash 412

Better than Sex 265
Bewitched 262
Big Al 106
Birds on a Shelf 162
Bitch I Won 346
Black Dagger 227
Blackjack 227
Black Market 105
Black Ops 115
Blackout 403
Black Raven 203
Black Ribbon 149
Black Tooth 420
Black Truth 119
Blarney Stone 259
Blind Ambition 163
Blind Deaf Old Goat 194
Blister in the Sun 414
Blockhead 412
Block Party 408
Blood on the Cracks 348
Blown Away 420
Blue Grouse 90
Blue Highway 147
Blue Suede Shoes 404
Blue-Tailed Skink 417
Bluto 352
Boar's Tusk 274
Bokeh Monster 274
Bold Deli Flavor 370
Bollocks 91
Bone-Eata' 94
Boneyard 273
Bookmark 209
Bottlecap 82
Bottle Rocket 146
Bottomless Column 325
Boxcar 134
Braille 154
Brand-X 333
Brave New World 228
Breathe the Air 402
Breitenbush Ears 288
Bridal Suite 222
Bride of Wyde 143
Broken Hand 203
Bronze Whale 203
Brother Mike 266

Brown Rice 28
BSD 23
Bucket o' Ribs 161
Buckets of Rain 431
Buckwheat 163
Buddha Belly 96
Buffalo Hunter 208
Bugs! 325
Bug Scum 277
Bulge Boogie 89
Bullah Bullah 206
Bulo Dancer 101
Bulo Point 99
Bungee's Crack 149
Burning Zone 49
Burrito 132
Butterfinger 147
Butterfly 60
Butt Shiner 168
By Hook or by Crook 399

C

Cabin Falls 236
Calf's Gash 50
Caligula 330
Callis Route 302
Calm Before The Storm 48
Camel Back 28
Campfire Route 382
Campus Wolfgang Gullich 95
Can't Dance 426
Cape Horn 140, 237
Cape Horn Falls 238
Captain Courageous 333
Captain Jim 115
Captain Winkie 400
Carl's Route 168
Cascade Curtain 234
Case of the Blues 366
Cassidy's Crack 408
Castle Canyon 58
Castle Crag's Direct 30
Catch Me If I Fall 71
Catch of the Day 239
Cathedral 45
Cattle Guard 101
Cattle Mutilation 110
Cattle Trough 101

Caveman 28
Central Oregon 373
Cerberus 89, 330
Chaco 121
Charlatan Salesman 258
Cheap Beer 420
Chicken Burrito 132
Chicken Legs 307
Chicken Pox 406
Chicken Richard 302
Chicken Rock 306
Chillin' out 225
Chimney 305
Chimney Face 324, 424
Chimney Face Left 424
Chimney Rocks 243
China Man 23
Chinquapin Corner 304
Choix des Dames 257
Chopper 411
Chubby Hubby 407
Chunky Monkey 407
Chunky Scoop 420
Cigar Rock 240
Classic Crack 424
Clavical Crack 400
Cleaned for Her Pleasure 354
Clean Sweep 417
Climbing Theme 28
Climbs with a Fist 101
Close Encounters 115
Coecoenut Bridge 265
Coe-Priestly 262
Coethedral 261
Collawash Cliff 266
Columbina 169
Committed Convenience 148
Compromising Positions 349
Confucious Says 273
Conga Line 144
Conga Variation 144
Conkling's Pinnacle 60
Conquistador 132
Conscious Haze 204
Conspicuous Arch 327, 330
Conspiracy Lake 118
Conspiracy Theory 118
Contrail Conspiracy 199

Cordwood 420
Cordwood Tower 420
Coriolis Effect 335
Cornered 404
Cornucopia 295
Cosmic Debris 112
Cosmic Journey 200
Coucher du Soleil 256
Couchmaster Shuffle 144
Count of Monte Cristo 194
Covert Research 118
Crackalicious 97
Crack Atowa 412
Crackerjack 332
Crankenstein 24
Crash Landing 109
Crash of the Titans 72
Crimp or Wimp 400
Critical Conundrum 39
Crooked Finger 203
Crop Circles 111
Crouching Climber Ridden Dragon 96
Crowds of Solitude 210
Crown Jewel 219
Crown Point 127, 219
Crows Feet 206
Cruiser 219
Cruisin' to a Bruisin' 400
Cryan's Shame 87
Crystal Ball 307
Crystallin Slab 256
Curly 420
Czech It Out 420

D

DaKind 106
Dalle de Cristal 256
Dangerous Toys 365
Dare 153
Dark Apron 153
Dark Side of the Moon 118
Darr Route 137
Dawg Daze 405
Dead Grouse 293
Death Star 115
Deception Crack 363
Deep Impact 401
Delicate Sound of Falling 95

Desert Dreaming 163
Desert of Reason 35
Desire Spire Pinnacle 124
Desperate Housewives 420
Digital Delight 412
Dilithium Crystals 116
Dirt In Your Eye 84
Dirty Deeds 24
Dirty Dog 420
Dismantled Fears 54
Djali 44
Doc Holiday 408
Doctors Patient 82
Dodge, Nicholas 1
Dod Route 312
Dodson 231
Dog Day Getaway 94
Dog House 222
Dog Show 400
Dog Spine 154
Dog Tooth Rock 283
Do It Again 26
Don't Call Me Ishmael 105
Don't Tread On Me 204
Do or Fly 425
Dorkboat 132
Double Eagle 257, 271
Double Trouble 256
D.P. 362
Dragon's Back 420
Drama Queen 409
Dreamcatcher 256
Dreamland 109
Dru's Cruise 359
Dru's Direct 359
Dunce 84
Dunlap 88
Dusty Devil 425

E

Eaglet 90
Earth First 109
East Arête 35, 135
East Couloir 141
East Face 314
East Face Direct 383
East Face Route 126
East Face South Tower 247

East Prow 317
East Ridge of South Chamber 33
East Route 130
East side Rock Climbs 65
East Wind 153
Eaten Alive 400
Eat Your Spinach 353
Ebb Tide 276
Eck-Rollings 293
Edge of Mordor 330
Eekwinocks 415
Eggs Overeasy 304
Eggs Overhard 304
Ego Extension 91
Eighteen Wheeler 412
Electric Blue 147
Elements of Style 366
Elephant Rock 281, 283
Elvis is Everywhere 424
Emerald City 25
EMF left 56
EMF middle 56
Enchilada ala Carte 133
End of the Line 169
Englund Direct 281
Enigma 199
Enola 47
Entrance Cracks 172
Entropic Gravity 69
Epiphany 404
Equinox 95
Erased Memory 110
Escalade 86
Esmeralda 42
ET 110
Eta Eva 362
Etched in Stone 411
Eternity 196
Even 79
Even Horizon 115
Event Gate 119
Excalibur 263
Exterminailer 399
Extra-Virgin 273
Extreme Makeover 360
Eye Of The Needle 84

F

Fab Slab 402
Face Farce 420
Face Lift 417
Face the Crook 399
Face the Facts 399
False Alarmageddon 367
Fame and Fortune 226
Fat Crack , 51
Fathers and Sons 420
Fat Rabbit 104
Feat Petite 400
Febmar Wall 420
Felsschlüpfer 90
Fifty-seven 50
Final Exam 415
Firearms 420
Fire Spire 140
First Contact 112
First Pinnacle 59
Fish for the Future 399
Fist-Fight 351
Fist-fighting Plumbers Area 350
Flaked Out 400
Foo Pinnacle 124
Forbidden Zone 48
Forest Circus Fiasco 168
Forest Fright 208
Forked Route 332
For Pete's Sake 78
Forthright 325
Fortune Cookie 52
Four Leaf Clover 259
Fractal Energy 226
Freak Show 133
Freddy's Dead 408
Fred Hart Lieback 303
Fred Hart Traverse 303
Free Bird 307
French's Dome 21
Fret Arête 424
Friend or Alien 111
Frogger 407
Frog Traverse 300
Frozen Embers 240
Full Circle 358
Fully Horizontal 134
Funkytown 94
Funny Trumpets Arête 401

G

Gathering Storm 222
Geek on a Leash 365
Geophagy 404
Geophysical 403
Get a Grip 405
Get It 168
Getting It Up for the Crack of Dawn 96
Getting Rich Watching Porn 133
Get Up and Stand Up 334
Giant's Direct 27
Giant's Staircase 26
Giant Steps 317
Gidrah 409
Gigantor 329
Gillette Arête 35
Gizzard 302
Global Warming 202
Glue Me Up Scotty 117
Goddess of Virtue 96
Gold 370
Golden Eagle 90
Golden Shower 27
Golden Spike 140
Gome Boy 395
Gonzo Pinnacle 315
Good for the Soule 367
Good Hearted Woman 238
Good Sport Route 94
Gorge Ice 211
Gorge Rock 125
Gothic Rock 382
Gothic Rocks 264
Grand Alliance 292
Gran Delusion 414
Granny's Got A Gun 48
Grass Crack 323
Gratitude 264
Gravity Waves 69
Great Pig Iron Dihedral 70
Great White Book 208
Grey Ghost 264
Griddle Cakes 200
Grits & Gravy 52
Groom Lake 118
Guillotine 79, 356
Guillotine Area 356
Gwenevere 346

Gypsy Dance 42

H

Hairy Tale 336
Hammerhead Shark 202
Hamunaptra 87
Hancock Tower 431
Hang 'em Higher 408
Hanging Chad 89
Hanging Curtain 237
Hangin' with the Hunch' 42
Hanz Crack 162
Hatchet Job 89
Hawaiian Slab 401
Headhunters 71
Heatstroke 379
Heatwave 153
Heinous Thing 420
Held Down 132
Heliotrope 106
Henpecked 420
Hen Rock 303
High Valley 422
High Voltage 22
Hillbilly Hot Tub 49
Hit and Run 354
Hogback Chimney 336
Ho' Lotta Shakin' 44
Hood River Pinnacle 120
Horizontal Delight 134
Horse Rock Pillar 320
Horsetail Falls 229
Horsethief butte 171
Hospital Corner 409
Hoss 118
Hostile Old Hikers 163
Hot Pockets 89
Hugo 45
Hunchback Wall 36
Hunch Sack 46

I

Ian's Route 329
Iceberg in a Sauna 196
Ice Cooler 226
Icon 153
Illumination Rock 29
Indian Summer 200, 412
Indirect East Arête 35

Infinite Regress 272
In Godzilla We Trust 96
Initiation 404
Inner Sanctum 146
Internal Combustion 420
Inukshuk 202
Inversion 406
Inversion Excursion 102
Iron Cross 417
Iron Maiden 32
Iron Mountain Spire 315
Itchy & Scratchy 168
It's All Good 89
It Taint Human 113

J

Jack and Jill 396
Jackie Chan 23
Jade 277
Java Jive 275
Jessie's Route 367
Jethro 51
Jet Stream 104, 238
Jet Stream Variation 105
Jet Wind 105
Jewel in the Crown 128
Jimmy Cliff 142
Jimmy's Favorite 144
Joe's Arete 420
John Harlin 91
Johnny Nowhere 409
Johnny's Got a Gun 412
Johnson-Watt route 266
Jon Pussman 46
Journey To The Sun 113
JP's Route 331
JRat Crack 103
Jugalicious 51
Jugular Vein 94
Juju Warrior 273
Junior Birdman 411
Just a Freakin' Rock Climber 163
Just Enough 420

K

K-9 Shanghai 88
Katanai Rock 138
Kestrel 90
King of the Moes 54

Kings of Rat 133
Kinzel Tower 60
Kirkpatrick Route 138
Kiwanis Crag 56
Klinger Springs 88
Knife-Fight 351
Know What I Mean 97
Kyles Big Adventure Gear 144

L

LaCamas PLug 251
Lady Slipper 420
Lamberson Butte 69
Lancaster Falls 235
Larry 420
La Siesta Tick Attack 425
Last Hurrah 425
Latent Genes 162
Latourrell Falls 219
Lava Flow 264
Laverne 45
Leadhead 35
Lean On Me 94
Learning to Fly 417
Left Ski Track 323
Le' Premie're 256
Lies and Deception 116
Life Shavings 226
Lightning Bolt Crack 73
Lights Over Phoenix 118
Line Dancer 101
Little Cougar Rock 134
Little Crow 206
Little Gray Men 111
Little Machu Pichu 430
Little Needle Rock 280
Little St. Pete's 138
Live Free or Die 206
Live Long and Prosper 115
Lively Up Yourself 417
Local Boy's Wall 420
Locked and Loaded 367
Loco Moco 273
Log Flume 161
Logisticon 69
Lonely Climax 210
Longtime Coming 409
Lord Frollo 40

Lorraine 406
Lost Art 348
Lost Wages 151
Lousy Putter 257
Lower Pillar 382
Lower Sore Thumb 140
Low Voltage 27
Luck of the Irish 259
Luna 110
Lunar Dreams 149
Lyle Tunnel Crag 170
Lyle West Crag 169

M

Machete 35
Magic 40
Magician 40
Maid in the Shade 417
Main Chimney 388
Major Tom 112
Makeover Band 359
Makin' Moonshine 277
Manic Madness 207
Mantle with Care 401
March Madness 33
Mark's Route 406
Marley's Route 412
Mars 111
Martini Rage 273
Mass Wasting 379
MC Direct 194
Measure of Pleasure 161
Meatloaf 49
Medussa 96
Megadike North 420
Megadike South 420
Mellow Drama 46
Men Are From Mars 119
Men in Black 109
Metamorphosis 39
Middle Chimney 388
Middle Sore Thumb 140
Middle Tower 383
Mighty Mite 148
Mighty Mouse 80
Minidike 420
Mirage 39
Mirage a' Trois 399

Mist Falls 223
Mists of Time 147
M&M's 415
Moe 420
Mojo Risin' 401
Molly's Route 168
Momma Bo Jomma 73
Money 380
Monkey on a Woodpile 420
Monster Crack 96
Monte Cristo Slab 185
Monty Piton 293
Moolack 337
Moonshiners Arête 53
Morgal Vale 329
Morning Thunder 420
Morning Wood Afternoon Delight 361
Morosoarus 96
Mosquito Butte 61
Moss Covered Funk 94
Mosserati 363
Mosserati Corner 362
Mothership 115
Mothership Supercell 39
Motional Turmoil 147
Moufot's Woof 401
Mountain Ears Route 396
Mouse in a Microwave 162
Moving to Manhatten 399
Mr. Clean 354
Mr. Denton on Doomsday 144
Mr. Flexible 411
Mr Hair of the Chode 51
Mt. Hood Regional Climbs 21
M.T.P. 410
Mud Crack 414
Multnomah Falls 226
Murky Water 42
Mushroom Band Area 352
My DNA 194
Mytosis 71
Mytosis Wall 71

N

Naked 147
Nancy's Run 238
Nasal Mozz 284
Needle Rock 279
Neophytes 69
Neuberger, Carl A. 1
Neutralized 276
Never-neverland 275
Never Neverland 295
New Chimney Column 325
New Chimney Jam 325
New Chimney Standard 325
Newton Pinnacle 69
New World Amphitheater 227
Niceline 148
Nieland Route 280
Nieland-Valenzuela route 253
Nightmare on Madrone Street 371
Night Music 153
Nip Tuck 361
No Balls 91
Noble Slabbage 401
Noodle Cracker 359
Nook and Cranny 104
North Arete 135
North Couloir 138
Northeast Face 376, 33
Northeast Ridge 33
Northern Lights 249
Northern Pearl 145
Northern Skylight 33
North Face 33, 127, 304, 312, 335
North Face Direct 141
North Face Jam Crack 299
North Forest 415
North Rabbit Ear 309
North Ravine 284, 290, 383
North Rib 61
North Ridge 315
NORTH SANTIAM REGION 279
North Talus Field 412
Northwest Face 304
Norwegian Queen 210
Nosferatu 96
No Star Slab 149
Not For Teacher 84
Notre Dame 44
Notta Slab 420
NPG 300
Nuggets 161
Nuked 101
Null Hypothesis 276

Nurse Ratchet 399
Nut Up 409
NW Face (Nieland-Valenzuela) 253

O

Oasis 40
OCD 163
OH8 162
Old Bologna 426
Old Chimney 324
Old Flakes 302
Olive Oil 354
One Flew Over the Cuckoo's Nest 352
One Half Shilling 260
One Note Samba 325
Oneonta Gorge 228
On My Face 405
On the Road to Shangri-La 372
Oot and Aboot 411
Opal's Arête 52
Open Space Plan 168
Open the Pod Bay Door HAL 115
Orange Crush 357
Oregon Yosemite 414
Organic Mist 220
Original 221
Orions Belt 249
Oroboros 96
Osprey 90
Outback BBQ 194
Outer Column Jam 323
Outer Limits 88
Out Of This World 111
Out There 420
Oz 25

P

Panorama 71
Park Her Here 26
Passing Lane 396
Paul's Route 168
PB Direct 55
Pearl's Jam 145
Pearly Gates Route 138
Pedestal 81
Pedestal Area 346
Peloton 40
Pencil Pusher 229
Penstemon 163

Pernicious Picklefest 209
Persistence Is Futile 43
Perverts in Paradise 367
Pesky Rodent 425
Peter Piper 230
Pete's Pile 74
Phadra 333
Phantom Gully 238
Philanthropy 23
Phish Food 415
Phlogistomat 412
Phoebus 43
Phone Home 110
Phoups 412
Pick Pocket 260
Pig Iron Wall 70
Pig Newton 70
Pig's Knuckles 48
Pigs Nipples 48
Pika Rock 293
Pikaville 295
Pillars of Hercules 129
Pirates Pinnacle 319
Pissfire 132
Plaid's Pantry 43
Plaidtastic 148
Play Palace 200
Pleasure Palace 354
Pledge Allegiance 350
Pledge Crack 350
Pledge Crack Area 349
Plumber Boy 415
Plumberette 56
Plumber's Crack 350
Plumbers Crack 104
Plum Butt 56
Poached 305
Point of Diminishing Returns 94
Poison Pill 69
Ponderosa 118
Ponytail 230
Pool Guy 357
Pop Quiz 83
Pororoca 273
Post Nasal Drip 229
Poultry Picnic 71
Power Child 96
Power & Politics 101

Prima Donna 294
Primal Institution 97
Probe 116
Progressive Climax 148
Prohibition 51
Propaganda 277
Psoriasis 27
Psycho Billy Cadillac 52
Psychotic Interlude 420
Ptero 162
Pumphauz 222
Pumpin' For The Man 87
Pumporama 23
Puppets Without Strings 409
Pushover 73

Q

Quantum Gravity 73
Quasar 206
Quasimodo 42

R

Rabbit Ears 141
Radical Sabbatical 346
Radioactive Wolves 294
Rad Plaid and Glad 265
Raging Sea 202
Raiders of the Lost Rock 103
Rally Race 403
Ramble On 87
Rapunzel's Back in Rehab 253
Rattler 160
Rattlesnake 163
Raven's of Odin 204
Raven's Revolt 206
Razmataz 124
Razorblade Pinnacle 34
Reckless Abandon 86
Reckless Rookie 257
Red 402
Red-headed Yeti 97
Redneck Knuckle Draggers 206
Redtail Arête 420
Red Zinger 420
Reed's Route 168
Regular Route 288
Resistance Is Futile 118
Retro Cognition 199
Return of Yoda 104

Right Roof Exit 246
Right Ski Track 323
Rime Dog 32
RIP Kurt Albert 95
Ripples 61
Risky Sex 168
Rites of Spring 305
River Dance 259
Rivers Edge 240
Road Face 22
Road Head 27
Road Kill 22
Road Rage 22
Roadview Wall 420
Rock Creek Crag 145
Rocketman 112
Rocket Ride 377
Rock Thugs 106
Rocktober Surprise 120
Rock Wren 90
Ron Love Verly 163
Roofatopia Dope 95
Rooster Hen & Chicks 267
Rooster Rock 125, 298
Roswell 112
RPM Overdrive 277
Runaway Weasel 265
RURP Traverse 128

S

Sacagawea's Route 168
Safety Dance 420
Salamander 221
Salathe Highway 264
Salmon 28
Salmon River Slab 28
Salmon Run 238
Samurai 49
Sanctum 74
Sands of Time 147
santiam pinnacle 314
Santiam Summits 279
Sasquatch 163, 351
Satisfaction 323
Sausalito 424
Scared Alive 365
Scene of the Crime 105
Schmitz-Caldwell Variation 377

Schmitz Route 140
Schoolroom 84
SCHOOLROOM CRACKS 82
Scorched Earth 294
Scorpio 149
Scorpion BBQ 49
Scum Suckers 346
Sea Hag Roof 52
SE Arête 244
Seasonal Anxiety 207
Second Pinnacle 59
Sendero De Sangre 372
Sendero Section 372
Separated at Birth 103
September Morn 204
SE Rib 285
Serpentine Arête 50
Seven Eleven 160
Seven Pearls 209
Sexy 380
Sfinks Crack 400
Shady Creek 226
Shafted 400
Shagadelic Groove 401
Shaken 96
Shanghai 333
Shangri-La 372
Shape Shifter 109
Shark Attack 221
Shasta's Spirit 378
Shepard Tower 388
Shepperds Smear 221
Shine 53
Shorty 168
Shorty Got Wolf 94
Sideways 349
Sidewinder 354
Sid's Slot 238
Sign Crack 325
Sign Face 325
Signs Preceding the End of the World 89
Silence of the Cams 102
Silence the Serenity 196
Silk Road 207
Silverstreak 24
Silver Streak 238
Single Wide 53
Sketchfest 420

Skinner Butte Columns 321
Skinny Hippie 400
Skookum Pinnacle 149
Sky's the Limit 200
Slanted and Enchanted 41
Slice of Pie 103
Slim Pickins 210
Slippery Dolphin 222
Slot Machine 372
Slow Dance 146
Sluice Box 161
Smackdown 407
Smokestack 316
Smoke Stack 424
Smokin' 83
Snack Time for Kea 404
Snapped it Off 403
Snazzic 225
Solar Flair 113
Solstice 94
Solstice Party 333
Sombrero 132
Something Else 404
Sophie 346
South Chamber 32
South Chimney 305, 246
South Crack 305
Southeast Face 302
Southeast Face Slab 306
Southeast Rib Direct 303
Southeast Slab 303
Southeast Slab Direct 306
Southern Cross 249
Southern Exposure 307, 369
Southern Skylight 33
South Face 126, 130, 286, 301, 314
South Face South Tower 247
South Rabbit Ear 311
South Ravine 291
South Ridge 135
South Santiam Region 297
South Talus Field 402
Southwest Crack 248
Southwest Face 127, 312, 378
South West Ridge 32
Space Cowboy 334
Spacy Face 425
Special Delivery 417

Sphinx 97
Spider 399
Spine Sender 332
Spiral Stairs 408
Spire Rock 285
Split Decision 401
Split Spire 283
Spring Breezes 168
Spring Cling 415
Spring Fever 415
Spring Mountain 393
Squall 259
Squatch's Travesty 208
Squeaky Alibi 60
Squirrel's Stew 168
Stack Rock 291
Stairs To The Stars 333
Standard North Face Route 299
Standard Route 138
S.T.A.R.D. 81
Stargate 116
Starship 119
Starvation Creek 236
Starvation Creek Area 235
Starvin' Marvin' 236
Static Cling 27
Steel and Stone 292
Steins Pillar 373
Stem-gem 420
Stems and Caps 353
Stems and Seeds 353
Stemulation 411
Steppin' Out 405
S#&t Eye 424
S#@t Fire 133
Sticky Fingers 307
Stinger 81
Stone Scared 293
St. Peters Dome 136
Straw Man 24
Streamlined 105
Summer Rules 306
Summertime Arête 409
Summit Scramble 244
Sunday's Best 196
Sunny Patina 176
Sunnyside Up 305
Sunset 256

Sunset Bluff 255
Sunset Bowl 73
Sunspot 113
Super Burrito 132
Supercalifragilistic 274
Superchron 198
Super Mario 353
SW Buttress 287
Sweetest Taboo 224
Sweet Pea 354
Swine of the Times 51

T

Tailgater 53
Take Me To Your Leader 110
Taken 95, 117
Tammy Jo Memorial Route 378
Tanner One 234
Tanner Two 234
TBA 403
Temptation 79
Termination 152
Test Tube 73
Thadallic 347
The Arête 331
The Borg 117
The Bump 140
The Bypass 156
The Cave Route 309
The Chain Gang 167
The Column 220
The Cover Up 111
The Dark Side 23
The Deer Hunter 224
The Dikes 418
The Direct 280
The Diving Board 399
The Dragons Spine 264
The Eagle Has Landed 110
The Easy Way 50
The Fang 53
The Final Shred 411
The First 256
The Gap 169
The Gingerbread Shortcut 264
The Goldband 367
The Grotto 366
The Last Dance 415

The Maverick 133
The Menagerie 297
The Middle Forest 404
The Move 144
The Pillar 223
The Plum Arête 56
The pod of god 403
The Point 250
The Rat Cave 130
Thermodynamics 276
The Short Bus 143
The Shuttler 168
The Siege 23
The South Forest 395
The Spur 300
The Steeple 265
The Steppes 153
The Stiffler 132
The Strand 240
The Swine 47
The Tallest Pygmy 40
The Truth Is Out There 115
The Watchman 147
The Wave 358
The Wormhole 116
Thick Enough to Screw 229
Thin Edge of Reality 162
Thin & Lovely 56
Third Pinnacle 59
Thirty-six Light Years 71
This ain't yo momma's five-nine 56
Thor's Hammer 289
Three Martini Lunch 45
Thunder Wall 258
Tibbet's Crack 48
Ticked 406
Tick Spray 407
Tic Talk 361
Tidewater 163
Tilting at Windmills 39
Times Tardy 84
Tin Man 25
Tin Tangle 25
Tipsy McStagger 51
Titanic Ego 277
To Boldly Bolt 114
Todd Skinner 95
Too Cool 52

Too Fat to Fly 426
Too Wet to Plow 426
Top O' the Bluff 259
Tornado 259
Tor the Hairy One 194
Tottering Tower 139
Tour de France 203
Toveline's Travesty 210
Tower Rock 252
Trad Dad 89
Trafalgar 72
Trafficosis 71
Transportation Routes 326
Trapped in Time 96
Tree Frog 249
Tree Nook 174
Trench Warfare 264
Tres Hombres 55
Tribes 81
Trick Wall 71
Trilobites 423
Triple Arthrodesis 402
Triple Threat 400
Trisha's Dilemma 424
Trix 404
Trouble With Tribbles 111
Trout Creek 384
Tsunami 259
Tuffnerd 133
Tumble Lake Area 279
Tumble Rock 282
Tunnel Vision 218
Turbocharged 278
Turkey Monster 312
Twenty Year Hangover 53
Twilight Zone 142
Twin Pillars 381
Twin Sisters Pinnacle 317
Twister 258, 415
Twitch 95
Two Beers and a Baby 356
Two Cheeks 424
Two Girls Mtn 317
Typhoon 258
Tyrolean Spire 141, 239
Tyrolean Tear 239

U

UFO 112
Ujahns Delight 265
Uluru 196
Unchained 332
Uncle Rick 27
Underdog 331
Under the Big Top 356
Unfinished Business 228
Unknown 128
Un-named 325
Unnamed Symphony 425
Unobtainium 273
Up an Alchemists' Sleeve 371
Up on a Pedestal 349
Upper Menagerie Wilderness 307
Upper Pillar 382
Upper Sore Thumb 140
Upper Trick Wall 73
Upskirt 262
Uranus Has Rings 112
Utopia 151

V

Van Golden Brown 405
Variation on Hit and Run 355
Velociraptor 275
Veranda 177
Vertical Frost 240
Vexation Variation 291
Victor 45
Vitruvian Man 272
Vrooom 275
Vulcan Mind Meld 113

W

Wage Slave 69
Wahkeena Falls 225
Walk on the Wild Side 198
Wanderer 404
Wankers Column 159
Warmnerd 133
War of the Worlds 109
Warp Pinnacle 121
Wasp Route 425
Water Buffalo 315
Water Heater 221
Water Ice Ratings 215
Waterpipe 220
Way Up 420

We Are Not Alone 117
Weather Pattern Cycle 214
Wedged Block 245
Wedged Block Right Exit 245
Weeble Pinnacle 121
Welcome to Spring Mtn 399
Welcome to the Swine 55
Wendell's Big Mistake 161
West Arete 135, 248
West Arête 30
West Chimney 128, 307
West Face 315, 316
West Face Crack 151
West Face Dihedral Direct 299
West Face of South Ear 311
West Gully 335
West Wind 154
Wet Spot 95
Where the Wild Things Are 352
Whipsaw 271
Whiskey 380
Whiskey River 367
White Lightning 53
Who's the Choss? 106
Widespread Panic 358
Wild Boar 274
Wild Boar Crag 269
Wild Hare 310
Wild Turkey 312
Wild West 304
Wind Dummy 163
Wind Mountain 151
Wind Tunnel 218
Windy Slab 152
Winema Pinnacles 134
Winter Sunshine 306
Wobbegong 199
Wolf Gang 94
Wolf Point 94
Wolf Rock 326
Workingman's Lack 372
Workman's Comp 152
World is Collapsing 74
Worth the Walk 417
Wyde Syde 147

X

Xenophobia 274

X-Marks Band 364
X-Marks the Spot 365
X-Spire 288

Y

Yay Climbing 371
Yellow Brick Road 27
Yeti's Betty 97
You Me & Everyone We Know 91
Young Jedi 109
You're Not Worthy 420
Yo Yo Draw 274

Z

Zabo's Delight 257
Zabo's Enchanteur 257
Zeno's Paradox 43
Zion Train 349
Zoo at Xanadu 276
Zucchini Route 128

"Good judgement comes from experience.
Experience comes from surviving bad judgement."

NW OREGON ROCK CLIMBS

Notes

Notes

Notes

Notes

Notes

www.ingramcontent.com/pod-product-compliance
Lightning Source LLC
Chambersburg PA
CBHW070521010526
44118CB00012B/1040